THE STRATEGIC ENVIRONMENTAL ASSESSMENT DIRECTIVE

The Strategic Environmental Assessment Directive (Directive 2001/42/EC) (SEA Directive) has been a lurking legal presence in EU and UK environmental law. Now, just over a decade since its implementation, the impacts of the SEA Directive are beginning to be felt throughout the UK, and more broadly throughout the European Union as a whole. These developments have been driven both by the expansive interpretation of the Directive's scope by the Court of Justice of the European Union and by a slow learning process about how this new type of regulation should be legally interpreted and applied. This edited collection is the first volume to reflect comprehensively on the emerging legal identity of SEA in the EU and UK. With contributions addressing the impact of the SEA Directive on the fields of town and country planning and European environmental law, the book is a comprehensive analysis of all aspects of the Directive, from its history and scope, to its impact on governmental policy and its implications in practice. The volume both reflects on key cases such as Case C-567/10 *Inter-Environnement Bruxelles* and *HS2*, and looks forward, as it considers and projects future legal implications of the SEA Directive. Written by a blend of distinguished academics and leading practitioners, it provides an in-depth critique and rounded appreciation of both the immediate practical effects of SEA and its wider impact on European and UK environmental law.

The Strategic Environmental Assessment Directive

A Plan for Success?

Edited by
Gregory Jones QC and Eloise Scotford

•HART•
OXFORD • LONDON • NEW YORK • NEW DELHI • SYDNEY

HART PUBLISHING
Bloomsbury Publishing Plc
Kemp House, Chawley Park, Cumnor Hill, Oxford, OX2 9PH, UK

HART PUBLISHING, the Hart/Stag logo, BLOOMSBURY and the Diana logo are trademarks of Bloomsbury Publishing Plc

First published in hardback, 2017
Paperback edition, 2019

A catalogue record for this book is available from the British Library.

Library of Congress Cataloging-in-Publication Data

A catalogue record for this book is available from the Library of Congress.

ISBN: HB: 978-1-84946-633-2
PB: 978-1-50993-015-9
ePDF: 978-1-78225-552-9
ePub: 978-1-78225-553-6

Typeset by Compuscript Ltd, Shannon

To find out more about our authors and books visit www.hartpublishing.co.uk. Here you will find extracts, author information, details of forthcoming events and the option to sign up for our newsletters.

FOREWORD

With just two exceptions, the chapters collected in this volume are based upon papers delivered at the Kingsland Conference II entitled *The Strategic Environmental Assessment Directive: A Plan for Success?* The conference, jointly co-organised by Francis Taylor Building, Temple and The Dickson Poon School of Law, King's College London, was held on 14 February 2014 at the London offices of King & Wood, Mallesons, SJ Berwin.

I was particularly pleased to be invited by the organisers (Gregory Jones QC and Dr Eloise Scotford) to take part in the conference as, in common with many other participants, I knew Christopher Kingsland well. Christopher would have been delighted by the quality of the papers and would have revelled in the discussions on law and policy that took place during the day. This series of conferences is a fitting memorial to him.

The organisers are to be congratulated on the timing of the conference. When they set the date, they could not possibly have known that it would be so shortly after the Supreme Court handed down its decision in *R (Buckinghamshire County Council) v Secretary of State for Transport* [2014] 1 WLR 324, or indeed the day after Lord Neuberger delivered his Freshfields lecture at Cambridge entitled 'The British and Europe'. In the event, it was hardly surprising that the decision of the Supreme Court in *HS2* (and, in particular, the criticism by Lord Neuberger and Lord Mance of the decision of the Fourth Chamber of the CJEU in Case C-567/10 *Inter-Environnement Bruxelles ASBL v Region de Bruxelles-Capitale* [2012] 2 CMLR 909) and the relationship of our domestic courts and the CJEU came to dominate the conference. This relationship is now likely to evolve further in light of the UK's referendum vote to leave the European Union in June 2016. The full legal implications of this vote have yet to be ascertained.

Those of us who were privileged to attend the conference heard a series of fine papers, which addressed both the practical issues arising from the SEA Directive and the wider constitutional issues raised by its impact on the policy-making function of governments of Member States. It is particularly pleasing that these papers are now available in a more permanent form to a wider public.

Rt Hon Lord Justice Lloyd Jones
The Royal Courts of Justice
The Strand
London WC1

PREFACE

With the exception of William Howarth's Chapter 12 and the Afterword, this volume is inspired by papers delivered at the second Kingsland Conference—*The Strategic Environmental Assessment Directive: A Plan for Success?*—held in London on 14 February 2014. We would like to thank Christine Copping and her team at the Centre for European Law, King's College London, and Deirdre Mahon at Francis Taylor Building, Temple for their great assistance in organising that conference. However, the chapters in this work seek to reflect the legal position as at 30 April 2016. It is the sister volume to *The Habitats Directive: A Developer's Obstacle Course?*, also published by Hart Publishing and based upon the first Kingsland Conference. Hart Publishing has been a great supporter of the Kingsland books and we are pleased this strong relationship has continued under new owner Bloomsbury Publishing. We thank the Hart team, Emily Braggins and her predecessor Rachel Turner, for their assistance and patience during the gestation of this book.

The conference and this book honour the late Lord Kingsland QC, a distinguished lawyer and politician. The book's topic is particularly apposite. Writing in 2009, Christopher Kingsland presciently noted that:

> Hitherto too often the planning system was overlooked as an instrument of environmental law. The [SEA] directive concerning the need for strategic environmental assessment of plans or programmes, is an ambitious step forward.[1]

We hope this volume will contribute to the understanding of the SEA Directive's role in plan making as well as foreshadowing its possible future steps forward.

Gregory Jones QC
St Mark's English Church
Florence
Italy
Oak Apple Day, 2016

Dr Eloise Scotford
Colliers Wood
London

[1] Andrew Waite, Tim Jewell, Gregory Jones and Valerie Fogleman, *Waite and Jewell: Environmental Law in Property Transactions*, 3rd edn (London, Bloomsbury Professional, 2009).

CONTENTS

CONTRIBUTORS

Stephen Ashworth is a Partner at Dentons in London in the planning and public law team. His practice concentrates on regeneration, residential and infrastructure projects, working for both the private and public sectors. He has market-leading experience on tariffs/infrastructure levies, affordable housing, CPOs and viability issues. He is recognised as a leading individual in the 2016 *Planning Magazine* survey.

Richard Caddell is Senior Research Associate and Nippon Foundation Senior Nereus Fellow at the Netherlands Institute for the Law of the Sea, Utrecht University, the Netherlands, and Lecturer in Law at Cardiff University, UK. He is also a member of the Academic Panel at Francis Taylor Building, Temple, London.

Jack Connah is a practising barrister specialising in planning, environmental, local government, public and property law at Francis Taylor Building, Temple, London. He is an elected member of the Constitutional and Administrative Bar Association Committee.

Denis Edwards is an Advocate in Scotland, of the Middle Temple Barrister at Law and a professional consultant in the Faculty of Law of the Chinese University of Hong Kong. He is a member of Francis Taylor Building, Temple, London and practises in all areas of public law, EU law and environmental law.

David Elvin QC is a member of the Bars of England and Wales and Northern Ireland, and practises in planning, environmental, local government, public and property law at Landmark Chambers. He has been involved in numerous cases concerning SEA, such as *Save Historic Newmarket*, the *HS2* litigation and *Ashdown Forest*, as well as many other environmental cases in the UK courts and the CJEU. He is a Recorder of the Crown Court, a Deputy High Court Judge (Administrative and Planning Courts), a part-time judge of the Upper Tribunal (IAC) and one of the Parliamentary Boundary Commissioners for England. He is joint General Editor of the *Planning Encyclopaedia*.

Elizabeth Fisher is Professor of Environmental Law at the Faculty of Law, Corpus Christi College, Oxford. She researches a range of topics in comparative environmental and administrative law. Her books include *Risk Regulation and Administrative Constitutionalism* (Hart Publishing, 2007) (winner of the 2008 SLS Peter Birks Book Prize) and (with Bettina Lange and Eloise Scotford) *Environmental Law: Text, Cases and Materials* (OUP, 2013). She is General Editor of the *Journal of Environmental Law*.

Valerie Fogleman was Natural Resources Law Fellow at Lewis & Clark Law School in Portland, Oregon, a Fellow at the University of Illinois College of Law and in private practice in Corpus Christi, Texas, prior to returning to England in 1992. She was subsequently Partner and Head of the Environment Group at Barlow Lyde & Gilbert (now Clyde & Co) and a consultant at Lovells (now Hogan Lovells). She is currently a consultant at Stevens & Bolton LLP and Professor of Law at Cardiff University School of Law and Politics. She advises clients on environmental, climate change, insurance, and health and safety law. Her work includes various projects (some with BIO by Deloitte) for the European Commission, including five projects on the Environmental Liability Directive. She is an Honorary Member of the Royal Institution for Chartered Surveyors, member and former Vice Chair of the City of London Law Society Planning and Environment Committee, member and former Council member of the United Kingdom Environmental Law Association and member of the Texas State Bar, the American Bar Association and the Association of Insurance and Risk Managers. She is listed as a leading environmental lawyer in the directories. She has written three books and over 200 articles on environmental and insurance law.

David Graham is a practising barrister specialising in planning, environmental, local government, public and property law at Francis Taylor Building, Temple, London. He is the author (with Gregory Jones) of 'Maritime Spatial Planning' in B Soyer and A Tettenborn (eds), *Offshore Contracts and Liabilities* (Routledge, 2014); and (with Charles George) 'After *Morge*: Where are We Now?' in G Jones (ed), *The Habitats Directive: A Developer's Obstacle Course?* (Hart Publishing, 2012). He is rated as one of the top planning barristers under the age of 35 by *Planning Magazine*.

Stephanie Hall is a practising barrister specialising in planning, environmental, local government, public and property law at Francis Taylor Building, Temple, London. Prior to coming to the Bar, she was involved in local government.

Rachael Herbert is an associate at Dentons in London, where she is a member of its planning and public law team. She joined the Dentons in August 2013 after working in Australia specialising in planning and environment work. She advises on all aspects of planning law, with a particular interest in major regeneration schemes, and has experience working for both public and private sector clients.

William Howarth is Professor of Environmental Law at the University of Kent. He is author, co-author or editor of 16 books relating to water and fisheries law, and author of over 100 reports, monographs and academic journal articles on diverse aspects environmental and ecological law. He is a member of the Committee of Fish Legal, is Honorary Legal Adviser to the Institute of Fisheries Management and is the Regional Representative for the International Association for Water Law.

Gregory Jones QC is a member of the Bars of England and Wales, Ireland and Northern Ireland. Practising in planning, environmental, local government, public and property law from Francis Taylor Building, Temple, London, he is identified as a leading silk in *Planning Magazine* and various directories. He has acted in many of the leading SEA Directive cases, including *Wakil* and *Cogent* in England and *Seaport* and *The Alternative A5 Alliance* in Northern Ireland. He is a Fellow of the Royal Geographical Society, the Centre of European Law, King's College, London, the Institute of Quarrying and the Linnean Society. He is a Legal Associate of the Royal Town Planning Institute (RTPI). His published work includes: G Jones (ed), *The Habitats Directive: A Developer's Obstacle Course?* (Hart Publishing, 2012); (with David Graham) 'Maritime Spatial Planning' in B Soyer and A Tettenborn (eds), *Offshore Contracts and Liabilities* (Routledge, 2014); and (with Robert McCracken and James Pereira) *Statutory Nuisance*, 3rd edn (Bloomsbury, 2012). In July 2015, he was appointed by the Irish government to chair the independent review of *An Bord Pleanála*, which reported in February 2016.

Richard Macrory CBE is one of the UK's most distinguished and experienced environmental lawyers, who has pioneered the development of the field of law. He was the UK's first professor of environmental law, and is Professor of Environmental Law at the Faculty of Laws, University College London. In 2006, he was appointed by the Cabinet Office to lead a Review on Regulatory Sanctions covering nearly all areas of business regulation. All the recommendations in his review were accepted by the government. Important new powers for regulators resulting from his review are now contained in the Regulatory Enforcement and Sanctions Act 2008.

Robert McCracken QC is Fellow of the Centre for European Law at King's College London, a Legal Associate of the RTPI and past Chairman of the United Kingdom Environmental Law Association. He is a barrister at Francis Taylor Building, Temple, London specialising in public, planning and environmental law. His wide experience includes the petrochemical industry, renewable and conventional power, water, retail and transport sectors, waste and contaminated land and statutory nuisance. He is recognised as a leading silk in Environment and Planning law by *Planning Magazine* and the leading directories. He is the co-author (with Gregory Jones and James Pereira) of *Statutory Nuisance*, 3rd edn (Bloomsbury, 2012).

Juliet Munn is a managing associate at international law firm King & Wood Mallesons and acts on both contentious and non-contentious planning and environmental matters for developers, landowners, interest groups and corporate bodies. She has acted on a number of matters involving the application of the SEA Directive, including the *HS2AA* and *Ashdown Forest* cases. She is an active member of the United Kingdom Environmental Law Association.

William Orbinson QC practises in Northern Ireland with an exclusive planning and environmental specialism. He represents development interests in major planning and development plan inquiries, appeals, enforcement appeals, prosecutions and judicial reviews. He acted for one of the challengers in the seminal *Seaport/Magherafelt* case and appeared in many of the subsequent challenges generated by that case to SEAs of draft development plans in Northern Ireland. He is a Legal

Associate of the RTPI. A founding member and past Chair of the Environmental and Planning Law Association for Northern Ireland (EPLANI), he is the Chair of the Planning Appeals Commission Users Group in Northern Ireland.

Colin Reid joined the University of Dundee in 1991 and has been Professor of Environmental Law since 1995. He has written widely on environmental issues, and 2016 saw the publication of his book *The Privatisation of Biodiversity?* He was the founding Convener of the Environmental Law Section of the Society of Legal Scholars, a founding member of the United Kingdom Environmental Law Association and is a member of the IUCN Environmental Law Commission, of the Law Society of Scotland's Environmental Law Sub-committee, and of the editorial boards of several leading academic journals. He regularly gives evidence to parliamentary committees at Holyrood and Westminster, most recently on the EU referendum.

Simon Ricketts is a partner and head of planning at international law firm King & Wood Mallesons. He has a wide planning, compulsory purchase and local government law practice, with particular experience in major mixed-use development in London, as well as urban extensions and new settlements in the rest of the country. A former barrister, he has been voted most highly rated planning solicitor in the country in *Planning Magazine*'s last seven annual surveys. He is co-author (with Duncan Field) of *Localism and Planning* (Bloomsbury, 2012).

Áine Ryall is Senior Lecturer at the School of Law, University College Cork, Ireland. She teaches and researches environmental law, EU law and tort law. Her research focuses in particular on environmental assessment, access to justice, environmental law enforcement, implementation of the Aarhus Convention and climate law. A qualified barrister, she is a member of the Aarhus Convention Compliance Committee and a member of the Avosetta Group of EU environmental law experts. She is a board member of the Irish Centre for European Law (ICEL) and a member of the Academic Panel of Francis Taylor Building, Temple, London.

Eloise Scotford is Senior Lecturer at The Dickson Poon School of Law, King's College London. She is author of *Environmental Principles and the Evolution of Environmental Law* (Hart Publishing, Oxford, 2017) and co-author (with Elizabeth Fisher and Bettina Lange) of *Environmental Law: Text, Cases and Materials* (OUP, 2013). Dr Scotford actively researches in the areas of climate change law and governance, waste regulation, air quality control, comparative environmental law and sustainable development. She is an associate member of Landmark Chambers, a visiting lecturer in environmental law at Bocconi University in Milan, a member of the Avosetta Group of EU environmental law experts, and Analysis Editor of the *Journal of Environmental Law*.

William R Sheate is Reader in Environmental Assessment, Imperial College London and Technical Director, Collingwood Environmental Planning. With over 30 years' experience in academia, consultancy and the voluntary sector, he is recognised internationally as an environmental assessment expert advising on compliance matters for judicial review. In 2014, he was Specialist Adviser to the House of Commons Environmental Audit Committee inquiry into HS2 and the environment. In 2015, he testified at the International Court of Justice in The Hague on behalf of the applicant in *Nicaragua v Costa Rica* (Border Road). He is a member of the Academic Panel of Francis Taylor Building, Temple, London.

Ned Westaway is a barrister specialising in environmental and planning law at Francis Taylor Building, Temple, London. He regularly talks and writes on environmental law and, in particular, is a co-author (with Gregory Jones and Roger Watts) of 'Why Central Craigavon was Wrongly Decided (and Other Problems with the Incorporation of the Strategic Environmental Assessment Directive into Domestic Law)' (2013) *Journal of Planning & Environment Law* 1074. He is also a visiting researcher at the UCL Centre for Law and the Environment. He is a trustee of the United Kingdom Environmental Law Association and acts as counsel for the Campaign for National Parks.

TABLE OF CASES

European Union

Alphabetical order

Chronological order

Hong Kong

International

Ireland

United Kingdom

United States of America

TABLE OF LEGISLATION

Australia

Canada

European Union

Directives

United States of America

International Conventions and Other Materials

Press Releases

INTRODUCTION

GREGORY JONES QC AND ELOISE SCOTFORD

Directive 2001/42/EC on the assessment of the effects of certain plans and programmes (the 'Strategic Environmental Assessment Directive' or 'SEA Directive') has been on the European statute books since 2001[1] and was implemented throughout the UK in 2004.[2] Just over a decade on and the legal impacts of this novel and ambitious Directive are finally being felt throughout the UK, as well as in the EU legal order more broadly. These developments have partly been driven by the expansive interpretation of the Directive's scope by the Court of Justice of the European Union (CJEU)[3] and partly by a slow process of learning about how this new type of regulation should be legally interpreted and applied. Whilst the SEA Directive is related to the more well-established process of environmental impact assessment (EIA), which applies to discrete projects (although even that process is fraught with legal complexity), strategic environmental assessment is a different and relatively unknown legal cousin.

This edited collection is the first volume to reflect comprehensively on the emerging legal identity of strategic environmental assessment (SEA) in the EU and the UK, and it identifies a range of reasons why that identity has been challenging to ascertain. Three reasons dominate the contributions of the volume, relating to the *context*, *purpose* and *ambiguity* of the SEA Directive. First, SEA in UK law and EU law is highly contextual. SEA—as an environmental assessment concept relating to public plans, policies and programmes—is not unknown in environmental policy generally.[4] However, as Elizabeth Fisher points out in Chapter 8, SEA is not a programmatic tool, but an 'ambiguous bundle of processes designed to reframe decision-making, which are embedded in wider legal cultures'. The

[1] Directive 2001/42/EC of the European Parliament and of the Council of 27 June 2001 on the assessment of the effects of certain plans and programmes [2001] OJ L197/30.

[2] The Environmental Assessment of Plans and Programmes Regulations 2004 SI 2004/1633; The Environmental Assessment of Plans and Programmes Regulations (Northern Ireland) 2004 SR 2004/280; The Environmental Assessment of Plans and Programmes (Scotland) Regulations 2004 SSI 2004/258; The Environmental Assessment of Plans and Programmes (Wales) Regulations 2004 WSI 2004/1656/W170.

[3] In particular, Joined Cases C-105/09 and C-110/09 *Terre wallonne ASBL and Inter-Environnement Wallonie ASBL v Région wallonne* [2010] ECR I-5611; and Case C-567/10 *Inter-Environnement Bruxelles ASBL* [2012] ECLI:EU:C:2012:159.

[4] See the contributions in this volume by Elizabeth Fisher (Ch 8) and William R Sheate (Ch 9) for a broader perspective on SEA.

legal context of SEA obligations is thus critical in determining their meaning and operation. In EU and UK law, that context is not uncontroversial. This is because the different legal cultures of the EU and the UK need to meet to determine and express the requirements of the SEA Directive, and because, even within UK law, there is a backdrop of legal traditions, doctrine and devolved power that must accommodate the Directive. In the former respect, Robert McCracken and Ned Westaway in Chapter 1 highlight the often 'tortuous' negotiations involved in introducing a new form of environmental assessment that EU Member States could live with, which sits uncomfortably between trends and requirements of public international law and the political compromises struck between the different EU legislative institutions in drafting the Directive. The legal culture of the UK does not make matters any simpler for interpreting and implementing the SEA Directive. For one thing, there is a weighty backdrop of constitutional law against which the Directive sits awkwardly. Lord Justice Lloyd Jones, former chair of the Law Commission and chair of one of the sessions at the second Kingsland Conference, kindly provides the Foreword to this book in which he perceptively observes that the SEA Directive case law, in particular *HS2*, has put a spotlight on wider constitutional issues between the UK and the EU. In Chapter 10, Eloise Scotford points out the troubling questions for UK public law that arise in light of the SEA Directive's incursion into policy-making and into the role of executive government. Furthermore, the devolved nature of environmental power across the UK has resulted in a fragmented approach to SEA throughout the UK. In Chapter 14, Colin Reid and Denis Edwards show that SEA has been embraced much more openly in Scotland and that the Scottish legislature has introduced regulation that not only complies with the Directive but also constructs a broader form of SEA. By contrast, William Orbinson notes in Chapter 15 that in Northern Ireland, the progressive and purposive approach adopted by the Northern Ireland high court in *Seaport*[5]—the first major SEA Directive case within the UK—has given way to the narrow (and almost certainly erroneous) approach adopted by its Court of Appeal in *Craigavon*.[6] Evolving SEA law thus reflects constitutional and political developments within Member States, as well as across the EU.[7]

Two other chapters in the book highlight the contextual nature of SEA. At one extreme, Richard Caddell in Chapter 13 shows how SEA in the offshore context has been ambitious and even foreshadowed the requirements of the Directive. In the offshore energy sector in particular, the UK government has been progressive and proactive in developing a form of SEA that sits at the heart of offshore development, albeit that its methodology is not beyond criticism. At the other end of

[5] *Seaport Investments Ltd's Application for Judicial Review, Re* [2008] Env LR 23 (HCNI); and Case C-474/10 *Department of the Environment for Northern Ireland v Seaport (NI) Ltd and Others* [2011] ECR I-10227 (CJEU). Note that the Draft Northern Area Plan 2016 and Draft Magherafelt Area Plan 2015 were also referred to the CJEU in Case C-474/10.

[6] *Central Craigavon Ltd's Application for Judicial Review, Re* [2011] NICA 17 (CANI).

[7] In relation to EU developments, Gregory Jones discusses the findings of the European Commission's First Progress Report in Ch 2.

the spectrum, Áine Ryall in Chapter 16 shows how the Irish approach to implementing the SEA Directive has been limited, narrow and potentially in breach of the Directive's goals. This is particularly due to 'wider, deeply rooted problems with environmental governance in Ireland' (politics again), lack of public engagement, and the courts' inaccessibility and approach to the Directive once judicial review actions are brought. In one sense, all the different legal contexts examined in the present volume provide scope for legal learning about the SEA Directive across cultures, since they are all grappling with, and fundamentally influenced by, the Directive. However, they also show how SEA is not a fixed and known legal phenomenon—it is still evolving in many contexts and is invariably shaped by them.

The second factor that has a determinative impact on the nature of SEA within legal contexts is the Directive's perceived purpose. If we look to Article 1 of the SEA Directive, it has a stated purpose:

> The objective of this Directive is to provide for a high level of protection of the environment and to contribute to the integration of environmental considerations into the preparation and adoption of plans and programmes with a view to promoting sustainable development, by ensuring that, in accordance with this Directive, an environmental assessment is carried out of certain plans and programmes which are likely to have significant effects on the environment.

However, as Elizabeth Fisher deftly points out in Chapter 8, more fine-tuning is required in thinking about the purpose of the SEA Directive. She shows that there are at least two ways of conceiving of the Directive's aim—involving either a 'narrow' or an 'expansive' approach to assessing 'upstream' planning processes—and that each of these purposes can result in different ways of interpreting the Directive. This is because the identified purpose of the Directive will fundamentally frame how decision-making involving strategic environmental assessment is undertaken in relation to 'plans and programmes'. In a related way, in Chapter 9, William Sheate shows how the identified purpose of SEA is central to appraising whether SEA is being done well, and whether legal decisions interpreting the Directive's requirements are properly capturing the aim and spirit of SEA processes. For Sheate, SEA is a key component of 'streamlining' all environmental assessment processes (including environmental impact assessment of projects), so that together they operate in a holistic way to ensure that different stages of development and project planning are appropriately assessed for their significant environmental impacts. SEA should fit into a model of 'tiering' environmental assessment so that 'the most relevant issues [are assessed] at the most appropriate level of detail relative to the level of decision-making'. A rigorous methodology is thus required to ensure that SEA processes contribute to assessing significant environmental impacts of plans and projects as effectively as possible, and legal decisions can only be defended if they tend towards this aim. In practical terms, as Jack Connah and Stephanie Hall note in Chapter 7, the Directive's aim has not been helped in practice by the UK government's claims that SEA and sustainability appraisals and SEAs are essentially the same thing. They are not—not least because, as Connah and Hall point out, sustainability appraisals are wider in their scope but shallower in their detail than the SEA procedure required by the Directive.

Third, and implicit in the two reasons so far discussed, the Directive itself leaves room for interpretation and argument about its interpretation. Its legal identity is thus up for grabs. As McCracken and Westaway point out in Chapter 1, the drafting of the SEA Directive was highly contentious and the key provisions that determine the scope of the Directive in Articles 2 and 3 present a 'convoluted picture'. This legal complexity was generated through the drafting process by a 'tension between the competing desires to have an integrated and holistic mechanism of environmental assessment and to define in advance exactly what plans and programmes required such assessment'. Valerie Fogleman examines in detail what is meant by a 'plan or programme' in Chapter 3, in part by tracing the origins of the SEA Directive from the groundbreaking National Environmental Policy Act 1969 in the USA.

Both legal and practical consequences flow from the Directive's textual uncertainty. In Chapter 4, Simon Ricketts and Juliet Munn examine the uncertainty relating to the key 'gateway' provision to the requirement to conduct an SEA, namely, whether the production of the plan or programme in question is 'required by legislative, regulatory or administrative Provisions'. As they point out:

> The most uncertainty has been caused by the use of 'required by' in relation to administrative provisions. Almost by definition an administrative provision will not 'require' anything, in the sense of rendering it legally obligatory.

Uncertainty over the scope of the Directive can have profound consequences for legal orders within Member States. As Eloise Scotford points out in Chapter 10, the broader the interpretation given to the Directive's provisions that relevant plans and programmes are 'required by legislative, regulatory or administrative provisions' and must 'set the framework' for future development consent, the broader the scope of the Directive, and the more extensive is the constitutional reordering imposed by the Directive in UK law. Big things can turn on the meaning of small but ambiguous phrases. Similarly, Stephen Ashworth and Rachel Herbert in Chapter 5 discuss the obligation to ensure that the public is given an 'early and effective' opportunity to participate in SEA processes, where what is 'early and effective' is undefined, but of critical practical importance to the Directive's model of environmental democracy.

In practice, the textual ambiguity of the Directive can have significant impacts for public decision-makers and developers. This can be seen in relation to the key requirement in conducting an SEA to consider alternatives. As David Elvin notes in Chapter 6, the ambiguity of this obligation has had some surprising consequences in decided cases. Reflecting on the Supreme Court's decision in *HS2*,[8] Elvin comments that the obligation to carry out an SEA:

> [A]ppears to exempt major infrastructure (which calls out for assessment of reasonable alternatives) from assessment if it is introduced by government as a matter of policy

[8] *R (Buckinghamshire County Council) v Secretary of State for Transport* [2014] UKSC 3; [2014] 1 WLR 324.

> only. The nature of the origin of the project has, with respect, little to do with the need to ensure environmental assessment of alternatives, which remains a key feature in understanding and minimising environmental harm.

The Supreme Court may have refused to make a reference to the CJEU in *HS2*, but, as Richard Macrory and Gregory Jones remind us in the Afterword, the ongoing proceedings in relation to *HS2* before the Aarhus Compliance Committee mean that the UK Supreme Court may not yet have had the last word on the matter.

The uncertain practical operation of the Directive is also felt in sectors that are in a grey area of the Directive's operation. Thus, Caddell in Chapter 13 highlights how novel offshore industries, such as carbon-capture-and-storage and fracking, sit uncomfortably within the framework of the Directive. Similarly, Gregory Jones and David Graham illustrate in Chapter 11 that the requirements of the SEA Directive can be difficult to identify and apply in relation to plans and programmes outside the field of town and country planning. The challenge is particularly acute where the subject matter is also governed by the requirements of another directive, such as the Water Framework Directive, as William Howarth points out in Chapter 12.

In summary, the chapters of this book show that the SEA Directive is a novel legal instrument, which has heralded a new era in environmental assessment in EU law, but without a clear direction as to its legal impact. Its legal nature is currently being worked out through disputes and decided cases, within various legal cultures and with various analytical standards being applied to test its progress. In one sense, this is all unsurprising. Environmental law is a hotbed for this kind of legal innovation, development and complexity. As Elizabeth Fisher has written elsewhere:

> ['E]nvironmental law' is directly concerned with 'hot situations' in which the agreed frames, legal and otherwise, for how we understand and act in the world are in a constant state of flux and contestation. As such, environmental law stands in stark contrast to those areas of law where actors, interests, preferences, and thus rights and responsibilities, can be easily identified and thus workable frames of legal action can operate. Environmental law is thus a subject in which 'reassured certainties give way to tormented complexities'.[9]

The volume captures a moment in time reflecting on the evolution of SEA in EU and national law. In another decade, Brexit notwithstanding, its arguments and reflections will no doubt need revisiting and we anticipate more fraught legal cases, political wrangling and adjustment of the legal status quo in getting to grips with the Directive. In the meantime, and despite its complexities, the Directive has important work to do in broadening the idea of environmental assessment in public development planning and in holding governments to account for their policies and plans where these have significant effects on the environment.

[9] Elizabeth Fisher, 'Environmental Law as "Hot Law"' (2013) 25(3) *Journal of Environmental Law* 347 (footnotes omitted).

Part I

Understanding the Strategic Environmental Assessment (SEA) Directive

1

The History and Context of the SEA Directive

ROBERT McCRACKEN QC AND NED WESTAWAY

Introduction

Strategic decisions are those that operate at a higher level and guide or determine subsequent events. The word 'strategy' derives from the Greek *strategos*: a military commander. Strategic appraisal may therefore be seen as part of the art of military (and civil) decision-making, and is as old as human enterprise. However, it was only in the latter part of the twentieth century that attempts were made to set down a statutory framework for making and reviewing administrative planning decisions, in part in response to the increasing environmental impacts of human enterprise.

To appreciate how and why this statutory framework has evolved, this chapter sets out the history and context of Directive 2001/42/EC on the assessment of the effects of certain plans and programmes on the environment, commonly known as the Strategic Environmental Assessment Directive (hereinafter 'the SEA Directive').[1] Interestingly, the word 'strategic' is nowhere contained within the Directive itself, although it represents a fundamental development in the strategic appraisal of development planning.

The SEA Directive must be understood in light of earlier Directive 85/337/EEC on the assessment of the effects of certain public and private projects on the environment (hereinafter 'the EIA Directive')[2] and as part of the ongoing environmental assessment agenda in development planning, which has led to a further recent

[1] Parliament and Council Directive 2001/42/EC of 27 June 2001 on the assessment of the effects of certain plans and programmes on the environment [2001] OJ L197/30.

[2] Council Directive 85/337/EEC of 27 June 1985 (now Directive 2011/92/EU as amended by 2014/52/EU) on the assessment of the effects of certain public and private projects on the environment [1985] OJ L175/40.

revision of the EIA Directive.[3] Major projects likely to have an impact on the environment are assessed under the EIA Directive, but that was always accepted to be limited in its scope; in particular, environmental impact assessment often takes place at a stage when options for significant change are limited. Decisions on the site of a project, or on the choice of alternatives, may already have been taken in the context of policies, plans or programmes set at a higher level, which project-level assessment is unable to influence.

The SEA Directive plugs this gap by requiring the environmental effects of a broad range of plans and programmes to be assessed at an earlier stage. In that regard, it is an important step forward in European environmental law. However, in a number of respects, the SEA Directive missed the opportunity to give full expression to the principle of strategic, holistic and integrated environmental assessment, apparent from the international context and historical background. This was largely due to the unwillingness of EU Member States to accept a broader remit to their obligation to assess policies, plans and programmes for their environmental effects. This chapter sets out the often tortuous negotiations that took place in developing and drafting the SEA Directive and explains the scope and effect of the resulting provisions of the Directive against that background.

Transatlantic Inspiration: NEPA 1969

The undoubted worldwide model for environmental assessment as a procedural tool in decision-making is the National Environmental Policy Act 1969 (NEPA 1969), a federal US instrument, sometimes described as an 'environmental Magna Carta',[4] signed on New Year's Day 1970. Virtually all international, regional, domestic and state or local measures on environmental impact assessment owe their inspiration to section 102 of NEPA. When the European Commission formally announced its intention of drawing up proposals on environmental impact assessment in its Second Environmental Action Programme of 1977, it acknowledged the debt owed to the US model.[5] It is therefore worth setting out the terms of section 102, which provides, so far as relevant:

> The Congress authorizes and directs that, to the fullest extent possible:
>
> …

[3] The current version of the EIA Directive is: European Parliament and Council Directive 2011/92/EU on the assessment of the effects of certain public and private projects on the environment [2012] OJ L28/1, as amended by European Parliament and Council Directive 2014/52/EU [2014] OJ L124/1.

[4] See, eg, Daniel R Mandelker, 'The National Environmental Policy Act: A Review of its Experience and Problems' (2010) 32 *Washington University Journal of Law & Policy* 293; see further Valerie Fogleman in Ch 3 of this volume.

[5] [1977] OJ C139/1.

(2) all agencies of the Federal Government shall—
  (A) utilize a systematic, interdisciplinary approach which will insure the integrated use of the natural and social sciences and the environmental design arts in planning and in decision making which may have an impact on man's environment;
  (B) identify and develop methods and procedures, in consultation with the Council on Environmental Quality established by title II of this Act, which will insure that presently unquantified environmental amenities and values may be given appropriate consideration in decision making along with economic and technical considerations;
  (C) include in every recommendation or report on proposals for legislation and other major Federal actions significantly affecting the quality of the human environment, a detailed statement by the responsible official on—
    (i) the environmental impact of the proposed action,
    (ii) any adverse environmental effects which cannot be avoided should the proposal be implemented,
    (iii) alternatives to the proposed action,
    (iv) the relationship between local short-term uses of man's environment and the maintenance and enhancement of long-term productivity, and
    (v) any irreversible and irretrievable commitments of resources which would be involved in the proposed action should it be implemented.

Prior to making any detailed statement, the responsible Federal official shall consult with and obtain the comments of any Federal agency which has jurisdiction by law or special expertise with respect to any environmental impact involved. Copies of such statement and the comments and views of the appropriate Federal, State, and local agencies, which are authorized to develop and enforce environmental standards, shall be made available to the President, the Council on Environmental Quality and to the public as provided by section 552 of title 5, United States Code, and shall accompany the proposal through the existing agency review processes.

Subsection (2)(C) further provides that copies of the statement must be circulated for comment to other federal agencies, to state and local governments and to the public. Further relevant provisions are set out in subsections (2)(D)–(H). Sub-section (2)(H), for example, provides that agencies must 'initiate and utilize ecological information in the planning and development of resource-oriented projects'.

Little distinction is made in the Act between different types of regulatory action. The requirement for an environmental statement applies to legislative recommendations or reports and to any other 'major Federal action' which may significantly affect environmental quality. It has a very broad scope.[6] Some guidance was given by the 1973 Guidelines on the Preparation of Environmental Impact

[6] This was confirmed in *Sierra Club v Marsh* 769 F 2d 868 (1st Cir 1985).

Statements, which included the following in the list of 'Types of actions covered by the Act':

(1) Recommendations or favourable reports relating to legislation, including requests for appropriations …
(2) New and continuing projects and program activities: directly undertaken by Federal agencies; or supported in whole or in part through Federal contracts, grants, subsidies, loans, or other forms of funding assistance … or involving a Federal lease, permit, license, certificate, or other entitlement for use.
(3) The making, modification, or establishment of regulations, rules, procedures, and policy.

The provisions of NEPA proved deceptively simple. They were the subject of a great volume of litigation in the US, both with regard to the scope and content of environment impact statements.[7]

The Environmental Impact Assessment Directive

The extensive litigation generated by NEPA led to understandable caution in the development of a European model of environmental assessment. The European Commission produced no fewer than 20 internal drafts before finally proposing a Directive in 1980.[8] Given that no express environmental Treaty basis for regulatory intervention existed at that time, the stated rationale for intervention was to avoid distortion of competition within the EEC by harmonising environmental controls.[9]

While the Commission's 1980 proposal was limited to the assessment of development projects, earlier drafts had covered a broader range of activities, including 'strategic'-level policies, plans and programmes.[10] There is no doubt that the intention of European policy-makers at the time was to bring forward further legislation to cover higher-level decisions and actions. The fourth recital to the proposed Directive indicated that EIA principles:

> [S]hould be introduced, with a view to improving good management of planning procedure governing private and public activities likely to have significant effects on the

[7] For examples of the volume of jurisprudence even in NEPA's early years, see Erica Dolgin and Thomas Guilbert (eds), *Federal Environmetal Law* (St Paul, West Publishing Co, 1974) 958.

[8] Nigel Haigh, *Manual of Environmental Policy: The EU and Britain* (Oxford, Elsevier, 1999) 11.2–5.

[9] For example, the ninth recital to the draft directive on environmental assessment (COM (80) 313 final) noted that the 'significant disparity between measures in force in the various Member States with regard to the assessment of environmental effects may create unfavourable competitive conditions and thereby directly affect the functioning of the common market'.

[10] See Stuart Bell, Donald McGillivray and Ole Pedersen, *Environmental Law*, 8th edn (Oxford, Oxford University Press, 2013) 488.

> environment: in particular, planning and decision-making with respect to individual projects, land use plans, regional development programmes, economic programmes including those in particular sectors.

This suggested that the EIA Directive, with its focus on the environmental impacts of individual projects, was but the first step in developing a programme of assessment for examining the likely environmental effects of public actions and social programmes.[11]

Towards the SEA Directive

Strategic environmental assessment (SEA) may therefore be seen as akin to EIA; it extends similar environmental assessment principles to earlier stages than those of individual projects, and potentially well beyond plans and programmes that are direct precursors to individual projects. As noted in Partidário and Clarke: 'In theory, SEA could be brought to bear on almost any action or non-action taken by a government, even national budgets and overall legislative agendas.'[12] The definition of SEA adopted by the European Environment Agency in its 1995 discussion paper is of more practical instruction:

> SEA is defined as environmental assessment of policies, plans and programmes, where a policy may … be considered as the inspiration and guidance for action, a plan as a set of co-ordinated and timed objectives for the implementation of the policy, and a programme as a set of projects in a particular area.[13]

Reference to the extension of environmental assessment beyond the project level was taken out of the EIA Directive, but remained a preoccupation of the Commission. The Fourth Environmental Action Programme of 1987 stated that EIA 'will also be extended, as rapidly as possible, to cover policies and policy statements; plans and their implementation; procedures; programmes (including both their overall objectives and their sub-elements), as well as individual projects'.[14]

Following the Single European Act of 1986, there was an explicit legal basis in the EC Treaty for Community policy on the environment. The general rolling out of environmental assessment was seen both as an essential application of the

[11] This stepwise approach to environmental assessment also suggests the different 'linear' (project-focused) and 'expansive' (relating to environmentally significant plans and programmes more broadly) approaches that might be taken to SEA: see further Elizabeth Fisher in Ch 8 of this volume.

[12] Maria Partidário and Ray Clarke (eds), *Perspectives on Strategic Environmental Assessment* (London, Lewis Publishers, 2000).

[13] European Environment Agency Discussion Paper, 'A Strategy for Integrated Environmental Assessment at the European Environment Agency' (Copenhagen, 1995).

[14] COM (86) 485 final; [1987] OJ C 328/1 [2.3.3].

principle of preventive action to avoid environmental damage and as a crucial tool for ensuring the integration of environmental requirements into the planning and execution of actions across the economic and social sectors.[15]

The reality of rolling out EIA to cover policies, plans and programmes proved tortuous. The Commission's initial proposals extended to policies as well as plans or programmes, but this approach was abandoned at the Edinburgh Summit in 1992 following a UK veto.[16] The momentum was recovered by the Commission's 1993 report on effectiveness of EIA, which concluded that:

> It is clear … that evaluation of the environmental impacts of certain projects is taking place too late in development planning and decision-making process. In effect this has the result of removing from consideration the possible adoption of alternatives both to the individual project under consideration as well as to its particular location or route (in the case of linear developments).[17]

This was followed up by a 1995 Commission study on the assessment of plans and programmes at the Member State level. What was required was to address the 'inherent limitation' in the EIA Directive by providing for the assessment of plans and programmes—a 'second phase' of the process that began in 1985 with the EIA Directive.[18] The Explanatory Memorandum to the 1996 proposal states baldly that: 'If the Community does not take any action the environmental assessment system established under Community law will remain incomplete.'[19]

What finally emerged from the further negotiations at the end of 1996 was nonetheless not a complete version; it contained a number of exemptions and only applied to formally adopted town and country planning documents.[20] This was transmitted to Council and Parliament on 25 March 1997. It was broadly welcomed by the Economic and Social Committee and the Committee of the Regions in their respective Opinions, although they expressed reservations about its lack of coordination and limited scope.[21] Parliament added its concerns after its first reading on 20 October 1998.[22] This led to an amended proposal from the

[15] Paragraph 1.2 of the Fourth Environmental Action Programme. The legal basis for EU legislation in environmental matters and for environmental integration is now found in arts 191(2) and 11 TFEU.

[16] See William Sheate, 'The EC Directive on Strategic Environmental Assessment: A Much-Needed Boost for Environmental Integration' (2003) 12(12) *European Environmental Law Review* 331, 333.

[17] Commission, 'Report from the Commission of the Implementation of Directive 85/337/EEC on the Assessment of the Effects of Certain Public and Private Projects on the Environment and Annexes for the Member States' COM (93) 28 final, April 1993, quoted in the SEA Directive Proposal (n 18) [1.12].

[18] Commission, 'Proposal for a Council Directive on the Assessment of the Effects of Certain Plans and Programmes on the Environment' COM (96) 511 final ('SEA Directive Proposal') [1.13].

[19] ibid [2.8].

[20] ibid.

[21] Opinion of the Economic and Social Committee on the 'Proposal for a Council Directive on the assessment of the effects of certain plans and programmes on the environment' [1997] OJ C287/101; Opinion of the Committee of the Regions on the 'Proposal for a Council Directive on the assessment of the effects of certain plans and programmes on the environment' [1998] OJ C64/63.

[22] Opinion of the European Parliament on the 'Proposal for a Council Directive on the assessment of the effects of certain plans and programmes on the environment' [1998] OJ C341/18.

Commission on 22 February 1999.[23] By December 1999, a Common Position had been reached by ministers from the then 15 Member States, and this was formally adopted by the Council on 30 March 2000.[24] The Common Position was communicated to Parliament, which proposed further amendments on 6 September 2000. Most of these amendments were accepted by the Commission, although it resisted what it perceived to be the removal of flexibility from the Common Position in a number of key areas.[25] Directive 2001/42/EC of the Parliament and Council was eventually promulgated on 27 June 2001. As noted by Tromans, the Directive's 'lengthy gestation period … is reflected in the complex drafting'.[26] Some of the more significant developments in the drafting process are discussed separately in the following sections.

The Legal Basis of the SEA Directive

An immediate issue was the legal basis for the SEA Directive. This was Article 130s(1) of the then EC Treaty (now Article 192(1) of the Treaty on the Functioning of the European Union (TFEU)), which required legislation to be passed by a qualified majority vote in Council and, following changes in the 1999 Treaty of Amsterdam, co-decision with Parliament. However, Article 130s(2) (now Article 192(2) TFEU) contained a derogation for measures affecting, among other things, town and country planning and land use. If the derogation applied, the unanimous approval of the Council would have been necessary, effectively giving the UK (or any other Member State) a veto on the proposal. However, the Commission and a majority of Member States concluded that the SEA Directive was concerned with the provision of information about environmental impacts rather than with town and country planning per se. The Explanatory Memorandum described the proposal as being a means of 'awareness raising of the authorities having a decisional power'.[27] At its first reading, Parliament rejected a proposal to amend the legal basis for the Directive.[28]

However, the Committee of the Regions called upon the Commission to reconsider whether Article 130s(1) was the appropriate legal basis given the 'broader picture' of social and economic issues engaged.[29] It may in fact have been justifiable

[23] COM (1999) 73 final.

[24] Common Position 25/2000/EC of 30 March 2000 adopted by the Council, with a view to adopting a Directive of the European Parliament and of the Council on the assessment of the effects of certain plans and programmes on the environment [2000] OJ C137/11 (hereinafter 'Common Position').

[25] COM (2000) 636 final. Two particular areas of disagreement were the ability for Member States to screen plans and programmes and the interaction with the EIA Directive, discussed below at nn 64–69 and in the accompanying text.

[26] Stephen Tromans, *Environmental Impact Assessment*, 2nd edn (London, Bloomsbury, 2002) 319.

[27] SEA Directive Proposal (n 18) [4.2].

[28] See the discussion in Haigh (n 8) 11.2–5.

[29] Opinion of the Committee of the Regions (n 21) [1.3].

to promote the SEA Directive on an economic market basis, as was done for the EIA Directive. The Explanatory Memorandum noted that 'in defining clearly … the conditions in which economic activities may be undertaken in the framework of the plan or the programme security will be increased and delays and additional costs at project level will be reduced'.[30]

The Nature and Objective of SEA

As Maine memorably observed in the context of the common law: 'So great is the ascendancy of the Law of Actions in the infancy of Courts of Justice, that substantive law has at first the look of being gradually secreted in the interstices of procedure.'[31] Procedure is often the very substance of environmental law and nowhere is this more true than in the area of environmental assessment.

Article 1 of the 1996 proposal stated that the objective of the Directive was 'to provide for a high level of protection of the environment by ensuring that an environmental assessment is carried out of certain plans and programmes and that the results of the assessment are taken into account during the preparation and adoption of such plans and programmes'. That essential objective—to 'plug the gap' in environmental protection—was uncontroversial and did not change during negotiations, although it was enhanced by reference to the principles of integration and sustainable development, first found in the 1996 recitals.[32]

It was never in doubt that the proposal was purely procedural, as is now explained in Recital (9). This reflected the US model. It was also important for the acceptability of the measure to Member States: the Explanatory Memorandum 'underlined that this Proposal is of a procedural nature' and that it does not allot any binding effect to a final decision.[33] As noted above, this was also important for justifying its legal basis as an environmental measure, but not one affecting (in a substantive way) land use or planning.

Interestingly, at its first reading, Parliament proposed a new Article 4b(2), namely that: 'Urban development plans should prohibit the construction of dwellings, campsite, farms and items of infrastructure in areas which are liable to flooding.'[34] The amendment, which would have given the SEA Directive a substantive edge, was not taken forward.

[30] SEA Directive Proposal (n 18) [1.11].

[31] Sir Henry Sumner Maine, *On Early Law and Custom* (London, John Murray, 1890) 389.

[32] The objective of the Directive is now further explained in the SEA Directive, recitals (4), (5) and (6).

[33] SEA Directive Proposal (n 18) [4.2].

[34] Opinion of the European Parliament (n 22).

The Scope of the SEA Directive: Plans and Programmes

The scope of the Directive is essentially set by the meaning of 'plans and programmes' in Article 2 of the SEA Directive and the assessment requirements in Article 3. However, as discussed further by Valerie Fogleman in Chapter 3 of this volume, these provisions essentially present a convoluted picture. This was caused by the tension between the competing desires to have an integrated and holistic mechanism of environmental assessment and to define in advance exactly what plans and programmes required such assessment. Those tensions manifest themselves in several different ways.

Subject Matter of Plans and Programmes

There was no question after 1992 of the SEA Directive applying to policies. The UK's influence in the 1996 proposal is also apparent in that it was restricted to 'town and country planning' plans and programmes, and modifications to them.[35] Two points may be noted in particular. First, while this fitted with the UK's system of spatial planning and development control, it would have been of far less effect in Member States where development is planned either more informally or from a more centralised and overarching perspective. The definition was stated to include plans in sectors such as transport, energy and tourism, yet, even in the UK, it would not have affected documents such as the Northern Ireland Programme for Government 2008–11, which was held to require SEA by Stephens J in the recent case on the A5 dual carriage link.[36] Second, it was perceived not to trespass on moves that had been taken at domestic level in the UK to require environmental appraisals of development plans.[37]

The Committee of the Regions criticised the limitation of the draft document to plans and programmes that referred specifically (or perhaps exclusively) to land use. It considered that plans and programmes that relate to 'any type of physical or spatial development or provision' should be subject to SEA.[38] Parliament proposed opening up the definition in Article 2 to all plans and programmes 'affecting the terrestrial and marine environment'.[39] In subsequent versions of the Directive, no general qualification in the definition of plans and programmes was maintained.

[35] ibid, art 2(a)(i).

[36] *Re Alternative A5 Alliance's Application for Judicial Review* [2013] NIQB 30; [2014] NI 96, 56. For Northern Ireland's experience of the SEA Directive, see further William Orbinson in Ch 15 of this volume.

[37] See, eg, Department of the Environment, *This Common Inheritance* (Cmd 1200, 1990); *Planning Policy Guidance 12: Development Plans* (London, HMSO, 1992) (emphasising the sustainability appraisals of plans); Department of the Environment, *Environmental Appraisal of Development Plans: A Good Practice Guide* (1993).

[38] Opinion of the Committee of the Regions (n 21) [4.2].

[39] Opinion of the European Parliament (n 22) (proposed amendment to art 2(a)(i)).

Instead, the method of adoption of plan or programme became relevant to how the SEA provisions applied, as is discussed further below. However, the Common Position included specific exemptions for three types of plans and programmes: (i) those whose sole purpose is to serve national defence or civil emergency; (ii) financial or budget plans and programmes; and (iii) plans and programmes co-financed under Council Regulations on the application of the EC Structural Funds or support for rural development.[40] These exceptions remain.

However, the omission of plans and programmes promoted by Community funds was widely criticised. In its final Opinion of 1999, the Committee of the Regions was disappointed: 'Although the Structural Fund guidelines do contain environmental criteria, these are not as rigorous as full environmental assessment and there is currently no requirement for public consultation.'[41] Parliament proposed an addition to the definition in Article 2 whereby all plans and programmes 'funded by the European Union' would require SEA.[42] A compromise was reached. The exemption for EC-funded measures was time limited. Only those brought forward under the 2000–06 or 2000–07 programming periods would avoid potential SEA.[43] The special treatment was in any event anomalous and it is hard to see why benefiting from European funding should avoid the application of European law. The Commission's statement on the Common Position stressed that 'there is no justification for legally exempting the EU Structural Funds from the scope of this Directive'.[44]

Method of Adoption of Plans and Programmes

The second way in which it was sought to cut down the range of plans and programmes caught by SEA was by restricting the application of the Directive to those that had been formally adopted. The 1996 proposal only applied to plans and programmes if they were 'subject to preparation and adoption by a competent authority or … prepared by a competent authority for adoption by a legislative act'.[45] This avoided SEA applying to informal documents prepared, for example,

[40] Common Position (n 24) art 3(8).

[41] Opinion of the Committee of the Regions on the amended proposal for Council Directive on assessment of the effects of certain plans and programmes on the environment [1999] OJ C374/9.

[42] Position of the European Parliament, adopted at second reading with a view to the adoption of European Parliament and Council Directive 2000/…./EC on the assessment of the effects of certain plans and programmes on the environment (1996/0304(COD) (6 September 2000) 5.

[43] See SEA Directive, art 3(9).

[44] Commission, 'Communication to the European Parliament concerning the Common Position of the Council on the amended Proposal for a European Parliament and Council Directive on the assessment of the effects of certain plans and programmes on the environment' SEC (2000) 568 final.

[45] SEA Directive Proposal (n 18) art 2(a)(i).

by consortia. It was also meant drawing a line between plans and programmes and the legislative procedure.

Again, the limitation was subject to criticism. The Committee of the Regions considered that:

> Many plans and programmes with potentially fundamental effects upon the environment are formulated and promulgated by the relevant governments or authorities or by agencies at arm's length from these, without the existence of a prescribed framework of the degree of formality envisaged in Article 2(a)(i).[46]

In hindsight, though, the articulation of a formal procedure in the 1996 proposal seems relatively straightforward. The Common Position both retained the requirement of preparation and adoption by an authority and added a further stipulation that plans and programmes be 'required by legislative, regulatory or administrative provisions', language that is retained in Article 2(a) of the SEA Directive.

The background to the new stipulation was discussed by Advocate General Kokott in *Inter-Environnement Bruxelles ASBL v Gouvernement de la Région de Bruxelles-Capitale* as follows:

> Neither the original Commission proposal nor an amended version of it included the condition that the plans and programmes covered must be required by law. After the proposal proved unsuccessful in this regard, the Commission, supported by Belgium and Denmark, proposed that the directive should at least apply to plans and programmes 'which are provided for in legislation or based on regulatory or administrative provisions'. The legislature did not take up those proposals either, however.
>
> Instead, the Council explained the rules that were eventually adopted, to which the Parliament did not object, in a common position which stated, including in the Italian version, that only plans and programmes that are required ('prescritti') are covered. Consequently, the Italian version of the directive must also be construed as meaning that it covers only plans or projects which are based on a legal obligation.
>
> In the light of the wording of the second indent of Article 2(a) of the SEA Directive and its drafting history, neither the general objective of European environmental policy, that is to say a high level of protection (Article 3(3) TEU, Article 37 of the Charter of Fundamental Rights of the European Union and Article 191(2) TFEU), nor the specific objective pursued by the SEA Directive, that is to say the environmental assessment of plans and programmes which are likely to have a significant effect on the environment (Article 1), leads to any other interpretation. It is true that plans and programmes which are not based on a legal obligation may also have significant effects on the environment. Indeed, their effects may be even more significant than those of compulsory plans. None the less, the legislature clearly did not intend such measures to require an environmental assessment.[47]

[46] Opinion of the Committee of the Regions (n 21) [4.4].

[47] Case C-567/10 *Inter-Environnement Bruxelles ASBL v Gouvernement de la Région de Bruxelles-Capitale*, Opinion of AG Kokott (17 November 2011) [18]–[20]. See further Elizabeth Fisher in Ch 8 of this volume.

The Court of Justice disagreed with this analysis, holding memorably that 'required' must in fact mean 'plans and programmes whose adoption is regulated by national legislative or regulatory provisions',[48] because it would have the effect of 'appreciably restricting the directive's scope' and 'would compromise [its] practical effect of the directive, having regard to its objective, which consists in providing for a high level of protection of the environment'.[49] However, it may be noted that the objective of the Directive had not changed appreciably between 1996 and 2001.

In *R (HS2 Action Alliance Ltd) v Secretary of State for Transport*, the UK Supreme Court preferred the Advocate General's 'impeccable analysis'[50] and considered that 'required' meant 'based on a legal obligation'[51] (although it did not refer the question for the Court of Justice's reconsideration as its resolution was not necessary to dispose of the case before it).

The practical effect of these high judicial decisions is that it is the third restriction on the scope of plans and programmes that require SEA—that they 'set the framework' for future project level consent—that has become most important.

Effect of Plans and Programmes

Whether or not a plan or programme sets a framework for subsequent decisions is an attractive way of defining measures requiring SEA as it is related to the actual likely consequences of the document. The 1996 proposal did not include the criterion, although it may have been thought that 'town and country planning' documents would normally have that effect. It was Parliament that first proposed restricting the definition of plans and programmes to those, inter alia, 'which set a general or sectoral framework for establishing subsequent land-use, resource-use or development consents which involve directly or indirectly the future implementation of projects within the meaning of Directive 85/337/EEC'.[52] This would have been in addition to plans and programmes 'which contain provisions on the nature, size, location or operating conditions of projects'. This relatively broad scope was included in the Commission's amended proposal of March 1999.[53]

Following further consideration, the Common Position moved the text from Article 2 (Definitions) to Article 3 (Scope), where a further distinction was made. Plans and programmes in the fields of agriculture, forestry, fisheries, energy and a number of other sectors which 'set the framework' for the consent of projects listed in the EIA Directive required *mandatory* SEA. Those that operated to determine 'the use of small areas at local level' only required SEA if Member States

[48] Case C-567/10 *Inter-Environnement Bruxelles ASBL* (CJEU, 22 March 2012) [31].
[49] ibid [30].
[50] *R (HS2 Action Alliance Ltd) v Secretary of State for Transport* [2014] UKSC 3 [177].
[51] ibid [176].
[52] Opinion of the European Parliament (n 21) (proposed amendment to art 2(a)(i)).
[53] See n 17.

considered, on a case-by-case basis, that they were likely to have significant effects—a process of screening. Screening also applied to all other plans and programmes which 'set the framework for future development consent of projects'—that is, where the plan or programmes fell without the listed sectors or the projects without the EIA Directive Annexes. The latter provision, at Article 3(4) of both the Common Position and the SEA Directive, has been described as a 'mopping-up clause'.[54] The Commission Communication accompanying the Common Position explains the rationale for the distinction:

> The scope of the application of the future Directive formed the key issue of the negotiations. In its amended proposal, the Commission, responding also to a request of the European Parliament, went for a rather broad scope for which an environmental assessment was mandatory for all plans and programmes … Only as regards minor modifications and certain plans and programmes at local level Member States were given the possibility of determining for themselves whether an environmental assessment was necessary or not. The result achieved by the Common Position is quite different. The Common Position clearly splits the scope of application into mandatory and non-mandatory parts resulting in a limitation of the plans and programmes covered.[55]

The same distinction was carried through to the SEA Directive. It may be rare that a plan or programme will set the framework for as yet undefined development, yet not be likely to have significant environmental effects, especially as 'likely' should probably (or at least could arguably) be understood in accordance with *Waddenzee* as meaning a mere possibility or risk.[56] However, a development plan document that, for example, sets criteria for minor residential extensions outside of conservation areas will undoubtedly 'set the framework' for development, but may on no real basis be likely to have a significant environmental impact.

A safeguard is provided in Article 3(7) whereby Member States must make public their conclusions for not requiring environmental assessment, including reasons. This amounts to a screening process, familiar at the project level for EIA development. However, unlike for EIA, there is little current practice, in the UK at least, of screening to determine whether or not SEA is required of plans or programmes.

Timing of Plans and Programmes

The 1996 proposal envisaged implementation by 31 December 1999 and would have applied to all plans and programmes adopted after that date. This led to a concern about plans and programmes that were in the pipeline before the Directive

[54] Joined Cases C-105/09 and C-110/09 *Terre Wallonne ASBL and Inter-Environnement Wallonie ASBL v Région Wallonne* [2010] ECR I-5611, Opinion of AG Kokott [103].

[55] Commission Communication (n 44).

[56] Case C-127/02 *Landelijke Vereniging tot Behoud van de Waddenzee v Staatssecretaris van Landbouw, Natuurbeheer en Visserij* [2004] ECR I-7405.

came into force and would not have complied with its provisions. The Common Position addressed this by excluding SEA for plans and programmes whose 'first formal preparatory act' occurred before the date for transposition. At its second reading, Parliament sought to cut down the scope of the exclusion by reinstating the requirement for SEA for plans and programmes begun before the transposition date but adopted or submitted for adoption more than 12 months after. That amendment was only partially accepted. Article 13 of the final Directive represents a compromise whereby the obligation to carry out SEA only applies to plans and programmes for which the first formal preparatory act was after 21 July 2004 (the date for transposition) provided that they were adopted or submitted to the legislative procedure no more than 24 months after then (so by 21 July 2006). However, a pipeline measure may still be adopted without SEA after 21 July 2006 if Member States 'decide on a case by case basis that this is not feasible [to submit it to SEA] and inform the public of their decision'. In a period of 24 months, it would normally be feasible to comply with the basic SEA procedure.

Relationship with the Habitats Directive

There had always been greater impetus and consensus in relation to the strategic assessment of measures likely to affect recognised biodiversity interests. As long ago as 1979, the preamble to the Berne Convention on the conservation of European wildlife and natural habitats recognised that the conservation of wild flora and fauna 'should be taken into consideration by the governments in their national goals and programmes'. Related initiatives were brought forward under the Ramsar Convention on wetlands of international importance[57] and the Bonn Convention on the conservation of migratory species.[58]

The 1992 UN Convention on Biological Diversity required Contracting Parties to integrate the principles of conservation and sustainable use of biological diversity into relevant plans, programmes and policies.[59] Article 14 covered impact assessment and required parties, among other things, to: 'Introduce appropriate arrangements to ensure that the environmental consequences of its programmes and policies that are likely to have significant adverse impacts on biological

[57] See, eg, 8th Meeting of the Conference of the Contracting Parties to the Convention on Wetlands (Ramsar, Iran, 1971), 'Resolution VIII.9: Guidelines for Incorporating Biodiversity-Related Issues into Environmental Impact Assessment Legislation and/or Processes and in Strategic Environmental Assessment' (2002, Valencia, Spain).

[58] 7th Meeting of the Conference of the Parties to the Convention on the Conservation of Migratory Species of Wild Animals, 'Resolution 7.2: Impact Assessment and Migratory Species' (2002, Bonn, Germany).

[59] Convention on Biological Diversity (Rio de Janeiro, 5 June 1992) 1760 UNTS 79, entered into force 29 December 1993, art 6(b).

diversity are duly taken into account.' These provisions were strengthened by a number of decisions of the Conference of the Parties on impact assessment.[60]

It was therefore logical that Article 6(3) of Directive 92/43/EEC on the conservation of natural habitats and of wild fauna and flora (hereinafter 'the Habitats Directive') required that appropriate assessment be undertaken of any 'plan or project' likely to have a significant effect on a European nature conservation site, without qualification or distinction.[61] For some reason, 'programmes' were not covered, although many programmes would also be plans, and the Court of Justice would be likely to adopt a purposive approach in the event of any doubt.

SEA represents an additional and potentially overlapping assessment tool to the Habitats Directive. The Commission's 1996 proposal excluded conservation management plans adopted pursuant to Article 6(1) of the Habitats Directive from SEA, but did not otherwise refer to the Habitats Directive. Following calls for procedural simplification, a recital was added to the Common Position to the effect that Member States could provide for a joint procedure of appropriate assessment and SEA where both are required.[62] At the same time, it was made clear that SEA was mandatory wherever a plan or programme had been determined to require appropriate assessment under Article 6 or 7 of the Habitats Directive.[63] Appropriate assessment is therefore fortified by the detailed procedural requirements of SEA when plans or programmes are at issue.

Relationship with the EIA Directive

More contentious was the relationship between SEA and EIA. Sheate comments that given the similarities between the two directives:

> [They] could be strengthened by one piece of consolidated legislation. However, politically, this was seen as too great a leap to be achieved at once, and the Commission was at pains to keep the draft SEA Directive entirely separate from amendments to the project EIA Directive during the 1990s.[64]

The Explanatory Memorandum to the 1996 proposal envisaged a relatively clean interaction between SEA and EIA: SEA could clarify the environmental conditions

[60] 4th Ordinary Meeting of the Conference of the Parties to the Convention on Biological Diversity, 'Decision IV/10: Measures for Implementing the Convention on Biological Diversity' (1998, Bratislava, Slovakia); Fifth Ordinary Meeting of the Conference of the Parties to the Convention on Biological Diversity, 'Decision V/18: Impact Assessment, Liability and Redress' (2000, Nairobi, Kenya).

[61] Council Directive 92/43/EEC on the conservation of natural habitats and of wild fauna and flora [1992] OJ L206/7.

[62] See now SEA Directive, recital 19.

[63] ibid, art 3(2)(b).

[64] Sheate (n 16) 333.

for project consent, so that EIA would 'be easier and in some cases maybe even unnecessary'.[65] That was unduly optimistic.

The Committee of the Regions and the Economic and Social Committee were both concerned about the overlap and the need to avoid duplication. Parliament went even further. One of the amendments proposed by Parliament in 1998 was that: 'Where a Member State provides that a plan or programme is to be drawn up for a project and that the procedure for drawing up this plan or programme already requires an environmental impact assessment to be carried out pursuant to Directive 85/337/EEC, the present Directive shall not be applicable.'[66] When that amendment was rejected, Parliament tried again in 2000, suggesting that Article 4(3) be amended to allow Member States to 'define the level at which' assessment will take place where plans and programmes form part of a hierarchy—that is, to choose whether environmental assessment be carried out at a plan or project level. This was firmly rejected by the Commission, which stated that it would 'strongly reduce the scope of the Directive and go against its objectives'.[67]

Instead of this, what came forward are rather weaker provisions on the tiering of assessments.[68] Article 5(2a) of the Commission's 1999 version provided that information in the environmental statement could 'take into account' the extent to which matters were more appropriately addressed at different stages of the decision-making process. The concern is reiterated throughout the subsequent proposals: duplication should, where appropriate, be avoided.[69] This applies both to the relationship between plans and projects and to different stages of the plan or programme process. The reality is that it will often not be 'appropriate' for strategic assessments to defer to project specific assessments or vice versa. That would risk creating gaps in the assessment and undermining the purpose of the SEA Directive. However, the text does leave a certain amount of discretion to Member State authorities as to how to integrate the different levels of assessment.[70]

Environmental Report

Unlike the EIA Directive, the 1996 proposal for SEA incorporated a definition of 'environmental assessment'. This was principally the preparation of an

65 SEA Directive Proposal (n 17) para 1.14.

66 Opinion of the European Parliament (n 21) (proposing a new art 4a).

67 Commission Opinion (n 25) 5.

68 The relationship between with the EIA Directive was considered in the Report from the Commission to the Council, the European Parliament, the European Economic and Social Committee and the Committee of the Regions on the application and effectiveness of the Directive on Strategic Environmental Assessment (Directive 2001/42/EC) COM(2009) 469 FINAL-September 2009, as to which see further Gregory Jones in Ch 2 of this volume.

69 See SEA Directive, recitals 9 and 19, arts 4(3), 5(2) and 11(2).

70 For the avoidance of any doubt, art 11(1) of the final Directive states that SEA 'shall be without prejudice to any requirements under Directive 85/337/EEC and to any other Community law requirements'.

environmental statement (as well as consultation upon it). Sheate comments that this was an 'important departure from the EIA Directive, where the Commission and Member States were at pains to avoid the requirement for a single document', which was in light of the litigious experience in the US.[71] The 1996 proposal also included express provisions for defining the scope of the environmental statement, again not something found within the EIA Directive, and an indicative Annex of information to be included. These were largely uncontroversial parts of the proposal, subject to various tweaks and additions, but (with the exception of alternatives, considered below) not fundamentally altered. The term 'environmental statement' was substituted with 'environmental report' in the Common Position, perhaps to avoid confusion with environmental statements produced to comply with the information requirements of EIA.

Another interesting departure from the EIA Directive is the inclusion of quality control and monitoring provisions. Quality control was a late amendment proposed by Parliament in 2000. Article 12(2) of the SEA Directive provides that: 'Member States shall ensure that environmental reports are of a sufficient quality to meet the requirements of this Directive and shall communicate to the Commission any measure they take concerning the quality of these reports.' The mechanism for quality control is left open and it is not clear how or when the obligation in Article 12(2) may be enforced. Parliament's additional stipulation that Member States 'prevent decisions being taken on the basis of an environmental report which does not comply with these requirements' was removed from the final version of the Directive.[72] To date, there has been no litigation focusing specifically upon this aspect.

Mandatory Consideration of Alternatives

Where a private developer promotes a particular development project, there is often limited scope for him seriously to consider alternative options. As noted in the Foreword to the Commission's Implementation Guidance, the assessment of projects often took place where the scope for making changes was limited: 'Decisions on the site of a project, or on the choice of alternatives, may have already been taken in the context of plans for a whole sector or geographical area.'[73] This had the potential to render EIA (a purely procedural exercise) meaningless. At a strategic level, greater scope for considering alternatives arises. Indeed, it has been suggested that one way of testing whether a plan or programme sets the

[71] Sheate (n 16) 344.

[72] Position of the European Parliament (n 42) 11.

[73] Commission, 'Guidance on the Implementation of Directive 2001/42/EC on the Assessment of the Effects of Certain Plans and Programmes on the Environment' (2003) (hereinafter 'Implementation Guidance') 1. The case law on 'alternatives' for the purposes of the SEA Directive has developed at a quick speed, as noted by David Elvin in Ch 6 of this volume.

framework for future development consent 'is to ask if it closes alternative options down'.[74] If this is the effect of a plan or programme, it should be assessed against those alternatives.

The Explanatory Memorandum to the 1996 proposal stated that: 'One particular benefit of bringing plans and programmes within the assessment system is that it will allow the issue of alternatives ... to be properly assessed. The issue of alternatives can only be properly assessed at the plan and programme level.'[75] The information a developer was then required to supply under the EIA Directive included: 'Where appropriate, an outline of the main alternatives studied ... and an indication of the main reasons for his choice.'[76] This was marginally strengthened in 1997 by its inclusion in Article 5(3) and the removal of the proviso 'where appropriate',[77] and this has been further strengthened in the most recent revision of the EIA Directive, which requires developers to include a description of 'reasonable alternatives ... which are relevant to the project and its specific characteristics' within environmental statements.[78]

The 1996 proposal on SEA was based upon the EIA text and, as with the 1985 EIA Directive, the only reference to alternatives was in the Annex of information to be included in environmental statements. Paragraph (f) of the Annex stipulated 'any alternative ways of achieving the objectives of the plan or programme which have been considered during its preparation (such as alternatives types of development or alternative locations for development) and the reasons for not adopting these alternatives'.[79] The failure to express the consideration of alternatives as a mandatory requirement appears out of step with the policy in the Explanatory Memorandum.

The drafting process provided the opportunity to enhance the requirement. Parliament's first opinion was primarily concerned with one particular alternative: the 'zero-option' that it suggested be considered in every case.[80] This was accepted, although it was rationalised and broadened in the Commission's 1999 draft so that the environmental statement included 'a description of the 'zero-option' and reasonable alternatives'. By the time of the Common Position, the requirement to identify, describe and evaluate 'reasonable alternatives' had found its way into Article 5(1) itself. The Common Position introduced at Article 5(1) the need to

[74] See Gregory Jones, Ned Westaway and Roger Watts, 'Why Central Craigavon was Wrongly Decided (and Other Problems with the Incorporation of the Strategic Environmental Assessment Directive into Domestic Law)' (2013) *Journal of Planning & Environment Law* 1074.

[75] SEA Directive Proposal (n 18) [1.8].

[76] EIA Directive, Annex III(2).

[77] European Parliament and Council Directive 2011/92/EU on the assessment of the effects of certain public and private projects on the environment [2012] OJ L28/1, art 5(3)(d).

[78] EIA Directive, as amended, art 5(1)(d).

[79] SEA Directive Proposal (n 18) 23.

[80] Parliament additionally proposed that there be 'a description of the "do-minimum" [alternative] and the best practical options': see n 22.

have regard to 'reasonable alternatives' and required an outline of the reasons for selecting those alternatives to be included in the environmental statement.[81]

The more extensive treatment of alternatives under the SEA process is a stand-out feature of the finalised SEA Directive. It is mandatory and onerous—'reasonable alternatives' must be considered. As noted in the Commission's 2003 Implementation Guide: 'The essential thing is that the likely significant effect of the plan or programme and the alternatives are identified, described and evaluated in a comparable way.'[82] In the UK, it has driven much of the litigation on SEA to date.[83]

Public Consultation and the Aarhus Convention

The genesis of SEA occurred prior to the development of an environmental justice agenda in Europe. By 1998, however, the UNECE Convention on Access to Information, Public Participation in Decision-Making and Access to Justice in Environmental Matters (hereinafter the Aarhus Convention) had been adopted. It entered into force on 30 October 2001 and was ratified by the EU on 17 February 2005. The Aarhus Convention set out minimum standards of public access to information about, and participation in, decision-making in relation to environmental matters. The definition of 'environmental information' in the Aarhus Convention includes 'administrative measures, environmental agreements, policies, legislation, plans and programmes' likely to affect the environment.[84] Significantly, Article 7 of the Aarhus Convention extended the requirement on parties to make arrangements for public participation to 'the preparation of plans and programmes relating to the environment'.

The 1996 SEA Directive proposal contained only basic provisions on public participation. An early call was made by the Economic and Social Committee in 1997 for 'greater precision in defining procedures and means of access, in order to ensure that all interested parties are properly consulted and are given time to prepare their comments'.[85] While specific amendments were brought forward to ensure that the EIA Directive aligned with the obligations in the Aarhus

[81] Common Position (n 24) Annex I(h).

[82] Implementation Guide (n 73) [5.12].

[83] eg, *HS2* (n 50) [44]–[45]; *Heard v Broadland District Council* [2012] EWHC 344 (Admin); [2012] Env LR 23. See also David Elvin in Ch 6 of this volume.

[84] Convention on Access to Information, Public Participation in Decision-Making and Access to Justice in Environmental Matters (Aarhus, 28 June 1998) 2161 UNTS 447; 38 ILM 517 (1999), in force 30 October 2001, art 2(3)(b). See also the terms of the requirements to disseminate such information in arts 5(3)(c) and 5(5)(a).

[85] Opinion of the Economic and Social Committee (n 21) [2.15].

Convention,[86] the intention with SEA was to draft it so that no such amendment was needed. By the time of the Common Position, substantial changes had been made to the consultation provisions so that the Commission could communicate to Parliament that the requirements were intended to be 'aligned with and transpose obligations coming from the second pillar [public participation] of the Aarhus-Convention'.[87]

Nevertheless, important parts of the consultation requirements in the SEA Directive had been subject to negotiation. First, Parliament had intervened to ensure that the 'public' was more broadly defined than in the initial proposal, which would have given Member States complete discretion as to the designation of the public to be consulted, depending on the stage of the decision-making process.[88] The definition of the public in Article 2(d) is now identical to that found in the Aarhus Convention and includes non-governmental organisations. Second, Parliament sought to bolster the procedural protections so that the public (together with statutory consultees) be given 'a reasonable amount of time' for consultation.[89] Article 6(2) now provides that the public 'be given an early and effective opportunity … to express their opinion on the draft plan or programme'. This chimes with Article 6(2) and (more importantly) with Article 6(4) of the Aarhus Convention.

It is open to question whether the SEA Directive represents a full transposition of Article 7 of the Aarhus Convention. Article 7 refers to plans and programmes generally, without the qualifications found in the Directive's definition and scope. More significantly, the SEA Directive does not reflect Article 9(2) of the Aarhus Convention, which provides for members of the public to challenge the substantive and procedural legality of any decision, act or omission subject to the provisions of Article 6 of that convention.

In fact, *restricting* the ability of the public to challenge plans and programmes appears to have been an early ambition of the SEA Directive's drafters. A striking feature of the 1996 proposal was Article 10(3), which provided as follows: 'No provision of this Directive shall give rise to a right to seek judicial review in respect of a legislative act by which a plan or programme has been adopted.'[90] The exclusory provision was not taken forward. However, while specific amendments were made to establish access for concerned members of the public to an independent review procedure of acts or omissions subject to the public participation provi-

[86] Parliament and Council Directive 2003/35/EC providing for public participation in respect of the drawing up of certain plans and programmes relating to the environment and amending with regard to public participation and access to justice Council Directives 85/337/EEC and 96/61/EC [2003] OJ L156/17.

[87] Commission Communication (n 44).

[88] Opinion of the European Parliament (n 21); Parliament's proposed amendment to art 6(4) was that the public 'directly or indirectly concerned by a plan or programme'.

[89] ibid (proposed amendment to art 6(2)).

[90] SEA Directive Proposal (n 18) 21.

sions of the EIA Directive,[91] this is noticeably lacking for SEA. This appears to be an omission: there should be express provision within the SEA Directive along the lines of Article 11 of the consolidated EIA Directive. Article 7 of the Aarhus Convention on public participation in strategic decision-making expressly applies to Article 6(3), (4) and (8), so Article 9(2) on access to justice must arguably at least have some direct application to strategic assessment. At present, there appears to be a gap in the compliance of the SEA Directive with the Aarhus Convention.[92]

International and Comparative Context

The international and comparative context is inescapable when considering both EIA and SEA. This chapter has already mentioned NEPA in the US, the UNECE Aarhus Convention, the UN Convention on Biological Diversity and other international nature conservation conventions. However, these represent only a fraction of a much broader international perspective relevant to the SEA Directive. The centrality of SEA to recent environmental protection measures is also apparent from some of the key international sources of environmental law and policy. Thus, paragraph 90 of the Overview to the Brundtland Report of 1987 states that: 'Governments must begin now to make the key national, economic, and sectoral agencies directly responsible and accountable for ensuring that their policies, programmes, and budgets support development that is economically and ecologically sustainable.'[93] Similarly, principle 17 of the 1992 Rio Declaration is that: 'Environmental impact assessment, as a national instrument, shall be undertaken for proposed activities that are likely to have a significant adverse impact on the environment and are subject to a decision of a competent national authority.'[94]

Environmental assessment was also included as a standard mechanism in many of the key international treaties. The 1982 UN Convention on the Law of the Sea required Member States to assess the potential effects of 'planned activities under their jurisdiction' that may cause pollution or significant change to the marine environment.[95] The 1992 UN Framework Convention on Climate Change

[91] See now EIA Directive, art 11.

[92] In *HS2*, Lord Carnwath considered the discrepancy and concluded that: 'The SEA Directive must be interpreted on its own terms. If this falls short of full compliance with the Aarhus Convention, it does not invalidate the Directive so far as it goes. It simply means that a possible breach of the Convention may have to be considered as a separate and additional issue. In the present case the point is academic because no such breach is alleged': *HS2* (n 50) [52].

[93] Report of the UN World Commission on Environment and Development, 'Our Common Future' (Brundtland, 1987).

[94] United Nations Rio Declaration on Environment and Development (13 June 1992), 31 ILM 874 (1992).

[95] United Nations Convention on the Law of the Sea (Montego Bay, 10 December 1982) 1833 UNTS 3, 21 ILM 1261 (1982), entered into force 16 November 1994, art 206.

required Member States to: 'Take climate change considerations into account, to the extent feasible, in their relevant social, economic and environmental policies and actions.'[96]

There are countless other examples. What is instructive is the broad scope of the assessment in each instance: the goal is to assess the environmental impacts of a wide range of actions, including policies. The international context does not provide a justification for the narrow definitions and pettifogging distinctions encountered in the SEA Directive. The Commission's original idea, as discussed above was more in tune with the essence of how SEA is understood internationally.

A harmful 'reverse influence' of the SEA Directive on international law in this respect can be seen in the post-2001 negotiations on the Kiev Protocol on Strategic Environmental Assessment (one of the few formal uses of that phrase) to the Espoo Convention on EIA in a transboundary context. Negotiations on the Protocol concluded in January 2003 and an extraordinary meeting of the Parties to the Espoo Convention adopted the Protocol on 21 May 2003 in Kiev.[97] Thirty-six states (including the UK) as well as the EU have signed the Protocol, and it entered into force on 10 July 2010. As noted by De Mulder, the start of negotiations was characterised by 'major scepticism' from the European group, who were keen to ensure that it did not go beyond the contents of the SEA Directive.[98] The approach succeeded. The definition of plans and programmes is identical to that in the SEA Directive. The provisions on screening and transboundary assessment also show their debt to the EU model. The SEA Directive therefore appears to have stifled the growth of the international thinking from which it is derived.

Conclusion

EIA was never intended to be the end point for EU legislative intervention on environmental assessment. Broader and strategic level assessment was seen as a necessary part of the agenda. The comparative and historical context shows that agenda to be much wider than the proposal that was eventually brought forward in the SEA Directive. Environmental assessment only works if it is operative at all levels. The rationale behind SEA is supported by the Court of Justice's radically purposive interpretation in *Inter-Environnement Bruxelles*, where it sought in effect to overcome one of the tensions in the incomplete regime that had so far been established.

[96] United Nations Framework Convention on Climate Change (New York, 9 May 1992) 1771 UNTS 107, 31 ILM 849 (1992), entered into force 21 March 1994, art 4(1)(f).

[97] Protocol on Strategic Environmental Assessment to the Convention on Environmental Impact Assessment in a Transboundary Context (Kiev, 21 May 2003), entered into force 11 July 2010.

[98] Jan De Mulder, 'The Expansion of Environmental Assessment in International Law: The Protocol on Strategic Environmental Assessment to the Espoo Convention' (2006) 18 *Environmental Law and Management* 269, 270–71.

At present, the agenda is stalled. The original idea was to extend environmental assessment to policies. From a broader perspective, applying to high-level operational measures is of the essence of SEA and is consistent with how environmental assessment was first conceived by the US Congress in 1970. As noted by Sheate, 'the logic of "tiering" ... is that SEA should also be applied to policy level decisions'.[99] Otherwise, there will remain gaps in assessment.

The current basis for extending SEA to policies is weak. Article 7 of the Aarhus Convention concludes that: 'To the extent appropriate, each Party shall endeavour to provide opportunities for public participation in the preparation of policies relating to the environment.' Article 13(1) of the Kiev Protocol is similarly limited,[100] although it is enhanced by the provision at Article 13(4) that each party must report to the Meeting of the Parties on the endeavours it has taken to extend SEA under the article. The Protocol is still relatively new and it is conceivable this will give some momentum to further discussions.

At the EU level, the Commission has recently reviewed the provisions of the EIA Directive. The revisions to the EIA Directive in light of that review include some features that may be inspired by the SEA Directive, such as a definition of the assessment process[101] and a wider scope for consideration of alternatives.[102] However, the 2012 EIA review made no suggestion of reform to or extension of strategic assessment.[103] Nor was there any consideration of streamlining EIA and SEA into a single Directive. In fact, and in contrast to the regular amendments and consolidations of the EIA Directive, there has been no significant amendment to the strategic assessment regime in Europe since the SEA Directive was introduced in 2001. This may stem from a desire not to upset the careful balance that was sought to be struck in its initial drafting. Whatever the reason, the convoluted nature of the Directive's provisions and the uncertainty as to its scope will not present the EU institutions with an easy task when they do come to update it.

99 Sheate (n 16) 342.

100 Kiev Protocol (n 97) ('Each Party shall endeavour to ensure that environmental, including health, concerns are considered and integrated to the extent appropriate in the preparation of its proposals for policies and legislation that are likely to have significant effects on the environment, including health').

101 EIA Directive, as amended, art 1(2)(g).

102 ibid, Annex IV(2).

103 COM (2012) 628 final.

2

The Transposition of the SEA Directive

GREGORY JONES QC*

> Whilst the concept of strategic environmental assessment is relatively straightforward, implementation of the Directive sets Member States a considerable challenge. It goes to the heart of much public-sector decision-making.
>
> Catherine Day, Director General—DG Environment[1]

Introduction

The transposition of the SEA Directive[2] has not been without its problems. Initially, there was a slow take-up by Member States, with a majority failing to transpose the Directive before the prescribed deadline of 21 July 2004.[3] In fact, only nine out of the then 25 Member States transposed the Directive in time. As a consequence, in December 2004, 15 non-communication infringement procedures were opened by the Commission for failure to adopt the legislation transposing the SEA Directive and, subsequently, five Member States were condemned by the European Court of Justice (ECJ) for failing to transpose it.

The reluctance of some Member States to transpose the Directive may, in part, be explained by the Directive's legislative history. The Directive was adopted solely

* The author is grateful to the inspiration for this chapter provided by Sibylle Grohs—DG Environment, European Commission in her presentation to the second Kingsland Conference, 14 February 2014. However, all views expressed herein remain those of the author.

[1] From the foreword to the European Commission's guidance document 'Implementation of Directive 2001/42 on the assessment of the effects of certain plans and programmes on the Environment', http://ec.europa.eu/environment/archives/eia/pdf/030923_sea_guidance.pdf.

[2] Directive 2001/42/EC of the European Parliament and of the Council of 27 June 2001 on the assessment of the effects of certain plans and programmes.

[3] Article 13(1).

under Article 175(1) of the EC Treaty,[4] notwithstanding and controversially, it touches upon land use planning.[5] The main rule on the legislative adoption procedure is that measures are generally adopted under the co-decision procedure (Article 175(1)). However, in politically sensitive areas, which include 'measures affecting town and country planning' (Article 175(2)) in which Member States have not been able to accept the co-decision procedure unanimously, the co-decision-making process does not apply. Accordingly, by way of a derogation from paragraph 1, measures mentioned in paragraph 2 have to be enacted unanimously.[6] The adoption of the Directive solely under Article 175(1) thus also resulted in heavily negotiated texts within the SEA Directive, such as those that took place in respect of Article 2(a), defining the categories of plans and programmes caught by the requirements of the Directive.[7]

The First Progress Report

Article 12(3) of the Directive required the Commission to send a first report on its application and effectiveness to the European Parliament and the Council before 21 July 2006.[8] Article 12(3) also stated that, with a view to integrating environmental protection requirements, such a report should, if appropriate, be accompanied by proposals for amendment, in particular on the possibility of extending its scope to other areas/sectors and other types of plan and projects. However, by the time the 2006 deadline arrived, few Member States had actually transposed the Directive. Accordingly, the Commission took the view that it would not be useful to produce a report at that time. Furthermore, it considered that delaying production of the Report would have the added advantage of enabling it also to

[4] Now contained substantially in art 192 of the Treaty on the Functioning of the European Union.

[5] For an examination of the arguments in relation to the correct legal basis for the adoption of the SEA Directive, see further Simon Marsden, *Strategic Environmental Assessment in International and European Law: A Practitioner's Guide* (London, Earthscan, 2008) 207–08.

[6] The second subparagraph of para 2 opens up the possibility of moving to qualified majority voting by unanimous decision.

[7] The drafting history of art 2(a) was expressly considered by Advocate General Kokott in Case C-567/10 *Inter-Environnement Bruxelles ASBL Pétitions-Patrimoine ASBL Atelier de Recherche d'Action Urbaines ASBL v Gouvernement de la Région de Bruxelles-Capitale* [2012] 2 CMLR 909. This is discussed in further detail later in this chapter, and by Gregory Jones and David Graham in Ch 11 and Elizabeth Fisher at Ch 8 of this volume.

[8] The report drew on the study commissioned by the Commission on the application and effectiveness of the SEA Directive (the COWI report: http://ec.europa.eu/environment/eia/pdf/study0309.pdf) as well as other sources, including Member States' responses to the Commission questionnaire on the application and effectiveness of the SEA Directive, the study commissioned by the Commission on 'The Relationship between the EIA and the SEA Directives' (2005), the *Handbook on SEA for Cohesion Policy 2007–2013* (2007, GRDP), the Commission's guidance on the implementation of Directive 2001/42/EC, (2003), and the Commission's experience of the implementation and enforcement of the SEA Directive and its application to the EU co-financed 2007–13 Programmes for the period.

include within the Report the experience of the recently joined Member States[9] of transposing the Directive. The First Progress Report[10] (hereinafter 'the Report') was eventually produced on 14 September 2009. By that time, all Member States had implemented the Directive,[11] but there had been no case law from the Court of Justice of the European Union (CJEU).

Scoping

Somewhat surprisingly, Member States indicated to the Commission that there were no problems with the scope of plans or programmes as defined in the SEA Directive. Most reported that their model was based on a combined approach, whereby the list of plans or programmes to be assessed was supplemented by a case-by-case approach to determine whether an assessment was needed. There were, however, differences between Member States with regard to which authority decides the outcome of the 'scoping' procedure.[12] Often it was the responsibility of the planning authority, after having consulted the environmental authority, but in other instances, it was left to the environmental authority. An examination as to whether the background discipline of the examining authority can be shown to influence the approach taken in scoping might prove a fruitful area of future research. The Report noted that in a few Member States, the 'scoping' procedure required public consultation, even though this is not, of course, an obligation under the Directive.

Data Quality and Detail

The transposing legislation adopted in each of the Member States laid down formal requirements to provide a description of the baseline situation in the Environmental Report accompanying the environmental assessment. However, Member States reported difficulties in identifying the correct scale of data and the level of detail required for the assessment.[13] The quality of data and the degree of detail necessary are obviously matters of great practical importance.[14] Giving guidance

[9] Those that had acceded in 2004 and 2007.

[10] Report from the Commission to the Council, the European Parliament, the European Economic and Social Committee and the Committee of the Regions on the application and effectiveness of the Directive on Strategic Environmental Assessment (Directive 2001/42/EC) COM(2009) 469 FINAL, September 2009, http://eur-lex.europa.eu/legal-content/en/TXT/?uri=CELEX%3A52009DC0469.

[11] Although Stephen Tromans suggests that transposition was 'in some cases incomplete or imperfect' in *Environmental Impact Assessment*, 2nd edn (London, Bloomsbury Professional, 2012) para 8.68.

[12] At para 3.3: Determination of the scope of the environmental report (art 5(4)).

[13] At para 3.4: Environmental report (art 5 and Annex I).

[14] See also C Fry, V McColl, P Tomlinson, R Eales and S Smith, 'Analysis of Baseline Data Requirements for the SEA Directive', Final Report (2002) http://www.southwest-ra.gov.uk/media/SWRA/Environment/Analysis_Baseline_Data_Requirements.pdf

is problematic because but the issues which arise are likely to be inherently case-specific, being obviously dependent on the particular subject matter of the plan or programme, as well as the position of the document in the hierarchy of plans or programmes. It is also a problem identified in respect of the EIA Directive. The amendments to the EIA Directive[15] seek to tackle this issue—not without some degree of controversy—by requiring that an environmental impact assessment report (as it will henceforth be known) will need to be undertaken by 'competent experts'. What is meant by 'competent experts' will be defined more clearly by individual Member States.

Identification of Alternatives

Some Member States had developed national guidelines to assist in the identification of reasonable alternatives, but the majority had not. Most national legislations did not provide a specific definition of 'reasonable alternatives' or prescribe a number of alternatives that must be assessed and had provided that the choice of 'reasonable alternatives' was to be determined by means of a case-by-case assessment and a decision. The exception was that all the Member States reported that the 'do-nothing' alternative had to be included in the environmental report on a mandatory basis. However, overall Member States reported that the consideration and identification of alternatives in the environmental report was giving rise to problems.[16] Indeed, in the years following the publication of the Report, this issue has continued to prove problematic. Certainly within the UK, as discussed by David Elvin,[17] the consideration of alternatives has resulted in a significant amount of litigation.

Consultation

There is no prescribed method of consultation set out in the SEA Directive. The Report found[18] that a wide range of methods were in fact used by the different Member States for consultation, such as public announcements, publication in official journals or the press, public meetings, internet surveys and questionnaires. In terms of the duration of the public consultation, only a few Member State had

[15] http://eur-lex.europa.eu/legal-content/EN/TXT/?uri=CELEX:52012PC0628.

[16] At para 3.5: Definition of reasonable alternatives (art 5(1)).

[17] See David Elvin in Ch 6 of this volume. On the historical background to the requirement to look at alternatives, see Robert McCracken and Ned Westaway in Ch 1 of this volume. For a detailed consideration of the case law in relation to alternatives.

[18] At para 3.6: Consultations (public, and environmental authorities) (art 6).

set fixed timeframes. Most Member States allowed for consultation periods of at least one month, while others decided on a case-by-case basis.[19]

Member States also reported that transboundary consultations in general went well, with an apparently 'high' level of satisfaction. The main issues concerned the lack of systematic translation of the documentation and the costs associated with the task of translation. Non-governmental organisations (NGOs) also complained that the consultation process often took place late in the process when the plan or programme was already well developed.

Monitoring

Article 10 of the Directive provides for the monitoring of significant environmental effects of the implementation of plans and programmes so that unforeseen adverse effects can be identified at an early stage and remedial action can be taken where necessary. Active monitoring can play an important role in establishing whether the environmental assessment has been effective and the assumptions made robust. Disappointingly, however, very few Member States reported that they had established monitoring methods or drawn up national guidance on how to establish monitoring indicators.

The Relationship Between the SEA and EIA Directives

The Report also considered the relationship between the SEA and EIA Directives.[20] The Foreword to the Commission's Guidance to the SEA Directive had already pointed out that environmental assessments carried out of projects by the EIA Directive took place 'at a stage when options for significant change are often limited. Decisions on the site of a project, or on the choice of alternatives, may already have been taken in the context of plans for a whole sector or geographical area'. The role of the SEA Directive, according to the Foreword, was to plug that gap: 'by requiring the environmental effects of a broad range of plans and programmes to

[19] In *Seaport (No 1), Re* [2007] NIQB 62; [2008] Env LR 23, Weatherup J had held that the Directive required Member States to specify a consultation period. This view was subsequently rejected by the CJEU upon its reference by the Court of Appeal of Northern Ireland in Case C-474/10 *Department of the Environment v Seaport (NI) Ltd and Others* [2011] ECR I-10227; [2012] Env LR 21, which held that Member States could specify the period of consultation on a case-by-case basis by administrative action. See further William Orbinson in Ch 15 of this volume for an examination of the circumstances of the *Seaport* reference to the CJEU, which might explain the different approach taken by the CJEU.

[20] Environmental Impact Assessment Directive 2011/92/EU of 13 December 2011 on the assessment of the effects of certain public and private projects on the environment (codification), can be found at http://ec.europa.eu/environment/eia/pdf/EIA_Directive_informal.pdfhttp://eur-lex.europa.eu/LexUriServ/LexUriServ.do?uri=OJ:L:2012:026:0001:0021:EN:PDF.

be assessed, so that they can be taken into account while plans are actually being developed, and in due course adopted'. The Report echoed this theme by reflecting upon the 'complementary' aspects of the two Directives. It described the 'SEA' as 'upstream' and as something that identifies the best options at an early planning stage. By contrast, the 'EIA' is 'downstream' and refers to 'the projects that are coming through at a later stage'. The Report stated that, at least in theory, an overlap of the two processes should be unlikely to occur. However, it also pointed out that the following different areas of potential overlaps in the application of the two Directives had in fact been identified, namely; where large projects are made up of sub-projects or where projects have more than local significance; Projects that require amendments of land use plans (which will require strategic environmental assessment before a developer can apply for development consent and undertake the environmental impact assessment; and plans or programmes which set binding criteria for the subsequent development consent of projects, so-called hierarchical linking between the SEA and the EIA Directives ('tiering').

The Report identified that the boundaries between what constitutes a plan, a programme or a project are not always clear,[21] and that there may be some doubts as to whether the 'subject' of the assessment meets the criteria of either or both of the Directives. In this regard, the Report found that the definitions of some project categories listed in Annex II of the EIA in relation to changes in land use are not clear and could create confusion with the SEA. The Report found that Member States had chosen different approaches to resolve potential shortcomings resulting from overlapping procedures ranging from joint procedures in specific cases to informal coordination between the competent authorities. However, many Member States often felt that they did not have sufficient experience to properly identify and assess any overlapping issues. Due to this lack of experience in the implementation of the SEA Directive, many Member States stressed the need for coordination of both procedures. The Report suggested that could be done by means of guidance documents to be drawn up in cooperation with Member States.

Interestingly, the Report gave consideration as to whether it would be a good idea to merge the EIA and SEA Directives 'in order to clarify their interrelationship and boost their complementarity and efficiency through a holistic environmental assessment process'. However, it noted that very few Member States were in favour of merging the two Directives, preferring that each process should be completely separate in its own right, because they viewed the two Directives as complementary measures which addressed different stages and processes.[22]

[21] See further Stephen Tromans, 'The Meaning of "Any Plan or Project" under Article 6(3)' in Gregory Jones (ed), *The Habitats Directive: A Developer's Obstacle Course?* (Oxford, Hart Publishing, 2012) ch 5.

[22] It is has been suggested that the Court's judgment in Case C-36/98 *Spain v Council of the European Union* [2001] ECR I-779 offers support for the view that any amendment of the SEA Directive or consolidation with the EIA Directive would require unanimity under art 175(2) Treaty on European Union. see Marsden (n 5) 208.

Accordingly, whilst the Report initially considered that merging the two 'may appear to be an attractive option', having taken the views of the Member States and the limited experience in the application of the SEA Directive into account, the Report recommended that it was not appropriate at that time to merge the two processes. Instead, it suggested that better coordination and coherence could be achieved by correcting the inconsistencies between the provisions of the two Directives and clarification of the definitions of problematic project categories in the EIA Directive, by amending the latter and/or through the development of guidance as explained above. The possibility of merging the two Directives was reconsidered as part of the twenty-fifth anniversary review of the EIA Directive. In the consultation exercise,[23] of the 1,365 replies, 29 per cent were in favour of merger, 50 per cent against and 21 per cent had no opinion on the matter. Accordingly, the merger of the two Directives was not pursued in the proposed amendments to the EIA Directive.[24] So notwithstanding some obvious benefits in terms of consistency and cost saving a merger is unlikely in the foreseeable future.

The Habitats Directive and the Biodiversity Action Plan

Member States took the view that there were no major problems to report concerning its relationship with Article 11(2) of the SEA Directive, which provides for co-coordinated or joint assessment procedures. Indeed, they reported that they have taken steps to avoid duplication and overlapping, mainly by means of a coordinated approach, which was preferred by Member States to a joint approach. However, the views of the Member States may not always reflect the actual reality, and the Report noted that NGOs had raised concerns about this issue.[25] Furthermore, with regard to the Biodiversity Action Plan (BAP), many Member States simply felt that the provisions of the SEA are sufficient and take its substance into account. Indeed, the Report itself drew attention to the fact that the European Commission's own 2008 mid-term Report on the implementation of the BAP[26] revealed that the EU was highly unlikely to meet its 2010 target of halting biodiversity decline (as indeed proved to be the case). The mid-term Report had stressed the need for further progress in ensuring that strategic environmental assessments and environmental impact assessment are systematically conducted

[23] http://ec.europa.eu/environment/eia/pdf/results_consultation.pdf.

[24] www.europarl.europa.eu/sides/getDoc.do?type=TA&reference=P7-TA-2014-0225&language=EN&ring=A7-2013-0277.

[25] See David Elvin in Ch 6 of this volume for a discussion of the potential difficulties involved in the obligations to examine alternatives under the SEA Directive and the Habitats Directive highlighted by the Court of Appeal's judgment in *Ashdown Forest Economic Development LLP v Wealden District Council* [2015] EWCA Civ 681.

[26] COM(2008)864.

in relation to environmentally sensitive interventions funded by Member States and the European Community (EC).

The SEA Protocol

The Espoo Convention on EIA in a Transboundary Context—to which the EC had acceded—was supplemented by the SEA Protocol.[27] The Protocol was adopted by an extraordinary meeting of the parties[28] to the Espoo Convention held on 21 May 2003 during the Ministerial 'Environment for Europe' Conference in Kiev. It was subsequently signed by 36 states and the 'European Community', as it was then known. A total of 16 signatories were needed to ratify it. At the time of the Report, it had been ratified by only 10 signatories. The Report acknowledged that the entry into force of the SEA Protocol may result in changes having to be made to the SEA Directive. It noted, in particular, that:

> [T]he SEA Protocol goes further than the SEA Directive, in that it also encourages potential application to certain policies and legislative proposals. The fact that the SEA Directive does not apply to policies which set the framework of P&P makes it necessary to consider the possible inclusion of policies and legislation in the application of the Directive as an option for the future.

The Protocol subsequently came into force on 11 July 2010. The Report noted that some of these amendments could be incorporated as part of the review of the EIA Directive, for instance, through amendments to its Annexes.

Perceived Benefits

Member States reported an increased transparency in decision-making brought about by the Directive's involvement of several levels of society. They also noted that it resulted in a better integration of environmental considerations into decisions, thereby 'greening' plans and programmes. Member States felt that the process has increased compliance with other EU requirements in sector-specific environmental legislation.

Some Member States highlighted the need for further guidance, in particular on the interpretation of certain key concepts of the Directive (screening criteria,

[27] www.unece.org/env/eia/sea_protocol.html. For an examination of the differences between the SEA Directive and the SEA Protocol, see Gernot Stoeglehner and Gerald Wegerer, ' The SEA-Directive and the SEA-Protocol Adopted to Spatial Planning: Similarities and Differences' (2006) 26(6) *Environmental Impact Assessment Review* 586.

[28] www.unece.org/env/eia/meetings/mop_ex1.html.

identification of alternatives, coordination mechanisms and/or joint procedures for fulfilling the requirements for assessment under other Directives, and specific guidance on the link between SEA and EIA). It was also felt that EU guidance on the consideration of better integration of climate change and biodiversity issues in SEA Directive could be developed by the Commission in cooperation with the Member States.[29]

The Report's Conclusion

The Report found that the overall picture of the application and effectiveness of the SEA Directive across all Member States was varied in terms of the institutional and legal arrangements of the SEA procedure, and in terms of how Member States themselves perceived the Directive's role. It concluded that this diverse picture also determined the way in which Member States viewed the benefits and drawbacks of the Directive, and what measures they considered were likely to improve its implementation and effectiveness.

The general findings of the Report suggested that the application of the SEA Directive was in its infancy. It was felt that further experience was needed before deciding on whether the Directive should be amended and, if so, how this should be done. The Report observed that Member States seemed to prefer stability in the legislative requirements in order to allow SEA systems and processes to settle down and provide the opportunity to establish robust ways of using SEAs to improve the planning process. The next evaluation report was intended to be prepared in 2013 but that date has been missed.

Overall, it was concluded that the SEA Directive contributed to the systematic and structured consideration of environmental concerns in planning processes and better integration of environmental considerations upstream. In addition, by means of its requirements (environmental report, consultation and information of the authorities and public concerned etc), it ensured better and harmonised planning procedures, and contributed to transparent and participatory decision-making processes.

In 'Appraisals of Sustainability and the New National Policy Statements: Opportunities Missed and Challenges to Come?'[30] published in January 2010, the authors addressed the Commission's First Progress Report, noting that:

> The Commission reports draw heavily upon the views and reporting of Member States themselves so caution is needed in the interpretation, especially given the focus on

[29] See the subsequently adopted 'Guidance on Integrating Climate Change and Biodiversity into Strategic Environmental Assessment' (2013), http://ec.europa.eu/environment/eia/pdf/SEA%20 Guidance.pdf.

[30] Report for the Royal Society for the Protection of Birds (RSPB) and the World Wildlife Fund (WWF) prepared by Ric Eales, William Sheate and Indre Vaizgelaite

implementing the Directive and SEA procedures rather than the quality of assessments, changes to plans and wider benefits. The experience of applying the SEA Directive is still in its infancy.

Early Case law

Important clarification on the interpretation of the Directive came from the CJEU as the first preliminary references began to arrive. The first cases tended to focus on the difficulties in defining plans and programmes.

Terre Wallonne and Inter-Environnement-Wallonie

Terre Wallonne and Inter-Environnement-Wallonie,[31] addressed the question as to whether the Walloon government's amendments to its water law in line with the Nitrates Directive[32] amounted to a strategic plan or programme within the meaning of the SEA Directive. The Walloon government had adopted the contested order in pursuance of Article 5 of the Nitrates Directive. That order amended Bo ok II of the Environment Code, which formed the Water Code, as regards the sustainable management of nitrogen in agriculture.[33] NGOs challenged the order, seeking its annulment before the Conseil d'Etat for a failure to comply with the SEA Directive. The Conseil d'Etat referred the case to the CJEU. The CJEU held that, as a result both of the characteristics they displayed and of the actual intention of the EU legislature, action programmes are 'plans and programmes' within the meaning of Directive 2001/42.

Furthermore, according to the Court, as regards the content of action programmes, it was apparent from Article 5 of the Nitrates Directive, in conjunction with Annex III thereto, that those programmes were to contain specific, mandatory measures that cover, in particular, periods during which the spreading of certain types of fertiliser was to be prohibited, the capacity of storage vessels for livestock manure, spreading methods[34] and the maximum quantity of livestock manure containing nitrogen that could be spread. The Court held that in the

[31] Joined Cases C-105/09 and C-110/09 *Terre Wallonne and Inter-Environnement-Wallonie* [2010] ECR 1-5611.

[32] Council Directive 91/676/EEC of 12 December 1991 concerning the protection of waters against pollution caused by nitrates from agricultural sources, http://eur-lex.europa.eu/LexUriServ/LexUriServ.do?uri=CELEX:31991L0676:EN:HTML.

[33] In the judgment of 22 September 2005 in Case C–221/03 *Commission v Belgium* [2005] ECR I–8307 the CJEU held that, by failing to adopt within the relevant time limit the measures needed for the full and correct implementation of Directive 91/676, Belgium had failed to fulfil its obligations under that directive.

[34] See Case C-416/02 *Commission v Spain* [2005] ECR I-7487.

context of environmental assessment provided for by the EIA Directive, the national authorities must take into account not only the direct effects of the planned works, but also the environmental impact liable to result from the use and exploitation of the end product of those works.[35] The Court held that in particular in the case of installations for intensive rearing, such an environmental assessment must envisage the impact of the installations on water quality.[36]

Accordingly, the CJEU concluded that an action programme adopted pursuant to Article 5(1) of the Nitrates Directive was in principle a plan or programme covered by Article 3(2)(a) of the SEA Directive since it constituted a 'plan' or 'programme' within the meaning of Article 2(a) of the SEA Directive and contained measures which must be complied with in order for consent to be granted for carrying out projects lists in Annexes I and II to the EIA Directive. It was ultimately left to the domestic court to rule on the issue. In due course, the Conseil d'Etat confirmed this view by ruling that the nitrates amendment was in fact such a measure.

Inter-Environnement Bruxelles and Others v Gouvernement de la Région de Bruxelles-Capitale

Inter-Environnement Bruxelles ASBL Pétitions-Patrimoine ASBL Atelier de Recherche d'Action Urbaines ASBL v Gouvernement de la Région de Bruxelles-Capitale[37] is of interest not just in terms of the approach to the interpretation of the SEA Directive, but also as part of the CEJEU's canon of judicial interpretation. The main issue in the case concerned the question as to whether the Directive applied to plans or programmes which had been adopted voluntarily. In paragraphs 16–20 of her Opinion, Advocate General Kokott was able to discover 'the real intention of the legislature'. Having rejected wider definitions, the Council had adopted a common position[38] in which it explained that the words that were eventually adopted, to which the Parliament did not object, meant that only plans and programmes that are 'required' to be adopted were covered by Article 2(a). The Advocate General therefore concluded at paragraph 30 that: 'In short, the word "required" in Article 2(a) of the SEA Directive must be construed as meaning that that definition does not include plans and programmes which are provided for by legislative provisions but the drawing up of which is not compulsory.'

The CJEU took a different approach to the Advocate General. It did not refer expressly to the analysis of the drafting history by the Advocate General, but it did

[35] Case C-2/07 *Paul Abraham v Region Wallone* [2008] ECR I-01197 and Case C-142/07 *Ecologistas en Acción-CODA* [2008] ECR I-6097.

[36] *Commission v Spain* (n 34).

[37] *Inter-Environnement Bruxelles ASBL* (n 7).

[38] [2000] OJ C137, 11 (at 20).

note, at paragraph 26, that the Belgian, Czech and UK governments had submitted: 'that it is apparent not only from the wording of Article 2(a) of Directive 2001/42 but also from the Directive's *travaux preparatoires* that the European Union legislature did not intend to make administrative and legislative measures that are not required by rules of law subject to the environmental impact assessment procedure established by the directive'. The CJEU did not say that this submission was wrong, as it related to what had been the actual intention of the legislature, but instead it held, at paragraph 30, that 'such an interpretation of Article 2(a) of Directive 2001/42, by appreciably restricting the Directive's scope, would compromise, in part, the practical effect of the Directive, having regard to its objective, which consists in providing for a high level of protection of the environment'.

It is apparent that in this instance, the Court rejected the notion of original intendment as advanced by some Member States and Advocate General Kokott. Indeed, it went further than what may be said to be even a purposive approach. It was plain from the *travaux preparatoires* that it was not the purpose of the Directive to apply to voluntary plans. This judgment is a therefore a good example of the CJEU adopting a teleological as opposed to a mere 'purposive' approach to the interpretation of EU law.[39] It is true that the two approaches are similar, and 'teleological' is often defined as the interpretation of legislative provisions in the light of the purpose, values and the legal, social and economic goals these provisions aim to achieve, but, as Advocate General Miguel Poiares Maduro explained:

> Teleological interpretation in EU law does not refer exclusively to a purpose driven interpretation of the relevant legal rules. It refers to a particular systemic understanding of the EU legal order that permeates the interpretation of all its rules.[40]

This approach tends to be applied most often by the CJEU in instances where it is seeking to bolster a new piece of EU law or else to establish the robustness of EU law in a new field of application. Accordingly, the judgment in *Inter-Environnement Bruxelles and Others v Gouvernement de la Région de Bruxelles-Capitale* may be seen as a clear message that the CJEU believes that the scope of the Directive should be interpreted widely so that, subject to few exceptions, all plans and programmes that are likely to have significant effects on the environment should be subject to environmental assessment.[41]

Nomarchiaki Aftodioikisi Aitoloakarnanias

By a number of legislative acts, Greece sought the partial diversion of the upper waters of the river Achekoos in western Greece to another river, the Pinio. This

[39] See further Oreste Pollicino, 'Legal Reasoning of the Court of Justice in the Context of the Principle of Equality between Judicial Activism and Self-restraint' (204) 5(3) *German Law Journal* 289.

[40] Miguel Poiares Maduro, 'Interpreting European Law: Judicial Adjudication in a Context of Constitutional Pluralism' (2007) 1(2) *European Journal of Legal Studies* 5.

[41] See further Ch 8 of this volume for Elizabeth Fisher's analysis of the Court's expansive 'upstream' approach to its interpretation of the SEA Directive.

would serve irrigation needs, produce electricity and supply local towns with water. Numerous organisations and local authorities opposed the project. In *Nomarchiaki Aftodioikisi Aitoloakarnanias*,[42] the Simvoulio tis Epikrateias, the Greek Council of State, referred a number of questions to the CJEU on the interpretation of a range of environmental directives, including, in particular, whether a project for the partial diversion of the waters of a river must be regarded as a plan or programme falling within the scope of the SEA Directive.

The CJEU noted that in order to establish whether a project falls within the scope of SEA Directive, it is necessary to consider whether that project is a plan or a programme within the meaning of Article 2(a) of that directive. Under the second paragraph of Article 2(a) of the SEA Directive, only plans and programmes required by legislative, regulatory or administrative provisions are to be regarded as 'plans and programmes' within the meaning of that directive. The Court found that in this case, it was not evident that the project in question constituted a measure which defined criteria and detailed rules for the development of land and which subjected the implementation of one or more projects to rules and procedures for scrutiny.[43]

Valciukiene v Pakruojo rajono savivaldybe

The reference to the CJEU in *Valciukiene*[44] arose from a challenge to decisions to allow intensive pig-rearing facilities in Lithuania. One of the issues was whether national legislation could create exemptions from the SEA Directive, in this case exemptions directed at smaller-scale developments and where there was limitation on the extent of activities. The national law on land planning in this case directed assessment only at 'economic activities' that affected the environment and provided exemptions for proposals that included only one economic activity.

The Court stressed that it was the likely significant effect on the environment that had to be looked at rather than whether economic activity was anticipated. A 'small-scale' exemption was capable of being lawful provided it was linked to the test of whether significant environmental effects were likely. The obligations of both the SEA and EIA Directives were mandatory, but the Court acknowledged that it was possible that a single study could meet the requirements of both of them. There is no obligation to have a joint and coordinated approach to the two directives. The interrelation of the EIA and SEA directives is also helpfully examined in this judgment. It is presently seen as a two stage process in the UK, for example, but the judgment in *Valciukiene* indicates that this is not a mandatory approach.[45]

[42] Case C-43/10 *Nomarchiaki Aftodioikisi Aitoloakarnanias* [2013] Env LR 453.

[43] See Case C-567/10 *Inter-Environment Bruxelles and Others* [2012] ECR I-0000, paragraph 30.

[44] Case C-295/10 *Valciukiene v Pakruojo rajono savivaldybe* [2012] Env LR11.

[45] This judgment and the potential for overlap between a 'project' governed by the EIA Directive and a 'plan or programme' covered by the SEA Directive was considered by the Supreme Court in *Walton v Scottish Ministers* [2012] UKSC 44; [2013] 1 CMLR 28; 2012 GWD 34-689; [2013] Env LR 16, as to which see further Colin Reid and Denis Edwards in Ch 14 of this volume.

Plans and Programmes Co-financed by the EU

Whilst Article 3(9) of the SEA Directive excluded plans and programmes co-financed by the EU in the funding period 2000–06, future plans are required to undergo SEA. This became a requirement for the programmes for the funding period 2007–13 and covered environmentally relevant 'Funds: Cohesion Funds, Agriculture and Transport in the form of Trans European Networks (TEN-T)'. SEA compliance is a prerequisite for Commission approval.

The 'Ex ante conditionalities' are described in Article 19 of Regulation (EC) 1303/2013 and guidance has been produced in respect of its application to the various funds. The specific conditionalities described in detail in the Annexes also cover compliance with other environmental directives, such as requiring water pricing regimes and waste management plans to be put in place. For transport infrastructure, a project can only be allocated TEN-T funding if the development in question is supported by an SEA-compliant plan.

Conclusion

The next European Commission implementation progress report is now promised for 2016 rather than 2013 as was originally intended, although by the end of September 2016 no further report had been published. Work on the revision of the EIA Directive should already provide some clarification on climate change methodologies, biodiversity and integration of the SEA Protocol. There should also be more clarification on the treatment of alternatives. Accordingly, the next progress report should be more informative since it will be able to draw on more substantial experience. Whether there will be the sort of SEA streamlining powerfully advocated by William Sheate seems unlikely.[46] However, the work which has been done to date does appear to support the view developed by Eloise Scotford[47] that upon 'a closer examination of the Directive, and its potential scope in constituting and limiting, and in some cases requiring judicial review of, government policy shows that its impact on issues of English public law can be significant'. If correct, such impacts would not be limited only to English public law, but would also embrace the constitutional systems of the other Member States.[48]

[46] See Ch 9 of this volume.

[47] See Ch 10 of this volume.

[48] See, eg, the impact of the SEA Directive in Ireland, as discussed by Áine Ryall in Ch 16 of this volume.

3

Plans and Programmes Under the SEA Directive

VALERIE FOGLEMAN

Introduction

The Strategic Environmental Assessment Directive ('the SEA Directive') requires an environmental assessment to be carried out for 'certain plans and programmes which are likely to have significant effects on the environment in the [EU]'.[1] The fundamental purpose of the Directive is to ensure that environmental effects are considered when a plan or programme is proposed and before its adoption in order to provide for a high level of protection of the environment.[2] The SEA Directive complements the Environmental Impact Assessment Directive ('the EIA Directive')[3] by requiring consideration of environmental effects before a 'project' under the EIA Directive is proposed and thus before the location and other characteristics of the project have already been determined.

This chapter discusses the meaning of 'plans and programmes' under the SEA Directive and analyses activities that fall within that term.

Background

The concept of carrying out an environmental assessment for plans and programmes prior to the proposal of projects pursuant to them pre-dates the SEA Directive and, indeed, the EIA Directive.

[1] Directive (EC) 2001/42 on the assessment of the effects of certain plans and programmes on the environment, recital 4 [2001] OJ L197/30.

[2] SEA Directive, art 1; see Case C-567/10 *Inter-Environnement Bruxelles ASBL v Région de Bruxelles-Capitale* [2012] 2 CMLR 909, para 30; Treaty on the Functioning of the European Union (TFEU), art 191(2).

[3] Directive (EU) 2011/92 on the assessment of the effects of certain public and private projects on the environment [2012] OJ L26/1.

The National Environmental Policy Act

The concept began in the US under the National Environmental Policy Act of 1969 (NEPA),[4] which requires federal agencies to assess the environmental impacts of proposed 'major Federal actions significantly affecting the quality of the human environment'.[5] NEPA is landmark legislation that ushered in the 'environmental decade' in the US, during which a substantial number of federal environmental legislation was enacted. NEPA was soon followed by mini-NEPAs in States throughout the US and environmental assessment legislation around the world.[6]

NEPA is procedural, not substantive. In other words, a federal agency must take a 'hard look' at the environmental effects of proposed major actions before carrying them out.[7] If the agency then decides to carry out a proposed action regardless of those effects, NEPA does not preclude it from doing so.[8]

The first case to determine that an environmental assessment should be carried out for a programme occurred early in NEPA's history. In 1973, the District of Columbia Circuit Court of Appeals ruled in *Scientists' Institute for Public Information, Inc v Atomic Energy Commission* that an environmental assessment was required for a research programme concerning the liquid metal fast breeder reactor.[9] The Atomic Energy Commission had considered that NEPA did not require it to analyse the entire research and development programme for the new technology, but, instead, to prepare only a 'detailed statement'[10] (called an environmental impact statement (EIS)) for each facility constructed under the programme. The Court of Appeals disagreed and concluded 'that NEPA requires impact statements for major federal research programs ... aimed at development of new technologies which, when applied, will significantly affect the quality of the human environment'.[11] The court stated that 'crystal ball' gazing is not required.[12]

[4] Public Law No 91-190, 83 Stat 852 (1970), 42 USC ss 4321–47.

[5] 42 USC s 4332(C).

[6] See Nicholas A Robinson, 'International Trends in Environmental Impact Assessment' (1992) 19 *Boston College Environmental Affairs Law Review* 591, 597 and Appendix 1 (listing jurisdictions adopting environmental impact assessment legislation); International Study of the Effectiveness of Environmental Assessment, Final Report, 'Environmental Assessment in a Changing World: Evaluating Practice to Improve Performance' (June 1996) 25, s 2.2.2 (prepared by Barry Sadler).

[7] See *Baltimore Gas & Electric Co v Natural Resources Defense Council, Inc*, 462 US 87, 97 (1983); *Kleppe v Sierra Club*, 427 US 390, 410 fn 21 (1976).

[8] See *Robertson v Methow Valley Citizens Council*, 490 US 332, 351 (1989) ('it would not have violated NEPA if the Forest Service, after complying with the Act's procedural prerequisites, had decided that the benefits to be derived from downhill skiing at Sandy Butte justified the issuance of a special use permit, notwithstanding the loss of 15 percent, 50 percent, or even 100 percent of the mule deer herd. Other statutes may impose substantive environmental obligations on federal agencies, but NEPA merely prohibits uninformed—rather than unwise—agency action').

[9] *Scientists' Institute for Public Information, Inc v Atomic Energy Commission*, 481 F 2d 1079 (DC Cir 1973).

[10] ibid 1085; see 42 USC s 4332(C).

[11] *Scientists' Institute* (n 9) 1091.

[12] ibid 1086.

Instead, the assessment of 'the anticipated environmental effects of [the] proposed action is subject to a rule of reason'.[13] Thus, a federal agency:

> [N]eed not foresee the unforseeable, but by the same token neither can it avoid drafting an impact statement simply because describing the environmental effects of and alternatives to particular agency action involves some degree of forecasting … one of the functions of a NEPA statement is to indicate the extent to which environmental effects are essentially unknown. It must be remembered that the basic thrust of an agency's responsibilities under NEPA is to predict the environmental effects of proposed action before the action is taken and those effects fully known. Reasonable forecasting and speculation is thus implicit in NEPA.[14]

The conclusion that NEPA requires an EIS for some programmes, as well as actions that are not on a programmatic or policy level, meant that the US Congress did not enact—or need to enact—separate legislation to require preparation of programmatic EISs. Instead, the regulations under NEPA, which were promulgated in 1978, include, as a 'major federal action', the adoption 'of programs, such as a group of concerted actions to implement a specific policy or plan [and] systematic and connected agency decisions allocating agency resources to implement a specific statutory program or executive directive.'[15] These programmes are subject to the same criteria as any other major federal action. A federal agency in the US must therefore prepare a programmatic EIS when it proposes a programme that may significantly affect the human environment.[16] If a programmatic EIS is prepared, site-specific EISs may be 'tiered' from it.[17] A programmatic EIS is not the same as a comprehensive EIS; the latter is prepared for connected, cumulative and similar actions when the similarities warrant discussion within the same EIS.[18]

[13] ibid 1092.

[14] ibid.

[15] 40 CFR s 1508.18(b)(3); see ibid s 1502.4(b).

[16] See *Kleppe v Sierra Club*, 427 US 390, 414–15 (1976) ('respondents' contention as to the relationships between all proposed coal-related projects in the Northern Great Plains region does not require … one comprehensive impact statement covering all before proceeding to approve specific pending applications … there exists no proposal for regionwide action that could require a regional impact statement').

[17] See 40 CFR s 1508.28 ('"Tiering" refers to the coverage of general matters in broader [EISs] (such as national program or policy statements) with subsequent narrower statements or environmental analyses (such as regional or basinwide program statements or ultimately site-specific statements) incorporating by reference the general discussions and concentrating solely on the issues specific to the statement subsequently prepared. Tiering is appropriate when the sequence of statements or analyses is: (a) From a program, plan, or policy [EIS] to a program, plan, or policy statement or analysis of lesser scope or to a site-specific statement or analysis. (b) From an [EIS] on a specific action at an early stage (such as need and site selection) to a supplement (which is preferred) or a subsequent statement or analysis at a later stage (such as environmental mitigation). Tiering in such cases is appropriate when it helps the lead agency to focus on the issues which are ripe for decision and exclude from consideration issues already decided or not yet ripe'); see generally Valerie Fogleman, *Guide to the National Environmental Policy Act; Interpretations, Applications, and Compliance* (Westport, CT, Quorum Books, 1990) 141–42.

[18] 40 CFR s 1508.25(a).

The EIA Directive

The EU followed the lead of the US in 1985 by adopting legislation to require the preparation of environmental assessments for proposed projects.[19] Such legislation was not new in the EU; some Member States, including Denmark, Finland, the Netherlands and the UK, had already adopted legislation or guidance on the consideration of environmental effects for proposed projects.[20] Like NEPA, the EIA Directive is procedural; it requires consideration of the environmental effects of specified proposed projects, but does not require substantive changes to be made to a project regardless of the findings and conclusions of the assessment. As in the US, however, in many cases, the environmental assessment results in beneficial changes that would not otherwise have been made.

The EIA Directive defines the word 'project' as 'the execution of construction works or of other installations or schemes [and] other interventions in the natural surroundings and landscape including those involving the extraction of mineral resources'.[21] This definition does not include the policy, or programmatic, decision that may pre-date the proposal for the project. By the time that a project is proposed, a plan or programme that results in significant effects on the environment may already have been adopted.[22] For example, an environmental assessment carried out when development consent is being considered for a road may be too late to assess the environmental effects of its construction at a different location. By that time, the corridor in which the road is to be located may have already been determined.[23]

The gap in the EIA Directive for consideration of the environmental effects of plans and programmes that precede 'projects' soon became evident.[24] However, the gap was intentional. In particular, the UK had opposed the European Commission's initial proposal for the EIA Directive because, among other things, the

[19] Council Directive (EEC) 85/337 on the assessment of the effects of certain public and private projects on the environment [1985] OJ L175/40 (now (EC) 2001/42). There are many differences between NEPA, the EIA Directive, and the SEA Directive. It is beyond the scope of this chapter to discuss these differences.

[20] See Barry Sadler, 'A Framework Approach to Strategic Environmental Assessment: Aims, Principles and Elements of Good Practice' in *Proceedings of International Workshop on Public Participation and Health Aspects in Strategic Environmental Assessment* (ed J Dusik), 11, 12 (Szentendre, Regional Environmental Center for Central and Eastern Europe, 2001); see also RAA Verheem and JAMN Tonk, 'Strategic Environmental Assessment: One Concept, Multiple Forms' (2012) 18(3) *Impact Assessment and Project Appraisal* 177, 179.

[21] EIA Directive, art 1(2)(a).

[22] See Joined Cases C-105/09 and C-110/09 *Terre Wallonne ASBL v Région Wallonne* [2010] ECR I-5611, Opinion of AG Kokott, paras 31–32.

[23] ibid, para 33.

[24] See Christopher Wood and Mohammed Dejeddour, 'Strategic Environmental Assessment: EA of Policies, Plans and Programmes' (1992) 10(1) *Impact Assessment* 3.

proposal went beyond UK planning legislation.[25] Denmark had also objected to inclusion of development projects subject to authorisation by Parliament in the proposal on the grounds of infringement of sovereignty.[26]

The gap in the EIA Directive was significant because the purely procedural nature of the Directive could have resulted in it becoming ineffective for projects for which a decision on their location or other characteristics had already been made.[27] In 1989, the Commission began internal preparations for an SEA Directive. The preparations proved to be lengthy. In 1991, the Commission failed to agree on the draft proposal.[28] In 1993, it commented, in a report on the application and effectiveness of the EIA Directive, that many decisions had already been made by the time that a project was proposed.[29] In 1995, the Commission began work again on the SEA Directive, resulting in the submission of a proposal in 1996.[30] In 2001, following lengthy debates between the Commission, the Council and the European Parliament, the gap was filled by the EU's adoption of the SEA Directive.[31] The SEA Directive operates at a strategic level, even though neither the word 'strategy' nor the word 'strategic' appears in the Directive itself.[32]

There are, naturally, major differences between the EIA Directive and the SEA Directive. For example, the EIA Directive requires the preparation of 'an outline of the main alternatives studied by the developer and an indication of the main

[25] See Nigel Haigh, 'Environmental Assessment—The EC Directive' (1987) *Journal of Planning & Environment Law* 4, 8–9; see also Malcolm Grant, 'Implementation of the EC Directive on Environmental Impact Assessment' (1989) 4 *Connecticut Journal of International Law* 463, 469 ('new provision in [the EIA] Directive allows Member States to integrate environmental impact assessment into the existing procedures for granting consent to projects, thus establishing the right of Britain to implement the EC Directive through amendments to its existing town and country planning system'); ibid 473 ('[the] principal conclusion of the working party set up by the Department of the Environment to examine the problems of implementation was that "the requirements of the Directive can be met within the context of the existing planning system without imposing significant new burdens on either developers or planning authorities"' (quoting Department of the Environment, Implementation of the European Directive on Environmental Assessment, para 5 (1986) (consultation paper)).

[26] See Haigh (n 25) 9.

[27] See Gregory Jones, Ned Westaway and Roger Watts, 'Why Central Craigavon was Wrongly Decided (and Other Problems with the Incorporation of the Strategic Environmental Assessment Directive into Domestic Law)' (2013) *Journal of Planning & Environment Law* 1074, 1075, referring to *Central Craigavon Ltd v Department of the Environment for Northern Ireland* [2011] NICA 17 (CA). See further William Orbinson in Ch 15 of this volume.

[28] See Lieselotte Feldmann, 'The European Commission's Proposal for a Strategic Environmental Assessment Directive: Expanding the Scope of Environmental Impact Assessment in Europe' (1998) 18 *Environmental Impact Assessment Review* 3, 4.

[29] See ibid (referring to Report from the Commission of the Implementation of Directive 85/337/EEC on the Assessment of the Effects of Certain Public and Private Projects on the Environment and Annexes for the Member States COM (93) 28 final, vol 3, April 1993.

[30] See ibid 5 (referring to Proposal for a Council Directive on the assessment of the effects of certain plans and programmes on the environment COM (96) 511 final).

[31] See text accompanying n 37.

[32] See Commission, 'Implementation of Directive 2001/42 on the assessment of the effects of certain plans and programmes on the environment' 2, fn 2 (21 July 2001) (SEA Directive Guidance). http://ec.europa.eu/environment/archives/eia/pdf/030923_sea_guidance.pdf

reasons for his choice, taking into account the environmental effects'.[33] In contrast, the SEA Directive requires 'the likely significant effects on the environment of implementing the plan or programme, and reasonable alternatives taking into account the objectives and the geographical scope of the plan or programme [to be] identified, described and evaluated'.[34] It is not therefore permissible to carry out an environmental assessment that meets only the requirements of the EIA Directive in order also to comply with the SEA Directive. Unless a coordinated or joint assessment is carried out to meet the requirements of both Directives, separate environmental assessments must be carried out.[35] The differences have inevitably led to disputes as to whether a proposal is subject only to the EIA Directive and not the SEA Directive.

The extent of the scope of plans and programmes under the SEA Directive is not a model of clarity. This is due, in part, to the different positions taken by the then 15 Member States when the EU adopted the Directive. The Commission's proposal for the Directive defined the terms 'plan' and 'programme' to:

(i) refer only to town and country planning plans and programmes
  — which are subject to preparation and adoption by a competent authority or which are prepared by a competent authority for adoption by a legislative act, and
  — which are part of the town and country planning decision-making process for the purpose of establishing the framework for subsequent development consents and
  — which contain provisions on the nature, size, location or operating conditions of projects.

(ii) include modifications of existing plans and programmes as described in point (i).

The Commission noted that: 'This definition includes town and country planning plans and programmes in sectors such as transport (including transport corridors, port facilities and airports), energy, waste management, water resource management, industry (including extraction of mineral resources), telecommunications and tourism.'[36]

In 1999, when the Council finally began discussing the proposal, a large split was revealed between Member States that wanted the scope of plans and programmes to be narrow and precisely defined, and those that wanted a broad scope. An agreement on the extent of the scope was reached only at the last minute and only by excluding additional plans and programmes from those that had already been excluded during the Council's consideration of the Commission's proposal. The differences even led the Commission to disagree with the common position,

[33] EIA Directive, art 5(3)(d).

[34] SEA Directive, art 5(1).

[35] Case C-295/10 *Genovaitė Valčiukienė v Pakruojo rajono savivaldybė* [2011] ECR I-8819, para 63.

[36] Commission, 'Proposal for a Council Directive on the assessment of the effects of certain plans and programmes on the environment' COM (96) 511 final, art 2(a).

leading to further negotiations on the extent of the scope before the Directive's adoption on 30 March 2000.[37]

Definition of Plans and Programmes

The SEA Directive sets out the following 'definition' of the term 'plans and programmes':

> plans and programmes, including those co-financed by the European Community, as well as any modifications to them:
>
> — which are subject to preparation and/or adoption by an authority at national, regional or local level or which are prepared by an authority for adoption, through a legislative procedure by Parliament or Government, and
> — which are required by legislative, regulatory or administrative provisions.[38]

There are exclusions for 'plans and programmes the sole purpose of which is to serve national defence or civil emergency [and] financial or budget plans and programmes'.[39]

The term 'plans and programmes' must be construed broadly[40] in line with its objective rather than its literal wording.[41] Thus, it is sufficient for there to be a legislative, regulatory or administrative power to prepare a plan or programme; a duty to do so is not necessary.[42] Although the above 'definition' has a 'clear core meaning', its extent is unclear.[43] The definition is, for example, circular in that

[37] Commission, 'Opinion of the Commission pursuant to Article 251(2)(c) of the EC Treaty, on the European Parliament's amendments to the Council's common position regarding the proposal for a Directive of the European Parliament and of the Council on the assessment of the effects of certain plans and programmes on the environment; amending the proposal of the Commission pursuant to Article 250(2) of the EC Treaty' COM(2000) 636 final, 5, s 3.3; see Lieselotte Feldmann, Marc Vanderhaegen and Charles Pirotte, 'The EU's SEA Directive; Status and Links to Integration and Sustainable Development' (2001) 21 *Environmental Impact Assessment Review* 203, 206.

[38] SEA Directive, art 2(a).

[39] ibid, art 3(8); see SEA Directive Guidance 19, s 3.62 (commenting on difference with the EIA Directive, which does not apply to 'projects serving national defence purposes' and which does not include the term 'the sole purpose of which').

[40] *Inter-Environnement Bruxelles ASBL* (n 2) para 37.

[41] *Walton v Scottish Ministers* [2012] UKSC 44, [2013] 1 CMLR 28 [20] (Lord Reed). See further Elizabeth Fisher in Ch 8 of this volume on the extent to which the CJEU's interpretation of the SEA Directive goes beyond even a purposive approach.

[42] *Inter-Environnement Bruxelles ASBL* (n 2), para 28; see Christoph Sobotta, 'Species Protection in the Environmental Assessment—Assembling the Puzzle' (2013) 10(3) *Journal for European Environmental and Planning Law* 233, 240 (the CJEU concluded that '"required by legislative, regulatory or administrative provisions" … includes plans and programmes whose adoption is *regulated* by national legislative or regulatory provisions').

[43] See Jonathan Robinson and David Elvin, 'The Environmental Assessment of Plans and Programmes' (2004) *Journal of Planning & Environment Law* 1028, 1030.

it defines a 'plan and programme' as a 'plan and programme'. Further, it is not really a definition. Rather, it qualifies the term 'plan and programme' to state that requirements specified in the term must be fulfilled.[44] In other words, a plan or programme must be 'subject to preparation and/or adoption by the prescribed authorities' and be 'required by legislative, regulatory or administrative provisions'.[45] The focus is thus, unlike the EIA Directive, on the entity that prepares the plan or programme and 'its mandate for doing so, rather than the content of the [plan or programme]'.[46]

The issue as to whether an EU co-financed 'plan or programme' falls within the definition of 'plans and programmes' under the SEA Directive does not tend to arise.[47] Some co-financed programmes require conformance to the SEA Directive.[48] For example, the guidelines for construction of the Trans-European Transport Network (TENT) specifically refer to the SEA Directive.[49] As a general rule, programmes co-financed by the European Regional Development Fund and the Cohesion Fund require an environmental assessment under the SEA Directive, whilst those co-financed by the European Social Fund do not.[50]

The terms 'plan' and 'programme', as stated by the European Commission in its guidance on the SEA Directive, are not synonymous. Instead, they are 'capable of a broad range of meanings which at some points overlap'.[51] The guidance further states that: 'The name alone ("plan", "programme", "strategy", "guidelines", etc) will not be a sufficiently reliable guide: documents having all the characteristics of a plan or programme as defined in the Directive may be found under a variety of names.'[52] The Commission considers that a rigorous distinction between the two terms is unnecessary to determine the main characteristics of either term.[53]

[44] See *Walton v Scottish Ministers* (n 41) para 19 (Lord Hope).

[45] See SEA Directive Guidance (n 32) 5, s 3.2 (quoting SEA Directive, art 2(a)).

[46] William Sheate, Helen Byron, Suzan Dagg and Lourdes Cooper, 'The Relationship between the EIA and SEA Directives; Final Report to the European Commission (Contract No ENV.G.4./ETU/2004/0020r, August 2005), 5, s 3.2.1.

[47] See Vassilia Theophilou, Alan Bond and Mat Cashmore, 'Application of the SEA Directive to EU Structural Funds: Perspectives on Effectiveness' (2010) 30 *Environmental Impact Assessment Review* 136; Alexandra Jiricka and Ulrike Pröbstl, 'The Role of SEA in Integrating and Balancing High Policy Objectives in European Cohesion Funding Programmes' (2013) 38 *Environmental Impact Assessment Review* 44.

[48] SEA Directive, art 11(3); see N Lee and F Walsh, 'Strategic Environmental Assessment: An Overview' (1992) 7(3) *Project Appraisal* 126, 127.

[49] See Regulation (EU) No 1315/2013 on Union guidelines for the development of the trans-European transport network, art 36, OJ L348/1 (20 December 2013) (current version) ('environmental assessment of plans and projects shall be carried out in accordance with the Union law on the environment, including Directives 92/43/EEC, 2000/60/EC, 2001/42/EC, 2009/147/EC and 2011/92/EU'); see also Environmental Resources Management, 'Strategic Environmental Assessment of Transport Corridors: Lessons Learned Comparing the Methods of Five Member States', s 2.3 (January 2001) (prepared for European Commission, DG Environment).

[50] Commission, 'The Programming Period 2014–2020 Monitoring and Evaluation of European Cohesion Policy: Guidance Document on Ex-ante Evaluation', 17, Annex 1, 23–24 (January 2013).

[51] See SEA Directive Guidance (n 32) 5, s 3.3.

[52] ibid.

[53] ibid.

The guidance includes examples of 'plans' in some Member States, such as 'land use plans setting out how land is to be developed, or laying down rules or guidance as to the kind of development which might be appropriate or permissible in particular areas, or giving criteria which should be taken into account in designing new development'. Such proposals also include waste management plans and water resources plans provided they meet other criteria set out in the SEA Directive.[54] They do not include ad hoc measures that do not constitute 'an organised and coordinated system'.[55]

The guidance also includes examples of 'programmes', including plans that cover 'a set of projects in a given area, for example a scheme for regeneration of an urban area, comprising a number of separate construction projects', such as an integrated transportation programme that is 'planned to take the place of independent programmes for road, airport, harbour and coastal defence projects'.[56] Other examples in some Member States include proposals that precede a town and country plan and that may include an inquiry into whether a plan is needed, appropriate and feasible.[57]

Categories of Plans and Programmes

The SEA Directive sets out the following categories of 'plans and programmes' for which an environmental assessment must be carried out. The two main categories are plans and programmes:

> (a) which are prepared for agriculture, forestry, fisheries, energy, industry, transport, waste management, water management, telecommunications, tourism, town and country planning or land use and which set the framework for future development consent of projects listed in Annexes I and II to [the EIA Directive, or]
> (b) which, in view of the likely effect on sites, have been determined to require an assessment pursuant to Article 6 or 7 of [the Habitats Directive].[58]

These categories are followed by a subcategory for plans and programmes 'which determine the use of small areas at local level and minor modifications' to them.[59] Finally, there is a 'mopping up' category[60] of any plan or programme that does not

[54] ibid 6, s 3.5.
[55] ibid 6, s 3.5 and fn 7 (quoting Case C-387/97 *Commission v Greece* [2000] ECR I-5047, para 76).
[56] ibid 6, s 3.6.
[57] ibid.
[58] SEA Directive, art 3(2); see Council Directive (EEC) 92/32 on the conservation of natural habitats and of wild fauna and flora [1992] OJ L206/7 ('the Habitats Directive'). A consolidated version was issued on 1 January 2007.
[59] SEA Directive, art 3(3).
[60] *Terre Wallonne ASBL* (n 22) Opinion of AG Kokott, para 103.

satisfy the criteria in the two main categories.[61] This category may include plans or programmes that are not covered by the EIA Directive.[62]

The term 'development consent' is defined by the EIA Directive as 'the decision of the competent authority or authorities which entitles the developer to proceed with the project'.[63] If a plan or programme falls into any of the above categories, the SEA Directive sets out minimum procedural rules concerning the environmental report that must be prepared to describe and evaluate 'the likely significant effects on the environment of implementing the plan or programme, and reasonable alternatives taking into account the objectives and the geographical scope of the plan or programme', a consultation process.[64] The environmental report is taken into account in the assessment process as are the results of consultations, with communication of the decision that is adopted following the assessment.[65]

Projects that Set the Framework for Future Development Consent

The first category of plans and programmes consists of a broad description of sectors in which there are 'projects' listed in Annexes I and II of the EIA Directive with the proviso that a 'project' must be listed in those Annexes. Thus, as with the EIA Directive, this category does not apply to a project that is not listed in Annex I or II of the EIA Directive even if the project significantly affects the environment.[66] The first category further requires the 'plan or programme' to 'set the framework for future development consent' for such projects.[67]

The determination of whether a plan or programme falls within this category thus involves the following issues:

— Is the plan or programme 'prepared for agriculture, forestry, fisheries, energy, industry, transport, waste management, water management, telecommunications, tourism, town and country planning or land use'?
— Does the plan or programme 'set the framework for future development consent'?
— Does the plan or programme concern a 'project listed in Annexes I and II to [EIA Directive]'?[68]

An issue that is not relevant is whether the plan or programme is likely to have significant effects on the environment. If a plan or programme falls within the above

[61] SEA Directive, art 3(4).
[62] See Sobotta (n 42) 241.
[63] EIA Directive, art 1(2)(c).
[64] SEA Directive, art 5(1); see ibid, art 3(1).
[65] See ibid 2(b).
[66] See Sobotta (n 42) 240 (citing Case C-156/07 *Salvatore Aiello v Comune di Milano* [1996] ECR I-5215, para 34; Case C-275/98 *Brussels Hoofdstedelijk Gewest* [2011] ECR I-1753, para 25).
[67] SEA Directive, art 3(2)(a).
[68] ibid.

category, it is automatically considered to have a likely significant environmental effect.[69]

The answer to the first issue is relatively easy. For example, the Court of Justice of the European Union (CJEU) easily determined that an action plan to determine vulnerable zones under the Nitrates Directive was prepared for agriculture.[70] The answer to the third issue is also easy due to the direct reference to the list of projects in Annexes I and II of the EIA Directive. The answer to the second issue, however, may be difficult.

The SEA Directive does not define the term 'set the framework for future development consent'.[71] A study on the implementation of the Directive found that 18 Member States did not define or interpret the term either.[72] The study indicated overlaps between 'plans and programmes' under the SEA Directive and 'projects' under the EIA Directive.[73] Examples include projects to restructure rural land holdings, to use uncultivated land or semi-natural areas for intensive agriculture, to reclaim land from the sea, and infrastructure projects, especially industrial and urban development projects. Another example is zoning plans in the Netherlands that may simultaneously be subject to both Directives.[74] The overlaps have resulted, among other things, in environmental assessments being carried out under the EIA Directive before, or simultaneously with, plans and programmes under the SEA Directive.[75]

In its guidance on the SEA Directive, the European Commission stated that:

> The words ['set the framework for future development consent'] would normally mean that the plan or programme contains criteria or conditions which guide the way the consenting authority decides an application for development consent. Such criteria could place limits on the type of activity or development which is to be permitted in a given area; or they could contain conditions which must be met by the applicant if permission is to be granted; or they could be designed to preserve certain characteristics of the area concerned (such as the mixture of land uses which promotes the economic vitality of the area).[76]

The Commission referred to a similar term in Annex II of the SEA Directive that refers to: 'The characteristics of plans and programmes, having regard, in particular, to—the degree to which the plan or programme *sets a framework for projects*

[69] SEA Directive Guidance (n 32) 10, s 3.22.

[70] Joined Cases C-105/09 and C-110/09 *Terre Wallonne ASBL v Région Wallonne* [2010] ECR I-5611, para 56.

[71] See SEA Directive Guidance (n 32) 10, s 3.23.

[72] See COWI A/S, Study concerning the report on the application and effectiveness of the SEA Directive (2001/42/EC), final report, 56, s 5.3.4 (Report No p-67683-a, prepared for the European Commission, DG ENV, April 2009)

[73] See ibid, 103–05, s 6.2.

[74] ibid, 104, s 6.2.

[75] ibid, 104–05, s 6.2.

[76] SEA Directive Guidance (n 32) 10–11, s 3.23.

and other activities, either with regard to the location, nature, size and operating conditions or by *allocating resources*'.[77] (emphasis added)

The Commission stated that the undefined word 'resources' can include financial, natural or perhaps also human resources, commenting that a 'generalised allocation of financial resources' is probably insufficient to 'set the framework'.[78] The Commission further stated that conditions as to how consent is granted is also required, either by setting out a future course of action, limiting the types of potentially available solutions or other specific and identifiable conditions.[79] Legally binding conditions for future development consents would also be sufficient,[80] as could sectoral plans and programmes that identify the location of subsequent developments in the specified sector, depending on the extent to which they condition future decisions on projects.[81] The Commission commented that an environmental assessment is more likely to be required for a legally binding plan or programme because it would 'set the framework more strictly than non-binding plans or programmes', as would plans or programmes with a single or main purpose compared to those with different purposes and issues.[82]

The issue as to whether certain activities are a plan or programme came before the CJEU in *Terre Wallonne ASBL v Région Wallonne*.[83] The case involved the implementation of the Nitrates Directive, under which land that drains into specified waters must be designated as vulnerable zones. Codes of good agricultural practice must be established for such zones in order to reduce 'water pollution caused or induced by nitrates from agricultural sources and [to prevent] further such pollution'.[84] The purpose of the Directive is to prevent water pollution from nitrates entering—and polluting—water. Pollution occurs when, for example, more manure is spread on land than can be taken up by the crops. Farmers may engage in excessive spreading because not only does the spreading fertilise crops, it also disposes of manure, a practice that economically benefits farmers.[85] The implementation of the Nitrates Directive had had a substantial effect on the Walloon Region of Belgium because 42 per cent of land in the Region was included in vulnerable zones and 54 per cent of productive agricultural land was affected by the Directive.[86]

The CJEU concluded that an action programme for the sustainable management of nitrogen in agriculture in the Region was a plan or programme.[87] It stated

[77] SEA Directive, Annex II, point 1.

[78] SEA Directive Guidance (n 32) 11, s 3.25.

[79] ibid.

[80] ibid 11, s 3.27.

[81] ibid 11, s 3.28.

[82] ibid 16, s 3.51.

[83] *Terre Wallonne ASBL* (n 70), para 23.

[84] Council Directive (EEC) 91/676 concerning the protection of waters against pollution caused by nitrates from agricultural sources [1991] OJ L375/1, art 1 ('the Nitrates Directive').

[85] See *Terre Wallonne ASBL* (n 22) Opinion of AG Kokott, para 3.

[86] See *Terre Wallonne ASBL* (n 70) para 23.

[87] ibid, para 55.

that, whereas all legislative measures that concern the protection of water from nitrate pollution from agricultural sources are not a plan or programme, 'the mere fact that such a measure is adopted by legislative means does not exclude it from the scope of [the SEA Directive]'[88] if it includes specified measures and actions that Member States must implement and monitor to combat nitrate pollution, a requirement for competent authorities periodically to review whether such measures and actions are appropriate and, if necessary, to revise action programmes.[89]

The action programme established by the Walloon Region was 'subject to preparation by an authority at national, regional or local level or [was] prepared by an authority for adoption, through a legislative procedure by Parliament or Government, and [was] required by legislative, regulatory or administrative provisions'.[90]

In discussing whether the action programme 'set the framework for future development consent of projects listed in Annexes I and II to [the EIA Directive]',[91] the CJEU noted that the programme was indisputably prepared for agriculture,[92] as well as including measures for intensive rearing installations, as specified in Annexes I and II.[93] The CJEU stated that the Nitrates Directive provided for measures, compliance with which could be a requirement for consent for projects listed in Annexes I and II of the EIA Directive,[94] further commenting that there was discretion in the Nitrates Directive concerning measures for the storage of livestock manure in respect of 'the consent that *may* be granted for carrying out [Annex I and II projects]'.[95] (emphasis added)

In her Opinion in *Terre Wallonne ASBL*, Advocate General Kokott had discussed the meaning of the term 'framework'.[96] She stated that the term 'must reflect the objective of taking into account the environmental effects of any decision laying down requirements for the future development consent of projects even as that decision is being taken'.[97] She further stated that the issue concerned the influence that requirements of plans and programmes must have on individual projects in order to 'set a framework'.[98] She rejected the notion that a framework must determine the location, nature or size of a project because a proposal for such a requirement by the Netherlands and Austria when the legislation that became the SEA Directive was being considered had not been accepted.[99] She also rejected the

88 ibid, para 41.
89 ibid (referring to characteristics set out in ibid, para 36).
90 ibid, para 35.
91 SEA Directive, art 3(2)(a).
92 *Terre Wallonne ASBL* (n 70) para 44.
93 ibid, para 49 (referring to point 17 of Annex I and point 1e of Annex II of the SEA Directive).
94 ibid, para 53.
95 ibid, para 55; see Nitrates Directive, Annex II, art A.5
96 *Terre Wallonne ASBL* (n 22) Opinion of AG Kokott, para 60.
97 ibid.
98 ibid, para 61.
99 ibid, para 62.

similar notion that a project must implicitly or explicitly be subject to a plan or programme because a proposal for this requirement by the Czech Republic had also not been accepted.[100] Instead, she considered that the degree of influence is flexible and thus the term 'framework' has a broad concept that 'does not require any conclusive determinations, but also covers forms of influence that leave room for some discretion'.[101]

Advocate General Kokott also referred to Annex II of the SEA Directive, which sets out criteria for determining the likely significance of effects on the environment.[102] Point 1 refers to: 'The characteristics of plans and programmes, having regard, in particular, to … the degree to which the plan or programme sets a framework for projects and other activities, either with regard to the location, nature, size and operating conditions or by allocating resources.'[103] She concluded that the use of the term 'in particular' means that each indent can be considered in terms of varying intensity or not at all.[104] She summarised by stating that 'a plan or programme sets a framework in so far as decisions are taken which influence any subsequent development consent of projects, in particular with regard to location, nature, size and operating conditions or by allocating resources'.[105] Although the CJEU did not endorse Advocate General Kokott's discussion, neither did it expressly reject it.[106]

The CJEU subsequently concluded in *Nomarchiaki Aftodioikisi Aitoloakarnanias v Ipourgos Perivallontos, Khorotaxias kai Dimosion Ergon* that a project for the partial diversion of the upper waters of the River Acheloos in western Greece in order to generate power was not a plan or programme.[107] Although the project concerned water management, as specified in the SEA Directive,[108] the court concluded that it was not evident that the project was a measure that defined 'criteria and detailed rules for the development of land'.[109] The court disagreed with Advocate General Kokott that management plans under the Water Framework Directive[110] must, in principle, be plans or programmes.[111] However, as Lady Hale subsequently commented, the issue decided by the CJEU in *Terre Wallonne*

[100] ibid, para 63.
[101] ibid, para 65.
[102] ibid, para 66.
[103] SEA Directive, Annex II, point 1.
[104] *Terre Wallonne ASBL* (n 22) Opinion of AG Kokott, para 66.
[105] ibid, para 67.
[106] See *R (on the Application of HS2 Action Alliance Ltd) v Secretary of State for Transport* [2014] UKSC 3; [2014] 1 WLR 324 [149] (Lady Hale).
[107] Case C-43/10 *Nomarchiaki Aftodioikisi Aitoloakarnanias v Ipourgos Perivallontos, Khorotaxias kai Dimosion Ergon* [2013] Env LR 453, para 96.
[108] SEA Directive, art 3(2)(a).
[109] *Nomarchiaki* (n 107) para 95 (referring to *Inter-Environnement* (n 2) para 30).
[110] Directive (EC) 2000/60 establishing a framework for Community action in the field of water [2000] OJ L327/1.
[111] *Nomarchiaki* (n 107) para 96 (referring to Opinion of AG Kokott, para 157).

and *Nomarchiaki*, was whether a project was a 'plan or programme', not whether the plan or programme 'set the framework'.[112]

Advocate General Kokott proposed further guidance on the meaning of 'plans or programmes' in *D'Oultremont v Région Wallonne*, a case that involves whether an order in the Walloon Region of Belgium containing provisions on the construction and operation of wind power installations must be preceded by a strategic environmental assessment.[113] Advocate General Kokott proposed that the term 'plans and programmes' could relate to the general development of areas or land; they do not have to relate to a specific area.[114] She further proposed that it is sufficient for plans or programmes 'to lay down criteria and detailed rules of some form'; they do 'not have to lay down *the* criteria and detailed rules for the development of land'.[115] Finally, she proposed that an order that contains provisions concerning safety, inspection, restoration of the site and financial collateral, which refers to noise levels by reference to spatial planning legislation, and which prescribes part of the framework for 'Installations for the harnessing of wind power for energy production (wind farms)' under the EIA Directive, must be classified as a 'plan or programme' under the SEA Directive.[116]

The UK Supreme Court has also ruled on whether a plan or programme falls within the SEA Directive. In 2014, in *R (on the Application of HS2 Action Alliance Ltd) v Secretary of State for Transport*, the court concluded that a command paper for the HS2, the proposed high-speed rail link between London and Birmingham,[117] is not a plan or programme. The command paper confirmed the Coalition government's strategy to construct the high-speed railway, summarised the government's decisions, reviewed responses to the 2011 public consultation on the proposals and set out next steps to be carried out.[118]

The issue was not whether HS2 is a transport project under the EIA Directive, which it indisputably is; rather, the issue was whether the command paper 'set the framework for future development consent'.[119] Lord Carnwath discussed *Terre*

[112] *HS2* (n 106) [149] (Lady Hale).

[113] *D'Oultremont v Région Wallonne* Case C-290/15, Opinion of AG Kokott (14 July 2016) para 26.

[114] ibid, para 45.

[115] ibid, para 57 (emphasis original).

[116] ibid, para 84(3) (referring to EIA Directive, annex II(3)(i)).

[117] Department for Transport, *High Speed Rail: Investing in Britain's Future—Decisions and Next Steps* (Cm 8247, 2012).

[118] See *HS2* (n 106) [10] (Lord Carnwath). This chapter does not discuss whether an environmental report was 'required by … administrative provisions' (SEA Directive, art 2(a)) because that is the subject of another chapter.

[119] See *HS2* (n 106) [38] (Lord Carnwath); see also [125] (Lord Sumption) ('The main reason why the command paper cannot require an environmental assessment under the SEA is that it is nothing more than a proposal. Naturally, the fact that it is a government proposal and appears in a command paper makes it influential in the broader sense that I have mentioned above. It means it is politically more likely to be accepted. But the command paper does not operate as a constraint on the discretion of Parliament. None of the factors which bear on the ultimate decision whether to pass the hybrid bill into law have been pre-empted, even partially. I accept that this means that governments may in some cases be able to avoid the need for an environmental assessment by promoting specific legislation authorising development').

Wallonne ASBL, Inter-Environnement and *Nomarchiaki*,[120] concluding that a plan or programme must influence a development decision in the sense that it constrains subsequent consideration and prevents 'appropriate account from being taken of all the environmental effects which might otherwise be relevant'.[121] He stated that the command paper:

> [I]s a very elaborate description of the HS2 project, including the thinking behind it and the government's reasons for rejecting alternatives. In one sense, it might be seen as helping to set the framework for the subsequent debate, and it is intended to influence its result. But it does not in any way constrain the decision-making process of the authority responsible, which in this case is Parliament.[122]

Lord Sumption agreed, commenting that the command paper was not a constraint on Parliament's discretion.[123] Lady Hale also concluded 'that the "framework" has to be one which those granting such consent must at the very least take into account'.[124]

The Court of Appeal in Northern Ireland has also ruled on the SEA Directive. In a decision concerning whether a planning policy statement (PPS) 'set the framework for future development consent', the court concluded in *Central Craigavon Ltd v Department of the Environment for Northern Ireland* that a PPS is not a plan because it:

> [D]oes not lay down anything that would fall within what we would normally understand to be a framework or cadre, Rahmen or quadro in the French, German or Italian texts, these latter words indicating a frame. What it does do is to indicate that the material planning considerations to be taken account of were the contribution of the application to [the area's] Regional Development, consideration of the development's impact on Belfast City Centre and other retail centres and the provisions of policy RRP1 and 'detailed policy in a prevailing development plan.[125]

In a critique of *Central Craigavon,* Gregory Jones, Ned Westaway and Roger Watts commented that the PPS had 'set out the policies of the Department on particular aspects of land-use planning [that] apply to the whole of Northern Ireland [and] their contents will be taken into account in preparing development plans and are also material to decisions on individual planning applications and appeals'.[126]

[120] ibid [10].
[121] ibid [40] (Lord Carnwath).
[122] ibid [38] (Lord Carnwath).
[123] ibid [125] (Lord Sumption).
[124] ibid [150] (Lady Hale).
[125] *Central Craigavon Ltd v Department of the Environment for Northern Ireland* [2011] NICA 17 (CA) [43].
[126] Jones, Westaway and Watts (n 27) 1082 (quoting Planning Policy Statement 1, para 33 (Northern Ireland PPS1)).

Requirement for Appropriate Assessment Pursuant to the Habitats Directive

Any plan or programme that has been determined to require an 'appropriate assessment' under the Habitats Directive because it is likely to have an effect on a proposed site of community importance (SCI) under the Habitats Directive or a special protection area (SPA) designated under the Birds Directive automatically falls within the SEA Directive.[127] The obligation to carry out an environmental assessment under the SEA Directive does not mean that an appropriate assessment under the Habitats Directive need not be carried out. The obligations are separate and fulfil different purposes.[128]

This category of plans and programmes typically applies to proposed projects such as corridors to construct roads that affect Natura 2000 sites.[129] In contrast to the EIA Directive, which requires an assessment depending on the type of project, this category focuses on the area to be affected by a plan or programme.[130] Perhaps the most notorious case was the proposed construction of the Via Baltica through protected sites in the Rospuda River Valley in northeast Poland.[131] An environmental assessment was finalised in 2008 and the Via Baltica was re-routed in 2009, but not before roads in the area had been constructed.[132]

The determination whether a 'plan or project', a term that is not defined in either the Habitats Directive or the Birds Directive, is 'likely to have significant effects', either individually or in combination with other plans or projects,[133]

[127] Directive (EC) 2009/147 on the conservation of wild birds [2010] OJ L20/7. SACs and SPAs form the Natura 2000 network of protected areas that covers over 18 per cent of the land area of the EU. See (January 2014) Natura 2000, 35, 8–9.

[128] See Nicolas de Sadeleer, 'The Appropriate Impact Assessment and Authorisation Requirements of Plans and Projects Likely to Have Significant Impacts on Natura 2000 Sites' (2013) 1+2 *Environmental Law Network International Review* 7, 21.

[129] See *Terre Wallonne ASBL* (n 22) Opinion of AG Kokott, para 91.

[130] See William Sheate, Helen Byron, Suzan Dagg and Lourdes Cooper, 'The Relationship between the EIA and SEA Directives; Final Report to the European Commission' (Contract No ENV.G.4./ETU/2004/0020r, August 2005) 5, s 3.3.1.

[131] The strategic environmental assessment was recommended under the Bern Convention before Poland became a Member State of the EU on 1 May 2004. See Convention on the Conservation of European Wildlife and Natural Habitats, Standing Committee, 30th Meeting, Construction of the 'Via Baltica' in Poland; Report by the NGOs (6–9 December 2010); 'Commission Asks the European Court of Justice to Order Poland Not to Start Road Construction in Rospuda Valley' (press release, IP/07/1191, 30 July 2007); see Birdlife International, OTOP, WWF, CEE Bankwatch Network, Background Note, Brussels, June 2006,' Via Baltica—Not This Way!', bankwatch.org/documents/via_baltica_issue_paper 0606.pdf.

[132] See, eg the Rospuda Case, Białystok (2012), www.natura2000.efort.pl/pliki/2012/rospuda_case.pdf; Environmental and Social Data Sheet, Project Name Augustow Bypass, Project No 20130205 (26 July 2013), www.eib.org/infocentre/register/all/48501113.pdf.

[133] Habitats Directive, art 6(3).

is decided objectively on a case-by-case basis.[134] The CJEU has ruled that an appropriate assessment must be carried out for any plan or project that is not directly connected with, or necessary to, the management of a special area of conservation if the possibility of harm cannot be excluded on the basis of objective information.[135] In such a case, there must remain 'no reasonable scientific doubt as to the absence of such effects'.[136] In effect, the CJEU concluded that the word 'likely' means 'possible'[137] and that the term 'likely to have significant effects' means 'may have significant effects'.[138]

As with a plan or programme in respect of projects under Annexes I and II of the EIA Directive, there is no need to determine whether a plan or programme that concerns a 'plan or project' under the Habitats Directive is likely to have significant effects on the environment; the plan or project is automatically considered to have a likely significant environmental effect.[139] Thus, the issue as to whether there is an obligation to carry out an environmental assessment under the SEA Directive 'is necessarily limited to the question as to whether it can be excluded, on the basis of objective information, that the plan or project will have a significant effect on the site concerned'.[140]

Use of Small Areas at a Local Level

An environmental assessment must be prepared for plans and programmes 'which determine the use of small areas at local level [but] only where the Member States

[134] Managing Natura 2000 Sites 33, s 4.4.1 ('[it is] clear that what may be significant in relation to one site may not be in relation to another').

[135] Case C-127/02 *Landelijke Vereniging tot Behoud van de Waddenzee v Staatssecretaris van Landbouw, Natuurbeheer en Visserij* [2004] ECR I-7405, para 44.

[136] ibid, para 67; see also *Terre Wallonne ASBL* (n 22) Opinion of AG Kokott, para 94. The competent authority may agree to a proposed plan or project only if it will not adversely affect the integrity of the site. There is an exception for plans or projects that must be carried out for 'imperative reasons of overriding public interests', in which case a Member State must take compensatory measures. Habitats Directive, art 6(4); see Case C-127/02 *Landelijke Vereniging tot Behoud van de Waddenzee v Staatssecretaris van Landbouw, Natuurbeheer en Visserij* [2004] ECR I-7405, para 4; see also Niamh O'Sullivan, 'Combating Biodiversity Loss: An Analysis of Compensatory Measures under the Habitats Directive' (2010) 13 *Trinity College Law Review* 33, 39–54 (analysing concept of compensatory measures).

[137] See Robert McCracken, 'EIA, SEA and AA, Present Position: Where are We Now?' (2010) *Journal of Planning & Environment Law* 1515, 1520.

[138] Case C-258/11 *Sweetman v An Bord Pleanála* [2013] 3 CMLR 16, Opinion of AG Sharpston, para 47 ('*possibility* of there being a significant effect on the site will generate the need for an appropriate assessment … There is no need to *establish* such an effect; it is … merely necessary to determine that there *may* be such an effect' (emphasis in original)); see also Case C-258/11 *Sweetman v An Bord Pleanála* [2013] 3 CMLR 16, para 48 (destruction of only part of site is sufficient for integrity of site to be adversely affected).

[139] See *Terre Wallonne ASBL* (n 22) Opinion of AG Kokott, paras 47–54.

[140] Case C-177/11 *Sillogos Ellinon Poleodomon kai Khorotakton v Ipourgos Perivallontos, Khorotaxias kai Dimosion Ergon* (CJEU, 21 June 2012), para 24.

determine that they are likely to have significant environmental effects'.[141] A plan falls within this provision regardless of whether it involves a single economic activity. Thus, a plan to construct an intensive pig-rearing complex with capacity for 4,000 pigs did not fall outside the SEA Directive simply because it concerned only one economic activity.[142]

The Commission's guidance states that the word 'small' should probably be decided on a case-by-case basis due to differences between Member States. It noted that 'a careful exercise of judgement' is necessary, commenting that the type of plan or programme envisaged by the SEA Directive 'might be a building plan which, for a particular, limited area, outlines details of how buildings must be constructed, determining, for example, their height, width or design'.[143] The Commission also noted that the term 'local' implies a contrast with national or regional levels of government and that an entire local authority cannot be excluded unless it is small.[144] In other words, as in the EIA Directive, the threshold for determining whether there is a plan or programme may not be based solely on size.[145]

If a plan or programme falls within this category, there is no automatic conclusion that it is likely to have significant environmental effects. A Member State must make this determination either by a case-by-case examination, specifying the types of plans or programmes, or a combination of both approaches. Regardless of the methodology selected, the determination must take into account relevant criteria for determining the likely significance of effects in Annex II of the SEA Directive,[146] in particular, characteristics of the plan or programme, its effects and the area likely to be affected by it.[147] The three types of criteria are based on the screening mechanisms in the EIA Directive. The first mechanism, as its name states, examines a plan or programme on an individual basis. The second mechanism envisages a general determination based on plans and programmes of the same kind, with the potential for application of the third mechanism in some cases.[148]

Minor Modifications to a Plan or Programme

The SEA Directive provides that 'minor modifications to plans and programmes … shall require an environmental assessment'.[149] As with the use of small areas at

[141] SEA Directive, art 3(3).
[142] Case C-295/10 *Genovaitė Valčiukienė v Pakruojo rajono savivaldybė* [2012] Env LR 283, para 39.
[143] SEA Directive Guidance (n 32), 12, s 3.33.
[144] ibid, 13, s 3.34.
[145] ibid 13, s 3.35 (citing Case C-392/96 *Commission v Ireland* [1999] ECR I-5901, para 72).
[146] See *Inter-Environnement Bruxelles ASBL* (n 2) para 5 (quoting SEA Directive, art 3(5)).
[147] Case C-295/10 *Genovaitė Valčiukienė v Pakruojo rajono savivaldybė* [2012] Env LR 283, para 46.
[148] SEA Directive Guidance (n 32), 14–15, ss 3.40–47.
[149] SEA Directive, art 3(3).

a local level, a determination as to whether a proposal is likely to have significant environmental effects is required.[150]

The reason for requiring assessments for modifications is, as the Commission stated in its guidance to the SEA Directive, because land use plans tend to be modified when they become outdated rather than new plans being prepared. Excluding modifications would therefore restrict the scope of the SEA Directive.[151] The Commission further stated that a plan or programme may be modified as a result of consultation, reconsideration of elements of the plan or programme, or changes in the state of the environment, with even minor modifications resulting in significant environmental effects.[152]

The CJEU ruled on this category in *Inter-Environnement Bruxelles ASBL v Région de Bruxelles-Capitale*, which involved the repeal of a provision in the Brussels Town and Country Planning Code that provided for consultation by governmental entities and the public in the preparation or modification of an environmental report, but not in the repeal of a land use plan.[153] The CJEU concluded that the procedure for the partial or total repeal of a land use plan fell, in principle, within the SEA Directive; thus, the procedure was subject to an assessment as to whether it had a likely significant effect on the environment.[154] The Court reasoned that 'the provisions which delimit the directive's scope, in particular those setting out the definitions of the measures envisaged by the directive, must be interpreted broadly'.[155] It referred to the EIA Directive, stating that the modification of a project under that directive is subject to the same requirements as a project.[156]

The Court did not conclude that all partial or total repeals of a land use plan are subject to the SEA Directive. Instead, it stated that if a repealed measure is part of a hierarchy of town and country planning measures that establish 'sufficiently precise rules governing land use', has been subject to an environmental assessment and 'it may reasonably be considered that the interests [designed to be protected by the EIA Directive] have been [sufficiently] taken into account', the measure is not subject to the SEA Directive.[157] If, however, a repealed measure does not satisfy the above criteria, it is subject to the SEA Directive because it modifies the framework for assessing whether it may give rise to significant effects on the environment.[158]

[150] ibid; see *Terre Wallonne ASBL* (n 22) Opinion of AG Kokott, para 51.

[151] SEA Directive Guidance (n 32) 7, s 3.9.

[152] ibid 7–8, s 3.10.

[153] *Inter-Environnement Bruxelles ASBL* (n 2) para 12.

[154] ibid, para 43.

[155] ibid, para 37.

[156] See Case C-72/95 *Aannemersbedrijf PK Kraaijeveld BV v Gedeputeerde Staten van Zuid-Holland* [1996] ECR I-5403, paras 39–40.

[157] *Inter-Environnement Bruxelles ASBL* (n 2), para 42.

[158] ibid, para 39.

In her Opinion in the case, Advocate General Kokott had stated that if a plan or programme has set the framework for future development consent of projects by imposing limits on the projects, the repeal of a plan or programme in the framework necessarily gives rise to significant effects on the environment. She gave the example of a land use plan that allows the construction of a 20,000 square metre building. Repeal of the plan to allow the construction of a 44,000 square metre office building would extend the framework for development consents for office buildings, with the result that removal of the restrictions may have an effect on the environment.[159]

The modification must affect or modify the legal or administrative framework for the future development consent of projects. In this respect, the UK Supreme Court held in a case involving the construction of a road network around Aberdeen that even if transport strategies adopted by two local authorities as part of a scheme was a plan or programme,[160] the decision to enlarge the road construction project was not the modification of a plan or programme because it altered a specific project that continued to require development consent; it did not alter a plan or programme.[161]

Conclusion

The SEA Directive is still in its infancy. Although Member States were directed to transpose it by 21 July 2004, it was not until 2009 that it had been transposed in all Member States.[162] Even then, some Member States had not fully transposed it.[163]

[159] ibid, Opinion of AG Kokott, paras 40–41.

[160] *Walton v Scottish Ministers* (n 41) para 62 (Lord Reed: 'sufficient to say that it appears to me to be arguable that the [scheme or strategies] formed a plan or programme within the meaning of the Directive'); para 99 (Lord Carnwath: 'I should register my serious doubts [that the scheme was itself a plan or programme] even accepting the flexible approached required by the European authorities').

[161] ibid, paras 69 (Lord Reed), 99 (Lord Carnwath), 149 (Lord Hope).

[162] Report on the application and effectiveness of the Directive on Strategic Environmental Assessment (Directive 2001/42/EC) 2, s 2 COM (2009) 469 final (14 September 2009).

[163] See 'Environment: Commission Asks Belgium and Portugal to Comply with EU Legislation on Strategic Environmental Assessments' (press release, IP/10/1564, 24 November 2010); 'Environment: Commission Asks Slovakia to Comply with EU Legislation on Strategic Environmental Impact Assessments' (press release, IP/11/176, 16 February 2011); 'Environment: Commission Asks Lithuania to Comply with EU Legislation on Strategic Environmental Impact Assessments' (press release, IP/11/306, 14 March 2011); 'Environment: Commission Prompts Finland to Comply with Waste and Environmental Assessments Legislation' (press release, IP/11/1268, 26 October 2011); 'Environment: Commission Asks Sweden to Comply with EU Legislation on Strategic Environmental Impact Assessments' (press release, IP/12/294, 22 March 2012); 'Environment: Commission Asks Slovakia to Comply with EU Legislation on Strategic Environmental Impact Assessments and Packaging Waste' (press release, IP/12/295, 22 March 2012).

As this chapter discusses, the definition of a plan and programme has led to problems. In its 2009 report on the application and implementation of the SEA Directive, the Commission recognised such problems, commenting that:

> In particular, the boundaries between what constitutes a plan, a programme or a project are not always clear, and there may be some doubts as to whether the 'subject' of the assessment meets the criteria of either or both of the Directives. In this regard, the definitions of some project categories listed in Annex II of the EIA in relation to changes in land use are not clear, and could create confusion with the SEA.[164]

The Commission also commented that:

> Consideration could be given to *merging the EIA and SEA Directives* in order to clarify their interrelationship and boost their complementarity and efficiency through a holistic environmental assessment process. While this may appear to be an attractive option, very few [Member States] recommended merging the two Directives; they stressed that each process should be completely separate in its own right, because the two Directives are complementary and address different stages and processes (emphasis in original).[165]

The Commission considered that inconsistencies between both Directives could be resolved by correcting them, clarifying the overlapping projects/plans and programmes, and by issuing guidance.[166] Experience since 2009 has shown that the need for such guidance—or an alternative means of dealing with the continuing difficulties in defining a plan and programme—has grown in urgency.

[164] Report from the Commission to the Council, the European Parliament, the European Economic and Social Committee and the Committee of the Regions on the application and effectiveness of the Directive on Strategic Environmental Assessment (Directive 2001/42/EC) 6, s 4.1 COM (2009) 469 final (14 September 2009). This report is further discussed by Gregory Jones in Ch 2 of this volume.

[165] ibid.

[166] ibid 7, s 4.1.

4

The Meaning of 'Required by Legislative, Regulatory or Administrative Provisions'

SIMON RICKETTS AND JULIET MUNN

Introduction

Others in this volume have explained the gestation of, and intentions behind, the SEA Directive.[1] The SEA regime is intended to require assessment of the environmental effects of plans and programmes, which have a strategic role in the development process, at a point in the preparation of these documents where options are still open. It addresses what would otherwise be an inevitable limitation of the EIA Directive: that by the time the likely significant environmental effects of proposed project come to be assessed, the policy background that has determined important characteristics of that project have often already been set in stone.

Article 2(a) sets out the categories of 'plans and programmes' to which the Directive applies:

> '[P]lans and programmes' shall mean plans and programmes, including those co-financed by the European Community, as well as any modifications to them:
>
> (i) which are subject to preparation and/or adoption by an authority at national, regional or local level or which are prepared by an authority for adoption, through a legislative procedure by Parliament or Government, and
>
> (ii) which are required by legislative, regulatory or administrative provisions.

Both of the limbs of this test must be met for the SEA Directive to apply. This chapter will only consider the second limb.

[1] Directive 2001/42/EC of the European Parliament and of the Council of 27 June 2001 on the assessment of the effects of certain plans and programmes on the environment. For a history of the SEA Directive, and for its transposition within the various Member States, see, eg, Robert McCracken and Ned Westaway, and Gregory Jones in Chs 1 and 2, respectively, of this volume.

As with other aspects of the SEA Directive, its application in practice is beset with difficulties arising from its deceptively simple terms, nuances in the official languages of the European Union (EU)[2] and the variety of activities of the Member States, governed by wide-ranging domestic legal requirements as well as constitutional and political arrangements.

The position may have been more straightforward had Article 2(a) remained limited in the way envisaged in the *travaux preparatoires*[3] in referring:

> only to town and country planning plans and programmes:–
>
> — which are subject to preparation and adoption by a competent authority or which are prepared for adoption by a legislative act; and
> — which are part of the town and country planning decision-making process for the purpose of establishing the framework for subsequent development consents; and
> — which contain provisions on the nature, size, location or operating conditions of projects.

Given that the objective of the SEA Directive is to 'contribute to the integration of environmental considerations into the preparation and adoption of plans and programmes with a view to promoting sustainable development' (Article 1), it might be thought that the phrase 'required by legislative, regulatory or administrative provisions' would be given a wide meaning in the interests of promoting sustainable development. However, this is not necessarily the approach taken by Member States, faced with what may appear to be bureaucratic procedures that threaten the timely delivery of politically sensitive projects—the *HS2* case being a recent example.[4]

It is of note that, unlike with the previous eco-towns programme (where the government voluntarily accepted the need to carry out strategic environmental assessment (SEA) in relation to its programme for identifying potential locations for eco-towns),[5] the government has firmly taken the stance (now supported by the Supreme Court) that its decision to proceed with the HS2 high-speed rail programme did not engage the requirements of the SEA Directive.[6] This approach has not helped with the confusion as to when Article 2(a) will be applied, considering

[2] For a brief consideration of those varying nuances, see Jonathan Robinson and David Elvin QC 'The Environmental Assessment of Plans and Programmes' (2004) *Journal of Planning and Environmental Law* 1032 at fns [18] and [19].

[3] 'Proposal for a Council Directive on the assessment of the effects of certain plans and programmes on the environment, Official Journal C 129, 25/04/1997 P. 0014.

[4] *HS2 Action Alliance and Others v Secretary of State of Transport* [2014] UKSC 3.

[5] *Bard Campaign v Secretary of State for Communities and Local Government* [2009] EWHC 308 (Admin).

[6] *HS2 Action Alliance and Others v Secretary of State of Transport* [2014] UKSC 3. For the Scottish experience of dealing with similar issues, see further Colin Reid and Denis Edwards in Ch 14 of this volume. Plainly, the extent to which the courts are prepared to give wide interpretations to the preconditions for an SEA requirement is relevant to the debate explored by Eloise Scotford in Ch 9 of this volume, namely, the extent to which the SEA Directive operates as a control to government environmental policy.

the formality of the 'plan or programme' in question in the *HS2* case, particularly when compared to the revocation of regional strategies and the introduction of National Policy Statements for which a number of 'voluntary' SEAs were carried out.[7]

The most uncertainty has been caused by the use of 'required by' in relation to administrative provisions. Almost by definition, an administrative provision will not 'require' anything in the sense of rendering it legally obligatory. As was noted by Advocate General Kokott in her Opinion in *Inter-Environnement Bruxelles*,[8] the Commission had proposed that the SEA Directive should apply to plans and programmes 'which are provided for in legislation or based on regulatory or administrative provisions'.[9] However, that more precisely worded proposal was not taken up by the EU legislature.

There is also the overlap with the requirement that the plan or programme should 'set the framework for future development consent'. How tightly should 'set the framework' be defined when the framework setting is by way of an administrative provision, with the inherent complication that the resultant framework will necessarily not be a legislative one, but one that is more in the nature of administrative statement or policy?

Implementation in the UK

The SEA Directive is implemented in the UK as follows:

- in England: the Environmental Assessment of Plans and Programmes Regulations 2004;
- in Wales: the Environmental Assessment of Plans and Programmes Regulations (Wales) 2004;
- in Scotland: the Environmental Assessment (Scotland) Act 2005; and
- in Northern Ireland: the Environmental Assessment of Plans and Programmes Regulations (Northern Ireland) 2004.

In England, Wales and Northern Ireland, the reference to 'required by legislative, regulatory or administrative provisions' is simply adopted from the SEA Directive. However, in Scotland, SEA is applied to all public sector strategies, plans and programmes likely to have significant environmental effects, regardless of whether

[7] Gregory Jones QC, Ned Westaway and Roger Watts, 'Why Central Craigavon was Wrongly Decided (and Other Problems with the Incorporation of the Strategic Environmental Assessment Directive into Domestic Law)' (2013) *Journal of Planning and Environmental Law* 1074.

[8] Case C-567/10 *Inter-Environnement Bruxelles ASBL v Région de Bruxelles-Capitale* [2012] 2 CMLR 30; [2012] Env LR 30.

[9] ibid, para 18.

they are required by legislative, regulatory or administrative measures and regardless of whether they set a framework for future development consents.

In September 2005, the then Office of the Deputy Prime Minister published 'A Practical Guide to the Strategic Environmental Assessment Directive',[10] which sets out an indicative list of the types of plans or programmes which, in its view, were subject to the SEA Directive. This list is non-exhaustive and includes documents such as:

— Local Plans;
— National Park Plans (Scotland);
— Local Development Documents;
— Local Housing Strategies;
— Local Transport Plans; and
— National Park Management Plans.

This guidance has not been updated to take into account subsequent changes to planning legislation such as the Planning Act 2008 (national policy statements) and the Localism Act 2011 (neighbourhood plans).

The Second Limb of Article 2(a)

The terms 'legislative' and 'regulatory' provisions are relatively self-explanatory. However, 'required by' and 'administrative provisions' have led to protracted debate in a series of cases. We take these in turn.

'Required by'

The European Commission[11] guidance to the term 'required' in Article 2(a) asserts that this test will not be met if a plan or programme arises from legislation which is couched in permissive terms (ie, that the authority *may* prepare a plan rather than *shall* prepare a plan) or if the authority decides to prepare a plan of an activity which is unregulated, but that if an authority is not required to draw up a plan unless certain preconditions are met, once such preconditions have been met, and if the plan or programme meets the other requirements of the legislation, the plan will be subject to the requirements of the SEA Directive. The guidance goes on to

[10] 'A Practical Guide to the Strategic Environmental Assessment Directive—Practical Guidance on Applying European Directive 2001/42/EC "on the Assessment of the Effects of Certain Plans and Programmes on the Environment"', Office of the Deputy Prime Minister, September 2005.

[11] Commission Guidance on SEA, Implementation of Directive 2001/42 on the assessment of certain plans and programmes on the environment, paragraph 3.15.

state that it is open to Member States within their national systems to go further than the minimum requirements of the SEA Directive and it would be possible for an authority to carry out SEA on plans or programmes which do not meet the legislative test.

Inter-Environnement Bruxelles

The meaning of 'required by … legislative provisions' was considered by the Court of Justice of the European Union (CJEU) in *Inter-Environnement Bruxelles.*[12] This case concerned an order amending the Belgium Town and Country Planning Code, which the applicants alleged was incompatible with the SEA Directive as it did not require an environmental report to be drawn up for the total, or partial, repeal of a specific land use plan. The CJEU was asked by the Belgium Cour Constitutionelle (Constitutional Court) to consider whether 'the SEA Directive covers plans or programmes which are provided for in legislative provisions but the adoption of which is not compulsory, or whether that directive applies only where these is a legal obligation to draw up a plan'.

In her Opinion on the case, Advocate General Kokott considered this question by comparing the provision in the different language versions of the SEA Directive.[13] She identified that almost all of the language versions of Article 2(a) refer to plans or programmes which 'must' be prepared or 'are required'. Therefore, plans or programmes which are governed by law but which do not have to be adopted would not be covered by such an interpretation. Only the Italian version of the SEA Directive provides for a slightly different approach. This version refers to plans and programmes which are 'provided for' ('previsti') rather than 'required' by law—language which doesn't appear to be as restrictive as other versions of the SEA Directive. However, the Advocate General concluded that, based on the intention of the SEA Directive and the background to its adoption, the Italian version of the SEA Directive must be held to apply only to plans or projects the adoption of which is based on a legal obligation. She went on to recognise that 'plans and programmes which are not based on a legal obligation may also have significant effects on the environment. Indeed these effects may be even more significant than those of compulsory plans. Nonetheless, the legislature clearly did not intend such measures to require an environmental assessment'.[14]

One of the reasons put forward by the Member States in support of the Advocate General's interpretation was that if an SEA was required during the preparation of voluntary plans and programmes, there is a risk that Member States would simply elect not to adopt them in order to avoid the requirements of the Directive.

[12] *Inter-Environnement Bruxelles ASBL* (n 8).
[13] ibid, Opinion of Advocate General Kokott delivered on 17 November 2011.
[14] ibid, para 20.

However, Advocate General Kokott held that each plan or programme must be assessed on its own merits regardless of whether its preparation is voluntary or compulsory and concluded that:

> In short, the word 'required' in Article 2(a) of the SEA Directive must be construed as meaning that that definition does not include plans and programmes which are provided for by legislative provisions but the drawing up of which is not compulsory. Plans or programmes which may under certain conditions be prepared voluntarily are covered by that definition only in cases where there is an obligation to draw them up.[15]

The referred question was then considered by the CJEU, which disagreed with the Advocate General's opinion for the following reasons:

> [25] According to the applicants in the main proceedings, a mere literal interpretation of [Article 2(a)], which would exclude from the scope of Directive 2001/42 plans and programmes that are only provided for by legislative, regulatory or administrative provisions, would entail the dual risk of not requiring the assessment procedure for land development plans which normally have major effects on the territory concerned and of not ensuring uniform application of the directive in the Member States' various legal orders, given the differences existing in the formulation of the relevant national rules.
>
> [26] The Belgian, Czech and United Kingdom Governments submit, on the other hand, that it is apparent not only from the wording of Article 2(a) of Directive 2001/42 but also from the directive's travaux préparatoires that the European Union legislature did not intend to make administrative and legislative measures that are not required by rules of law subject to the environmental impact assessment procedure established by the directive.
>
> [27] The European Commission considers that, where an authority is subject to a legal obligation to prepare or adopt a plan or programme, the test of being 'required' within the meaning of Article 2(a) of Directive 2001/42 is met. That is prima facie so, in its view, in the case of the plans that must be adopted by the Brussels-Capital Region.
>
> [28] It must be stated that an interpretation which would result in excluding from the scope of Directive 2001/42 all plans and programmes, inter alia those concerning the development of land, whose adoption is, in the various national legal systems, regulated by rules of law, solely because their adoption is not compulsory in all circumstances, cannot be upheld.
>
> [29] The interpretation of Article 2(a) of Directive 2001/42 that is relied upon by the abovementioned governments would have the consequence of restricting considerably the scope of the scrutiny, established by the directive, of the environmental effects of plans and programmes concerning town and country planning of the Member States.
>
> [30] Consequently, such an interpretation of Article 2(a) of Directive 2001/42, by appreciably restricting the directive's scope, would compromise, in part, the practical effect of the directive, having regard to its objective, which consists in providing for a high level of protection of the environment (see, to this effect, Case C-295/10 *Valčiukienė*

[15] ibid, para 30.

> *and Others* [2011] ECR I-0000, paragraph 42). That interpretation would thus run counter to the directive's aim of establishing a procedure for scrutinising measures likely to have significant effects on the environment, which define the criteria and the detailed rules for the development of land and normally concern a multiplicity of projects whose implementation is subject to compliance with the rules and procedures provided for by those measures.
>
> [31] It follows that plans and programmes whose adoption is regulated by national legislative or regulatory provisions, which determine the competent authorities for adopting them and the procedure for preparing them, must be regarded as 'required' within the meaning, and for the application, of Directive 2001/42 and, accordingly, be subject to an assessment of their environmental effects in the circumstances which it lays down.
>
> [32] It follows from the foregoing that the answer to the second question is that the concept of plans and programmes 'which are required by legislative, regulatory or administrative provisions', appearing in Article 2(a) of Directive 2001/42, must be interpreted as also concerning specific land development plans, such as the one covered by the national legislation at issue in the main proceedings.

The CJEU therefore interpreted the term 'required by legislative provisions' so as to include plans and programmes the adoption of which is not compulsory (and thus not 'required' in any ordinary sense of the term), but where adoption is 'regulated' by national legislative or regulatory provisions. This analysis, as opposed to that of Advocate General Kokott, creates uncertainty when determining in which circumstances SEA needs to be carried out. However, it does widen the scope of the Directive from an otherwise restrictive interpretation. Extending the scope of Article 2(a) in this manner also allows modifications and repeals of plans and programmes (which are very rarely 'required' in the restrictive sense) to be subject to SEA. If such actions were excluded from the SEA Directive, there would, in principle, be nothing to prevent Member States from implementing plans with minor environmental effects and then making significant modifications to them further down the line.[16] This purposive approach[17] was adopted in the CJEU in the case of *Attikis*,[18] which made it clear that the intention of the SEA Directive is for it to apply to modifications of plans and programmes which fall within Article 2(a), even where the Directive was not in force at the time that the original plan or programme came into force.

[16] See further William Orbinson in Ch 15 of this volume; and Jones, Westaway and Watts (n 7).

[17] As to whether this approach may go beyond even what is ordinarily regarded as a 'purposive' approach, see Elizabeth Fisher in Ch 10 of this volume.

[18] Case C-473/14 *Attikis v Ipourgos Perivallontos* [2015] All ER (D) 69 (Sep). See further Lorenzo Squintani 'On the Difference between Repealing Plans with Modifying Plans under the Strategic Environmental Assessment Directive' [2016] *Journal for European Environmental & Planning Law* [2016] 13(1), 102–03.

Central Craigavon

The Northern Ireland courts grappled with the issue of the interpretation of Article 2(a) in a case known as *Central Craigavon*.[19] The case was ultimately settled before its scheduled hearing date in the Supreme Court, but the judgment in the Court of Appeal (Northern Ireland) provides some clarity on the UK courts' approach to the question of the definition of 'required by'. The case involved the issue of a new draft planning policy statement in relation to retail planning matters which proposed relaxing existing controls on out-of-town retail development. The policy statement was not subject to SEA. The Court held that the draft policy statement was not required by legislative, regulatory or administrative provisions on the basis that:

> A draft PPS proposing to alter an earlier PPS is not something which the Department was obliged to produce. It is a statement of evolving departmental policy thinking. While the DOE is required to formulate and coordinate policy for securing the orderly and consistent development of land and the planning of that development, the ongoing duty to formulate policy did not oblige the DOE to introduce draft PPS5 or to produce it in the form which it did. It represents a policy choice and, at this stage, it is a preliminary policy choice which will not be finalised until the consultation process is exhausted.[20]

Although this judgment pre-dated *Inter-Environnement Bruxelles*, it is perhaps indicative of the UK courts' sceptical approach to a wider interpretation of the term 'required'. Nonetheless, Orbinson must be correct when he states that in the light of the judgment of the CJEU: 'The [Northern Ireland] Court of Appeal's view on the meaning of "required" is unsustainable.'[21]

Walton v Scottish Ministers

The CJEU judgment in *Inter-Environnemental Bruxelles* was noted by the UK Supreme Court in *Walton v Scottish Ministers*.[22] This involved a road scheme in Aberdeenshire which was proposed by NESTRANS, a partnership between Aberdeen City Council and Aberdeenshire Council, and subsequently promoted by the Scottish Ministers. The Ministers then amended the scheme to include a section of the road known as the Fastlink. The appellants argued that the amendment was a modification to a 'plan or programme' and therefore triggered the SEA Directive. The Court held that the Fastlink did not fall within the SEA Directive as it did not alter the development consenting framework for the particular road network. Some scepticism as to the CJEU's approach may perhaps be noted in Lord Reed's judgment:

[19] *Central Craigavon Ltd v Department of the Environment for Northern Ireland* [2011] NICA 17.
[20] ibid, para 37.
[21] See William Orbinson in Ch 15 of this volume.
[22] *Walton v Scottish Ministers* [2012] UKSC 44,

> [61] It might be argued with some force that none of these documents has been shown to have been 'required by legislative, regulatory or administrative provisions' as stipulated by the second indent of Art 2(a), *even according the term 'required' the width of meaning given to it in Inter-Environnement Bruxelles* (para 31). It might also be argued that NESTRANS, at least, was not an 'authority' within the meaning of the first indent, since it was established voluntarily and did not exercise any statutory functions. On the other hand, it might be argued that the documents 'set the framework for future development consent of projects', as explained by Advocate General Kokott in her opinion in *Terre Wallonne* (points 64, 65), and were therefore likely to have significant effects on the environment. In those circumstances, it might be argued that a purposive interpretation of the Directive would bring the documents within its scope.
>
> [62] For reasons which I shall explain, it does not appear to me to be necessary to reach a concluded view on these questions. It is sufficient to say that it appears to me to be arguable that the MTS, or the local transport strategies which formed its constituent parts, formed a plan or programme within the meaning of the Directive. The question whether the decision to construct the Fastlink constituted a modification to a plan or programme can be considered on the hypothesis that the MTS (or its constituent documents) comprised such a plan or programme. (emphasis added)

Lord Carnwath appeared equally sceptical:

> [99] On the first point, like Lord Reed, I am content to proceed on the assumption that the MTS, as approved by NESTRANS in March 2003, was itself such a 'plan or programme'. However, I should register my serious doubts on the point, even accepting the flexible approach required by the European authorities. I note from that the passage from *Inter-Environnement Bruxelles ASBL and ors v Région de Bruxelles-Capitale* quoted by Lord Reed (para 22) refers to regulation of plans and programmes by provisions 'which determine the competent authorities for adopting them and the procedure for preparing them'.

There is little in-depth analysis of the SEA Directive, still less a desire to apply a purposive or *teleological* approach. As Reid and Edwards state: 'The Supreme Court's decision does not deal at any length with the fundamental purposes of the SEA Directive, which are aired more extensively in *HS2*. But *Walton* does lay the judicial groundwork for *HS2* and, with hindsight, there is little by way of surprise in the latter decision in the light of *Walton*.'[23]

The HS2 Cases

The issue next came before the UK courts in the *HS2* case.[24] This case concerned the question as to whether the UK government's decision to promote a proposed high-speed train line from London to the north of the UK, announced in a January 2013 Command Paper entitled *High Speed Rail: Investing in Britain's*

[23] See Colin Reid and Denis Edwards in Ch 14 of this volume.

[24] *HS2 Action Alliance and Others* (n 4).

Future—Decisions and Next Steps (hereinafter 'the DNS'), should have been preceded by SEA.

The appellants argued that the DNS was a 'plan or programme' under the SEA Directive as it was 'required' by the 'administrative provisions' within a March 2010 Command Paper[25] that set out the government's 'proposed strategy' for the 'development of a core high speed rail network linking London to Manchester and Leeds via Birmingham'[26] with northward high-speed connections. The Command Paper described the Y-shaped network that was (and still is) proposed. As to the procedure, the Command Paper stated that 'powers to deliver this proposed high speed network should be secured by a single Hybrid Bill, to be introduced subject to public consultation, environmental impact assessment and further detailed work on funding and costs'.[27] If the appellants' contentions were correct, SEA, considering and consulting upon all the reasonable alternatives to the programme set out in the DNS, should have been carried out prior to the publication of the DNS.

At first instance, Mr Justice Ouseley accepted that the March 2010 Command Paper could be considered to be an 'administrative provision'.[28] However, he held at paragraph 68 of his judgment that 'the mere fact that there is some prior administrative action cannot of itself satisfy the language of the Directive. A mere statement of intent, or of policy, by Government that it will produce a plan is not a requirement on Government, in any sense, that it produce a plan. A real degree of formality, control and non-statutory administrative need for a process culminating in a decision is required'. These characteristics, he found, did not apply to the government's March 2010 Command Paper, which on his analysis had simply announced the government's intention to proceed with the creation of a high-speed rail strategy. Ouseley J considered that the Command Paper 'contained no requirements in any sense of that word. The government was entirely free to change its mind'.[29]

However, this interpretation was rejected by the Court of Appeal. In Lord Justice Sullivan's dissenting judgment, he held that:

> [181] The fact that the 2010 Command Paper was a statement of Government policy on High Speed Rail (see para 69 of Ouseley J's judgment) does not mean that this particular policy statement did not 'require', in the sense in which the Court of Justice interpreted that word in the *Inter-Environnement Bruxelles* case (see para 162(2) above), the preparation of a document which was in due course produced in the form of the DNS in which, following the process of public consultation described in the policy statement,

[25] 'High Speed Rail', Presented to Parliament by the Secretary of State for Transport by Command of Her Majesty March 2010.

[26] ibid, foreword.

[27] ibid 9.

[28] *Buckinghamshire County Council and Others v Secretary of State for Transport* [2013] EWHC 481 (Admin), para 67.

[29] ibid, para 70.

the Government's decisions on the matters identified in the policy statement would be announced in accordance with the process which was set out in the statement.

[182] The fact that the Government could (subject to any issues of legitimate expectation, e.g. as to the nature and extent of the proposed consultation process) change or abandon the process at will (see para 72 of Ouseley J's judgment) does not mean that the DNS which was in fact prepared and adopted by the Government in accordance with the process described in the 2010 Command Paper was not 'required' by that process. Governments may abandon plans or programmes that are 'required' by administrative rather than legislative provisions while they are in preparation or even after they have been adopted, but the mere possibility that this may happen does not place a plan or programme outside the scope of the SEA Directive if it has in fact been prepared and adopted in accordance with an administrative requirement. While there were some alterations to the procedure set out in the 2010 command paper, e.g. the decision to proceed with two hybrid Bills rather than one, the process described in the 2010 Command Paper was, in substance, followed by the Government in its preparation and adoption of the DNS. For these reasons, I conclude that an SEA was required.

The Master of the Rolls and Richards LJ in their majority judgment stated that they shared these concerns in relation to these aspects of Ouseley J's reasoning and that if they had found that the DNS were a plan or programme, they would be inclined to find that the DNS should be treated as having been 'required by administrative provisions' within the meaning of Article 2(a) of the SEA Directive, 'adopting an appropriately broad and purposive interpretation of the provision'.[30] The case then proceeded to the Supreme Court. The HS2 Supreme Court Panel was made up of seven justices[31] and their Lordships' judgment was handed down in five sections:

— Lord Carnwath (with whom Lord Neuberger, Lord Mance, Lord Kerr, Lord Sumption and Lord Reed agreed) on SEA Directive issues;
— Lord Reed (with whom all the other justices agreed) on those grounds relating to the Environmental Impact Assessment (EIA);[32]
— Lady Hale on SEA Directive issues;
— Lord Sumption (with whom Lord Neuberger, Lord Mance, Lord Kerr and Lord Reed agreed) on SEA Directive issues; and
— Lord Neuberger and Lord Mance (with whom the other justices agreed) on issues that the Court considered felt arose more generally from the European case law which they had been asked to consider.

[30] *HS2 Action Alliance & Others v Secretary of State for Transport*, [2013] EWCA Civ 920, para 71.

[31] The Supreme Court Rules state that more than five justices should sit on a panel if: the Court is being asked to depart, or may depart, from a previous decision; the case is of high constitutional importance; the case is of great public importance; where there is a conflict between decisions in the House of Lords, the Judicial Committee of the Privy Council and/or the Supreme Court has to be reconciled; or a case raising an important point in relation to the European Convention on Human Rights.

[32] Directive 2001/92/EU.

Lord Carnwath stated that he was prepared to proceed on the assumption that Sullivan LJ's findings that the DNS was 'required' by the March 2010 Command Paper were correct or 'at least that there is a referable issue on the meaning of that part of the definition'.[33] However, as a result of finding that the Command Paper did not 'set the framework for future development consent', a reference was not necessary.

The final section of the judgment, that of Lord Neuberger and Lord Mance (with whom the other members of the Court agreed), takes the opportunity to address issues that arose out of decisions of the CJEU in *Inter-Environnement Bruxelles*, which the Court 'found problematic and which call for some further observations'.[34] In particular, in respect of the SEA Directive, the justices set out their disagreement with the 'expansive'[35] interpretation of 'required' adopted by the CJEU in *Inter-Environnement Bruxelles*, which they considered to be contrary to the intention of the EU legislature. In particular, their Lordships concurred with Advocate General Kokott's interpretation of the meaning of 'required', calling her analysis 'impeccable'.[36]

After praising the Advocate's General's approach, the Court then went on to criticise the findings of the CJEU in the following terms, stating that if no CJEU decision on the point had been in existence, the UK Supreme Court would undoubtedly have adopted a similar interpretation to the Advocate General. In reaching this conclusion, their Lordships state that:

> [187] Had the meaning of article 2(a) come before the Supreme Court without there being any European Court of Justice decision to assist, we would unhesitatingly have reached the same conclusion as Advocate General Kokott, and for the reasons she (as well as the Governments and the Commission represented before the Fourth Chamber) so convincingly gave. We would, like her, have concluded that that 'the legislature clearly did not intend plans and programmes not based on a legal obligation to require an environmental assessment, even though they might have significant effects on the environment [AG20].
>
> [188] We would also have regarded this as clear to the point where no reference under the CILFIT principles was required. The reasons given by the Fourth Chamber of the Court of Justice would not have persuaded us to the contrary. While they allude, in the briefest of terms, to the fact that the Governments made submissions based on the clear language of article 2(a) and on the legislative history, they do not actually address or answer them or any other aspect of Advocate General Kokott's reasoning.
>
> [189] In the result, a national court is faced with a clear legislative provision, to which the Fourth Chamber of the European Court of Justice has, in the interests of a more complete regulation of environmental developments, given a meaning which the European legislature clearly did not intend. For this reason, we would, had it been necessary, have

[33] *HS2 Action Alliance & and Others v Secretary of State of Transport* [2014] UKSC (n 4), para 23.
[34] ibid, para 158.
[35] ibid, para 141.
[36] ibid, para 177.

> wished to have the matter referred back to the European Court of Justice for it to reconsider, hopefully in a fully reasoned judgment of the Grand Chamber, the correctness of its previous decision.

Accordingly, the case law is in a highly unsatisfactory position with the Supreme Court at odds with a binding decision of the CJEU, albeit with the Supreme Court being able to find that SEA was not required for HS2 on the basis of its analysis of 'setting a framework' in the context of Parliament's constitutional position.

'Administrative Provisions'

The Guidance from the former Office of the Deputy Prime Minister[37] sets out characteristics of those plans which may be 'required by administrative provisions'. Such plans are likely to be 'publically available, prepared in a formal way, probably involving consultation with interested parties. The administrative provision must have sufficient formality such that it counts as a "provision" and it must also use language that plainly requires rather than just encourages a plan or a programme to be prepared'.[38]

The Commission's SEA Guidance states that:

> Administrative provisions are formal requirements for ensuring that action is taken which are not normally made using the same procedures as would be needed for new laws and which do not necessarily have the full force of law. Some provisions of 'soft law' might count under this heading. Extent of formalities in its preparation and capacity to be enforced may be used as indications to determine whether a particular provision is an 'administrative provision' in the sense of the Directive. Administrative provisions are by definition not necessarily binding, but for the Directive to apply, plans and programmes prepared or adopted under them must be *required* by them, as is the case with legislative or regulatory provisions.[39] (Emphasis as original)

Lord Carnwath, when considering the meaning of 'administrative provisions' in *Walton*,[40] stated that:

> [99] There may be some uncertainty as to what in the definition is meant by 'administrative', as opposed to 'legislative or regulatory', provisions. However, it seems that some level of formality is needed: the administrative provisions must be such as to identify both the competent authorities and the procedure for preparation and adoption. Given the relatively informal character of the NESTRANS exercise, it is not clear to me what 'administrative provisions' could be relied on as fulfilling that criterion.

37 'A Practical Guide to the Strategic Environmental Assessment Directive' (n 10).

38 ibid, para 2.6.

39 Commission Guidance on SEA, Implementation of Directive 2001/42 on the assessment of certain plans and programmes on the environment, para 3.16.

40 *Walton v Scottish Ministers* (n 22).

In *HS2*, it was accepted that a Command Paper, a government document formally presented to Parliament, could be considered to be an 'administrative provision'. The formality required for an 'administrative provision' was considered by Lindblom J (as he then was) in the case *of West Kensington Estate Tenants and Residents Association and Another v Hammersmith and Fulham London Borough Council and Another.*[41] This case concerned an action brought by a residents' group against the London Borough of Hammersmith and Fulham's proposals to demolish two housing estates for the redevelopment of Earl's Court. One of the grounds on which the claimants relied was that the Earl's Court and West Kensington Opportunity Area Joint Supplementary Planning Document adopted by Hammersmith and Fulham London Borough Council should have been subject to SEA.

The preparation of a supplementary planning document, as set out in regulation 2(1) of the Town and Country Planning (Local Development) (England) Regulations 2004 is not mandatory under the statutory provisions for the preparation of local development documents and development plan documents. However, the judge held that:

> [179] Applying a broad interpretation to the concept of requirement by an administrative provision, I think that the SPD was required in that sense. In several places in their core strategies LBHF and RBKC announced their intention to prepare a supplementary planning document. The need for guidance in a supplementary planning document was acknowledged in policy FRA 1 and in paras 7.113, 7.131 and 8.7 of LBHF's core strategy and in paras 10.4.4, 26.2.1 and 26.3.2 of RBKC's (see paras 30 and 32 to 35 above). Paragraph 7.113 of LBHF's core strategy says that guidance on the regeneration of the Opportunity Area will be 'by means of an area planning framework in the form of a Supplementary Planning Document…'. Paragraph 7.131 says that the SPD 'is testing alternative quantums of development … and will provide more detailed guidance'. Paragraph 8.7 says that the SPD 'will provide more guidance on factors that will determine capacity'. And paras 26.2.1 and 26.3.2 of RBKC's core strategy, respectively, look to the SPD as a means of considering the 'full development capacity and exact disposition of uses across the Opportunity Area' and providing 'a framework for a coordinated and phased development' in it. All of these passages in the core strategies make clear what the local planning authorities were going to do to provide detailed guidance supplementing the policies and provisions of the development plan, and thus finish the framework of policy and guidance within which proposals for development in the Opportunity Area would be considered. It follows that the framework of policy and guidance required the SPD if it was to be complete. The core strategies said as much. I think this is enough to amount to a requirement in an administrative provision within the ambit of art 2(a) of the SEA directive.

[41] *West Kensington Estate Tenants and Residents Association and Another v Hammersmith and Fulham London Borough Council and Another* [2013] EWHC 2834 (Admin).

Interaction Between the SEA Directive and the Aarhus Convention

Article 7 of the Convention on Access to Information, Public Participation in Decision-Making and Access to Justice in Environmental Matters (hereinafter the Aarhus Convention), to which the UK is a signatory, provides that:

> Each Party shall make appropriate practical and/or other provisions for the public to participate during the preparation of plans and programmes relating to the environment, within a transparent and fair framework, having provided the necessary information to the public. Within this framework article 6, paragraphs 3, 4 and 8, shall be applied. The public which may participate shall be identified by the relevant public authority, taking into account the objectives of this Convention. To the extent appropriate, each Party shall endeavour to provide opportunities for public participation in the preparation of policies relating to the environment.

It was argued by the appellants in *HS2* that Article 2(a) of the SEA Directive should be given a broad purposive meaning in order for it to satisfy the requirements of the Aarhus Convention. Article 7 of the Convention applies to all 'plans and programmes relating to the environment', until there is no requirement for these plans or programmes to be 'required by legislative, regulatory or administrative provisions'.

It is of note that the Public Participation Directive (Directive 2003/35/EC) which amended European environmental legislation to ensure its compliance with the Aarhus Convention did not amend the SEA Directive, as it was already considered to be compliant with the public participation requirements of the Aarhus Convention.[42] The appellants in *HS2* argued that this assumption of compliance must mean that any plan or programme for the purpose of Article 7 of the Aarhus Convention must also be a plan or programme for the purposes of the SEA Directive.

Lord Justice Sullivan, in his dissenting Court of Appeal judgment, agreed with this interpretation of the SEA Directive, stating that:

> [178] I am troubled by the conclusion of the Master of the Rolls and Lord Justice Richards that because the DNS does not in their view set the framework for future development consent it is difficult to see how Article 7 of Aarhus can have been intended to apply to it. We know that the Government did, in fact, engage in a comprehensive consultation exercise prior to the adoption of the DNS (see paragraphs 84–109 above). In my judgment, a conclusion that even if there had been no consultation prior to the adoption of the DNS there would have been no breach of Article 7 of Aarhus would not be in accordance with the purposive interpretation of EU environmental legislation that has been consistently adopted by the CJEU.

[42] See recital (10) and art 2(5) of the Public Participation Directive.

The Supreme Court, however, disagreed. Lord Carnwath stated:

> [52] To my mind there is a more fundamental objection to Mr Elvin's argument. There is no reason to assume that article 7 and the SEA Directive are intended to cover exactly the same ground. The differences in wording are clear and must be assumed to be deliberate. Indeed the UNECE guidance on the Convention (*The Aarhus Convention: An Implementation Guide* 2nd Ed 2013 p 118–119) accepts that its reference to plans and programmes relating to the environment is broader than the equivalent definition in the SEA Directive. The SEA Directive must be interpreted and applied in its own terms. If this falls short of full compliance with the Aarhus Convention, it does not invalidate the directive so far as it goes. It simply means that a possible breach of the Convention may have to be considered as a separate and additional issue. In the present case the point is academic because no such breach is alleged.

This reasoning follows that given by Advocate General Kokott in her opinion in *Inter-Environnment Bruxelles*:

> [22] At the hearing, *Inter-Environment Bruxelles and Others* also relied on the public participation provided for in Article 7 of the Aarhus Convention and Article 2 of Directive 2003/35/EC. Under that convention, the public is to be given the opportunity to participate in all plans and programmes relating to the environment, but an environmental report is not expressly required. If it were the case that the SEA Directive transposed that international law obligation in its entirety in respect of the European Union, there would be good reason to apply it above and beyond the wording of the SEA Directive, that is to say to all plans and programmes relating to the environment.
>
> [23] However, the SEA Directive does not contain any indication that it is designed to transpose Article 7 of the Aarhus Convention. Rather, recital 10 in the preamble to Directive 2003/35 shows that, in this regard, the Convention is to be transposed only in relation to plans and programmes under European Union law—more specifically by Directive 2003/35 in relation to certain measures but, in future, by specific rules laid down in the relevant legislative act. Article 2(5) of Directive 2003/35 simply makes it clear that an environmental assessment in accordance with the SEA Directive is sufficient from the point of view of public participation.
>
> [24] The objectives of Article 7 of the Aarhus Convention do not therefore justify an interpretation of the SEA Directive that is contrary to the recognisable intention of the legislature.

So we appear to have arrived at a position where the SEA Directive plainly does not satisfy the requirements of the Aarhus Convention, given that the SEA Directive does not apply to any plan or programme which is not 'required by legislative, regulatory or administrative provisions'. It remains to be seen whether the EU is accordingly in breach of its responsibilities under the Aarhus Convention by not giving it full effect or whether a separate ground of challenge will arise in relation to plans or programmes where (as with *HS2*), there is real doubt as to whether or not the 'required by legislative, regulatory or administrative provisions' test is satisfied. These issues have now come before the Aarhus Compliance Committee.[43]

Conclusion

Unnecessary confusion has been caused by the drafting of the second limb of Article 2(a). The very concept of a plan or programme that is 'required' by an administrative provision leads to difficulties. Furthermore, the antipathy of the UK Supreme Court to the broadening of the meaning of 'required' from what it assumes was originally intended is plain in *Walton* and scathing in *HS2*. When one again considers the objective of the SEA Directive and, indeed, the obligations imposed by the Aarhus Convention (which is mercifully free of this troublesome phrase), would the Directive's legislators really have taken issue with the CJEU's approach in *Inter-Environnement Bruxelles* or with the suggestion that it is appropriate and common sense for the programme for HS2 to be treated as required by administrative provisions in the form of a formal, considered, definitive and prescriptive parliamentary Command Paper?

[43] See further Richard Macrory and Gregory Jones in Ch 17 of this volume.

5

The Meaning of 'Early and Effective Opportunity' for Consultation

STEPHEN ASHWORTH AND RACHAEL HERBERT

Introduction

General experience shows that public consultation, especially when organised at an early stage of planning and when understood as a process, contributes to a higher acceptance of the plan and programme, and therefore to the early identification and resolution of conflicts.[1]

This chapter considers the consultation procedure under European Directive 2001/42 of the European Parliament and of the Council of 27 June 2001 on the assessment of the effects of certain plans and programmes on the environment (hereinafter 'the SEA Directive') and, more particularly, the requirement under Article 6(2) of the SEA Directive for there to be an 'early and effective opportunity' for people to express an opinion on a proposed plan or programme. The SEA Directive and its 'early and effective opportunity' requirement was transposed into domestic law in the UK in 2004 through a series of regulations.[2] Neither the SEA Directive nor the UK regulations set out in detail what needs to be done to achieve an 'early and effective opportunity' for consultation, instead leaving it the subject of much interpretation. The SEA Guidance has done little to take things further. Fortunately, the courts have, in recent times, shown some leadership. The

[1] Commission of European Communities, Report from the Commission to the Council, the European \Parliament, the European Economic and Social Committee and the Committee of the Regions on the application and effectiveness of the Directive on Strategic Environmental Assessment (Directive 2001/42/EC), Brussels, 14 September 2009, COM(2009) 469 final, [3.6], http://eur-lex.europa.eu/LexUriServ/LexUriServ.do?uri=CELEX:52009DC0469:EN:NOT.

[2] Environmental Assessment of Plans and Programmes Regulations 2004 (SI 2004/1633); Environmental Assessment of Plans and Programmes Regulations (Northern Ireland) 2004 (Statutory Rule 2004/280); Environmental Assessment of Plans and Programmes (Scotland) Regulations 2004 (Scottish SI 2004/258); and Environmental Assessment of Plans and Programmes (Wales) Regulations 2004 (Welsh SI 2004/1656 (W170)).

decisions in *Cogent Land LLP v Rochford District Council and Bellway Homes Ltd*[3] and *Re Seaport Investments Ltd's Application for Judicial Review*[4] helpfully explain what they consider an 'early and effective opportunity' to mean in practice. This chapter considers the detailed wording of the SEA Directive and UK regulations in relation to consultation, including what it does not say. It will then explore how European and UK Guidance and the courts have sought to interpret and apply what is meant by 'early and effective opportunity' in the SEA Directive.

What Are the Consultation Requirements Under the SEA Directive?

Article 6 of the SEA Directive prescribes the consultation requirements:

Article 6—Consultation

1. The draft plan or programme[5] and the Environmental Report[6] prepared in accordance with Article 5 shall be made available to the authorities referred to in paragraph 3 of this Article and the public.[7]
2. The authorities referred to in paragraph 3 and the public referred to in paragraph 4 shall be given *an early and effective opportunity* within appropriate timeframes to express their opinion on the draft plan or programme and the accompanying Environmental Report before the adoption of the plan or programme or its submission to the legislative procedure.
3. Member States shall designate the authorities[8] to be consulted which, by reason of their specific environmental responsibilities, are likely to be concerned by the environmental effects of implementing plans and programmes.
4. Member States shall identify the public for the purposes of paragraph 2, including the public affected or likely to be affected by, or having an interested in, the decision-making subject to this Directive, including relevant non-governmental organisations,

[3] *Cogent Land LLP v Rochford District Council and Bellway Homes Ltd* [2012] EWHC 2542 (Admin) [2013] 1 P & CR 2; [2013] JPL 170

[4] *Re Seaport Investments Ltd's Application for Judicial Review* [2008] Env LR 23 (HCNI) and Case C-474/10, [2012] Env LR 21 (CJEU).

[5] 'Plans and programmes' are defined in art 2(a) as meaning 'plans and programmes, including those co-financed by the European Community, as well as any modifications to them which: (1) are subject to preparation and/or adoption by an authority at national, regional or local level; or (2) are prepared by an authority for adoption, through a legislative procedure by Parliament or Government; and in either case (3) are required by legislative, regulatory or administrative provisions'.

[6] 'Environmental Report' is defined in art 2(c) to mean the part of the plan or programme documentation containing the information required in art 5 and Annex I.

[7] 'Public' is defined in art 2(d) as meaning one or more natural or legal persons and, in accordance with national legislation or practice, their associations, organisations or groups.

[8] These authorities are typically defined by the Member States as ministries or specialised environmental agencies at different levels (national/regional/local), but climate change issues typically require a different and often broader perspective, including authorities responsible for the energy, transport, water management, health and economic sectors.

such as those promoting environmental protection and other organisations concerned.

5. Detailed arrangements for the information and consultation of the authorities and the public shall be determined by Member States.

Article 6 does not specify the method or procedure for the release of information to designated authorities and the identified public under Article 6(5), nor does it detail the means for consultation or what constitutes an 'appropriate timeframe' or period for consultation.[9] The absence of this detail is not an oversight; it is consistent with the broad drafting style of European Commission directives.[10] The SEA Directive seeks to establish the principles and the purpose of consultation only, leaving the detailed arrangements for Member States to determine. The intent is that Member States will be able to adopt wide-ranging and innovative measures which are tailored to the 'Plan or Programme' in question.[11] For example, a Member State could choose to implement the customary consultation practices of requiring opinions in writing and/or conducting a public hearing, or may instead choose to set other less conventional methods for consultation.

Articles 8 and 9 of the SEA Directive make it clear that any opinions expressed on the SEA information (i.e. draft plan or programme and Environmental Report) are to be taken into account during the preparation of the plan or programme and before the decision making body consider the plan or programme to be in final form The wording of Articles 6–9 of the SEA Directive establish the following minimum requirements for Member States in relation to 'early and effective opportunity' consultation:[12]

— The plan or programme is to be 'made available to the designated authorities and the public'. This suggests that wide consultation is to be promoted.
— The words 'given an early and effective opportunity to express their opinions' must mean being consulted on in advance of the plan or programme being adopted or being submitted to the legislative procedure.
— The Environmental Report must be available before the plan or programme is adopted.
— The opinions of the 'designated authorities' must be sought when deciding on the scope and level of the information to be included in the Environmental Report.

[9] European Commission, DG ENV Study concerning the report on the application and effectiveness of the SEA Directive (2001/42/EC) Final report April 2009, paragraph 5.13, p 89, http://ec.europa.eu/environment/eia/pdf/study0309.pdf.

[10] R McCracken, 'EIA, SEA and AA, Present Position, Where are We Now?' (2010) *Journal of Planning and Environmental Law* 1518.

[11] European Union Preparatory Acts, Proposal for a Directive of the European Parliament and of the Council providing for Public Participation in respect of the drawing up of certain plans and programmes relating to the environment and amending Council Directives 85/337/EEC and 96/61/EC, OJ C 154E, 29/05/2001, 123 at [6.12(13)].

[12] I Gilder 'The Impact of the SEA Directive' (2010) *Journal of Planning and Environmental Law* 712, 714.

- The length of time for any consultation must be 'appropriate'.
- The 'designated authorities' who have a right to express their opinions on a proposed plan or programme are those that are likely to be concerned by the environmental effects of such, due to their specific environmental responsibilities.
- It is those members of the public identified as being concerned by the plan or programme who are to be given the right to express their opinions.
- The decision-making body is obliged to take due account of the outcome of the consultation to ensure that the environmental consequences of the proposed plan or programme are identified and assessed before its adoption or submission.

UK Transposition of the Consultation Requirement of the SEA Directive

The SEA Directive has been transposed into domestic law in the UK through the following four Regulations:

- The Environmental Assessment of Plans and Programmes Regulations 2004 (hereinafter 'the England Regulations').
- The Environmental Assessment of Plans and Programmes Regulations (Northern Ireland) 2004 (hereinafter 'the Northern Ireland Regulations').
- The Environmental Assessment of Plans and Programmes (Scotland) Regulations 2004 (hereinafter 'the Scotland Regulations').
- The Environmental Assessment of Plans and Programmes (Wales) Regulations 2004 (hereinafter 'the Wales Regulations).

The consultation provisions of the above four Regulations (the UK Regulations) are generally consistent with each other, except that the England Regulations,[13] refer to an 'effective opportunity' and not an 'early and effective opportunity' as stated in the Northern Ireland Regulations. Notably, none of the UK Regulations stipulate what is necessary to ensure that there is an 'effective opportunity' for designated authorities or the public to express their opinion on the SEA information. Regulations 12 and 13 of the England Regulations state:

> 12— Preparation of Environmental Report
>
> (1) Where an environmental assessment[14] is required by any provision of Part 2 of these Regulations, the responsible authority shall prepare, or secure the preparation of, an Environmental Report in accordance with paragraphs (2) and (3) of this regulation.

[13] The Regulations for Scotland and Wales are essentially the same as the England Regulations.

[14] 'Environmental assessment' is defined in art 2(b) of the SEA Directive to mean 'the preparation of an Environmental Report, the carrying out of consultations, the taking into account of the

(2) The report shall identify, describe and evaluate the likely significant effects on the environment of–
   (a) implementing the plan or programme; and
   (b) reasonable alternatives taking into account the objectives and the geographical scope of the plan or programme.
(3) The report shall include such of the information referred to in Schedule 2 to these Regulations as may reasonably be required, taking account of–
   (a) current knowledge and methods of assessment;
   (b) the contents and level of detail in the plan or programme;
   (c) the stage of the plan or programme in the decision-making process; and
   (d) the extent to which certain matters are more appropriately assessed at different levels in that process in order to avoid duplication of the assessment.
(4) Information referred to in Schedule 2 may be provided by reference to relevant information obtained at other levels of decision-making or through other EU legislation.
(5) When deciding on the scope and level of detail of the information that must be included in the report, the responsible authority shall consult the consultation bodies.
(6) *Where a consultation body wishes to respond to a consultation under paragraph (5), it shall do so within the period of 5 weeks beginning with the date on which it receives the responsible authority's invitation to engage in the consultation.* (emphasis added)

13— Consultation procedures

(1) Every draft plan or programme for which an Environmental Report has been prepared in accordance with regulation 12 and its accompanying Environmental Assessment ('the relevant documents') shall be made available for the purposes of consultation in accordance with the following provisions of this regulation.
(2) As soon as reasonably practicable after the preparation of the relevant documents, the responsible authority shall–
   (a) send a copy of those documents to each consultation body;
   (b) take such steps as it considers appropriate to bring the preparation of the relevant documents to the attention of the persons who, in the authority's opinion, are affected or likely to be affected by, or have an interest in the decisions involved in the assessment and adoption of the plan or programme concerned, required under the Environmental Assessment of Plans and Programmes Directive ('the public consultees');
   (c) inform the public consultees of the address (which may include a website) at which a copy of the relevant documents may be viewed, or from which a copy may be obtained; and
   (d) invite the consultation bodies and the public consultees to express their opinion on the relevant documents, specifying the address to which, and the period within which, opinions must be sent.
(3) *The period referred to in paragraph (2)(d) must be of such length as will ensure that the consultation bodies and the public consultees are given an effective opportunity to express their opinion on the relevant documents.* (emphasis added)

Environmental Report and the results of the consultations in decision-making and the provision of information on the decision in accordance with Articles 4 to 9'.

(4) The responsible authority shall keep a copy of the relevant documents available at its principal office for inspection by the public at all reasonable times and free of charge.
(5) Nothing in paragraph (2)(c) shall require the responsible authority to provide copies free of charge; but where a charge is made, it shall be of a reasonable amount. (emphasis added)

In comparison, Regulations 11 and 12 of the Northern Ireland Regulations provide that:

11— Preparation of Environmental Report

(1) Where an environmental assessment is required by any provision of Part II, the responsible authority shall prepare, or secure the preparation of, an Environmental Report in accordance with paragraphs (2) and (3).
(2) The report shall identify, describe and evaluate the likely significant effects on the environment of–
  (a) implementing the plan or programme; and
  (b) reasonable alternatives taking into account the objectives and geographical scope of the plan or programme.
(3) The report shall include such of the information referred to in Schedule 2 that may reasonably be required, taking account of–
  (a) current knowledge and methods of assessment;
  (b) the contents and level of detail in the plan or programme;
  (c) the stage of the plan or programme in the decision-making process; and
  (d) the extent to which certain matters are more appropriately assessed at different levels in that process in order to avoid duplication of the assessment.
(4) Information referred to in Schedule 2 may be provided by reference to relevant information obtained at other levels of decision-making or through other Community legislation.
(5) When deciding on the scope and level of detail of the information that must be included in the report, the responsible authority shall consult the consultation body.
(6) *Where the consultation body wishes to respond to a consultation under paragraph (5), it shall do so within the period of 5 weeks beginning with the date on which it receives the responsible authority's invitation to engage in the consultation.* (emphasis added)

12— Consultation procedures

(1) Every draft plan or programme for which an Environmental Report has been prepared in accordance with regulation 11 and its accompanying Environmental Report ('the relevant documents') shall be made available to the consultation body and to the public in accordance with the following provisions of this regulation.
(2) As soon as reasonably practicable after their preparation, the responsible authority shall send a copy of the relevant documents to the consultation body and invite it to express its opinion on the relevant documents within a specified period.
(3) The responsible authority shall also–
  (a) within 14 days of the preparation of the relevant documents, publish in accordance with paragraph (5), or secure the publication of, a notice–
    (i) stating the title of the plan, programme or modification;
    (ii) stating the address (which may include a website) at which a copy of the relevant documents may be inspected or from which a copy may be obtained;

(iii) inviting expressions of opinion on the relevant documents; and

(iv) stating the address to which, and the period within which, opinions must be sent;

(b) keep a copy of the relevant documents available at its principal office for inspection by the public at all reasonable times and free of charge; and

(c) publish a copy of the relevant documents on the authority's website.

(4) *The periods referred to in paragraphs (2) and (3)(a)(iv) must be of such length as will ensure that those to whom the invitation is extended are given an early and effective opportunity to express their opinion on the relevant documents.* (emphasis added)

(5) Publication of a notice under paragraph (3)(a) shall be by such means as will ensure that the contents of the notice are likely to come to the attention of the public affected by, or likely to be affected by, or having an interest in, the draft plan or the programme.

(6) Nothing in paragraph (3)(a)(ii) shall require the responsible authority to provide a copy of the documents concerned free of charge; but where a charge is made, it shall be of a reasonable amount. (emphasis added)

While the Member States are required to transpose the requirements of the SEA Directive into domestic law, there is no requirement for it to be identical to the SEA Directive. In fact, to do so would mean that certain procedural issues purposely left by the European Commission for the Member States to define would remain unanswered. Notwithstanding that, the guiding principle[15] is to ensure that (save in exceptional circumstances) the UK complies with, at least, the minimum requirements set out in the European directive being transposed. Prudent practice suggests that the European directives should be read together with national legislation. Although limited, there is a risk in following the letter of the domestic laws only, without reference to a European directive, because the domestic legislation is subordinate to the directive[16] and must be disapplied to the extent that it cannot be so construed.[17] Therefore, while a failure correctly to transpose a European directive into domestic law can result in the domestic law not applying and the European directive having direct effect, it is an accepted principle that the transposing legislation must so far as possible be interpreted in a way which is compatible with the relevant European directive.[18]

[15] Transposition Guidance: How to Implement European Directive Effectively', revised April 2013, https://www.gov.uk/government/uploads/system/uploads/attachment_data/file/229763/bis-13-775-transposition-guidance-how-to-implement-european-directives-effectively-revised.pdf.

[16] Town and Country Planning (Environmental Impact Assessment) (England and Wales) Regulations 1999 (SI 1999/293), as amended by the Town and Country Planning (Environmental Impacts Assessment) (Amendment) (England) Regulations 2008 (SI 2008/2335).

[17] *R v Durham City Council ex p Huddleston* [2000] 1 WLR 1484; Case C-201/02 *R (on the Application of Wells) v Secretary of State for Transport, Local Government and the Regions* [2004] ECR I-723; Case C-290/03 *R (on the Application of Barker) v Bromley London Borough Council* [2006] QB 764; McCracken (n 10).

[18] In accordance with the canon of 'convergent construction' enunciated by Sedley LJ in *R v Durham City Council ex p Huddleston* (n 17) 1490 [10]; Case C-106/89 *Marleasing SA v La Comercial Internacional de Alimentacion SA* [1990] ECR I-4135 [8]; McCracken (n 10); *Cogent Land LLP v Rochford District Council and Bellway Homes Ltd* [2012] EWHC 2542 (Admin); [2013] 1 P & CR 2; (2013) *Journal of Planning and Environmental Law* 170 [69].

In comparing the SEA Directive with the England Regulations, the following points can be made. First, as stated above, the England Regulations do not make specific reference to an early opportunity to express an opinion—only an 'effective opportunity' in regulation 13(3). However, in regulation 13(2), the England Regulations make it clear that the responsible authority must, as soon as reasonably practicable after preparing the plan or programme and the accompanying Environmental Report, invite the consultees to express their opinion. Second, the England Regulations do not promote a wide consultation of the plan or programme and instead take a more reserved position, requiring the authority to only 'take such steps as it considers appropriate to bring the preparation of the report' to the attention of the public under regulation 13(2)(b).[19] Third, the England Regulation stipulates the method for the public to express their opinion, that being by written submission to a particular address within the time period. Fourth, the reference to an 'effective opportunity' in the England Regulations is more aligned with the timeframe provided to a consultee to prepare their submissions on a draft plan or programme and less about the stage in the process where consultation should occur.

An analysis of the Northern Ireland Regulations suggests that its provisions essentially mirror that of the England Regulations with the following exceptions. The Northern Ireland Regulations make specific reference to an 'early and effective opportunity' and not just an 'effective opportunity'. The Northern Ireland Regulations require a notice to be published within 14 days of the relevant documents having been prepared so that the existence of the relevant documents is brought to the attention of the public at large. The England Regulations make no reference to a public notice, but do require the responsible authority to take such steps as it considers appropriate to bring the preparation of the relevant documents to the attention of the persons who are likely to be concerned by them. The Northern Ireland Regulations invite the public at large to express their opinion on the plan or programme, not just those persons whom the responsible authority identifies as being concerned by the plan or programme. The invitation for the public at large to express their opinion goes beyond the requirements of both the SEA Directive and the England Regulations and promotes widespread consultation.

The UK Regulations are sufficiently compatible with and do not contradict the consultation requirements of the SEA Directive. However, they do not provide any great insight into or clarification on what the words an 'early and effective opportunity' should be taken to mean.

[19] Gilder (n 12).

Guidance on 'Early and Effective Opportunity' for Consultation

As neither the SEA Directive nor the UK Regulations make 'early' and 'effective' defined terms, the ordinary and natural meaning of these words should be used. The *Oxford English Dictionary* provides the following definitions for 'early' and 'effective':

- 'early'[20] means 'not far on in a period, development or process of evolution; being the first stage'; and
- 'effective'[21] means (1) 'having a definite or desired effect'; (2) 'powerful in effect; impressive'; and (3) 'actually usable; realisable; equivalent in its effect'.

Article 8 of the United Nations Economic Commission for Europe Protocol of SEA (UNECE 2003),[22] a supplement to the Aarthus Convention, states:

> Article 8—Public Participation
>
> (1) Each party shall ensure *early, timely and effective opportunities* for public participation, *when all optionsare open*, in the strategic environmental assessment of plans and programmes.
>
> ...
>
> 4. Each party shall ensure that the public referred to in paragraph 3 has the opportunity to express its opinion on the draft plan or programme and the Environmental Report within a *reasonable timeframe*. (emphasis added)

Similar to the literal dictionary definition, the words 'given an early and effective opportunity to express their opinion' would, as guided by the UNECE 2003, suggest that consultation should occur early in the decision-making process for the plan or programme, before any strategic decisions are made.[23] The Court of Appeal decision in *R (Morge) v Hampshire County Council*[24] illustrates the importance of a using a purposive approach focusing not only on the substance of legislation (i.e. its words) but also preambles.[25] Therefore, the preamble to the SEA Directive, together with its other articles, should, in applying the purposive

[20] HG Fowler and FG Fowler, *The Concise Oxford Dictionary of Current English, Eighth Edition* (London, BCA, 1991) 369.

[21] ibid 374.

[22] The Protocol supplements the 1991 Convention on Environmental Impact Assessment in a Transboundary Context and acknowledges the 1998 Convention on Access to Information, Public Participation in Decision-Making and Access to Justice in Environmental Matters (hereinafter 'the Aarhus Convention')

[23] R Therivel, *Strategic Environmental Assessment in Action* (London, Earthscan, 2004) 33–34 and 226.

[24] *R (Morge) v Hampshire County Council* [2010] EWCA Civ 608

[25] McCracken (n 10).

approach,[26] be considered when interpreting what an 'early and effective opportunity' means in practice. The objective of the SEA Directive is:

> [T]o provide for a high level of protection of the environment and to contribute to the integration of environmental considerations into the preparation and adoption of plans and programmes with a view to promoting sustainable development, by ensuring that, in accordance with this Directive, an environmental assessment is carried out of certain plans and programmes which are likely to have significant effects on the environment.[27]

The preamble to the SEA Directive declares that:

> In order to contribute to more transparent decision making and with the aim of ensuring that the information supplied for the assessment is comprehensive and reliable, it is necessary to provide that authorities with relevant environmental responsibilities and the public are to be *consulted during the assessment of plans and programmes and that appropriate timeframes are set, allowing sufficient time for consultations*, including the expression of opinion.[28]
>
> …
>
> Where the implementation of a plan or programme prepared in one Member State is likely to have a significant effect on the environment of other Member States, provision should be made for the Member States concerned to enter into consultations for the relevant authorities and the public to be informed and enabled to express their opinion.[29]
>
> …
>
> The Environmental Report and the *opinions expressed* by the relevant authorities and the public, as well as the results of any transboundary consultation, should be *taken into account during the preparation of the plan or programme and before its adoption or submission to the legislative procedure.*[30] (emphasis added)

Other articles in the SEA Directive are relevant to the issue of consultation. Article 2(b) defines 'Environmental Assessment' to mean 'the preparation of an Environmental Report, the carrying out of consultations, the taking into account of the Environmental Report and the results of the consultations in decision-making and the provision of information on the decision in accordance with Articles 4 to 9'. Article 5(1) provides that 'where an Environmental Assessment is required under Article 3(1), an Environmental Report shall be prepared in which the likely significant effects on the environment of implementing the plan or programme, and reasonable alternatives taking into account the objectives and the geographical scope of the plan or programme, are identified, described and evaluated. The

[26] For further discussion on the purpose approach, see, eg, Gregory Jones and David Graham in Ch 11 and Elizabeth Fisher in Ch 8 of this volume.

[27] SEA Directive, art 1.

[28] SEA Directive Preamble, para 15.

[29] ibid, para 16.

[30] ibid, para 17.

information to be given for this purpose is referred to in Annex 1'. Annex 1 sets out a number of matters, including at sub-paragraph (h) an outline of the reasons for selecting the alternatives dealt with and a description of how the assessment was undertaken, including any difficulties (such as technical deficiencies or lack of know-how) encountered in compiling the required information. Article 12(2) requires Member States to ensure 'that Environmental Reports are of a sufficient quality to meet the requirements of this Directive'.[31]

Accordingly, it can be said that the preamble and other articles of the SEA Directive give practical assistance in the interpretation of 'early and effective' consultation because they reinforce the idea that the opinions received during consultation and the information in the Environmental Report should be taken into account during the preparation of the plan or programme before it is finalised and adopted.

The Impact of the SEA Protocol and the Aarhus Convention

It has been argued that the definition of 'plan' in the SEA Directive, the EU Protocol on Strategic Environmental Assessment[32] (hereinafter 'the SEA Protocol') and the Aarhus Convention are similar and, as such, any plan or programme that falls under the SEA Directive should also meet the standards of both treaties.[33] Article 8 of the SEA Protocol provides that:

> (1) Each Party shall ensure *early, timely and effective opportunities for public participation, when all options are open*, in the strategic environmental assessment of plans and programmes.
>
> …
>
> (4) Each Party shall ensure that the public referred to in paragraph 3 has the opportunity to express its opinion on the draft plan or programme and the Environmental Report *within a reasonable timeframe*. (emphasis added)

[31] It was subsequently explained in *Save Historic Newmarket Ltd v Forest Heath District Council* [2011] EWHC 606 (Admin) [2011] JPL 1233; [2011] NPC 35, QBD (Admin) [12] that 'quality involves ensuring that a report is based on proper information and expertise and covers all the potential effects of the plan or programme in question. In addition, since one of the purposes of the Directive is to allow members of the public to be consulted about plans or programmes which may affect them, the report should enable them to understand why the proposals are said to be environmentally sound. To that end, the report must not only be comprehensible but must contain the necessary information required by the Directive'.

[32] This came into force on 11 July 2010.

[33] Article 15 of the SEA Protocol states that 'the relevant provisions of this Protocol shall apply without prejudice to the UNECE Conventions on Environmental Impact Assessment in a Transboundary Context and on Access to Information, Public Participation in Decision-Making and Access to Justice in Environmental Matters'.

It was the Aarhus Convention that introduced compulsory public participation in environmental decision-making[34] and its consultation requirements are remarkably similar to the SEA Protocol.

Articles 6 and 7 of the Aarhus Convention states as follows:

> Article 6
>
> …
>
> Article 6(3): the public participation procedures shall include reasonable timeframes for the different phases, *allowing sufficient time for informing the public* in accordance with paragraph 2 above *and for the public to prepare and participate effectively during the environmental decision-making.*
>
> Article 6(4): Each Party shall provide for *early public participation, when all options are open and effective public participation can take place.*
>
> …
>
> Article 6(8): *Each Party shall ensure that in the decision due account is taken of the outcome of the public participation.*
>
> Article 7
>
> Each Party shall make appropriate practical and/or other provisions for the public to participate during the preparation of plans and programmes relating to the environment, within a transparent and fair framework, having provided the necessary information to the public. Within this framework, Article 6, paragraphs 33,[35] 4[36] and 8[37] shall be applied. The public which may participate shall be identified by the relevant public authority, taking into account the objectives of this Convention. To the extent appropriate, each Party shall endeavour to provide opportunities for public participation in the preparation of policies relating to the environment.[38] (emphasis added)

It has been said that the intent of Article 6 of the SEA Directive was to implement the consultation requirements of Articles 6 and 7 of the Aarhus Convention. However, as is evident in the wording of the articles above, the consultation requirements in Article 6 of the SEA Directive are not as clear, certain or prescriptive as those contained in the Aarhus Convention or the SEA Protocol. Read together, the SEA Protocol and the Aarhus Convention establish the following minimum requirements for consultation and participation:

[34] D Obradovic, 'EC Rules on Public Participation in Environmental Decision-Making Operating at the European and National Levels' (2007) 32(6) *European Law Review* 829, 843; United Nations Economic Commissions for Europe (UNECE), 'Convention on Access to Information, Public Participation in Decision-Making and Access to Justice in Environmental Matters' (1999) 38 *International Legal Materials* 3, 517.

[35] This sets timeframes for public participation procedures.

[36] This requires public participation to take place early on in the process.

[37] Parties must ensure that the plan or programme takes due account of public participation.

[38] Aarhus Convention, art 7, www.unece.org/fileadmin/DAM/env/pp/documents/cep43e.pdf.

— that the public that may participate are to be identified;
— all necessary information, such as an Environmental Report, must be provided to assist the public in arriving at and expressing their opinions;
— participation is to occur when all options are open, which means during the preparation of the plan or programme and in advance of the plan or programme being adopted;
— reasonable timeframes for participation are to be set; and
— there is an obligation on the decision-making body to take due account of the outcome of the public participation to ensure that the environmental consequences of the proposed plan or programme are identified and assessed before the adoption of the relevant plan or programme.

Similar to the SEA Directive, neither the SEA Protocol nor the Aarhus Convention specifies a definition for what constitutes a reasonable timeframe for consultation. In this way, EU Member States are given the discretion to prescribe a minimum timeframe for public participation, but also have the ability to set a longer timeframe if the complexity of the plan or programme demands it.[39] The SEA Protocol and the Aarhus Convention make clear that participation is to take place when all options are open. Critically, the words of the SEA Directive, specifically 'before the adoption of the plan … or its submission to the legislative procedure', do not necessarily require consultation to take place when all options are open. The SEA Directive takes a different approach to the other material and appears to accept, implicitly at least, that 'political and commercial pressures may effectively foreclose certain technical options'.[40] The report of the European Network of Environmental Law Organizations has suggested that the wording of Article 6(2) of the SEA Directive should be amended to comply with both the SEA Protocol and the Aarhus Convention. In particular, it proposed revisions to the 'early and effective' requirement so that Article 6(2) would read as follows:

> The authorities referred to in paragraph 3 and the public referred to in paragraph 4 shall be given an early and effective opportunity *when all options are open and* within appropriate timeframes to express their opinion on the draft plan or programme and the accompanying Environmental Report before the adoption of the plan or programme or its submission to the legislative procedure. *As a minimum, the public should be given 60 days to participate in the preparation of the plan or programme. When setting the timeframes, Member States shall take into account the complexity of the planning procedure and the objective of effective public participation.*[41]

[39] European Network of Environmental Law Organisations [2012], 'Legal analysis on the conformity of the SEA Directive with the provisions stated under the Aarhus Convention and the Espoo Convention, SEA', Justice and Environment, 12, 13, 18, http://www.oekobuero.at/images/doku/seaanalysis 2012.pdf

[40] European Network of Environmental Law Organisations [2012] 'Legal analysis on the conformity of the SEA Directive with the provisions stated under the Aarhus Convention and the Espoo Convention: SEA', Justice and Environment, 13. http://www.oekobuero.at/images/doku/seaanalysis2012.pdf

[41] ibid.

Prior to concluding the Aarhus Convention, the EC had already put in place some measures intended to foster public participation in environmental decisions.[42] The EC's minimum standards and general principles for consulting interested parties were as follows:

- clear content on the process: all communications relating to consultation should be clear and concise and should include all necessary information to facilitate responses;
- consultation target groups: when defining the target group(s) in a consultation process the Commission should ensure that the relevant parties have an opportunity to express their opinions;
- publications: the Commission should ensure adequate awareness-raising publicity and adapt its communication channels to meet the needs of all target audiences. Without excluding other communication tools, open public consultations should be published on the internet and announced at the 'single access point';[43]
- time limits for participation: the Commission should provide sufficient time for planning and responses to invitations and written contributions. The Commission should strive to allow at least eight weeks for receipt of responses to written public consultations and 20 working days' notice for meetings; and
- acknowledgement and feedback: receipt of contributions should be acknowledged. Results of open public consultation should be displayed on a website linked to the single access point on the internet.[44]

These minimum standards are helpful in understanding the origins of the 'early and effective' consultation requirement in the SEA Directive and, importantly, how this ambition was to have been applied, together with the other general principles of consultation, including, openness, accountability, effectiveness and coherence.

European Commission Guidance

In 2001, the European Commission issued guidance on the implementation of the SEA Directive entitled 'Implementation of Directive 2001/42 of the Assessment

[42] Obradovic (n 34) 840–41; Council Decision on the conclusion, on behalf of the European Community, of the Convention on access to information, public participation in decision-making and access to justice in environmental matters [2005] OJ L124/1. The European Community signed the Convention in 1998.

[43] Commission of the European Communities [2002] 'Communication from the Commission: Towards a Reinforced Culture of Consultation and Dialogue—General Principles and Minimum Standards for Consultation of Interested Parties by the Commission', 20. http://ec.europa.eu/governance/docs/comm_standards_en.pdf;; Obradovic, (n 34) 840–41.

[44] Commission of the European Communities [2002], 'Communication from the Commission: Towards a Reinforced Culture of Consultation and Dialogue—General Principles and Minimum

of the Effects of Certain Plans and Programmes on the Environment' (hereinafter 'EC Guidance'). The EC Guidance is worth consulting as it provides useful background on how the provisions of the SEA Directive evolved, including what constitutes 'early and effective' consultation. While the EC Guidance is not binding[45] and may be out of date,[46] it offers a helpful insight into the intent of the European Commission when drafting a particular article and should be considered alongside the facts of each case in deciphering what the words 'early and effective opportunity' actually call for. The following passages of the EC Guidance were cited by counsel in arguments before the courts in *Cogent* and *Seaport* concerning consultation:

— Paragraph 4.2—As a matter of good practice, the Environmental Assessment of plans and programmes should influence the way the plans and programmes themselves are drawn up. While a plan or programme is relatively fluid, it may be easier to discard elements which are likely to have undesirable environmental effects than it would be when the plan or programme has been completed. At that stage, an Environmental Assessment may be informative but is likely to be less influential. Article 4(1) places a clear obligation on authorities to carry out the assessment during the preparation of the plan or programme.
— Paragraph 5.11—The obligation to identify, describe and evaluate reasonable alternatives must be read in the context of the objective of the Directive which is to ensure that the effects of implementing plans and programmes are taken into account during their preparation and before their adoption.
— Paragraph 5.12—In requiring the likely significant environmental effects or reasonable alternatives to be identified, described and evaluated, the Directive makes no distinction between the assessment requirements for the drafted plan or programme and for the alternatives. The essential thing is that the likely significant effects of the plan or programme and the alternatives are identified, described and evaluated in a comparable way. The requirements in Article 5(2) concerning the scope and level of detail for the information in the report apply to the assessment of alternatives as well. It is essential that the authority or Parliament responsible for the adoption of the plan or programme as well as the authorities and the public consulted, are presented with an accurate picture of what reasonable alternatives there are and why they are not considered to be the best option.
— Paragraph 4.6—If the assessment of a plan or programme at a later stage of the process uses the findings of the earlier assessment, those findings must be

Standards for Consultation of Interested Parties by the Commission', 19–22. http://ec.europa.eu/governance/docs/comm_standards_en.pdf; Obradovic (n 34) 840–41.

[45] Paragraph 1.5 of Implementation of Directive 2001/42/EC on the Assessment of the Effects of Certain Plans and Programmes on the Environment, http://ec.europa.eu/environment/archives/eia/pdf/030923_sea_guidance.pdf and Ouseley J in *Heard v Broadland District Council* [2012] EWHC 344 (Admin) [69] makes it clear that the EC Guidance is only the view of the Commission and is not of a source of law.

[46] McCracken (n 10) 1519.

up to date and accurate for them to be used in the new assessment. They will also have to be placed in the context of the assessment. If these conditions cannot be met, the later plan or programme may require a fresh or updated assessment, even though it is dealing with matter which was also the subject of the earlier plan or programme.

- Paragraph 4.7—It is clear that the decision to reuse material from one assessment in carrying out another will depend on the structure of the planning, the contents of the plan or programme, and the appropriateness of the information in the Environmental Report, and that decisions will have to be taken case by case. They will have to ensure that comprehensive assessments of each element of the planning process are not impaired, and that a previous assessment used at a subsequent stage is placed in the context of the current assessment and taken into account in the same way. In order to form an identifiable report, the relevant information must be brought together: it should not be necessary to embark on a paper-chase in order to understand the environmental effects of a proposal. Depending on the case, it might be appropriate to summarise earlier material, refer to it, or repeat it. But there is no need to repeat large amounts of data in a new context in which it is not appropriate.
- Paragraph 7.4 of the EC Commission Guidance, which relates to the definition of 'Environmental Assessment' in Article 2(b) of the SEA Directive states that 'this definition clearly states that consultation involved is an inseparable part of the assessment. Further, the results of the consultation have to be taken into account when the decision is being made. If either element is missing, there is, by definition, no Environmental Assessment in conformity with the Directive. This underlines the importance that is attached to consultation in the assessment.'
- Paragraph 7.9—The timeframe [for participation] needs to be laid down in legislation and that Member States are to be free to determine its duration so long as it meets the requirement to give an 'early and effective' opportunity for responses. Experiences with the EIA Directive and other consultation procedures will give Member States information about the timeframes needed.
- Paragraph 7.10—Different timeframes may be appropriate for different types of plan or programme but care should be taken to allow sufficient time for opinions to be properly developed and formulated on lengthy, complex, contentious or far reaching plans or programmes. Adequate time will also be needed for the planning authority to take these views into account before deciding on the plan or programme. Sometimes requests for additional information may be made and the timeframe for consultation may also need to take into account the time for the responsible authority to respond.[47]

[47] The authors are grateful to Gregory Jones QC, who appeared in both cases and who confirmed the passages of the EC Commission Guidance which were cited in the skeleton arguments and oral submissions before the courts.

UK Guidance

The UK government issued its own guidance in September 2005, 'A Practical Guide to the Strategic Environment Assessment Directive' (hereinafter the 'Practical Guide'),[48] in relation to its interpretation and implementation of the SEA Directive into domestic law through the UK Regulations. Paragraphs from the Practical Guide that are relevant to the issue of consultation are included below:

— Paragraph 5.D.1—The Environmental Report must be made available at the same time as the draft plan or programme, as an integral part of the consultation process, and the relationship between the two documents clearly indicated.
— Paragraph 5 5.D.2—... Responsible Authorities must ensure that the public and the Consultation Bodies are given an early and effective opportunity within appropriate timeframes to express their opinion.
— Paragraph 3.3—Consultation with the public at earlier stages (e.g. when considering the scope of the Environmental Report) can provide useful information and public and stakeholder opinions on issues relevant to the plan or programme and the SEA. This can also help to avoid issues arising later which might delay the preparation of the plan or programme.
— Paragraph 3.14—Responsible Authorities must allow enough time for consultation when preparing for the plan or programme and the Environmental Report. It may be helpful to produce an outline of how consultation is to be conducted, making clear how the Directive's requirements will be met (normally as part of the wider consultation strategy for the plan or programme) ...
— Paragraph 3.15—Effective consultation needs appropriate skills, knowledge and experience. The form of consultation and the participation of individuals and organisations will vary depending on the nature and scale of the plan or programme. It is important to ensure that participants are involved at appropriate levels.
— Paragraph 3.16—Some consultees will want to become active participants, while others may only wish to be kept informed, or to be involved through participatory events or written consultation ... consultees are not a homogenous group and ... [care should be taken to allow them] ... to indicate how they wish to be involved.

The Approach of the Courts

There are two main authorities which consider the consultation requirements of the SEA Directive. These decisions outline how the courts interpret and apply

[48] 'A Practical Guide to the Strategic Environmental Assessment Directive', https://www.gov.uk/government/uploads/system/uploads/attachment_data/file/7657/practicalguidesea.pdf

the UK Regulations and the SEA Directive, as influenced by the various guidance documents, and helpfully explain how designated authorities should act when preparing and consulting on a new plan or programme.

Seaport

In *Seaport*, two draft plans for Northern Ireland entitled 'Draft Northern Area Plan 2016' and 'Draft Magherafelt Area Plan 2015' (hereinafter 'the Plans') were challenged by the applicants[49] because, allegedly, they had been subjected to inadequate strategic environmental assessment.[50] In the main proceedings,[51] the High Court found for the applicants and determined that the Northern Ireland Regulation did not adequately implement a number of the requirements from the SEA Directive. In particular, Weatherup J held that Article 6(3) of the SEA Directive had not been properly transposed by the Regulation 4 of Northern Ireland Regulation because there needed to be separation between the responsible authority and the consultation body, which had not been achieved through the Environmental and Heritage Service Seeking input from the Planning Service, a separate divisions of the same Department.[52] He determined that it was necessarily implicit in Articles 5(4) and 6(3) that there be consultation with an authority with relevant environmental responsibilities that was also external to the responsible body.[53] Weatherup J also found that the absence of an actual time period for consultation in regulation 12 of the Northern Ireland Regulation did not properly transpose Article 6(2) of the SEA Directive.[54] In contrast, the Department was of the view that no duty of consultation arose under the SEA Directive because the Department was fully possessed of relevant expertise and responsibilities, and there was no obligation to create a new environmental authority for consultation purposes in order to meet its environmental responsibilities (which could be discharged within its existing structures).[55] The Department appealed to the Court of Appeal and, after hearing

[49] The first applicant was Seaport Investments Ltd, a property development company based in Portballintrae, County Antrim. The second applicants were Magherafelt District Council and five property development companies operating in the Magherafelt area.

[50] G Jones, 'Strategic Environmental Assessment: The Seaport Investments Case' (2008) 20 *Environmental Law and Management* 282.

[51] *Re Seaport Investments Ltd's Application for Judicial Review* [2007] NIQB 62 (QBD (NI)). In this case, the High Court found that the Member State should be required to specify the time limit in the transposing legislation under art 6(2) of the SEA Directive and that the Member State could not delegate the responsibility for laying down the time limit in each case to the authority responsible for the plan.

[52] *Re Seaport Investments Ltd's Application for Judicial Review* (HCNI) (n 4) [H5 1.] and [15].

[53] ibid.

[54] ibid [H7, 3] and [15].

[55] ibid [13]–[14].

the argument for two days, the Court of Appeal decided to refer two issues for preliminary reference to the European Court of Justice (ECJ) asking:

(a) whether, Article 6(3) of the SEA Directive required a designated authority to create or designate a new authority for the purposes of consultation, despite the designated authority being the body which would ordinarily be consulted on in connection with the preparation of the Environmental Report and the adoption of that plan; and
(b) whether Article 6(2) of the SEA Directive, required that the national transposing legislation lay down precisely the 'appropriate timeframes' within which the authorities designated and the public affected or likely to be affected for the purposes of Article 6(3) and (4) should be able to express their opinions.[56]

In the interim, the Department entered into settlement with the other parties. As a consequence, the other parties were not represented before the ECJ.[57]

In response, to the two issues, the ECJ (Fourth Chamber) ruled that:

> '…in circumstances such as those in the main proceedings, Article 6(3) of the SEA Directive does not require that another authority to be created or designated for the purposes of consultation, provided that, within the authority usually responsible for undertaking consultation on environmental matters and designated as such, a functional separation is organised so that an administrative entity internal to it has real autonomy, meaning, in particular, that it is provided with administrative and human resources of its own and is thus in a position to fulfil the tasks entrusted to authorities to be consulted as provided for in Article 6(3) of the SEA Directive and, in particular, to give an objective opinion on the plan or programme envisaged by the authority to which it is attached'.[58]

> '…Article 6(2) of SEA Directive must be interpreted as not requiring that the national legislation transposing the Directive to lay down precise periods within which the authorities designated and the public affected or likely to be affected (for the purposes of Articles 6(3) and (4) of the SEA Directive) are to express their opinions on a particular draft plan or programme and on the Environmental Report upon it. Nevertheless, Article 6(2) of the SEA Directive does not preclude such periods from being laid down on a case-by-case basis by the authority which prepares the plan or programme. In that situation, Article 6(2) of the SEA Directive requires that the period actually laid down must be sufficient to allow the designated authorities and public an effective opportunity to express their opinions in good time'.[59]

[56] Case C-474/10 *Department of the Environment for Northern Ireland v Seaport (NI) Ltd* [2011] ECR I-10227; [2012] Env LR 21; ECJ (4th Chamber) [H2]; Jones (n 50) 288.

[57] See further on this aspect William Orbinson's comments on the *Seaport* case in Ch 15 in this volume.

[58] Case C-474/10 *Department of the Environment for Northern Ireland v Seaport (NI) Ltd* [2011] (n 56) [43].

[59] ibid [50].

This decision helped to establish what could be considered an appropriate timeframe for consultation (for the purposes of Article 6(a) of the SEA Directive). In particular, it made it clear with regards to the timeframe questions that:

— the national legislation of Member States does not need to set what is an 'appropriate timeframe' for designated authorities to express their opinions about a proposed plan or programme.[60] However, there is also nothing which precludes a Member State from prescribing a minimum or mandatory timeframe for consultation. For example, six- and eight-week periods were considered acceptable in the main proceedings; and
— the national legislation of Member States can pass to the authority proposing the plan or programme the power to itself lay down the timeframe for the consultation, provided that the period set for each individual consultation is sufficient to allow it an effective opportunity to express its opinion in good time on that draft plan or programme and on the Environmental Report upon it.[61]

In relation to Article 6(3) of the SEA Directive and what is required in order for consultation with the designated authority to be 'effective', the ECJ in *Seaport* found that:

— the authority to be consulted can be an administrative entity internal to the designated authority provided that it is in a position to fulfil the tasks entrusted to it. This requires, as a minimum, a functional separation so that the administrative entity internal to it has real autonomy. This requires the entity to be provided with administrative and human resources of its own so that can give an objective opinion on the plan or programme;[62]
— the authority to be consulted must have specific environmental responsibilities and proven skills in that regard;[63]
— the designated authority should be consulted or informed at the various stages of the process of preparation, adoption and implementation of the plan or programme; and
— the purpose of consulting the designating authority (due to its specific environmental responsibilities or the likelihood of it being concerned by the environmental effects of the plan or programme being implemented) is to ensure:
  - o the soundness of the Environmental Report—that it robustly takes due account of the environmental effects and objectively considers reasonable alternatives to the proposed plan or programme,[64]

[60] ibid [44].
[61] ibid [46].
[62] ibid [34],[35], [38], [41] and [42].
[63] ibid [34].
[64] ibid [35].

- that the authority preparing the plan or programme is properly perceiving the environmental effects of it at each of the various stages,[65] and
- the environmental effects of the plan or programme are assessed on reliable and comprehensive information.[66]

Further guidance can be taken from Advocate General Bot who opined that:

> Consultation is not solely a right. It is also a duty, namely the duty to protect and improve the quality of the environment by expressing concerns and by assisting the authorities responsible for preparing plans to take due account of those concerns and by adopting the best decisions.[67]
>
> All of the provisions of the Directive bear witness to the EU legislature's intention to respect those rights [established under the Aarhus Convention]. The legislature sets up a procedural framework which makes it possible to ensure, at each stage of the preparation and adoption of a plan, that the environmental concerns of the authorities and the persons affected by those projects are genuinely taken into account. In particular, the aim is to ensure that the information supplied for the environmental assessment is comprehensive and reliable.[68]
>
> …
>
> Consultation of the authorities is intended to take place from the first stages of the preparation of the plan right through to its adoption. First of all, the authorities express their views on the need for an environmental assessment of the plan in question (Article 3(6) of the Directive). Next, they must be consulted on the scope and level of detail of the information to be included in the Environmental Report (Article 5(4) of the Directive). Finally, they must express their opinion on that report and on the draft plan or programme (Article 6(2) of the Directive).[69]
>
> …
>
> The essence of the consultation procedure is therefore that an authority with responsibility for environmental matters should provide an opinion which is informed and which is, above all, directly concerned with the environmental effects of the plan. That procedure must make it possible to obtain an opinion, at each stage, not only as to the need for an environmental assessment, but also as to the actual content of the report on the environmental effects and the draft plan. The authority designated for the purposes of consultation must therefore be able to provide up-to-date information of real value. It must also be in a position to criticise the evaluations and choices made by the authority responsible for preparing the plan, by suggesting modifications and alternative solutions on the basis of its own knowledge and areas of competence.[70]

[65] ibid [36].
[66] ibid [36].
[67] ibid [AG28].
[68] ibid [AG29].
[69] ibid [AG30].
[70] ibid [AG31].

> That authority must, of necessity, be a body which is separate from and independent of the planning authority, this being the only guarantee that the consultation procedure will be credible and effective.[71]
>
> ...
>
> It is accepted that the Directive does not bring about a full harmonisation of environmental assessment procedures and, in particular, of the consultation procedure. As is made clear by recital 8 in the preamble and Article 6(5) of the Directive, the European Union legislature intended to lay down a minimum framework, leaving the specific details concerning consultation of the authorities and the public to be laid down by the Member States.[72]
>
> That approach has the advantage of avoiding excessive inflexibility in the procedure by permitting the authority responsible for the plan to specify a period which can take into account the nature, scale and complexity of the plan. In that connection, it must be observed that the scope of the Directive is extremely wide because, pursuant to Article 3, it covers such widely different sectors as agriculture, energy, industry, telecommunications and indeed tourism. Apart from the diverse nature of the draft versions which may *be drawn up, each plan has, in my view, specific characteristics and for that reason merits separa* te examination within a timeframe which must be appropriate. It seems to me that the authority responsible for the plan is best placed to determine that timeframe.[73] (emphasis added)
>
> In the present case, I find that the Department of the Environment for Northern Ireland laid down a period of eight weeks for the draft Northern Area Plan 2016 and one of six weeks for the draft Magherafelt Area Plan 2015, in accordance with reg. 12 of the 2004 Regulations. Those periods appear sufficient because they enabled the authorities and the public who were consulted to submit more than 5,250 representations concerning the first project and more than 5,300 representations with regard to the second. As the United Kingdom Government points out in its observations, if in a given case the consultation bodies or the public consider that the timeframe set is too short, an *extension can*, under national law, *be requested and, if it is refused, legal proceedings by way of judicial review can be brought on the basis that the period allowed for consultation was inadequate.*[74] (emphasis added)

In arriving at his decision in the main proceedings, Weatherup J also remarked about purpose and preparation process for the Environmental Report in connection with the development of the plan or programme, stating that:

> The scheme of the Directive and the Regulations clearly envisages the parallel development of the Environmental Report and the draft plan with the former impacting on the development of the latter throughout the periods before, during and after the public consultation. In the period before public consultation the developing Environmental Report will influence the developing plan and there will be engagement with the consultation body on the contents of the report. Where the latter becomes largely settled, even

[71] ibid [AG32].
[72] ibid [AG46].
[73] ibid [AG48].
[74] ibid [AG50].

> though as a draft plan, before the development of the former, then the fulfilment of the scheme of the Directive and the Regulations may be placed in jeopardy. The later public consultation on the Environmental Report and draft plan may not be capable of exerting the appropriate influence on the contents of the draft plan.[75]
>
> …
>
> Once again the Environmental Report and the draft plan operate together and the consultees consider each in the light of the other. This must occur at a stage that is sufficiently 'early' to avoid in effect a settled outcome having been reached and to enable the responses to be capable of influencing the final form. Further this must also be 'effective' in that it does in the event actually influence the final form. While the scheme of the Directive and the Regulations does not demand simultaneous publication of the draft plan and the Environmental Report it clearly contemplates the opportunity for concurrent consultation on both documents.[76]

Analysis of *Cogent*

In *Cogent*,[77] the High Court had to consider what was required for there to be an adequate SEA in a multi-stage development plan adoption process and whether earlier defects in the SEA process were capable of being rectified through an addendum report, provided it was published prior to the adoption of the draft plan. The allegations by the claimant, Cogent Land LLP, relevant to the discussion concerning 'early and effective' consultation are as follows:

— The 2008 Revised Core Strategy Preferred Options draft preferred West Rochford as a general location for housing along with 10 other general locations. Under Policy H2 of that draft, East Rochford (where the claimant owned freehold land) was identified as an 'Alternative Option' to the 'other Rochford' location. This was the first time in the Core Strategy process that any general development locations had been preferred and the first time that identified alternative locations had been rejected. Accordingly, the affected public were entitled (applying the provisions of the Regulations and the SEA Directive) to look to the Sustainability Appraisal (SA)/SEA accompanying the draft plan to understand why such a preference was being expressed in relation to reasonable alternatives and to examine the evidence upon which such a preference was based. However, the SA/SEA which accompanied the Preferred Options document did not allow the public this early and effective engagement.[78]

[75] *Northern Ireland, Re Seaport Investments Ltd's Application for Judicial Review* [2008] Env LR 23 [47].
[76] ibid [49].
[77] *Cogent Land LLP v Rochford District Council and Bellway Homes Ltd* (n 3).
[78] ibid [86].

- The July 2011 Addendum failed to meet the requirements of the England Regulations and the SEA Directive in a number of ways.[79]
- Even if the Addendum complied as a matter of fact with the England Regulations and the SEA Directive, as a matter of law, it was incapable of curing defects from the earlier stages of the process.[80]

On the evidence, the Court refused the claimant's application and held that the adopted plan was lawful. It adequately complied with the SEA Directive and England Regulations as a result of the Addendum. This case illustrates that whilst there is a genuine and procedural need for public consultation in the unfolding of options, the courts will adopt a rational approach where failings in the SEA have subsequently been rectified and adequate consultation has since been achieved (before the adoption of the plan or programme) despite the original defect.

This decision establishes that 'early and effective' engagement requires the SEA accompanying the draft plan to adequately set out the reasons for an authority preferring the alternative selected (and rejecting other reasonable alternatives) and to critically examine the evidence upon which such a preference was based.[81] Even though the SEA Directive and UK Regulations only require one compliant Environmental Report to be made available for the purposes of consultation, neither expressly precludes the use of an addendum or later reports to cure a deficiency or supplement an earlier report. Effective consultation calls for the draft plan and any accompanying 'environmental information' be made available so as full a picture as possible is consulted on.[82] The Court also held that if a plan-making process is carried out such that earlier stages and critical decisions could not be revisited (such as the principles being decided first and later stages providing the details), then an adequate SEA would have to have been carried out at those earlier stages, not just at the end of the plan-making process.[83] As a matter of law, defects from an earlier stage in the plan process may be capable of being cured;[84] however, to do so will require critical decisions from earlier stages to be revisited and a compliant SEA to be carried out. An addendum report must be a genuine exercise rather than an exercise of fine-tuning or a 'bolt-on consideration of an already chosen preference' to justify decisions that have already been made.[85]

[79] ibid [91]
[80] ibid [108].
[81] ibid [86].
[82] ibid [126].
[83] 'Case Comment: *Cogent Land LLP v Rochford District Council and Bellway Homes Ltd*: Strategic Environmental Assessment Directive 2001/42—Environmental Assessment of Plans and Programmes Regulations 2004—later addendum' (2013) *Journal of Planning & Environment Law* 170–192 [140].
[84] *Cogent Land LLP v Rochford District Council and Bellway Homes Ltd* (n 3) [127].
[85] ibid [102].

The Court stated that whilst it is good practice to carry out the SEA as the plan is being formulated[86] (rather than preparing a draft plan after several stages and then assessing its effect), what is absolutely critical is that an adequate SEA is properly carried out in compliance with the SEA Directive and the England [Member States] Regulations before the plan's adoption. As such, earlier errors may, depending on the legal and factual circumstances, be capable of being cured by later (addendum) reports and consideration. Furthermore, Singh J found that the SEA Directive and the England Regulations were drafted in contemplation of a single draft plan or programme being produced with an accompanying Environmental Report and that it would be subject to just one round of consultation before a decision was made. In reality, the adoption of a development plan document often involves several stages of consultation. While there is no express requirement for an SEA to be carried out as the plan is being formulated, the SEA Directive and the England Regulations require the SEA process to be properly carried out before the plan's adoption. In practice, this may mean that Directive-compliant Environmental Reports are to be prepared at each stage of a plan-making process if earlier plan-making stages could not be revisited.[87] In arriving at his decision, Singh J noted:

> Under ground 4 the claimant relies, first, upon the language of regulation 13 [of the England Regulations], which requires 'every draft plan … and its accompanying Environmental Report' (prepared in accordance with the Regulations) to be made available for the purposes of consultation by informing the public 'as soon as reasonably practicable' of where documents may be viewed. However, in my judgment, this does not have the effect contended for by the claimant, that the Addendum was incapable as a matter of law of curing any earlier defects in the process. It means simply that the draft plan, and any accompanying Environmental Report there happens to be, must be available for public consultation as soon as reasonably practicable. This is a timing provision. It does not prescribe the content of the report. Still less does it have the effect that if, for some reason, the accompanying report was not wholly adequate at that time, it cannot be supplemented or improved later before adoption of the plan, for example by way of the Addendum in the present case.[88]
>
> 'Strategic Environmental Assessment' is not a single document, still less is it the same thing as the Environmental Report: it is a process, in the course of which the Directive and the Regulations require production of an 'Environmental Report'. Hence, Article 2(b) of the SEA Directive defines 'environmental assessment' as: 'the preparation of the Environmental Report, carrying out consultations, the taking into account of the Environmental Report and the results of the consultations in the decision making and the provision of information on the decision in accordance with Articles 4 to 9'.[89]

[86] ibid [86].

[87] 'Case Comment: *Cogent Land LLP v Rochford District Council and Bellway Homes Ltd*: Strategic Environmental Assessment Directive 2001/42—Environmental Assessment of Plans and Programmes Regulations 2004—later addendum' (2013) *Journal of Planning & Environment Law* 170–192 [140].

[88] *Cogent Land LLP v Rochford District Council and Bellway Homes Ltd* (n 3) [111].

[89] ibid [112].

Although Articles 4 and 8 of the Directive require an 'environmental assessment' to be carried out and taken into account 'during the preparation of the plan', neither Article stipulates when in the process this must occur, other than to say that it must be 'before [the plan's] adoption'. Similarly, while Article 6(2) requires the public to be given an 'early and effective opportunity … to express their opinion on the draft plan or programme and the accompanying Environmental Report', Article 6(2) does not prescribe what is meant by 'early', other than to stipulate that it must be before adoption of the plan. The Regulations are to similar effect: Regulation 8 provides that a plan shall not be adopted before account has been taken of the Environmental Report for the plan and the consultation responses.[90]

… the claimant's primary argument seeks to extend the principles in *Forest Health*[91] and *Heard*[92] beyond their proper limit. Those were both cases where the court was satisfied that no adequate assessment of alternatives had been produced prior to adoption of the plans in those cases. Although they comment (understandably) on the desirability of producing an Environmental Report in tandem with the draft plan, as does *Seaport*, neither is authority for the proposition that alleged defects in an Environmental Report cannot be cured by a later document … the claimant's approach would lead to absurdity, because a defect in the development plan process could never be cured.[93]

… an analogy can be drawn with the process of Environmental Impact Assessment where it is settled that it is an:[94] 'unrealistic counsel of perfection' to expect that an applicant's environmental statement will always contain 'the full information' about the environmental impact of a project. The Regulations are not based upon such an unrealistic expectation. They recognise that an environmental statement may be deficient, and make provision through the publicity and consultation processes for any deficiencies to be identified so that the resulting 'environmental information' provides the local planning authority with as full a picture as possible. There will be cases where the document purporting to be an environmental statement is so deficient that it could not reasonably be described as an environmental statement as defined by the Regulations … but they are likely to be few and far between.

The judgment of Singh J in *Cogent* has clarified that in relation to the phrase 'parallel development', Weatherup J did not intend to lay down a general and absolute rule, but was simply stressing that whether or not the scheme of the Regulations and SEA Directive is breached will depend on the facts of each case.[95] He also confirmed that the SEA Directive and the England [Member State] Regulations do not require the 'simultaneous' publication of a draft plan and the Environment Report.[96] Rather, the intent is for the Environmental Report to be prepared

[90] ibid [113].
[91] *Save Historic Newmarket Ltd v Forest Heath District Council* (n 31).
[92] *Heard v Broadland District Council* (n 45).
[93] *Cogent Land LLP v Rochford District Council and Bellway Homes Ltd* (n 3) [124] and [125].
[94] ibid [126].
[95] ibid [118].
[96] ibid [121].

alongside the relevant plan or programme so that it can properly inform the consultees and the public about the environmental consequences of the plan or programme before the expiry of the consultation period and it being adopted.

How Are *Seaport* and *Cogent* Judgments Being Applied, if at all?

The lessons from *Cogent* and *Seaport* in relation to the behaviours that are required to ensure there is an 'early and effective opportunity' should be implemented by authorities during the preparation, consultation and adoption of various plans and programmes. The *Seaport* decision has been cited in a number of judgments,[97] but has only been treated as a significant citation in *Save Historic Newmarket Ltd v Forest Heath District Council*,[98] which is explored further below. In contrast, *Cogent* has been applied is two judgments,[99] but is yet to be treated as a significant citation. Notwithstanding this, the teachings from *Cogent* have been discussed and expanded upon in the decisions of *No Adastral New Town Ltd v Suffolk Coastal District Council*[100] (where *Cogent* was applied) and *Kendall v Rochford District Council*[101] (where *Cogent* was mentioned).

In *No Adastral*, the Court of Appeal held, in dismissing the appeal of the local residents' action group and applying *Cogent*, that there was no evidence to support the group's argument that consultation had not been real or that the local authority had approached the results of the consultation with a closed mind. The Court of Appeal agreed with the findings of Patterson J, deciding that any prior deficiencies with the SEA process had been cured before the plan was adopted,[102] because the pre-submission draft development plan included an updated Sustainability Appraisal, which dealt with the environmental implications on all alternative areas and the reasons why alternative sites were rejected.[103]

In *Kendall*, Lindblom J was asked to consider whether a breach of the consultation requirements of the SEA Directive, which gave rise to no real prejudice,

[97] *West Kensington Estate Tenants and Residents Association v Hammersmith and Fulham London Borough Council* [2013] EWHC 2834 (Admin), *QBD) see [194]–[195]; *DB Schenker Rail (UK) Ltd v Leeds City Council* [2013] EWHC 2865 (Admin) (QBD) [71]–[78]; *McGinty v Scottish Ministers* [2013] CSIH 78; [31], [39], [52]–[53]; *Shadwell Estates Ltd v Breckland District Council* [2013] EWHC 12 (Admin) (QBD) [74]–[78].

[98] *Save Historic Newmarket Ltd v Forest Heath District Council* (n 31).

[99] *Satnam Millennium Ltd v Warrington Borough Council* [2015] EWHC 370 (Admin) (QBD); *No Adastral New Town Ltd v Suffolk Coastal District Council* [2015] EWCA Civ 88; [2015] Env LR 28.

[100] *No Adastral New Town Ltd v Suffolk Coastal District Council* (n 99).

[101] *Kendall v Rochford District Council* [2014] EWHC 3866 (Admin); [2015] Env LR 21.

[102] ibid [59].

[103] ibid [46]–[60].

was sufficient cause for the development plan to be quashed, either in part or full by the court. The allegation of interest was that which concerns to the procedural integrity or the plan-making process. The question was whether the 'affected public' were given the opportunity to express their opinions on the draft allocations, plan together with 'the accompanying environmental report', before the plan was adopted. The requirements Regulation 13 of the England Regulations and Article 6 of the SEA Directive were what was considered. Significantly, there was no suggestion in this case that:

— the local authority had omitted to send copies of the draft allocations plan and the sustainability appraisal to the 'consultation bodies' or that it failed to invite any of them to express its opinion on those documents;
— there was no environmental assessment within the definition in Article 2(b) of the SEA Directive;
— the content of the environmental report prepared for the draft allocations plan (in the form of the sustainability appraisal) was lacking;
— any of 'the likely significant effects on the environment' was missed or inadequately described and evaluated; and
— the selection and treatment of 'reasonable alternatives' were insufficient or unclear.

The Local Authority breach was not related to its use of its website to consult, but, instead, its failure to announce and carry out its consultation by some other means (in addition to its website), which would have included those without internet access.[104] At paragraph 92, Lindblom J explained what he thought 'early and effective' consultation meant, saying:

> 'As is explicit in article 6(2) and implicit in regulation 13(2)(d) and (3), the opportunity given to the public to express their opinions on the documents, including, perhaps most importantly, their opinions on the assessment of alternative allocations in the sustainability appraisal, had to be not merely an 'early' opportunity but also an 'effective' one. *It would only have been an effective opportunity if those being consulted were conscious of it and able to act on it in time.* For the 'consultation bodies' and for those 'public consultees' whom the council consulted proactively the opportunity to comment was, I am sure, *both early enough—coming as it did at a stage when the proposals in the draft plan were still evolving—and effective. For individual members of the public it would have been early enough if they were aware of it. So the crucial question is whether, for them, it was an effective opportunity in that particular respect.* In my view it was not. An individual member of the public would only have been aware of the council's consultation on the draft plan together with the sustainability appraisal, and able to act on it, if he had discovered it for himself on the website or found out about it in some other way, and there was still time for him to submit his comments before the deadline.' (emphasis added)

[104] *Kendall v Rochford District Council* (n 101) [92]–[95].

Despite finding that the local authority had, failed to comply with its consultation requirements, by using only its website to announce and carry out its consultation on the affected public,[105] Lindblom J refused to exercise his discretion to quash the development plan. In his view, it 'would be disproportionate, and wrong' in the circumstances of the case to do so because the 'errors were not such as to vitiate either the environmental assessment itself or the plan-making process as a whole'. His reasons for this decision are best explained as follows:

> This does not mean that there was no breach of the SEA directive, only that any harm done by the breach that did occur was, in my view, fully repaired within the plan-making process itself and well before the plan's eventual adoption. The breach, such as it was, did not result in Mrs Kendall or anyone else being denied the substance of any right arising under European law. It did not frustrate the essential aim of the SEA directive, expressed in article 1, 'Objectives'—namely 'to provide a high level of protection of the environment and to contribute to the integration of environmental considerations into the preparation and adoption of plans and programmes with a view to promoting sustainable development, by ensuring that … an environmental assessment is carried out'.

The court held, that it did not constitute a substantial failure to allow Mrs Kendall or anyone else to participate in the process, or to have their say within it—as is envisaged in two of the recitals:

> (15) In order to contribute to more transparent decision making and with the aim of ensuring that the information supplied for the assessment is comprehensive and reliable, it is necessary to provide that authorities with relevant environmental responsibilities and the public are to be consulted during the assessment of plans and programmes, and that appropriate time frames are set, allowing sufficient time for consultations, including the expression of opinion.

And:

> (17) The environmental report and the opinions expressed by the relevant authorities and the public … should be taken into account during the preparation of the plan or programme and before its adoption or submission to the legislative procedure.[106]

In *Save*, the court was satisfied that the council had failed to comply with the requirements of the SEA Directive and the England Regulations to carry out an adequate strategic environmental assessment of the adopted Forest Heath Core Strategy because the final assessment report did not contain an assessment of all that it should have, namely the other alternatives. While there was an SEA, the rejection of alternatives occurred when the proposal for an urban extension to the northeast of the town was at a very much smaller scale than that which was ultimately adopted in the Forest Heath Core Strategy.[107] The court noted that the

[105] The website along with additional means should have been used so as to have included those without internet access.

[106] *Kendall v Rochford District Council* (n 101) [121].

[107] PG Tucker, 'Legal update' (2011) *Journal of Planning and Environmental Law* 13 Supp (Occasional Paper), OP94-122 [OP108].

planning process is an iterative one and, while an authority may reject alternatives at an early stage of the process and not revisit them later, this is only possible if the reasons given for dismissing the alternative options were made known and remain valid despite any change in circumstances, and the consultees are able to know from the assessment accompanying the Forest Heath Core Strategy what those reasons were. In arriving at its decision, the court explained that:

— it was not possible for the consultees of the Forest Heath Core Strategy to know from the final report what the reasons were for rejecting other alternatives to the proposed location of the urban development or why a significant increase to the size of the residential development made no difference to the council's earlier assessment;[108]
— despite earlier reports being published during the planning process, these reports did not provide sufficient justification for the dismissal of other alternatives and, in any event, the final assessment report accompanying the Forest Heath Core Strategy did not refer to the relevant passages of these earlier reports to identify for the consultees other alternatives that had been considered, the reasons for dismissing them and why they remained valid.[109]

In his judgment, Collins J also helpfully explained that:

> [T]he final report may rely on earlier material but must bring it together so that it is identifiable in that report. This is consistent with the requirement that members of the public must be able to involve themselves in the decision-making process and for that purpose receive all relevant information. It cannot be assumed that all those potentially affected would have read all or indeed any previous reports (in the context of this claim previous environmental assessments).[110]
>
> The process adopted is … described as iterative. Thus it is open to an authority to reject alternatives at an early stage of the process and, provided that there is no change of circumstances, to decide that it is unnecessary to revisit them.[111]
>
> It is clear from the terms of Article 5 of the SEA Directive and the guidance from the Commission that the authority responsible for the adoption of the plan or programme as well as the authorities and public consulted must be presented with an accurate picture of what reasonable alternatives there are and why they are not considered to be the best option (See Commission Guidance paragraphs 5.11 to 5.14). Equally, the environmental assessment and the draft plan must operate together so that consultees can consider each in the light of the other. That was the view of Weatherup J in the Northern Irish case *Re Seaport Investments Ltd's Application for Judicial Review.*[112] However that does not mean that when the draft plan finally decided on by the authority and the accompanying environmental

[108] *Save Historic Newmarket Ltd v Forest Heath District Council* (n 31) [40].
[109] ibid.
[110] ibid [15].
[111] ibid [16]
[112] *Re Seaport Investments Ltd's Application for Judicial Review* (n 4).

assessments are put out to consultation before the necessary examination is held there cannot have been during the iterative process a prior ruling out of alternatives. But this is subject to the important proviso that reasons have been given for the rejection of the alternatives, that those reasons are still valid if there has been any change in the proposals in the draft plan or any other material change of circumstances and that the consultees are able, whether by reference to the part of the earlier assessment giving the reasons or by summary of those reasons or, if necessary, by repeating them, to know from the assessment accompanying the draft plan what those reasons are.[113]

What Is the Impact of *Save, No Adastral* and *Kendall*?

Save explains that an authority can reject reasonable alternatives at an early stage of the process and then rely on this decision moving forward, provided its reasons for doing so are communicated (to the responsible authority, the consultees and public) in an Environmental Report and that there is no material change in circumstances which would warrant this decision being reconsidered. The Environmental Report which accompanies the draft plan must clearly identify the reasons for any reasonable alternatives being rejected by either referring to an earlier assessment report or by repeating the reasons in the final assessment report, depending on the circumstances. If an authority chooses to reject reasonable alternatives at an early stage of the process, it must be careful to ensure that consultees and/or the public are provided the reasons and opportunity to express an opinion on whether or not the dismissal of alternatives was adequate.

The decision in *No Adastral* makes it clear that the failure to carry out an SEA at the early stages of plan preparation can be remedied by a later SEA and that the critical question is whether the authority was fully informed about the environmental implications on the alternative areas and the results of the public consultation when deciding to proceed with a plan or programme. Even if there is a consultation breach, *Kendall* clarifies that this need not necessarily be fatal to the plan or programme if the breach gave rise to no real prejudice and there was no basis on which to conclude that the outcome of the plan-making process would have been different if the breach had not occurred.

113 ibid [17].

Conclusion

There will be more court discussion of the meaning, in practice, of the phrase 'early and effective opportunity' in relation to consultation on a plan or programme. The SEA Directive is inconsistent, at least in part, with the Aarhus Convention requirements. The English Regulations, by omitting any reference to 'early', are flawed. The decisions of *Seaport*, *Cogent*, *No Adastral*, *Kendall* and *Save* provide some helpful clarification and show that the courts will take a pragmatic approach, judging the consultation process on its merits. This, however, begs the real question, which is whether there is genuinely early and effective consultation on plans and programmes. The answer is 'probably not', even when benchmarked against the standards applied in the cases mentioned, and 'certainly not' if plans are being examined and reviewed in a participative, devolved and more inclusive planning system.

6

The Role of Alternatives in the SEA Directive

DAVID ELVIN QC*

> Consideration of reasonable alternatives can vary between assessments and plans, and can be challenging for both the practitioner and the plan-maker. Alternatives have been a focus for several legal challenges within the UK, and so it is important to ensure reasonable alternatives are meaningfully considered. More positively, reasonable alternatives should be recognised as an opportunity to minimise environmental problems and enhance the environmental benefits of the plan.
>
> Strategic Environmental Assessment Guidance (Government of Scotland)[1]

Introduction

Since Directive 2001/42/EC on the assessment of the effects of certain plans and programmes on the environment ('the SEA Directive') was transposed[2] into domestic law a decade ago by the Environmental Assessment of Plans and Programmes Regulations 2004 ('the SEA Regulations'),[3] the requirement that the

* I am grateful to Heather Sargent of Landmark Chambers for her assistance with this chapter.

[1] See www.gov.scot/Resource/0043/00432344.pdf, para 3.21.

[2] See further Gregory Jones in Ch 2 of this volume on the transposition of the SEA Directive by the Member States.

[3] Its proposal and legislative history preceded the formal amendment of other aspects of EU environmental assessment law following the Aarhus Convention, carried out by Directive 2003/35/EC, which did not apply to SEA. However, there seems little doubt that the Commission intended the SEA Directive to be Aarhus compliant, especially with art 7. See the Commission SEA Guidance, below, to this effect at [7.3] and s III of the Statement of Reasons for the Common Position on the draft SEA Directive: 'The renewed emphasis on the concept of integration of environmental considerations in the definition and implementation of other activities, as well the acknowledgement of the principles of the Aarhus Convention on access to information and public participation in decision-making were also inspirational elements for the more recent work by Council on the proposal.' In the context of the *HS2* litigation, however, contrast Lord Carnwath in *R (Buckinghamshire County Council and Others)*

likely significant effects on the environment of 'reasonable alternatives' to the proposed plan or programme be assessed has proven to be a fertile source of challenge before the courts and a stumbling block for many plan-makers. After explaining the legal framework which governs the assessment of alternatives as part of the strategic environmental assessment (SEA) process, this discussion will first examine the effect of domestic judgments which have dealt with the issue and will then compare the duty to assess alternatives in SEA with the duty imposed in the Environmental Impact Assessment (EIA) context.[4]

Legal Framework

In the SEA Directive, the requirement to consider alternatives to the proposed plan or programme is imposed by Article 5(1) in the following terms:

> Where an environmental assessment is required under Article 3(1), an environmental report shall be prepared in which the likely significant effects on the environment of implementing the plan or programme, and reasonable alternatives taking into account the objectives and the geographical scope of the plan or programme, are identified, described and evaluated. The information to be given for this purpose is referred to in Annex I.

Article 5 provides that:

> 2. The environmental report prepared pursuant to paragraph 1 shall include the information that may reasonably be required taking into account current knowledge and methods of assessment, the contents and level of detail in the plan or programme, its stage in the decision-making process and the extent to which certain matters are more appropriately assessed at different levels in that process in order to avoid duplication of the assessment.
> 3. Relevant information available on environmental effects of the plans and programmes and obtained at other levels of decision-making or through other Community legislation may be used for providing the information referred to in Annex I.

Also relevant are Article 6 of the SEA Directive, which requires public consultation on the environmental report before the adoption of the plan or programme concerned, and Article 7, which provides for transboundary consultation where significant effects on the environment in another Member State are likely. Article 9(1)(b) requires Member States to make available, upon the adoption of the plan

v Secretary of State for Transport [2014] 1 WLR 324 [52] with Sullivan LJ's dissent in the Court of Appeal [2013] PTSR 1194 [175]–[177]. The Aarhus Compliance Committee in July 2014 declared admissible complaints against the UK and the EU relating to HS2 and SEA, which are currently pending before the Committee, an oral hearing having been held in March 2016.

[4] This will change when the amendments made to Directive 2011/92/EU by Directive 2014/52/EU (16.4.14) which must be transposed with effect on 16 May 2017.

or programme, a statement summarising, inter alia, the reasons for choosing the plan or programme as adopted, in the light of the other reasonable alternatives dealt with.

Annex I(h) to the SEA Directive provides that:

> The information to be provided under Article 5(1), subject to Article 5(2) and (3), is the following:
>
> …
>
> (h) an outline of the reasons for selecting the alternatives dealt with, and a description of how the assessment was undertaken including any difficulties (such as technical deficiencies or lack of know-how) encountered in compiling the required information.

Interpreting the Duty to Assess Alternatives

General Considerations

There is as yet no Court of Justice of the European Union (CJEU) authority on the interpretation of the duty to assess reasonable alternatives.[5] There is, however, guidance from the European Commission[6] ('the Commission Guidance') on the issue, although it does not have the force of law.[7] There is also joint guidance, 'A Practical Guide to the Strategic Environmental Assessment Directive', issued by the four UK authorities in 2005, which is more limited in scope and detail than the Commission Guidance and which explains the process through a series of stages (see Stage B2, 'Developing Strategic Alternatives' and Appendix 6).

The purpose of SEA is made clear from Article 1 and from the Commission Guidance, and the role of reasonable alternatives should be approached from the perspective of that purpose. As the Commission Guidance states at [5.11]:

> The obligation to identify, describe and evaluate reasonable alternatives must be read in the context of the objective of the Directive which is to ensure that the effects of

[5] Compare the requirements under the US National Environmental Policy Act (NEPA) passed by Congress in 1969 and overseen by the Council on Environmental Quality (CEQ). Section 102 requires federal agencies to incorporate environmental considerations in their planning and decision-making, more specifically through the preparation of detailed statements assessing the environmental impact of and alternatives to major federal actions significantly affecting the environment (EISs). These also require the assessment of alternatives. Regulation 1502.14 of the CEQ's NEPA Regulations is more prescriptive in its requirements for the assessment of alternatives than the SEA Directive. On the influence of the NEPA on the development of the SEA Directive more generally, see Robert McCracken and Ned Westaway in Ch 1 of this volume and also Valerie Fogleman in Ch 3 of this volume.

[6] *Implementation of Directive 2001/42 on the Assessment of the Effects of Certain Plans and Programmes on the Environment* (2003), see below.

[7] See, eg, Ouseley J in *Heard v Broadland District Council* [2012] Env LR 23 [69].

implementing plans and programmes are taken into account during their preparation and before their adoption.

Most significantly, the requirement that alternatives be assessed as part of the SEA process has been considered on several occasions by domestic courts, most recently by the Supreme Court in the litigation over the HS2 proposals.[8] See, in particular, *Save Historic Newmarket Ltd v Forest Heath District Council*[9] and *Heard v Broadland District Council*[10] followed in *HS2* by Ouseley J,[11] with the endorsement of the Court of Appeal[12] at [72] and [183]–[185].

The resulting domestic jurisprudence addresses the following questions in relation to the scope of the duty to assess alternatives, which it is convenient to consider in turn:

- Which alternatives is it necessary to assess in order to comply with the requirements of the SEA Directive and the SEA Regulations?
- To what level of detail must the selected alternatives be assessed?
- To what extent must reasons be given for (i) the selection of alternatives for assessment and (ii) the rejection of the selected alternatives in favour of the proposed plan or programme as adopted?
- What format must the assessment of reasonable alternatives to the proposed plan or programme take?
- What are the consequences of a failure to satisfy the requirements of the SEA Directive and the SEA Regulations as regards the assessment of reasonable alternatives?

Which Alternatives *Must* Be Assessed?

The most immediate question that arises in considering the duty to assess alternatives is what is meant by 'reasonable alternatives taking into account the objectives and the geographical scope of the plan or programme' and, more specifically, what constitutes a *reasonable* alternative?

In the *Study concerning the report on the application and effectiveness of the SEA Directive (2001/42/EC)*[13] (April 2009), it was noted that:

> It is characteristic that the reported national legislations do not provide for a distinct definition of 'reasonable alternatives', but the definitions/choice of 'reasonable alternatives'

[8] *R (Buckinghamshire County Council) v Secretary of State for Transport* [2014] 1 WLR 324.

[9] *Save Historic Newmarket Ltd v Forest Heath District Council* [2011] JPL 1233.

[10] *Heard* (n 7).

[11] *R (Buckinghamshire County Council) v Secretary of State for Transport* [2013] EWHC 481 (Admin).

[12] Court of Appeal [2013] PTSR 1194. The issue was not contested by the Secretary of State before the Supreme Court.

[13] http://ec.europa.eu/environment/eia/sea-support.htm. The Report was produced by the Danish consultancy COWI. See further Gregory Jones in Ch 2 of this volume, at n 7.

> is left to a case-by-case assessment and decision. Some Member States have developed general national guidelines referring to the understanding of the function alternatives and the logic behind the requirements of alternatives.[14]

The UK Guidance is more general:

> 5.B.4 In conducting SEA, Responsible Authorities must appraise the likely significant environmental effects of implementing the plan or programme and any reasonable alternatives. It is normal practice when developing a plan or programme to propose different ways of fulfilling its objectives. In the UK the term 'options' is often used. Each alternative can be tested against the SEA objectives, with positive as well as negative effects being considered, and uncertainties about the nature and significance of effects noted. This will often be an iterative process, with the alternatives being revised as part of the SEA to enhance positive effects and reduce negative ones.
>
> 5.B.5 Alternatives considered often include scenarios termed 'no plan or programme' and 'business as usual'. It is important to be clear what these alternatives mean in relation to a particular plan or programme.

By way of contrast, the US NEPA Regulations[15] (1978) impose an apparently more rigorous duty, recognising that the assessment of alternatives is a key aspect of environmental assessment:

> §1502.14 Alternatives including the proposed action
>
> This section is the heart of the environmental impact statement. Based on the information and analysis presented in the sections on the Affected Environment (§1502.15) and the Environmental Consequences (§1502.16), it should present the environmental impacts of the proposal and the alternatives in comparative form, thus sharply defining the issues and providing a clear basis for choice among options by the decision maker and the public. In this section agencies shall:
>
> (a) Rigorously explore and objectively evaluate all reasonable alternatives, and for alternatives which were eliminated from detailed study, briefly discuss the reasons for their having been eliminated.
> (b) Devote substantial treatment to each alternative considered in detail including the proposed action so that reviewers may evaluate their comparative merits.
> (c) Include reasonable alternatives not within the jurisdiction of the lead agency.
> (d) Include the alternative of no action.
> (e) Identify the agency's preferred alternative or alternatives, if one or more exists, in the draft statement and identify such alternative in the final statement unless another law prohibits the expression of such a preference.
> (f) Include appropriate mitigation measures not already included in the proposed action or alternatives.[16]

[14] Section 5.8 p. 76.

[15] *40 CFR Parts 1500–08*, http://energy.gov/sites/prod/files/NEPA-40CFR1500_1508.pdf.

[16] See the CEQ's Guidance *ENVIRONMENTAL JUSTICE Guidance Under the National Environmental Policy Act* at https://www.energy.gov/sites/production/files/2015–02/documents/ej_guidance_nepa_ceq/293.pdf.

A helpful starting point in ascertaining which alternatives must be assessed is provided by paragraphs 5.13 and 5.14 of the Commission Guidance:

> 5.13. The text of the Directive does not say what is meant by a reasonable alternative to a plan or programme. The first consideration in deciding on possible reasonable alternatives should be to take into account the objectives and the geographical scope of the plan or programme. The text does not specify whether alternative plans or programmes are meant, or different alternatives within a plan or programme. In practice, different alternatives within a plan will usually be assessed (e.g. different means of waste disposal within a waste management plan, or different ways of developing an area within a land use plan). An alternative can thus be a different way of fulfilling the objectives of the plan or programme. For land use plans, or town and country planning plans, obvious alternatives are different uses of areas designated for specific activities or purposes, and alternative areas for such activities. For plans or programmes covering long time frames, especially those covering the very different future, alternative scenario development is a way of exploring alternatives and their effects …
>
> 5.14. The alternatives chosen should be realistic. Part of the reason for studying alternatives, is to find ways of reducing or avoiding the significant adverse environmental effects of the proposed plan or programme. Ideally, though the Directive does not require that, the final draft plan or programme would be the one which best contributes to the objectives set out in Article 1. A deliberate selection of alternatives for assessment, which had much more adverse effects, in order to promote the draft plan or programme would not be appropriate for the fulfilment of the purpose of this paragraph. To be genuine, alternatives must also fall within the legal and geographical competence of the authority concerned.

Two points emerge with particular clarity from the guidance. First, the reference to 'alternatives' in Article 5(1) of the SEA Directive is not only—or even, it would seem, primarily—a reference to alternative plans or programmes to the plan or programme proposed. Rather, it encompasses alternative proposals which would secure the objectives of the plan or programme proposed *within that plan or programme*. This is also emphasised by the UK Guidance above. Second, it is not legitimate to select a set of alternatives which have obviously more significant adverse effects than the plan or programme as proposed in a bid to promote the latter. The UK Guidance underlines the need to consider both positive and negative effects.

The requirement that alternatives to particular policies within the proposed plan or programme be considered was first emphasised domestically by Mitting J in *St Albans City and District Council v Secretary of State*.[17] The claimants sought to challenge the adoption by the Secretary of State of a revision of the East of England Plan, on the ground that certain policies affecting Hemel Hempstead, Welwyn Garden City and Hatfield should be quashed because the environmental report had not 'identified, described and evaluated' reasonable alternatives to those policies such that a proper SEA had not been undertaken. Mitting J held that:

> The policies decide that house building should occur on such a scale in and around the three towns as to require the erosion of the metropolitan green belt around them.

[17] *Albans City and District Council v Secretary of State* [2010] JPL 70.

> Although acceptance of the need to accommodate economic pressures on the outskirts of London necessarily involves extensive house building and some erosion into the green belt in the London Arc, it may not be inevitable that that must occur in around [sic] the three towns.
>
> Article 5.1 and Regulation 12(2) required that reasonable alternatives to the challenged policies be identified, described and evaluated before the choice was made. The environmental report … did not attempt that task. It should have done so and the Secretary of State should not have decided to adopt the challenged policies until that had been done. The consequence of omitting to comply with the statutory requirement is demonstrated by the outcome. A decision has been made to erode the metropolitan green belt in a sensitive area *without alternatives to that erosion being considered.* It is no answer to point to the requirement in the policies for green belt reviews to be undertaken at the local development framework stage. All that will do is to determine where within the district of the three towns erosion will occur, not whether it should occur there at all. (emphasis added)

The requirement to assess *reasonable* alternatives does not require that every conceivable alternative be assessed, and to do so at each stage in the process was made clear in *Heard* at [67] and the Commission Guidance at [5.14].

In *R (Chalfont St Peter Parish Council) v Chiltern District Council,*[18] the Parish Council sought to quash a policy within the District Council's Core Strategy in relation to strategic housing allocation on a particular site. The Parish Council had put forward a 'land swap' proposal pursuant to which an existing primary school would move to the allocation site and the site vacated by the primary school would be developed for housing. The Deputy High Court Judge[19] held that the land swap proposal had never been considered as a deliverable policy by the District Council, but that the District Council had in that respect been entitled to rely upon the submissions received from the County Council to the effect that there was no policy or plan which would make the land swap proposal a realistic possibility. The District Council was under no duty to go behind the County Council's statement and take its own view on the available material since it was only the County Council (as the education authority) that could make the land swap proposal deliverable. The Deputy Judge held that the District Council was entitled to decide not to treat the land swap proposal as a 'reasonable alternative':

> In the words of Ouseley J. in the *Broadland* case it was a 'non-starter' and it was reasonable for the Defendant to treat it as such. A key element of Core Strategy proposals is that they must be 'deliverable'. There was ample evidence upon which the Defendant could form the view that the Claimant's land swap proposal was not deliverable.

The range of alternatives which it is necessary to consider in order to satisfy the requirement that 'reasonable alternatives' be assessed may also vary depending on the scope of the proposed plan or programme. In *DB Schenker Rail (UK) Ltd*

[18] *R (Chalfont St Peter Parish Council) v Chiltern District Council* [2013] EWHC 1877 (Admin), especially at [36]–[38].

[19] Judge Foster.

v Leeds City Council,[20] the claimants sought to challenge the adoption of the Natural Resources and Waste Local Plan by the defendant on the ground, inter alia, that the sustainability appraisal undertaken for the plan failed to appraise the use of the claimants' sites for any other purpose. Judge Belcher, sitting as a deputy High Court Judge, considered that:

> [N]o one reading the SA could fail to appreciate that it was addressing limited areas of policy (Natural Resources and Waste) alongside the other DPDs referred to … which were considering the broader issues such as housing, employment opportunities etc.

She therefore accepted the defendant's submission that:

> [A] thematic plan such as the NRWLP does not have to consider alternatives such as housing, provided that the thematic plan forms part of a series of relevant documents, one or more of which consider the alternatives such as housing, and provided that the series of documents are considered together, or to use the SA terminology, 'acting cumulatively'.

Indeed, it might be thought that the alternatives only had to address the content and purpose of the plan in question, namely resources and waste, rather than include matters not intended to be promoted by the plan at all.[21]

The claimants in *DB Schenker* also challenged the SA on the ground that it failed to consider the option of 'doing nothing', ie, not safeguarding the relevant sites at all. Judge Belcher rejected that argument.[22] She held:

> When the whole purpose of the SA and the policies was to safeguard the land for the future uses identified, is it necessary to consider as an alternative the very obvious situation that, if not safeguarded, the sites may well be lost for that purpose? I am of the view that something as self-evident as that cannot properly be said to amount to an alternative use which needs to be considered in the SA.

Finally, in relation to the question of which alternatives it is necessary to assess in order to satisfy the requirements of the SEA Directive and the SEA Regulations, whilst in *HS2*[23] at first instance Ouseley J rejected the contention that the SEA Directive applied to the Government 'Decision and Next Steps' paper under challenge,[24] he found that had it applied, there had been a failure to assess reasonable alternatives.[25] However, he nevertheless held that alternative *objectives* for the proposed plan or programme did not have to be assessed:

> The [SEA Directive] requires the environmental report to contain an outline of the reasons for selecting the alternatives dealt with. That selection is made taking into account the objectives of the plan. Alternative objectives do not have to be explained nor, for these

[20] *DB Schenker Rail (UK) Ltd v Leeds City Council* [2013] EWHC 2865 (Admin).
[21] See Ouseley J in *HS2*, below.
[22] *DB Schenker* (n 20) [74].
[23] [2013] EWHC 481 (Admin) at [162]–[165].
[24] *High Speed Rail: Investing in Britain's Future—Decisions and Next Steps*, Cm 8247, 2012.
[25] Above, at [110]–[172].

> purposes, the reasons why the objectives are thought worth achieving. It is alternative ways of meeting the objectives which are the focus of the SEA.[26]

The effect on the range of alternatives that must be evaluated of the absence of any requirement that alternative *objectives* be considered, as opposed to considering alternative ways of meeting those objectives, is evident from the remainder of that paragraph:

> The Government concluded that alternative strategies for motorways or a new conventional or enhanced existing rail network were not capable of meeting the plan objectives set for high speed rail. It is obviously a contestable view as to whether those objectives should be met, or can be met to a large extent by means other than a new high speed rail network. These alternative strategies could not, however, have constituted reasonable alternatives to the plan for assessment in the SEA, since they are incapable by their very nature of meeting all the objectives for a new high speed rail network.

What Level of Detail is Required for the Assessment of Selected Alternatives?

The Commission Guidance makes it clear that the level of detail required of the assessment of the likely significant environmental impacts of reasonable alternatives is the same as the level of detailed required in relation to the proposed plan or programme:

> 5.12. In requiring the likely significant environmental effects of reasonable alternatives to be identified, described and evaluated, the Directive makes no distinction between the assessment requirements for the drafted plan or programme and for the alternatives. The essential thing is that the likely significant effects of the plan or programme and the alternatives are identified, described and evaluated in a comparable way. The requirements in Article 5(2) concerning scope and level of detail for the information in the report apply to the assessment of alternatives as well. It is essential that the authority or parliament responsible for the adoption of the plan or programme as well as the authorities and the public consulted, are presented with an accurate picture of what reasonable alternatives there are and why they are not considered to be the best option. The information referred to in Annex I should thus be provided for the alternatives chosen. This includes for example the information for Annex I(b) on the likely evolution of the current state of the environment without the implementation of the alternative. That evolution could be another one than that related to the plan or programme in cases when it concerns different areas or aspects.

In *Newmarket*, Collins J held the report had to make it clear to consultees the basis on which alternatives had been rejected and choices had been made:

> 40. In my judgment … the final report accompanying the proposed Core Strategy to be put to the inspector was flawed. It was not possible for the consultees to know from

[26] Above, at [162].

> it what were the reasons for rejecting any alternatives to the urban development where it was proposed or to know why the increase in the residential development made no difference. The previous reports did not properly give the necessary explanations and reasons and in any event were not sufficiently summarised nor were the relevant passages identified in the final report. There was thus a failure to comply with the requirements for the Directive and so relief must be given to the claimants.

The level of detailed required when assessing alternatives in the context of an 'iterative' plan-making process was considered by Ouseley J in *Heard v Broadland District Council*,[27] following the approach in *Newmarket*. Ouseley J accepted that:

> [T]he plan-making process permits the broad options at stage one to be reduced or closed at the next stage, so that a preferred option or group of options emerges; there may then be a variety of narrower options about how they are progressed, and … that too may lead to a chosen course which may have itself further optional forms of implementation. It is not necessary to keep open all options for the same level of detailed examination at all stages (67).

However, at each stage of the plan-making process, the preferred option and the alternatives under consideration must all be assessed to the same level of detail in the environmental report:

> 71. There is no express requirement in the directive … that alternatives be appraised to the same level as the preferred option … it seems to me that, although there is a case for the examination of a preferred option in greater detail, the aim of the directive, which may affect which alternatives it is reasonable to select, is more obviously met by, and it is best interpreted as requiring, an equal examination of the alternatives which it is reasonable to select for examination alongside whatever, even at the outset, may be the preferred option.

Where no alternatives were considered, it is necessary to explain the reason for selecting a single option:

> 70. Even more so, where a series of stages leads to a preferred option for which alone an SA is being done, the reasons for the selection of this sole option for assessment at the final SA stage are not sensibly distinguishable from reasons for not selecting any other alternative for further examination at that final stage. The failure to give reasons for the selection of the preferred option is in reality a failure to give reasons why no other alternatives were selected for assessment or comparable assessment at that stage. This is what happened here. So this represents a breach of the directive on its express terms.

Indeed, this approach is consistent with the Commission Guidance:

> 5.12. In requiring the likely significant environmental effects of reasonable alternatives to be identified, described and evaluated, the Directive makes no distinction between the assessment requirements for the drafted plan or programme and for the alternatives.

[27] *Heard* (n 7).

Footnote 14, which follows the above sentence, adds:

> Compare Article 5(3) and Annex IV of the EIA Directive which require the developer to provide an outline of the main alternatives studied and an indication of the main reasons for his choice taking into account the environmental effects.

Indeed, the primary obligation in the environmental report in Article 5 (and regulation 12) is the same for both the implementation of the plan and the reasonable alternatives, namely 'to identify, describe and evaluate' their likely significant environmental effects.

Ouseley J's observation that the aim of the SEA Directive 'may affect which alternatives it is reasonable to select' is interesting. He observed that it will be legitimate to discount certain potential alternatives as falling outside the set of 'reasonable alternatives' to the proposed plan or programme *having regard to the aim of the SEA Directive*, but that the alternatives which *are* selected for assessment (as 'reasonable' alternatives in the light of the aim of the SEA Directive) must then be assessed to the same level of detail as the proposed plan or programme.

The Extent of the Duty to Give Reasons

Much attention has been paid by domestic judgments to the question of the extent to which the SEA Directive and the SEA Regulations require reasons to be given for (i) the selection of alternatives for assessment and (ii) the rejection of the alternatives assessed, in favour of the proposed plan or programme as adopted.

The first issue is whether the use of 'outline' in Annex I limits the extent of the duty to identify and evaluate alternatives[28] and should be considered against the primary requirement in Article 5(1), which applies the same duty to identify, describe and evaluate both the plan and the reasonable alternatives.

The reason for the structure of the SEA Directive can be seen from the changes made during the legislative process where the assessment of reasonable alternatives always formed part of the requirements for SEA. The *travaux preparatoires* show that the original proposal for the Council Directive[29] did not include alternatives in draft Article 5 (which also included some of the provisions now found in Annex I), but only in Annex I:

> (f)[A]ny alternative ways of achieving the objectives of the plan or programme which have been considered during its preparation (such as alternative types of development or alternative locations for development) and the reasons for not adopting these alternatives.

[28] See Sales J (as he then was) in *Ashdown Forest Economic Development LLP v Secretary of State* [2014] EWHC 406 (Admin) [92]–[94], though this appears to be directed only at the extent of the reasons.

[29] OJ 97/C 129/08 Proposal for a COUNCIL DIRECTIVE on the assessment of the effects of certain plans and programmes on the environment (COM (96) 511 final, 4 December 1996).

The Explanatory Memorandum stated:

> *5.5 Article 5 and Annex* describe the information that has to be provided where an assessment is required. The competent authority (that is, the competent authority which is responsible for adopting the plan or programme or the authority which is responsible for submission to the legislative procedure) has to provide the information listed in the Annex in such detail as may reasonably be required for the purpose of assessing the environmental effects of implementing the plan or programme. (emphasis added)

The requirement was retained but amended in the Common Position (EC) No 25/2000 of 30 March 2000, where the primary alternatives provisions were moved from Annex I to Article 5 in terms equivalent to those now found in the SEAD with the following comments in the Statement of Reasons:

> Article 5—Environmental report
>
> The Article was reformulated by retaining the principal requirements, including as regards the assessment of reasonable alternatives, while a detailed description of the content of the report, including additional elements, was set out in Annex I.
>
> Annex I—Information to be provided—the report
>
> This Annex has been made more concise and at the same time more complete.

The objectives, the language and history of the SEAD therefore underline the importance of having regard to the primary duty in Article 5, which provides the clear basis, it is suggested, for the approach taken in *Newmarket*[30] and *Heard.*[31]

The duty to assess alternatives is transposed into domestic law by regulation 12 of the SEA Regulations, which insofar as is relevant is in the following terms:

> (1) Where an environmental assessment is required by any provision of Part 2 of these Regulations, the responsible authority shall prepare, or secure the preparation of, an environmental report in accordance with paragraphs (2) and (3) of this regulation.
> (2) The report shall identify, describe and evaluate the likely significant effect on the environment of–
> (a) implementing the plan or programme; and
> (b) reasonable alternatives taking into account the objectives and the geographical scope of the plan or programme.
> (3) The report shall include such of the information referred to in Schedule 2 to these Regulations as may reasonably be required, taking account of–
> (a) current knowledge and methods of assessment;
> (b) the contents and level of detail in the plan or programme;
> (c) the stage of the plan or programme in the decision-making process; and

[30] *Save Historic Newmarket Ltd* (n 9).
[31] *Heard* (n 7).

(d) the extent to which certain matters are more appropriately assessed at different levels in that process in order to avoid duplication of the assessment.

(4) Information referred to in Schedule 2 may be provided by reference to relevant information obtained at other levels of decision-making or through other EU legislation.

The relevant paragraph of Schedule 2 to the SEA Regulations is paragraph 8:

> An outline of the reasons for selecting the alternatives dealt with, and a description of how the assessment was undertaken including any difficulties (such as technical deficiencies or lack of know-how) encountered in compiling the required information.

The reference to 'outline', it is suggested, simply qualifies the reasons given and should not limit the identification, description and evaluation process.

Secondly, as to the reasons for preferring the proposed plan or programme adopted, it will be recalled that Article 9(1)(b) of the SEA Directive requires a statement to be made available upon the adoption of the plan or programme summarising, inter alia, the reasons for choosing the plan or programme as adopted 'in the light of the other reasonable alternatives dealt with'.

The requirement that an outline of the reasons for *selecting* the alternatives dealt with be given was considered by Ouseley J in *Heard*. Concluding that the requirement had not been met, he held that:

> No doubt there are some possible alternatives which could be regarded as obvious non-starters by anyone, which could not warrant even an outline reason for being disregarded. The same would be true of those which obviously could not provide what RS required, or which placed development in an area beyond the scope of the plan or the legal competence of the Defendants. But that is not the case here.[32]

Where an iterative process of plan or programme making was followed, an outline of the reasons for the selection of the options to be taken forward for assessment at each stage was required, albeit that that outline could legitimately be left to the final report.[33]

As noted above, in *Chalfont St Peter*, a potential 'reasonable alternative' (the land swap proposal which the judge held that the defendant had been entitled to view as undeliverable) was found to be a 'non-starter' in the sense of Ouseley J's judgment in *Heard.*

Turning to consider the decisions of domestic courts in relation to the requirement that reasons be given for preferring the proposed plan or programme as adopted, in *Save Historic Newmarket Ltd v Forest Heath District Council*,[34] Collins J held that it was open to a planning authority to adopt an iterative process of plan-making, ie, 'to reject alternatives at an early stage of the process and, provided

[32] ibid [66].
[33] ibid [67].
[34] *Save Historic Newmarket Ltd* (n 9).

that there is no change of circumstances, to decide that it is unnecessary to revisit them'.[35] However, the authority responsible for the adoption of the plan or programme as well as the authorities and public consulted had to be presented with 'an accurate picture of what reasonable alternatives there are and why they are not considered to be the best option'.[36] The proposition that 'a prior ruling out of alternatives' during the iterative process could legitimately take place was:

> [S]ubject to the important proviso that reasons have been given for the rejection of the alternatives, that those reasons are still valid if there has been any change in the proposals in the draft plan or any other material change of circumstances and that the consultees are able, whether by reference to the part of the earlier assessment giving the reasons or by summary of those reasons or, if necessary by repeating them, to know from the assessment accompanying the draft plan what those reasons are.

In view of the nature of SEA and the iterative approach to the making of plans and programmes, it is not surprising that in *No Adastral New Town Ltd v Suffolk Coastal District Council*,[37] Patterson J rejected the contention that such a multi-stage process itself fell foul of the criticism that it was a 'paper-chase', where the environmental report had properly referenced the earlier consideration of alternatives, applying *Newmarket*:

> Although the claimant criticises that document and that in August 2011, which also went out for consultation, on the basis that they create an unacceptable paper chase the situation is very different from the case of *Berkeley v Secretary of State for the Environment* [2000] 3 WLR 420 which the claimant relies upon. In that case there was no environmental assessment at all. In the instant case there was a complete reference back to earlier documents and the reasons for rejecting earlier options.[38]

Having considered the extent of the obligation to give reasons for the selection of alternatives to be considered, Ouseley J in *Heard* went on to address the extent of the duty to give reasons for the selection of the preferred option. He observed that such a duty was not an express requirement of the SEA Directive or of the SEA Regulations, but held that:

> [69] … an outline of reasons for the selection of alternatives for examination is required, and alternatives have to be assessed … all for the purpose of carrying out, with public participation, a reasoned evaluative process of the environmental impact of plans or proposals. A teleological interpretation of the directive, to my mind, requires an outline of the reasons for the selection of a preferred option, if any, even where a number of alternatives are also still being considered. Indeed, it would normally require a sophisticated and artificial form of reasoning which explained why alternatives had been selected for examination but not why one of those at the same time had been preferred.

[35] ibid [16].

[36] ibid [17].

[37] *No Adastral New Town Ltd v Suffolk Coastal District Council* [2014] EWHC 223 (Admin) [129] (iv), upheld by the Court of Appeal: [2015] Env LR 28.

[38] *Save Historic Newmarket Ltd* (n 9) [40].

[70]Even more so, where a series of stages leads to a preferred option for which alone an SA is being done, the reasons for the selection of this sole option for assessment at the final SA stage are not sensibly distinguishable from reasons for not selecting any other alternative for further examination at that final stage. The failure to give reasons for the selection of the preferred option is in reality a failure to give reasons why no other alternatives were selected for assessment or comparable assessment at that stage. This is what happened here. So this represents a breach of the directive on its express terms.[39]

Finally, depending on the circumstances of the draft plan and the assessment, the court may be willing to allow a considerable degree of latitude to the planning authority in its consideration of alternatives. In *Ashdown Forest Economic Development LLP v Secretary of State*,[40] Sales J took a broad approach to the assessment of reasonable alternatives even though an authority adopted a lower housing figure than objectively justified because research on the alternatives (and their impact on a SAC/SPA) was needed and known, but had not yet been undertaken. Further, in considering the alternatives for a policy limiting development within specified distances of the SAC/SPA, it was sufficient for the authority to have referenced a report by Natural England considering the issue generally by reference to other locations (though only intended as a habitats assessment). It is an approach that does not sit comfortably with that of Ouseley J in *Heard* and might be regarded as weakening the important protections which a consideration of reasonable alternatives confers in securing clearer knowledge of the environmental implications of the options and thus better decision-making.

The Court of Appeal[41] disagreed with Sales J. Richards LJ held that in adopting Policy WCS12, the council had failed to comply with the requirements of the SEA Directive. This was because no regard had been given to whether there were reasonable alternatives to the 7 km SANGS zone that ought to be subject to environmental assessment alongside the council's preferred approach. The difference between the purpose of the Habitats screening exercise and the requirements of SEA were underlined. Contrary to the judgment of Sales J, it could not be said that the Habitats Screening Assessment prepared in conjunction with the draft Core Strategy had considered the reasonable alternatives since its sole focus had been whether the 7 km SANGS zone would avoid the risk of harm to the Ashdown Forest SAC/SPA and thus avoid the need for appropriate assessment pursuant to the Habitats Directive and the Conservation of Habitats and Species Regulations 2010. It was not the function of the Habitats screening exercise to consider alternatives and therefore it did not follow its conclusions that there were no alternative means of ensuring the necessary protection of the forest.

Richards LJ held:

45. First, it was not the function of the Habitats Regulations Assessment to consider alternatives. What mattered for the purposes of that assessment was that the Core Strategy

[39] *Heard* (n 7) [69] and [70].

[40] *Ashdown Forest Economic Development LLP v Secretary of State* [2014] EWHC 406 (Admin).

[41] [2016] PTSR 78.

> should not lead to any adverse effects on the integrity of the Ashdown Forest SPA. The avoidance and/or mitigation measures recommended in it were put forward in accordance with the precautionary principle with the aim of eliminating the risk of adverse effects. They were considered to meet that aim. It does not follow that there were no alternative means of ensuring the necessary protection of the SPA.
>
> 46. Sales J. took the view, at para. 108 of his judgment, that on a fair reading of the Habitats Regulations Assessment three alternatives had been canvassed: a 5 km zone in accordance with the Thames Basin Heaths precedent, a 7 km zone, and a 15 km zone. With respect, and as already indicated at para. 27 above, I do not accept that the report can be read in that way. The report did not consider the 5 km as an alternative to a 7 km zone but simply as the starting point for a process of extrapolation leading to the 7 km zone. Nor was there was any suggestion of a 15 km zone as an alternative: a 15 km radius was simply used in the course of the process of extrapolation leading to the 7 km zone.
>
> 47. Sales J.'s alternative analysis, at para. 109 of his judgment, is that if the report is to be read just as a principled set of reasons for choosing a 7 km zone, 'the reasons given explain clearly why that solution was chosen and, by clear implication, why other solutions were not chosen'. Again, I respectfully differ from the judge's view. It comes back to the same point about the purpose of the Habitats Regulations Assessment and the nature of the exercise undertaken in it. It was sufficient that the measures recommended in it, including the 7 km zone, would eliminate the risk of adverse effects on the Ashdown Forest SPA. The reasons why the 7 km zone would serve that purpose did not amount by necessary implication to reasons why there were no alternative means of ensuring the necessary protection of the SPA. The report did not state or suggest that nothing short of a 7 km zone would suffice or that no other measures were possible. The report simply explained why a 7 km zone was considered.

Thus, it is clear from the balance of domestic authorities that assessment must be made and reasons must be given both for (i) the selection of alternatives for assessment and (ii) the selection of a preferred option. The requirement that reasons be given is particularly important where an iterative process is undertaken.

What Form Must the Assessment of Reasonable Alternatives Take?

Paragraph 4.6 of the Commission Guidance explains that where certain aspects of a plan or programme have been assessed at an earlier stage of the planning process and the plan-maker wishes to use the findings of that earlier assessment at a later stage of the process, that approach will be legitimate if the earlier findings remain up to date and accurate and those findings are placed in the context of the new assessment. However, paragraph 4.7 of the Commission Guidance emphasises (echoing Lord Hoffmann in *Berkeley*) that:

> In order to form an identifiable report, the relevant information must be brought together: it should not be necessary to embark on a paper-chase in order to understand

> the environmental effects of a proposal. Depending on the case, it might be appropriate to summarise earlier material, refer to it, or repeat it. But there is no need to repeat large amounts of data in a new context in which it is not appropriate.

In *Newmarket*, Collins J noted[42] that the second half of paragraph 4.7 permitted the final report to rely on earlier material, but required it to be brought together so that it was identifiable in the final report. He observed that paragraph 4.7 was consistent with the requirement that members of the public must be able to involve themselves in the decision-making process and for that purpose receive all relevant information, for it could not be assumed that all those potentially affected would have read all (or indeed any) previous reports.

In *Heard*, Ouseley J observed that Article 5(2) of the SEA Directive permitted the decision as to what information was reasonably required to take account of 'the contents and level of detail in the plan … its stage in the decision-making process and the extent to which certain matters are more appropriately assessed at different levels in that process'. He accepted that, whilst an iterative process was legitimate, a description of what alternatives were examined and why had to be available for consideration *at each stage*. This could be carried out by reference back to earlier documents, so long as the reasons given there remained sound, but the earlier documents had to be organised and presented in such a way that they could readily be ascertained and no paper chase was required to find out what had been considered and why it had been rejected.[43]

The decision in *DB Schenker*[44] provides an example of reliance successfully being placed upon reasons given in a different document rather than in the Sustainability Appraisal itself. The Deputy Judge held that:

> Provided the reasons for the rejection of alternative uses … is fully and properly explained and the document which does so is fully and properly identified in the SA … (and is a document freely available to consultees), the fact that the information is contained in a different document and not set out again in this SA does not, in my judgment, mean that this SA fails to consider the alternative uses. The contrary approach argued for … would effectively mean either that all DPDs relating to a given area would have to contain duplicate SA material or that it is impossible, in practical terms, to have separate thematic DPDs and that everything must be in one DPD. In my judgment neither alternative is sustainable.

In *R (West Kensington Estates Tenants and Residents Association) v Hammersmith and Fulham London Borough Council*,[45] the claimants challenged the Earl's Court and West Kensington Opportunity Area Joint Supplementary Planning Document (SPD). Lindblom J (as he then was) held that the SEA conducted for the SPD was

42 *Save Historic Newmarket Ltd* (n 10) [15].

43 At [12], with reference to the judgment of Collins J in *Newmarket* (n 9).

44 *DB Schenker* (n 20) [70].

45 *R (West Kensington Estates Tenants and Residents Association) v Hammersmith and Fulham London Borough Council* [2013] EWHC 2834, especially at [193]–[194].

an adequate and lawful assessment sufficient to complement the SEA, which had been undertaken for the London Plan and relevant core strategies. He accepted the submission that the requirements of the SEA Directive and the SEA Regulations had, in substance, been fully complied with and noted that 'substantial compliance' with the requirements of the SEA Directive was sufficient by reference to *Commission v Germany*[46] and *R (Edwards) v Environment Agency*:[47]

> In the process in which the SPD was prepared there was neither any legal requirement nor any justification for a duplication of the assessment already undertaken in the SEA for the core strategies … Alternatives had been considered and assessed in the sustainability appraisals prepared for the core strategies. It would have been inappropriate for the SPD to introduce new or different options that had not been ventilated during the plan-making process itself. The SPD did not add to the options already considered during the plan-making process. Nor did it favour an option previously rejected. The SEA undertaken for it did not need to repeat the work done in the SEA for the core strategies or reiterate the description of that assessment. The same applies to the local planning authorities' consideration of cumulative effects.

Finally, in this respect, it is established that defects in an environmental report can be cured by a later document, provided that it is not the case that *no* adequate assessment of alternatives was produced prior to the adoption of the relevant plan or programme: *Cogent Land LLP v Rochford District Council.*[48]

However, it is suggested that this approach can only be taken so far. Since the requirement is to consult concurrently on both the draft plan and report, and to do so at an early and effective stage, if the flaw has prevented consultation on the assessment at the relevant stage, then this is unlikely to be curable at a later stage, eg, following adoption. Such an approach would be inconsistent with the purposes of consultation and assessment and would run contrary to Article 6 (see below).

Consultation on Alternatives

The importance of public engagement in the SEA process is clear. As with EIA, the assessment of a plan or programme is not merely a question of the process in producing the environmental report, but the plan is also to be tested against the opinions of those to be consulted. This is made clear by the definition of

[46] Case C-431/92 *Commission v Germany* [1995] ECR I-2189.

[47] *R (Edwards) v Environment Agency* [2008] Env LR 34.

[48] *Cogent Land LLP v Rochford District Council* [2013] 1 P & CR 2 [124], approved by the Court of Appeal in *No Adastral New Town Ltd v Suffolk Coastal District Council* [2015] Env LR 28. See, further, the following section.

'environmental assessment' in Article 2(b) and the duty under Article 4[49] not to adopt until the environmental assessment required has been carried out:

> '[E]nvironmental assessment' shall mean the preparation of an environmental report, the carrying out of consultations, the taking into account of the environmental report and the results of the consultations in decision-making and the provision of information on the decision in accordance with Articles 4 to 9.

It is interesting to compare this with Sullivan J.'s characterisation of EIA in *R (Blewett) v Derbyshire County Council*:

> [39] This process of publicity and public consultation gives those persons who consider that the environmental statement is inaccurate or inadequate or incomplete an opportunity to point out its deficiencies. Under reg. 3(2) the local planning authority must, before granting planning permission, consider not merely the environmental statement, but 'the environmental information', which is defined by reg. 2 as 'the environmental statement, including any further information, any representations made by any body required by these Regulations to be invited to make representations, and any representations duly made by any other person about the environmental effects of the development'.[50]

The importance of the role of the public was emphasised by Lord Hoffmann in *Berkeley v Secretary of State*[51] in terms which are equally reflective of the SEA Directive:

> The directly enforceable right of the citizen which is accorded by the Directive is not merely a right to a fully informed decision on the substantive issue. It must have been adopted on an appropriate basis and that requires the inclusive and democratic procedure prescribed by the Directive in which the public, however misguided or wrongheaded its views may be, is given an opportunity to express its opinion on the environmental issues.

Further, Article 6 and reg. 13 require that the draft plan and report be consulted upon concurrently so that an effective consultation can be conducted: see Weatherup J in *Re Seaport Investments*.[52] This includes the identified and evaluated reasonable alternatives, and the evaluation of those in the report differs, for obvious reasons, from the reasons given once the plan is adopted under Article 9 and regulation 16. Patterson J, whilst still adopting this approach in *No Adastral New Town Ltd v Suffolk Coastal District Council*, was willing to consider the question with a degree of flexibility:

> 118 The wording of the domestic Regulations, read in the context of the Directive, make it clear that the environmental assessment of a draft plan should be an ongoing process. The objective is to ensure that the environmental effects of emerging policies can be taken into account while plans are actually being 'developed'. To enable that to occur the process of preparing the environmental report should start, as the Commission says in

[49] SEA Regulations, reg 8.

[50] *R (Blewett) v Derbyshire County Council* [2004] Env LR 29 [39].

[51] *Berkeley v Secretary of State* [2001] 2 AC 603, 615.

[52] *Re Seaport Investments* [2008] Env LR 23 [46]–[52].

its guidance, as early as possible, and ideally, at the same time as the preparation of the plan or programme.

119 That does not mean that there is an absolute rule that the plan and the environmental report proceed in parallel so that there is a requirement for simultaneous publication of the draft plan and environmental report. What it does mean though, in my judgement, is that there should be an integrated process whereby the environmental report assesses the emerging plan and the subsequent iteration of that plan has regard to the contents of the environmental report and public consultation on both documents. Whilst there is some flexibility in the process the objective of the Directive can only be met properly by taking into account an environmental report on the environmental effects of the policies in a draft plan as the policies develop. What is required may vary according to the plan being promoted and the stage that it has reached.[53]

In the Court of Appeal, Richards LJ, applying *Cogent Land*,[54] rejected the argument that the consultation that had taken place was unreal and therefore incapable of curing the earlier deficiency:

57. In my judgment, that line of argument is untenable. I can see no evidential basis for the proposition that the November 2011 consultation was not a real consultation or that the Council approached the results of the consultation with a closed mind. The very fact that the meeting of the Council on 15 December 2011 included debate on a motion calling for reconsideration of the preferred option in the light of further assessments shows that the issue was still a live one at that time. The fact that the motion was defeated does not begin to show a closed mind on the part of those voting against it. There is nothing whatsoever to suggest that the decision taken by the Council at that meeting to submit the draft CS for examination by the inspector was anything other than a genuine decision reached after due consideration of the November 2011 SA and the responses to the consultation on it.

58. The second strand to NANT's factual argument is a contention that the documentation consulted on in November 2011 did not sufficiently identify the reasons for rejecting the alternatives to Area 4 as locations for the allocation of 2000 dwellings. It is said that the SA involved too much of a 'paper chase', referring back to previous documents, and in any event that cross-reference to previous flawed decisions did not save the position.

59. Again I cannot accept the argument. It is true that the November 2011 SA did refer back to previous documents … All this was done, however, in a manner that was perfectly intelligible, and the material specifically included the January 2010 appraisal of the impact of an allocation of 2,000 dwellings on each of the five options originally considered. I agree with Patterson J that there was no unacceptable paper chase and that consultees were made well aware of the reasons for rejecting the alternatives to Area 4. I also agree with the judge that when the Council made the decision to proceed with the CS, it was fully informed about the environmental implications on all alternative areas and of the results of the public consultation on the effect of 2000 dwellings on all five of the original option areas. The judge was right to find that the earlier deficiencies in the SEA process had been cured.

[53] *No Adastral New Town Ltd v Suffolk Coastal District Council* (n 37) [118]–[120].
[54] See also *Satnam Millennium Ltd v Warrington Borough Council* [2015] Env LR 30.

The Consequences of a Failure to Fulfil the Duty to Assess Reasonable Alternatives

In *St Albans*,[55] having concluded that the challenged policies were beyond the appropriate power because the requisite assessment of reasonable alternatives had not been undertaken, Mitting J considered whether the policies ought to be quashed. He acknowledged the 'highly inconvenient' consequences of quashing the policies, but held (at [22]) that he was either bound by, or preferred to follow, Lord Hoffmann's observations in *Berkeley*.[56]

Lord Hoffmann observed that the relevant statutory provision, in providing that the court 'may' quash an ultra vires planning decision, clearly conferred a discretion upon the court. However, he doubted whether, consistently with its obligations under European law, it was open to the court to exercise that discretion so as to uphold a planning permission which had been granted contrary to the EIA Directive. He continued:

> To do so would seem to conflict with the duty of the court under article 10 (ex article 5) of the EC Treaty to ensure fulfilment of the United Kingdom's obligations under the Treaty. In classifying a failure to conduct a requisite EIA for the purposes of section 288 as not merely non-compliance with a relevant requirement but as rendering the grant of permission ultra vires, the legislature was intending to confine any discretion within the narrowest possible bounds. It is exceptional even in domestic law for a court to exercise its discretion not to quash a decision which has been found to be ultra vires … Mr. Elvin was in my opinion right to concede that nothing less than substantial compliance with the Directive could enable the planning permission in this case to be upheld.

Mitting J considered that Lord Hoffmann's observations applied with equal force to SEA and quashed the challenged policies. Despite the strictures placed by Lord Carnwath in *Walton v Scottish Ministers*[57] on treating *Berkeley* as a general prescription for dealing with breaches of EU law, Mitting J's approach is consistent with that set out by Lord Carnwath:

> 139. Where the court is satisfied that the applicant has been able in practice to enjoy the rights conferred by the European legislation, and where a procedural challenge would fail under domestic law because the breach has caused no substantial prejudice, I see nothing in principle or authority to require the courts to adopt a different approach merely because the procedural requirement arises from a European rather than a domestic source.[58]

[55] A statutory application for review under s 113 of the Planning and Compulsory Purchase Act 2004 challenging the adoption of a development plan.

[56] At 616D to E.

[57] *Walton v Scottish Ministers* [2013] PTSR 51.

[58] ibid [139]. See also Lord Hope at [156]. Note that in Hong Kong, the courts have followed *Berkeley*, but there the juridical foundation of the law is the Environmental Impact Assessment Ordinance, Cap 499, not EU law: see, eg, *Shiu Wing Steel Ltd. v Director of Environmental Protection* [2006] 3 HKLRD 33.

Lord Carnwath revisited the exercise of the court's discretion in *R (Champion) v North Norfolk District Council*,[59] where he also considered the decision of the CJEU in *Gemeinde Altrip v Land Rheinland-Pfalz (Vertreter des Bundesinteresses beim Bundesverwaltungsgericht intervening)*,[60] which he found consistent with the Supreme Court's own dicta in *Walton v Scottish Ministers*. He held at [58] that those authorities left it:

> [O]pen to the court to take the view, by relying 'on the evidence provided by the developer or the competent authorities and, more generally, on the case file documents submitted to that court' that the contested decision 'would not have been different without the procedural defect invoked by that applicant'. In making that assessment it should take account of 'the seriousness of the defect invoked' and the extent to which it has deprived the public concerned of the guarantees designed to allow access to information and participation in decision-making in accordance with the objectives of the EIA Directive.
>
> 59. Judged by those tests I have no doubt that we should exercise our discretion to refuse relief in this case. In para 52 of its judgment, the Court of Appeal summarised the factors which in its view entitled the authority to conclude that applying the appropriate tests, and taking into account the agreed mitigation measures, the proposal would not have significant effects on the SAC. That, admittedly, was in the context of its consideration whether the committee arrived at a 'rational and reasonable conclusion', rather than the exercise of discretion. However, there is nothing to suggest that the decision would have been different had the investigations and consultations over the preceding year taken place within the framework of the EIA Regulations.
>
> 60. This was not a case where the environmental issues were of particular complexity or novelty. There was only one issue of substance: how to achieve adequate hydrological separation between the activities on the site and the river. It is a striking feature of the process that each of the statutory agencies involved was at pains to form its own view of the effectiveness of the proposed measures, and that final agreement was only achieved after a number of revisions. It is also clear from the final report that the public were fully involved in the process and their views were taken into account. It is notable also that Mr Champion himself, having been given the opportunity to raise any specific points of concern not covered by Natural England before the final decision, was unable to do so. That remains the case. That is not to put the burden of proof on to him, but rather to highlight the absence of anything of substance to set against the mass of material going the other way.

In *Gemeinde Altrip*, the CJEU had held that not all procedural defects should lead to the conclusion that there had been a breach of the EIA Directive:

> 49. … it is unarguable that not every procedural defect will necessarily have consequences that can possibly affect the purport of such a decision and it cannot, therefore, be considered to impair the rights of the party pleading it. In that case, it does not appear that the

[59] *R (Champion) v North Norfolk District Council* [2015] 1 WLR 3710. There the specific context was compliance with the EIA and Habitats Directives and their transposing regulations.

[60] Case C-72/12 *Gemeinde Altrip v Land Rheinland-Pfalz (Vertreter des Bundesinteresses beim Bundesverwaltungsgericht intervening)* [2014] PTSR 311.

objective of Directive 85/337 of giving the public concerned wide access to justice would be compromised if, under the law of a member state, an applicant relying on a defect of that kind had to be regarded as not having had his rights impaired and, consequently, as not having standing to challenge that decision.

50. In that regard, it should be borne in mind that article 10a of that Directive leaves the member states significant discretion to determine what constitutes impairment of a right: see the *Bund für Umwelt* case [2011] ECR I-3673, para 55.

51. In those circumstances, it could be permissible for national law not to recognise impairment of a right within the meaning of sub-paragraph (b) of article 10a of that Directive if it is established that it is conceivable, in view of the circumstances of the case, that the contested decision would not have been different without the procedural defect invoked.

52. It appears, however, with regard to the national law applicable in the case in the main proceedings, that it is in general incumbent on the applicant, in order to establish impairment of a right, to prove that the circumstances of the case make it conceivable that the contested decision would have been different without the procedural defect invoked. That shifting of the burden of proof onto the person bringing the action, for the application of the condition of causality, is capable of making the exercise of the rights conferred on that person by Directive 85/337 excessively difficult, especially having regard to the complexity of the procedures in question and the technical nature of environmental impact assessments.

53. Therefore, the new requirements thus arising under article 10a of that Directive mean that impairment of a right cannot be excluded unless, in the light of the condition of causality, the court of law or body covered by that article is in a position to take the view, without in any way making the burden of proof fall on the applicant, but by relying, where appropriate, on the evidence provided by the developer or the competent authorities and, more generally, on the case file documents submitted to that court or body, that the contested decision would not have been different without the procedural defect invoked by that applicant.

54. In the making of that assessment, it is for the court of law or body concerned to take into account, inter alia, the seriousness of the defect invoked and to ascertain, in particular, whether that defect has deprived the public concerned of one of the guarantees introduced with a view to allowing that public to have access to information and to be empowered to participate in decision-making in accordance with the objectives of Directive 85/337.

55. As regards, in the second place, the condition that a substantive legal position of the applicant should be affected, the fact remains that the national court has not itself provided any details of what constitutes that condition and that nothing in the grounds of the order for reference enables the court to determine whether examining that condition would be useful for resolving the dispute in the main proceedings.

It is therefore clear from *Walton* and *Champion* that the court will examine the evidence to determine whether or not the substance of the rights deriving from the Directive has been satisfied and whether the defect in the individual case has any consequence.[61] The caveat that *Gemeinde Altrip* makes is that requiring an applicant to prove that the decision would have been different but for the defect in that case could make the exercise of the rights excessively difficult and would thus not meet the requirements for national procedural autonomy.[62] However, the approach of the UK courts,[63] which does not place a burden on the applicant in such circumstances, but considers the evidence to determine whether relief should be granted, appears to be compliant with the CJEU's requirements. Indeed, in practical terms, if a claimant establishes that an error of law has occurred, it will usually be the defendant or the interested party who is seeking to establish that relief should be withheld.

The Duty to Assess Alternatives: A Comparison with EIA

The Commission's *Report on the Effectiveness of the Directive on Strategic Environmental Assessment* (2009)[64] considered the complementary functions of SEA and EIA at section 4.1:

> The two Directives are to a large extent complementary: the SEA is 'up-stream' and identifies the best options at an early planning stage, and the EIA is 'down-stream' and refers to the projects that are coming through at a later stage.

In contrast to the duty to assess alternatives imposed by the SEA Directive and Regulations, in the EIA context, the developer is currently required simply to provide:

> [A]n outline of the main alternatives studied and an indication of the main reasons for the choice made, taking into account the environmental effects.

See Article 5 (1) and (3) of the EIA Directive,[65] paragraph 2 of Annex IV to the EIA Directive and Article 2(1) of and Schedule 4 to the EIA Regulations.[66]

As Lord Carnwath observed in *HS2*,[67] the reasons for this difference between the SEA and the EIA regimes are not obvious and:

[61] See *McGinty v Scottish Ministers* 2014 SC 81, where the Inner House of the Court of Session declined to quash for failures in consultation on Scottish national planning policy where the failure did not have a substantial effect, and issues of need and location of a power station would be considered as an open question in the project EIA ([55]–[59]).

[62] See, eg, Case C-201/02 *R (Wells) v Secretary of State* [2004] ECR I-723 [62]–[70].

[63] For examples of cases where the court has refused to exercise the discretion not to quash, see, eg, *Satnam Millennium Ltd* (n 54); and *R (Devon Wildlife Trust) v Teignbridge District Council* [2015] EWHC 2159 (Admin).

[64] COM(2009) 469 final, 14 September 2009. See further Gregory Jones in Ch 2 of this volume.

[65] Directive 85/337/EC on the assessment of the effects of certain public and private projects on the environment, subsequently codified by Directive 2011/92/EU.

[66] The Town and Country Planning (Environmental Impact Assessment) Regulations 2011.

[67] *R (HS2 Action Alliance Limited & Others) (Appellant) v The Secretary of State for Transport and another* [2014] 1 WLR 324 [44].

> [M]ay simply reflect the different stages at which the two exercises are carried out. At the earlier stage of strategic assessment neither the proposed plan nor the alternatives will need to have been worked up to the same degree of detail as will be appropriate at the EIA stage. At the latter stage to require an equivalent degree of detail for the rejected alternatives may be seen as unduly burdensome.

It is suggested that the purpose of SEA is to ensure that the 'pass is not sold' (to use the language of Ouseley J in *HS2*) on consideration of reasonable alternatives which might be better options in environmental terms before the project stage is reached. This concept does not appear to have been considered as a means of evaluating project-specific environmental impacts at the time of the original EIA Directive.

An alternative explanation is that, having regard to the objective of preventing deleterious environmental consequences, the 'earlier' SEA stage is simply considered to be the more appropriate stage at which to assess alternatives. The Explanatory Memorandum to the Commission's original proposal for the SEA Directive[68] explains that:

> 1.7. By the time that an application for development consent for a project is being considered by a competent authority many important decisions will already have been taken which will partly determine the outcome of the development consent process …
>
> 1.8. One particular benefit of bringing plans and programmes within the assessment system is that it will allow the issue of alternatives … to be properly assessed. The issue of alternatives can only be properly assessed at the plan and programme level.

Similarly, the Foreword to the Commission Guidance notes that at the EIA stage, options for significant change are often limited and that decisions on the choice of alternatives may already have been taken in the context of plans for a whole sector or geographical area.

An example of the shortcomings of the requirements relating to the assessment of alternatives in the EIA context is provided by the discussion of the House of Lords Select Committee on the Crossrail Bill.[69] The Spitalfields Small Business Society petitioned for the adoption of a 'Route B' for Crossrail and asserted before the Committee that Route B should have been treated as a 'main alternative' within the meaning of the EIA Directive, arguing that the failure to include it in the environmental statement rendered the process non-compliant with the Directive and thus unlawful.

The Select Committee observed that the EIA Directive[70] obliged the developer to set out in the Environmental Statement the main alternatives which he had studied. It noted that 'much discussion' of Route B had been available for a substantial period and that the route had been one of three alignments considered in a report produced by London Underground Limited in 2001. However, even at

[68] COM(96) 511 final.
[69] 1st Special Report of Session 2007–08, 102–04.
[70] Currently Annex IV.2: 'An outline of the main alternatives studied by the developer…'

that stage, Route B had not been thought to be a viable option and the promoters had abandoned further consideration of Route B. The Committee concluded that Route B had 'undoubtedly' never been presented as a main alternative and had never been considered as such by the promoters. There was therefore no requirement on them under the EIA Directive to 'write up' Route B in the ES.

In the Commission's Report *On the Application and Effectiveness of the EIA Directive*,[71] the issue of alternatives in EIA was considered:

> 3.2.2. Quality of the EIA process
>
> Experience with implementation shows that some issues are often raised in EIA procedures. With regard to alternatives, the Directive includes among the information to be provided in the EIA documentation 'an outline of the main alternatives studied by the developer and an indication of the main reasons for his choice'. Some MS have introduced a legal obligation to consider specific alternatives, while others have not. The competent authorities and the public may also contribute to the selection of alternatives for assessment. The assessment of alternatives in EIA procedures is usually a difficult issue. It may be necessary to specify what should be required under the provisions of the Directive, e.g. by introducing the obligatory assessment of alternatives or by specifying a range of alternatives (such as the 'do-nothing' alternative) to be studied.

The Commission, however, clearly regarded the absence of a more consistent approach to assessing alternatives to be a shortcoming of the EIA Directive. In October 2012, it published a proposal for the amendment of the existing EIA Directive,[72] which included provisions that mirrored the stricter SEA alternatives duty. The final text of Directive 2014/52/EU[73] inserting a new Article 5.1.d and Annex IV.2[74] into the EIA Directive together impose the duty to include:

> (d) a description of the reasonable alternatives studied by the developer,[75] which are relevant to the project and its specific characteristics, and an indication of the main reasons for the option chosen, taking into account the effects of the project on the environment.
>
> 2. A description of the reasonable alternatives (for example in terms of project design, technology, location, size and scale) studied by the developer, which are relevant to the proposed project and its specific characteristics, and an indication of the main reasons for selecting the chosen option, including a comparison of the environmental effects.

Although the Commission's Presentation of the new Directive[76] states that the duty is mandatory, unhappily this is not reflected in the wording 'studied by the developer' that also appears in the current and original EIA Directives. The provisions appear to re-impose, albeit in more detail, a duty to provide information

[71] COM(2009) 378 final, 23 July 2009.
[72] COM(2012) 628 final.
[73] OJ L 124/1. To be transposed by 16 May 2017: art 2(1) of the 2014 Directive.
[74] Article 1.5 of the 2014 Directive.
[75] Similarly, in the French version, 'une description des solutions de substitution raisonnables qui ont été examinées par le maître d; ouvrage', similarly reflecting the current 'qui ont été examinées par le maître d'ouvrage'.
[76] http://ec.europa.eu/environment/eia/pdf/Revised%20EIA.pdf.

concerning alternatives that the developer has studied rather than imposing a mandatory duty to study. The change in wording appears to have been made by the Parliament in its amendments of 9 October 2013 (which it sent back to the competent committee), then in its first reading position on 12 March 2014, which was subsequently accepted by the Council. However, though the wording was amended, the objective appears unchanged. The report on the draft proposal,[77] which first included the 'studied by the developer' amendments noted in the Explanatory Report:[78]

> In addition, the proposal introduces the mandatory assessment of reasonable alternatives to a project.

This is reflected in Recital (31) to the new Directive:

> The environmental impact assessment report to be provided by the developer for a project should include a description of reasonable alternatives studied by the developer which are relevant to that project.

Unfortunately, it seems inevitable that this amendment will be productive not of clarity, but of further litigation.

Conclusion

Unlike the slow emergence of understanding of EIA, the legal parameters of the duty to consider reasonable alternatives were recognised at an early stage following the transposition of the Directive into UK law. There is now a significant body of authority on their consideration, selection, assessment and consultation, although unsatisfactory issues remain, the greatest of which are perhaps the limitations on the duty to undertake SEA itself present in the Directive. This appears to exempt major infrastructure (which calls out for assessment of reasonable alternatives) from assessment if it is introduced by government as a matter of policy only. The nature of the origin of the project has, with respect, little to do with the need to ensure environmental assessment of alternatives, which remains a key feature in understanding and minimising environmental harm.

[77] A7-0277/2013, 22 July 13.
[78] ibid 71/132.

7

From SA to SEA: Sustainability Appraisals and Strategic Environmental Assessment

JACK CONNAH AND STEPHANIE HALL

Introduction

Without intending to be definitive, there are three important features of the modern, plan-led, planning ecosystem that permeate the whole process of development management: sustainable development; the use of assessments; and integrated decision-making.

The first of these is sustainable development. The concept of sustainable development provides the modern planning system's lodestar. It is the key component of the National Planning Policy Framework (NPPF). The NPPF makes it clear at the outset that the 'purpose of planning is to achieve sustainable development'. The whole of what follows in the NPPF is then dedicated to setting out what is necessary to achieve sustainable development. The NPPF gives a broad definition of sustainable development in paragraph 7, where it is said that:

> There are three dimensions to sustainable development: economic, social and environmental. These dimensions give rise to the need for the planning system to perform a number of roles:
>
> — an economic role—contributing to building a strong, responsive and competitive economy, by ensuring that sufficient land of the right type is available in the right places and at the right time to support growth and innovation; and by identifying and coordinating development requirements, including the provision of infrastructure;
>
> — a social role—supporting strong, vibrant and healthy communities, by providing the supply of housing required to meet the needs of present and future generations; and by creating a high quality built environment, with accessible local services that reflect the community's needs and support its health, social and cultural well-being; and
>
> — an environmental role—contributing to protecting and enhancing our natural, built and historic environment; and, as part of this, helping to improve biodiversity, use natural resources prudently, minimise waste and pollution, and mitigate and adapt to climate change including moving to a low carbon economy.

Outside of the confines of the NPPF, these 'three pillars' or 'triple bottom-lines' are commonly accepted to be the components of sustainable development.[1]

The next feature is assessments. Having established what sustainable development requires, how is a decision-maker to get the information necessary to assess whether and what extent a development or a plan or programme contributes to the attainment of sustainable development? While sustainable development may be lodestar, without a modern-day compass, that lodestar would be very easy to miss. In the modern world of plan-led planning, the compass which only pointed in one direction has been replaced: the acronymic assessment is king.[2] Development plans and the like are increasingly accompanied by what is often, to those unfamiliar with the process, a bewildering number of assessments, each with their own acronym: ESs, AAs, TAs and SAs rule the roost. Far from giving a binary, yes or no answer, they tend to provide an overview that then has to be put before the decision-maker to inform his or her decision.

Third, there is the concept of integrated decision-making.[3] The problem with the use of assessments is readily apparent—not only do they not ordinarily provide the answer, but quite often different assessments may also point the decision-maker in different directions. Although most practitioners are familiar with the requirements of the various types of assessment required, those assessments tend to be, to a large extent, separate exercises. There may, for instance, be only a limited overlap between assessments focusing on social impacts compared to those focusing on environmental impacts. This separation is exacerbated by the fact that often experts skilled in one field will not be experienced in another, or may have a natural predisposition to emphasising their own areas of expertise. This can require separate teams of consultants. The concept of integrated decision-making responds to this natural trend towards the separation of the key sustainable development factors by attempting to integrate their consideration so that sight of one is not lost in pursuit of another. It follows that the use of multi-disciplinary teams of consultants and experts should be used to ensure that the links between the three pillars of sustainable development are not lost sight of or, worse, not recognised at all.[4] This is especially important given that it appears that there is now a trend towards local authorities outsourcing strategic environmental assessment (SEA)/ sustainability appraisals (SAs) preparation rather than preparing in-house.[5]

[1] T Hacking and P Guthrie, 'A Framework for Clarifying the Meaning of Triple Bottom-Line, Integrated and Sustainability Assessment' (2008) 28 *Environmental Impact Assessment Review* 73, 77.

[2] See B Dalal-Clayton and B Sadler, *Sustainability Appraisal: A Review of International Experience and Practice*. First Draft of a work in progress, International Institute for Environment and Development (2004, p.8), referring to an 'alphabet soup of acronyms'.

[3] See, for instance, J Ravetz, 'Integrated Assessment for Sustainability Appraisal in Cities and Regions' (2000) 20 *Environmental Impact Assessment Review* 31.

[4] Hacking and Guthrie (n 1) 80.

[5] R Thérivel and F Walsh, 'The Strategic Environmental Assessment Directive in the UK: 1 Year Onwards' (2006) 26 *Environmental Impact Assessment Review* 663, 668. Compare with the earlier

Of course, this is but one aspect of integration. In their survey, Hacking and Guthrie refer to three forms of integration.[6] First, the type of integration identified above is horizontal integration, bringing together different categories of impacts. Second, there is vertical integration, bringing together separate assessments carried out at different stages of the process. Third, there is then the need to integrate these horizontal and vertical elements into the decision-making process itself. Integration is therefore a multi-layered concept.

Bearing in mind these three features, this chapter considers the extent to which SAs meet the requirements of the SEA and, in so doing, contribute to the process of integrated assessment, leading to a decision-making process that produces decisions promoting and attaining sustainable development.

This chapter first sets out the legal frameworks governing SEAs and SAs, before considering the differences between the two, and the scope for and benefits of producing SEA-compliant sustainability appraisals. It concludes with some suggestions for practitioners faced with the decision of how best to produce sustainability appraisals.

Strategic Environmental Assessment

The requirement to carry out SEA was introduced on 21 July 2004 by European Union (EU) Directive 2001/42/EC on the assessment of the effects of certain plans and programmes on the environment (hereinafter 'the Directive'). The requirement applies to plans and programmes where their preparation commenced after the Directive came into force. As directives largely leave implementation and transposition of their requirements to the Member States, the UK enacted the Environmental Assessment of Plans and Programmes Regulations 2004 (hereinafter 'the Regulations'). However, the Regulations largely copy the wording of the Directive word for word (with some amendments reflecting the various statutory bodies that are required to be consulted). Given this approach, in this chapter, unless otherwise stated, we refer to directly to the source provisions in the Directive itself.

The Planning Practice Guidance (PPG) explains the purpose of the Directive as follows:

> The Strategic Environmental Assessment Directive is a European Union requirement that seeks to provide a high level of protection of the environment by integrating environmental considerations into the process of preparing certain plans and programmes.

findings of R Thérivel, 'Strategic Environmental Assessment of Development Plans in Great Britain' (1998) 18 *Environmental Impact Assessment Review* 39, 45.

[6] Hacking and Guthrie (n 1) 74.

A fully account is provided by Article 1 of the Directive, which sets out the objectives of the Directive:

> The objective of this Directive is to provide for a high level of protection of the environment and to contribute to the integration of environmental considerations into the preparation and adoption of plans and programmes with a view to promoting sustainable development, by ensuring that, in accordance with this Directive, an environmental assessment is carried out of certain plans and programmes which are likely to have significant effects on the environment.

We have here an explicit recognition of the SEA's role both in providing an *assessment* and in ensuring an integrated decision-making process (although at this stage the Directive talks only of integrating *environmental* considerations into the process). The Directive then defines what is meant by 'plan and programmes' in Article 2(a):

> '[P]lans and programmes' shall mean plans and programmes, including those co-financed by the European Community, as well as any modifications to them:
>
> — which are subject to preparation and/or adoption by an authority at national, regional or local level or which are prepared by an authority for adoption, through a legislative procedure by Parliament or Government, and
>
> — which are required by legislative, regulatory or administrative provisions.

Although Article 1 provides that it is only for plans and programmes likely to have significant effects on the environment that require an SEA, Article 3(2) makes SEA mandatory for *all* plans or programmes:

> (a) which are prepared for agriculture, forestry, fisheries, energy, industry, transport, waste management, water management, telecommunications, tourism, town and country planning or land use and which set the framework for future development consent of projects listed in Annexes I and II to Directive 85/337/EEC, or
>
> (b) which, in view of the likely effect on sites, have been determined to require an assessment pursuant to Article 6 or 7 of Directive 92/43/EEC.

There are therefore two broad categories of plan or programme within the Article 2(a) definition that require SEA: those that are likely to have significant environmental effects; and those that fall within Article 3(2). If the plan or programme in question falls into those categories, then the requirements of the Directives are triggered. The Directive then defines what is meant by 'environmental assessment' or, more accurately, *strategic* environmental assessment in Article 2(b):

> '[E]nvironmental assessment' shall mean the preparation of an environmental report, the carrying out of consultations, the taking into account of the environmental report and the results of the consultations in decision-making and the provision of information on the decision in accordance with Articles 4 to 9.

There are therefore four components or stages to strategic environmental assessments: an environmental report; consultation; taking into account the report and consultations; and the provision of information. Article 4(1) makes it clear that the environmental assessment as a whole shall be 'carried out during the preparation of a plan or programme and before its adoption or submission to the legislative procedure'.

For our purposes, it is the first element—the environmental report—with which we are primarily concerned (although the other three elements cannot be discarded as they are integral parts of the SEA process). As to the required content of the environmental report, it is to Article 5 and Annex 1 of the Directive to which we must turn. Article 5 sets out four requirements:

1. An environmental report must identify, describe and evaluate the likely significant effects on the environment of implementing the plan or programme, and reasonable alternatives taking into account the objectives and the geographical scope of the plan or programme, are identified, described and evaluated. The information required for this is set out within Annex I.
2. The environmental report must include the information that may reasonably be required taking into account current knowledge and methods of assessment, the contents and level of detail in the plan or programme, its stage in the decision-making process and the extent to which certain matters are more appropriately assessed at different levels in that process in order to avoid duplication of the assessment.
3. Relevant information available on environmental effects of the plans and programmes and obtained at other levels of decision-making or through other Community legislation may be used for providing the information referred to in Annex I.
4. The authorities referred to in Article 6(3) shall be consulted when deciding on the scope and level of detail of the information which must be included in the environmental report. Article 6(3) provides, in turn, that Member States shall designate the authorities to be consulted which, by reason of their specific environmental responsibilities, are likely to be concerned by the environmental effects of implementing plans and programme.

Annex I then provides that the information to be provided under Article 5(1) is as follows:

(a) an outline of the contents, main objectives of the plan or programme and relationship with other relevant plans and programmes;
(b) the relevant aspects of the current state of the environment and the likely evolution thereof without implementation of the plan or programme;
(c) the environmental characteristics of areas likely to be significantly affected;
(d) any existing environmental problems which are relevant to the plan or programme including, in particular, those relating to any areas of a particular environmental importance, such as areas designated pursuant to Directives 79/409/EEC and 92/43/EEC;
(e) the environmental protection objectives, established at international, Community or Member State level, which are relevant to the plan or programme and the way those objectives and any environmental considerations have been taken into account during its preparation;
(f) the likely significant effects (1) on the environment, including on issues such as biodiversity, population, human health, fauna, flora, soil, water, air, climatic factors, material assets, cultural heritage including architectural and

archaeological heritage, landscape and the interrelationship between the above factors;

(g) the measures envisaged to prevent, reduce and as fully as possible offset any significant adverse effects on the environment of implementing the plan or programme;

(h) an outline of the reasons for selecting the alternatives dealt with, and a description of how the assessment was undertaken including any difficulties (such as technical deficiencies or lack of know-how) encountered in compiling the required information;

(i) a description of the measures envisaged concerning monitoring in accordance with Article 10;

(j) a non-technical summary of the information provided under the above headings.

(1) These effects should include secondary, cumulative, synergistic, short, medium and long-term permanent and temporary, positive and negative effects.

The European Commission's Guidance on the Directive states that the obligation to identify, describe and evaluate reasonable alternatives must be read in the context of the objective of the Directive.[7] As set out above, this is to ensure that the effects of implementing plans and programmes are taken into account during their preparation and before their adoption. In requiring the likely significant environmental effects of reasonable alternatives to be identified, described and evaluated, the Directive makes no distinction between the assessment requirements for the drafted plan or programme and for the alternatives.

The Directive is vague as to the practicalities of producing the required assessment and in essence the requirement is simply that an environmental report be produced with all of the relevant effects considered. In other words, the requirements of the Directive are aimed at the procedural rather than the substantive. As Stephen Tromans QC identifies, the fact that significant environmental effects are identified and assessed does not mean that those effects will be avoided. Instead, the intention of the Directive is to ensure that there is a report which identifies the effects and takes them into account.[8] In a similar vein, Brown and Thérivel state that:

> Our conceptual definition of SEA is thus a process directed at providing the proponent (during policy formulation) and the decision-maker (at the point of policy approval) with a holistic understanding of the environmental and social implications of the policy proposal, expanding the focus well beyond the issues that were the original driving force for new policy.[9]

[7] Implementation of Directive 2001/42 on the Assessment of the Effects of Certain Plans and Programmes on the Environment (23 September 2003), §5.11.

[8] S Tromans QC, *Environmental Impact Assessment*, 2nd edn (London, Bloomsbury Professional, 2012) 317.

[9] A Brown and R Thérivel, 'Principles to Guide the Development of Strategic Environmental Assessment Methodology' (2000) 18(3) *Impact Assessment and Project Appraisal* 184.

Further, Article 4(2) of the Directive provides as follows:

> Article 4 General Obligations
>
> 1. …
> 2. The requirements of this Directive shall either be integrated into existing procedures in Member States for the adoption of plans and programmes or incorporated into procedures established to comply with this Directive.

Article 4(2) therefore provides that the requirements under the Directive may be fulfilled as part of an existing procedure within a Member State, but it does not require a whole new procedure to be adopted. The emphasis can thus be said to be on substantial compliance rather than the precise form of the report produced.

The flexibility of SEA has been noted by other commentators, such as Brown and Thérivel, who state that:

> SEA must be seen as an overarching concept rather than as a unitary technique, housing within it a family of tools, with different members being appropriate for different types and different stage, of PPP [plans, policies and programmes] planning, development and review … No one SEA methodology will apply to all strategic actions and in all socio-political contexts: we must begin to think in terms of an array of SEA tools from which the appropriate ones can be selected to meet the needs of particular circumstances.[10]

Having established the broad outlines of what SEA requires, we now consider the home grown sustainability appraisal before considering whether, and how, the SA can meet the requirements of the SEA, as well, of course, of whether it should.

Sustainability Appraisals

This chapter addresses sustainability appraisals only within the UK[11] and, more specifically, England.[12] The legislative framework covering SAs is considerably more spartan than the SEA framework. Whereas the SEA Directive sets out detailed prescriptive provisions concerning the content of SEAs, section 39(2) of the Planning and Compulsory Purchase Act 2004 simply confirms the centrality of sustainable development in the planning system. It requires that anybody exercising a function in relation to local development documents must 'exercise the function with the objective of contributing to the achievement of sustainable

[10] ibid 186.

[11] The term 'sustainability appraisal' of course has the potential to mean different things to those in different jurisdictions: see Hacking and Guthrie (n 1) 73–74.

[12] A good overview of the different guidance that pertains to the SEA Directive in each of the UK's four countries can be found in Thérivel and Walsh (n 5) 665. More particularly in terms of the differences with the UK of the transposition of the requirement for public involvement to be 'early and effective', see Stephen Ashworth and Rachael Herbert in Ch 5 of this volume.

development'. Section 19(5) of the Act sets out a specific requirement of this general duty, requiring that in preparing local development documents:

> (5) The local planning authority must also–
> (a) carry out an appraisal of the sustainability of the proposals in each development plan document;
> (b) prepare a report of the findings of the appraisal.

The SA is the product of that requirement. It should be noted that although the current legal framework for SAs is to be found within the 2004 Act, SAs have in fact been in existence for considerably longer and in fact pre-date the SEA Directive. SA was therefore well established at the time the SEA Directive entered into force.[13]

In light of the paucity of legislative guidance, the role of the SA is beguiling simply: drawing on the definition in the NPPF, an SA is to promote sustainable development by assessing the extent to which the plan to which it relates will achieve or contribute to the three elements of sustainable development outlined in the NPPF, namely: environmental, economic and social objectives. It therefore goes beyond being a way of 'avoiding negative impacts, to also proactively enhancing positive impacts, and then [doing] this in a manner that contributes to [sustainable development]'.[14]

A good working definition of SA was provided in PPG11 on Regional Planning, which provided that sustainability appraisals are:

> [A] systematic and iterative process undertaken during the preparation of a plan or strategy, which identifies and reports on the extent to which the implementation of the plan or strategy would achieve the environmental, economic and social objectives by which sustainable development can be defined, in order that the performance of the strategy and policies is improved.[15]

The PPG amends this slightly, but retains the key elements of that definition:

> A sustainability appraisal is a systematic process that must be carried out during the preparation of a Local Plan. Its role is to promote sustainable development by assessing the extent to which the emerging plan, when judged against reasonable alternatives, will help to achieve relevant environmental, economic and social objectives.[16]

Despite the emphasis there on the systematic nature of the process, there is actually very little guidance on the process, both in terms of its methodology and

[13] R Thérivel, *Strategic Environmental Assessment in Action* (London, Earthscan, 2004) 65.

[14] Hacking and Guthrie (n 1) 82.

[15] See also Steven P Smith and William R Sheate, 'Sustainability Appraisal of English Regional Plans: Incorporating the Requirements of the EU Strategic Environmental Assessment Directive' (2001) 19(4) *Impact Assessment and Project Appraisal* 264–65.

[16] http://planningguidance.planningportal.gov.uk/blog/guidance/strategic-environmental-assessment-and-sustainability-appraisal/strategic-environmental-assessment-and-sustainability-appraisal-and-how-does-it-relate-to-strategic-environmental-assessment.

substance, compared to that found in the equivalent SEA documentation. While it is clear that it should be a holistic, or 'theme integrated',[17] approach to the three pillars of sustainable development, there is little indication of how this holistic approach can best be realised.

The Interaction Between SA and SEA

It follows that an essential consideration when drawing up planning documents is their effect on the environment and people's quality of life, both now and in the future. To help assess these affects, SA and SEA are carried out alongside the preparation of these plans to ensure that social, environmental and economic issues are taken into account at every stage so that sustainable development is delivered on the ground. Indeed, Brown and Thérivel explicitly recognise this crossover in stating that: 'The intention of SEA is moving policy … towards sustainable outcomes.'[18] As the SA pre-dated the SEA, the introduction of SEAs raised the question of how best to approach what essentially seemed to replicate something that was already, to some extent, assessed—namely the environmental consequences of a plan or programme. There was a variety of options available.

Thérivel sets out five options that were available.[19] In summary, these five options reduce to three broad approaches. First, the two systems could simply be superimposed on top of each other, resulting in a deeper emphasis on environmental matters only. Second, the SEA methodology could have been applied to social, economic and environmental issues, resulting in a deeper emphasis on all three elements of sustainability appraisal.[20] Third, the two systems could have been kept separate.

Smith and Sheate also considered how the requirements of SEA and SA could best be reconciled. In a similar vein to Thérivel, they set out four options:[21] first, at one extreme, SAs could have been discarded in favour of SEAs alone, second, the prevailing approach to SAs could have continued with SEAs being addressed through a separate process; third, the economic and social aspects to SA could have been hived off, leading to SEAs and Economic and Social Appraisals (ESAs); finally, SAs could evolve to incorporate and meet the requirements of SEA.

It was the latter approach that largely prevailed. Indeed, in Smith and Sheate's study, this was the approach that was favoured by the experts and practitioners they interviewed.[22] The guidance issued by the government on the SEA Directive promoted a wide and deep approach fulfilling the SEA approach across the three

17 Hacking and Guthrie (n 1) 80.

18 Brown and Thérivel (n 9) 184.

19 Thérivel (n 13) 64–66.

20 This was also the approach advocated by Brown and Thérivel (n 9) 186.

21 Smith and Sheate (n 15) 268. See further William Sheate's views on how the SEA process could be effectively 'streamlined' in Ch 9 of this volume.

22 Smith and Sheate (n 15) 269.

sustainability criteria.[23] It is not hard to see why this approach was adopted. As Brown and Thérivel explain, the integration of SEA and SAs helps to ensure a more ready acceptance of the SEA process by ensuring a smoother fit with existing practice.[24] An integrated approach is also more likely to result in sustainable development, and a wide and deep approach, porting across SEA requirements in relation to the environment, has the potential to strengthen conclusions relating to social and economic aspects.[25]

Furthermore, a quick scan of recent case law where SAs and/or SEAs have been considered also reveals a tendency for plan-makers to produce combined or integrated SAs and SEAs; for instance, in *No Adastral New Town Ltd v Suffolk Coastal District Council*, Richards LJ noted that:

> In line with that policy guidance, the sustainability appraisals (SAs) in this case were intended to meet not only the requirements of the 2004 Act and related regulations but also the environmental assessment requirements of the SEA Directive and implementing regulations.[26]

The 'policy guidance' Richards LJ was referring to for once makes the government's position on the matter clear. The PPG repeats the government's earlier guidance[27] in stating that:

> Sustainability appraisals incorporate the requirements of the Environmental Assessment of Plans and Programmes Regulations 2004 (commonly referred to as the 'Strategic Environmental Assessment Regulations'), which implement the requirements of the European Directive 2001/42/EC (the 'Strategic Environmental Assessment Directive') on the assessment of the effects of certain plans and programmes on the environment. Sustainability appraisal ensures that potential environmental effects are given full consideration alongside social and economic issues.[28]

In a similar vein, paragraph 165 of the NPPF provides that:

> Planning policies and decisions should be based on up-to-date information about the natural environment and other characteristics of the area including drawing, for example, from River Basin Management Plans. Working with Local Nature Partnerships where appropriate, this should include an assessment of existing and potential components of ecological networks. A sustainability appraisal which meets the requirements of the European Directive on strategic environmental assessment should be an integral part of the plan preparation process, and should consider all the likely significant effects on the environment, economic and social factors.

[23] Office of the Deputy Prime Minister, 'A Practical Guide to the Strategic Environmental Assessment Directive' (2005), §4.6. See also Thérivel (n 13) 66 and 68.

[24] Brown and Thérivel (n 9) 186 and 187.

[25] Smith and Sheate (n 15) 275–276.

[26] See, for instance, *No Adastral New Town Ltd v Suffolk Coastal District Council* [2015] EWCA Civ 88 [14].

[27] Now cancelled by the PPG, but previously available at: http://planningguidance.planningportal.gov.uk/blog/guidance/strategic-environmental-assessment-and-sustainability-appraisal/what-is-a-sustainability-appraisal-and-how-does-it-relate-to-strategic-environmental-assessment.

[28] ibid.

This almost reflects the approach adopted in PPS12: Local Spatial Planning, which the NPPF replaced. PPS12 provided, admittedly in rather more emphatic terms:

> 4.40 Sustainability appraisal fully incorporates the requirements of the European Directive on Strategic Environmental Assessment. Provided the sustainability appraisal is carried out following the guidelines in the A Practical Guide to the Strategic Environmental Assessment Directive and the Plan-Making Manual there will be no need to carry out a separate SEA.

What the NPPF recognises more clearly than did PPS12 is that formally speaking, SEA and SA are separate processes. It is one thing to say that SAs *can* meet the requirements of SEA, but it is quite another to say that they *do*.

The SEA Directive, as set out above, is heavily prescriptive. It provides detailed guidance both on the content of SEAs and the consultation requirements and also on the methodology. This prescriptive nature, which it applies only to environmental matters, contributes to SEAs being narrow, but deep, in their scope. They set out to assess environmental considerations, and that is what they do. Indeed, this is a conclusion supported by Thérivel, who has also concluded that the requirements of SEA are narrower but considerably deeper than the requirements of an SA.[29]

SAs on the other hand are directed towards a much broader objective—sustainable development—and their preparation and contents are considerably less prescribed than their SEA counterparts. While SEA may perhaps be said to be primarily concerned with the methodology by which conclusions regarding the environmental impact of a plan or programme are arrived at, by contrast, SAs are more focused on the objectives pursued by sustainable development than the process by which the plan or programme's contribution to those objectives is assessed.[30] In this sense, the primary purpose of an SA is to assess and evaluate a plan or programme's contribution to the objectives of sustainable development and, in doing so, to help to identify any room for enhancing that contribution. SAs are therefore broader in their scope, but potentially shallower[31] in terms of the process due to the less prescriptive methodologies employed.

Therefore, can it properly be said that, as the government claims, the completion of a SA will discharge the duties pursuant to the SEA Directive? That seems to be the position adopted in the new NPPG where, despite the NPPG recognising that the SEA and SAs are 'tools used at the plan-making stage to assess the likely effects of the plan when judged against reasonable alternatives', it then goes on to amalgamate the two:

> A sustainability appraisal of the proposals in each Local Plan is required by section 19 of the Planning and Compulsory Purchase Act 2004 and incorporates the required strategic environmental assessment.[32]

[29] Thérivel (n 13) 65, describing the SEA Directive approach as being 'narrow-but-deep'.
[30] Smith and Sheate (n 5) 268.
[31] Thérivel (n 13) 65, describing sustainability appraisals as being 'shallow-but-wide'.
[32] http://planningguidance.planningportal.gov.uk/blog/guidance/strategic-environmental-assessment-and-sustainability-appraisal/strategic-environmental-assessment-and-sustainability-appraisal-and-how-does-it-relate-to-strategic-environmental-assessment

While an SEA focuses on environmental matters, an SA is broader, considering also social and economic matters which may pull in different directions from an exclusively environmental approach. It does not follow that an SA must incorporate the requirements of the SEA Directive to be a valid SA. However, as the NPPF makes clear, it is desirable that it does and, indeed, it should do so in order to meet the NPPF's requirements. Moreover, an approach that combines the two matches well with the notion of integrated decision-making at the heart of the modern planning system.

So far, so good. As long as the SA meets the SEA criteria, the decision-maker is presented with a process that ticks both boxes, and one less acronym enters into the equation. However, one question inevitably arises: as SA already explicitly incorporates an environmental element as one of the three components of sustainable development, what can an SEA add to the process that is not already provided for? While it is tempting to say that the SEA requirements simply set out what is required to be considered in the environmental component of the sustainable development trinity, that answer—focusing on the environmental element—itself raises a further question that goes to the heart of what SAs and SEAs are trying to achieve.

An SA makes no judgmental distinction between the three elements of sustainable development. Neither does the NPPF. There is no indication of which element is to be 'preferred' or, indeed, whether there should even be a preferred element. In this sense, the purpose of the SA is to be a neutral document, appraising the plan against the requirement to promote sustainable development. SAs therefore represent a form of horizontal integration, ensuring that environmental, economic and social considerations are all assessed alongside each other and are all given equal weight, such that none inherently takes priority over any other.[33]

This is very different from SEA. By its very nature, an SEA does not comprise an economic or a social element. Instead, as Article 1 of the Directive makes patently clear, an SEA is primarily a way of ensuring that environmental issues are given sufficient consideration in the decision-making process by raising the profile of environmental issues[34] by ensuring first that there is sufficient and adequate environmental information, and second that that information is specifically taken in account in the decision-making process. By their very nature, therefore, SEAs cannot help but prioritise environmental considerations above others.

The plan-maker is therefore left with something of a dilemma. There is an inescapable overlap between SA and SEA. The environmental aspects of both will require and draw upon the same expertise, data and conclusions, so it makes very little sense to use that common basis to produce two separate documents with slightly different aims and intentions. However, at the same time, there is something of an inescapable tension between the environmental-only requirements

[33] Smith and Sheate (n 15) 266.
[34] ibid.

of SEA and the broader, sustainable development requirements of SA. How then should that tension be released, while still allowing the production of a document that meets both sets of requirements?

Producing an SEA-compliant SA

It is necessary, but not in our view sufficient, for the environmental component of the SA to meet the SEA criteria. That of course is the right starting point, for if it fails to do so, there is no question of the SA obviating the need for an SEA. However, it is not enough to leave the exercise there, for to do so would inherently unbalance the horizontally integrated process that characterises an SA by potentially elevating environmental considerations such that the whole process might not be one that could properly be characterised as horizontally integrated at all. This would manifestly fail to comply with one of the main themes of the modern planning system and would risk compromising the attainment of sustainable development.

The converse concern is also legitimate. By looking at the three pillars of sustainable development together, there is the danger that environmental concerns are marginalised compared to the social and economic concerns.[35]

Government guidance on SEA considers how best to integrate SEA with SA. It suggests that 'it may be helpful to look out for':

— Opportunities to optimise information collection processes so that information collected can be used to satisfy all appraisal requirements.
— Consistency amongst objectives used.
— Compatibility of information generated through forecasting and prediction techniques to generate comparable results, e.g. between social, economic and environmental information.
— Integrating staging of assessment to create a single process wherever possible, taking advantage of synergies.
— Facilitating transparency in decision making through analysis techniques that generate comparable findings.[36]

The same guidance provides that:

> Responsible Authorities wishing to cover the full range of sustainable development issues in their assessments are free to broaden the scope of the assessment to include social and economic effects of their plans and programmes in addition to environmental effects. The Environmental Report required by the SEA Directive can be included in an assessment report on the wider effects of the plan or programme, such as a Sustainability

[35] Hacking and Guthrie (n 1) 77.

[36] See www.gov.uk/government/uploads/system/uploads/attachment_data/file/7657/practicalguidesea.pdf.

> Appraisal Report. However it must clearly show that the Directive has been complied with, for example by signposting to enable the components that meet the requirements for the Environmental Report to be readily identified.

These are primarily methodological matters and integrating the SEA methodology may prove to be problematic in practice. An SEA may be seen as substantially similar to an Environmental Impact Assessment (EIA) under the EIA Directive (85/337/EEC);[37] however, as Brown and Thérivel point out,[38] even established EIA methodologies may fall short of the mark when looked at in terms of strategic plans and programmes for SEA purposes. They state that:

> Clearly, grafting SEA on to existing PPP formulation procedures will not be achieved by attempting to translate existing project-based EIA legislation, procedures and format, upstream [to SEA]. Thus, new methodologies and procedural requirements, specifically for SEA will be required.[39]

Therefore, it is worth considering whether their warning regarding EIA may be equally applicable in the SA context. Here, Smith and Sheate have noted:

> The sustainability appraisal process set out in the DETR Guide and the requirements of the SEA Directive arguably differ in terms of their overall aims and certainly in terms of their procedural and methodological requirements.[40]

Methodology is of course crucial, but it is necessary to go further. There are two necessary steps to produce not only an SA that complies with the SEA, but an SA that does so while remaining a proper SA and not devaluing social and economic considerations.

First, it is necessary for the SA to apply the same rigour that the SEA requires be applied to the environmental component to the economic and social components. This can be termed 'technique integration'.[41] To return to the theme picked up earlier in this chapter which stated that SEAs are narrow but deep and SAs are broad but shallow, it is necessary to increase the depth of SAs to match SEAs across all three elements of sustainable development. This will ensure that economic, social and environmental issues are all addressed with the same level of rigour. There will inevitably be some difficulty in this:

— First, the SEA Directive is clearly framed with environmental considerations in mind and its provisions do not always readily transpose themselves to the economic and social fields—indeed, they may sometimes point away from an approach that considers economic and social factors. For instance, the statutory list of consultees that the SEA legislation requires to be consulted

[37] See Hacking and Guthrie (n 1) 77.
[38] Brown and Thérivel (n 9).
[39] ibid 186.
[40] Smith and Sheate (n 15) 265.
[41] Hacking and Guthrie (n 1) 78–79.

obviously does not include bodies with social or economic remits. Those responsible for compiling SAs should therefore be encouraged to reach out to non-statutory bodies with social and economic remits alongside the formally recognised environmental consultees.[42] There is also often more data available in relation to environmental matters than social and economic matters, and the data that is available is often easier to quantify and present. It may therefore be difficult providing sufficient background data to support economic and social projections, although this is a deficiency that should reduce over time as social and economic forecasting matures (something that the approach advocated in this chapter to SAs would help to foster).

— Second, it would then be necessary to determine where the balance lies and how much weight should be accorded to each of the three components of sustainable development. So long as the first stage has been complied with and there is a sufficient and comparable evidence base upon which the exercise can be carried out, the SA would not be so unbalanced that it risks leading to a conclusion that inherently prioritises environmental matters. Sustainable development is about more than solely the environment, and an approach heavily influenced by the SEA may risk losing sight of that.

Second, having carried out assessments of equal depth to a plan or programme's economic, social and environmental impacts, in order to avoid undermining the goal of SEA, it is necessary to carry out a balancing, or weighing exercise, of the three components to ensure that appropriate consideration is given to each in the overall assessment and to assess the trade-offs between the three.[43] Although SA may be value neutral between its three components, a good SA will help to reconcile the three strands of sustainable development. A plan or programme that successfully contributes to social and economic objectives but undermines environmental objectives in an area where the environment is especially highly prized could hardly be said to contribute to sustainable development. A balancing exercise therefore introduces something of a safeguard to ensure that environmental issues are given a weighting which ensures that they are not automatically overshadowed by economic and social considerations, but there can be no default position that environmental matters trump economic and social factors in all cases. In assessing whether a plan or programme contributes to sustainable development, each factor needs to be considered alongside the others.

There may be concerns over the extent to which this weighing approach accords with the emphasis that the SEA Directive places on environmental considerations. But in an approach that will be familiar to public law practitioners, the requirement of the SEA is only for the environmental report to be 'taken into account' during the plan or programme's preparation. It says nothing of what the decision-maker should do having taken it into account. It is trite law that, in planning

[42] Smith and Sheate (n 15) 271.
[43] Hacking and Guthrie (n 1) 81.

terms, while what is a material consideration is a matter of law, the weight that the decision-maker places on those considerations is, broadly speaking, a matter for him or her. There is therefore nothing inconsistent with the SEA Directive in taking an SA-based balancing approach to environmental, social and economic information.

Conclusion

The position then is that it is very easy to produce an SA that complies fully with the SEA. The difficulty arises in ensuring that the resulting SA is not so unbalanced, either in terms of its evidence base or priorities, by focusing on environmental matters that it then fails to give the same level of consideration to the other two key elements of sustainable development. It then risks moving away from being an SA to being simply an SEA with an appraisal of economic and social elements appended—an *almost* SA.

Perhaps another question arises. Will there ever be a case where it is sufficient to produce an SA that does *not* comply with the SEA? Clearly, as we have set out above, there are advantages in making an SA SEA-compliant in terms of the depth and robustness of the end product, but that depth comes with an extra cost both financial and in terms of time.[44] The question of whether that cost is outweighed by the benefits will be one for the plan-maker. After carrying out this balancing exercise, there will be times when an SA may be carried out, but as the SEA Directive is not triggered, the decision is taken to produce a non-SEA-compliant SA—the recent challenge to HS2 provides a good example of where the SA did not comply with the SEA and (according to the Supreme Court at least) did not need to do so.[45] By contrast, the challenge to the Earl's Court and West Kensington Opportunity Area Joint Supplementary Planning Document provides an illustration of an SA that was held to substantially comply with the requirements of the SEA. Substantial compliance of course being the test that was laid down in *Commission v Federal Republic of Germany*.[46]

Conversely, a perhaps more unusual situation could arise where an SA is *not* required, but an SEA is. A good example would be a neighbourhood plan, which, while not engaging section 19 of the Planning and Compulsory Purchase Act 2004, may require an SEA if the plan were to have significant environmental effects. In the same way that carrying out a non-SEA-compliant SA could have cost benefits, so could carrying out a SEA that did not address economic and social factors as it would require only one experience set to compile. That said, given that sustainable

[44] Thérivel and Walsh (n 5) 671–672.

[45] *R (Buckinghamshire County Council) v Secretary of State for Transport* [2014] UKSC 3.

[46] Case C-431/92 *Commission v Federal Republic of Germany* [1995] ECR I-2189 and see as applied in *R (Edwards) v Environment Agency* [2008] Env LR 34.

development lies at the heart of the planning system, the benefits of carrying out a fully SEA-compliant SA even where one may not be legally required should not be forgotten.

Ultimately, both SEA and SA are flexible processes. The nature of both will be influenced by the plan or programme subject to assessment, with larger, wider-reaching programmes requiring larger and wider-reaching assessments than more localised (either geographically or spatially) programmes. As Brown and Thérivel explain, SEA is an 'overarching concept rather than … a unitary technique' and 'we must begin to think in terms of an array of SEA tools from which the appropriate one(s) can be selected to meet the needs of the particular circumstances'.[47] This flexibility in the processes leaves a large amount of discretion to the plan-maker.

The decision as to how to approach SEA and sustainability appraisal in any given case will therefore be one for the plan-maker. It should have been clear from the discussion above that even where only an SEA is required or where only a SA is necessary, there are in fact benefits in terms of the information base and robustness of the conclusions to carrying out a process that is compliant with both. A good example of this might be where a plan or programme is proposed for a underdeveloped region, where social and economic matters would benefit from the greater and more robust evidence base that an approach based on SEA would provide. Conversely, the plan-maker may decide that in a relatively affluent area, the extra costs involved in providing a deeper level of social and economic evidence may not be justified.[48] Whatever approach is adopted, it is imperative that it is an integral part of the plan-making process. This much is required for SEAs by Article 4(1) of the Directive, and the same approach should be taken for sustainability appraisals. It is only by integrating the SEA/SA into the overall plan-making procedure that the full benefits of SEA/SA will be realised.

It might therefore be that a new acronym is necessary: SEESA (Strategic Environmental, Economic and Social Assessment) or even perhaps SSA (Strategic Sustainability Assessment), but whatever the acronym, taken together and conducted fully, SEA and SA provide a mechanism and a framework for reconciling, integrating and balancing the three components of sustainable development at the heart of modern planning. SEA-compliant SAs should therefore be encouraged, even where they are not legally necessary.

[47] Brown and Thérivel (n 9) 186 and 185.
[48] See Hacking and Guthrie (n 1) 77–78.

Part II

Examining the Purpose and Impact of the SEA Directive

8

Blazing Upstream? Strategic Environmental Assessment as 'Hot' Law

ELIZABETH FISHER

Introduction

Directive 2001/42/EC of the European Parliament and of the Council of 27 June 2001 on the assessment of the effects of certain plans and programmes (hereinafter 'the SEA Directive')[1] like many other techniques in environmental law, is often characterised as a 'tool' for decision-making.[2] Such a characterisation is deeply misleading for three reasons. First, the Directive does not merely aid decision-making, but also reframes it by requiring the assessment of, and consultation about, environmental impacts 'upstream' in public decision-making processes.[3] The common label given to the processes mandated by the Directive (and similar laws in other jurisdictions)—'strategic environmental assessment' (SEA)—reflects this reframing agenda.[4] Second, the label 'tool' gives the impression that SEA is a fixed and rigid technique when it is not. There is a rich and varied discourse concerning SEA's nature and purpose,[5] and there is a range of different SEA regimes

[1] Directive 2001/42/EC of the European Parliament and of the Council of 27 June 2001 on the assessment of the effects of certain plans and programmes [2001] OJ L197/30.

[2] Jo Treweek et al, 'Principles for the Use of Strategic Environmental Assessment as a Tool for Promoting the Conservation and Sustainable Use of Biodiversity' (2005) 7 *Journal of Environmental Assessment Policy and Management* 173; Margaret Desmond, 'Strategic Environmental Assessment (SEA): A Tool for Environmental Decision-Making' (2007) 40 *Irish Geography* 63.

[3] Commission, 'Report on the Application and Effectiveness of the Directive on Strategic Environmental Assessment (Directive 2001/42/EC)' COM (2009) 469 final, 11.

[4] Olivia Bina, Tabatha Wallington and Wil Thissen, 'SEA Theory and Research: An Analysis of the Early Disourse' in Barry Sadler et al (eds), *Handbook of Strategic Environmental Assessment* (London, Earthscan, 2011).

[5] Ibid; and Olivia Bina, 'A Critical Review of the Dominant Lines of Argumentation on the Need for Strategic Environmental Assessment' (2007) 27 *Environmental Impact Assessment Review* 585.

in practice.[6] Even a single SEA regime such as the SEA Directive can be simultaneously interpreted as having different purposes. Third, describing SEA as a tool gives the impression that, while it is an aid to environmental protection, it does not interact with other features of legal and policy-making frameworks. As Bina and others point out, much of the discourse concerning SEA has historically ignored the context in which it applies.[7] Yet environmental law cannot be properly understood without exploring how it relates to the legal cultures of which it is part.[8] This is particularly so in relation to SEA because the reframing it entails is so significant. SEA then is not so much a tool as an ambiguous bundle of processes designed to reframe decision-making, which are embedded in wider legal cultures.

So far, so academic. Those more interested in the legal application of SEA may find all of the above an exercise in tedious 'theorising' (and you may still be wondering about the curious title of this chapter). Any annoyance at the conceptual babble may be particularly acute due to the fact that the implementation of SEA has given rise to a range of tricky legal questions and conundrums in practice, particularly concerning the scope of the Directive and how and when it applies.[9] Yet the trickiness of those legal questions is directly related to the conceptual complexities of the Directive. The purpose of this chapter is thus to show that by understanding the conceptual nature of SEA, we can begin to understand the complexities in its legal application.

This chapter is structured as follows. The first section shows how SEA is an example of 'hot' law in that its purpose is to reframe interrelationships between legal actors and how those actors understand their responsibility for environmental protection. This reframing occurs through SEA applying 'upstream' to a decision that concerns the authorisation of an activity. However, many decision-making processes can lie upstream and the second section shows how the upstream nature of the SEA Directive can be understood in linear or expansive terms. The third, fourth and fifth sections briefly illustrate how linear and expansive ideas of the Directive can shape its judicial interpretation and implementation. The third

[6] See, eg, the regimes under the Environmental Protection Conservation Act 1999 (Australia) and the SEA Protocol to the UNECE Espoo Convention on EIA in a Transboundary Context. Note many of these are SEA-type processes: see Resource Management Act 1991 (New Zealand) and programmatic environmental impact statements under the National Environmental Policy Act 1969 (US). See further Sadler et al (n 4) pt 1.

[7] Bina, Wallington and Thissen (n 4).

[8] Elizabeth Fisher, 'Unpacking the Toolbox: Or Why the Public/Private Divide is Important in EC Environmental Law' in Mark Freedland and Jean-Bernard Auby (eds), *The Public Law/Private Law Divide: Une Entente Assez Cordiale?* (Oxford, Hart Publishing 2006). The significance of taking into account all features of a legal culture can be seen in Elizabeth Fisher, Bettina Lange and Eloise Scotford, *Environmental Law: Text, Cases and Materials* (Oxford, Oxford University Press 2013) Pts II and III.

[9] eg, *Walton v Scottish Ministers* [2012] UKSC 44 (raising issues of standing and procedural autonomy); *HS2 Action Alliance Ltd, R (on the Application of) v The Secretary of State for Transport* [2014] UKSC 3 (EU interpretative practices, role of command papers, preliminary references). See also Ch 5 by Stephen Ashworth, Ch 3 by Valerie Fogelman, and Ch 4 by Simon Ricketts and Juliet Munn in this volume.

section considers this effect in relation to how Articles 2 and 3 of the Directive have been judicially interpreted by the Court of Justice of the European Union (CJEU), the fourth section focuses on how the Directive was interpreted as part of the *HS2* litigation and the fifth section examines how such differing understandings of the Directive influence remedies.

Before continuing, let me make three caveats. The first is that this chapter is not an exhaustive analysis of linear and expansive approaches to the SEA Directive and how such approaches interact with EU and UK legal culture. There is simply not room for that. Second, as will become obvious, it is difficult to discuss SEA without discussing environmental impact assessment (EIA).[10] This is because they are both conceptually and doctrinally linked due to the fact that both are similar legal techniques. Third, I should stress that my aim is not to damn or praise the SEA Directive or linear or expansive interpretations of it. Rather, it is to move past depictions of SEA as a simple regulatory 'tool' towards a more nuanced debate that explores the different ways in which law can frame the exercise of public power.[11]

SEA, 'Hot' Situations and 'Hot' Law

Environmental law often operates in 'hot' situations and thus is itself 'hot' law.[12] 'Hot' situations arise because the agreed frames, legal or otherwise, for how we understand and act in the world are in a constant state of flux and contestation due to scientific uncertainty, differing normative values and difficulties in identifying interrelationships between parties.[13] The role of law in such circumstances is to provide a workable frame for action. Those frames are usually legislative and administrative in nature,[14] and often involve the significant reframing of decision-making processes in terms of their scope, what they take into account and who they involve.[15] The history of environmental law shows that the development of such frameworks is neither easy nor linear.[16]

[10] Now codified in European Parliament and Council Directive 2011/92/EU on the assessment of the effects of certain public and private projects on the environment [2012] OJ L28/1, as amended by European Parliament and Council Directive 2014/52/EU [2014] OJ L124/1 (hereinafter 'the EIA Directive').

[11] A point also explored in Fisher (n 8).

[12] Elizabeth Fisher, 'Environmental Law as "Hot" Law' (2013) 25 *Journal of Environmental Law* 347. The concept of 'hot situations' is drawn from the work of Michel Callon. See Michel Callon, 'An Essay on Framing and Overflowing: Economic Externalities Revisited by Sociology' in Michel Callon (ed), *The Laws of the Markets* (Oxford, Blackwell, 1998).

[13] Callon (n 12) 260.

[14] Eloise Scotford and Jonathan Robinison, 'UK Environmental Legislation and its Administration in 2013—Acheivements, Challenges and Prospects' (2013) 25 *Journal of Environmental Law* 383.

[15] Elizabeth Fisher, 'Framing Risk Regulation: A Critical Reflection' (2013) 4 *European Journal of Risk Regulation* 125.

[16] Fisher (n 12) 352–53.

In thinking about environmental law as hot law, heat is a relative concept, as is the concept of reframing.[17] Some environmental problems are less hot than others and the way in which environmental law frames decision-making can vary in terms of how much new laws are perceived to depart from existing frames. For example, statutory nuisance can be understood as a less 'hot' area of environmental law than climate change law—a fact flowing from the nature of the problems to which each area of the law is responding.[18]

SEA is a particularly 'hot' example of environmental law. This is best illustrated by seeing how it developed from EIA. EIA, as first introduced in the US under the National Environmental Policy Act 1969 (NEPA), was an 'action-forcing' device that was designed to make decision-makers take environmental problems more seriously.[19] As Judge Leventhal of the District of Columbia Circuit of the US Federal Court of Appeals noted, it was one of a number of statutes that 'set the law ablaze'.[20] The EU and its Member States, like many other legal cultures, developed their own versions of EIA—all of which aimed to reconfigure decision-making processes in relation to granting permission for activities or projects.[21] In all cases, EIA required decision-makers to think about the environmental consequences of their actions and therefore to take ex ante responsibility for them. This is one of the reasons why EIA is often understood as 'reflexive' law.[22] However, this process of reconfiguration and reframing could mean different things. Thus, for example, EIA could be understood as instituting scientific, bureaucratic or deliberative processes.[23] Reconfiguration of EIA through decision-making has also brought its own set of legal complexities.[24]

Furthermore, by the early 1990s, it was appreciated that this process of reconfiguring was not always effective, because EIA occurred close to the end point of decision-making.[25] For environmental consequences to be taken *genuinely* into

[17] ibid 351.

[18] Compare Fisher, Lange and Scotford (n 8) ch 9; and Chris Hilson, 'It's All About Climate Change, Stupid: Exploring the Relationship between Environmental Law and Climate Law' (2013) 25 *Journal of Environmental Law* 359.

[19] Harold Leventhal, 'Environmental Decision Making and the Role of the Courts' (1974) 122 *University of Pennsylvania Law Review* 509, 509.

[20] ibid 509–10.

[21] For an overview, see Christopher Wood, *Environmental Impact Assessment: A Comparative Review*, 2nd edn (Upper Saddle River, NJ, Prentice Hall, 2003).

[22] Eric Orts, 'Reflexive Environmental Law' (1995) 89 *Northwestern University Law Review* 1227; Jane Holder, *Environmental Assessment: The Regulation of Decision-Making* (Oxford, Oxford University Press, 2005).

[23] Fisher, Lange and Scotford (n 8) 848–50.

[24] In the UK and EU, see, for example: *Berkeley v Secretary of State for the Environment* [2001] 2 AC 603 (implementation); Case C-287/98 *Luxembourg v Linster* [2000] ECR I-6917 (direct effect); and Case C-201/02 *R (Wells) v Secretary of State for Transport Local Government and the Regions* [2004] ECR I-723 (remedies).

[25] Stephen Dovers, 'Too Deep a SEA? Strategic Environmental Assessment in the Era of Sustainability' in Stephen Dovers and Simon Marsden (eds), *Strategic Environmental Assessment in Australasia* (Sydney, Federation Press, 2002).

account, they needed to be considered 'upstream' in the decision-making process. SEA was thus developed as a means of ensuring such upstream consideration. However, 'upstream' can mean many things. Thus, it often refers to the need to consider environmental impact earlier in time[26] and/or higher up the decision-making hierarchy.[27] In both cases, it is referring to a rugged and wide landscape of legal, political, administrative and policy processes.

This is best illustrated by thinking about the geography of a river. Take, for example, the River Thames. Even its very physical presence covers a large geographical space. The river itself is 215 miles long[28] and includes the following tributaries—'the Churn, the Thame, the Colne, the Leach, the Windrush, the Evenlode, the Cherwell, the Kennet, the Ver, the Wey, the Mole, the Medway, the Lea and the Roding'.[29] Its estuary is 'also a mysterious, and an ambiguous place. Where does the river end and the sea begin?'[30]

On such a river (and let us not forget the Thames is relatively small compared with other river systems in the world), 'upstream' can mean many different things. For example, there are many different points upstream from Westminster Bridge. Lambeth Bridge is directly upstream from it and that upstream relationship is easily navigable by walking from one point to the other. The upstream relationship is also observable—not only can you see one from the other, but if you drop something in at Lambeth Bridge, you should be able to see it flow under Westminster Bridge. In contrast, Oxford is upstream from Westminster Bridge, but that upstream relationship is over a longer distance and requires charting the river as it meanders over many miles. Burford, which sits on the River Windrush, is even further upstream. The upstream nature of Oxford and Burford is also not easily observable. Moreover, the geographical entity of the Thames is embedded in a varied and diverse natural and human landscape with the 'paraphernalia of life both ancient and modern clustered around its banks'.[31]

The idea of something lying 'upstream' is thus ambiguous, requires a reframing process more ambitious than in EIA, and can potentially entail a wide swathe of decision-making processes. What exactly SEA must reconfigure is by no means clear. Earlier and higher-up decision-making may shape later decision-making outcomes, but the relationship between the two will not be like charting water flows. This is particularly so when the paths between upstream and downstream decision-making are not always legally well charted.[32] While the relationship

[26] eg, *Walton* (n 9) [12]; *Save Historic Newmarket Ltd v Forest Heath District Council* [2011] EWHC 606 [16].

[27] Bina, Wallington and Thissen (n 4).

[28] Peter Ackroyd, *Thames: Sacred River* (London, Vintage Books, 2008) 3.

[29] ibid 43.

[30] ibid 395. I would like to thank Colin Reid for his discussion about estuaries. The ambiguity of estuaries has of course been litigated in the UK: see *R v Secretary of State for the Environment ex p Kingston upon Hull City Council* [1996] Env LR 248.

[31] Ackyroyd (n 28) 5.

[32] *Walton* (n 9) [14].

between planning permission and development plans in the planning regime is a legally well-trodden path—a little akin to the relationship between Westminster and Lambeth Bridges—the same is not true of other types of plans and programmes that lie upstream from final decision-making outcomes. Thus, in some legal contexts, the legal relationship between stages of decision-making can be ambiguous, developing, or contested.[33] It is more akin to the relationship between Burford and Westminster Bridge. This is not only in terms of the upstream relationship being over a longer distance, but also because other tributaries—actors, decision-making considerations, decisions, policies and events—will flow into the river. These 'tributaries' will affect the final decision made.

Linear and Expansive Interpretations of the Directive

While I appreciate the analogy between SEA and rivers has its limits, the discussion above makes clear that to talk in terms of SEA applying to 'upstream' processes not only requires further interpretation and elaboration, but also that 'upstream' can refer to different things. Indeed, the very rich legal and academic discourses concerning SEA reflects two distinct understandings of what lies 'upstream' of final decision-making for SEA purposes.[34] Moreover, these two different understandings can result in two different ways of construing the purpose of the SEA Directive. These two understandings are best understood as two different ways in which SEA is 'strategic': linear and expansive.

First, SEA can be understood as being strategic in linear terms by setting a strategic environmental assessment approach in relation to *projects* that will ultimately require an EIA or similar legally defined environmental assessment. In other words, SEA is strategic because it is ensuring that the environmental impacts of projects that will need an EIA (or some other form of legally mandated environmentally assessment) are considered (and ideally prevented) as early as possible in the decision-making processes that precede that project. SEA thus exists in a strategically *linear* relationship to the environmental impacts of particular projects. It lies directly upstream from those projects, and the stream between them is a close one and usually reinforced by a legal framework. This linear relationship might be best thought of as akin to the relationship between Lambeth Bridge and Westminster Bridge.

[33] Compare the role of 'plans and programmes' in planning law in *Cala Homes (South) Ltd v Secretary of State for Communities & Local Government* [2011] EWHC 97 (Dear Chief Planning Officer letters); *Cala Homes (South) Ltd v Secretary of State for Communities and Local Government* [2010] EWHC 2866 (regional strategies); *Walton* (n 9) (local government strategy); and *HS2* (n 9) (Command Papers).

[34] Bina, Wallington and Thissen (n 4).

The SEA Directive is capable of being understood in such linear terms. Take, for example, Article 3, which delimits the scope of the Directive by listing the plans and programmes to which it relates. The 'certain' plans and programmes' listed in Article 3(2)–(4) can all be understood as directly relating to projects that are themselves likely to have significant effects on the environment. Thus, Article 3(2) states:

> 2 Subject to paragraph 3, an environmental assessment shall be carried out for all plans and programmes,
> (a) which are prepared for agriculture, forestry, fisheries, energy, industry, transport, waste management, water management, telecommunications, tourism, town and country planning or land use and which set the framework for future development consent of projects listed in Annexes I and II to Directive 85/337/EEC, or
> (b) which, in view of the likely effect on sites, have been determined to require an assessment pursuant to Article 6 or 7 of Directive 92/43/EEC.

SEA applies upstream to *projects* that have been *legally* recognised as situations where there is a potential for environmental impact. Thus, Article 3(2) concerns projects that would be caught by the assessment obligations of the EIA Directive and the Habitats Directive.[35]

The fact that there is no obligation akin to the overarching obligation in Article 2(1) in the EIA Directive (which has been understood to have 'wide scope and broad purpose')[36] reinforces the idea that the SEA Directive exists in a linear relationship with projects. Article 3(1) of the SEA Directive is explicitly limited by Article 3(2)–(4), while Article 2(1) of the EIA Directive contains a general obligation to consider environmental assessment in relation to all projects that are likely to have significant effects. The 'General Obligations' in Article 4 of the SEA Directive also only relate to the projects listed in Article 3. Likewise, Article 4(3) explicitly seeks to avoid duplication in cases where there are decision-making 'hierarchies' and this reinforces the linear vision of decision-making. SEA is a strategy to target the environmental impacts of individual projects earlier and higher up in relation to established decision-making processes.

Yet the SEA Directive is also capable of being understood of pursuing a quite different 'strategic' approach. A second way in which SEA can be understood as strategic is in more *expansive* terms—SEA is not just strategic in relation to EIA projects and other projects with a legally identified environmental risk, but also in relation to environmental protection more widely. SEA is thus about reframing decision-making so as to achieve a deeper and more environmentally sustainable approach to public decision-making writ large.[37] On this basis, the upstream decision-making reconfigured by the SEA framework is more broadly understood.

[35] And note the limitation in art 3(3).

[36] Case C-72/95 *Aannemersbedrijf PK Kraaijeveld BV v Gedeputeerde Staten Van Zuid-Holland* [1996] ECR I-5403 [31], [39].

[37] On SEA and deeper forms of sustainability, see Dovers (n 25).

It is not just decision-making that directly impacts on EIA projects or projects likely to have significant effects in other legally defined ways, but is decision-making that can also lead to other downstream environmental impacts. This might be thought of as SEA trying to catch in its scope everything significant upstream for any environmental effect downstream.

From a more expansive perspective, the fact that the SEA Directive primarily applies to the plans and programmes in Article 3(2)–(4) is more a matter of practical convenience. Article 3(1) may not have the breadth of Article 2(1) of the EIA Directive, but it is still capable of broad interpretation, particularly in light of Article 3(4), which requires Member States to determine whether 'plans or programmes … which set the framework for future development consent of projects, are likely to have significant effects'. This obligation is potentially wide-reaching. On this expansive interpretation, the guiding force behind the Directive is Article 1, which states:

> The objective of this Directive is to provide for a high level of protection of the environment and to contribute to the integration of environmental considerations into the preparation and adoption of plans and programmes with a view to promoting sustainable development, by ensuring that, in accordance with the Directive, an environmental assessment is carried out of certain plans and programmes which are likely to have significant effects on the environment.

This more expansive vision of the Directive is reinforced by various paragraphs of the Preamble and in particular Recitals 4 and 5 in the Preamble, which state:

> (4) Environmental assessment is an important tool for integrating environmental considerations into the preparation and adoption of certain plans and programmes which are likely to have significant effects on the environment in the Member States, because it ensures that such effects of implementing plans and programmes are taken into account during their preparation and before their adoption.
>
> (5) The adoption of environmental assessment procedures at the planning and programming level should benefit undertakings by providing a more consistent framework in which to operate by the inclusion of the relevant environmental information into decision making. The inclusion of a wider set of factors in decision making should contribute to more sustainable and effective solutions.

The Directive can thus be understood as reflecting the integration and sustainable development principles set out in Article 11 of the Treaty on the Functioning of the European Union (TFEU) and Article 37 of the Charter of Fundamental Rights.

This rough sketch shows that the SEA Directive is not just a simple tool—the wording can be understood in different ways and as having different purposes. It is capable of being interpreted both as a linear and expansive strategy—each interpretation emphasising, and reflected in, different aspects of the Directive. As is the case with most pieces of legislation, the Directive is not a framework grounded on a single theory.[38] It reflects a mixture of hopes and expectations concerning

[38] Borrowing from Sunstein's analysis of constitutional adjudication, we might think of it as an 'incompletely theorized agreement'. See Cass Sunstein, *Legal Reasoning and Political Conflict* (Oxford, Oxford University Press, 1996).

SEA. This ambiguity is of course a feature of much legislation, but is a particularly strong feature of environmental legislation in 'hot' situations because the legislation itself is creating a new framework for action.

In relation to SEA, how much a departure that new framework is from conventional legal frames will vary depending on whether you start with a linear or expansive understanding. A linear understanding is more conventional because, as a more strategic approach to the environmental impact of *projects*, it can be easily understood as an extension of traditional planning law frameworks that focus on project approval. In contrast, an expansive understanding of SEA requires far more rethinking of public decision-making because it is concerned with environmental impacts writ large. Or, to return to my river analogy, a linear approach is concerned with environmental impacts at Westminster Bridge, while an expansive approach is concerned with environmental impacts across the whole of the Thames River Basin. It is far easier to understand how the former will be legally implemented than the latter.

Linear and expansive interpretations of SEA will affect nearly all aspects of how SEA is put into operation. Thus, while both linear and expansive SEA mandate a legal procedure that encompasses a process of assessment, reporting, consultation and decision-making, these different processes will mean different things.[39] In particular, a linear approach to SEA will involve a more tightly focused set of assessment and consultation procedures, with fewer and more specific considerations being taken into account. It is also the case that linear and expansive models of SEA have different aims. Thus, linear SEA can be still understood to be focusing on significant effects of certain individual projects, while a more expansive notion of SEA is aiming for a more fundamental shift in how the environment is factored into decision-making.

My interest, however, is in the judicial interpretation of the SEA Directive by the CJEU and the UK courts. The next two sections illustrate how linear and expansive interpretations of SEA shape its judicial application, providing brief examples from the two most commonly litigated issues in relation to the Directive—the scope of the Directive and the question of remedies. In both cases, it must be remembered that the interpretation and operation of the SEA Directive is embedded in both UK and EU legal culture. This is not an environmental regulatory tool operating in splendid isolation. As Maduro notes:

> The methods of interpretation used by courts as well as their institutional and value choices reflect (or ought to reflect) a certain systemic understanding of the normative preferences and institutional constraints of the legal order in which those courts operate.[40]

[39] Bina, Wallington and Thissen (n 4).

[40] Miguel Maduro, 'Interpreting European Law: Judicial Adjudication in a Context of Constitutional Pluralism' (2007) 1(2) *European Journal of Legal Studies* 1.

Thus, it has been generally recognised that the CJEU has taken a more purposive approach to the SEA Directive than the UK courts. But that is only one aspect of the point Maduro is making above. Interpretative method is not just about how purposive or literal an interpretation is, but also concerns how any particular interpretation relates to other aspects of a legal culture. How the SEA Directive is interpreted will depend on what other legal doctrine and ideas exist in the EU and the UK legal order, and on the significance of any particular interpretation of the Directive for those legal orders.

Interpreting the Scope of the Directive in the CJEU

One of the most litigated questions in relation to the SEA Directive has concerned the type of documents to which it applies. This is primarily a question of the Directive's scope and concerns the definition of 'plans and programmes' in Article 2(a) and the provisions in Article 3. Article 2(a) states that:

> '[P]lans and programmes' shall mean plans and programmes, including those co-financed by the European Community, as well as any modifications to them:
>
> — which are subject to preparation and/or adoption by an authority at national, regional or local level or which are prepared by an authority for adoption, through a legislative procedure by Parliament or Government, and
> — which are required by legislative, regulatory or administrative provisions;

Article 3(2) was extracted above, but much of the focus has been on Article 3(4), which states:

> Member States shall determine whether plans and programmes, other than those referred to in paragraph 2, which set the framework for future development consent of projects, are likely to have significant environmental effects.

Unlike Article 3(2), which refers to legal and physical categories of documents, these articles are phrased in conceptual terms and thus are in need of interpretation.

The litigation concerning the interpretation of the SEA Directive's scope is a good example of an environmental law 'setting the law ablaze',[41] as it illustrates how 'hot' law and legal culture intertwine. The Directive creates a new frame that cuts across conventional decision-making frameworks, but it is an ambiguous frame, which means that Articles 2(a) and 3 are open to a range of legitimate interpretations.[42] At the same time, the ways in which the Directive is interpreted will be significantly shaped by the norms, doctrines and ethos in a legal culture.

[41] Leventhal (n 19).
[42] See *Walton* (n 9) [61] recognising two lines of argument.

The blaze is only intensified by the practical significance of the question. If the SEA Directive applies, it imposes a series of obligations that can lead to a range of significant consequences for a diverse group of public and private parties. These consequences not only relate to the plans and programmes and the projects to which they relate, but also to how decision-making is understood. Just as with the EIA Directive,[43] there is thus a strong incentive to litigate the question of scope and, in doing so, to directly raise the question of the nature of the frame created by the SEA Directive. This kind of legal question is really asking what it means to say that SEA operates 'upstream'. In the case law, both linear and expansive judicial interpretations of Articles 2(a) and 3 answer this question. This is best illustrated by several examples from the CJEU and the UK courts.

Two interesting points can be gleaned from an examination of these cases and are considered in this and the following sections. The first point, considered in this section, is that the SEA Directive is capable of being interpreted in both linear and expansive terms. The second point, which is the focus of the next section, is that an expansive interpretation of the Directive does potentially require a more radical reframing of existing decision-making structures within national legal cultures.

In *Terre Wallonne ASBL*,[44] the question arose as to whether an action programme under the Nitrates Directive fell within the scope of the SEA Directive,[45] partly because it 'set the framework for future development consent of projects subject to the EIA Directive' and thus Article 3(2)(a). The legal measure in question was also legislative in nature and thus the Belgian government argued that it was not covered by the Directive because it was not a plan or programme 'required by' legislative, regulatory or administrative provisions.[46]

In her Opinion, Advocate General Kokott began the analysis with what appears to be a very linear approach to SEA, stressing its relationship to the EIA Directive.[47] Likewise, she noted in discussing the objectives of the Directive that:

> The application of the EIA Directive revealed that, at the time of the assessment of projects, major effects on the environment are already established on the basis of earlier planning measures … Whilst it is true that those effects can thus be examined during the environmental impact assessment, they cannot be taken fully into account when development consent is given for the project. It is therefore appropriate for such effects on the environment to be examined at the time of preparatory measures and taken into account in that context.[48]

[43] See Fisher, Lange and Scotford (n 8) ch 19.

[44] Joined Cases C-105/09 and C-110/09 *Terre Wallonne ASBL and Inter-Environnement Wallonie ASBL v Région Wallonne* [2010] ECR I-5611.

[45] Council Directive 91/676/EEC of 12 December 1991 concerning the protection of waters against pollution caused by nitrates from agricultural sources [1991] OJ L375/1.

[46] *Terre Wallonne ASBL and Inter-Environnement Wallonie ASBL v Région Wallonne* (n 44) [23].

[47] ibid [2].

[48] ibid [32]. See also the routing example she gives in [33].

The upstream nature of SEA is thus largely framed in terms of its relationship to projects that subsequently need an EIA.

However, a more expansive understanding of the upstream nature of SEA drives AG Kokott's analysis in the case. She refers to Article 1 and stresses that a range of different plans and programmes may be within the SEA Directive's scope because they 'stipulate how projects are to be implemented'.[49] She concludes:

> Significant effects on the environment can therefore be taken fully into account only if they are assessed in the case of all preparatory measures which may result in projects subsequently implemented having such effects.[50]

This leads her to conclude that legislative measures are subject to the SEA Directive and this expansive interpretation is reinforced by the fact that there is no explicit exclusion of legislative measures in Article 2(a) as there was at the time under the EIA Directive.[51] The reference to 'required by legislative, regulatory or administrative provisions', on her interpretation, thus excludes: 'Freely taken political decisions on legislative proposals.'[52]

A more expansive approach can also be seen in how AG Kokott interprets other aspects of the Directive. She concludes, for example, that the specific provisions defining which plans and programmes are covered by the Directive are putting the 'possibility of significant effects on the environment in concrete terms', thus fulfilling the requirement in Article 3(1) that plans and programmes likely to have significant environmental effects are subject to SEA.[53] Likewise, in interpreting the concept of a 'framework' in Article 3(2)(a), she states:

> Plans and programmes may, however, influence the development consent of individual projects in very different ways and, in so doing, prevent appropriate account from being taken of environmental effects. Consequently, the SEA Directive is based on a very broad concept of 'framework'.[54]

AG Kokott reinforces this expansive interpretation, describing Article 3(5) as requiring Member States to consider the 'degree' to which a plan or programme 'sets the framework'. On this expansive view, the SEA Directive catches 'forms of influence that leave room for some discretion'[55]—or, to put it another way, it catches more than what *directly* sets the framework.

[49] ibid [34].

[50] ibid [35].

[51] ibid [40]. See the previous EIA Directive, as codified in Directive 2011/92/EU [2012] OJ L26/1, art 1(4). The exclusion is more complex than it may appear: see Case C-128/09 *Boxus* [2011] ECR I-9711. As with the SEA case law, that complexity arises from the 'hot' nature of EIA. It should be noted that the SEA Directive has since been amended, and the exclusion of EIA for legislative approvals of projects is now less absolute in its terms and more limited: see EIA Directive (n 10) art 2(5).

[52] *Terre Wallonne ASBL and Inter-Environnement Wallonie ASBL v Région Wallonne* (n 44) [41]. As the action programme in this case is required under the Nitrates Directive, the Directive does apply.

[53] ibid [48].

[54] ibid [64].

[55] ibid [65].

The CJEU is less explicit in its analysis, but running through its judgment in *Terre Wallonne* can be seen an expansive approach, starting with its reference to Article 1 of the SEA Directive. The Court notes that 'the fundamental objective of that directive is, where plans and programmes are likely to have significant effects on the environment, to require an environmental assessment to be carried out at the time they are prepared and before they are adopted'.[56] It also finds that action programmes under the Nitrates Directive are within the scope of the Directive, noting that:

> [T]hey embody a comprehensive and coherent approach, providing practical and coordinated arrangements covering vulnerable zones and, where appropriate, the entire territory, for the reduction and prevention of pollution caused by nitrates from agricultural sources.[57]

Action programmes would thus have a significant effect on the environment.

Whilst an expansive approach can thus be seen in *Terre Wallonne*, the outer limits of that approach were still open to question. In *Inter-Environnement Bruxelles ASBL*, AG Kokott concluded that the SEA Directive did not apply to plans or programmes that were 'voluntary' due to the reference to them being 'required' in Article 2(a).[58] While her approach was still expansive, she felt constrained by the text as agreed by the Member States. She also noted that neither the general objective of EU environmental policy nor the specific objective of the Directive would change that result.[59] She was thus recognising that an expansive approach must be interpreted against the background of EU legal culture and the way in which directives were developed in that culture.

The CJEU came to a different conclusion—'required' meant 'regulated'.[60] For them, to conclude that it meant 'required' would run counter to the SEA Directive's aim of establishing a procedure for scrutinising measures likely to have significant effects on the environment, these measures being understood to define the criteria and the detailed rules for the development of land and normally concerning a multiplicity of projects whose implementation is subject to compliance with the rules and procedures provided for by those measures.[61]

For the CJEU, an expansive upstream approach predominated. This expansive approach can also be seen in relation to the other interpretative issue considered in the case—whether the repeal of a plan and programme is within the scope of the SEA Directive as a 'modification' of a plan or programme that is otherwise subject to the Directive. Both AG Kokott's Opinion and the CJEU's judgment found

[56] ibid [32].

[57] ibid [47].

[58] Case C-567/10 *Inter-Environnement Bruxelles ASBL*, Opinion of AG Kokott (17 November 2011), ECLI:EU:C:2011:755 [20]–[30].

[59] ibid [20].

[60] Case C-567/10 *Inter-Environnement Bruxelles ASBL* (CJEU, 22 March 2012), ECLI:EU:C:2012:159 [31].

[61] ibid [30].

that the repeal of a plan or programme amounted to a modification and was thus within the Directive's scope.[62]

It is important to note that the CJEU is doing more than just engaging in purposive interpretation. This is a common description of its legal activity,[63] and the approach taken in these cases has also been understood in these terms.[64] Yet to describe the CJEU's approach as purposive gives the impression that the SEA Directive can be understood as having only one purpose. The point here is that the approach in these cases is to give the Directive an expansive interpretation.[65] The reasons for this approach are various, but they all reflect aspects of EU legal culture. In *Terre Wallonne ASBL*, the most obvious reason for an expansive approach is that the measure in question—an action programme under the Nitrates Directive—does not easily fit into a linear understanding of the SEA Directive. Under an expansive approach, there can also be ambiguity—hence the divergence of approach between the Advocate General and the Court in *Inter-Environnement Bruxelles ASBL*. This divergence does not necessarily reflect the Court giving a more purposive interpretation to the Directive than the Advocate General. Rather, the Court and the Advocate General have divergent 'systemic understanding[s] of the normative preferences and institutional constraints'[66] that should guide their interpretation. For AG Kokott, the focus was upon the Directive as a legal instrument negotiated by the Member States. By contrast, the Court focused on the Directive as an effective legal device that operates according its own legal integrity.

Interpreting the Scope of the SEA Directive in the UK Courts: The *HS2* Litigation

Analysing different interpretative approaches to the SEA Directive also shows that an expansive approach to the Directive requires a more radical rethinking about how environmental impacts are factored into all environmental decision-making. SEA, on this basis, creates a very new frame that is far more likely to 'set the law ablaze'. This can be seen most obviously in the *HS2* litigation.[67] The practical

[62] *Inter-Environnement Bruxelles ASBL*, Opinion of AG Kokott (n 58) esp [53]; *Inter-Environnement Bruxelles* (n 60) paras 38–41.

[63] This is particularly in the environmental field. See Justine Thornton, 'Twenty Five Years of Domestic Case Law' (2013) 25 *Journal of Environmental Law* 531.

[64] *Walton* (n 9) [61].

[65] See also more recently Case C-473/14 *Attikis v Ipourgos Perivallontos* ECLI:EU:C:2015:582 (10 September 2015) [43], which considers the questions of hierarchy and modification.

[66] Maduro (n 40).

[67] *R (Buckinghamshire County Council and Others) v Secretary of State for Transport* [2013] EWHC 481; *HS2 Action Alliance Ltd and Others v Secretary of State for Transport* [2013] EWCA Civ 920; and *HS2* (n 9).

implications of the Directive can be seen quite starkly in the context of this litigation by a national court, which is not just considering the questions of a preliminary ruling but also other aspects of a dispute involving the SEA Directive.

As Lady Hale noted in the Supreme Court, she did not find the *HS2* case an 'easy case'.[68] In *HS2*, the question in relation to the SEA Directive was whether *High Speed Rail: Investing in Britain's Future—Decisions and Next Steps*[69] (known as the 'DNS') fell within the scope of the Directive. Determining the issue required consideration of whether it 'set the framework for future development consent' (Article 3(2)(a)) and whether it was 'required by … administrative provisions' (Article 2(a)). As we shall see, these phrases are capable of linear and expansive interpretations. Thus, for example, from a linear perspective, Article 3(2)(a) primarily catches town planning instruments, such as development plans, which *explicitly* set the conditions for development. On an expansive approach, the phrase catches any public law activity that substantially influences a final decision.

Before considering these different interpretations informing the literature on SEA, it is also important to note that the case has been primarily of interest to legal scholars (so far) for the discussion in the Supreme Court concerning the constitutional law principle of parliamentary privilege and UK legal understandings of the hierarchical relationship between EU and UK law.[70] These issues are not the direct focus of this chapter. However, it is significant to note that these issues arise because of the 'hot' nature of SEA. By creating a new frame for action, the SEA Directive cuts across existing frames for action and, by doing so, requires consideration of how the Directive and the existing constitutional order interrelate. The 'hot' nature of the Directive and the implications of it being 'hot' are particularly obvious because of the expansive approach to the Directive taken by the CJEU, as seen above, which widens the scope of the Directive's application. Yet, while the approach taken by the UK courts is primarily, but not completely, more linear in approach (as discussed below), it does not mean that the type of constitutional issues considered by the Supreme Court in *HS2* could not arise under a linear approach—it is just that, under a linear approach, the Directive is less likely to raise issues for conventional decision-making structures.

Turning back to Article 3(2)(a) and Article 2(a), Ouseley J in the Divisional Court in *HS2* can be seen to take a linear approach to the SEA Directive. His starting point for analysis is to focus on development consent. He states:

> The purpose of SEA is to ensure that the decision on development consent is not affected by earlier plans which through the framework, the rules or criteria or policies they

[68] *HS2* (n 9) [130].

[69] (Cm 8247, 10 January 2012).

[70] ibid [78]–[79] and [203]–[210]. Note that the EIA Directive also gave rise to these issues: see *Boxus* (n 51). See further Mark Elliott, 'Reflections on the HS2 Case: A Hierarchy of Domestic Constitutional Norms and the Qualified Primacy of EU Law', *UK Constitutional Law Blog* (23 January 2014), http://ukconstitutionallaw.org; Alison Young, 'Wilkommen zum Constitutional Pluralism', *UK Constitutional Law Blog* (17 February 2014), http://ukconstitutionallaw.org, for a discussion of these issues.

> contain, weigh one way or another against the application when the earlier plans have not themselves been assessed for likely significant environmental effects. The significant environmental effects have to be assessed at a time when they can play their full part in the decision; they cannot be left unassessed so that the development decision is made when the framework in the plan has sold the pass. A plan framework tilts the balance, creates presumptions, and urges weight to be given to various factors.[71]

The important point here is that a plan 'tilts the balance', 'creates presumptions' and 'urges weight' *in relation to a specific decision*. Ouseley J notes:

> The very concept of a framework, rules, criteria or policy, which guide the outcome of an application for development consent, as a plan which requires SEA even before development project EIA, presupposes that the plan will have an effect on the approach which has to be considered at the development consent stage, and that that effect will be more than merely persuasive by its quality and detail, but guiding and telling because of its stated role in the hierarchy of relevant considerations. That simply is not the case here.[72]

The fact that the decision-maker for the final 'development consent' of the HS2 rail project was Parliament meant that such a hierarchy did not exist.[73] This is because inherent in Parliament's legal identity is its sovereign nature—it cannot be bound by other institutions. There can be no 'setting the framework' for a development consent where the consent is to be considered and made by Parliament. This is an example of where the approach to interpreting the SEA Directive involves more than just characterising it as literal or purposive. As Maduro notes, any interpretation must secure the 'coherence and integrity' of a particular legal order.[74] Thus, Ouseley J was ensuring coherence and integrity within the UK constitutional order by interpreting the Directive consistently with ideas of parliamentary sovereignty. The problem of course is that the Directive, as 'hot law', can be understood to require a reframing of that order.

In the Court of Appeal, the majority judgment of the Master of the Rolls and Richards LJ also took a linear approach. While the majority expressly cited Article 1 and paragraphs (4) and (5) of the Preamble,[75] they also cited the Commission's Guidance document concerning implementation of the SEA Directive, which stressed that the role of the Directive was to 'plug … the gap' created by the downstream nature of the EIA Directive.[76] Their analysis, which agrees with Ouseley J's conclusion, can be seen as linear, particularly with its focus on 'legal influence'—that is, in order for a framework to 'set the framework', it must legally 'narrow … the discretion which the decision-maker would otherwise enjoy'.[77]

[71] *R (Buckinghamshire County Council and Others) v Secretary of State for Transport* (n 67) [93].
[72] ibid [96].
[73] ibid [95].
[74] Maduro (n 40) 3.
[75] *HS2 Action Alliance Ltd and Others v Secretary of State for Transport* (n 67) [23]–[24], [35].
[76] ibid [32].
[77] ibid [55]. See also [51]. Note that they do concede that there may be cases where a plan or programme is a 'sufficient potent factual influence': [55]. But this recognition only reinforces the importance they place on direct legal influence.

In contrast, Sullivan LJ, dissenting in the Court of Appeal, took an expansive approach to the same question. He stressed the need for a purposive approach to the SEA Directive in light of its aim of providing a 'high level of protection' for the environment.[78] Thus, he stated, after considering *Terre Wallonne* and *Inter-Environnement Bruxelles*:

> [T]he overarching principle that emerges from both cases is that the terms in the [SEA Directive]—'plans and programmes', 'modifications', 'required' and 'framework'—should all be given a broad and flexible meaning to ensure that the objective of the EU legislature, to provide for a high level of protection for the environment is achieved, and the practical effect of the Directive is not compromised.[79]

This is a very different purpose from interpreting it as a complement to EIA for development consents and it leads to Sullivan LJ's conclusion that the DNS did indeed set the framework in this case. He concluded that the DNS document would 'influence' Parliament's final decision on HS2, particularly taking into account the 'dual role' of the government as both policy-maker (drafting the relevant policy plans concerning HS2) and comprising Members of Parliament who will also vote on the final decision to allow the HS2 project to proceed or not.[80] Through this expansive approach, Sullivan LJ recognised that the Directive could require a significant reframing of decision-making. In relation to the Directive, he argued for the 'need to look at the substance, rather than the constitutional form, of the decision-making process'.[81] This may be seen as hot law in action—by creating new frames of action, the existing frames of the existing legal order are challenged. This is even when those existing frames of action are constitutionally entrenched. An expansive interpretation of the Directive is more likely to challenge the existing order due to the fact that the new framework is working towards a different aspiration (preventing environmental degradation) from the conventional order (separation of powers). Saying this is not to comment on the legitimacy of either an expansive interpretation of the Directive or of the existing constitutional order, but rather to note that the 'hotter' the law, the more likely that such a conflict will arise.

In the Supreme Court, Lord Carnwath can be seen to take a linear approach to the SEA Directive, particularly in his general discussion of the Directive that emphasises its interrelationship with the EIA Directive.[82] He also noted that: 'The purpose [of the SEA Directive] is more specific, that is to prevent major effects on the environment being predetermined by earlier planning measures before the EIA stage is reached.'[83] His discussion of CJEU authorities also emphasised those

[78] ibid [161]–[162].
[79] ibid [163].
[80] ibid [173].
[81] ibid [174].
[82] *HS2* (n 9) [34].
[83] ibid [35].

aspects of the EU case law that stress how the plans or programmes covered by the Directive directly relate to development. In discussing AG Kokott's Opinion in *Terre Wallonne ASBL*, he noted that her analysis emphasises that, for a plan of programme to fall under the Directive, 'the critical factor was that consideration of certain environmental effects would in practice be excluded altogether'.[84] Likewise, he highlighted that the CJEU in *Inter-Environnement Bruxelles ASBL*, in discussing whether the repeal of a programme was within the scope of the Directive, 'define[d] the criteria and the detailed rules for the development of land'.[85] Lord Carnwath's conclusion that the DNS did not 'set the framework'—because it 'does not in any way constrain the decision-making process of the authority responsible, which in this case is Parliament'[86]—flows from this linear interpretation. On this basis, the Directive covers only those 'upstream' plans and programmes that *directly* frame downstream effects.

Lord Sumption also understood the SEA Directive in linear terms. Thus, he stated:

> The effect of the SEA Directive is that where the grant or refusal of development consent for a specific project is governed by a policy framework regulated by legislative, regulatory or administrative provisions, the policy framework must itself be subject to an environmental assessment. The object is to deal with cases where the environmental impact assessment prepared under the EIA at the stage when development consent is granted is wholly or partly pre-empted, because some relevant factor is governed by a framework of planning policy adopted at an earlier stage.[87]

SEA can thus only be understood in terms of particular projects. For a plan or programme to fall within the scope of the Directive:

> It must at least limit the range of discretionary factors which can be taken into account in making that [final consent] decision, or affect the weight to be attached to them.[88]

The DNS did not fall into this category because, for Lord Sumption, it was 'nothing more than a proposal'.[89] This is consistent with a linear approach in which there needs to be a strong relationship between upstream and downstream processes.

In contrast, Lady Hale in *HS2* struggled with the ambiguity of the Directive's purpose. Thus, her initial analysis was in more expansive terms. Her starting point was not with a particular 'development consent', but with the general (and clearly correct) assumption that the development will have 'a major impact on the environment'.[90] She cited paragraphs 4 and 5 of the Preamble and noted that

84 ibid [25].
85 ibid [27]. See also the discussion at [28].
86 ibid [38].
87 ibid [122].
88 ibid [123].
89 ibid [125].
90 ibid [130].

the conclusion in this case may remove certain categories of project from the SEA Directive.[91] She also noted the importance of understanding that specific CJEU rulings concerned particular phrases in the Directive, none of which had finalised which approach should be taken to interpreting the Directive's fundamental 'setting the framework' requirement.[92] While she considered the question of whether a preliminary reference was needed, she finally decided it was not, for a range of factors. The second of these factors was that:

> [T]he aim of the Directive is not to ensure that all development proposals which will have major environmental effects are preceded by a strategic environmental assessment; rather, it is to ensure that future development consent for projects is not constrained by decisions which have been taken 'upstream' without such assessment, thus pre-empting the environmental assessment to be made at project level.[93]

She thus concluded by characterising the role of the SEA Directive in linear terms.

The above analysis of cases relating to the SEA Directive is not exhaustive.[94] Nor do I pretend that my analysis is any more than a sketch with a broad brush. What can be seen from it is that the judicial application of the Directive is tricky. The legal questions the Directive raises partly flow from its ambiguity, which allows room for both linear and expansive interpretative approaches to be taken. Thus, how Articles 2 and 3 should be interpreted will be directly influenced by what is understood as the purpose of the Directive, which includes the extent to which it is seen to require a reframing of environmental decision-making. The different possible approaches to interpreting the Directive not only raise questions about which plans and programmes fall into the scope of Article 2(a), but also how those plans legally relate to downstream activity. To talk of a 'purposive' interpretation of the Directive thus begs the question.

What can also be seen is that the process of interpretation is embedded in UK and EU legal culture. This is not only in terms of what is a legitimate mode of interpretation,[95] but also in terms of the types of legal questions that arise. These range from structural questions such as the interaction between different EU environmental law regimes[96] and the role of parliaments[97] to specific issues such as the repeal of plans and programmes[98] and the building of major infrastructure

[91] ibid [131], [153].

[92] ibid [149].

[93] ibid [155].

[94] See also Case C-463/11 *L v M* (18 April 2013); ECLI:EU:C:2013:247Case C-295/10 *Valčiukienė and Others* [2011] ECR I-8819; Case C-43/10 *Nomarchiaki Aftodioikisi Aitoloakarnanias and Others v Ipourgos Perivallontos, Khorotaxias kai Dimosion Ergon and Others* (CJEU, 11 September 2012) ECLI:EU:C:2012:560; *Walton* (n 9).

[95] See *HS2* (n 9) (Lord Mance and Lord Neuberger).

[96] *Terre Wallonne ASBL* (n 44).

[97] *HS2* (n 9).

[98] *Inter-Environnement Bruxelles ASBL* (n 58).

projects.[99] By 'setting the law ablaze', the impact of SEA (and EIA for that matter) is not localised. It forces lawyers and courts to consider a range of different optins.

Remedies

Linear and expansive interpretations of the SEA Directive will also shape what is understood to be an appropriate remedy for its breach. This is because, under the EU principles of procedural autonomy, the remedies provided by national courts must be equivalent and effective.[100] What is held to be 'effective' will be determined by what is understood as the strategic nature of the Directive. Linear and expansive understandings will yield different results. This can be illustrated with a few examples.

In *Inter-Environnement Wallonne ASBL*,[101] the question before the court was what was the consequence of a procedural breach of the Directive. AG Kokott took an expansive approach to the question. Her starting point was Article 1[102] and she stressed that the 'inclusion [by SEA] of a wider set of factors in decision-making will contribute to more sustainable and effective solutions'.[103] On this basis, the benefit of SEA was that a measure (that is, a relevant plan or programme) subject to assessment will be 'more favourable for the protection of the environment' in general terms.[104] If that is the case, then an expansive interpretation 'supports at first sight suspending the further implementation of a measure lacking an assessment'.[105] But AG Kokott also went on to note that such a suspension may in some regulatory structures result in 'more serious effects on the environment than the measure invoked incorrectly' and that this would 'contradict the objectives of the SEA Directive'.[106] Thus, making the SEA Directive effective is making its general objective of a 'high level of protection' effective.

The Grand Chamber agreed with this conclusion and, in doing so, also stressed the significance of Article 1 of the Directive,[107] as well as the referring court's reference to a 'high level of protection' in Article 191 TFEU.[108] The Chamber also

[99] *Walton* (n 9); *HS2* (n 9).

[100] Case C-432/05 *Unibet (London) Ltd and Unibet (International) Ltd v Justitiekanslern* [2007] ECR I-2271.

[101] Case C-41/11 *Inter-Environnement Wallonne ASBL and Terre Wallonne ASBL v Région Wallonne* (CJEU, 28 February 2012).

[102] ibid, Opinion of AG Kokott (8 December 2011) [10]. Also note the reference to Preamble (4) and (5) at [11].

[103] ibid [37].

[104] ibid [39]–[40].

[105] ibid [40].

[106] ibid [42].

[107] *Inter-Environnement Wallonne* (n 101) para 40.

[108] ibid [55].

fleshed out the nature of the obligation of the court in more detail by setting out four conditions—each of which had as its purpose environmental protection.[109]

This expansive approach to remedies can also be seen in the more recent decision of *L v M*.[110] Thus, AG Wathelet, after putting forward quite an expansive interpretation of the Directive, concluded in relation to remedies that:

> In the context of actions claiming irregularity or omission of environmental assessments, national courts must therefore be able to adopt, subject to the limits of procedural autonomy, measures that are appropriate for preventing a project from being implemented in the absence of an environmental assessment required under the SEA Directive.[111]

There was also reference to the principle of effective judicial protection.[112] The court came to the same conclusion, but it was perhaps less expansive in its approach, citing the effectiveness of Article 3(1), (4) and (5) as particularly important.

What can thus be seen from these cases is that the nature of the remedy flows from what is understood to be the purpose of the SEA Directive. In these cases, it is the expansive approach to defining the Directive that drives the analysis. A linear approach would arguably direct the analysis in a different way.

The nature of this linear approach can be seen through a brief discussion of *Walton*.[113] One of the arguments before the Court in that case was that the discretion of the Court in relation to the available remedy would depend on whether it was a breach of EU or UK law.[114] Lord Carnwath's analysis can be understood as consisting of two steps. In the first step, he recognised, as many others have, the relationship between remedies and the effectiveness of EU law. After an analysis of the different remedial frameworks and doctrines in domestic and EU law, he thus stated that:

> As *Wells* makes clear, the basic requirement of European law is that the remedies should be 'effective' and 'not less favourable' than those governing similar domestic situations. Effectiveness means no more than that the exercise of the rights granted by the Directive should not be rendered 'impossible in practice or excessively difficult'. Proportionality is also an important principle of European law.[115]

Thus, Lord Carnwath rightly emphasised that the SEA Directive, having its source in EU law, did not dictate a certain remedy; rather, the question of effectiveness required consideration of the 'rights granted under the Directive'.

In relation to the SEA Directive, this exercise is less about determining precise rights and more about an analysis of its purpose. If the purpose is understood

[109] ibid [59]–[62].
[110] *L v M* (n 94).
[111] ibid, Opinion of AG Wathelet (19 December 2012) [69].
[112] ibid [70].
[113] *Walton* (n 9).
[114] ibid [104], [116].
[115] ibid [138].

differently, then so will the concepts of effectiveness and 'rights granted under the Directive'. Linear and expansive understandings of SEA will thus lead to different understandings of remedies. The cases above show that the CJEU has taken an expansive approach. If a more linear approach were taken, focusing on the effectiveness of the Directive in relation to a particular project, then a different approach to remedies may be taken.

This linear approach can be seen in the second step of the judgment of Lord Carnwath in *Walton*, where he conceptualised the issue of effectiveness in relation to the specific project in a manner akin to the UK common law approach to granting remedies in cases of breaches of procedural fairness.[116] Accordingly, he noted that where 'the court is satisfied that the applicant has been able in practice to enjoy the rights conferred by the European legislation' and 'where a procedural challenge would fail under domestic law because the breach has caused no substantial prejudice', there would be no need for a remedy.[117] Under this linear approach, the question of effectiveness is considered in relation to a specific project and not in relation to environmental protection writ large. That said, it still leaves open the question of what a linear approach to remedies entails as it may not be a completely conventional rights-based approach.[118]

Conclusion

In a blog post on the *HS2* Supreme Court judgment, Adam Tomkins suggested that:

> The [EIA and SEA] directives themselves pose no challenge to the lawfulness of the Government's processes for implementing HS2. That challenge arises only by virtue of the ways in which the directives have been interpreted—that is to say, wilfully misinterpreted—by the CJEU.[119]

Tomkins is of course focusing on the constitutional aspects of the *HS2* judgment and he appears to be presuming that both Directives are capable of only one interpretation or are at least capable of yielding 'correct' and 'incorrect' interpretations. Such a view is relatively common and arguably stems from the perception that SEA and EIA are simple tools that do not require any reconfiguration of public decision-making. While the image of environmental law as a 'toolkit' has many appealing features, this chapter has shown that it is also a misguided one. Both

[116] ibid [112], [139].

[117] ibid [139].

[118] Compare ibid [124]–[133] (Lord Carnwath's analysis of *Berkeley* (n 24)) with Lord Hoffmann's judgment in *Berkeley*. See also *R (on the Application of Wells)* (n 23).

[119] Adam Tomkins, 'The Supreme Court's Welcome Attack on the Court of Justice', 23 January 2014, http://britgovcon.wordpress.com/2014/01/23/the-supreme-courts-welcome-attack-on-the-court-of-justice.

these legal forms are examples of 'hot law' that 'set the law ablaze'. SEA is an ambiguous idea, the 'upstream' nature of the Directive can be understood in linear and expansive terms, and the judicial application of it is embedded in EU and UK legal culture. The variation in judicial interpretation of its scope and remedies reflects all these factors. A similar situation can be seen in relation to EIA.[120]

This chapter can only be a sketch and there is scope for a far more careful charting of the issues highlighted, particularly in relation to how the interpretation of the SEA Directive is influenced by other aspects of a legal culture. However, the chapter has shown that SEA is not just a tool that is cleanly inserted into existing legal structures—an app for the environmental age. Likewise, the issues raised in the litigation concerning the Directive are not just a product of the interface between EU and UK legal orders. Rather, the Directive is about reframing decision-making and it is that fact which gives rise to the 'technical' issues of legal interpretation considered above.

Highlighting this is not an act in criticising the SEA Directive or the judges who have found themselves adjudicating on disputes about how the Directive applies. Rather, it is about explaining why this Directive has raised a set of quite diverse and interesting legal questions and is likely to continue to do so. The Directive is an example of where the creation of a 'frame of law' for a 'hot situation'[121] is by no means a straightforward task. The frame itself is open to interpretation, as is the way it interacts with EU and UK legal culture. In this sense, the SEA Directive has, in Judge Leventhal's terms, 'set the law ablaze'.[122]

120 Fisher, Lange and Scotford (n 8) 848–50.
121 Callon (n 12).
122 Leventhal (n 19).

9

'Streamlining' the SEA Process

WILLIAM R SHEATE

Introduction

A dictionary definition of 'streamlining' is to: 'Make (an organization or system) more efficient and effective by employing faster or simpler working methods.'[1] In current parlance, and in relation to environmental assessment, streamlining is often a euphemism for speeding up the planning process by reducing the burden of assessment on proponents and authorities. It is frequently uttered in the same breath as commentaries that blame delays on infrastructure delivery upon the lengthy planning process and objections by members of the public, often derogatorily labelled as NIMBYs.[2] It is used as justification to curtail public participation and the length of time taken to reach a decision. However, NIMBYism is a perfectly legitimate position for an individual or groups of individuals to take, even though it is one that is often derided as selfish and involves action that fails to recognise the wider public interest. In fact, such people have a much more immediate and legitimate interest in why and how a decision is to be made that will affect their life forever. It is entirely appropriate that they may seek to use the planning system and environmental assessment processes as a proper means of seeking accountability of the proponents and decision-makers associated with that development.[3]

In this chapter I seek to advance the case for the reclamation of the word 'streamlining' from the negative connotations it has acquired. I look at the concept of streamlining in a positive way as a means of enhancing effective environmental assessment, through the best use of strategic environmental assessment (SEA) and the way it relates to project level assessment—environmental impact assessment (EIA). In so doing, it draws significantly on the principles of 'tiering' viz, the nested

[1] *Oxford Dictionaries* (Oxford, Oxford University Press, 2014), www.oxforddictionaries.com.

[2] 'Not In My Back Yard'.

[3] See especially William R Sheate, 'Purposes, Paradigms and Pressure Groups: Accountability and Sustainability in EU Environmental Assessment 1985–2010' (2012) 33 *Environmental Impact Assessment Review* 91.

relationship between different levels of SEA and EIA. This chapter considers some of the recent drivers for streamlining—political, policy and legal—and then illustrates this process by looking in some depth at two case studies. The first of these case studies concerns national policy statements and national development projects (NDPs) where there is at least in theory an explicit tiering process between SEA and EIA, and also where arguably there have been some actual attempts at streamlining. The second case study is High Speed 2 (HS2). This is an illustration of a distinct failure to deliver an effectively tiered and streamlined process—all while there was great apparent government concern to deliver the infrastructure as quickly as possible. This chapter then concludes with what lessons can be learnt for delivering better SEA though streamlining, whilst at the same time recognising that streamlining does not have to mean less SEA. Indeed, a properly tiered SEA may mean more but more focused SEA.

Drivers for SEA and Decision-making

Streamlining of environmental assessment is often focused on decisions around projects—particularly major infrastructure projects. Concerns about the length of time taken to reach consent decisions on infrastructure are often focused on public objection to such proposals, such as those for electricity transmission lines, nuclear power stations, road and rail, and wind farms. Governments seek to speed up decision-making, for example, through setting time limits, in an attempt to curtail the time taken by public consultation/engagement processes.[4] But this is often a vain attempt at curbing so-called NIMBYism, not least because it fails to recognise the simple fact that controversial projects or programmes are controversial because they are controversial. Indeed, it is often a *lack* of strategic planning (and SEA) that leads to such adversarial conflict as projects follow a 'decide, educate, announce, defend' (DEAD) approach to their promotion. As I have commented elsewhere, in such contexts, NIMBYism is a perfectly legitimate strategy by local communities to hold decision-makers and proponents to account.[5]

A number of European countries have seen efforts at streamlining of environmental assessment processes, although what is meant by 'streamlining' varies greatly. For some, 'streamlining' means speeding up decision-making, saving time and reducing delays and costs, while for others, it means making the process more efficient and timely. These are not necessarily mutually exclusive, but more a matter of emphasis, sometimes ideological. A more efficient process in the short term

[4] See, eg, Commission, 'Proposal for a Regulation of the European Parliament and of the Council on guidelines for trans-European energy infrastructure and repealing Decision No 1364/2006/EC' COM (2011) 658 final.

[5] See especially Sheate (n 3).

may not necessarily be a quicker process overall, for example, if a curtailing of public consultation processes ultimately results in more conflict and a greater likelihood of legal challenge.[6] This section considers the approaches to EA streamlining that have taken place in the Netherlands, the UK and the EU, highlighting, in particular, the important role that economic growth has played as the overarching driver behind efforts to speed up decision-making and reduce perceived burdens on developers.

In the Netherlands, the main drivers for streamlining haves been in part a reaction against the perceived burden of environmental assessment (running counter to the long-standing reputation of the Netherlands as a strong-hold of environmental assessment), but also a move away from rigid, comprehensive procedures in SEA and EIA to a more selective application to fewer mandatory planning elements (plans, programmes and projects) and the desire to promote post-recession economic growth. Thus, changes were made to EIA and SEA legislation within the Act to Modernise Environmental Assessment, which came into force on 1 July 2010.[7] A raft of instruments has since been adopted to assist the development of renewable energy production, as part of a move to stimulate the national economy, with a particular focus on sustainability, energy and innovation.[8] Greater clarity has already been demanded in relation to wind farm projects where disputes have halted several proposals. This initiated the formulation of a National Policy Plan in this area to provide the strategic context for decisions on projects, providing a good example of how an attempt to deliver energy projects more quickly actually resulted in a slowing down of the approval process, thus demanding a more strategic approach to where such projects should be located.[9]

In the UK, key drivers over recent years for streamlining planning and environmental assessment processes have been a combination of political and ideological desire to unfetter the market, such as in the case of housing and infrastructure development, and the pressure on governments to promote economic growth because of the financial crisis between 2007 and 2013. Again, this materialised most obviously in relation to large infrastructure projects, particularly with the

[6] William R Sheate, and Richard P Eales, 'Effectiveness of European National SEA Systems: How are They Making a Difference?', in Barry Sadler and Jiri Dusik (eds), *European and International Experience of Strategic Environmental Assessment: Recent Progress and Future Prospects* (London, Earthscan, 2016).

[7] Veronica ten Holder, 'Twenty-Five Years of EA in the Netherlands. Views and Experiences 2012' (Series no 11, The Netherlands Commission for Environmental Assessment, 2012) http://api.commissiemer.nl/docs/mer/diversen/views_experiences_2012_p4-9.pdf.

[8] Norton Rose, 'Memorandum on the Dutch Recovery Act' (2010), www.nortonrose.com/knowledge/publications/27719/memorandum-on-the-dutch-recovery-act;

Norton Rose 'European Renewable Energy Incentive Guide—The Netherlands' (2012), www.nortonrose.com/knowledge/publications/66148/european-renewable-energy-incentive-guide-the-netherlands.

[9] Maeve Smyth, 'Streamlining Environmental Assessment for Priority EU Energy Infrastructure Projects: Progress or Retreat?' (unpublished MSc Environmental Technology thesis, Imperial College London Centre for Environmental Policy, September 2012).

introduction of the Planning Act 2008, which introduced a new fast-track process for approving nationally significant infrastructure projects (NSIPs). As part of that process, the government introduced national policy statements (NPSs) for a range of key infrastructure sectors, which seek to establish the priorities for delivering national sectoral policy and against which the decisions on NSIPs are judged by the Planning Inspectorate.[10] Ostensibly, this was an attempt to separate out responsibility for actual decisions (often controversial ones) on major infrastructure away from direct government involvement, devolving it to a non-departmental body—now the Planning Inspectorate—while the government set the framework through the NPSs. Originally, the intention of the Planning Act 2008 in creating the Infrastructure Planning Commission (IPC) was for the IPC to make the decision. Since the IPC's abolition, the Planning Inspectorate now advise on the decision, but the final decision rests with the Secretary of State. In reality, the NPS process allows the government to draw the decision-making framework very narrowly indeed, sometimes even to the point of identifying actual development projects in the NPS, which leaves little scope for discretion when it comes to the NSIP process itself. SEA is required on the NPSs, although the government uses a wider process called Appraisal of Sustainability (AoS), which is supposed to meet the requirements of the SEA Directive,[11] but also addresses social and economic aspects of proposed infrastructure plans, as well as environmental aspects. NPSs are therefore seen as 'plans or programmes' for the purposes of applying the SEA Directive and set the framework for projects likely to be subject to EIA.[12] The term 'Appraisal of Sustainability' refers solely to those assessments undertaken for NPSs, though in all other respects, they are the same as Sustainability Appraisals (SAs) undertaken for spatial plans in the UK and need to be screened for applicability of the SEA Directive.[13] EIA, according to the EIA Directive, is applied to the NSIPs themselves with requirements for pre-application consultation and there is a one-year time limit on the application process itself from receipt of the application to the final decision.[14]

[10] Originally this function rested with a newly created Infrastructure Planning Commission before its abolition.

[11] Directive 2001/42/EC of the European Parliament and of the Council on the assessment of the effects of certain plans and programmes on the environment [2001] OJ L197/30 (hereinafter 'the SEA Directive').

[12] ibid, art 3(2)(a).

[13] For an analysis of the relationship of SAs with SEA, see Jack Connah and Stephanie Hall in Ch 7 of this volume.

[14] Directive 2011/92/EU of the European Parliament and of the Council on the assessment of the effects of certain public and private projects on the environment (codification) [2012] OJ L26/1, as amended by European Parliament and Council Directive 2014/52/EU [2014] OJ L124/1 (hereinafter 'the EIA Directive'). Section 98(1) of the Planning Act 2008 (as amended) makes provision of six months for examination; s 107(1) provides for three months for the Planning Inspectorate to make a recommendation and a further three months for the Secretary of State to make a decision (ie, 12 months in total).

The Planning Act 2008—through NPSs and NSIPs—introduced some genuine benefits for citizen engagement, particularly the need for at least two rounds of pre-application consultation. The National Grid, as a developer of electricity transmission networks, choose to do three rounds of pre-application consultation, because it makes sense to it to engage with local communities as early and as fully as possible at the scoping stage of EIA rather than just on the Environmental Statement (ES) produced by the infrastructure developer. It has learned the hard way that early public consultation is effective and ultimately more efficient, after a lengthy 10-year process of seeking consent for a 90 km strategic connection in North Yorkshire from 1990 to 2000.[15]

In 2009, the UK government published a number of draft NPSs, which provided an important opportunity to reflect on how SEA was being implemented in the UK, particularly with respect to strategic actions at the national level. An important question (explored later on in this chapter) is whether the desire to speed up the decision-making process, one of the motivations for the NPSs, may compromise the environmental assessments or Appraisals of Sustainability being undertaken and particularly whether they may fail to comply with the requirements of the SEA Directive. If this is the case, then the speeding up of decision-making may actually not happen, even though it was the intention of the NPS. If NPSs and NSIPs end up being challenged in the courts, there can be no assumption that the planning process itself and the delivery of infrastructure will necessarily be any quicker in the long run. In 2014, the Coalition government undertook an overarching review of the Nationally Significant Infrastructure Planning Regime, which focused on improving the pre-application phase and further streamlining of consents.[16] The outcome of this review was never very clear, but there continues to be an ongoing ideological campaign by the government against the perceived burden of the planning system, and therefore also EA. The new Conservative government in 2015, for example, created a National Infrastructure Commission as an interim measure to advise HM Treasury on future major infrastructure needs. As part of its general drive to reduce bureaucracy and unnecessary administration (through its Red Tape Challenge), the government published the National Planning Policy Framework (NPPF) in 2012,[17] which sought to remove some 1,000-plus pages of planning guidance (through Planning Policy Statements and Guidance) and distil it down into around 50 pages. It is notable that the Department of Communities and Local Government (DCLG) has since found the need to provide supplementary online guidance through National Planning Practice Guidance (NPPG),[18] so

[15] See especially William R Sheate, 'Electricity Generation and Transmission: A Case Study of Problematic EIA Implementation in the UK' (1995) 5 *Environmental Policy and Practice* 17; and Sheate (n 3) for a more detailed description and analysis of the North Yorkshire Power lines case.

[16] See www.redtapechallenge.cabinetoffice.gov.uk/themehome/planning-administration.

[17] DCLG, 'National Planning Policy Framework' (2012) (hereinafter 'NPPF'), www.gov.uk/government/publications/national-planning-policy-framework--2.

[18] See National Planning Practice Guidance, http://planningguidance.planningportal.gov.uk.

maybe some detail was needed after all! The NPPF includes a presumption in favour of 'sustainable development', in the absence of a current approved local authority development plan. Clearly this leaves much for interpretation and was designed explicitly to facilitate easier development: 'Development that is sustainable should go ahead, without delay—a presumption in favour of sustainable development that is the basis for every plan, and every decision.'[19]

In short, the experience of the Planning Act 2008 scheme to date and recent spatial planning reforms is that streamlining of EA processes in the UK is primarily concerned with speeding up decision-making.

The picture in the EU is slightly different. Again there is regulation that seeks to organise and promote large-scale transboundary EU infrastructure projects, but any streamlining of the EA processes involved operates only at the individual project level, despite the strategic aims of the EU scheme overall. In short, there are no established SEA processes to streamline. The main EU regulatory scheme for promoting infrastructure development is found in the EU TEN-E Regulation 347/2013[20] and associated guidance streamlining environmental assessment procedures for energy infrastructure Projects of Common Interest (PCIs),[21] which draw significantly on the experience of the Planning Act 2008 in the UK. The TEN-E Regulation operates at the project level and seeks to facilitate the rapid delivery of key transboundary electricity transmission projects (PCIs). However, although PCIs are identified strategically at the EU level, so far this takes place in the absence of a formal preceding SEA process. While the Regulation allows for frontloading of public participation in the spirit of the Aarhus Convention[22]—to seek to deliver early and effective participation—there is no EU-wide electricity network plan as such to which SEA could be applied. This is despite the fact that the very existence of a PCI list effectively and deliberately sets the priority for the development of those projects, but without an SEA of their overall and combined implications. There are national-level 10-year transmission infrastructure plans produced by the transmission system operators (TSOs), but these are not statutory and to date have not been systematically subject to SEA, and in any case they are limited only to Member State boundaries, whereas PCIs have a transboundary focus. There was an attempt to undertake an EU-wide SEA of long-term electricity transmission infrastructure through an EU 7th Framework Programme funded

[19] Ministerial Foreword, NPPF (n 17), http://planningguidance.planningportal.gov.uk/blog/policy/ministerial-foreword.

[20] Regulation 347/2013/EU on guidelines for trans-European energy infrastructure and repealing Decision No 1364/2006/EC and amending Regulations (EC) No 713/2009, (EC) No 714/2009 and (EC) No 715/2009 [2013] OJ L115/39.

[21] Commission 'Streamlining Environmental Assessment Procedures for Energy Infrastructure Projects of Common Interest (PCIs)' (2013), http://ec.europa.eu/energy/infrastructure/environmental_assesment_en.htm.

[22] UNECE Convention on Access to Information, Public Participation and Access to Justice in Environmental Matters (Aarhus, 28 June 1998) 2161 UNTS 447; 38 ILM 517 (1999), in force 30 October 2001.

project known as e-Highway 2050—the electricity superhighway to 2050,[23] which looked at a range of scenarios for future electricity transmission architecture and undertaking a voluntary Strategic Environmental and Sustainability Assessment (SESA).[24] However, this was very high level and voluntary, and there is no equivalent EU-wide top-down plan to the national 10-year plans that could address the assessment deficit that currently exists above the decision to designate a potential project as a PCI. This is not just an assessment deficit, but also a democratic and accountability deficit—a consequence of seeking to speed up decisions on key infrastructure in the absence of SEA.

Streamlining of environmental assessment in itself is no bad thing, since it can, and should, make the process of decision-making and project approval more efficient, including by frontloading public participation to help deliver 'early and effective' participation in decision-making, which can help avoid consultation fatigue of stakeholders. For example, non-governmental organisations (NGOs) and Transmission System Operators (TSOs) have jointly signed up to the European Grid Declaration on Electricity Network Development and Nature Conservation in Europe—'a coalition of Europe's 29 largest environmental NGOs and grid operators pledged to work in partnership to ensure that the goals of grid modernisation and environmental protection can be achieved side by side'.[25] But streamlining can be a euphemism for deregulation and effectively eviscerating the objectives of environmental assessment legislation.[26] Even if that is not the intention, although it may be, it can be the consequence of acting in a piecemeal way with a narrow focus on faster infrastructure delivery and economic development.

Tiering Environmental Assessment

The problematic direction towards the streamlining of environmental assessment processes seen in the above EU and Member State developments suggests that a deeper understanding of effective SEA processes is needed. From a theoretical point of view, tiering is critical to understanding effective SEA—it is a well-established principle in relation to SEA design, implementation and public participation in SEA procedures. The idea of 'tiering' involves assessing the most

[23] See www.e-highway2050.eu/e-highway2050.

[24] The author was a member of the eHighway2050 SESA project team.

[25] Renewables Grid Initiative (RGI), 'European Grid Declaration on Electricity Network Development and Nature Conservation in Europe' (2011), http://renewables-grid.eu/documents/eu-grid-declaration.html.

[26] Canada is notable for its recent reform of the Canadian Environmental Assessment Act (CEAA), streamlining processes to the extent that some see the Canadian EA system—once heralded as a role model—to have been 'gutted'. See RB Gibson, 'In Full Retreat: The Canadian Government's New Environmental Assessment Law Undoes Decades of Progress' (2012) 30(3) *Impact Assessment and Project Appraisal* 179, 186.

relevant issues at the most appropriate level of detail relative to the level of decision-making.[27] Data requirements are quite different at the strategic and project levels—more qualitative in the former and more quantitative in the latter. Uncertainty varies too. There is a high level of uncertainty at the strategic level and a much lower level of uncertainty at the project level. And, critically, many more options are still open at strategic levels compared to the project level, where many options may have been foreclosed by earlier decisions.[28] The tiering of assessments therefore relates directly to the tiered hierarchy of plans, programmes and projects.[29] Tiering makes sense because environmental assessment at a strategic level is a fundamentally different process from that at a project level. In most cases, the appropriate data simply will not be available when things are at a strategic planning stage and, even if they were, there would be a serious risk of data overload in the planning process as a whole. Further, the level of detail would be meaningless given the levels of uncertainty and issues most pertinent at a higher strategic level.

The purpose of tiering is thus closely linked to the scope of the assessment: what are the most important issues, what are the boundaries and the relationships to other plans and programmes and levels of assessment, and what are the options/alternatives available? In this respect, Sheate et al highlight, presciently as it turns out, that the existence of the two EIA and SEA EU Directives:

> [C]reates a degree of dissonance between the legal relationship of the EIA and SEA Directives, and the theoretical and practical relationships between EIA and SEA. Theory suggests consistent tiering from SEA at higher levels down to project level is desirable … Legally, under the two Directives, EIA or SEA are required only if the project or PP [plan or programme] meets the specific requirements of the relevant Directive … Consequently many plans that might have significant effects on the environment may still not meet the SEA Directive screening criteria and so may not be subject to SEA, even though theory and practice might indicate that they should be subject to an SEA process.[30]

This has now come very much to the fore, most notably as a result of the Supreme Court decision in the case of *HS2*,[31] which concerned a judicial review challenge to

[27] Luis E Sánchez and Solange S Silva-Sánchez, 'Tiering Strategic Environmental Assessment and Project Environmental Impact Assessment in Highway Planning in São Paulo, Brazil' (2008) 28 *Environmental Impact Assessment Review* 515; Thomas B Fischer, Christopher Wood and Carys Jones, 'Policy, Plan, and Programme Environmental Assessment in England, the Netherlands, and Germany: Practice and Prospects' (2002) 29 *Environment and Planning B: Planning and Design* 159; J Ivan Scrase, and William R Sheate, 'Integration and Integrated Approaches to Assessment: What Do They Mean for the Environment?' (2002) 4 *Journal of Environmental Policy and Planning* 275.

[28] William R Sheate, Helen Byron, Suzan Dagg and Lourdes Cooper, 'The Relationship between the EIA and SEA Directives' (Final Report to the European Commission DG Environment, Contract No ENV.G.4./ETU/2004/0020r, August 2005), http://ec.europa.eu/environment/eia/eia-support.htm, 16.

[29] Ivan Scrase, 'Strategic Environmental Assessment of Grid Development Plans and Programmes' (2012) RSPB, UK (15 June 2012).

[30] Sheate, Byron, Dagg and Cooper (2005), n 28, 82.

[31] *R (on the Application of HS2 Action Alliance Ltd) v Secretary of State for Transport and Others* [2014] UKSC 3.

the proposed high-speed rail line between London and the West Midlands and on to Manchester and Leeds. Of all the large-scale infrastructure schemes for which one might expect an SEA to be required, the Supreme Court found that it did not meet the screening criteria for the SEA Directive. This case suggests that the 'tiering' of SEA and EIA in UK law (and possibly EU law) is not working optimally from a theoretical perspective.

However, as well as the scope of the assessment, an additional and equally important theoretical function of SEA, relevant to the relationship between SEA and EIA, is accountability.[32] Tiering of assessment through the hierarchy of plans and programmes allows proponents and decision-makers to be held accountable for their actions at the appropriate decision-making level, through a transparent process and through public participation at key stages of each decision-making process, recognising that that there will often be different 'publics' at different tiers of decision-making. For example, NGOs may be more able to engage with high-level strategic plans that do not have an immediate and obvious impact at the local level, whereas local groups and people directly affected will engage more immediately in a project or development that will affect their personal property or livelihood directly through EIA. This theoretical function of accountability is now legally enshrined in SEA processes due to Article 7 of the Aarhus Convention, which requires that parties to the Convention 'make appropriate practical and/or other provisions for the public to participate during the preparation of plans and programmes relating to the environment, within a transparent and fair framework, having provided the necessary information to the public. Within this framework, article 6, paragraphs 3, 4 and 8, shall be applied'.[33] This obligation is at least partly implemented in EU law by Article 6(2) of the SEA Directive, through its requirements for the public to be given an early and effective opportunity to express their opinion before the adoption of a draft plan or programme.[34] The EU Commission Guidance on the SEA Directive refers to the requirement in Article 6(4) of the Aarhus Convention: 'Each Party shall provide for early public participation, when all options are open and effective public participation can take place.'[35] A critical point here, in thinking about designing effective 'streamlined' SEA processes, is the requirement to call for relevant public views when all options are open.

[32] See generally Sheate (n 3) for a wider discussion of environmental assessment and accountability.

[33] Article 6(3) refers to timeframes for the public to engage; art 6(4) provides for early and effective participation; and art 6(8) requires that the outcome of the public participation is taken into account in the decision on the plan or programme.

[34] For the gaps in implementing art 7 of the Aarhus Convention in the SEA Directive, see Robert McCracken and Ned Westaway in Ch 1 of this volume.

[35] Commission, 'Guidance on the Implementation of Directive 2001/42/EC on the Assessment of the Effects of Certain Plans and Programmes on the Environment' (2003) (hereinafter 'Implementation Guidance') 36.

Article 7 of the Aarhus Convention goes on to elaborate on the need for a fair and transparent framework for the preparation of plans and programmes relating to the environment, which is further elaborated by *The Aarhus Convention: An Implementation Guide*:

> The reference to a transparent and fair framework emphasizes that the public must have opportunities to participate effectively. To do so the public must be able to use rules that are applied in a clear and consistent fashion, which in turn requires the implementation of a transparent and fair framework. Article 1 helps to clarify the intention behind this provision. Article 1 states that one objective of the Convention is to guarantee rights in respect of public participation in decision-making. For rights to be guaranteed, a transparent and fair framework must be in place, both for decision-making itself and to afford affected members of the public the possibility to uphold the standards of decision-making processes by challenging procedures and decisions.[36]

This last point is fundamental to ensuring accountability—the ability of the public to uphold standards of decision-making by challenging procedures and decisions during the planning and assessment process through participation as well as final recourse to access to justice.[37] Therefore, any attempt at streamlining SEA procedures must not undermine the public's ability to seek accountability of promoters and decision-makers alike through the assessment process, and this should apply at all stages of the decision-making process. Article 6(3) of the Aarhus Convention makes clear that public participation procedures shall include reasonable timeframes for the different phases of decision-making. The *The Aarhus Convention: An Implementation Guide* recognises that tiering may exist and that public participation may occur at different decision levels:

> In complex cases where public participation may take place at several points in the decision-making process, the reference to different phases may also be taken to refer to phases in the overall decision-making process. Thus, Parties must ensure that all stages of the decision-making where public participation takes place include time frames that allow for the effective implementation of the related requirements in article 6, including time for the public to digest the information provided in the notification according to paragraph 2, time to seek additional information from the public authorities identified in the notification, time to examine information available to the public, time to prepare for participation in a hearing or commenting opportunity and time to participate effectively in those proceedings.[38]

In addition, the Office of the Deputy Prime Minister's Guidance on SEA elaborates on what is meant by 'effective' public participation, adding a further useful point about the levels at which participation should take place, by recognising that:

[36] UNECE, *The Aarhus Convention: An Implementation Guide* (2nd edn) 184 (Geneva, UNECE, 2013).

[37] See Sheate (n 3).

[38] UNECE (2013), n 36, 143–44.

> Effective consultation needs appropriate skills, knowledge and experience. The form of consultation and the participation of individuals and organisations will vary depending on the nature and scale of the plan or programme. It is for example often difficult for local representative groups to take a regional perspective, when their work and interests are focused on a particular locality. Similarly, bodies represented at the regional level may not always be familiar with local issues. It is important to ensure that participants are involved at appropriate levels.[39]

The Aarhus Compliance Committee, in a report on a landfill waste case in Lithuania, draws out the relevance of tiering explicitly to delivering early and effective participation:

> The requirement for 'early public participation when all options are open' *should be seen first of all within a concept of tiered decision-making, whereby at each stage of decision-making certain options are discussed and selected with the participation of the public and each consecutive stage of decision-making addresses only the issues within the option already selected at the preceding stage.* Thus, taking into account the particular needs of a given country and the subject matter of the decision-making, each Party has a certain discretion as to which range of options is to be discussed at each stage of the decision-making. Such stages may involve various consecutive strategic decisions under article 7 of the Convention (policies, plans and programmes) and various individual decisions under article 6 of the Convention authorizing the basic parameters and location of a specific activity, its technical design, and finally its technological details related to specific environmental standards. Within each and every such procedure where public participation is required, it should be provided early in the procedure, when all options are open and effective public participation can take place.[40]

Therefore, in order to be both effective and efficient (in terms of resources and costs), a streamlined SEA process needs to recognise the valuable role that effective and targeted public participation can play in informing decision-making. This is because ultimately all decisions in the planning and development context are political, and so the public's opinion will ultimately have a strong degree of resonance with politicians. To ignore that fact, such as by trying to shorten or curtail the time available for public participation, is likely to be counter-productive, not least since an aggrieved public is likely to resort to the only final recourse available: legal challenge. The next section explores some examples where SEA implementation, or non-implementation, has indeed been counter-productive, providing useful practical lessons for designing streamlined SEA practices that are likely to be more effective.

[39] Office of the Deputy Prime Minister, 'A Practical Guide to the Strategic Environmental Assessment Directive' (London, ODPM, 2005) [3.15].

[40] Aarhus Compliance Committee, ACCC/C/2006/16, Report ECE/MP.PP/2008/5/Add.6 re: Lithuania (4 April 2008) [71]. (emphasis added)

Streamlining SEA through Tiering: Limits in UK Practice

This section looks at two different, though related, UK examples where SEA processes were less than optimal. The first example relates to key UK planning documents where there were problems associated with specific projects being prematurely identified in strategic plans, thus subverting the important tiering role of SEA practices and thereby undermining effective public participation and meaningful consideration of alternatives. The second example is a case study, examining more closely the *HS2* case and showing how SEA is undermined when a project effectively determines the associated plan. Over recent years, the UK government has increasingly recognised the value of strategic planning in a number of sectors and the need for some form of SEA alongside that planning process. However, the application of SEA to these national-level policy statements, plans and programmes has not been without controversy. Through the examples analysed, this section argues that the government has missed an important opportunity to deliver both more effective and more streamlined SEA processes, and that this missed opportunity has been primarily because of either a lack of understanding of the real value of SEA or a wilful intention to circumvent SEA by seeking to avoid its influence or to avoid it altogether. Whatever the reason, there is clearly scope for improvement in 'streamlining' SEA in the UK.

The Dangers of Plans Identifying Projects: National Policy and Key Infrastructure

The Planning Act 2008 has already been identified above as a significant piece of national British legislation that sought to speed up the consent process for nationally significant infrastructure and to reduce delays in the planning process and in implementation. The first tranche of NPSs in 2009 (for Energy Infrastructure, Nuclear Power and Ports) adopted an approach similar to that already trialled by the Eco-towns Planning Policy Statement[41] and Eco-towns Programme[42] in

[41] DCLG, 'PPS—Eco-towns—A Supplement to Planning Policy Statement 1', https://www.gov.uk/government/publications/eco-towns-planning-policy-statement-1-supplement.

[42] DCLG 'Eco-towns: Sustainability Appraisal and Habitats Regulations Assessment of the Draft Planning Policy Statement—eco-towns Statement' (2009), http://webarchive.nationalarchives.gov.uk/20120919132719/www.communities.gov.uk/publications/planningandbuilding/ecotownsstatement#.

2008–09, and by the draft National Planning Framework 2 in Scotland in 2008. All these documents exhibited common failings with respect to the SEA Directive, even though the government accepted in these cases that the SEA Directive did at least apply. The primary failing was the inadequate consideration of reasonable alternatives, as required by Article 5(1) of the SEA Directive, and consequently the lack of opportunity for the public to participate in an early and effective manner when all options were open.

The Eco-towns Draft Planning Policy Statement and Programme

The Eco-towns draft Planning Policy Statement (PPS), published for consultation in November 2008, set out what the UK government considered 'the UK's toughest ever green standards for new development', including achieving 'zero carbon' status across all the buildings in a planned eco-town and allocating 40 per cent of the area within the town to be green space.[43] The draft PPS also pledged that individual eco-towns would need to submit planning applications in the same way as any other major development proposal.

SA (incorporating SEA) was applied to the draft Eco-towns PPS and to the Eco-towns Programme, which contained the shortlist of potential eco-town locations in England. An earlier consultation exercise had been undertaken in April 2008 by the DCLG. It had sought views from the public and interested parties on the preliminary shortlist of 15 potential sites to go forward for further study, following an early call from the government for developers to come forward with proposals for possible locations for eco-towns in July 2007. Although the government conducted separate SAs/SEAs for the draft PPS and the Programme,[44] there was still, arguably, a failure to consider 'reasonable alternatives' in the SEA process for both appraisals,[45] as required under Article 5(1) of the SEA Directive. The reality of implementation has been that while the Eco-towns PPS was published in 2009, the Eco-towns Programme had been much reduced to the point that it had largely disappeared from public view—many developers withdrew their support because they felt it did not help their relationships with local communities[46]—even before

[43] 'Draft Planning Policy Statement: Eco-towns—Consultation' (November 2008), http://webarchive.nationalarchives.gov.uk/20120919132719/http://www.communities.gov.uk/archived/publications/planningandbuilding/ppsecotowns.

[44] 'Eco-towns: Sustainability Appraisal and Habitats Regulations Assessment of the Draft Planning Policy Statement' (November 2008) available at http://webarchive.nationalarchives.gov.uk/20120919132719/http://www.communities.gov.uk/publications/planningandbuilding/ppssustainabilityappraisal; 'Eco-towns: Sustainability Appraisal and Habitats Regulations Assessment of the Eco-towns Programme', http://webarchive.nationalarchives.gov.uk/20120919132719/http://www.communities.gov.uk/publications/planningandbuilding/sustainabilityappraisalintro.

[45] William R Sheate, 'Report to BARD Campaign' (2008), https://www.researchgate.net/publication/302441913_%27Review_of_Eco-towns_SA_Reports%27_to_BARD_Campaign_-_Stop_Middle_Quinton_Eco-town.

[46] Sheate (n 3) 97.

the Coalition government eventually scrapped the programme along with top-down housing targets. In practice, the experience of eco-towns planning has thus involved a failed policy process in which SEA was incompletely performed, arguably undermining public acceptance of planned eco-towns. Notably, the government is currently trying to revive the concept of 'new settlements' for housing, which are planned from a strong base of community support.[47]

National Policy Statements

Hot on the heels of eco-towns, in 2009, the UK government published a number of draft NPSs, including for energy and ports. The draft NPSs were each subject to an AoS, which also sought to comply with the SEA Directive. One overarching NPS appraisal was prepared for the energy sector, with four technical annexes. A separate NPS for new nuclear power stations was prepared with a separate appraisal. All of these were produced by the UK's Department of Energy and Climate Change with the appraisals undertaken by a number of consultants. A Ports NPS and its AoS were produced by the Department for Transport, supported by consultants. There were similarities in these processes to the SEA process undertaken for the National Planning Framework 2 (NPF2) in Scotland, considered in the following subsection.[48] In 2011, the Energy NPSs were completely redrafted and new AoSs undertaken and published, following major criticism of earlier versions[49] and re-evaluation by the new Coalition government in 2010. Efforts were then made in the new Energy NPS AoS to at least consider and assess other reasonable alternatives. This was effectively an admission that the first attempt was likely to have been non-compliant with the SEA Directive.

Common criticisms in relation to SEA in these cases included, among other things: the failure to consider and assess reasonable alternatives, the failure to undertake compliant assessment of cumulative and synergistic effects, and the failure to undertake proper early and effective public participation. The Scottish NPF2 illustrates these generic problems particularly well.

[47] See recent government pronouncements on 'locally-led garden cities': Press Release, 'Government Offers Support for Locally-led Garden Cities' (14 April 2014), www.gov.uk/government/news/government-offers-support-for-locally-led-garden-cities. Note that the first such announcement in relation to Ebbsfleet in Kent is largely a re-announcement of development that has been long in the pipeline, but was suspended by the recession of 2007–13.

[48] William R Sheate, Richard Eales and Indre Vaizgelaite, 'Appraisals of Sustainability and the New National Policy Statements: Opportunities and Challenges to Come?' (Final Report to RSPB and WWF by Collingwood Environmental Planning) (RSPB, 2010).

[49] ibid.

National Planning Framework 2 (Scotland)

In 2008, the NPF2 set out the strategy for Scotland's spatial development to 2030. The NPF2 focus was on promoting 'sustainable economic growth' while also having clear environmental objectives. It set out a broad vision for planning in Scotland and created a class of priority NDPs, the inclusion of which in the NPF2 signalled a desire to see those projects delivered. However, the process of arriving at those NDPs appeared far from logical, given that the list started out with only nine projects, and then became a wish list of some 52 projects, before being finalised at 14 projects. As part of the preparation of the NPF2, the Scottish government carried out an SEA.[50] Environmental assessment was particularly important in this planning process, considering the deep conflicts between environmental concerns (such as climate change and biodiversity loss) and the economic imperatives supporting the nominated NDPs. Compliance with the SEA Directive was a challenge in the SEA process, particularly the relationship between the strategy and the NDPs, which resulted in a legal challenge. The main problems were associated with a failure to ensure early and effective public participation when all the options were open, particularly whether the *Edinburgh Gazette*, an official online publication with which most members of the public are unlikely to be very familiar, counted as advertising in the local area. This called into question the lawfulness of the NDP selection process itself and was subject to scrutiny by a judicial review, initially in November 2010,[51] and subsequently appealed to the Supreme Court in 2013,[52] in relation to the proposed Hunterston coal-fired power station and transshipment centre (one of the final 14, but not the original nine NDPs).

Two types or levels of alternatives were considered in the SEA for NPF2, neither of which appeared particularly coherent (or indeed 'reasonable'), given the nature of the strategic action that the SEA was assessing. The first were high-level 'alternatives' representing four thematic scenarios—economic, sustainability, communities and connectivity along with a 'Business as Usual' scenario—each of which represented a selection of policy options. The second level were National Development 'alternatives', representing a number of energy, transport or environmental infrastructure projects. However, as the NPF2 process and SEA unfolded, there appears to have been even less logic to the way in which these projects might have been considered alternatives—could they really have been considered alternatives to each other when they were so disparate?

A fundamental problem illustrated by this approach to alternatives is the gap between 'strategic scenarios' and 'national development projects'—that is, there was no sectoral or programme level of assessment, or assessment of spatial

[50] Scottish Government, 'National Planning Framework 2: Discussion Draft January 2008' (2008) www.scotland.gov.uk/Topics/archive/National-Planning-Policy/npf/NPF2Archive.

[51] *McGinty v Scottish Ministers* [2011] CSOH 163.

[52] *McGinty v Scottish Ministers* [2013] CSIH 78.

alternatives. The NPF2 SEA attempted to do both high-level policy assessment and low-level (but superficial) project assessment simultaneously. It is therefore not surprising that it did not really accomplish either very satisfactorily.[53] The reality here is that the strategic planning process ended up being driven by the desired projects rather than the other way around, constraining the nature of what might be considered to be 'reasonable' alternatives and potentially raising a question as to whether the SEA Directive is being circumvented by such an approach. There were also serious issues of the lack of accountability in the decision-making process when a project is labelled a 'national development' project with no effective assessment of alternatives to that project. By the time that EIA is undertaken on such a project, strategic alternatives to it have already been ruled out by the earlier 'strategic' decision and the public have effectively been excluded from participating in an 'early and effective' manner in that process, arguably contrary to the requirements of both the SEA Directive and the Aarhus Convention. The NPF2 designation of NDPs established the need for a particular development and therefore prevented the introduction of further evidence at a later stage that might otherwise have challenged need. This is particularly because NPF2 (and its successor NPF3) is a material consideration in the planning consent process—even though the plan does not itself authorise the project, it can effectively restrict consideration of locational alternatives at the project EIA stage. The defining character of the NPF2, however, is that it is both a national plan *and* a national programme of local projects. As such, the SEA is seeking to assess the significant effects of both non-spatial national strategic policies and highly spatial projects for which no real assessment of alternatives is provided. This is a confused, rather than a streamlined, SEA process.

In *McGinty v Scottish Ministers*,[54] the NPF2 process was legally challenged, highlighting the confused nature of the SEA process undertaken in relation to the NPF2. The case concerned the selection of Hunterston as a location for a coal-fired power station and transshipment centre, which was identified as an NDP under NPF2. Alternative locations for this project were at no point assessed. The petitioner in the case argued that he had been excluded from participating in the supplementary assessment consultation process when the list of national developments had been extended from nine to 52 (eventually finalised at 14) because he had not been made aware (because of inadequate publicity) that the NPF2 might have had local implications through an NDP at Hunterston, an area he frequented as a keen birdwatcher. The decision to include Hunterston in the final list of 14 national developments was a very significant decision, given that it established a level of priority to its development. The Supreme Court, however, rejected

[53] Richard P Eales and William R Sheate, 'Effectiveness of Policy Level Environmental and Sustainability Assessment: Challenges and Lessons from Recent Practice' (2011) 13 *Journal of Environmental Assessment Policy and Management* 39.

[54] *McGinty v Scottish Ministers* (n 52).

the appeal, finding, inter alia, that advertising in the *Edinburgh Gazette* met the requirements of the Scottish SEA Act 2005 for advertising in a newspaper circulating in the local area and therefore also met the requirements of the SEA Directive (and Article 7 of the Aarhus Convention).[55] This would seem to be a much narrower interpretation than that provided by the Aarhus Compliance Committee in relation to the obligation in Article 6(2) of the Convention to inform the public in an 'adequate, timely and effective manner'.[56]

This inclusion of the NDPs without effective public participation would also seem to run contrary to the requirements of Article 6(4) of the Aarhus Convention for early participation 'when all options are open and effective public participation can take place' and therefore, arguably, contrary to the SEA Directive requirements for early and effective participation under Article 6(2) of the Directive. This would seem, on the face of it, to have the effect of circumventing the very purposes of both the SEA and EIA Directives, which are to ensure that plans, programmes *and* projects are assessed for their likely significant effects before decisions about whether they are adopted or approved are made, and that the public have an early and effective opportunity to express their opinions on the draft plans/proposals and environmental reports before those decisions happen. The relationship between the requirements of the SEA Directive and the requirements of the EIA Directive is a complex one,[57] but the lack of assessment and consultation on alternative options for the candidate NDPs as part of the NPF2 SEA process—and for Hunterston in this particular case—raises genuine concerns of potential non-compliance with the SEA Directive. This is particularly because there was no environmental assessment of alternative locations at the strategic level. This then resulted in members of the public having no opportunity to question the location, or consider alternative locations, at the project EIA level. The opportunity to undertake that EIA-level assessment was prevented by the location and need having been accepted in the NPF2. Overall, this was a case of dysfunctional environmental assessment tiering and an ineffective SEA process.

The latest review of the NPF—NPF3—was finally approved in June 2014 after Scottish government response to Scottish parliamentary scrutiny. Notably, Hunterston is no longer in the final list of 14 national developments; however, a similar approach of designating NDPs still exists for the new NPF3.[58]

[55] Section 16(4) of the Environmental Assessment (Scotland) Act 2005 (known as the SEA Act) requires: 'Publication of a notice under subsection (2)(a) shall be by such means (including publication in at least one newspaper circulating in the area to which the plan or programme relates) as will ensure that the contents of the notice are likely to come to the attention of the public (a) affected by or likely to be affected by; or (b) having an interest in the plan or programme.'

[56] See discussion of this issue in the *The Aarhus Convention: An Implementation Guide* (2nd edn) 135–36 and ACCC/C/2006/16 (Lithuania) (n 48) para 67.

[57] Sheate et al, 'The Relationship between the EIA and SEA Directives' (n 28).

[58] Scottish Government, 'National Planning Framework 3: A Plan for Scotland: Ambition, Opportunity, Place' (2014), www.scotland.gov.uk/Topics/Built-Environment/planning/NPF3-SPP-Review/NPF3.

Piecemeal Is Not Strategic: The Case of HS2

In the case of HS2, again the proposed project ended up defining the preferred plan in the absence of (and undermining the possibility of conducting) an effective SEA. However, in this case, the UK government did not accept the need for conducting an SEA and partly avoided any strategic assessment by breaking the planning of the project up into phases. This case is another highly political case in which SEA processes were undermined, and this was found to be lawful due to a narrow construction of the SEA Directive's requirements.

Planning for HS2 has been under way since January 2009, when High Speed Two Limited (HS2 Ltd) was set up by the previous (Labour) government with the principal aim of advising on the development of proposals for a new railway from London to the West Midlands and potentially beyond. HS2 Ltd's scope included advising on a potential route or routes, indicative costs and benefits, and possible financing, and managing the design of the potential route or routes.[59] HS2 Ltd's report, which was presented to the Secretary of State for Transport at the end of December 2009, concluded that there was a strong case for a new London to Birmingham line and set out a recommended route which left London via Ruislip, crossed the Chilterns in the Aylesbury direction, partly in a tunnel, and approached Birmingham on an alignment between Coventry and Kenilworth.[60]

In March 2010, the UK government published its command paper *High Speed Rail* in which it set out its case for a new 'Y' high-speed rail network to link London to Birmingham, Manchester, the East Midlands, Sheffield and Leeds, with connections onto existing tracks so that direct high-speed train services could be operated from the outset to cities such as Glasgow, Edinburgh, Newcastle and Liverpool.

The command paper stated that 'HS2 Ltd's recommended route for a London-Birmingham high speed line ("High Speed Two"), which would run from a rebuilt Euston station in London to a new Birmingham City Centre station at Curson/Fazeley Street, is viable, subject to further work on reducing specific impacts on the local environment and communities'.[61] Two clear phases of HS2 became apparent: Phase 1, which would span from London to Birmingham; and Phase 2, which would span from Birmingham to Manchester and Leeds. The Command

[59] Letter dated 14 January 2009 from the Department for Transport to High Speed Two Ltd, 'The Role and Funding of High Speed Two Ltd', http://webarchive.nationalarchives.gov.uk/20121107103953/http://www.dft.gov.uk/publications/hs2-remit.

[60] High Speed Two Ltd, 'High Speed Rail: London to West Midlands and Beyond: A Report to Government by High Speed Two Limited' (Department for Transport, 2010), http://webarchive.nationalarchives.gov.uk/+/http:/www.dft.gov.uk/pgr/rail/pi/highspeedrail/hs2ltd/hs2report.

[61] Department for Transport, *High Speed Rail* (Cm 7827, 2010) 8, www.gov.uk/government/uploads/system/uploads/attachment_data/file/228887/7827.pdf.

Paper also set out that the government's proposed consultation, scheduled for the autumn of 2010, would cover three key issues:

— HS2 Ltd's detailed recommendations for a high-speed line from London to the West Midlands;
— the strategic case for high-speed rail in the UK; and
— the government's proposed strategy for an initial core high-speed rail network, the 'Y'-shaped line and beyond (to Scotland).

Following the May 2010 General Election, the new government's Coalition Agreement adopted the Command Paper, stating that it would:

> [E]stablish a high speed rail network as part of our programme of measures to fulfil our joint ambitions for creating a low carbon economy. Our vision is of a truly national high speed rail network for the whole of Britain. Given financial constraints, we will have to achieve this in phases.[62]

The Command Paper therefore represented the policy of the Coalition government in 2010.[63]

In October 2010, the then Secretary of State again announced the government's commitment to HS2 and declared that the government would consult in early 2011 on a strategic high-speed rail network, including:

the government's preferred route for the first leg between London and Birmingham (Phase 1); and
— the government's preferred option for Phase 2 of HS2 north of Birmingham, comprising separate legs from the West Midlands to each of Manchester (to connect to the West Coast Mainline) and Leeds (to connect to the East Coast Mainline).[64]

Following the 2011 consultation process, the government produced a White Paper in January 2012, *High Speed Rail: Investing in Britain's Future—Decisions and Next Steps (DNS)*,[65] that outlined its approach to the planned HS2 project, including its preferred routes for the project. It also provided that the proposals for HS2 would be subject to the hybrid bill procedure—a legislative process by which Parliament adopts legislation by a combination of both public and private bill procedures. It was legally significant in this case that any approval for the HS2 project would thus be granted by way of specific legislative act rather than being considered as a large infrastructure project through the planning system. Accordingly, pursuant to

62 HM Government, *The Coalition: Our Programme for Government* (London, Cabinet Office, 2010) 34.

63 The UK government from 2010 to 2015.

64 Department for Transport Press Release, 'Proposed High Speed Rail Network North of Birmingham Confirmed' (4 October 2010), www.dft.gov.uk/news/press-releases/dft-press-20101004-2.

65 Department for Transport, *High Speed Rail: Investing in Britain's Future—Decisions and Next Steps* (Cm 8247, 2010) 118.

what was then Article 1(4) of the EIA Directive,[66] a full EIA would be undertaken in conjunction with the introduction of the hybrid bill. Even though Article 1(4) seemingly exempted projects adopted by specific acts of national legislation, it did so only on the basis that the objectives of the EIA Directive were already met by the legislative process—if the process did not already meet those objectives, then the exemption could not apply and thus EIA would be required.[67] Consequently, Parliamentary Standing Orders SO 27A and SO 224A were passed, which are supposed to ensure the hybrid bill process meets the objectives of the EIA Directive, including the requirements for public consultation.[68] SO224A also allows for public petitions by those affected against specific elements of the bill and for supplementary environmental information (addenda to the Environmental Statement) to be consulted on as for the Environmental Statement. Parliament as competent authority can request further information as it requires and changes to the route, plans etc would need to be assessed and consulted on, otherwise the government would be likely to be in breach of the Parliamentary Standing Orders. Detailed site surveys on the chosen route would be undertaken for the EIA. The UK government therefore did not consider it appropriate to undertake any further site surveys on the various route options at the AoS stage, which was a more strategic-level assessment, though only in relation to Phase 1 (and separately at a much later stage to Phase 2), but not in relation to the whole HS2 project (or programme as it could be viewed).

Following successive legal challenges, HS2 ended up in the Supreme Court,[69] which found that the SEA Directive did not apply to HS2, in relation to the DNS document in particular. This was principally because the project would be promoted through the hybrid bill procedure. The Supreme Court found that SEA was not required because the DNS document was not a plan required by 'legislative, regulatory or administrative provision' *and* that 'set the framework for development consent' for projects subject to the EIA Directive. This was despite

[66] Council Directive 85/337/EEC of 27 June 1985 on the assessment of the effects of certain public and private projects on the environment [1985] OJ L175/40. See now EIA Directive (n 14) art 1(5), according to which Member States can only exempt a project adopted by a specific legislative act from the Directive's requirements in a more limited manner and, importantly, the objectives of the Directive must still be met.

[67] The argument hinged on the interpretation of the word 'since' in what was then art 1(4): 'This Directive shall not apply to projects the details of which are adopted by a specific act of national legislation, *since* the objectives of this Directive, including that of supplying information, are achieved through the legislative process'. (emphasis added) The CJEU, in a series of judgments (Case C-435/97 [1999] ECR I-5613; Case C-287/98 [2000] ECR I-6917), severely limited the scope of the exemption, referring in particular to the need to ensure that information provision to Parliament was equivalent to that which would occur when an application is submitted to a competent authority in an ordinary consent procedure.

[68] SO 27A makes provision for the deposit of an Environmental Statement and SO 224A makes provision for public consultation on the environmental statement, and for an independent assessor to summarise the consultation responses for Parliament, and for similar consultation on any subsequent supplementary information.

[69] *HS2* (n 31).

the finding in *Inter-Environnement Bruxelles* that 'required' needs to be interpreted broadly, in line with the intentions of the Directive.[70] The Court found that the DNS (even if it were an administrative provision) could not set the framework for Parliament's ultimate decision on whether to proceed with the project because Parliament is sovereign and is not able to be influenced by the DNS decision. Parliament can do as it likes:

> The DNS would have no legal influence on Parliament, which was not obliged to comply with it or even to have regard to it in reaching its decision. Nor was it appropriate or possible for the court to assess the degree of influence the DNS was likely to have as a matter of fact on Parliament's decision-making process.[71]

This reasoning is highly questionable.[72] However, without rehearsing the lengthy legal arguments over whether or not the SEA Directive applied on the particular facts of *HS2*,[73] the Supreme Court's ruling shows that there is a risk that a narrow interpretation of plan or programme can result in major development plans or schemes not made subject to SEA, even though theoretically and logically one would expect them to be.[74] The High Speed Strategy would seem to be just such a scheme. As Lady Hale commented in *HS2*:

> HS2 will be the largest infrastructure project carried out in this country since the development of the railways in the 19th century. Whatever the economic and social benefits it may bring, it will undoubtedly have a major impact upon the environment. There has never been a full environmental assessment of HS2 as against the alternative ways of developing the railway system … One might have thought that it was the object of [the SEA Directive] to ensure that such an assessment took place.[75]

From a theoretical perspective, the logical place to start with environmental assessment in relation to HS2 would be a high-level SEA (with low level of detail) of the proposed strategy and options/alternatives to that strategy. The consultation

[70] Case C-567/10 *Inter-Environnement Bruxelles ASBL etc v Région de Bruxelles-Capitale* (CJEU, 22 March 2012) [29]–[32].

[71] *HS2* (n 31) [31].

[72] The notion that Parliament is sovereign is fine in principle, but that by extension it is not influenced by government or the preceding strategic AoS process (in which Parliament had no role) makes little sense in practice. One has only to have witnessed the 2nd Reading debate on the Phase 1 hybrid bill (*Hansard*, 28 April 2014, coll 557–678), and the subsequent debate on the select committee motion (*Hansard*, 29 April 2014, coll 705–74), to see the extent to which government relied on the previous strategic process, and the absence of any mechanism by which Parliament can challenge the process that led up to the hybrid bill. Parliament is faced with a narrowly defined route, and that is all it can adjudicate over. See *R (HS2 Action Alliance Ltd) v Secretary of State for Transport* [2013] EWCA Civ 920 [173]–[174] (Sullivan LJ).

[73] See the chapters by Simon Ricketts & Juliet Munn (Ch 4), Eloise Scotford (Ch 10) and Valerie Fogleman (Ch 3) of this volume.

[74] See Sheate et al (n 31) 69 ('problems are likely to occur where higher level decisions (e.g. at policy level) that have not been subjected to SEA, have constrained the consideration in SEA of as wide a range of options as possible or have already foreclosed many decisions. This means that only limited options are then available for project development and EIA').

[75] *HS2* (n 31) [130]–[131].

in February 2011 was undertaken on the strategy as a whole—the consultation document sought feedback on the whole strategy, including Phase 1 and Phase 2. But the AoS assessment information provided to the public related *only* to Phase 1. Consequently, the public were provided with an inconsistent level of information on which to comment effectively on the *whole* strategy and all the elements of the strategy. Some communities were severely disadvantaged by having far less information about their areas (such as West Midlands to Leeds/Manchester) than others, and/or it was difficult for the public to assess the overall environmental impact of the whole strategy on the basis of the partial information provided. In the event that the SEA Directive was not applicable (and, indeed, even if it were), the public were provided with only partial information for part of the strategy—they were therefore unable to participate in an 'early and effective manner' in the 2011 consultation process leading to the publication of the DNS document. The fact that the Phase 2 AoS was to be consulted on at a later stage is irrelevant, since this was after the decision on the strategy as a whole had been made, and therefore that consultation would have no opportunity to influence the original strategic decision. Indeed, the Supreme Court, and the Appeal Court and High Court before it, recognised that the AoS for Phase 1, consulted on with the strategy as a whole, would not have met the requirements of the SEA Directive had the SEA Directive applied,[76] because the strategy included Phases 1 and 2, while the AoS covered only Phase 1; moreover, nor did the AoS properly consider reasonable alternatives.[77]

The two HS2 planning stages—Phase 1 and Phase 2—could theoretically be approached in a number of ways, following a high-level SEA of the overall strategy. Plan or programme-level SEAs could have been undertaken for each phase followed by EIA of each phase to coincide with the hybrid bill procedure. However, given the nature of SEA and EIA, there needs to be a decision-making process to which the assessment is tied. In the case of SEA, this is the adoption or approval of a plan/programme—the DNS document was just such a decision-making process for the HS2 strategy as a whole and, indeed, appears to be the only 'decision' made apart from the hybrid bills. There would appear to be no formal decision process to apply an SEA or AoS to the individual phases of the planning process. It may have been expedient to do an AoS for each phase, in light of the way in which the Department for Transport brought forward Phase 1 and Phase 2 incrementally in stages, but there is little logic in undertaking an AoS or SEA only in relation to the separate phases. The Phase 1 AoS may have informed the February 2011 consultation and decision-making process, but, in the absence of a Phase 2 AoS at the same time, it could only ever provide a *partial* assessment. The London to West Midlands section of HS2 (Phase 1)—and the level of detailed work

[76] ibid [133].

[77] See David Elvin in Ch 6 of this volume

undertaken for it—effectively pre-selected the route of the whole of HS2 and the entire high-speed rail strategy without any environmental assessment of reasonable alternatives, such as alternative strategic routes or the upgrading of existing rail infrastructure to meet the objectives of increasing capacity and relieving congestion and of promoting high-speed rail. Moreover, by setting the strategy for Phase 2 but not assessing its impacts, the government, it could be argued, has engaged in 'salami-slicing' (splitting up of elements of a plan or project). This is contrary to the purpose and application of the SEA Directive (had it applied) and the Habitats Directive (where Article 6(3) of the Habitats Directive (as amended)[78] requires an appropriate assessment of the implications for the site's conservation objectives of a plan or project affecting a designated site), since it has failed to assess the environmental impacts of the whole plan prior to approving it. In *Waddenzee*,[79] the Court of Justice of the European Union (CJEU) confirmed that the principles under the EIA Directive apply to the Habitats Directive and, in that context, Commission Guidance has advised against salami-slicing, having regard to *Commission v Ireland*[80] and *Commission v Spain*.[81] The Phase 2 AoS at a later (post-decision) stage would appear to inform no formal decision-making process at all.

Note that there is, however, a consent or decision-making process for EIA for each phase, since each phase is to go through its own hybrid bill process. The separate phases have separate consent processes at the project level and therefore for EIA. This is because the hybrid bill process provides consent only in terms of project construction, not in terms of adoption of a plan. Figure 9.1 summarises this unsatisfactory picture of how environmental assessment was in fact carried out in the HS2 planning and decision-making process.

If we consider what would have been a logical theoretical or practitioner approach to environmental assessment in this case, irrespective of the legal interpretation of SEA requirements, such an approach would have been to undertake a high-level assessment (SEA or AoS) of the overall high-speed strategy. This would have been followed by an EIA for each phase to go alongside each hybrid bill process, if that was the strategy and route that emerged from the consultation and SEA process. This kind of approach is set out in Figure 9.2. As Figure 9.2 indicates, the challenge here is to ensure that cumulative effects are properly addressed in relation to Phase 1 and Phase 2. Phase 1 will establish the route alignment for Phase 1 but also termini, including where Phase 2 will start, and so will have a knock-on effect on Phase 2 and beyond, and also future additions, such as a connection to

[78] Council Directive 92/43/EEC of 21 May 1992 on the conservation of natural habitats and of wild fauna and flora [1992] OJ L206/7.

[79] Case C-127/02 *Landelijke Vereniging tot Behoud van de Waddenzee and Nederlandse Vereniging tot Bescherming van Vogels v Staatssecretaris van Landbouw* [2004] ECR I-7405.

[80] Case C-392/96 *Commission v Ireland* [1999] ECR I-5901.

[81] Case C-227/01 *Commission v Spain* [2004] ECR I-8253. See also Commission, 'Interpretation of Definitions of Certain Project Categories of Annex I and II of the EIA Directive' (2008), http://ec.europa.eu/environment/eia/eia-support.htm.

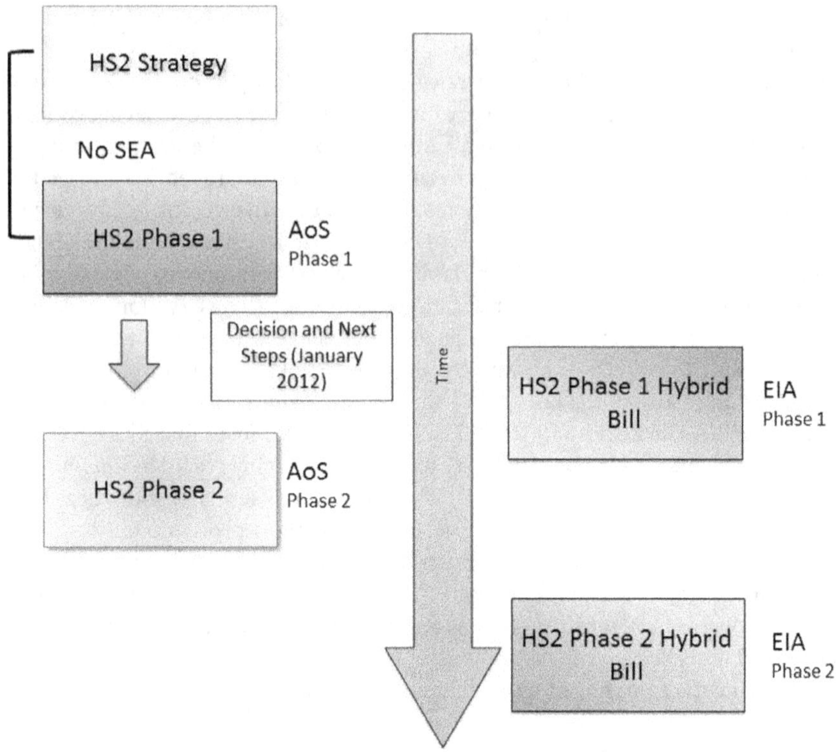

Figure 9.1: The 'SEA' Process that Took Place for HS2 and its Relationship to EIA

HS1 (the high speed link from London to the Channel Tunnel), which was left out of the hybrid bill for Phase 1 at the last minute before second reading. In parallel to both SEA and EIA, Habitats Regulations Assessment (HRA) needs to be undertaken to screen for whether a full appropriate assessment is needed should the conservation status of a European Natura 2000 designated site be adversely affected.[82] A good practice approach would be to provide an intermediate 'overview EIA' for Phases 1 and 2 together, which assesses the whole project, including cumulative effects across the two phases, at an appropriate level of detail, using something like the French system's *appreciation generale* (and that is capable of being updated over time), followed by separate detailed EIAs for each phase. This recognises that the project needs to be assessed as a whole as *un programme de travaux*—that is, as a single project or programme of works, with the detail left to individual phase EIAs.

[82] The Conservation of Habitats and Species Regulations 2010 (SI 2010/490) implement the Habitats Directive and establish the need to undertake HRA screening and appropriate assessment.

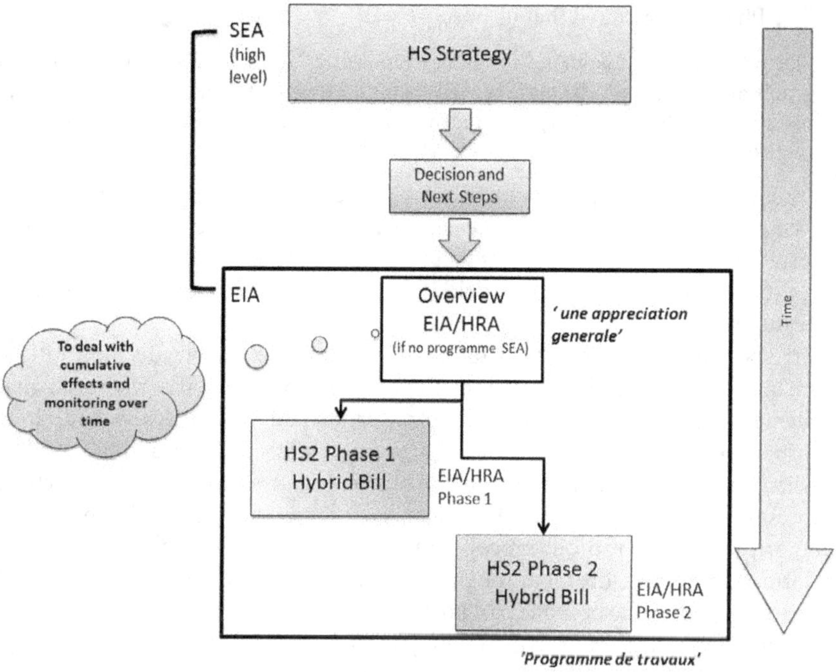

Figure 9.2: A Logical Tiered SEA and EIA Process for HS2

There is therefore little logic in not undertaking an AoS or SEA for the overall HS2 strategy while undertaking incremental AoS/SEAs for Phase 1 and Phase 2, followed by separate EIAs for Phase 1 and Phase 2. This suggests an unfortunate (or maybe wilful) misunderstanding by the Department for Transport of the purpose of environmental assessment and an undue reliance on a *de minimis* approach to SEA. Undertaking an AoS only for each phase meant that the overall strategic decisions about whether a high-speed strategy was appropriate, and where and how that strategy should be implemented, were never assessed for their environmental impact. Economic appraisal may have been undertaken, but no high-level assessment of the environmental impact of strategic alternatives was provided as part of the critical consultation process in February 2011. The assessment was immediately focused down at the programme or project level, at a level of detail that focused on the mitigation of impacts rather than their avoidance, contrary to the mitigation hierarchy,[83] and all principles of good EA practice.

[83] The mitigation hierarchy is widely recognised in both the EIA and SEA Directives through the need to 'avoid, prevent or reduce and, if possible, offset likely significant adverse effects on the environment' (EIA Directive, art 5(1)(c)) and 'prevent, reduce and as fully as possible offset any significant adverse effects' (SEA Directive 2001/42/EC, Annex I(g)). The hierarchy means that all efforts should be directed towards seeking to avoid adverse effects in the first place, and only then to reduce them and finally to remedy or mitigate residual effects.

The Phase 1 AoS stated that its purpose was:

> [T]o provide design guidance to the development of route (and station) options; to enable differentiation to be made between options in terms of their sustainability performance relative to each other; and to identify mitigation that can improve the preferred route option that became the proposed scheme.[84]

Consequently, it did not attempted to assess the likely significant environmental effects of strategic alternatives to the national high-speed strategy as laid out in the consultation document. There was therefore no assessment of 'reasonable alternatives' to the plan as required by Article 5(1) of the SEA Directive and as established by case law.[85]

Irrespective of the rights or wrongs of the Supreme Court's decision in law, Parliament was faced simply with the hybrid bill along with the Environmental Statement submitted at the time of its introduction and which was open for public consultation subject to Parliamentary Standing Orders SO 27A and SO 224A.[86] Parliament had no role in the strategic planning and AoS (non-SEA Directive) process prior to the hybrid bill. As Parliament is sovereign—and as the competent authority in the hybrid bill process—then in principle, it could have requested information on measures that sought to avoid, reduce or remedy environmental impacts as part of the bespoke parliamentary EIA process (maybe not completely different alternative routes, but certainly modifications to the route and design standard should be within the remit of the principle of the bill).[87] However, while Parliament could have required HS2 to provide information Parliament felt necessary to allow it to properly evaluate and scrutinise the hybrid bill proposals, the principles of the bill were promoted by the government and only allowed for petitions and amendments in relation to the broad route alignment proposed in the bill. Of course, Parliament could have rejected the bill outright, but that takes no cognisance of how Parliament works in practice.[88] In effect,[89] the

[84] Nick Geilser, 'HS2 London to the West Midlands Appraisal of Sustainability Appendix 1—The Appraisal Process: A Report for HS2 Ltd' (Booze-Temple, 2011) [8.1.2].

[85] eg, *Save Historic Newmarket v Forest Heath District Council* [2011] EWHC 606 (Admin); *City and District Council of St Albans and Hertfordshire County Council v Secretary of State for Communities and Local Government* [2009] EWHC 1280 (Admin).

[86] UK Parliament (n 68).

[87] For example, Parliament could have asked about an assessment of modifications to the route that sought to avoid rather than mitigate/compensate for habitat loss, such as a slower speed route (similar to HS1 speed) that might allow some wildlife sites and ancient woodland to be avoided by adjustment and realignment, particularly given the justification by HS2 Ltd and the Department for Transport that HS2 is no longer principally about speed and more about capacity. There was no assessment of such modifications in the environmental assessment.

[88] The author was Specialist Adviser in the inquiry relating to the House of Commons Environmental Audit Committee, *HS2 and the Environment* (13th Report, London, The Stationery Office, 2014).

[89] It will be interesting to see the outcome of the ongoing HS2 challenge before the Aarhus Compliance Committee discussed by Richard Macrory and Gregory Jones in Ch 17 of this volume.

proponent—the Department for Transport in this case—was able to set the rules by which the competent authority (Parliament) makes its decision. The strategic process undertaken prior to the Phase 1 hybrid bill inevitably shaped the way in which the final route would be approved, whatever the Supreme Court may say. Moreover, Parliament had had no role whatsoever in the preceding strategic process and so had no opportunity to influence that process[90] or to put Phase 1 in a wider context. In short, the parliamentary EIA process was no substitute for the deficient SEA earlier in the HS2 planning process. By the time Parliament came to consider the matter, strategic options and considerations were effectively foreclosed. The piecemeal, hybrid bill parliamentary processes employed by the government effectively subverted the principles of effective SEA and environmental assessment more generally.

Conclusion

Sometimes more is less. In the case of SEA, we should not assume that doing fewer SEAs, or trying to combine multiple-level assessments into one SEA, will necessarily streamline and simplify the assessment process. In some cases it may do the opposite, particularly if it leads to failures to assess certain elements properly, such as alternative options or cumulative effects (and therefore risks of legal challenge), or to prevent the public from being able to engage in an early and effective way when they can genuinely influence the decision-making process. A much better understanding of the purpose of SEA—and particularly of tiering of environmental assessment—is needed among authorities and within government if we are to deliver genuinely streamlined SEA that also helps to promote effective SEA. Stakeholders themselves often demand streamlining because of the demands consultation processes make upon them. More focused and relevant consultation processes through properly tiered SEA could also encourage better participation.

The point of tiering—undertaking the appropriate level of assessment at the appropriate level of decision-making—is to avoid duplication while ensuring that options and alternatives are properly considered, along with their environmental effects, at a point where a decision can still be influenced. This is a critical element of the Aarhus Convention and the reason why public participation should be early and effective. Irrespective of whether the SEA Directive applies, the Aarhus Convention provides an important baseline standard for determining whether the process was transparent and fair, and an early and effective mechanism for ensuring accountability of environmental decision-making.

90 House of Commons Environmental Audit Committee (n 88) [83].

From a theoretical perspective and as a matter of good SEA practice, if not from a legal perspective, there could be a useful role for voluntary SEA, inasmuch as a commitment to undertake genuine SEA, even when it is not legally required, might offer the opportunity to address the problems seen where the SEA Directive is deemed legally not to apply, but when logically it should. While, for HS2, the government did undertake a form of voluntary SEA—AoS—it did so in an illogical way. It was in too much of a hurry to get to a decision on route alignment, rather than willing to spend a little more time on getting the overall strategy right in the first place and establishing wider consensus on the role that high-speed rail should play in the nation's transport policy. Had it done so, we may have ended up with a very different HS strategy, one which might have not included the current proposed route alignments, which could have been less controversial overall and which ultimately might have taken less time to deliver both consent and implementation for a high-speed network. But we shall never know.

10

SEA and the Control of Government Environmental Policy

ELOISE SCOTFORD

Introduction

Directive 2001/42/EC on the assessment of the effects of certain plans and programmes on the environment[1] is a novel kind of legal instrument. In broad terms, it extends the well-established concept of environmental assessment by applying it to certain government plans and programmes, and it reconfigures its requirements, making them more demanding in some respects.[2] However, as European legislative debates around the precise formulation of the SEA Directive reveal, it is politically contentious.[3] This is because it does not merely extend the application of an existing environmental regulatory tool, it also makes inroads into the inner workings of national governments in areas that are arguably beyond the competence of the EU institutions. It makes a move that is controversial not only in terms of EU competence,[4] but also for its potential constitutional implications in Member State legal orders. This latter point was made plain in the decision of the UK Supreme Court in *R (HS2 Action Alliance Ltd) v Secretary of State for Transport and Another*,[5] in which the Court was at pains to discern and decide how the application of the SEA Directive did not (and could not) impede parliamentary sovereignty in the UK.[6] This chapter reflects on this controversial legal picture in

[1] Parliament and Council Directive 2001/42/EC on the assessment of the effects of certain plans and programmes on the environment [2001] OJ L197/30 (hereinafter the 'SEA Directive').

[2] Particularly by requiring rigorous assessment of alternative options to a proposed plan or programme: SEA Directive, art 5(1) (although see below n 84).

[3] See Robert McCracken and Ned Westaway in Ch 1 of this volume.

[4] Thus, for example, it modifies processes for formulating plans for land use, infrastructure policy and water management: SEA Directive, art 3(2) and 3(4).

[5] *R (HS2 Action Alliance Ltd) v Secretary of State for Transport and Another* [2014] UKSC 3 ('*HS2*').

[6] See eg ibid [38]–[39] (Lord Carnwath). Notably the Court was even more exercised over the constitutional issues raised by the prospect of reviewing parliamentary processes for their compatibility with the EIA Directive (Parliament and Council Directive 2011/92/EU on the assessment of the effects of certain public and private projects on the environment [2012] OJ L26/1 at the time, see n 84). See Denis Edwards, 'HS2—The First Spike' (2014) 26(2) *Journal of Environmental Law* 319.

UK law in two ways. First, it considers how the Directive is in fact unremarkable in environmental law—the next section examines how the Directive is one of many ways in which environmental law constitutes and limits policy relating to environmental matters. However, it does present an interesting example of how this phenomenon occurs, and the third section of the chapter considers how the extent of the SEA Directive's constitutive and limiting impact on policy is determined by its judicial interpretation. Second, the chapter reflects on the public law significance of the SEA Directive, examining the extent to which it challenges or informs public law concepts and debates. More than the Directive's controversial potential to control parliamentary decision-making, the fourth section of the chapter argues that a particularly notable public law dimension of the Directive concerns its limiting of governmental and executive power.

Environmental Law and Policy

Environmental law, as a subject, provides a legal context in which questions, and arguably answers, about the nature of law are different. It is not a single body of doctrine, supervised primarily by courts and characterised (solely) by bipolar disputes between individuals or even by criminal prosecutions brought by the state. It is a much messier legal context. This is particularly because environmental law concerns a wide body of regulation and administrative activity that governs environmental problems.[7] Much environmental law is thus concerned with regulatory strategy—some of which is *sui generis* and even 'non-legal'[8]—and with the constitution of public administration.[9] Within this regulatory domain, *policy* has a pervasive role in informing administrative decision-making and in constituting environmental regimes. As a significant feature of administrative decision-making, policy is also controlled by law, so that it is itself legally constituted in significant ways. The SEA Directive is a prominent example of generating this latter effect.

What Is Environmental Policy?

In general, environmental policy is not a monolithic concept. At its broadest, 'environmental policy' refers to a course of action adopted to secure, or that tends to

[7] Thus, most environmental law claims that go to court in the UK are public law disputes that challenge administrative discretion and decision-making.

[8] Elizabeth Fisher et al, 'Maturity and Methodology: Starting a Debate about Environmental Law Scholarship' (2009) 21(2) *Journal of Environmental Law* 213, 225.

[9] Elizabeth Fisher, *Risk Regulation and Administrative Constitutionalism* (Oxford, Hart Publishing, 2007).

secure, a state of affairs in relation to environmental matters that is conceived to be desirable.[10] However, this jurisprudential definition does not begin to suggest the full array of policy at work or otherwise implicated in environmental law.[11] 'Policy' in environmental law comes in all shapes and sizes—including ministerial statements and central government policy papers that set the overarching direction of environmental and planning regulation, local development plans required under planning statutes, regulator-generated guidance for industry concerning their compliance with environmental regulation, technical reference documents on best industrial practice generated at the EU level, and statutory guidance required by particular regimes (such as land contamination) to fill in the detail of their operation. All these different forms of 'policy' need to be viewed in their own terms in order to identify and appraise their legal roles and effects.

The Legal Effects and Legal Constraint of Environmental Policy

As indicated above, there are two broad ways in which different kinds of policy are relevant or implicated in environmental law. First, some policy has legal effects.[12] These legal effects might be prescribed by the statutory framework that empowers the formulation of a relevant policy,[13] they might arise as a matter of administrative law doctrine,[14] or they might arise simply because, in practice, policy instruments contain important regulatory and technical details that dictate how an environmental regime in fact works. Thus, policy instruments can act as a primary source of legal obligations for those who are subject to a relevant regime,[15] and they can also control acts of administrative decision-making to which they relate as a matter of public law. In the latter sense, government is regularly held to account for failing to comply with its own policy.[16] Similarly, policy documents are fundamental to the legal operation of the English planning regime, since a range of policies (including the National Planning Policy Framework (NPPF), National Infrastructure Statements and Local Development Plans) must be taken into account in planning decisions as they are relevant.[17] Even evolving planning policy

[10] Adapting the definition in Neil MacCormick, *Legal Reasoning and Legal Theory* (Oxford, Clarendon Press, 1994) 261.

[11] *Bushell v Secretary of State for the Environment* [1981] AC 75, 98.

[12] See further Elizabeth Fisher, Bettina Lange and Eloise Scotford, *Environmental Law: Text, Cases and Materials* (Oxford, Oxford University Press, 2013) Ch 11.

[13] eg, Waste (England and Wales) Regulations 2011, SI 2011/988, reg 15(2).

[14] *Tesco Stores Ltd v Dundee City Council* [2012] UKSC 13.

[15] eg, BAT Reference documents under the EU integrated pollution prevention and control regime (see http://eippcb.jrc.ec.europa.eu/reference; Directive 2010/75/EU on industrial emissions (integrated pollution prevention and control) [2010] OJ L334/17, art 14(3)).

[16] eg *R (Manchester Ship Canal) v Environment Agency* [2012] EWHC 1643 (QB).

[17] Town and Country Planning Act 1990, s 70(2); Planning and Compulsory Purchase Act 2004 (PCPA), s 38(6).

can be found to have legal effects on decision-making in the planning regime.[18] And whilst policies are not treated as being as legally binding as statutes,[19] much depends on the nature of the policy in determining its legal effects—including who issued the policy document,[20] how well considered was its formulation[21] and whether the policy leaves room for judgment.[22] Overall, environmental policy instruments have a range of legal effects, the precise nature of which can involve a close exercise in legal analysis that takes into account the statutory and decision-making context, as well as the nature of the relevant policy itself.

Second, rather than having legal effects (or as well as having such effects), some policy is constituted or constrained by law. Thus, when policy is created under a statutory regime, it will be legally constructed by the terms of the legislation that empowers its creation.[23] Such policy will be susceptible to challenge by way of judicial review if it does not conform to the relevantly applicable statutory framework on the grounds of illegality or the failure to take into account relevant considerations.[24] Beyond this, legal constraints on *high-level strategic policy* of government on environmental issues are of particular note. However, it is a basic constitutional principle, central to administrative law, that evaluating the merits of high-level policy is beyond the proper scope of judicial review and that its review on grounds of legality should be very limited.[25] In the environmental sphere, high-level policy is subject to legal constraints in at least three ways.

First, in some cases, the courts have undertaken intensive judicial review in relation to high-level government policy. By applying judicial review principles broadly and purposively in some cases, courts have extended 'legality' review to cover the substance of policy decisions made by government, where these have

[18] *Cala Homes (South) Ltd v Secretary of State for Communities and Local Government* [2011] EWCA Civ 639.

[19] *Tesco Stores* (n 14) [19]. See also *R v Derbyshire County Council ex p Woods* [1998] Env LR 277, 288–89, 290–92 (recognising that policies are different from statutes when it comes to their legal interpretation).

[20] ibid.

[21] *Manchester Ship Canal* (n 16) [93] and generally.

[22] *Tesco Stores* (n 14) [18]. See further Eloise Scotford and Jonathan Robinson, 'UK Environmental Legislation and its Administration in 2013—Achievements, Challenges and Prospects' (2013) 25(3) *Journal of Environmental Law* 383, 397–99.

[23] eg s 78YA of the Environmental Protection Act 1990—in relation to contaminated land regime statutory guidance—indicates not only what should be included in the guidance in terms of content (detailed provisions on defining and identifying contaminated land, and identifying the appropriate persons responsible for remediation), but also the procedure for formulating the guidance, including consultation requirements and parliamentary approval. Aspects of policy may also be constructed by other, related pieces of legislation: eg Conservation of Habitats and Species Regulations 2010, SI 2010/490, regs 39, 102, 103, 106.

[24] Such a challenge might also be made in relation to policy otherwise shaped by a statutory regime: *Dimmock v Secretary of State for Education* [2007] EWHC 2288 (Admin).

[25] *R v Secretary of State for the Environment ex p Hammersmith and Fulham London Borough Council* [1991] UKHL 3, 12.

an environmental dimension.[26] Second, administrative law doctrine may require that environmental policy is to be developed in a certain way. Thus, full public consultation will be legally required when the government has promised this.[27] Third, some high-level policy is also subject to statutory requirements and constraint, particularly when made under highly prescriptive legislation such as the Climate Change Act 2008[28] or under provisions implementing EU environmental legislation. In this third sense, there is a range of EU law constraints on high-level UK government policy relating to the environment, which both require and shape the substance of particular strategic environmental policies,[29] and which require environmental assessments in relation to some policies when they are likely to have significant environmental effects, as in the case of the SEA Directive. It is this latter kind of constitutive impact or 'constraint' with which this chapter is directly concerned, but, as seen here, it is part of a larger legal picture relating to environmental policy. In combination, these various constraints render a significant body of government policy subject to legal obligation and scrutiny, although the precise impact of any legal oversight should not be presumed. If any of the legal requirements outlined above are enforced in court, much will depend on the intensity of any judicial review undertaken in determining whether government decision-makers have met these legal obligations in creating or applying a particular environmental policy.

In sum, UK environmental law relies on policy to do all sorts of things that a UK lawyer, particularly a constitutional lawyer or theorist, might initially baulk at.[30] By acting as an effective source of legal obligation in some cases and coming under review by the courts even when made at a high strategic level, environmental policy challenges the influential Dworkinian view that policy and law are properly separate concepts.[31] This is not a legal domain where matters of policy—even

[26] *R v Secretary of State for Foreign Affairs ex p The World Development Movement* [1995] 1 All ER 611. See AH Hammond, 'Judicial Review: The Continuing Interplay between Law and Policy' [1998] *Public Law* 34.

[27] *R (Greenpeace) v Secretary of State for Trade and Industry* [2007] EWHC 311. It might also be argued that the public should be fully consulted in relation to the formulation of any strategic UK environmental policy since art 7 of the Aarhus Convention, to which the UK is a signatory, requires this: ibid [49]; *cf HS2* (n 5) [52] (Lord Carnwath concluding that the Aarhus Convention was not directly helpful in interpreting the public participation requirements of the SEA Directive).

[28] See ss 4–10 of the Climate Change Act 2008 in relation to government carbon budgets.

[29] eg river basin management plans required under Council and Parliament Directive 2000/60/EC establishing a framework for Community action in the field of water policy [2000] OJ L327/1, art 13; action programmes required under Council Directive 91/676/EEC concerning the protection of waters against pollution caused by nitrates from agricultural sources [1991] OJ L375/1, art 5; and waste management and prevention programmes required under Council and Parliament Directive 2008/98/EC on waste and repealing certain Directives [2008] OJ L312/3 (Waste Framework Directive), arts 28 and 29. Also note the binding effect of the waste hierarchy in the Waste Framework Directive (art 4) on UK waste policy.

[30] Environmental law is not necessarily special in this respect. See eg, the complex role of policy in immigration law: eg, *R (Pankina) v Secretary of State for the Home Department* [2010] 3 WLR 1526.

[31] Ronald Dworkin, *Taking Rights Seriously* (rev ed, London, Duckworth, 1978) 22–28, 84–85.

understood in the more limited, elevated sense of 'high-level strategic policy'—are left purely to the discretion of government or Parliament. However, this state of affairs is not a simple legal picture or a descriptive fait accompli. As indicated above, the precise legal effects of, and limits to, environmental policy are variable—they depend on the particular type of environmental policy and the particular legal control mechanism or issue at stake. Furthermore, there are important public law questions to be asked about whether this legal picture presents an acceptable state of affairs. The following sections consider these two issues in the context of the SEA Directive: examining the actual legal limits imposed by the Directive in relation to the environmental policy of government and considering their public law implications.

The Mechanism of the SEA Directive in Constituting and Limiting Environmental Policy

In determining the legal impact of the SEA Directive in relation to environmental policy, the first thing to note is that the Directive is not a wholesale programme for subjecting all 'strategic' environmental policy to environmental assessment;[32] it is a more limited and precise legal mechanism. In particular, it requires environmental assessment (meeting the requirements of Articles 4 and 5 of the Directive) to be undertaken for public 'plans or programmes'[33] that:

— are *required* by legislative, regulatory or administrative provisions;[34]
— are *likely to have significant environmental effects*;[35] and
— *set the framework* for future development consent of projects.[36]

In particular, the SEA Directive requires an assessment of all plans and programmes that relate to agriculture, forestry, fisheries, energy, industry, transport, waste management, water management, telecommunications, tourism, town and country planning and land use, where such plans 'set the framework' for approving projects listed in Annexes I or II of the Environmental Assessment Directive.[37] An assessment under the SEA Directive is also required for plans or

[32] As Lord Carnwath and Lady Hale point out in *HS2*, the word 'strategic' does not actually appear in the text of the Directive, although it is commonly used to describe it in shorthand: *HS2* (n 5) [35], [131].

[33] ie plans and programmes 'which are subject to preparation and/or adoption by an authority at national, regional or local level or which are prepared by an authority for adoption, through a legislative procedure by Parliament or Government': SEA Directive, art 2(a).

[34] ibid.

[35] ibid, art 3(1).

[36] ibid, art 3(2) and (4).

[37] ibid, art 3(2)(a), subject to the exception in art 3(3), ie, cases where a plan or programme determines the use of small areas at a local level or involves minor modifications to the plans and

programmes determined to require an assessment under Article 6 or 7 of Directive 92/43/EEC,[38] whether or not they 'set the framework' for future consent decisions.[39] Otherwise, Member States need to determine whether a relevant plan or programme that sets the framework for future development consent decisions is likely to have significant environmental effects on a case-by-case basis and/or by specifying certain types of plans and programmes.[40] Two categories of government policy are excluded from the scope of the SEA Directive: plans or programmes solely aimed to serve national defence or civil emergency; and financial or budget plans and programmes.[41] Beyond this, identifying what kinds of government policy are in fact caught by the Directive involves a delicate exercise in interpretation of the Directive.[42] This section undertakes this interpretive exercise in order to get an accurate picture of what governmental policy falls within the scope of the Directive, before considering the overall effect of the Directive in constituting and constraining such government policy.

What Kinds of Government Policy Fall Within the Directive?

In determining the extent to which government policy is subject to the SEA Directive, there are two main points of statutory interpretation to consider. First, when is a plan or programme 'required by legislative, regulatory or administrative provisions'? The more broadly this phrase is defined, the more government policy will be covered. To date, the interpretation of this phrase by courts has been ambiguous and not finally resolved, at least in the UK courts. Second, similar challenges of interpretation arise in determining what kinds of plans and programmes 'set the framework' for future consent decisions, which again affect the scope of the Directive. This requirement is not just ambiguous, it also raises difficult questions about the timing of the Directive's application. Furthermore, at least in UK law, the identity of the future consent decision-maker—in particular, whether they are a Member of Parliament or part of the executive—has a significant impact on whether a relevant 'plan or programme' will be subject to the Directive's assessment obligations.

programmes included in art 3(2), unless a Member State determines they are likely to have significant environmental effects.

[38] Council Directive 92/43/EEC on the conservation of natural habitats and of wild fauna and flora [1992] OJ L206/7 (hereinafter 'the Habitats Directive').

[39] SEA Directive, art 3(2)(b), subject to the same art 3(3) exception.

[40] ibid, art 3(4).

[41] ibid, art 3(8).

[42] This is not an easy exercise, as several of the chapters in this volume highlight. See in particular the chapters by Stephen Ashworth and Rachael Herbert (Ch 5), David Elvin (Ch 6), Valerie Fogelman (Ch 3) and Simon Ricketts and Juliet Munn (Ch 4).

'Required by Legislative, Regulatory or Administrative Provisions'

Advocate General Kokott in *Terre Wallonne* indicated that the requirement in Article 2(a) that a plan or programme be 'required by legislative, regulatory or administrative provisions' meant that 'freely taken political decisions on legislative proposals are not therefore subject to the obligation to carry out assessments'.[43] If her position is correct, then policies that are adopted on the sole initiative of the legislature (or one assumes on the initiative of the executive, whether or not in legislative form) would be immune from the requirements of the SEA Directive. However, even in this scenario, many plans and programmes would be caught by the Directive, at least in the English and UK context, since many policy documents are required by legislative provisions. Thus, for example, Part IIA of the Environmental Protection Act 1990, establishing the contaminated land regime, operates on the basis that statutory guidance is issued in accordance with the requirements of section 78YA. More comprehensively, the Planning and Compulsory Purchase Act 2004 requires a suite of planning policy documents to be drawn up by local planning authorities as their 'local development scheme'.[44] Another example, in which legislation requires the development of more cross-cutting policy that is likely to have significant environmental effects, is the obligation on the government to set carbon budgets under the Climate Change Act 2008.[45] This latter example shows how the 'required by' limit of the SEA Directive does not exempt highly political and strategic government policy from the scope of the Directive, even on a strict interpretation of the term, considering the extensive statutory construction of policy in the UK.

Beyond these straightforward cases, there are other kinds of government policy that are likely to have significant effects on the environment, but that are not strictly 'required by' legislative measures. It is debatable whether these fall within the scope of the SEA Directive. For instance, what of policy documents likely to have significant effects on the environment, which are empowered, rather than required, by legislation (such as ministerial guidance on the application of the waste hierarchy and waste collection requirements under the Waste (England and Wales) Regulations 2011)?[46] Or similar policy documents that are regulated but not required by legislation (such as National Policy Statements for 'specified descriptions of development' that may be designated by a minister under the Planning Act 2008)?[47] Or that are required by *other* policy documents (such as 'Travel Plans' under the National Planning Policy Framework)?[48] On one view, all

[43] Case C-567/10 *Inter-Environnement Bruxelles ASBL v Gouvernement de la Région de Bruxelles-Capitale*, Opinion of AG Kokott [2013] ECLI:EU:C:2013:219, para 41.

[44] PCPA, s 15. See also Regulatory Enforcement and Sanctions Act 2008, ss 63–65.

[45] Climate Change Act 2008, s 4(1)(a).

[46] SI 2011/988, reg 15(2).

[47] Planning Act 2008, s 5.

[48] Department of Communities and Local Government, *National Planning Policy Framework* (2012) [36].

these kinds of policy instruments fall without the SEA Directive since they are not strictly 'required' by legislative, regulatory or administrative provisions.[49] However, the picture is not that clear-cut, in light of Court of Justice of the European Union (CJEU) case law. Recognising that other such policy documents might still have significant effects on the environment, the CJEU in *Inter-Environnement Bruxelles* rejected 'a mere literal interpretation of [the] provision' in Article 2(a). In line with the Directive's objective to provide for a high level of environmental protection, the Court held that:

> [P]lans and programmes whose adoption is *regulated* by national legislative or regulatory provisions [or presumably administrative provisions], *which determine the competent authorities for adopting them and the procedure for preparing them*, must be regarded as 'required' within the meaning [of Article 2(a)].[50] (emphasis added)

This expansive approach to the meaning of 'required' reflects the purposive interpretation of many environmental provisions by the CJEU[51] and it considerably widens the scope for government policy potentially to fall within the scope of the SEA Directive. In *HS2*, Lady Hale indicated the possible breadth of the CJEU's formulation above, in that 'administrative provisions' regulating the procedure for preparing plans or programmes could include the government's Consultation Principles,[52] which apply to all forms of Whitehall policy-making. This leaves out of account the CJEU's requirement that the provisions should also 'determine the competent authorities for adopting' relevant plans and programmes, but such a provision would certainly cover forms of government policy that government actors are *empowered* by statute or policy to make (such as the waste guidance or National Policy Statements mentioned above). All that would seem to fall outside this definition is UK government policy that is generated on the initiative of government, in relation to which there are no administrative, regulatory or legislative provisions indicating who should adopt the relevant policy (albeit that there do exist administrative provisions relating to the process of its formulation). However, as Lord Carnwath pointed out in *HS2*, we have no definitive understanding of 'administrative provisions',[53] which at its widest could mean all principles of public law, including constitutional conventions concerning the power of government to introduce policy and propose legislation. Such a broad understanding would bring *all* government policy within the scope of the Directive, at least to the extent it is 'regulated' by 'legislative, regulatory or administrative provisions'.

[49] This is the view of Lords Mance and Neuberger in *HS2* (n 5).

[50] Case C-567/10 *Inter-Environnement Bruxelles* [2013] ECLI:EU:C:2013:510, para 31.

[51] eg Joined Cases C-418/97 and C-419/97 *Arco Chemie Nederland Ltd v Minister Van Volkshuisvesting* [2000] ECR I-4475; Case C-371/98 *R v Secretary of State for the Environment, Transport and the Regions; ex p First Corporate Shipping Ltd* [2000] ECR I-9235; Case C-127/02 *Landelijke Vereniging tot Behoud van de Waddenzee v Staatssecretaris van Landbouw, Natuurbeheer en Visserij* [2004] ECR I-7405.

[52] UK Cabinet Office, 'Consultation Principles: Guidance' (2013), formerly the Government's 'Code of Practice on Consultation' (2008).

[53] *HS2* (n 5) [21].

Rather than tackling this interpretive issue directly, the Supreme Court in *HS2* avoided deciding it, in light of its finding that the government policy document at issue in that case did not relevantly 'set the framework' for future consent of projects. However, the *HS2* litigation did provide diametrically opposed views on the issue. The majority in the Court of Appeal suggested that if a plan or programme 'set the framework' for future consent decisions, it was difficult to say that it was not 'required by administrative provisions'.[54] It is challenging to see the logic in this position, but it has the potential to strip the requirement in Article 2(a) of all meaning, which is quite the opposite of what it was intended to do (as highlighted by AG Kokott's point above).[55] At the other end of the spectrum, Lords Neuberger and Mance were strongly of the view that the CJEU had clearly got this issue wrong in *Inter-Environnement Bruxelles*: 'in the interests of a more complete regulation of environmental developments, [the Court has given the legislative provision] a meaning which the European legislature clearly did not intend'.[56] Their Lordships would like to see a fresh reference to the CJEU on the matter.[57] Whichever way future interpretation of this provision goes, it will have an impact on the scope of government policy included in the Directive and on the extent to which executive policy-making processes are subject to the requirements of the Directive.

Setting the Framework for Future Development Consent

Like the provision that a plan or programme must be 'required by legislative, regulatory or administrative provisions', the requirement that a plan or programme 'set the framework' for future development consent of projects[58] has proved to be an interpretive challenge. Competing judicial interpretations of 'setting the framework' have included: 'being determinative' of future development consents, 'setting criteria' for their determination, or being more loosely 'influential' in the determination of such consents. In this way, the Court of Appeal in *HS2* saw there being a 'spectrum' of 'influence' of relevant plans and programmes, which could be caught by the SEA Directive, including potent factual influence as well as legal influence.[59] In the Supreme Court, Lord Carnwath saw the matter more narrowly, finding

[54] *R (HS2 Action Alliance Ltd) v Secretary of State for Transport* [2013] EWCA Civ 920 [71].

[55] Lords Neuberger and Mance point out the 'striking' legislative history of the SEA Directive that led to this wording, including the rejection of a Commission proposal that had no provision for plans and programmes to be 'required by' law, and also a revised proposal which qualified that such plans or programmes must be '*provided* for in legislation or based on regulatory or administrative provisions': *HS2* (n 5) [178]. (emphasis added)

[56] ibid [189].

[57] ibid.

[58] This is a requirement for all applications of the SEA Directive except where an assessment is required under the Habitats Directive, as set out above: see nn 37–40 and accompanying text.

[59] *R (HS2 Action Alliance Ltd)* (n 54) [54]. Note Lord Carnwath's approval of counsel's argument that the Court of Appeal's 'influencing' test should be qualified so that the influence 'must be such as to *constrain* subsequent consideration, and to prevent appropriate account from being taken of *all the environmental effects* which might otherwise be relevant': *HS2* (n 5) [40]. (emphasis added)

that a plan or programme should set 'limits on the scope of things that can be considered' in a future development consent decision in order to 'set the framework' for such a decision.[60] He saw this interpretation of EU law as being 'acte clair', driven by the core purpose of the Directive:

> One is looking for something which does not simply define the project, or describe its merits, but which *sets the criteria* by which it is to be determined by the authority responsible for approving it. The purpose is to ensure that the decision on development consent is not *constrained* by earlier plans which have not themselves been assessed for likely significant environmental effects.[61] (emphasis added)

However, even on this narrower view, with which all members of the Supreme Court essentially agreed, this includes a wide range of strategic government policy. This is because, in English administrative law terms, 'setting the criteria' that bind future decision-makers translates legally into setting material considerations that a future decision-maker must take into account where relevant (or not take into account where irrelevant). Considering the extent to which policy documents have legal effects in administrative law terms, as discussed in the previous section, this means that a wide range of policy documents could still be seen to 'set a framework' for future development consent. As Lord Sumption recognised in *HS2*, there are many different kinds of environmental policy with different kinds of legal effects:

> The legal effect of these general policies may be weaker or stronger. In some cases development consent must be given or refused in accordance with the policy subject to limited exceptions, while in others the obligation of the planning authority is only to have regard to or take account of it.[62]

This recognises and confirms two aspects of environmental policy discussed in the previous section: the terms of the SEA Directive recognise that policy documents concerning the environment have legal effects (so that they 'set the framework' for future decisions), but these effects can vary depending on the nature of the policy instrument at issue.

The wide impact of this interpretation of the 'setting the framework' requirement can be seen by way of example. On Lord Carnwath's reasoning, at least the following would come within the scope of the SEA Directive in relevantly setting the framework for future development consent decisions: planning policy documents of all types (local development schemes, the NPPF, National Policy Statements and the like) in relation to planning decisions,[63] waste and water management plans in relation to any related infrastructure planning consent or environmental permit, and potentially any government policy that is considered to

[60] *HS2* (n 5) [49].
[61] ibid [36].
[62] ibid [121].
[63] *Inter-Environnement Bruxelles* (n 50) confirms this.

be a material consideration in administrative law terms for making a consent decision. It is notable that land use and town planning policies, in particular, are seen to be the 'paradigm' case falling within the Directive's scope.[64] Even in this case, the impact of the Directive's application is significant. This is because planning policies, even if quite formalised in the English planning system, are highly politicised documents that concern issues in relation to which Member States are reluctant to cede competence.[65] The Directive's oversight of their formulation represents a significant inroad into domestic policy-making and control over land use by EU measures. This has significant political and legal consequences as it seems to shift the balance of policy-making power between the EU and its Member States.

However, there are two relevant limits to the scope of the SEA Directive introduced by the 'setting the framework' requirement, at least in the UK governmental context and particularly in relation to highly strategic government policy. The first limit concerns *who* the subsequent decision-maker for development consent is and the second concerns the *timing* of the policy document that is suggested to set the framework. Lord Carnwath's reason for finding that the *Decision and Next Steps* document at issue in *HS2* (the 'DNS', which committed the government to its proposed HS2 strategy and set out a procedure for protecting its planned route and empowering its approval)[66] did not set the framework for the decision to approve the final HS2 project was that the DNS was more like a planning application, since it contained extensive information about the options for the proposal and its merits, but crucially did not constrain the ultimate decision-maker who would have to approve the scheme.[67] It set the terms of the debate, but it did not set the framework for the final decision by constraining it. This was particularly so because *Parliament* was the ultimate decision-maker in relation to the HS2 scheme. As the majority highlighted in the Court of Appeal: 'Parliament is constitutionally sovereign and free to accept or reject statements of Government policy as it sees fit, and the court should not seek to second-guess what Parliament will do.'[68] Lord Carnwath agreed: 'Formally, and in reality, Parliament is autonomous, and not bound by any "criteria" contained in previous government statements.'[69] This indicates that the constitutional supremacy and independence of Parliament was critical in determining whether or not the DNS 'set the framework' in the *HS2*

[64] *R (HS2 Action Alliance Ltd)* (n 54) [170].

[65] Treaty on the Functioning of the European Union, art 192(2)(b).

[66] UK Government, *High Speed Rail: Investing in Britain's Future—Decisions and Next Steps* (Cm 8247, 2012).

[67] *HS2* (n 5) [37].

[68] *R (HS2 Action Alliance Ltd)* (n 54) [56]. See also *R (Buckinghamshire County Council, HS2 Action Alliance and Others) v Secretary of State for Transport* [2013] EWHC 481 (Admin) [95] (Ouseley J).

[69] *HS2* (n 5) [39]; *cf* Sullivan LJ in dissent in the Court of Appeal, who found there was no clear distinction between the government's role as promoter of the scheme and its role in the parliamentary decision-making process. The government has a dual role: 'Parliament is constitutionally distinct from the executive, but members of the Government are members of Parliament': *R (HS2 Action Alliance Ltd)* (n 54) [173].

case. This finding sets a bright-line limit to the application of the SEA Directive in relation to policies and related consent decisions that are so 'controversial and politically sensitive' that they are ultimately decided by Parliament.[70]

However, Parliament as subsequent decision-maker is the easy case for determining whether the SEA Directive applies, when put in such constitutional terms. What about when the subsequent decision-maker is a planning minister or a local government planning authority or other administrator/regulator? Presumably, in that case, a policy statement such as the DNS could have set the framework for a future consent decision, rendering the SEA Directive applicable. Sullivan LJ made this point in the Court of Appeal, which counsel for the government had accepted.[71] For the HS2 project, development consent for such a nationally significant project could have been sought through the development consent procedure for nationally significant infrastructure projects under the Planning Act 2008 or by an order for a scheme of national significance under the Transport and Works Act 1992. Either way, the DNS would have 'set the framework' in that it would have been a material consideration that the decision-maker would have been obliged to take into account when considering ultimately whether to approve the scheme by either route.

The second limit (or complexity) that arises from the SEA Directive's 'setting the framework' requirement relates to timing, particularly in relation to multi-stage decision-making processes for project consent, which come after a long gestation period in background policy development. The Directive is designed to apply and intervene in this kind of process before the final consent decision, if 'major effects on the environment [are] *predetermined* by earlier planning measures'.[72] (emphasis added) But the exact moment at which it will apply can be difficult to pinpoint. In a complex and multi-stage policy and decision-making process, it might be hard to discern at what point in a series of government White Papers, other Command Papers, Ministerial Statements and National Policy Statements there is a certain document that constrains a final decision as to whether a particular sewage treatment plant, a bridge, a power plant, an airport or a train line will go ahead. The stories of airports and nuclear policy over the last decade or so certainly suggest that final project outcomes are not always obvious or predetermined by strategic governmental decision-making processes, even when there may be administrative law constraints in relation to how those kinds of governmental policy should evolve.[73] Outside the more structured strategic planning documents mandated by statute, such as National Policy Statements under the Planning Act 2008, it will not always be obvious (and will no doubt depend on the facts) whether the government

[70] *R (HS2 Action Alliance Ltd)* (n 54) [56].

[71] ibid [151].

[72] *HS2* (n 5) [35].

[73] eg *Greenpeace* (n 27). See also *R (London Borough of Hillingdon) v Secretary of State for Transport* [2010] EWHC 626 (Admin).

has effectively constrained future consent decision-making through issuing a policy statement. This is a challenging position for the government when devising high-level policies relating to national infrastructure and land use planning, in relation to which there are multiple, often conflicting socio-political considerations, where policy positions can change through debate and discussion, and for which the government believes it (or Parliament) has ultimate decision-making power.[74]

It is an even more challenging position for the courts, in a constitutional sense, in considering when to intervene in such complex policy and decision-making processes. This difficulty is highlighted by the fact that the courts are uncomfortable in intervening to test the legality of strategic decision-making processes that are ongoing and politically sensitive.[75] The likelihood of this kind of intervention is somewhat minimised by Lord Carnwath's finding that mere influence on final decision-making, even in the form of potent arguments put forward for a particular proposal, is not enough for a government policy to fall within the SEA regime.[76] However, as set out above,[77] the Directive's 'setting the framework' requirement seems to depend, in English law at least, on the extent to which policy documents and statements are legally material and relevant considerations in relation to final consent decisions (rather than on whether they predetermine the environmental impacts of a final project, for instance). As set out in the previous section, English law has increasingly recognised the legal effects of environmental policy instruments in administrative law terms, although the extent of their legal relevance varies depending on who issued the relevant policy, how well considered it was and so on. However, on its current judicial interpretation, the SEA Directive does not seem to recognise that certain plans or programmes may 'set the framework' to different degrees—it seems that any legal effect will do.[78] For multi-stage policy and decision-making processes, this suggests that the precise point at which the SEA Directive might bite in such a process can be unpredictable and might not reflect the point at which key environmental impacts of a project are most fully constrained and predetermined. A problematic scenario thus arises in that if the government seeks to gives some assurance of the direction of travel for a particular strategic project, for example, concerning a major road network, an airport or a planned rail link, it becomes more likely that the Directive might apply to require assessment of the planned project when the government is of the view that its shape and conditions are not yet set but are still open to discussion

[74] And the government might need flexibility not to predetermine the final result politically, particularly if there is a change of government.

[75] See *Hillingdon* (n 73); *HS2* (n 5) (particularly in relation to the EIA challenge at this stage of the process of considering and finalising the parameters of the HS2 project: see Lord Reed [93]–[97]).

[76] *HS2* (n 5) [41]: 'A test based on the potency of the influence could have the paradoxical result that the stronger the case made in favour of a proposal, the greater the need for strategic assessment.'

[77] See nn 60–64 and accompanying text.

[78] *cf HS2* (n 5) [121] (Lord Sumption).

and change through policy development. Legal challenges at such points might be unhelpful in the ongoing process of debate relating to a future project and they might fail to pursue the central purpose of the Directive, which is to ensure that environmental impacts are assessed when they are actually decided 'upstream' in a decision-making process.[79]

How the Directive Constitutes and Constrains Government Policy

The discussion so far shows that the SEA Directive potentially applies in relation to a wide range of government policy documents. If that is the case, it then constitutes and constrains that policy and related political decision-making in a number of ways. As the previous section highlighted, these are not unusual impacts in environmental law. First, the Directive constitutes policy by prescribing part of the process for its formulation—a prescribed environmental assessment needs to be carried out during the preparation of the relevant plan or programme,[80] which requires the preparation of an environmental report:

> [I]n which the likely significant effects on the environment of implementing the plan or programme, and reasonable alternatives taking into account the objectives and the geographical scope of the plan or programme, are identified, described and evaluated.[81]

The report, along with the draft plan or programme, must then be made available to certain authorities and the public for comment.[82] The outcome of that consultation and the report itself must then be taken into consideration in the adoption of the final plan or programme, thus constraining its final formulation.[83]

In one sense, these requirements simply add to the process of policy-making. They do not directly prescribe the substantive outcome of an SEA process as it feeds into the design of a plan or programme. However, as the *HS2* litigation showed, conducting an SEA can add time, which can be politically and financially costly or significant. Furthermore, it requires a deeper fleshing out of 'reasonable alternatives'.[84] Article 5 of the SEA Directive requires that reasonable alternatives are identified and evaluated in an SEA environmental report, which must then be taken into account in finalising the relevant plan or programme.[85] This raises the possibility of irrational decision-making—that is, decision-making that is open to legal challenge—if the government pursues a plan or programme where

[79] ibid [155] (Lord Carnwath). See also Elizabeth Fisher in Ch 8 of this volume.

[80] SEA Directive, art 4(1).

[81] ibid, art 5(1).

[82] ibid, art 6.

[83] ibid, art 8.

[84] ibid, art 5(1); *cf* the requirement to consider alternatives under the EIA Directive at the time of the *HS2* litigation: Parliament and Council Directive 2011/92/EU on the assessment of the effects of certain public and private projects on the environment [2012] OJ L26/1, art 5(3)(d). Note that the EIA Directive has since been made more demanding in this respect: see now art 5(1)(d) after Directive 2014/52/EU [2014] OJ L124/1.

[85] ibid, art 8.

there exist other 'reasonable' alternatives (taking into account the objectives and the geographical scope of the relevant plan or programme)[86] that are less environmentally damaging. This apparently procedural requirement to consider alternatives can thus act as a substantive constraint on the formulation of strategic government policy, affecting a plan or programme's final shape.[87] This is the main reason why the appellants in the *HS2* litigation were so concerned to have the project subject to strategic environmental assessment, so that reasonable alternatives to the proposed HS2 rail route would have to be considered and, if found to be feasible and less environmentally harmful, ideally adopted.

The extent of this substantive constraint on policy-making may not be quite so significant in light of the Supreme Court's apparent acceptance that the alternatives required to be considered by an SEA environmental report would need to achieve the same end as the proposed plan or programme (in the case of *HS2*, constructing a new high-speed rail network over the designated area of the UK).[88] In this respect, much depends on how the 'end' of a plan or programme is defined and who has the authority to identify that goal. However, overall, the SEA process does, in a real way, limit and constrain how a government can introduce and decide on policy matters that come within the scope of the SEA Directive.

Public Law Implications and Reflections

So why does all this matter? In one sense, the mechanism of the SEA Directive is a novel and interesting legal development, which is a tricky legal puzzle to get to grips with. It's good business for environmental lawyers to have knotty legal instruments like this to figure out. However, for the English lawyer more generally, the Directive has notable implications, particularly in public law terms. This final section sets out three ways (and there are no doubt more) in which the Directive is remarkable as a matter of public law, indicating how the potential scope of the Directive challenges principles or informs debates in English public law. These relate to the role of law in controlling executive power, the constitutional

[86] ibid.

[87] This hybrid procedural/substantive character is not confined to SEA. There are also different ways of framing the understanding of EIA, which for example, can be seen as a process that can embody a range of different environmental values and politics rather than simply being an instrumental procedure. See Fisher, Lange and Scotford (n 12) 847–53.

[88] *HS2* (n 5) [47]–[48] (Lord Carnwath accepting the view of Ouseley J below, unchallenged in the Supreme Court); *cf* Habitats Directive (n 38) art 6(4), where 'alternative solutions' is interpreted by the Commission to include doing nothing if the impact on protected sites or species is particularly significant, as well as considering 'alternative locations or routes, different scales or designs of development, or alternative processes': Commission, 'Guidance Document on Article 6(4) of the "Habitats Directive" 92/43/EEC' (2007/2012) 6.

and institutional competence of the courts, and the impact of EU law on the public law of the UK.

First, the most startling aspect of the Directive is the fact that its very premise is to make inroads into the policy-making function of government. It is not surprising that it was a controversial measure to pass in the EU legislature. And while the Directive does not apply in relation to *all* government plans and programmes that will have major environmental effects (although there was some judicial dismay in *HS2* that it does not do so),[89] the analysis in the previous section shows that it has an extensive reach, particularly in an era of highly structured and open policy-making at Whitehall. This legal intrusion into executive policy-making is constitutionally remarkable, an implication which was masked (or avoided) in the *HS2* litigation due to the ultimate decision-maker in that case being Parliament. Whilst, in one sense, there is nothing contentious about ministers or executive actors being subject to legislative constraint (in this case the Environmental Assessment of Plans and Programmes Regulations 2004),[90] it is the nature of this legislative constraint implementing the SEA Directive that is constitutionally significant, in that it limits the power of government to set policy. In doing so, it defines and partly resets the balance of UK executive power. In 1998, Eric Barendt described the powers of the executive, within the constitutional settlement of the UK, as follows:

> The executive is not only the most powerful, but it is the most difficult of the three branches of government to explain. In the first place, it is hard to describe exactly what are executive *functions*. They are much more varied than legislative and judicial functions. The choice of Prime Minister, the formation of governments, the dissolution of Parliament, the making of treaties, and the conduct of war all involve executive decisions. The *preparation of general economic and social policy*, as well as its detailed administration, are equally executive functions.[91] (emphasis added)

Other scholars have similarly highlighted the wide-ranging powers of the executive. In 1964, Birch argued that the UK had in fact shifted from a Westminster (parliamentary) form of government to a Whitehall form of government.[92] More recently, Diana Woodhouse has emphasised the scope of policy-making power

[89] *HS2* (n 5) [134] (Lady Hale). See also Sullivan LJ in the Court of Appeal, who concluded: 'the "High Speed Rail Strategy" set out in the DNS is a prime candidate for an SEA if the objectives of the Directive, to provide for a high level of protection for the environment, and to ensure that certain plans and programmes which are "likely to have significant effects" on the environment are subject to an SEA, are not to be frustrated. The Respondent was not able to identify any current UK project which is likely to have more significant effects on the environment': *R (HS2 Action Alliance Ltd)* (n 54) [164].

[90] SI 2004/1633. This is the rule of law: see Albert Venn Dicey, *Introduction to the Study of the Law of the Constitution*, 10th edn (London, MacMillan & Co, 1959) 327.

[91] Eric Barendt, *An Introduction to Constitutional Law* (Oxford, Oxford University Press, 1998) 107–08.

[92] AH Birch, *Representative and Responsible Government: An Essay on the British Constitution* (Toronto, University of Toronto Press, 1964).

that now exists beyond the reach of ministerial responsibility to Parliament.[93] However, the SEA Directive moves in the reverse direction, curtailing the policy-making freedom of the executive and subjecting it to legal constraint. Thus, even where the government or a particular minister is not acting under statutory mandate in proposing and developing a policy, as it has the power to do, the SEA Directive may well apply to construct and limit the process of government in *developing* that policy rather than in simply applying it.[94] If it was already difficult to explain the functions of the executive,[95] the SEA Directive seems to have made matters more complicated and to have reduced to some extent the powers of one branch of government in the UK.[96]

This impact is highlighted by the extent to which the SEA Directive, and judicial oversight of it, can be construed to apply in advance of the final formulation of governmental policy that has any environmental impact and dimension (which covers quite a lot of policy areas). The whole point of the Directive is to prevent predetermined decisions that will have significant effects on the environment, but, in achieving that aim, the Directive has scope to intervene in politically sensitive processes. As seen in the previous section, this gives rise to some legal complexities about the timing at which such intervention should take place, particularly since not all policies will pre-empt or constrain ultimate project consent decisions, but the Directive certainly provides a lever for judicial intervention in policy-making processes to test their legality at a developmental stage. This kind of legal impact is not something that public lawyers have spent a lot of time thinking about. The extensive theorising that has gone into thinking about public law in the courts has mainly concerned judicial review challenges in relation to discrete administrative decisions,[97] rather than being concerned with legally testing the path of governmental policy formulation and decision-making as it goes along, including considering its substantive formulation. If nothing else, the Directive, and its potential for triggering judicial review claims, opens up new ground for public lawyers in thinking about the nature of judicial review and administrative law.

However, this also leads to the second key public law issue that the SEA Directive challenges: the constitutional and institutional competence of the courts. Any normative statement as to the proper constitutional role of the courts requires a

[93] Diana Woodhouse, 'Ministerial Responsibility' in Vernon Bogdanor (ed), *The British Constitution in the Twentieth Century* (Oxford, Oxford University Press, 2003).

[94] See the second section of the chapter for how the latter already happens in environmental law.

[95] See the related complexity in analysing the concept of ministerial responsibility: Woodhouse (n 93).

[96] *cf* Lords Neuberger and Mance on the EIA Directive: 'Nothing in the Directive suggests that it is aimed at excluding either political involvement or reasoning based on political policy decisions from planning decisions. On the contrary, the recognition that projects may legitimately be approved by specific legislative act constitutes express recognition of the legitimacy of such factors': *HS2* (n 5) [209].

[97] See eg Jeffrey Jowell, 'Of Vires and Vacuums: The Constitutional Context of Judicial Review' in Christopher Forsyth (ed), *Judicial Review and the Constitution* (Oxford, Hart Publishing, 2000).

particular theoretical approach to be taken to the UK state, which then informs the appropriate balance of power between the courts, Parliament and the executive.[98] To the extent that a defensible constitutional model of the UK state provides that the courts have no constitutional competence in expressing views on social or economic issues, or on any matters of 'policy',[99] the role of the courts in reviewing government plans or programmes may appear problematic. However, one may argue that there is nothing improper with the courts enforcing the requirements of the Environmental Assessment of Plans and Programmes Regulations 2004—their legislative imprimatur can properly be upheld by the courts by way of judicial review. As Dicey pointed out: '[Executive p]owers, however extraordinary, which are conferred or sanctioned by statute, are never really unlimited, for they are confined by the words of the Act itself and, what is more, by the interpretation put upon the statute by the judges.'[100] However, the more broadly the requirements of the Directive are interpreted (how far 'administrative' provisions are construed and what the full extent of measures are that might 'set the framework' for future consent decisions), the more that the courts may be involved in resetting policy-making. If not expressing a view on policy matters, they may well be involved in discounting the significance of the executive's views and function, which does seem like a shift in their constitutional role, arguably beyond the limits of their constitutional competence.

Whichever model of the state, and of the rule of law, sets that constitutional frame, it is more straightforward to argue that the SEA Directive redefines the 'institutional competence' of the courts.[101] Simply put, in reviewing the lawful formulation of a plan or programme under the Directive, the courts will be able to test and check one aspect of substantive input into plans and programmes—that concerning their environmental effects—where those plans and programmes have multiple social aspects and involve polycentric decision-making processes. In this way, the institutional competence of the courts is being both widened (by widening the scope of what constitute reviewable 'legal' issues) and reoriented (towards the consideration of substantive environmental issues).

The third public law issue—more a debate—which is informed by the SEA Directive concerns the impact of EU law on English and UK public law. If the above two impacts are indeed being felt on the English constitutional landscape—the increased legal control of executive power and a reframing of the constitutional

[98] Carol Harlow and Richard Rawlings, *Law and Administration*, 3rd edn (Cambridge, Cambridge University Press, 2009) 1. The existence of different normative models can also lead to a 'somewhat disconnected heap of [intellectual] activities' in theorising about UK constitutional law: Geoffrey Marshall, 'The Constitution: Theory and Interpretation' in Vernon Bogdanor (ed), *The British Constitution in the Twentieth Century* (Oxford, Oxford University Press, 2003).

[99] *R (Hammersmith & Fulham London Borough Council) v Secretary of State for the Environment* [1991] AC 521; Jowell (n 97) 330; *cf* Timothy Endicott, *Administrative Law*, 3rd edn (Oxford, Oxford University Press, 2015) ch 7.

[100] Dicey (n 90) 413.

[101] See Jowell (n 97) 330.

(and institutional) competence of the courts—then that means that EU law, through the SEA Directive, is impacting on the constitutional architecture of English law. The difficult UK public law cases that have dealt with the clash of EU and UK constitutional orders to date have focused primarily on threats posed by EU legislative measures to the supremacy of Parliament.[102] The impact of the SEA Directive examined in this chapter shows that there are other aspects of the UK constitutional order—in particular the nature and role of the executive—which are susceptible to change by the implementation of EU law. The lawfulness, or at least the constitutional understanding, of this influence is yet to be fully worked out.[103] Yet again, environmental law challenges us to think about public law concepts in a different light and to reframe our legal analysis accordingly.

Conclusion

The recognition of the important role of policy in environmental law is not surprising for the environmental law scholar or practitioner, but it is one that raises quite fundamental questions about the nature of law in relation to environmental problems and that might be more surprising (or at least interesting) to a constitutional lawyer. Environmental law is not merely an applied law subject; it reflects new insights about other legal areas and even shapes them. This chapter has shown that this is particularly the case in relation to the SEA Directive. This might not seem obvious from a first glance at the Directive and its purpose, as Lady Hale states in *HS2*:

> [T]he aim of the Directive is not to ensure that all development proposals which will have major environmental effects are preceded by a strategic environmental assessment; rather, it is to ensure that future development consent for projects is not constrained by decisions which have been taken 'upstream' without such assessment, thus pre-empting the environmental assessment to be made at project level.[104]

However, a closer examination of the Directive, and its potential scope in constituting, limiting and in some cases requiring judicial review of government policy, shows that its impact on issues of English public law can be significant. This raises questions about the proper roles of the executive and the courts, and the constitutional impact of EU law in the UK legal order. In short, this chapter argues that environmental law offers a different and challenging legal perspective for thinking about fundamental questions of public law.

[102] *R (Factortame Ltd and Others) v Secretary of State for Transport* [1990] UKHL 13; *Thoburn v Sunderland City Council* [2002] EWHC 195 (Admin).

[103] *cf* the constitutional issues raised in *HS2* in relation to the EIA Directive: see *HS2* (n 5) (Lord Reed in particular); and Edwards (n 6).

[104] *HS2* (n 5) [155].

Part III

SEA Beyond Town and Country Planning

11

SEA of Non-Town and Country Planning Plans or Programmes

GREGORY JONES QC AND DAVID GRAHAM

> The 'holy grail' is a situation where SEA is more closely integrated into the planning process ... to the point where there is no longer a differentiation between SEA and planning, where sustainability issues are effectively considered and where SEA ultimately leads to political change.[1]

Introduction

The town and country planning regime is the regulatory regime most naturally associated with strategic environmental assessment (SEA). However, the SEA Directive[2] is intended to catch a wide variety of 'plans and programmes' and not just those related to town and country planning. Indeed, the broad philosophy underlying the SEA process logically applies across all spheres of policy-making and planning. This chapter examines the scope of the SEA Directive in respect of its application to other types of plans and programmes not directed related to town and country planning. The chapter focuses particularly on the transport and water resources management sectors, although the relationship between the SEA Directive and the Water Framework Directive[3] is addressed in greater detail by William Howath in Chapter 12 of this volume.

[1] Monica Fundingsland Tetlow and Marie Hanusch, 'Strategic Environmental Assessment—The State of the Art' (2012) 30(1) *Impact Assessment and Project Appraisal* 15, 17.

[2] Directive 2001/42/EC of the European Parliament and of the Council of 27 June 2001 on the assessment of the effects of certain plans and programmes on the environment.

[3] Directive 2000/60/EC of the European Parliament and of the Council of 23 October 2000 establishing a framework for Community action in the field of water policy.

Sectors Caught

The starting point for ascertaining the identity of the various sectors covered by the SEA Directive is the text of Article 3 of the Directive, and Article 3(2) in particular, which, subject to exclusion of minor matters,[4] requires that an environmental assessment be carried out for all plans and programmes 'which are prepared for agriculture, forestry, fisheries, energy, industry, transport, waste management, water management, telecommunications, tourism, town and country planning or land use and which set the framework for future development consent of projects listed in Annexes I and II to Directive 85/337/EEC [hereinafter "the EIA Directive"]; or which, in view of the likely effect on sites, have been determined to require an assessment pursuant to Article 6 or 7 of Directive 92/43/EEC [hereinafter "the Habitats Directive"]'. The reference to the consent framework for Environmental Impact Assessment (EIA) projects means that it also is necessary to read Article 3 alongside the EIA Directive, Article 1(2)(a) of which defines 'project' to mean 'the execution of construction works or of other installations or schemes, [or] other interventions in the natural surroundings and landscape including those involving the extraction of mineral resources'. However, only the types of plans or programmes which are EU funded or require adoption in the terms of Article 2 of the SEA Directive are caught. It should be noted that sectoral plans for what might be called 'social infrastructure'—schools and universities, hospitals and clinics, prisons, museums, libraries and so on—are not included within Article 3(2). Those sorts of developments would, if they feature at all, fall within 'urban development projects' for the purposes of the EIA Directive. It may be fair to assume that ordinarily these activities tend to have less potential to cause ecological harm than some more extensive uses of land, but they can include significant projects nonetheless. Such plans and programmes will in any case be caught by Article 3(4) to the extent that they are thought likely to have significant effects, and so need to be considered as potentially subject to SEA.

Plans or Programmes Requiring Assessment under the Habitats Directive

The inclusion in Article 3(2) of the SEA Directive of the plan or programmes requiring appropriate assessment (AA) under the Habitats Directive[5] might be thought an oddity because even where an AA may subsequently prove that there is unlikely to be any adverse effect on the integrity of a protected site, the Member

[4] Plans or programmes relating to small areas of land at a local level and minor modifications of existing plans as set out in art 3(3).

[5] See generally G Jones (ed), *The Habitats Directive: A Developer's Obstacle Course?* (Oxford, Hart Publishing, 2012) and, in particular, Chs 9 and 10.

State is, on the face of it, required to consider and assess alternatives anyway under the SEA Directive. A criticism may thus be made that it is disproportionate to require an assessment of alternatives on habitat-related grounds before the Habitats Directive assessment process has been undergone. Nonetheless, there is, in fact, some logic in assessing strategic alternatives before embarking upon an AA of a particular plan. The AA might be extremely resource-intensive and if it concluded that there *was* harm to the protected site, this might then leave the public authority without having worked out whether there were less damaging alternative solutions that would have been acceptable in relation to protected habitats and species, and hence unable to properly consider the derogation tests. Furthermore, the criticism may also be met by the inbuilt flexibility in Article 5 of the SEA Directive, which allows the scope and detail of the actual assessment to depend upon the objectives of the plan, the 'stage in the decision-making process and the extent to which certain matters are more appropriately assessed at different levels in that process'.[6]

What is a Plan or Programme Setting the Framework for Development Consent?

The ambit of the term 'plans or programmes', beyond general land use plans for town and country planning, was considered in the Lithuanian case of *Genovaitė Valčiukienė*.[7] The defendant district council had approved detailed plans for two intensive pig-rearing complexes, each with a capacity for 4,000 pigs and a reservoir capable of holding 10,000 litres of slurry, in the spring of 2006. The basis for the claimant's challenge was that no SEA had been carried out. Under Lithuanian law, a plan that covered a small area of land and related to only one economic sector was exempt from SEA. The Fourth Chamber of the European Court of Justice (ECJ) held that the Lithuanian law was contrary to the SEA Directive by exempting, a priori, plans for single economic sectors, without reference to the environmental impacts of the plans. The Court also stated:

> [P]lans such as those at issue in the main proceedings … in practical terms … set … the framework for the implementation of projects listed in … Directive 85/337.

[6] In *Ashdown Economic Development LLP v Secretary of State for Communities and Local Government, Wealden District Council and South Downs National Park Authority* [2014] EWHC 406 (Admin) [90]–[91], Sales J considered that 'the necessary choices to be made are deeply enmeshed with issues of planning judgment, use of limited resources and the maintenance of a balance between the objective of putting a plan in place with reasonable speed … and the objective of gathering relevant evidence and giving careful and informed consideration to the issues to be determined. The effect of this is that the planning authority has a substantial area of discretion as to the extent of the inquiries which need to be carried out to identify the reasonable alternatives which should then be examined in greater detail'. The judgment was reversed on appeal ([2015] EWCA Civ 681), but on other grounds.

[7] Case C-295/10 *Genovaitė Valčiukienė and Others v Pakruojo rajono savivaldybe and Others* [2011] ECR I-08819.

It is significant that the ECJ found that detailed plans about just two specific facilities within a local district in Lithuania were plans that 'set … the framework for the implementation of projects'. The judgment indicates that so long as a plan has an impact on 'major projects', it is to be treated as potentially within the scope of the Directive.[8]

There are, we can postulate, two principal categories of plan that will 'set the framework for future development consent' of such projects. The first is the sort of 'plan or programme' that generates demand for, or removes restrictions on, projects of a particular kind, while not going so far as to specify where the works are needed. This will include, for instance: a political choice to favour the extraction of a particular natural resource; a particular means of transport; a particular type of activity which requires its own facilities; a type of agricultural crop; or generation of energy in a particular way. These plans and programmes may end up having a determining influence on spatial development and the projects that follow them. The second type of sectoral plan that would be caught is one that does have a degree of spatial specificity and where what is at issue is the choice of broad locations for future projects, even though the need for, or desirability of, those projects is not at issue. This is where one encounters a degree of overlap with 'town and country planning'. Categories of plan would include routeing plans for infrastructure such as energy transmission lines or highways, decisions to defend areas of land from flooding, and the locations for facilities.

Influence

Commission v UK[9] concerned whether non-binding statutory development plans required assessment under the Habitats Directive, and the European Court of Justice ruled that they did because they were required to be taken into account and could have great influence on development decisions so as to significantly affect the environment.[10] It might be objected that the Habitats Directive refers in the same breath to 'plans and projects' as requiring 'appropriate assessment', whereas the SEA Directive refers to plans and programmes, but not to projects. However, the same principles had also clearly underpinned the reasoning of Advocate General Kokott in the earlier *Terre Wallonne* case, which specifically concerned the SEA Directive.[11]

[8] ibid [38] and [42]. The Court did recognise (at [45]–[48]) that the plans at issue were potentially capable of falling within the scope of art 3(3), whereby plans which determine the use of small areas at local level require SEA only where the Member States 'determine that they are likely to have significant environmental effects'.

[9] Case C-6/04, *Commission v UK* [2005] ECR I-09017.

[10] ibid [51]–[56].

[11] Joined Cases C-105/09 and C-110/09, *Terre Wallonne ASBL and Inter-Environnement Wallonie ASBL v Région Wallonne* [2010] ECR I-05611; [2011] Env LR D8.

In *Terre Wallonne*, a Belgian court asked whether SEA was required for a legislative order comprising an action programme established under Article 5 of the Nitrates Directive[12] to protect water quality in 'vulnerable zones'.

Advocate General Kokott referred to the objective of the SEA Directive, which was 'to provide for a high level of protection of the environment and to contribute to the integration of environmental considerations into the preparation and adoption of plans and programmes', and stated that her approach was therefore to 'ensure that measures likely to have significant effects on the environment undergo an environmental assessment'. She noted:

> The application of the EIA Directive revealed that, at the time of the assessment of projects, major effects on the environment are already established on the basis of earlier planning measures ... It is therefore appropriate for such effects on the environment to be examined at the time of preparatory measures and taken into account in that context. An abstract routing plan, for example, may stipulate that a road is to be built in a certain corridor. The question whether alternatives outside that corridor would have less impact on the environment is therefore possibly not assessed when development consent is subsequently granted for a specific road-construction project. For this reason, it should be considered, even as the corridor is being specified, what effects the restriction of the route will have on the environment and whether alternatives should be included.[13]

She went on to state:

> Area-related plans may specify with varying degrees of accuracy where the implementation of certain projects is permissible. But measures which stipulate how projects are to be implemented may similarly have significant effects on the environment. Thus a (fictitious) set of rules permitting the discharge of untreated manure from intensive livestock installations directly into natural waters would have significant effects on the environment. Significant effects on the environment can therefore be taken fully into account only if they are assessed in the case of all preparatory measures which may result in projects subsequently implemented having such effects. Accordingly, the interpretation of the terms 'plan' and 'programme' must be broad enough to include legislation.[14]

The Advocate General here perceived that the SEA Directive was aimed at creating a means for consideration of strategic alternatives before a project is implemented.

The third strand to the Advocate General's reasoning concerned the language of Article 2(a) and the first indent of the first point of Annex II of the SEA Directive.[15] A 'framework' did not have to be determinative so long as it was

[12] Council Directive 91/676/EEC of 12 December 1991 concerning the protection of waters against pollution caused by nitrates from agricultural sources.

[13] *Terre Wallonne ASBL* (n 11) [AG29]–[AG32].

[14] ibid [AG34]–[AG35].

[15] ibid [AG43].

influential and: 'Consequently, the SEA Directive is based on a very broad concept of 'framework.' The plan would set a framework 'insofar as decisions are taken which influence any subsequent development consent of projects, in particular with regard to location, nature, size and operating conditions or by allocating resources', though that list of factors was 'not exhaustive' and a plan might possibly do none of these things, but still be covered. The 'objective [was] making all preliminary decisions for the development consent of projects subject to an environmental assessment if they are likely to have significant effects on the environment'.[16]

This seems an extremely broad interpretation indeed, because many environmental laws affect the allocation of resources and the manner in which projects are to be operated. Examples would include air and water quality standards or carbon-trading schemes.

Significantly in the light of subsequent case law, the Advocate General considered that 'a comprehensive obligation to assess the environmental impact of laws is precluded if only because the second indent of Article 2(a) of the SEA Directive extends only to plans and programmes which are *required* by legislative, regulatory or administrative provisions. Freely taken political decisions on legislative proposals are not therefore subject to the obligation to carry out assessments'.[17] On the facts, the Advocate General considered that since the Nitrates Directive required Action Programmes to be drawn up, the Belgian law was subject to SEA.

The Court of Justice held that a Nitrates Action Programme was a 'plan or programme' as it was required by legislative provisions and was subject to the Public Participation Directive. The Court ruled that it was apparent from the full title of the Nitrates Directive 'that action programmes are prepared for the agricultural sector'. It then examined the 'content and purpose' of the action programmes, finding that they 'involve a global examination, at the level of vulnerable zones, of the environmental issues linked to nitrate pollution from agricultural sources, and that they put in place an organised system designed to provide a general level of protection against such pollution'. It relied on the 'comprehensive … specific, mandatory measures' in the programme.[18] It found that compliance with sets of measures specified in action programmes 'can be a requirement for issue of the consent that may be granted for projects'.[19] It concluded that 'it must be held that the action programme is to be regarded, in respect of those measures, as setting the framework for future development consent of projects' listed in the EIA Directive.[20] The judgment did not go so far as to endorse the Advocate General's full reasoning, but then it was unnecessary to do so. The test for what determinations by public authorities will be caught by the Directive accordingly remains unclear.

[16] ibid [AG61]–[AG67].
[17] ibid [AG41].
[18] ibid [48].
[19] ibid [53].
[20] ibid [54].

Requirement for the Plan or Programme and the Degree of Influence Required

The language of the definition of 'plans and programmes' in Article 2(a) is enigmatic insofar as it includes only those 'required by legislative, regulatory or administrative provisions'. It remains an open question as to what is meant by 'regulatory or administrative provisions' which were presumably to be distinguished both from each other and from instruments with the force of law.[21] It is difficult to see how a plan or programme can be 'required' by a mere policy commitment which does *not* have the force of law, although that appears to have been envisaged in the reference to 'regulatory or administrative provisions'.

A narrow interpretation was taken in the domestic *Central Craigavon* case.[22] This concerned Northern Irish Planning Policy Statement 5 (PPS5), which was entitled *Retailing in Town Centres*. The Northern Ireland Court of Appeal sought to distinguish the *Terre Wallonne* case. It endorsed[23] the English judgment of Lindblom J (as he then was),[24] who had ruled that mere 'advice' that something was already a material consideration, and that 'freely taken decisions on legislative proposals' were not themselves plans or programmes and did not themselves alter the content of existing plans and programmes. The Northern Irish Court of Appeal was also at pains to confine the conclusion in *Terre Wallonne* to its specific factual context. It stated: 'In the context of that case there was no question but that the relevant action programme contained a high degree of detailed precision as to the steps to be taken under the programme introduced pursuant to the Nitrates Directive. Insofar as the Advocate General may have suggested that anything which might influence a subsequent development consent constituted a framework we would respectfully differ from that conclusion. She was not … addressing anything other than whether the particular programme fell within Article 2(2). The ECJ accepted that it did and did not consider it necessary to adopt the wording of the Advocate General's formulation.'

Subsequent to the *Central Craigavon* case, the ECJ decided *Inter-Environnement Bruxelles*,[25] holding that 'plans and programmes whose adoption is regulated by national legislative or regulatory provisions, which determine the competent authorities for adopting them and the procedure for preparing them, must be regarded as 'required' [and subjected to SEA]'.[26] While to that extent, the Court

[21] This issue is discussed in detail by Simon Ricketts and Juliet Munn in Ch 4 of this volume.

[22] *Central Craigavon Ltd's Application for Judicial Review, Re* [2011] NICA 17 (CANI).

[23] ibid [41]–[43].

[24] *Cala Homes (South) Ltd v Secretary of Communities and Local Government* [2011] EWHC 97 (Admin) [92]–[101].

[25] Case C-567/10 *Inter-Environnement Bruxelles ASBL and Others v Région de Bruxelles-Capitale* [2012] 2 CMLR 30.

[26] ibid [31].

departed from the *Central Craigavon* reasoning, it also appeared to pronounce upon the intendment of the EU legislature in using the phrase 'plans or programmes', referring to:

> [T]he directive's aim of establishing a procedure for scrutinising measures likely to have significant effects on the environment, which define the criteria and the detailed rules for the development of land and normally concern a multiplicity of projects whose implementation is subject to compliance with the rules and procedures provided for by those measures.[27]

This formulation simultaneously relaxed the criterion that plans or programmes were 'required' and arguably circumscribed the scope of such plans or programmes to 'measures … which define the criteria and the detailed rules for the development of land'.

Contractual Measures

The phrase 'regulatory or administrative provisions' may also be intended to catch schemes that are contractual and are entered into voluntarily, such as regulatory or procurement agreements with particular industries. The most relevant case on this issue is *Abraham*.[28] This concerned whether an agreement between public authorities and a private undertaking amounted to a 'project' requiring assessment under the EIA Directive. The agreement was signed with a view to having that undertaking operate an airport with a runway, featuring an exact description of infrastructure work to be carried out on the runway, and the construction of a control tower so as to permit large aircraft to fly 24 hours per day and 365 days per year, and providing for 24-hour flights. It was argued that the contract was not a formally required step for development consent. Advocate General Kokott considered that the agreement was not itself a 'project', but fell to be treated as part of the consent procedure for the airport upgrading works that it contemplated, and hence was potentially subject to EIA. She reasoned that the Directive:

> would not be able to achieve its aim if the decision on a project were *de facto* already taken before any formal consent procedure was initiated. The agreement should therefore be regarded as the first stage of a consent procedure carried out in several stages if and in so far as it limits the discretion of the competent national authorities in subsequent consent procedures. It cannot therefore only matter whether the discretion is formally unimpaired, as several of the parties claim. It is questionable whether an independent and impartial administrative decision taking full account of any environmental impact assessment and of public participation can be made if the bodies with political responsibility have decided clearly in favour of the project. Liability for damages as a

[27] ibid [28].

[28] Case C-2/07 *Abraham v Terre Wallonne* [2008] ECR I-1197; [2008] Env LR 32.

> result of failure to obtain consents—as might be provided for under … the agreement—may also limit discretion.[29]

The ECJ took rather a more restrictive view of 'development consent', holding that this meant 'a decision of the competent authority which entitles the developer to proceed with the project'.[30] The Advocate General's reasoning about agreements limiting an authority's discretion might, though, arguably apply to contractual agreements with developers, suppliers or other interested parties that have the effect of 'setting a framework' for subsequent development consents. For instance, an agreement in principle to procure only certain types of control systems or aircraft might have the effect of limiting what kind of airport facility was acceptable.

The SEA Directive in Practice: Transport

Inter-agency or International Agreements and Investment Plans

In principle, if a binding agreement between the state and a private person may amount to a 'plan or programme' as in *Abraham*, then it seems to follow that an agreement between two public authorities within or between states might also potentially count as a plan setting a framework for development consent.

In the Northern Irish case of the Alternative A5 Alliance judicial review, a claim was brought to quash a decision by the Northern Irish Minister for Regional Development to approve a new 85 km dual-carriageway trunk road in parallel with the existing route, at a cost of £800 million. At a North-South Ministerial Council in July 2007, an inter-governmental decision had been made to progress a major programme providing a dual-carriageway standard road serving the north-west of the island with a contribution of £400 million from the Irish government. In September 2007, the Ministerial Council issued a communiqué stating, under the heading 'Strategic transport Planning', that they 'agreed to … a management structure for the A5 project'. In January 2008, the Northern Irish Executive ratified its 'Investment Strategy for Northern Ireland 2008–2018', which purported to '[set] out the framework with which we will create a sustainable 21st century infrastructure' and identify 'priority areas for investment in the years ahead'. It stated that 'key milestones will include … opening the A5 … dualling scheme'. Its 'Investment Delivery Plan for Roads' was published in April 2008, which was premised on the delivery of the A5 dual-carriageway project. The 'Northern Ireland Programme for Government 2008–2018' also included a commitment to 'progress plans to extend dual carriageways on the western corridor (A5)'.[31]

[29] ibid [AG76]–[AG78].

[30] ibid [25].

[31] See *Re Alternative A5 Alliance's Application for Judicial Review* [2013] NIQB 30 [18]–[26] for the factual background. Robert McCracken and Ned Westaway in Ch 1 of this volume point out that in the

Mr Justice Stephens sitting in the Northern Irish High Court upheld the applicants' submissions that the Investment Strategy, Investment Delivery Plan and Programme for Government all amounted to 'plans or programmes', and furthermore rejected the submissions that they came within the exception for 'financial or budget plans or programmes' provided for by Article 3(8) of the SEA Directive. While no reasoning for that latter finding was given, it appears from the judgment that at the time of publication of these documents, the exact route was not known, and the timing and cost of the works had not been fixed. He was not asked to rule on the inter-ministerial council determination, but the reasoning applies equally to that initial commitment to proceed.

Mr Justice Stephens considered[32] that a 'plan or programme normally concerns a multiplicity of projects but this is not an absolute requirement', a conclusion that inevitably follows from the decision in the *Genovaitė Valčiukienė* case. The judge reasoned in reliance upon *Inter-Environnement Bruxelles* that a 'plan or programme which "might" influence subsequent development consent does not set a framework. To set a framework a plan or programme has to prospectively influence a development consent and has to define criteria and the detailed rules for the development of land. However the degree of detail may be limited by the high strategic level of the plan or programme'.[33] In his judgment, it was clear from the intention at the time of drafting and from the way that these documents had subsequently been treated by planning inspectors that they had set a criterion for subsequent consent to any project, namely that it must be a dual carriageway serving the corridor and ruling out all other options.[34]

It might be argued that the UK Supreme Court (UKSC) has taken a different approach from the High Court in *A5 Alliance* in Northern Ireland and from the CJEU, in relation to whether a plan about a single project requires SEA. In *Walton v Scottish Ministers*,[35] the UKSC considered the Scottish Ministers' approval of a scheme to alter the route of a proposed western peripheral road (WPR) near Aberdeen to take in a new stretch called Fastlink. It ruled that the WPR was not a 'plan or programme' but a project, as it was 'a specific development' and not 'a document setting the framework for future development consent of projects'.[36] *Walton* appears difficult to reconcile with the rulings in *A5 Alliance* and *Genovaitė Valčiukienė*, which each related to a specific development.

1996 draft version of the SEA Directive, the UK had sought to restrict the application of the Directive to 'town and country planning' plans and programmes, and modifications to them. They correctly note that as then drafted, '[the SEA Directive] would not have affected documents such as the Northern Ireland Programme for Government 2008–2011, which was held to require SEA by Stephens J in the recent case on the A5 dual carriage link'.

32 ibid [125].

33 ibid [130].

34 ibid [137]–[140].

35 *Walton v Scottish Ministers* [2012] UKSC 44; [2013] PTSR 51.

36 ibid [65]–[66].

The UKSC adopted a similar approach in relation to the proposed High Speed Two (HS2) rail link, which was to run between London, Birmingham, Leeds and Manchester.[37] By a Command Paper ('the DNS'),[38] the government had announced its intention to promote HS2 and set out a strategy for the promotion, construction and operation of the rail link. The DNS had proposed that hybrid bills be passed by Parliament to grant development consent in the form of deemed planning permission. The claimants contended that the proposals required SEA of alternatives before approval. The UKSC treated the proposed rail link as a 'project' and considered that plans and proposals for it would not amount to 'plans' unless they constrained the discretion of the decision-maker in granting or withholding consent.

The reasoning of Lord Sumption JSC[39] was that before it requires SEA:

> [T]he policy framework must operate as a constraint on the discretion of the authority charged with making the subsequent decision about development consent. It must at least limit the range of discretionary factors which can be taken into account in making that decision, or affect the weight to be attached to them. Thus a development plan may set the framework for future development consent although the only obligation of the planning authority in dealing with development consent is to take account of it. In that sense the development plan may be described as influential rather than determinative. But it cannot be enough that a statement or rule is influential in some broader sense, for example because it presents a highly persuasive view of the merits of the project which the decision maker is perfectly free to ignore but likely in practice to accept. Nor can it be enough that it comes from a source such as a governmental proposal or a ministerial press statement, or a resolution at a party conference, or an editorial in a mass circulation newspaper which the decision-maker is at liberty to ignore but may in practice be reluctant to offend.

The UKSC ruled that the DNS was 'a very elaborate description of the HS2 project, including the thinking behind it and the Government's reasons for rejecting alternatives. In one sense, it might be seen as helping to set the framework for the subsequent debate, and it is intended to influence its result. But it does not in any way constrain the decision-making process of the authority responsible, which in this case is Parliament'.[40] The constitutional supremacy of Parliament therefore led the Court to reject the argument that the DNS amounted to a document setting a framework or criteria for the subsequent project.[41] The UKSC's approach was

[37] *R (Buckinghamshire County Council) v Secretary of State for Transport* [2014] UKSC 3 [2014] 1 WLR 324. Colin Reid and Denis Edwards in Ch 14 of this volume suggest that: 'In the light of the Supreme Court's subsequent decision in *HS2*, it is unlikely that, if the point had required to be determined in *Walton*, that the original proposals for the WPR would have been a plan or programme under the Directive.'

[38] *High Speed Rail: Investing in Britain's Future—Decisions and Next Steps* (Cm 8247, January 2012).

[39] *R (Buckinghamshire County Council)* (n 37) [123], concurred in by the majority of the Justices. These issues may well be revisited in the ongoing proceedings before the Aarhus Compliance Committee, which are discussed by Richard Macrory and Gregory Jones in the Afterword to this volume.

[40] ibid [38] per Lord Carnwath JSC.

[41] ibid [39]–[41] per Lord Carnwath JSC.

followed by the Court of Appeal when it rejected the submission that 'safeguarding directions' for HS2 amounted to 'plans or programmes' for the purpose of the Directive.[42] The Secretary of State had made directions which required certain procedural steps to be followed, as regards consultation, for planning applications made within a specified zone. The purpose of the directions was to prevent further development consents being granted that could interfere with the construction or operation of the rail link, or increase the cost of the project. However, they did not amount to a veto and did not themselves contain any criteria for judging future projects. The Secretary of State had a power to make a further direction prohibiting development if the local planning authority were minded to grant planning permission, which direction could be the subject of appeal. The Court of Appeal found that the safeguarding directions reflected rather than shaped the HS2 project and did not themselves specify any policy criteria for approving or rejecting applications:

> While it is highly likely that on appeal the Secretary of State for Communities and Local Government would place considerable weight on the three objectives that are set out in the guidance notes and the directions themselves … he would not be doing so because they are the stated aims of the directions. The three objectives would be weighty planning considerations because of the national importance which the Government attaches to the implementation of the HS2 project, as evidenced by the fact that it is promoting the hybrid Bill.

Furthermore, the Court of Appeal considered that 'it is not realistic to describe the directions which take their shape from a project which is being pursued (in the absence of any plan or programme) in a hybrid Bill, and whose sole purpose is to ensure that the implementation of that project is not prejudiced by other developments, as some form of "plan or programme" in their own right'.[43]

The result accordingly was that the HS2 project was allowed to proceed without having required strategic alternatives to be publicly, comprehensively and transparently examined, even though, objectively speaking, the rail link required planning and programming before it could be built. Furthermore, the planned HS2 project itself, even before consent had been granted, was a material consideration in determining other planning applications. In the absence of criteria referring to the proposed rail link in an existing formally prepared land use development plan, the courts considered that the planning authority was entitled to give decisive weight to the objectives of facilitating the HS2 project. As a result, the proposed rail link would have knock-on effects in social, economic and environmental terms. The objective of the Directive, in requiring the impact of mooted projects to be considered at the strategic planning stage rather than just when they were individually consented, was undermined.

[42] *R (HS2 Action Alliance Ltd) v Secretary of State for Transport* [2014] EWCA Civ 1578; [2015] PTSR 1025.

[43] ibid [19]–[21] per Sullivan LJ.

One could argue that the adverse environmental effects would be limited insofar as the UKSC's reasoning narrowly related to projects promoted in Parliament. However, it is precisely the largest and costliest projects that tend to be consented by primary legislation. Furthermore, the reasoning of the UKSC that a plan does not 'set a framework' unless it constrains the discretion of the decision-maker is of potentially broader application. Lord Sumption acknowledged that a statutory development plan sets a framework because it must be taken account of, even though it does not limit the range of other considerations that a decision-maker is free to have regard to, nor preclude him assigning greater weight to them. The distinction between a statutory development plan and the plan for the rail link is that the latter is only potentially capable of being thought relevant and is not a mandatory material consideration in every case. However, in practice, in our view it would often be irrational, unfair or unreasonable for a public authority to fail to have regard to proposals for another project nearby, in particular where that other project is widely accepted to be of major significance. In that event, the decision-maker considering an application will be under a legal duty to have regard to the significant proposed project. Hence, the effect of the HS2 judgments is that even where the planned major scheme will inevitably be a material consideration in determining other applications for development consent, it will not itself require assessment unless there is a document formally setting mandatory criteria for those other applications. This is most unfortunate, because there can be little doubt that strategic assessments of alternatives can make a practical difference.

An instructive case study of the advantages of rigorous strategic assessment and the dangers of embarking upon a project without one is that of Lisbon,[44] which is served by an airport located within the urban area at Portela.

In 1971, the authorities proposed relocating the airport on plains south of the Tagus which had been opened up by a bridge that had opened in 1966. Five alternative sites to the south of the city were considered for a four-runway project and a preferred location at Rio Frio was identified, but the oil crisis of the early 1970s resulted in the project being suspended. Nevertheless, local town planners continued to base their spatial plans around the proposed Rio Frio airport.[45]

In 1982, a larger study was carried out in respect of 12 sites, in which environmental considerations were marginal, and the results of the previous study were not examined. The study concluded that a military airbase at Ota, lying about 40 km to the north of Lisbon, would be most suitable. Lack of funding prevented

[44] The following synthesis derives from Maria R Partidario and Miguel Coutinho, 'The Lisbon New International Airport: The Story of a Decision-Making Process and the Role of Strategic Environmental Assessment' (2011) 31(3) *Environmental Impact Assessment Review* 361; João de Abreu e Silva, Jorge Gonçalves, Marcos Correia and Susana Marreiros, 'Airport Planning Process: The Case of the New Lisbon Airport' (2015) 99 *Finisterra* 63; and Miguel Cotinho and Maria Partidario, 'The New Lisbon International Airport: The History of a Decision-Making Process', paper delivered at the 28th International Association for Impact Assessment (Perth, 2008).

[45] De Abreu e Silva et al (n 44) 71.

the relocation project from progressing. In the 1990s, environmental impact assessments were carried out for alternative proposals at Rio Frio and Ota. There was not a single comparative assessment of the two projects and nor were alternative configurations within each site studied. The Rio Frio site was rejected as it would require the removal of protected habitat containing more than 50,000 cork trees and would interrupt an ecological corridor.[46] The Ota proposal influenced the infrastructure proposals in local spatial development plans, so that 'the regional planning process was not leading but mainly followed the location decisions proposed by the airport location technical studies'.[47] However, Ota was a smaller site such that only two runways could be built there rather than the three or four that had previously been proposed at Rio Frio. The site was windier, had drainage problems and had difficult terrain.[48]

Owing to the high costs of construction and the small capacity benefit of relocating to Ota airbase, the Confederation of Portuguese Industry commissioned its own strategic study. The aim was to assess not particular proposals for airport infrastructure, but rather strategic sites for an airport. Instead of first selecting sites and then assessing their fitness for purpose, this study used geographical information systems to identify and then winnow out available sites based on criteria including connectivity and infrastructure, ecological criteria, physical features and pollution. This was published in 2007 and identified Campo Tiro de Alcochete, another Portuguese Air Force facility. The private initiative prompted the Ministry of Public Works to approve a comparative study with open terms of reference, comparing Alcochete and Ota against seven objective criteria: air safety, use of resources, biodiversity, spatial planning policy, competitiveness and financial feasibility. This included an economic cost–benefit analysis. It transpired that in terms of safety of air navigation, Alcochete was a superior site.[49] From 2009, regional spatial plans were built around the new airport being located at Alcochete.[50]

With the financial crash and the Portuguese debt crisis, the proposals for relocating the airport were again put on hold. Substantial investment has instead been made in enhancing the capacity of the current Portela facility with a new terminal and metro link, such that in 2013, the Secretary of State for Transport rejected the need to build another airport at all.[51] What we can see in the Lisbon example is a

[46] Partidario and Coutinho (n 44) 362.
[47] De Abreu e Silva et al (n 44) 73–74, quotation at 73.
[48] Partidario and Coutinho (n 44) 362–63.
[49] ibid 364–65.
[50] De Abreu e Seilva et al (n 44) 74.
[51] '"O novo aeroporto de Lisboa é na Portela", diz secretário de Estado dos Transportes' and 'Aeroporto de Lisboa com novo terminal e area comercial', *Publico*, 17 July 2013, http://fugas.publico.pt/Noticias/323025_aeroporto-de-lisboa-com-novo-terminal-e-area-comercial; www.publico.pt/economia/noticia/o-novo-aeroporto-de-lisboa-e-na-portela-diz-secretario-de-estado-dos-transportes-1600497.

planning and transport system that was project-led rather than strategic in conception. The result was a misdirection of resources and a delay in investment to improve the infrastructure. In the UK, we can observe a similar pattern of project-led planning, with resultant delays to capacity improvements and misdirection of resources, not just at the national level of HS2 but also at a much more local level.

Alternatives

Whether and how alternatives are taken into account is a critical aspect of assessing whether a project can be properly justified. One particular example of project-led planning has been proposals for 'park and ride' and similar public transport link schemes. Prior to 2012, government policy in England and Wales was supportive of such schemes, whose aims included accommodating parking requirements without taking urban land, encouraging modal shift from cars to public transport, reducing traffic congestion, reducing overall carbon emissions and air pollution, and supporting the economic vitality of traditional urban centres.[52] The relevant policy guidance stated: 'Schemes need to be subject to robust assessment, including consideration of alternative sites, the impact on local amenity, and travel impacts, including traffic reduction and generation.'[53] However, appraisal at public inquiries tended to focus on the scheme under examination.[54] There is evidence that approved edge-of-urban-area park-and-ride schemes have tended to result in system-wide increases in traffic by increasing traffic outside the urban area more than traffic is decreased within the urban area. Such schemes may also damage other public transport routes by abstracting passengers and threatening the viability of the existing public transport infrastructure.[55]

At a public inquiry, it usually falls to objectors to a scheme, if any, to raise evidence of more suitable alternatives. It is extremely difficult for objectors to a scheme at a public inquiry to replicate the kind of detailed strategic assessment of alternatives that a team of professional experts would carry out under the SEA Directive. Nor, in most cases, will objectors or planning inspectors have the technical expertise to interrogate the conclusions drawn in an environmental impact assessment at the project stage. If there is a worked-up project being put forward at an inquiry that meets identified and undisputed needs or objectives, then the

[52] Graham Parkhurst and Jeremy Richardson, 'Modal Integration of Bus and Car in UK Local Transport Policy: The Case for Strategic Environmental Assessment' (2002) 10 *Journal of Transport Geography* 195, 195–96.

[53] Department for Communities and Local Government, *Planning Policy Guidance 13: Transport* (London, The Stationery Office, January 2011), paragraph 60. Earlier 2001 guidance was in similar terms.

[54] Parkhurst and Richardson (n 52) 198. See also Ch 6 of this volume for David Elvin's discussion of the limitations imposed upon the range of alternatives examined under the SEA Directive.

[55] Parkhurst and Richardson (n 52) 201–03.

absence of worked-up alternatives to meet the same objectives would tend to count in favour of the project's approval even where alternatives would be more efficient, less environmentally damaging or better value for money.

A second weakness of the SEA Directive is that even where a systematic assessment of alternatives to a particular transport scheme is carried out, the objectives may be so narrowly defined that optimal solutions are not examined. The Directive requires consideration of 'reasonable alternatives taking into account the objectives and the geographical scope of the plan or programme'.[56] In the case of HS2, the brief was not improving transport efficiency between northern and southern England, but was narrowly defined as being the creation of a new high-speed rail line between defined cities. The project's opponents advocated the examination of 'new motorways or enhancements to the existing ones, and rail alternatives in the form of a new conventional rail network or enhancements to the existing networks or a lower but still high speed network'.[57] Ouseley J was constrained to rule: 'It is obviously a contestable view as to whether [the] objectives should be met, or can be met to a large extent by means other than a new high speed rail network. These alternative strategies could not, however, have constituted reasonable alternatives to the plan for assessment in the SEA, since they are incapable by their very nature of meeting all the objectives for a new high speed rail network.'[58] This ruling was endorsed by the Supreme Court.[59]

The discretion accorded under the SEA Directive to plan-makers to determine the objectives of their plans and programmes can allow them to ignore or give no weight to the purpose of protecting the environment at the stage of specifying objectives, as well as when choosing between assessed alternatives. Finnveden and Akerman have documented that the objectives of the Swedish Road Administration's national infrastructure plan for the period 2010 to 2021 did not include minimising climate change impacts, environmental harm or promoting sustainable development. While the assessed options would in any event be appraised against those criteria as part of the assessment process, the environmental report noted that performance against environmental quality objectives was negative and the plan itself stated that economic efficiency had guided the choice of the decision-makers.[60] This outcome is to be expected, on occasion, given that the Directive dictates procedural rather than substantive environmental outcomes.

[56] Article 5(1).

[57] *R (Buckinghamshire County Council) v Secretary of State for Transport* [2013] EWHC 481 (Admin) [160] per Ouseley J.

[58] ibid [162].

[59] *R (Buckinghamshire County Council) v Secretary of State for Transport* [2014] UKSC 3 [47]–[48] per Lord Carnwath JSC.

[60] Göran Finnveden and Jonas Akerman, 'Not Planning a Sustainable Transport System' (2014) 46 *Environmental Impact Assessment Review* 53.

While it is beyond the scope of this chapter to examine this in detail, it is noteworthy that a study of 45 English town and country planning 'core strategies' has found SEA to have had a minimal positive impact on environmental protection:

> SEA does not seem to be leading to core strategies that achieve a high level of protection of the environment. This is probably due to the need to achieve other sustainability objectives. However, the SA/SEAs do not explain how or why these tradeoffs are being made; they are not justifying why environmental protection is not being achieved. As such, they are not leading to effective outcomes.[61]

It has also been held that plan alternatives whose approval is beyond the competence of the planning authority need not be considered a reasonable alternative.[62] Accordingly, where a proposed project spans multiple local authority areas or requires approval by a Transport and Works Act Order rather than a local authority, it may not be considered within a statutory Local Transport Plan.

Even where there is a duty to examine 'reasonable alternatives' under the SEA Directive, it is left to the plan-making authority to decide what alternatives are 'reasonable' because they are feasible and adequately meet the objectives that it has set itself.[63] There is no obligation to consult the public for suggestions as to what the objectives or the reasonable alternatives might be. Moreover, alternatives to the plan are to be examined, but not necessarily alternatives to every individual component of a plan.[64]

Alternatives often take the form of generic options rather than packages of measures that are worked up in as much detail as the initially preferred option. A 2011 study of seven statutory local transport plans adopted in the northwest of England found their environmental reports to be of barely satisfactory quality: 'For the most part, only do nothing or business as usual scenarios were compared with plan implementation. Rarely were other options considered (for example, in the case of … Merseyside … options related to funding and environmental sustainability). Furthermore, reasons for selecting reasonable options and alternatives were insufficiently explored.'[65] A recent comprehensive study of practice in the Republic of Ireland examined 40 environmental reports (20 land use plans and 20 sectoral plans), surveyed 11 national practitioners and academics, and interviewed a further seven. It reported 'narrowly defined alternatives', as well as 'alternatives

[61] Riki Therivel, Gemma Christian, Claire Craig, Russell Grinham, David Mackins, James Smith, Terry Sneller, Richard Turner, Dee Walker and Motoko Yamane, 'Sustainability-Focused Impact Assessment: English Experiences' (2009) 27(2) *Impact Assessment and Project Appraisal* 155, 163.

[62] *Heard v Broadland District Council* [2012] EWHC 344 (Admin) [10].

[63] *Ashdown Forest Economic Development LLP v Secretary of State for Communities and Local Government and Wealden District Council* [2015] EWCA Civ 681; [2016] Env LR 2 [37], [42] and [50] per Richards LJ.

[64] *Heard v Broadland District Council* [2012] Env LR 23 [71]: *R (Buckinghamshire County Council)* (n 57) [165]; *R (Friends of the Earth) v Welsh Ministers* [2015] EWHC 776 (Admin) [85]–[86], [88]–[89] and [106] per Hickinbottom J.

[65] Thomas B Fischer, 'Identifying Shortcomings in SEA Practice' (2012) 81(6) *Town and Country Planning* 281, 285.

that are neither genuine nor realistic, and which are often retrofitted to support an already identified preferred option' and 'generally poor collaboration [with] the general public in alternative identification, assessment and selection'. It found that 'current practice is generally to develop and document about three alternatives in the eventual [environmental report]', where 'the preferred SEA alternative is usually easily identifiable or already known'. Often, the public and statutory consultees were only able to comment after alternatives had been identified and assessed.[66]

The authors' own experience at the 2014 public inquiry into proposals for a trolleybus line in Leeds was that the SEA Directive had exerted a very limited practical impact upon the 'upstream' transport planning process. The proposal there was for the creation of a new public transport system to be known as 'New Generation Transport' (NGT). This was to initially comprise a 15 km-long electric trolleybus line with overhead power cables running from north to south through the city centre, serving 27 dedicated stops and incorporating two park-and-ride car parks.[67] The scheme was promoted by way of an application for a Transport and Works Act Order, listed building consent and deemed planning permission.

The project had been originally conceived to follow the route that had been safeguarded for a proposed 'Supertram' project that had been cancelled for financial reasons. The route of this previous scheme had not been subject to SEA and had pre-dated the implementation of the SEA Directive. The unitary development plan contained policies safeguarding the route and was examined in 1999. At that time, the examining inspector had not examined alternatives, but had taken the view that:

> Detailed proposals for ST [Supertram] will be subject to the requirements of the Transport and Works Act including a public inquiry … It is … for the T&W Act inquiry to consider the detailed merits of the ST proposals for the … corridors, including no doubt comparisons with other forms of PT [public transport].[68]

The NGT project was promoted by Leeds City Council and the West Yorkshire combined transport authority. It was proposed that it would be funded largely using central government funds, and an initial funding application was made in 2009. The specification of alternative bus-based options in submissions made to support the finding bid was, it was conceded at the public inquiry, not done as part of an open-minded study to maximise the potential value of such options at a stage when all options were open, but to justify funding in support of the strategic decision that had already been made to promote the trolleybus project.[69]

[66] Ainhoa González, Rik Thérivel, John Fry and Walter Foley, 'Advancing Practice Relating to SEA Alternatives' (2015) 53 *Environmental Impact Assessment Review* 52, 53–55.

[67] Mott MacDonald, *Leeds Trolley Vehicle System Order Environmental Statement, Non-Technical Summary* (September 2013) 3–5 and 11, www.persona.uk.com/LTVS/core_docs/A-08a.pdf.

[68] *Leeds Unitary Development Plan Inspector's Report* (February 1999), Ch 6, paras 159.1 and 160.16, www.persona.uk.com/LTVS/core_docs/D-Dox/D-2-5.PDF.

[69] Authors' transcript of proceedings on 19 June 2014; see the authors' Closing Submissions on behalf of First West Yorkshire Ltd at 113–14 (inquiry document FWY159), www.persona.uk.com/LTVS/I-OP_INQDOX/OBJ1604/FWY159.pdf. In the event, the inspector's recommendation to refuse to make the order and the consequential listed building and conservation areas consents was adopted

Strategic assessment of local plans subsequent to the transposition of the Directive had not re-examined alternatives to the route[70] or appraised alternative means of achieving the scheme's objectives of reducing congestion, such as improvements to conventional bus services.[71] Those drafting the subsequent Core Strategy local plan in 2011 and 2012 had incorporated emerging plans for the trolleybus line, which by that stage was being worked up in detail by the project team, rather than examining afresh the strategic alternatives to a trolleybus project.

Whatever the merits of the trolleybus proposals themselves, it is apparent that as in Lisbon, successive large-scale infrastructure projects had determined the shape of the strategic local transport plans and spatial plans without the strategic alternatives having been considered afresh in a systematic and wide-ranging way.

Flooding and Water Resource Management

If the practical impact of the SEA Directive in the transport sector has been small, its implementation in the sphere of water resources management shows up another weakness, which is the failure of the procedure to engage the general public in strategic-level decisions and thereby generate a sense of buy-in to eventual outcomes.

There is a consensus in the literature that broader and more participatory SEA processes tend to result in more effective assessment processes with more credible and widely accepted outcomes.[72] A startling example was provided by the English winter flooding of 2014. A total of 800,000 homes were left without electricity for as long as a week, while 17,000 acres of the Somerset Levels were flooded for more than a month. Within the Levels, the village of Muchelney with around

by the Secretaries of State. Interestingly, part of the reasoning was that not all alternatives had been adequately explored. This is therefore perhaps an example of where much time and money would have been saved if the alternatives had been properly explored at a strategic higher level. See decision letter at https://www.gov.uk/government/publications/leeds-trolley-vehicle-system-order-decision-letter and the inspector's report at https://www.gov.uk/government/publications/leeds-trolley-vehicle-system-order-inspectors-report.

[70] Some significant departures from the Supertram route were made for the final NGT project along part of its length, but different alternative routes were not the subject of strategic assessment during the plan-making.

[71] For instance, the environmental report for the West Yorkshire Local Transport Plan 2011–2026 specified three 'high level' alternative overall strategies that focused respectively upon maintaining existing assets, reducing carbon emissions and reducing congestion across the whole West Yorkshire area. See *West Yorkshire Local Transport Plan Integrated Sustainability Assessment Report* (January 2011) Ch 7, www.wymetro.com/uploadedFiles/WYMetro/Content/aboutmetro/Local_Transport_Plan/ISA-MainReport.pdf.

[72] Hens Runhaar and Peter Driessen, 'What Makes Strategic Environmental Assessment Successful Environmental Assessment? The Role of Context in the Contribution of SEA to Decision-Making' (2007) 25(1) *Impact Assessment and Project Appraisal* 2, 3–6.

200 residents was entirely cut off by floodwaters.[73] There was particular local anger and surprise about the policies of the Environment Agency not to dredge the River Parrett and to protect towns at the expense of farmland, resulting in national media attention.[74] At the time, one relevant management document was the Parrett Catchment Flood Management Plan, with a 50–100-year long-term time horizon. It had designated the Somerset Levels as a policy area 'where we will take action with others to store water or manage run-off in locations that provide overall flood risk reduction or environmental benefits'.[75] The policy had been to intentionally 'redistribute' floodwaters such that some locations with fewer assets at risk would suffer increased flooding in order to provide net benefits across the catchment.[76]

Had local people been aware of this policy, it might not have come as a surprise that the farmland in question was not being defended. It may be that the euphemistic language in the plan, with references to storage and redistribution, was not helpful. The Catchment Flood Management Plan had been through an SEA process, although the plan asserted that it did not fall within the scope of the SEA legislation. If one delves into Appendix B to the main environmental report, which contained a total of 276 pages, one finds a straightforward rationale:

> We selected these policies because alternative options would have resulted in unacceptable increases in flood risk to urban areas in particular to Taunton and Bridgwater. Directed flooding on the Somerset Levels and Moors has the potential to enhance already significant nature conservation interest … as well as reducing the speed of floodwater and intensity of flooding elsewhere in the catchment.[77]

The objectives of the previous, pilot draft plan had been consulted upon many years earlier in 2003,[78] although that work was not repeated in 2008. The draft plan had been subject to public consultation in 2008, but only after the alternative options had been selected and assessed. The post-adoption statement declared, under the heading 'alternatives', that: 'There are six generic flood risk management policies that could have been used. Each was assessed against a range of criteria and objectives during the scoping stage.'[79] It is striking that these were described

[73] Graham Norwood, '2014 Floods: How Have Britain's Towns Recovered?', *Daily Telegraph*, 17 January 2015, www.telegraph.co.uk/finance/property/11350709/2014-floods-how-have-Britains-towns-recovered.html. See also '10 Key Moments of the UK Winter Storms', *BBC News*, 17 February 2014, www.bbc.co.uk/news/uk-26170904.

[74] Resulting in a combative response by Lord Smith, the Chairman of the Environment Agency, in 'Difficult Choices as Flood Waters Rise', *Daily Telegraph*, 2 February 2014.

[75] Environment Agency, *Parrett Catchment Flood Management Plan Summary Report* (December 2009) 10 (map 3) and 11.

[76] ibid 18–19.

[77] Environment Agency, *Parrett Catchment Flood Management Plan Consultation Draft*, Appendix B, 8 (March 2008).

[78] ibid, Appendix B, 5–6.

[79] Environment Agency, 'Post-adoption Statement: The Parrett Catchment Flood Management Plan', https://www.gov.uk/government/uploads/system/uploads/attachment_data/file/295643/Parrett_Catchment_Flood_Management_Plan_Post_adoption_statement.pdf.

as 'generic' and not as genuine options that had been under serious consideration. The generic alternative policies were then turned into scenarios for modelling, that were put together using specific policy assumptions notwithstanding that the plan itself was ostensibly the highest-level plan which was not intended to dictate any specific measures to achieve its objectives.[80] The assumptions made as to on-the-ground development were summarised, but not set out transparently.[81] Accordingly, the modelled scenarios were both highly speculative and difficult for members of the public to comment on intelligently during the consultation, even assuming that they had been aware of the consultation and had been able to obtain and study all the documents. Jilberto perceived that 'SEA practice devotes most of its efforts and large amounts of resources to simulate a future scenario to be able to identify … the projects … that it will cause … to create a listing of expected outcomes of the plan or programme and subsequently to estimate their environmental effects'. However, as he notes, 'predicting multiple layers of decisions deriving from the strategic PPP [plan, programme or policy] in question is not the intrinsic objective of the strategic decisions subject to SEA', which is rather to create a framework for decision-making. It is simply impossible to make an accurate estimate about the environmental effects of a plan that will influence numerous independent discretionary decisions taken lower down the hierarchy. Jilberto persuasively argues that effective SEAs need not attempt to provide 'data', but that so long as they proceed on a sound understanding of systems, processes and causal mechanisms, they can score policy options against each other in a qualitative way.[82]

In addition to the inherent difficulty in predicting the impact of high-level strategies, the SEA of flood risk plans will also suffer from uncertainties in the science. Meteorological data series reliably date back decades or hundreds of years, which makes predicting the return periods of infrequent events using the historical record extremely difficult, particularly when extreme events may cluster together.[83] Moreover, the climate is a dynamic system that is constantly changing, and the potential extent and local impacts of global warming are notoriously uncertain.[84] As a result, modelling used to predict flood risk may be unable to

[80] Environment Agency (n 75) Appendix B, 11 and 20–21.

[81] ibid, Appendix B, summary tables such as that on 37.

[82] RH Jilberto, 'Strategic Environmental Assessment: The Need to Transform the Environmental Assessment Paradigms' (2007) 9(2) *Journal of Environmental Policy and Management* 211, especially 214 and 217.

[83] Oliver Moody, Paul Simons and David Brown, 'After the Deluge, Another Storm Brews over Causes', *The Times*, 8 December 2015, 8.

[84] The resolution of the UK Meteorological Office's Hadley Centre modelling for the Intergovernmental Panel on Climate Change's Fifth Assessment Report was between 208 km × 139 km at the equator and 120 km × 139 km at 55 degrees of latitude. See www.metoffice.gov.uk/research/modelling-systems/unified-model/climate-models/hadgem2.

helpfully forecast the risk of extreme events. After numerous episodes of flooding in early December 2015, the deputy director of operations at the Environment Agency stated that the rainfall was 'an unprecedented event' which was 'beyond the forecasts and beyond the models'.[85]

There has been scant published systematic research into how strategic assessment of flood risk management plans and programmes has been conducted. However, a very recent study of four local authority spatial plans[86] in England and Scotland is not encouraging in its conclusions. The authors report 'inappropriate simplification' and 'overreliance on uncertain data [that] may result in false precision being attributed to flood risk data'.[87] The plans each included a presumption against development in areas of flood risk areas which necessarily relied upon flood risk data, and also contained an implicit assumption that other areas were safe from flooding. The authors found that the 'evidence suggests that SA and SEA do not specifically promote a holistic, whole system response, or promote improved resilience to mitigate uncertainties in data'.[88] Instead, it found that 'generic attenuation approaches' were favoured, along with delay for greater information at a 'lower or site-specific scale' when confronted with uncertainty, rather than proposing proactive steps to improve resilience.[89]

The Flood Risk Directive[90] requires by Article 3(2)(b) that Member States 'identify certain coastal areas or individual river basins and assign them to a unit of management', which may be the 'river basin district' referred to in Article 3(1) of the Water Framework Directive.[91] It requires the Member States to conduct a preliminary assessment for each unit of management utilising historic flooding information and to identify those areas 'for which potential significant flood risks exist or might be considered likely to occur'.[92] For each unit of management, 'flood risk maps' and 'flood hazard maps' must be drawn up. Flood hazard maps have to show predicted extent, depth and flow velocity of floodwaters in three different scenarios: high probability floods, medium probability floods (more than or equal to 100 years' return period) and extreme events. Flood risk maps must show the population and economic activity that will be affected, as well as

[85] Quoted in David Brown and Callum Jones, 'Spending on Flood Defences Has Been Cut by £116m This Year', *The Times*, 8 December 2015, 9.

[86] Samuel Hayes, Adam Barker and Carys Jones, 'Flood Management Consideration in Sustainability Appraisal and Strategic Environmental Assessment in England and Scotland' (2014) 16(3) *Journal of Environmental Assessment Policy and Management* 1450025-1 to 1450025-23.

[87] ibid 1450025-14. The lack of general data in respect of onshore SEA may be contrasted with the amount of data collected in respect of offshore SEA, as noted by Richard Caddell in Ch 13 of this volume.

[88] ibid 1450025-16.

[89] ibid 1450025-18.

[90] Directive 2007/60/EC of the European Parliament and of the Council of 23 October 2007 on the assessment and management of flood risks.

[91] Directive 2000/60/EC of the European Parliament and of the Council of 23 October 2000 establishing a framework for Community action in the field of water policy.

[92] Directive 2007/60/EC, arts 4 and 5(1).

installations that might cause pollution if flooded.[93] The legislation defines 'flood risk' as 'the combination of the probability of a flood event and of the potential adverse consequences for human health, the environment, cultural heritage and economic activity associated with a flood event'.[94] The Flood Risk Directive then requires that 'flood risk management plans' be drawn up on the basis of the hazard maps and risk maps, coordinated for each unit of management, by 22 December 2015, and reviewed every six years.[95]

The Flood Risk Directive requires that plans 'establish appropriate objectives for the management of flood risks for the areas identified … focusing on the reduction of potential adverse consequences of flooding for human health, the environment, cultural heritage and economic activity, and, if considered appropriate, on non-structural initiatives and/or on the reduction of the likelihood of flooding' and 'shall include measures for achieving the objectives'. The plans must 'take into account relevant aspects such as costs and benefits, flood extent and flood conveyance routes and areas which have the potential to retain flood water, such as natural floodplains, the environmental objectives of Article 4 of Directive 2000/60/EC, soil and water management, spatial planning, land use, nature conservation, navigation and port infrastructure'. Furthermore, they are required to 'address all aspects of flood risk management focusing on prevention, protection, preparedness, including flood forecasts and early warning systems and taking into account the characteristics of the particular river basin or sub-basin'. The Flood Risk Directive states that the plans 'may also include the promotion of sustainable land use practices, improvement of water retention as well as the controlled flooding of certain areas in the case of a flood event'.[96]

Crucially, Article 10(2) provides, 'Member States shall encourage active involvement of interested parties in the production, review and updating of the flood risk management plans'. This ought to ensure that persons who may be adversely affected by the plans (for instance, by 'directed flooding'), are aware of this prospect and can made representations or move away from the area accordingly, rather than being surprised, hurt and angry when extreme weather events occur.

In England, the Flood Risk Directive has been transposed by the Flood Risk Regulations 2009.[97] These provide for lead local flood authorities (LLFAs), which are either unitary authorities or county councils.[98] The Environment Agency (EA) is tasked with producing flood risk maps, flood hazard maps and assessment reports in relation to each river basin district. Each LLFA is tasked with making preliminary assessment reports in relation to its own local area, in consultation

[93] ibid, art 6.
[94] ibid, art 2(1).
[95] ibid, arts 7 and 14.
[96] Ibid, art 7(2) and (3).
[97] Flood Risk Regulations 2009, SI 3402/2009.
[98] ibid, reg 9.

with the EA.[99] Both the EA and the LLFA are under a duty to identify areas that they consider are threatened with a 'significant' flood risk, for which the LLFA must go on[100] to prepare hazard maps and risk maps in respect of its own areas. In the event that the LLFA disagrees with the EA about which local areas are at 'significant' risk, it may refer the matter to a minister for a determination.[101] The maps are to be reviewed by the EA, which may suggest modifications, but the LLFA is not obliged to adopt such modifications. However, the risk and hazard maps produced by an LLFA do have to be 'consistent' with the hazard plans produced by the EA for the river basin district.[102] The Regulations require the EA rather than the individual LLFAs to publish the maps.[103] The EA must produce a flood risk management plan for areas at significant risk within a river basin district and the LLFA must do likewise for its area.[104]

These Flood Risk Regulations appear to involve the EA and the local authorities in a degree of duplication of effort, although the system appears to be designed to ensure that each is a check upon the work of the other. We may question whether Article 10(2) of the Directive has been adequately transposed, for regulation 27(7) merely states that the LLFA and the EA must 'consult' the public.

We may well ask whether flood risk management plans are not plans setting a framework for development consent. For instance, there is no statutory duty imposed upon local planning authorities to have regard to flood risk management plans when determining planning applications. However, any policies intended to guide built development are required by the Planning and Compulsory Purchase Act 2004 to be comprised in statutory local development documents with their own statutory consultation procedures.[105] Spatial planning measures may well be relevant to achieving the objectives of the flood risk management plan, and its objectives are in turn likely to be relevant to planning. The final plans may well end up including requirements for engineering projects to defend against flooding or giving a steer towards citing particular types of development in some areas in preference to others. It may be difficult during the early planning stage, when options are still open, to know whether the final plan will need to relate to development projects or not. Accordingly, it would appear to be prudent to prepare the plans with an SEA.

Somerset County Council published its 'Local Flood Risk Management Strategy' and purported to assess it under the SEA Directive in March 2013. The SEA did

[99] ibid, regs 9 and 10.

[100] Pursuant to ibid, regs 19 and 20.

[101] ibid, regs 13 and 14.

[102] ibid, regs 20(6) and 21(3).

[103] ibid, reg 22.

[104] ibid, regs 26 and 27.

[105] Section 17(3) of the Planning and Compulsory Purchase Act 2004 provides that: 'The local planning authority's local development documents must (taken as a whole) set out the authority's policies (however expressed) relating to the development and use of land in their area.' The procedures are found in the Town and Country Planning (Local Planning) (England) Regulations 2012, as amended,

consult the public at the stage of selecting options, unlike that for the Catchment Flood Management Plan. The environmental report assessed seven measures as 'alternative … strategic options', plus a 'do nothing' option. The approaches were:

1. Establishing and maintaining effective partnerships with key organisations and local communities …
2. Improving the evidence base and understanding of the local flood risk to ensure that limited resources are targeted in the areas of highest risk and vulnerability.
3. Prioritise actions to address local flooding including empowering local communities and land owners to take action themselves in order to be prepared for and limit the impacts of flooding.
4. Raise awareness of flood risk through targeted, effective communication …
5. … encouraging best practice for maintenance of assets …
6. Avoiding increasing the flood risk by preventing inappropriate development …
7. Work in partnership to deliver cost effective flood risk management measures which take a catchment wide approach and contribute to wider social, economic and environmental outcomes.

It was implausible to include a 'do nothing' option when there was a statutory duty to implement a flood risk management plan addressing numerous mandatory objectives. The other so-called 'alternatives' were themselves generic and also complementary rather than genuine alternatives to each other; it would be unrealistic to expect a strategy to include only one of them rather than a mixture of all of them.

A tentative conclusion to draw from the example of the River Parrett is therefore that the SEA procedures for the various flood-risk management plans were insufficiently clear and rigorous to lend legitimacy to the eventual plan.

Flood risk management plans are not the only area of water resource management in which SEA must play a role. The Water Framework Directive provides at recital (26) that Member States should aim to achieve the objective of 'good water status by defining and implementing the necessary measures within integrated programmes of measures, taking into account existing Community requirements'. Article 13 of the Water Framework Directive requires Member States to ensure that a river basin management plan is produced for each river basin lying within their territory, and is reviewed and updated every six years. Article 14 requires Member States to 'encourage the active involvement of all interested parties in the implementation of this Directive, in particular in the production, review and updating of the river basin management plans'. It requires that the public be

reg 5(1)(a) of which applies s 17 to 'any document prepared by a local planning authority individually or in cooperation with one or more other local planning authorities, which contains statements regarding … (i) the development and use of land which the local planning authority wish to encourage during any specified period; (ii) the allocation of sites for a particular type of development or use, (iii) any environmental, social, design and economic objectives which are relevant to the attainment of the development and use of land mentioned in paragraph (i); and (iv) development management and site allocation policies, which are intended to guide the determination of applications for planning permission'.

consulted upon the timetable and work programme for the plan, the significant water management issues that have been identified and the eventual draft plan. It requires that 'access shall be given to background documents and information used for the development of the draft river basin management plan', and that the public have six months to comment on the background documents. The mandatory minimum requirements ought to facilitate participation in what is bound to be a technical and wide-ranging exercise. Annex VI to the Water Framework Directive requires the basin management plans to include all 'measures required under' 11 directives.[106] Part B of Annex VI notes that Members States 'may choose to adopt' a non-exclusive list of possible 'supplementary measures' to ensure good water quality, to include 'emissions controls', 'codes of good practice', 'negotiated environmental agreements', 'abstraction controls', 'recreation and restoration of wetlands', 'construction projects', 'desalination plants', 'demand management measures' and 'artificial recharge of aquifers.' This means that the plans may (though strictly need not) include measures bearing upon development consent for projects. There is also a domestic law statutory duty upon those determining development consent applications to have regard, so far as the decision affects a river basin, to river basin management plans.[107] Accordingly, on any reasonable view, English river basin management plans will 'set a framework' for development consent of projects affecting a river basin and will need SEA.[108]

The EA published a set of revised river basin management plans on 30 October 2015.[109] River basin management planning is a fiendishly difficult task,[110] as it has to reconcile a variety of environmental objectives and requires the participation of numerous local authorities and stakeholders at different geographical scales.[111] There is also considerable divergence in approaches across Europe as to how to measure water quality and ecosystem health, in terms of sampling techniques, metrics and indicators, with the requirements of the Water Framework Directive

[106] Part A lists them: '(i) The Bathing Water Directive (76/160/EEC); (ii) The Birds Directive (79/409/EEC) (1); (iii) The Drinking Water Directive (80/778/EEC) as amended by Directive (98/83/EC); (iv) The Major Accidents (Seveso) Directive (96/82/EC) (2); (v) The Environmental Impact Assessment Directive (85/337/EEC) (3); (vi) The Sewage Sludge Directive (86/278/EEC) (4); (vii) The Urban Waste-water Treatment Directive (91/271/EEC); (viii) The Plant Protection Products Directive (91/414/EEC); (ix) The Nitrates Directive (91/676/EEC); (x) The Habitats Directive (92/43/EEC) (5); (xi) The Integrated Pollution Prevention Control Directive (96/61/EC).'

[107] Water Environment (Water Framework Directive) (England and Wales) Regulations 2003, reg 17. It is notable that there is no such provision in respect of flood risk management plans in the Flood Risk Regulations 2009.

[108] In Case C-43/10 *Nomarchiaki Aftodioikisi Aitoloakarnanias and Others* [2013] Env LR 21 [AG152], Advocate General Kokott opined that: 'It is beyond doubt that they are plans within the meaning of the SEA Directive.'

[109] www.gov.uk/government/consultations/update-to-the-draft-river-basin-management-plans.

[110] For a general discussion of the difficulties involved in integrated river basin management, see Bruce Hooper, 'Integrated Water Resources Management and River Basin Governance' (2003) 126 *Water Resources Update* 12.

[111] See Paula Orr, John Colvin and David King, 'Involving Stakeholders in Integrated River Basin Planning in England and Wales' (2007) 21(1) *Water Resources Management* 331.

having encouraged research into that subject.[112] It is also frequently difficult to estimate the degree of uncertainty of monitoring and sampling data owing to a lack of understanding of the ecosystems.[113] The Water Framework Directive's own criteria for status may also paint an insufficiently nuanced picture of an ecosystem, as status may be dragged down by a single poorly performing component.[114] Hering et al have concluded that while large amounts of data are being gathered about water bodies, it is not always well structured, comparable or of high quality.[115] The Water Framework Directive sets objectives in terms of ecological status rather than simple limits on pollutants or stress factors, which adds to the uncertainty for planners of hitting the objectives, since ecosystems differ in terms of their resilience and sensitivity to each pollutant or stressor.[116] Emerging risks such as climate change,[117] siltation, new toxic substances (eg, plastic microbeads)[118] and invasive alien species[119] are less well understood than more traditional stressors and pollutants.[120] All this inevitably impinges upon the effectiveness of SEA in informing a sound plan and requires strategies to be taken to estimate and compensate for uncertainties. However, as William Howath points out in Chapter 12 of this volume, the major differences concern the stated requirements for assessments under the Water Framework Directive and the comparative lack of these under the SEA Directive. We agree with Howath that this 'raises the question whether a more substantive kind of environmental assessment needs to be developed from the SEA procedures'.

On top of the scientific and technical uncertainties, a particularly fraught issue in river basin management is the 'social uncertainty' surrounding agricultural

[112] Daniel Hering, Angel Borja, Jacob Carstensen, Laurence Carvalho, Mike Elliott, Christian Feld, Anna-Stiina Heiskanen, Richard Johnson, Jannicke Moe, Didier Pont, Anne Lyche Solheim and Wouter van de Bund, 'The European Water Framework Directive at the Age of 10: A Critical Review of the Achievements with Recommendations for the Future' (2010) 408 *Science of the Total Environment* 4007, author's manuscript version accessed at http://nora.nerc.ac.uk/10073/2/N010073PP.pdf, 8–11 and 15–16.

[113] ibid 11–13.

[114] ibid 17–18.

[115] ibid 21–22.

[116] ibid 25–27 and 32.

[117] RL Wilby, HG Orr, M Hedger, D Forrow and M Blackmore, 'Risks Posed by Climate Change to the Delivery of Water Framework Directive Objectives in the UK' (2006) 32(8) *Environment International* 1043.

[118] Rachel Doughty and Marcus Eriksen. 'Plastic Pollution: The Case for a Ban on Microplastics in Personal Care Products' (2014) 27 *Tulane Environmental Law Journal* 277.

[119] Jochen Vandekerkhove, Ana Cristina Cardoso and Philip J Boon, 'Is There a Need for a More Explicit Accounting of Invasive Alien Species under the Water Framework Directive?' (2013) 4(1) *Management of Biological Invasions* 25; Momir Paunovic, Bela Csanyi, Predrag Simonovic and Katarina Zoric, 'Invasive Alien Species in the Danube' in *The Handbook of Environmental Chemistry* (Berlin, Springer, 2015).

[120] Hering et al (n 112) 32. See also Keren Raiter, Hugh Possingham, Suzanne Prober, and Richard Hobbs, 'Under the Radar: Mitigating Enigmatic Ecological Impacts' (2014) 29(11) *Trends in Ecology & Evolution* 635.

and development pressures and the future availability of funding.[121] The English EA has, for instance, experienced a rise in real-terms funding for flood defences of about three-quarters from 1997 to 2010, followed by a 20 per cent real-terms cut between 2010 and 2015.[122] The difficulty of accounting for political risk and the impact on SEA processes can clearly be seen in the case of the environmental report for the EA's proposed new river basin management plan for the Anglian River Basin District.[123] This stated:

> The draft plan presents a scenario of water body objectives that could be achieved in the long-term if all measures that give rise to more benefits than cost were implemented … It is unlikely that there will be sufficient funding available in the short term to deliver the proposed programme of measures in the scenario of the draft plan. Therefore choices will need to be made about which of the proposed water body objectives are achieved first and how improvements should be funded. The purpose of the consultation on the draft plan is to seek people's views on these choices to help inform a final plan of objectives.[124]

The environmental report stated that:

> The measures are set out [in the plan] as a package (or bundle) … and provide strategic options for addressing significant water management issues rather than detailed actions for specific water bodies … The proposed water body objectives in the draft plan are based on an assumption (or scenario) that they are achievable in the long-term if all measures that are technically feasible and worthwhile are implemented. This scenario means that no measures at this stage have been ruled out on the basis of affordability constraints.[125]

The alternatives that were assessed were four generic scenarios: (i) maintaining ongoing measures, but taking no new measures; (ii) measures aiming to prevent deterioration and meet the protected area objectives up to 2027; (iii) measures aiming at preventing deterioration and meeting the protected area objectives plus achieving all technically feasible improvements; (iv) measures aiming at preventing deterioration and meeting the protected area objectives plus all measures to improve status where the estimates benefits exceeded the costs.[126]

The work underlying the assessment, namely costing the various technically possible measures and determining their benefits and potential synergies so as to allow for the prioritisation of packages that work together, is a sensible way to

[121] See GT Raadgever, C Dieperink, P Driessen, A Smit and HFMW van Rijswick, 'Uncertainty Management Strategies: Lessons from the Regional Implementation of the Water Framework Directive in the Netherlands' (2011) 14(1) *Environmental Science and Policy* 64.

[122] Oliver Bennett and Sarah Hartwell-Naguib, 'Flood Defence Spending in England', House of Commons Library standard note SN/SC/5755 (November 2014) 3–4.

[123] Environment Agency, *Draft Update to the River Basin Management Plan for the Anglian River Basin District Environmental Report* (October 2014).

[124] ibid 9.

[125] ibid 14.

[126] ibid 18.

allow for the uncertainty in relation to long-term funding. Yet these scenarios are highly artificial. The first option, doing less than the minimum required, is not a lawful option. Assessing the third option is artificial if the plan-makers have already come to the view that the costs exceed the benefits of a course of action, although the inclusion of this scenario in the report might simply reflect a costing of all the technically feasible measures *before* the selection of the fourth scenario. The latter, assuming no funding constraints, is also unrealistic.

Conclusion

Whilst there are now numerous academic journals concerned with the technical, scientific and organisational aspects of environmental assessment, there have been few attempts to systematically examine SEA practice on a sector-by-sector basis within or between Member States, or to critically examine the case for redefining the definition of 'plans and programmes' requiring SEA. There is a tremendous amount of work required to appraise lengthy environmental reports and to investigate the effectiveness of SEA in respect of each plan or programme to which it has been, or could have been, applied. Nonetheless, we consider that such comprehensive studies are likely to prove extremely useful in understanding the efficacy and suitability of the current regulatory regime. In particular, we consider that an examination of the impact of the SEA Directive upon energy generation requires further research. It appears likely that the significant role of exempt budgetary subsidies and pecuniary incentives in determining the delivery of low-carbon energy has resulted in strategic decisions with major implications for the environment in terms of the eventual energy mix and the projects that will come forward for development consent, being taken without being informed by SEA work.

A systematic study of these questions is far beyond the scope of this chapter. Our brief survey has inevitably been highly selective, examining a small number of case studies across just two sectors. Nevertheless, we do feel that it is possible to draw some tentative conclusions from our review of the case law, literature and practical examples.

The first conclusion to draw is that the jurisprudence of the UKSC has allowed a gap in the procedural protection of environmental interests to remain in place. Where projects are planned and promoted, the initial plans for the projects are not treated as qualifying as plans requiring assessment under the SEA Directive because they do not expressly set criteria for the determination of the development consent for that project or for other projects. This means that very large-scale infrastructure schemes may be promoted without a mandatory examination of alternative options. Inevitably, this increases the risk that relatively poor-performing projects are promoted and that needless or disproportionate harm to the environment is caused. The consequences may be the costly destruction of natural assets or a waste of resources.[127]

The second tentative conclusion is that the strategic assessment of options too often tends to be based upon narrow a priori objectives or generic formulations of alternative courses of action that were not really realistic strategies.

A third tentative conclusion is that the SEA Directive has not succeeded in engaging the public, raising awareness of or lending legitimacy to the plans, programmes and projects examined. This may well be a corollary of the previous two points; if assessment exercises are avoided or are done in a perfunctory or formulaic manner, then that does not inspire the confidence of the general public. However, it may also be a function of other factors, such as a weak local press, poor publicity for consultations or a lack of interest amongst the public. The means of best engaging the public is a question that merits experimentation and research.

Fourth, it seems to us that in many cases too much is expected of SEA, insofar as it is not always able to provide the precise information that decision-makers expect when drawing up plans. Strategic planning is inevitably a high-level exercise, highly contingent upon future events and often based upon incomplete and contested scientific data. In many cases, decision-makers would be best served by clearer statements of the risks and uncertainties surrounding the impacts of a plan or programme, so that the plans and programmes can be designed with an inbuilt flexibility and in a sufficiently robust way to cope with projections differing from reality.

In summary, SEA has the potential to be a powerful tool in the development of sectoral plans and programmes, but it would appear that there is still some way to go before its full promise is fulfilled.

[127] It has been similarly argued by Eva Barrett that national renewable energy action plans adopted under art 4(1) of Directive 2009/28/EC of the European Council and of the Parliament of 23 April 2009 on the promotion of the use of energy from renewable sources ought properly to have required an SEA regardless of whether they were, as a matter of domestic law, a mandatory consideration in development consent applications, as they 'set the framework' for renewable energy projects. An Irish High Court claim is pending alleging that Ireland breached the SEA Directive by adopting an expensive policy encouraging onshore wind without an analysis of alternative renewable energy options. Eva Barrett, 'In Sowing the Wind, How Ireland Could Reap the Whirlwind'—A Case against Irish Wind Development(s)' (2015) 33(1) *Journal of Energy & Natural Resources Law* 59. It is difficult not to agree with the assessment of Áine Ryall in Ch 16 of this volume that in Ireland: 'Significant work remains to be done to improve implementation and embed SEA in national practice.'

12

The Strategic Environmental Assessment and Water Framework Directives

WILLIAM HOWARTH

Introduction[1]

Taking a step back from the detailed body of contemporary European Union (EU) environmental legislation (in which the Strategic Environmental Assessment Directive[2] and the Water Framework Directive[3] are placed), some introductory points may usefully be made about the evolutionary sequence that is illustrated. Broadly, the historical progression has been from 'primitive' approaches to environmental law, primarily grounded in the prohibition of environmentally unacceptable activities, towards a 'purposive' kind of environmental legislation, where the law is being used as a means of achieving a state of the environment that is generally regarded as satisfactory.[4] The shift is from the punishment of environmental wrongdoing, and making polluters pay for their harms, towards the encouragement of environmental 'rightdoing', as, for example, where obligations are imposed to meet EU environmental quality standards for water, air and land. Nonetheless, the chronological sequence is a 'cumulative' progression in the sense that purposive legislation has supplemented, rather than replaced, the outlawing of environmentally unacceptable activities.

[1] This chapter is based on a paper on "Assessment under the EU Strategic Environmental Assessment and the Water Framework Directives" delivered at the Law and Environment 2014 Conference held at University College Cork and earlier work on substance on procedure in environmental assessment published in J. Holder and D. McGillivray, Eds. Taking Stock of Environmental Assessment: Law, Policy and Practice (2007). The author is grateful to those who have commented on the work in its various forms.

[2] Directive on the assessment of the effects of certain plans and programmes on the environment (2001/42/EC) (hereafter 'the SEA Directive').

[3] Directive establishing a framework for Community action in the field of water policy (2000/60/EC) (hereafter 'the WF Directive').

[4] See further the discussion of the extent to which the approach to the interpretation of the SEA Directive goes beyond even a purposive approach by Elizabeth Fisher in Ch 8 of the volume.

The shift of emphasis from primitive to purposive approaches to environmental law is of profound significance in requiring consideration of not merely the appropriate legal reaction to past events, but also a testing of our anticipations of environmental futures. What state of water, air and land would presently count as environmentally satisfactory or, viewed more futuristically, what state of the environment would we regard as an acceptable bequest to future generations? In engaging with these kinds of questions, it becomes apparent that futurism involves gradations of predictability. Where it is known that a chemical is toxic, a *preventative* approach towards the entry of that chemical into watercourses is properly adopted. Alternatively, where a new substance has unknown, but potentially serious, impacts upon the environment, management of the possibility of adverse impacts is through the adoption of a *precautionary* approach towards assessment of the risk of harm. Hence, the overall direction in environmental legislative thinking is from reactions to past events to preactions in respect of future events. Amongst these anticipations of the future, legal recognition is given to the difference between preventing likely harms and taking a precautionary approach towards more remotely possible harms (or the management of risks).[5]

The cumulative progression from reaction to preaction in environmental law has placed ever-greater emphasis upon the assessment processes by which future harms and risks of harm are evaluated. Stripped of subject-specific detail, an 'assessment' process might be seen as the appraisal of the subject matter against some generally agreed set of valuation criteria. Justifications of value judgements resulting from assessment only succeed where they can be shown to rely upon higher norms which are shared by those who might seek to contest them. Hence, for most environmentalists, the key higher norm is the idea of sustainable development.[6] It follows that the central question in any kind of environmental assessment is the extent to which the outcomes of a present decision will contribute towards development which best meets the environmental and developmental needs to future generations. The problem, of course, is that we have no way of knowing what the needs of future generations will be. Beyond that, in most cases where a decision has to be made, sustainable development proves to be a rather nebulous or remote objective. More immediate and practicable criteria, such as meeting legislatively specified environmental quality standards, are needed as a means towards the ultimate goal. Nonetheless, the key point remains: that any

[5] Now see art 191(2) of the Treaty on the Functioning of the European Union, which sets out the principles of the environment policy of the EU, requiring EU policy on the environment to aim at a high level of protection and to be based on the precautionary principle and on the principles that preventive action should be taken, and that environmental damage should as a priority be rectified at source and that the polluter should pay.

[6] The literature on the concept of 'sustainable development' is vast, but a good starting point on its practical legal implications is A Ross, *Sustainable Development Law in the UK: From rhetoric to reality?* (2012).

'assessment' involves or assumes some generally accepted valuation criteria against which the subject of the assessment is measured.

The difficulty, so far as EU environmental law is concerned, is that whilst assessment requirements are frequently adopted as a response to environmental uncertainties, the valuation criteria against which these assessments are to be undertaken are often unstated and/or unclear, and are frequently left to depend upon background or context. For example, in the field of EU ecological law, the Habitats Directive requires that plans or projects that are likely to have a significant effect upon ecologically designated sites should be subject to an 'appropriate assessment'[7] of their implications with regard to the conservation objectives of a site.[8] In this context, the expression 'appropriate assessment' seems almost intentionally mysterious, begging the inevitable question: *appropriate* to what? It is only when the Habitats Directive is read as a whole that the values underlying the assessment become evident. Hence, the need for designated sites to be maintained at a 'favourable conservation status' and the need to maintain 'interity' or 'coherence' in the overall network of ecological sites (Natura 2000) provide the valuation criteria against which 'appropriate assessments' must be undertaken.[9] Even then, perhaps, terms like 'favourable conservation status' and 'ecological coherence' may open up further debates as to how these things are to be understood in specific contexts.

Although the underlying values that provide the basis for 'appropriate assessment' under the Habitats Directive are not made explicit, they are at least reasonably discoverable by investigation of the body of the Directive. However, in other instances where an 'assessment' is required under environmental legislation, the valuation criteria are less readily discoverable. In the extreme case, assessment processes become 'aimless' where there are no stated or discoverable valuation criteria or where no indication is provided as to the relevant factors in the assessment and the weight to be given to these. 'Aimlessness' is here understood in the literal sense of lacking clearly stated or discoverable aims (rather than the everyday sense of 'being worthless'). This is a particular problem in respect of EU legislation providing for environmental impact assessment (EIA) under the Environmental Impact Assessment Directive[10] and strategic environmental assessment (SEA) under the SEA Directive. By contrast, in other areas of EU environmental legislation, environmental assessment processes are far more explicit in specifying which factors are relevant to the assessment and what may count as an acceptable outcome to the assessment process. Placed at the extreme (explicit or stipulative) end of the

[7] See further S Tromans, 'The Meaning of "Any Plan or Project" under Article 6(3)' in G Jones (ed), *The Habitats Directive: A Developer's Obstacle Course?* (Oxford, Hart Publishing, 2012) 90–101.

[8] Habitats Directive (92/43/EEC), art 3(3).

[9] ibid, art 4(4). and see Case C-258/11 *Sweetman v An Bord Pleandla* CJEU 11 April 2013 [2015] Env LR 18.

[10] Originally, the Directive on the assessment of the effects of certain public and private projects on the environment (85/337/EEC) subsequently amended and codified as Directive 2011/92/EU and now amended as Directive 2014/52/EU (hereafter 'the EIA Directive').

spectrum of environmental assessment processes is the kind of assessment that is provided for under the EU WF Directive.

The discussion which follows compares and contrasts assessment processes under the SEA Directive and the WF Directive. The purpose of this is to highlight the major differences between the stated requirements for assessments under the WF Directive and the comparative lack of these under the SEA Directive.[11] Inevitably, this contrast raises the question whether a more substantive kind of environmental assessment needs to be developed from the SEA procedures. As a precursor to this discussion, the next section offers some observations on the forerunner to all kinds of EU environmental assessment: EIA under the EIA Directive. The Origins of Environmental Assessment in the EIA Directive.

The environmental assessment processes under both the SEA Directive and the WF Directive build upon assessment requirements inherited from the EIA Directive. The value of the legacy provided by the EIA Directive, in shifting EU environmental legislation in an anticipatory direction, cannot be overstated. As was noted soon after its adoption in 1985, the Directive was 'arguably the most significant of all the existing pieces of Community environmental legislation'.[12] Despite the passage of time, the special significance of the Directive remains in providing the foundation for an assessment methodology which has progressively expanded its remit.

In contrast to previous (pre-1985) sectoral environmental quality legislation concerning the protection of the different environmental media of water, air and land, the EIA Directive required the significant effects of a development project to be assessed across a challengingly wide range of possible impacts upon all environmental sectors and their living constituents, both human and non-human. The breadth of this cross-sectoral, or horizontal, exercise may well explain some of the early difficulties encountered by Member States in giving effect to obligations concerning EIA, particularly where national responsibilities for the environment were entrusted to different and sectorally specific authorities.[13] Nonetheless, the overall aim of EIA, that decision-makers should be fully informed of the environmental implications of authorising a development project, might be seen to justify the complexities involved. Information is vital in seeking to avoid, or mitigate, adverse impacts.

[11] For an examination of the application of the SEA Directive to other land use plans, see G Jones & D Graham at chapter 11 of this volume.

[12] R Macrory, 'Environmental Assessment: Critical Legal Issues in Implementation', in D Vaughan (ed), *Environment and Planning Law* (1991) 31.

[13] On the implementation difficulties and the cases before the Court of Justice of the European Union to which these gave rise, see European Commission, *Environmental Impact Assessment of Projects: Rulings of the Court of Justice* (2013); and for a discussion of national implementation issues, see S Tromans, *Environmental Impact Assessment* (2012).

Beyond its contribution to horizontal or holistic environmental legislation, the EIA Directive broke new ground in requiring a markedly greater degree of transparency and democratisation in environmental decision-making. The information gathered through the EIA process was not to be appropriated as the exclusive property of those entrusted with making development consent determinations.[14] EIA is perhaps the first EU recognition of a public right to be fully informed about the implications of a development project and to have access to sufficient information to enable participation in development-consenting procedures that determine the environmental quality of the localities in which ordinary citizens must live.[15] Inclusivity, through the provision of information to enable informed public participation in environmental decision-making, constitutes another dimension to EIA which, at the time of its initiation at least, set it apart from other branches of EU environmental law.[16]

Alongside the new departures in respect of horizontality and inclusivity, the EIA Directive may be seen as enacting an approach to environmental management that is potentially unlimited in its breadth. Accepting, as a general matter, that environmental assessment means subjecting certain kinds of decisions or actions to scrutiny with respect to their environmental implications, the question arises as to *what kinds* of decisions or actions should be subject to that requirement? On this, the form of environmental assessment initially adopted in the European Community must be seen as a rather timid compromise.[17] By comparison, 'environmental impact assessment', as understood in the US, encompassed a requirement that all agencies of Federal Government are to include, with every proposal for legislation and other major federal actions significantly affecting the quality of the human environment, a detailed statement by the responsible officials of the environmental impact of the proposed action.[18] Clearly, the 1985 European

[14] For a general discussion of the role of citizens in environmental decision-making, see J Steele, 'Participation and Deliberation in Environmental Law: Exploring a Problem-Solving Approach' (2001) 21(3) *Oxford Journal of Legal Studies* 415.

[15] See, for example, *Berkeley v Secretary of State for the Environment (Berkeley No 1)* [2000] AC 603, particularly the opinion of Lord Hoffmann, and contrast earlier decisions discussed in J Alder, 'Environmental Impact Assessment—The Inadequacies of English Law' (1993) 5(2) *Journal of Environmental Law* 203; and A Ward, 'The Right to an Effective Remedy in European Community Law and Environmental Protection: A Case Study of United Kingdom Judicial Decisions Concerning the Environmental Assessment Directive' (1993) 5(2) *Journal of Environmental Law* 221.

[16] Although subsequently see the Environmental Information Directive (90/313/EEC and 2003/4/EC) and the raft of EU and national measures seeking to give effect to the 1998 United Nations Economic Commission for Europe Convention on Access to Information, Public Participation and Decision Making and Access to Justice in Environmental Matters (hereinafter 'the Aarhus Convention').

[17] See C Wood, *Environmental Impact Assessment: A Comparative Review* (1996) 35, recounting the 'emasculation' of earlier versions of the EIA Directive.

[18] National Environmental Policy Act 1969 (US), s 102(c). On the influence of the National Environmental Policy Act 1969 on the SEA Directive, see further Robert McCracken and Ned Westaway in Ch 1 and Valerie Fogleman in Ch 3 of this volume.

Community version was considerably narrower in requiring environmental assessment only in respect of particular, public or private development projects, with no attempt to encompass all legislative and other major acts as required in the US.

The relatively limited version of environmental assessment adopted by the European Community under the original EIA Directive may be seen as politically expedient at the time it was adopted.[19] Nonetheless, in the light of experience of implementing the EIA process, it was inevitable that its limitations would come to be recognised. Determination of whether a particular project should be authorised is profoundly influenced by broader policies for land and other resource uses and a range of other environmental concerns. In many respects, these are at least as important as the project-specific and location-specific considerations upon which EIA tends to focus. When this constraint upon the EIA process is recognised, the shortcomings of project-specific approach towards environmental assessment become readily apparent.

The natural response to the limitations of EIA was to bring a wider range of factors into the assessment process. This was accomplished by the SEA Directive, which extended environmental consideration from the impacts of particular development projects to the assessment of environmental effects of the 'plans and programmes' under which they fell. With a view towards further promoting sustainable development, the preparation and adoption of plans and programmes is now the subject to a process of scrutiny as to the significant effects they are likely to have upon the environment. As will be seen, the scope of the 'plans and programmes' subject to SEA is extensive, though not always certain. Nonetheless, the progression from projects to plans and programmes, as the target for environmental assessment is a welcome enlargement of environmentally informed decision-making.

Despite this, it should be recognised that environmental assessment remains a less extensive requirement under EU law than under US federal law. In the EU, the policy-making and legislative processes have been particularly resistant to the application of environmental assessment as a legal requirement. However, the need for an 'impact assessment' methodology to improve the quality and coherence of the EU policy development process and to enable the more coherent implementation of sustainable development is accepted. The EU makes informal use of SEA at the level of the policy formulation and legislative enactment processes. Hence, all major legislative and other policy proposals that have a potential economic, social and/or environmental impact and/or require some regulatory measures for their implementation will be subject to a preliminary and, in some cases, extended assessment of their economic, environmental and/or social impacts

[19] See P Wathern, 'The EIA Directive of the European Community' in P Wathern (ed), *Environmental Impact Assessment: Theory and Practice* (1988) 192 for a discussion of the background to the adoption of the EIA Directive.

before adoption.[20] Recognising the increasing degree to which the formulation of policies and the enactment of legislation involves issues of political judgement, the potential for the further formalisation of environmental assessment requirements in these areas is likely to be limited.

In short, therefore, the adoption of the EIA Directive set EU environmental law on a new course which is distinguished from previous environmental law in respect of its horizontality and inclusivity. Moreover, it puts in place a forward-looking and purposive approach to environmental law which has gained momentum and become more broadly applied to other kinds of environmental decision-making. The SEA Directive and the WF Directive may thus be seen as inheritors of EIA methodology, but have reapplied it in markedly different ways and, as will be seen, illustrate environmental assessment being reinterpreted in ways which are profoundly different in terms of their procedural and substantive characteristics.

Assessment in SEA

The SEA Directive is extensively discussed elsewhere in this volume and warrants only the briefest of summaries of its content and mechanisms here to enable these to be compared and contrasted with provisions under the WF Directive. Hence, in brief, SEA involves the transmission of the environmental assessment process 'upstream' from assessment of projects (under the EIA Directive) to the assessment of plans and programmes. This involves the focus of attention being shifted from proposals for individual projects to the land use development and other plans which guide or determine whether individual projects, which may have a significant environmental impact, should be authorised.

The essential legal requirements are that SEA must[21] be undertaken in respect of a plan or programme which is likely to have significant environmental effects and, among other things, is prepared for stated purposes and sets the framework for future development consent for projects listed in Annex I or II of the EIA Directive, or is likely to have to have an effect on sites falling under the Habitats Directive.[22] Within this statement, five requirements may be identified: first, whether a plan or programme is likely to have significant environmental effects;

[20] See European Commission, Communication from the Commission on Impact Assessment, COM (2002), 276 final; and see J Holder, *Environmental Assessment: The Regulation of Decision Making* (2004) 164.

[21] Although an element of discretion is given to Member States to broaden this requirement under the obligation to determine whether plans and programmes other than those that are explicitly identified are likely to have significant environmental effects. See SEA Directive, art 3(4).

[22] ibid, arts 2 and 3(1). In relation to the Habitats Directive, this is a reference to the need for an 'appropriate assessment' of sites under art 6 or 7.

second, whether it is prepared for a stated purpose; third, whether 'it sets the framework for future development consent'; fourth, whether that future development consent relates to a project within Annex I or II of the EIA Directive; and, fifth, as an alternative to the fourth requirement, whether it is likely to have an effect upon certain protected habitats.

This concise summary suffices to show that, in most respects, SEA is concerned with secondary or derivative kinds of environmental impact. It is not the particular plan or programme under consideration that has the adverse environmental impacts, but rather the individual projects that are authorised by or undertaken in accordance with the plan or programme. In neither SEA nor EIA are explicit environmental values incorporated as requirements of the assessment process. Hence, SEA may be seen to have inherited the 'aimlessness' of EIA.

Assessment Under the WF Directive

The WF Directive establishes an EU strategy for water management at river basin level through a diverse range of mechanisms directed towards securing the good status of relevant waters and meeting other environmental objectives under the Directive. This raises a raft of challenging implementation issues which are not up for discussion here.[23] The narrower focus that is needed is upon the role of assessment and planning processes under the WF Directive, and the extent to which this involves a methodology that is comparable to assessment under the SEA Directive. In respect of this, a major innovation of the WF Directive is the introduction of approaches towards achieving satisfactory water quality that involve assessing and addressing impacts upon the aquatic environment and anticipating what must be done to realise specified environmental quality objectives within a stipulated timescale.

Centrally, under the WF Directive, the principal administrative obligation upon Member States is that of ensuring that a river basin management plan (RBMP) is produced for each river basin district lying entirely within its territory.[24] The elements of a RBMP, under Annex VII, encompass: a general description of the characteristics of the river basin district, and specified details concerning surface waters, groundwaters and significant human impacts; information concerning

[23] See generally W Howarth and D McGillivray, *Water Pollution and Water Quality Law* (2001) Ch 5; and, from the perspective of environmental non-governmental organisations, World Wide Fund for Nature and European Environmental Bureau, *'Tips and Tricks' for Water Framework Directive Implementation* (2004).

[24] WF Directive, art 13(1). In respect of international river basin districts falling entirely within the Community, coordination is to be ensured with a view to producing a single international river basin management plan, but where this is not done, RBMPs covering national territories are to achieve the objects of the Directive. See ibid, art 13(2).

protected areas; monitoring arrangements and information on the status of waters; a statement of environmental objectives; and information on the economic analysis of water use. Critically, an RBMP must include a summary of the Programme of Measures (PoMs) that are to be adopted and, by means of which, the environmental objectives of the Directive are to be achieved, and various specific details concerning particular measures.

PoMs are to be established for each river basin district and are to take into account the results of analyses of the characteristics of the river basin district, a review of the impact of human activity and an economic analysis of water use.[25] Hence, account needs to be taken of the most significant anthropogenic pressures on waters and assessments of the impacts of those pressures upon water quality.[26] PoMs also need to be established for the purpose of achieving the environmental objectives of the WF Directive.[27] Broadly, this means that deterioration in the status of waters should be avoided and that waters should be protected, enhanced and restored with the aim of achieving 'good status' for most waters by 2015.[28] However, various exceptions and qualifications are provided for in relation to artificial and heavily modified waters, and situations where less stringent objectives are justified for reasons of feasibility or disproportionate expense.[29]

The Contrast Between Procedure and Substance

Whilst the preceding discussion has outlined similarities between the SEA Directive and the WF Directive, insofar as both require certain kinds of assessment as a precursor to decision-making, a notable contrast exists between the procedural and substantive aspects of the two kinds of assessment procedures. In this context, 'procedure' refers to the activities needing to undertaken prior to making an administrative decision, whereas 'substance' relates to the permissible outcomes of the decision-making process. The critical distinction between these two Directives lies in the question whether, provided defined procedures are followed, anything prevents a final decision in which environmental concerns are overridden by social and/or economic or considerations. If specified environmental requirements need to be met, the process is substantive, whereas if they do not, the process is purely procedural. The key question therefore concerns the extent to which assessments under the SEA Directive and the WF Directive are procedural or substantive.

The critical significance of the procedure/substance distinction in relation to environmental assessment has been recognised for some time, particularly in the

25 ibid, art 11(1).
26 ibid, art 5 and Annex II, paras 1.4 and 5 (surface waters) and similarly para 2.3 (groundwaters).
27 ibid, art 11(1).
28 See the statement of the environmental objectives of the WF Directive later in this chapter.
29 WF Directive, art 4.

US, where EIA was first provided for under the National Environmental Policy Act 1969. The 'rise and fall' of substantive environmental assessment in this jurisdiction is pertinently recounted.[30] The early basis for inferring substantive content was that the obligation upon federal bodies to undertake EIA was capable of being read alongside environmental policy objectives that are articulated in an adjacent section of the Act. This states that the Federal Government is to:

> [U]se all practicable means and measures … in a manner calculated to foster and promote the general welfare, to create and maintain conditions under which man and nature can exist in productive harmony, and fulfil the social, economic and other requirements of present and future generations of Americans.[31]

In furtherance of this policy, the Federal Government is to:

> [U]se all practicable means consistent with other essential considerations of national policy, to improve and coordinate Federal plans, functions, programs and resources to the end that the Nation may [amongst other things] attain the widest range of beneficial uses of the environment without degradation, risk to health or safety, or other undesirable and unintended consequences.[32]

The critical issue arising from these provisions ishe extent to which the policy declaration, and the indication as to the manner of its implementation, gives rise to substantive obligations that must be met through the EIA process. Put the other way around, to what extent may EIA be used to reach outcomes that are contrary to the stated national policy?

The high-water mark in substantive judicial interpretation of EIA can be seen in the *Calvert Cliffs* decision,[33] where the argument was accepted that the environmental policy in the National Environmental Policy Act 1969 imposed substantive duties upon federal agencies. Hence, it was the proper role of the judiciary to review the merits of administrative decisions alongside the policy declaration. However, subsequent decisions have effectively extinguished substantive review by reasserting that only procedural rights are created by EIA requirements.[34] The decline of the substantive interpretation was sealed by a ruling of the Supreme Court affirming that EIA only has the narrower procedural purposes of ensuring that agencies consider environmental impacts and disclose relevant information to the public:

> NEPA does not mandate particular results, but simply prescribes the necessary process. If the adverse environmental effects of the proposed action are adequately identified and

[30] See also Holder (n 20) 250.

[31] National Environmental Policy Act 1969 (US), s 101(a).

[32] ibid, s 101(b).

[33] *Calvert Cliffs' Coordinating Committee v Atomic Energy Commission* 449 F 2d 1109 (DC Circ 1971).

[34] *Stryker's Bay Neighbourhood Council Inc v Karlen* 44 US 223 (1980); *Robertson v Methow Valley Citizens Council* 490 US 332, 104 Led 2d 351 (1989), also cited by Holder (n 20) 254.

evaluated, the agency is not constrained by NEPA from deciding that other values outweigh the environmental costs.[35]

In short, the argument for substantive interpretation of EIA requirements has come to nothing in the US. The issue for the present discussion is whether the same line of reasoning should apply in respect of environmental assessment under EU law, particularly under the SEA Directive and the WF Directive.

Procedure and Substance in the SEA Directive

The recitals to the SEA Directive note that European Community policy on the environment is intended to contribute to the preservation, protection and improvement of the quality of the environment, the protection of human health, and the prudent and rational utilisation of natural resources.[36] Reference is also made to the Fifth Environment Action Programme of the Community, emphasising the need for action in relation to the environment and sustainable development.[37] More broadly, the Directive may be seen as a means of furthering the overall tasks of the EU of promoting 'a harmonious, balanced and sustainable development of economic activities' and securing 'a high level of protection and improvement of the quality of the environment'.[38] However, the critical issue is whether any of these stated policy objectives, which are given as a prelude to the detailed content of the Directive, might be construed as requiring SEA to be undertaken in a substantive manner, so as to ensure that the outcomes of SEA are consistent with the stated policy objectives. On this, the answer is almost certainly in the negative. The stark affirmation that the SEA Directive is of a 'procedural nature'[39] seems to rule out any substantive content to SEA. Nonetheless, it is remarkable that a directive should go to such lengths to spell out its policy objectives whilst recognising that it provides no mechanisms to ensure that any of those objectives will actually be advanced to any extent by the content of the Directive. The language of the recitals turns out to be purely exhortatory and the body of the Directive 'aimless'.

'Aimless', again, needs to be understood in the sense of lacking mandatory environmental aims or values rather than being of no benefit. The benefit of SEA (or EIA) may be seen arising otherwise than through meeting minimum environmental standards in decision-making, for example, in securing

[35] Per Stephens J in *Robertson v Methow Valley Citizens Council* 490 US 332, 104 Led 2d 350.

[36] SEA Directive, Recital 1.

[37] ibid, Recital 2, referring to Fifth Environment Action Programme, *Towards Sustainability—A European Community programme of policy and action in relation to the environment and sustainable development* (1993), as supplemented by Council Decision 2179/98/EC affirming the importance of assessing the likely environmental effects of plans and programmes [1998] OJ L275, 10 October, 1.

[38] European Community Treaty, art 2; and now see Treaty on European Union, art 3.

[39] SEA Directive, Recital 9.

better-informed or more participative decision-making. Hence, the view may plausibly be maintained that more widely informed environmental decisions necessarily result in environmentally better outcomes, since environmental assessment requirements are a force for change in institutional cultures, requiring a better appreciation of the importance of environmental considerations. Likewise, the democratisation of environmental decision-making, through the provision of public information and encouraging public involvement, may be seen as a means of securing better protection of the environment. Despite the vigour with which these views have been presented by commentators, it remains an open question, which seems to be empirically unprovable either way, whether environmental assessment has actually resulted in environmentally better decisions than would have been reached if it did not exist.[40]

The converse (sceptical) view, in relation to EIA at least, is that assessment procedures have merely added legitimacy to decisions that involve an inbuilt bias towards those developers who use environmental statements to direct the flow of information in a pro-development direction.[41] Alternatively, participative procedures may be seen as open to domination by particular interest groups and inevitably failing to reflect the interests of future generations.[42] More sceptically still, the extreme view might be taken that the central premise upon which EIA is based, that detailed articulation of reasons for administrative decisions necessarily enhances the integrity of the decision-making process, is simply a 'dubious example of wishful thinking', put colourfully, 'nine parts myth and one part coconut oil'.[43]

Clearly, it is informative to ascertain that a particular project, plan or programme is likely to have environmentally catastrophic consequences, but the remarkable observation is that neither EIA nor SEA does anything to preclude the approval of the project, plan or programme, despite that finding. The lack of (probably unobtainable) hard evidence that environmental assessment actually produces environmentally better decisions and the absence of logically compelling reasons why it should produce such decisions make positioning oneself on the converts-to-sceptics spectrum of views largely a matter of faith. If there are benefits to environmental assessment, they are the incidental rather than the necessary results of the legal forms in which it has been established. The only incontrovertible way of showing that environmental assessment will necessarily produce environmentally better decisions is through the explicit incorporation of mandatory substantive environmental requirements upon decision-making.

[40] See, eg, European Commission, Report from the Commission on the implementation of Directive 85/337/EEC on the assessment of the effects of certain public and private projects on the environment COM(93)28, s 4.5 and Table 4.9.

[41] Holder (n 20) 285.

[42] Generally, on participation, see M Lee, *EU Environmental Law* (2005) Chs 5 and 6.

[43] JL Sax, 'The (Unhappy) Truth about NEPA' (1973) 26 *Oklahoma Law Review* 239.

Procedure and Substance in the WF Directive Assessment

A major advancement of the WF Directive, as compared with previous EU water legislation, was the introduction of approaches towards achieving satisfactory water quality that involve assessing and addressing impacts upon the aquatic environment, including those arising from a range of land-based activities, and anticipating what must be done to realise specified environmental and ecological quality objectives. Hence, the WF Directive adopts an environmental assessment methodology which allows direct comparisons with the SEA Directive, but applies that methodology in a way that demonstrates some striking points of contrast.

The form of environmental assessment provided for in the WF Directive requires RBMPs and PoMs to be prepared according to a formalised procedure based upon the gathering, analysis and application of specified kinds of information. In particular, Member States must ensure that for each river basin district, the following are undertaken: an analysis of its characteristics; a review of the impact of human activity on the status of surface waters and groundwater; and an economic analysis of water use.[44] These three kinds of 'assessment' must be carried out in accordance with the technical specifications set out in Annexes II and III to the Directive. Annex II sets out in some detail the principles that must be applied to the characterisation of surface waters, the type-specific reference conditions that are to be applied, and the identification of pressures and assessment of impacts. Annex III identifies the information that needs to be gathered, among other things, to make estimates of the volumes, prices and costs associated with the provision of water services. The overall impression is that a challengingly wide-ranging and detailed amount of environmental information needs to be gathered and analysed as a precursor to formulating the RBMPS and PoMs.

Perhaps most critically, the purpose of the assessments is to identify water bodies where individual, cumulative or synergistic impacts cause them to be at risk of failing to meet the environmental objectives of the WF Directive by the required deadline Concisely stated, this means that relevant waters must not fall below what is required for the following environmental objectives to be met:

- preventing deterioration of water quality;[45]
- protecting, enhancing and restoring waters with the aim of achieving good status (encompassing both good chemical status and good ecological status of surface waters) by 2015;[46]
- protecting, enhancing and restoring artificial or heavily modified waters with the aim of achieving good status by 2015;[47]

44 WF Directive, art 5.

45 ibid, art 1.a.i and b.i.

46 ibid, art 4.1.a.ii and b.ii.

47 ibid, art 4.1.a.iii.

— progressively reducing pollution by priority substances and phasing out emissions, discharges and losses of priority hazardous substances;[48]
— preventing or limiting inputs of pollutants into groundwaters;[49]
— reversing significant upward trends in the concentration of any pollutant in groundwater;[50] and
— complying with standards and objectives for protected areas by 2015, including objectives for areas for the abstraction of drinking water.[51]

This clear statement of the environmental objectives of the WF Directive sets out the aims against which assessments need to be made and the values that determine the acceptability of any RBMP or PoMs. Subject to various exceptions and conditions, the environmental objectives provide the substance that must be met through the assessment process under the Directive.

The Contrast on Substance

The most significant contrasts between the kinds of environmental assessment provided for under the SEA Directive and the WF Directive are in relation to the degree of substance provided for in respect of the outcomes of the respective assessment processes. Taking the SEA Directive first, the preamble recognises that the Directive seeks to harmonise different environmental assessment systems operating within Member States so that they 'contain a set of common procedural requirements'.[52] The purpose of adopting common minimum environmental assessment procedures across the EU is to include a wider set of factors in decision-making in order to 'contribute to more sustainable and effective solutions'.[53] However, it is far from clear how the SEA Directive procedures will guarantee any particular level of environmental protection. This is because the overriding obligation, that specified kinds of environmental information should only be 'taken into account' in environmental decision-making,[54] does not determine what weight should be given to significant environmental effects in the final decision.

An environmental report must provide information on the environmental protection objectives, established at the international, EU or Member State level, which are relevant to the plan or programme, and the way in which those objectives and any environmental considerations have been taken into account during its preparation.[55] Despite this, there is no mandatory requirement that the decision

[48] ibid, art 4.1.a.iv.
[49] ibid, art 4.1.b.ii.
[50] ibid, art 4.1.b.ii.
[51] ibid, arts 1.c and 7.
[52] SEA Directive, Recital 6.
[53] ibid, Recital 5.
[54] ibid, art 8.
[55] ibid, Annex I(e).

reached must be in conformity with these objectives. Hence, the identification of significant adverse environmental effects[56] of implementing a plan or programme does not prevent it being authorised in accordance with the SEA Directive. Notwithstanding a finding that a plan or programme is relevant to the implementation of other EU environmental legislation[57] and is likely to prevent or obstruct effective implementation of that other legislation, the SEA Directive provides no bar to the plan or programme being adopted. If the consequences of implementation are that other EU legislation is breached, implicitly, this matter is then left to be dealt with under the other legislation.

The lack of substance in the SEA Directive contrasts markedly with the emphasis upon the measures that are needed actually to achieve the environmental quality objectives in the WF Directive assessment and planning. Assessment of human impacts upon the aquatic environment is undertaken for an explicit purpose. Its aim is to ascertain how much adverse impacts need to be reduced in order to achieve specified environmental objectives within a stated timescale. An RBMP or a PoMs would therefore be unacceptable if it were not formulated in a manner likely to achieve those environmental objectives.[58] It would not be sufficient to embark upon a process of plan formulation that merely involved 'taking into account' the environmental objectives that need to be achieved. Moreover, the specification of environmental objectives under the WF Directive goes further than setting out the generalised requirements that were noted above as the 'environmental objectives' of the Directive. In various ways, the environmental objectives also relate to environmental quality standards that establish precise chemical and biological quality criteria that need to be realised if the environmental objectives of the Directive are to be met.

An appreciation of the ways in which the WF Directive assessment and planning is driven by environmental quality standards may be best illustrated by the requirement of 'non-deterioration' of water quality. As an environmental quality objective of the Directive, it has been noted that this means that implementation must be by measures that prevent the deterioration of the existing quality of surface and groundwaters.[59] Beyond that, the Directive states that implementation 'is to achieve a level of protection of waters at least equivalent to that provided in certain earlier acts', which are to be repealed once the relevant provisions of the WF Directive are fully implemented.[60] The broad implication is that where

[56] As determined by the 'significance criteria' under ibid, Annex II.

[57] As identified as a criterion of significance under ibid, Annex II, para 1.

[58] However, an issue remains as to whether the obligation on Member States is actually to meet the environmental objectives or merely to use their 'best efforts' to achieve those objectives: see D Grimeaud, 'Reforming EU Water Law: Towards Sustainability' (2001) *European Environmental Law Review* 41–51, 88–97, 125–35; and J van Kempen, 'Countering the Obscurity of Obligations in European Environmental Law: An Analysis of Article 4 of the European Water Framework' (2012) 24(3) *Journal of Environmental Law* 499.

[59] WF Directive, arts4(1)(a)i and 4(1)(b)i.

[60] ibid, Recital 51.

an environmental quality standard has been provided for in a previous water directive, at least equally stringent requirements are imposed by the WF Directive. More specifically, where pre-existing legislation requires a quality objective or standard to be met and this cannot be achieved by existing controls upon emissions, stricter conditions must be imposed to ensure that the objective or standard is met.[61] In part, this has the consequence that environmental quality standards established pursuant to the Aquatic Environment (or Dangerous Substances) Directive must be adhered to in implementing the WF Directive,[62] but the same approach also applies to 'other' existing legislation setting relevant objectives or quality standards.[63]

Beyond non-deterioration below existing water quality standards, the WF Directive incorporates mechanisms for the adoption of further water quality standards for substances that have not been provided for under previous legislation. Hence, the 'framework' character of the Directive envisages additional measures being adopted against pollution of water by individual pollutants or groups of pollutants presenting a significant risk to or via the aquatic environment.[64] Among other actions for this purpose, the Commission is bound to submit proposals for quality standards applicable to the concentrations of priority substances in surface water, sediments and biota.[65]

Although the environmental quality standards referred to above concentrate upon precisely determined parameters for maximum levels or particular pollutants which may be present in the aquatic environment, the exercise of standard setting is not limited to chemical parameters. The WF Directive also incorporates requirements for good ecological status of surface waters involving the determination of biological standards which must be met by relevant waters. The substantial challenge involved in securing good ecological status has become almost as precisely quantified as that involved in securing parameters relating to good chemical status.[66]

[61] ibid, art 10(3), which provides for a 'combined approach' to point and diffuse sources.

[62] The Dangerous Substances Directive (76/464/EEC) came to be referred to as the Aquatic Environment Directive 2006/11/EC (on pollution caused by certain dangerous substances discharged into the environment of the Community), but has been repealed under the WF Directive. The five 'daughter' Directives to the Dangerous Substances Directive, setting environmental quality standards for specific substances, are listed in Annex IV to the WF Directive.

[63] Although the WF Directive is not explicit as to what 'other' legislation is relevant here, it is possible that water quality standards provided for under the Agricultural Nitrates Directive (91/676/EEC) and the Drinking Water Quality Directive (80/778/EEC, as amended) might be examples that fall within this category.

[64] See WF Directive, art 16(1) on strategies against pollution of water.

[65] ibid, art 16(7). 'Priority' substances are identified in accordance with art 16(2) and are listed in Annex X. See ibid, art 2(30). See Decision No 2455/2001/EC of the European Parliament and of the Council establishing the list of priority substances in the field of water policy and amending Directive 2000/60/EC, establishing WF Directive Annex X. See also the Environmental Quality Standards Daughter Directive (2008/105/EC).

[66] Although see W Howarth, 'The Progression Towards Ecological Quality Standards' (2006) 18(1) *Journal of Environmental Law* 3, which expresses some reservations as to the basis for ecological valuation in setting ecological standards under the WF Directive.

In relation to both chemical and ecological status, precise quantified criteria are provided to determine what is required for RBMP or PoMs to be acceptable. The overriding point to be reiterated is that WF Directive assessment and planning is being undertaken for the purpose of actually realising explicit and precisely stated environmental objectives and standards, not merely 'taking into account' the need for a high level of protection of the environment, as is required in EIA or SEA.

Conclusion

The preceding discussion has drawn attention to the many points of similarity between the processes of assessment involved in formulating RBMPs and PoMs under the WF Directive and the requirements for SEA under the SEA Directive. On points of detail, many contrasts have been noted and, in respect of specificity, the WF Directive is markedly more explicit and stipulative as to the assessment procedures that need to be followed. Nonetheless, the overall similarities may be seen as greater than the differences. The WF Directive and the SEA Directive share admirably comparable and compatible environmental assessment methodologies.

However, the fundamental contrast between the WF Directive and the SEA Directive lies in the balance between procedure and substance. While assessment under the SEA Directive is entirely procedural in character, the WF Directive incorporates many points of substance which ensure that assessment and planning processes are directed towards ensuring that precisely stated environmental and ecological objectives and standards are actually met. The possibility that a faultless environmental scrutiny procedure could still lead to an environmentally unacceptable decision being reached is ruled out in the WF Directive assessment and planning processes. This is because the WF Directive procedures go beyond informing decision-makers of the existence of environmental factors which need to be 'taken into account'. They instruct decision-makers as to the weight to be attached to those factors. Certain outcomes of the WF Directive decision-making process are made unacceptable by the specification of mandatory thresholds, below which the environmental impact of an RBMP or a PoMs should not be allowed to fall.

If substantive environmental assessment can be implemented in the water sector, it seems difficult to see a reason why it should not be achieved in other sectors, or cross-sectorally through the EIA and SEA processes. Most simply, this might be accomplished, initially at least, by the incorporation of existing environmental objectives and standards from other EU environmental legislation as a threshold for acceptability of any project, plan or programme. This could be done by a relatively small change of wording to prohibit the approval or adoption of any project, plan or programme that involved contravention of other EU environmental legislation. Hence, whilst the existing wording of the SEA Directive merely requires account to be taken of the relevance of a plan or programme for the implementation of other Community environmental legislation,[67] this needs to be bolstered. The step needs to be taken from taking cognisance of existing environmental objectives and standards to *requiring* that they should actually be adhered to in the authorisation or adoption of any project, plan or programme. As has been seen, this step, from procedure into substance, has already been taken in WF Directive assessment and planning. The culmination of the argument is that suggestion that the same step should also be followed in respect of the EIA Directive and the SEA Directive.

Environmental standards should be seen as a means to an end rather than an end in themselves. In the longer term, the effectiveness of SEA must be measured by the extent to which it yields decisions which allow progress towards sustainable development. However, as has been noted, the difficulty with this objective is that criteria for what is to count as 'sustainable development' are notoriously inaccessible. Possibly, in the distant future, precise quantified criteria might be devised to assess the sustainability of proposed projects, plans or programmes. For the foreseeable present at least, adherence to environmental objectives and standards in decision-making is the most feasible option for progress. Arguably, the introduction of environmental standards as mandatory requirements for EIA and SEA is the next step in this progression.

[67] WF Directive, Annex II, para 1; and see also Annex I(e), which requires an environmental report to provide information on environmental protection objectives, established at the international, Community or Member State level, which are relevant to a plan or programme. Article 8 of the WF Directive requires these matters to be 'taken into account' before the adoption of a plan or programme.

13

Uncharted Waters: SEA in the UK Offshore Area

RICHARD CADDELL

Introduction

Despite its clear significance for the myriad economic, developmental and infrastructure policies of the Member States, the Strategic Environmental Assessment Directive[1] remains one of the more mysterious and underappreciated elements of European Union (EU) environmental law. This has proved to be especially true in the context of the offshore environment. Indeed, while the maritime implications of pertinent nature conservation and planning-orientated EU legislation have been overlooked generally,[2] there has been little consideration of the application of the principles of strategic environment assessment (SEA) within the marine environment worldwide[3] and virtually no evaluation of this issue in the specific case of the various EU seas. The lessons learned from SEA practices in the offshore environment, and their wider implications for 'certain plans and programmes' undertaken in both a marine and a terrestrial setting, have therefore been chronically neglected to date. This oversight is indeed regrettable for, as

[1] Directive 2001/42/EC of the European Parliament and of the Council on the Assessment of the Effects of Certain Plans and Programmes on the Environment [2001] OJ L197/30 (hereinafter 'the SEA Directive').

[2] On the challenges raised by the marine application of EU nature conservation law, see Richard Caddell, 'The Maritime Dimensions of the Habitats Directive: Past Challenges and Future Opportunities' in Gregory Jones QC (ed), *The Habitats Directive: A Developer's Obstacle Course?* (Oxford, Hart Publishing, 2012) 187.

[3] The current legal literature on offshore SEA has largely addressed the Arctic region, either holistically or in the context of individual jurisdictions. For a helpful overview in the specific context of Canada, see Meinhard Doelle, Nigel Bankes and Louie Porta, 'Using Strategic Environmental Assessments to Guide Oil and Gas Exploration Decisions: Applying Lessons Learned from Atlantic Canada to the Beaufort Sea' (2013) 22 *Review of European Community and International Environmental Law* 103. On multilateral commitments towards the application of SEA in this region, see Gunnar Sander, 'International Legal Obligations for Environmental Impact Assessment and Strategic Environmental Assessment in the Arctic Ocean' (2016) 31 *International Journal of Marine and Coastal Law* 88.

this chapter seeks to illustrate, particular EU Member States have demonstrated a largely unheralded history of innovation in addressing SEA concerns in relation to their offshore activities.

This chapter examines the SEA practices of the UK in respect of its key offshore industries, a sector that presents an intriguing case study of the practical implementation of the Directive. As this chapter demonstrates, while the UK authorities have been justifiably criticised for a 'somewhat schizophrenic approach to SEA'[4] in a terrestrial context, these principles were purposely introduced and applied in the national offshore energy sector a considerable period of time before the Directive entered into effect. Moreover, while little explored in the current legal literature, the UK offshore framework has since evolved organically into a sophisticated and innovative regime that is in many key respects considerably more advanced than its terrestrial counterpart. Accordingly, this proactive regulatory framework governing the UK offshore energy industries has generated extensive assessment experience that may be of considerable value in framing SEA-related practices in other sectors and jurisdictions. Indeed, as this chapter outlines, particular advances have been apparent in administering the SEA process and facilitating public and expert participation, which has been underpinned by a strong culture of institutional reflection to foster targeted improvements to SEA practices. Nevertheless, despite these laudable developments, as with terrestrial SEA practices, a number of shortcomings and challenges also have been encountered in the marine context, notably concerning the acquisition and management of environmental data and its practical application to the decision-making process. To this end, this chapter provides an appraisal of SEA practices in the UK offshore energy sector, evaluating the lessons that have been forthcoming to date and considering their implications for the further refinement of the offshore SEA process in respect of traditional and emerging marine industries.

Offshore Waters and SEA

What Are (UK) Offshore Waters?

As a matter of general international law, offshore waters are usually considered to encompass those situated between the seaward side of the territorial sea (which traditionally extends up to 12 nautical miles from the national baseline),[5] up to the

[4] William R Sheate, Helen J Byron and Steven P Smith, 'Implementing the SEA Directive: Sectoral Challenges and Opportunities for the UK and EU' (2004) 14 *European Environment* 73, 74.

[5] UN Convention on the Law of the Sea (10 December 1982) 1883 UNTS 396, 21 ILM 1261 (entered into force 16 November 1994) (hereinafter 'LOSC') art 3. National territorial seas nonetheless vary in size and some coastal states claim substantially more than 12 miles, an exercise ultimately in enterprising illegality. Other coastal states may claim significantly less, primarily for reasons of geography or by

outer limits of the exclusive economic zone (EEZ), which subsequently extends out to a maximum of 200 nautical miles to sea.[6] Technically speaking, however, the precise parameters of the UK offshore area have traditionally been rather more complex than this general model would suggest. The UK government formally established a national EEZ only as recently as 2014,[7] instead favouring a series of alternative jurisdictional designations, christened with varying nomenclature,[8] to regulate economic activities commonly associated with the exercise of EEZ powers within the 200-mile offshore limit. Accordingly, the prior concept of the 'offshore marine area' within which pre-2014 SEA procedures were conducted was instead framed by the parameters of UK fisheries jurisdiction.[9]

For the current purposes of UK law, the concept of offshore waters thereby generally excludes the territorial sea,[10] an area often referred to as 'coastal' or 'inshore' waters. Exceptionally, however, in the context of the marine energy sector, 'offshore activities' are construed as encompassing the entire sweep of the jurisdictional waters of the UK, including the territorial sea.[11] Hence, as far as UK energy production is concerned, all marine activities are inherently 'offshore' in nature. This position notwithstanding, as noted below, it is the current policy of the UK government to sanction energy development where possible solely within areas beyond the territorial sea and upon the UK continental shelf (UKCS).[12]

virtue of a judicial delimitation settlement or an agreement with neighbouring jurisdictions. The UK acceded to the LOSC on 25 July 1997.

[6] LOSC, art 57.

[7] Legal powers to rectify this rather convoluted position by reclassifying these waters as an orthodox EEZ were created under s 41(3) of the Marine and Coastal Access Act 2009. This was duly established under the Exclusive Economic Zone Order 2013, SI 2013/3161, and the UK EEZ entered into effect on 31 March 2014.

[8] These included a 'renewable energy zone' (Energy Act 2004, s 84), which was subsequently rescinded by the Exclusive Economic Zone Order 2013, and a 'pollution zone' (Merchant Shipping (Prevention of Pollution) (Limits) Regulations 1996, SI 1996/2128 and 1997 SI 1997/506). Neither concept was within the explicit contemplation of the LOSC, although coastal states do exercise sovereign rights over energy production and jurisdiction over the protection and preservation of the marine environment under art 56 of the Convention. This approach arguably represented an incomplete application of national EEZ powers and generated occasional legal complications in interacting with neighbouring jurisdictions: David Anderson, *Modern Law of the Sea: Selected Essays* (Leiden, Martinus Nijhoff Publishers, 2008) 460–76. Such difficulties should now accordingly be largely settled, although the prior consent of Denmark is still needed for renewable energy and gas storage projects undertaken adjacent to the limits of the jurisdictional waters of the Faroe Islands.

[9] Offshore Marine Conservation (Natural Habitats, etc) Regulations 2007, SI 2007/1842 (as amended), reg 2(2).

[10] Discrete powers over appropriate areas of the territorial sea are exercised by each of the devolved administrations. Powers over elements of the marine area that may eventually be remodelled as the UK EEZ can also be devolved to the nominated institutions of Scotland, Wales and Northern Ireland, respectively: Marine and Coastal Access Act 2009, s 41(4). Nevertheless, these are limited in scope: under s 113 of the 2009 Act, oil and gas activities remain the exclusive preserve of the central UK government.

[11] Petroleum Act 1998, s 10(7).

[12] The continental shelf of a coastal state 'comprises the seabed and subsoil of the submarine areas that extend beyond its territorial sea throughout the natural prolongation of its land territory to the outer edge of the continental margin, or to a distance of 200 nautical miles from the baselines from which the breadth of the territorial sea is measured where the outer edge of the continental

The distinction between inshore and offshore waters has a practical significance primarily in the context of EU fisheries. In this regard, the Member States have relinquished competence over fisheries management in their respective EEZs, but retain certain regulatory powers in respect of their territorial waters. Notably, the SEA Directive applies solely to the Member States; SEA is not a broad requirement for the EU institutions. Accordingly, there is currently no legal scope to subject offshore activities that fall under the competence of the EU, of which fishing is a prime example, to a prior SEA process. Despite some agitation towards revisiting this position during the renegotiation of the Common Fisheries Policy, especially given the extension of these broad competences to aquaculture activities, SEA considerations were omitted from the final terms of the legislation.[13] There is therefore little scope to advance fisheries SEAs within EU waters, aside from within inshore areas, as has been conducted by the UK authorities to a limited degree, and in the riverine industries of landlocked Member States, thereby missing an opportunity to promote a more strategic approach to fisheries management at an EU level.[14] Fisheries issues have nevertheless received consideration in the various SEAs that have been conducted for the offshore energy sector which, as noted below, have encompassed the full range of UK jurisdictional waters.

The Offshore Application of the SEA Directive

On a multilateral level, the Directive represents the primary source of SEA obligations applicable to the UK offshore area. While the LOSC prescribes a series of broad rights and duties incumbent in the use of ocean space, SEA obligations have not been expressly formulated within this instrument. The closest recognition of this concept within the LOSC, Article 206, requires parties to 'assess' as far as practicable the potential effects of planned activities under their jurisdiction or control

margin does not extend up to that distance': LOSC, art 76(1). In essence, marine energy production—especially in relation to hydrocarbons—is centred upon the national continental shelf; the EEZ regime addresses the water column as opposed to the ocean floor. A state may apply to claim an extended area of continental shelf of up to 360 nautical miles from the national baseline if particular geographical criteria are met: LOSC, art 76(4)–(10). Ownership of the continental shelf in the Hatton-Rockall area has yet to be resolved between the UK, Ireland, Denmark and Iceland, for which periodic quadrilateral discussions have been ongoing since 2001. Within the 12-mile territorial limit, the seabed constitutes a material part of the territorial sea and is accordingly subject to the sovereignty of the coastal state: LOSC, art 2(2).

[13] Regulation (EU) No 1380/2013 of the European Parliament and of the Council on the Common Fisheries Policy, amending Council Regulations (EC) No 1954/2003 and (EC) No 1224/2009 and repealing Council Regulations (EC) No 2371/2002 and (EC) No 639/2004 and Council Decision 2004/585/EC [2013] OJ L354/22 (as amended).

[14] The limited fisheries SEA experience that does exist on a global basis suggests that while individual legislation may be flawed in certain respects, it has nonetheless added a valuable tier of oversight to the process: Simon Marsden, 'Strategic Environmental Assessment and Fisheries Management in Australia: How Effective is the Commonwealth Legal Framework?' in Simon Marsden and Stephen Dovers (eds), *Strategic Environmental Assessment in Australasia* (Sydney, Federation Press, 2002) 47, 66.

where there are grounds for believing that they may cause 'substantial pollution' or 'significant and harmful changes to the marine environment'. Nevertheless, while the use of SEA would constitute an effective means of implementing Art 206, this provision stops short of formally requiring its application. Commentators have advocated a cautious interpretation of Art 206, noting that the drafters were unlikely to have considered SEA to have been a significant aspect of the planning process at the material time.[15] Indeed, SEA remains a far from universal feature in many coastal jurisdictions, and was a comparative novelty at the time at which the LOSC was negotiated. Moreover, while SEA is now more readily practised by an expanding number of coastal states, this trend has seemingly not been driven by a sense of multilateral obligation. Few treaties expressly mandate the use of SEA in the pursuit of marine resources and, as Johnstone observes, 'Under international law the evidence to support the duty to conduct SEAs as a binding legal obligation is sparse.'[16] Notwithstanding current regulatory intentions towards strengthening assessment practices in high seas areas,[17] SEA requirements have been primarily articulated within an optional protocol appended to the framework for environmental impact assessment.[18] Even then, this rather isolated instrument has generally proved unsuited to the demands of marine spatial planning due to contradictions in its subsequent listing process.[19]

The SEA Directive was broadly inspired by pioneering US Federal legislation and purports to expose certain plans and programmes undertaken by the Member States to an environmental assessment procedure before such initiatives are formally approved.[20] In this way, and in terminology highly familiar to offshore operators, the SEA process is considered to be the 'upstream' element of the environmental assessment process. SEA therefore prescribes a consideration of the best strategic options at a preliminary stage in the planning process, so as in principle to inform decision-making to ensure that the environmental integrity of national and transnational development projects is maintained.

[15] Sander (n 3) 109.

[16] Rachael Lorna Johnstone, *Offshore Oil and Gas Development in the Arctic under International Law: Risk and Responsibility* (Leiden, Brill, 2015) 172.

[17] Current developments towards the elaboration of a legally binding instrument to address the conservation needs of biodiversity beyond national jurisdiction envisage a central role for 'environmental impact assessment', although it is as yet unclear as to how significant a role (if any) will be allocated to SEA in this regard or how it will be implemented: see UN Document A/69/780 of 13 February 2015: Outcome of the Ad Hoc Open-ended Informal Working Group to study issues relating to the conservation and sustainable use of marine biological diversity beyond areas of national jurisdiction and co-chairs' summary of discussions.

[18] See the 2003 Protocol on Strategic Environmental Assessment to the Convention on Environmental Impact in a Transboundary Context (25 February 1991) 1989 UNTS 309, 30 ILM 800 (entered into force 10 September 1997) (hereinafter 'the Espoo Convention'). The UK is a signatory to the Protocol but has not yet ratified it, although the EU is a full party.

[19] Sander (n 3) 115.

[20] On the origins of the SEA Directive—and the political adjustments to its eventual scope—see Jane Holder, *Environmental Assessment: The Regulation of Decision Making* (Oxford, Oxford University Press, 2004) 60–64.

The Directive accordingly works in tandem with a series of other EU environmental assessment processes, notably those contemplated under the Environmental Impact Assessment Directive[21] and the Habitats Directive.[22] The SEA Directive mandates that an assessment should be undertaken in respect of any plan or programme that is explicitly identified within the Directive as being likely to have 'significant environmental effects'[23] or is otherwise considered by an individual Member State to require such a process.[24] To this end, two broad categories of plans or programmes are considered to require SEA. In the first instance, SEA is mandatory for all plans and programmes that are prepared for agriculture, forestry, fisheries, energy, industry, transport, waste management, water management, telecommunications, tourism, town and country planning or land use and, in addition to this criterion, 'set the framework for future development consent of projects' as required under the EIA Directive.[25] Second, SEAs are necessary where the plan or project, by virtue of its prospective impact upon protected areas established pursuant to EU nature conservation law, ought to be subject to the particular assessment process prescribed under Articles 6 and 7 of the Habitats Directive.[26] Member States are permitted derogations to these general requirements in respect of the use of small areas at a local level, and for minor modifications to be made to plans and programmes if their environmental effects are unlikely to be 'significant'.[27]

The issue of whether SEA is formally required in a particular context is therefore often a matter of considerable uncertainty. Questions may be raised as to whether a particular plan or programme ultimately sets a framework for future development consent, while the nomenclature attached to certain industrial initiatives by the national authorities may also require complex legal[28]—or, indeed,

[21] Council Directive 85/337/EEC of 27 June 1985 on the assessment of the effects of certain public and private projects on the environment [1985] OJ L175/40 (hereinafter 'the EIA Directive'). The Directive was substantively revised in April 2014: Directive 2014/52/EU of the European Parliament and of the Council of 16 April 2014 amending Directive 2011/92/EU on the assessment of the effects of certain public and private projects on the environment [2014] OJ L124/1. The new Directive entered into effect in May 2014.

[22] Council Directive 92/43/EEC on the conservation of natural habitats and of wild fauna and flora [1992] OJ L206/7 (hereinafter 'the Habitats Directive'). The application of the Habitats Directive to UK offshore waters was only recognised judicially in 2000: *R v Secretary of State for Trade and Industry ex p Greenpeace Ltd (No 2)* (2000) 2 CMLR 94 (QBD). Indeed, the 1994 version of the Offshore Marine Conservation (Natural Habitats, etc) Regulations had expressly confined the application to the Directive to the territorial sea, thereby imposing significantly fewer environmental constraints on offshore energy operators than is currently the case.

[23] SEA Directive, art 3(1).

[24] ibid, art 3(4).

[25] ibid, art 3(2)(a).

[26] ibid, art 3(2)(b).

[27] ibid, art 3(3).

[28] See Gregory Jones QC, Ned Westaway and Roger Watts, 'Why *Central Craigavon* was Wrongly Decided (and Other Problems with the Incorporation of the Strategic Environmental Assessment Directive into Domestic Law)' (2013) *Journal of Planning & Environment Law* 1074, 1078–81.

constitutional[29]—interpretation.[30] Likewise, Article 6 of the Habitats Directive is a notoriously poorly drafted provision,[31] which offers limited assistance to public authorities in determining whether their assessment obligations are engaged in respect of protected sites and species.[32] Given the potential for resultant loopholes, the SEA Directive does not elaborate further on the specific industrial activities and processes that may fall within its regulatory purview. The EU institutions have subsequently acknowledged that significant interpretive difficulties have been raised by the transposition of the Directive within the various Member States.[33] SEA requirements under the Directive accordingly constitute some of the more inscrutable procedural elements of EU environmental law.

Notwithstanding this general uncertainty, the Directive generates comparatively fewer interpretive difficulties at sea. Unlike the terrestrial context, the practical and commercial challenges incumbent in offshore operations ensure that relatively few industrial sectors are active in these waters. Beyond shipping activities, the primary offshore industries in UK waters are energy production and fishing, each of which is expressly within the contemplation of the SEA Directive (even if the latter is subject to an alternative regulatory approach due to the prevailing EU competences over this sector). In this context, the legal question is generally not whether an SEA is formally required, but whether it has been correctly and effectively implemented by the competent authorities in question.

Nevertheless, some questions remain in respect of the precise SEA requirements in relation to more nascent offshore industries, such as carbon capture and storage (CCS), deep-seabed mining and the controversial practice of hydraulic fracturing or 'fracking' of the seabed in the pursuit of shale gas. Some doubt was initially raised as to whether CCS falls within the ambit of the SEA Directive,[34] although an arguable case could be made that it constitutes 'waste management' for the purposes of SEA. The explicit application of pertinent environmental assessment requirements to CCS was subsequently confirmed through specific EU legislation

[29] Notably *R (on the Application of HS2 Action Alliance Ltd) v Secretary of State for Transport and Another* [2014] UKSC 3 [78]–[79].

[30] See in particular the contributions by David Elvin (Ch 6), Elizabeth Fisher (Ch 8), Simon Ricketts and Juliet Munn (Ch 4), Eloise Scotford (Ch 10) and Valerie Fogleman (Ch 3) in the current volume.

[31] André Nollkaemper, 'Habitat Protection in European Community Law: Evolving Conceptions of a Balance of Interests' (1997) 9 *Journal of Environmental Law* 271, 286.

[32] On this issue generally, see Stephen Tromans QC, 'The Meaning of "Any Plan or Project" under Article 6(3)' in Jones (n 2) 91.

[33] Commission, 'Report on the Application and Effectiveness of the Directive on Strategic Environmental Assessment (Directive 2001/42/EC)' COM(2009) 469 final, 11.

[34] Anton Ming-Zhi Gao, 'The Application of the European SEA Directive to Carbon Capture and Storage Activities: The Issue of Screening' (2008) 17 *European Energy and Environmental Law Review* 341, 343.

on the issue.[35] Prior to this, SEA was conducted on a proactive basis for CCS, evidenced, for example, in the Netherlands[36] and, as noted below, in the UK.

Likewise, the environmental assessment obligations associated with fracking have proved to be a matter of considerable uncertainty. Indeed, controversial loopholes under UK law have been exploited to evade environmental assessment processes for terrestrial fracking, with 'exploratory' endeavours, as opposed to commercial activities, not subject to these requirements.[37] The EU Commission has since issued a Recommendation stating that Member States 'should' subject such initiatives to a process of SEA.[38] This provision ultimately fell rather short of the moratorium on shale fracking advocated by the European Parliament and the current EU legal regime governing unconventional fossil fuels remains somewhat ambiguous.[39] Offshore fracking for shale gas has not yet proceeded, largely as a result of overriding commercial considerations. From an environmental assessment standpoint, however, the first ever offshore exploration licence was issued by the UK authorities in February 2014 and was subject to a preceding SEA.[40]

Deep-seabed mining rather exposes the territorial limitations of the SEA Directive, as well as the paucity of SEA practice at an international level. In recent years, the pursuit of deep-seabed mineral wealth has become more commercially viable, with a wide range of states keen to conduct or, alternatively, to sponsor extractive activities within the International Seabed Area (hereinafter 'the Area').[41]

[35] Directive 2009/31/EC of the European Parliament and of the Council on the geological storage of carbon dioxide and amending Council Directive 85/337/EEC, European Parliament and Council Directives 2000/60/EC, 2001/80/EC, 2004/35/EC, 2006/12/EC, 2008/1/EC and Regulation (EC) No 1013/2006 [2009] OJ L140/114, recital 17 and art 11(2). On the regulation of CCS in the North Atlantic region, see Susanna Much, 'The Emerging International Regulation of Carbon Storage in Subseabed Geological Formations' in Richard Caddell and D Rhidian Thomas (eds), *Shipping, Law and the Marine Environment in the Twenty-First Century* (Witney, Lawtext, 2013) 255.

[36] Joris Koornneef, André Faaij and Wim Turkenburg, 'The Screening and Scoping of Environmental Impact Assessment and Strategic Environmental Assessment of Carbon Capture and Storage in the Netherlands' (2008) 28 *Environmental Impact Assessment Review* 392, 410 (noting that environmental assessment obligations at the material time could nonetheless 'be interpreted ambiguously' in this context).

[37] Andreas Kotsakis, 'The Regulation of the Technical, Environmental and Health Aspects of Current Exploratory Shale Gas Extraction in the United Kingdom: Initial Lessons for the Future of European Union Energy Policy' (2012) 21 *Review of European Community and International Environmental Law* 282, 284.

[38] Commission Recommendation on minimum principles for the exploration and production of hydrocarbons (such as shale gas) using high-volume hydraulic fracturing (2014/70/EU) [2014] OJ L39/72.

[39] On these developments, see Elen Stokes, 'New EU Policy on Shale Gas' (2014) 16 *Environmental Law Review* 42. Ultimately, the EU may need to fall back on other elements of its competence, such as broader and more binding considerations of energy, environmental and possibly water policy to advance a more comprehensive regime to address fracking.

[40] 'Shale Gas Pioneer Plans World's First Offshore Wells in Irish Sea', www.bbc.co.uk/news/business-26157228.

[41] Defined as the 'seabed and ocean floor and subsoil thereof, beyond the limits of national jurisdiction': LOSC, art 1(1). The Area is managed by the International Seabed Authority. The first deep-sea mine appears likely to open in Papua New Guinea, following a sponsorship agreement concluded on 25 April 2014: Agreement reached on deep sea mining; www.bbc.co.uk/news/science-environment-27158883. The UK is currently considering its sponsorship options in this respect.

The jurisdictional parameters of the SEA Directive are limited to the 'environment in the Member States',[42] while transboundary consultation is restricted to impacts upon other Member States,[43] hence there is little explicit obligation to apply SEA to operations occurring in remote pockets of the high seas in locations significantly beyond EU boundaries. Such matters will instead be regulated by the International Seabed Authority (ISA), which is charged, inter alia, with assessing the environmental implications of activities in the Area.[44] Given that strong international obligations towards environmental impact assessment (EIA) have been established, both under the general rules of the ISA and by international courts,[45] SEA requirements may be considered likely to be rather more circumspect in this context in the mid-term future, a trend that has been reflected in recent domestic developments. Indeed, while national legislation governing deep-seabed mining remains in its comparative infancy, requirements towards SEA are nonetheless conspicuous by their current absence.[46]

Notwithstanding consideration of these specific activities, the long-term ecological health of the marine environment is not threatened solely by at-sea activities. Indeed, a significant proportion of marine degradation is attributable to land-based sources.[47] Hence, an integrated approach towards the protection of the offshore environment also necessitates consideration of the marine implications of land-based activities.[48] The projected impact of terrestrial development projects upon marine sites, both near-shore and offshore, may therefore also require consideration from an SEA perspective. While reasons of space and focus preclude an analysis of SEA practice in this regard in this chapter, the alleged necessity for assessments to gauge the impact of terrestrial plans and programmes upon

[42] SEA Directive, recital 4.

[43] ibid, art 7.

[44] LOSC, art 165(2)(e).

[45] Notably by the International Court of Justice in *Case Concerning Pulp Mills on the River Uruguay (Argentina v Uruguay)* [2010] ICJ Rep 14 [197] and the International Tribunal for the Law of the Sea in *Responsibilities and Obligations of States Sponsoring Persons and Entities with Respect to Activities in the Area* (ITLOS Case No 17, 1 February 2011) [141]–[150].

[46] As a case in point, on 20 August 2014, Tonga enacted the most comprehensive current legislation to regulate deep-seabed mining in the form of the Seabed Minerals Act 2014. Notwithstanding a vague commitment to 'employ best environmental practice' (s 2(2)(f)), the Act is silent on SEA requirements, although the role of EIA is emphasised throughout the legislation.

[47] Indeed, one of the leading judgments on SEA determined at an EU level, Joined Cases C-105/09 and C-110/09 *Terre Wallonne ASBL and Inter-Environnement Wallonie ASBL v Région Wallonne* [2010] ECR I-5611 concerned the implications of agricultural run-off into the water column, a notorious if indirect source of offshore pollution.

[48] Strong concerns over the impacts of land-based pollution on marine ecosystems have been raised by the UN's leading forum on the marine environment, the Joint Group of Experts on the Scientific Aspects of Marine Environmental Protection (GESAMP). Indeed, in its most recent global assessment of the impact of land-based pollution on the marine environment, while not explicitly referring to SEA by name, GESAMP considered that the 'incorporation of environmental considerations into all projects, policies, and programmes' constitutes a key strategic element in addressing this issue: GESAMP, *Protecting the Oceans from Land-Based Activities: Land-Based Sources and Activities Affecting the Quality and Uses of the Marine, Coastal and Associated Freshwater Environment* (Nairobi, UNEP, 2001) 78.

protected marine sites has already provided the basis for one recent (and unsuccessful) review of development frameworks in a UK coastal context.[49] It is unlikely to be the last such challenge to land-based activities with a marine bearing.

Offshore Energy Production and the SEA Directive

Given the breadth of assessment practice in this sector, offshore energy production represents the clearest example of the application of SEA principles to the marine environment of the UK. Three main energy industries have an active presence within national waters, to varying degrees of maturity: petroleum (oil and gas); renewable energy, especially in the form of offshore wind; and, prospectively, shale fracking. Each of these industries has, in recent years, been subject to SEA processes prior to the grant of an operative licence by the appropriate national authority.

The oil and gas sector is, by some considerable margin, the most mature offshore extractive industry in UK waters. Offshore hydrocarbon licensing has been within the contemplation of the UK authorities for over a century, first as an aspect of the domestic front during the First World War,[50] latterly regularised in peacetime[51] and now governed through the framework of the Petroleum Act 1998. The basic tenets of UK oil and gas law have altered remarkably little during this time: all petroleum deposits are vested in the Crown, which, through the appropriate government representative, may grant a licence to 'search, bore for and get' petroleum deposits either on land or at sea.[52] The first offshore licences were issued in 1964, for a period of 46 years, expiring in 2010. Licences are awarded through a competitive process of periodic 'Rounds', which are issued on an approximately biennial basis and have the overarching objective of ensuring maximum productivity and discouraging inactivity. The conduct of the operator is controlled on an essentially contractual basis, through mandatory adherence to a series of 'model clauses' imposed by the UK government within the licence. These obligations establish the core environmental commitments of the operator and vary in accordance with the type of operation undertaken and the location in which it is conducted. Until its formal dissolution in July 2016, the Department of Energy and Climate Change (DECC) fulfilled the role of the appropriate government representative and had exercised responsibility over the implementation of offshore SEA requirements

[49] *No Adastral New Town Ltd v Suffolk Coastal District Council and Secretary of State for Communities and Local Government* [2014] EWHC 223 (Admin). The case concerned the potential impact of a housing development upon a Natura 2000 site established in the Deben Estuary in respect of migratory waterbirds.

[50] Defence of the Realm Act 1914, as amended; Petroleum (Production) Act 1918, s 2.

[51] Petroleum (Production) Act 1934, s 2.

[52] Petroleum Act 1998, s 2(1).

since its inception in 2008. Oversight of future offshore SEA processes will accordingly be vested in the newly established Department for Business, Energy and Industrial Security (BEIS) which, at the time of writing, was at a preliminary stage in the process of subsuming the offshore responsibilities of the former DECC. Subsequent licences for oil and gas exploration and production, as well as CCS, are administered by the Oil and Gas Authority in the light of the environmental data generated by the SEA process.

Unlike the expanding—and controversial—terrestrial industry, commercial fracking has yet to be attempted in UK waters. In principle, offshore fracking in the UK will be governed by a materially similar licensing process to that of other hydrocarbons, subject to the ongoing development of specific rules and procedures for this nascent sector. In contrast, with regard to offshore windfarms, regulatory requirements vary with the operational capacity of the development in question. The establishment of an 'offshore generating station' capable of producing over 100 megawatts of energy[53] requires development consent.[54] Such initiatives will therefore be governed by the BEIS on the advice of the Planning Inspectorate.[55] Smaller developments are subject to approval by the Marine Management Organisation (MMO), although commercial considerations ensure that few proposed windfarms will be likely in practice to generate less than 100 megawatts. A marine licence is required for activities ancillary to windfarm construction,[56] which will be issued by either the Crown Estate, which manages the seabed up to the 12-mile territorial limit, or the MMO within its broad areas of jurisdiction.[57]

The emergence of a large-scale offshore energy sector neatly exemplifies the value of the SEA procedure to regulatory oversight and environmental management. The licensing procedure, especially as applied to hydrocarbons, involves the release of large portions of acreage upon the UKCS within particular geographical locations for exploration and exploitation. Until 2001, environmental oversight of these activities would essentially proceed *ex post facto*, with the successful operator subject to EIA requirements and tailored ecological obligations imposed under the model clauses for the specific area of operation. Beyond the appraisal of individual EIAs in particular marine locations, the decision to sanction wholesale industrial activity within any given licensable area would accordingly have been taken with minimal consideration of cumulative environmental impacts, effects upon

[53] Planning Act 2008, s 15.

[54] ibid, s 31.

[55] On these regulatory steps, see Olivia Woolley, 'Trouble on the Horizon? Addressing Place-Based Values in Planning for Offshore Wind Energy' (2010) 22 *Journal of Environmental Law* 223, 234–40. This framework streamlines the previous regime established under the Energy Act 2004; on this process, see Karen N Scott, 'Tilting at Offshore Windmills: Regulating Windfarm Development Within the Renewable Energy Zone' (2006) 18 *Journal of Environmental Law* 89, 97–99.

[56] Marine and Coastal Access Act 2009, s 66.

[57] Marine Scotland is responsible for licensing activities in Scottish inshore and offshore waters, while the devolved administrations of Wales and Northern Ireland exercise these powers within their respective jurisdictional waters.

species with an extended or idiosyncratic range or the wider ecological health of a maritime region, thereby providing little scope for meaningful strategic oversight. Although of limited concern in the early years of oil and gas licensing, the advancing offshore presence of the hydrocarbon industry has subsequently necessitated a more strategic approach to marine spatial planning. Norway was the first major offshore hydrocarbon producer to reject this piecemeal assessment in favour of a more integrated regional approach,[58] which was swiftly emulated by the UK. Nevertheless, in many marine regions—especially where industrial improvisation and ecological sensitivity maintain an uneasy coexistence—offshore operators largely continue to proceed on a project-by-project basis.[59] Indeed, despite the clear drawbacks of an individual project approach, even in jurisdictions that are favourably predisposed to the merits of SEA, 'large hydrocarbon programmes continue to unfold offshore without adequate strategic thinking'.[60]

As Long observes in the context of offshore windfarms in Irish waters, '[i]f implemented rigorously', SEA can be a vital mechanism for promoting effective marine planning and management, since it offers the scope to address the individual and cumulative impacts of proliferating development projects at a preliminary stage and provides a platform for effective stakeholder participation.[61] Nevertheless, few concerted studies have evaluated the rigour with which SEA processes have been applied in an offshore context and, accordingly, whether such projected advantages have ultimately been delivered. Even where regulators have established a clear framework for facilitating SEA, 'the opportunities and risks associated with SEA offshore are unclear and linkages between SEA and other forms of planning and impact assessment remain elusive'.[62] The energy licensing practices of the UK therefore provide a valuable opportunity to assess the development and performance of SEA as a regulatory tool as applied within a jurisdiction with a substantial offshore industrial presence.

[58] On the Norwegian arrangements, see Geir Ottersen et al, 'The Norwegian Plan for Integrated Ecosystem-Based Management of the Marine Environment in the Norwegian Sea' (2011) 35 *Marine Policy* 389. As a member of the European Economic Area (EEA), although not an EU Member State, Norway is also obliged to apply the SEA Directive.

[59] Courtney Fidler and Bram Noble, 'Advancing Strategic Environmental Assessment in the Offshore Oil and Gas Sector: Lessons from Norway, Canada and the United Kingdom' (2012) 34 *Environmental Impact Assessment Review* 12, 13.

[60] Bram Noble et al, 'Strategic Environmental Assessment Opportunities and Risks for Arctic Offshore Energy Planning and Development' (2013) 39 *Marine Policy* 296, 297. Indeed, consideration of SEA-style approaches was expressly omitted from a post-*Deepwater Horizon* review of the hydrocarbon licensing process in at least one major offshore energy jurisdiction: Will Amos, 'Development of Canadian Arctic Offshore Oil and Gas Drilling: Lessons from the Gulf of Mexico' (2011) 20 *Review of European Community and International Environmental Law* 39, 42–43.

[61] Ronán Long, 'Offshore Wind Energy Development and Ecosystem-Based Marine Management in the EU: Are the Regulatory Answers Really Blowing in the Wind?' in Myron H Norquist, John Norton Moore, Aldo Chircop and Ronán Long (eds), *The Regulation of Continental Shelf Development: Rethinking International Standards* (Leiden, Martinus Nijhoff Publishers, 2013) 15, 40.

[62] Noble et al (n 60) 297.

SEA of Offshore Energy Plans in the UK

SEA processes in the UK offshore energy sector significantly pre-date the application of the SEA Directive itself, which was introduced in 2001 and established a transposition deadline of 21st July 2004. In 1999, as part of the national 'Greening Government' initiative, the UK authorities were encouraged to undertake so-called 'environmental appraisals' of major plans and programmes to be approved under their auspices.[63] In this respect, the Department of Trade and Industry (DTI), the body then charged with oversight of the offshore energy sector, undertook to subject all future licensing Rounds for oil and gas to a prior process of SEA, pending the formal conclusion of the EU provisions. This new strategy was first implemented in 2001 in the government's Nineteenth Oil and Gas Round,[64] a process that addressed a comparatively modest geographical area formerly known as the 'White Zone' in the northern segment of Scottish waters, following agreement with Danish officials over the official seabed boundary between the UK and the Faroe Islands. A further three SEAs were conducted in the offshore area prior to the formal conclusion of the Directive: the Twentieth[65] and Twenty-First[66] Oil and Gas Rounds in 2002 and 2003, each of which engaged substantial areas of the North Sea (with SEA2 subsequently extended into the ecologically and economically significant Moray Firth area), and the Second Offshore Wind Leasing Round,[67] addressing windfarm development in three separate locations. With limited legislative guidance available at an EU level, these initial SEA processes involved a blend of practices adapted from comparable jurisdictions, elements of the prospective EU rules and principles, and a concerted degree of indigenous improvisation. Subsequently, SEAs have been conducted in respect of all further Oil and Gas Licensing Rounds,[68] while in 2009, SEA was applied to both

[63] These processes were subsequently re-termed 'sustainability appraisals' in the administrative vernacular. Despite these pioneering endeavours, the pre-Directive SEA initiatives were conducted on a voluntary basis and accordingly had 'none of the regulatory weight that gives EIA such importance': Stephen Jay, 'Strategic Environmental Assessment for Energy Production' (2010) 38 *Energy Policy* 3489, 3491.

[64] Strategic Environmental Assessment of the Deep Water Area along the UK and Faroese Boundary (19th Oil and Gas Round; 2001) (hereinafter 'SEA1'). This process was complemented by a separate academic exercise examining the 'holistic environmental assessment of UK offshore oil': Jay (n 63).

[65] Strategic Environmental Assessment of the Mature Areas of the Offshore North Sea (20th Oil and Gas Round; 2002) (hereinafter 'SEA2').

[66] Strategic Environmental Assessment of Parts of the Central & Southern North Sea (21st Oil and Gas Round; 2003) (hereinafter 'SEA3').

[67] Strategic Environmental Assessment of Three Strategic Regions Off the Coasts of England and Wales in Relation to a Second Round of Offshore Wind Leasing (2nd Wind Leasing Round; 2003) (hereinafter 'R2').

[68] Strategic Environmental Assessment of the Area North and West of Shetland and Orkney (22nd Oil and Gas Round; 2004) (hereinafter 'SEA4'); Strategic Environmental Assessment of Parts of the Northern and Central North Sea to the East of the Scottish Mainland, Orkney and Shetland (23rd Oil and Gas Round; 2005) (hereinafter 'SEA5'); Strategic Environmental Assessment of Parts of the Irish Sea (24th Oil and Gas Round; 2006) ('SEA6'); Strategic Environmental Assessment of the Offshore Areas to the West of Scotland (25th Oil and Gas Round; 2008) (hereinafter 'SEA7').

the hydrocarbon and offshore wind sectors as a strategic whole.[69] In 2011, this process was extended even further to address oil and gas, renewable energy and, for the first time, prospective CCS activities.[70] In early 2015, given that the time horizon for OESEA 2 extended for five years from its initial publication, a further offshore energy SEA process was launched,[71] which was concluded on 13 July 2016, a day prior to the formal closure of the DECC.

In assessing the broad outcomes of these initiatives, two core trends are apparent. In the first instance, it can be seen that offshore SEA has been generally friendly towards proposed marine licensing activities. Thus far, the SEA process has not discouraged development proposals, although it has assisted the regulatory authorities in identifying a series of locations within which—for now—licensing ought in principle to be precluded for reasons of environmental or socio-economic sensitivity. Moreover, the regulatory authorities have explicitly identified an overarching ethos for offshore licensing practices, with the DECC having advanced a broad commitment towards adopting a precautionary approach to offshore industrial activities,[72] alongside a general presumption against locating installations within inshore areas, especially in relation to extractive industries and, where feasible, renewable energy activities.[73] Nevertheless, as discussed below, concerns may be raised that the current application of SEA in the UK offshore environment has been characterised by a tacit bias towards development and, arguably, a somewhat laissez-faire approach to precautionary management in the face of chronic shortfalls in baseline data in sanctioning the release of acreage for offshore energy development and a limited assessment of alternatives to the proposed development strategies.

Second, the application of SEA by the national authorities[74] in the UK offshore environment has been an evolutionary process, with experiences from earlier and

[69] Strategic Environmental Assessment of UK Offshore Waters and Territorial Waters of England and Wales (26th Oil and Gas Round and 3rd Wind Leasing Round; 2009) (hereinafter 'OESEA').

[70] Strategic Environmental Assessment of UK Offshore Waters and Territorial Waters of England and Wales (27th and 28th Oil and Gas Rounds; 2011) (hereinafter OESEA 2').

[71] UK Offshore Energy Strategic Environmental Assessment: Future Leasing/Licensing for Offshore Renewable Energy, Offshore Oil and Gas, Hydrocarbon Gas and Carbon Dioxide Storage and Associated Infrastructure (hereinafter OESEA 3'). The 29th Oil and Gas Round was accordingly launched by the Oil and Gas Authority on 27 July 2016, following the conclusion of OESEA 3.

[72] This was first mandated within SEA1, where: 'In the absence of conclusive data, which is unlikely to be forthcoming for technical and ethical reasons, a precautionary approach is justified': DTI, *Strategic Environmental Assessment of the Former White Zone: Volume Three—Assessment* (London, DTI, 2001) 64. This broad approach has been maintained in the recommendations of all subsequent SEA initiatives.

[73] This principle was most explicitly iterated during the OESEA processes: see Recommendation 3 of OESEA, Recommendation 4 of OESEA 2 and Recommendation 3 of OESEA 3. Few energy projects have as yet been sanctioned within the territorial sea. Nevertheless, given that licensing decisions will be dependent essentially upon the location of marine resources, as well as topographical, hydrographical and oceanographic conditions, there is by no means a prohibition on permitting industrial access to territorial waters. This position is complicated by the various devolution settlements where powers over these activities have been vested to a greater or lesser extent in the national administrations.

[74] The 11 separate SEA processes initiated thus far in the UK offshore environment have been instituted by a number of different government bodies. Having conducted the assessment processes for

more experimental SEA initiatives having informed and improved successive procedures in subsequent licensing Rounds. This laudable commitment to regular reflective practice has resulted in a series of significant procedural and practical refinements, especially in coordinating SEA methodologies, fostering improvements in data generation and management and in promoting a strong culture of institutional learning and a generally inclusive approach towards public and expert participation. The various offshore SEA initiatives have also been of considerable practical utility in framing the subsequent stages of the licensing procedure by advancing a series of operative recommendations in respect of future activities. These recommendations have evolved from somewhat vague and rudimentary 'bulletpoint' conclusions in earlier SEAs into clear and targeted proposals within later SEA initiatives to facilitate environmental monitoring of the area in question, to address gaps in the knowledge base and to improve further the offshore SEA machinery in general. To this extent, the SEA process can be seen as a broadly productive addition to the overarching regulatory framework, which has helped to facilitate a more coordinated approach to the licensing procedure, notwithstanding apparent difficulties in the management and processing of information and in tracking the ultimate progress of individual SEA initiatives.

Approval, Uncertainty and the Limits of Precautionary Management

A central purpose of SEA in the context of an eventual licensing process is to indicate the core areas of sensitivity and the major environmental impacts likely to ensue from the plan or programme in question, so as to concentrate industrial activities within areas of lesser ecological concern. To this end, the offshore SEA initiatives have identified a series of common environmental pressures raised by prospective energy licensing, including the physical presence of installations, increased vessel traffic and an enhanced risk of pollution, both as a byproduct of drilling and the prospect of oil spills. Nevertheless, although the SEA processes have identified a series of ecological risks, a considerable degree of uncertainty has been raised concerning the threats posed by the prospective activities in question, both as isolated sources of potential environment harm and in terms of their cumulative and combined effects.

In this respect, as an individual ecological concern, the myriad SEA documentation has consistently identified ocean noise as the most significant and pernicious byproduct of purported marine energy development, although the treatment of

SEAs 1–6 and R2, the DTI was disbanded in June 2007 and was briefly replaced with the Department of Business, Enterprise and Regulatory Reform (BERR), under whose auspices SEA7 was performed. All subsequent initiatives (OESEA, OESEA 2 and OESEA 3) have been undertaken by the DECC.

this issue within the SEA processes has been decidedly mixed. Despite being a relatively poor conductor of heat and light, the ocean is a highly efficient medium through which to transmit sound. While a considerable degree of ambient sound is ever-present within the marine environment, strong concerns have been raised in recent years over the proliferation of anthropogenic marine noise and its impacts upon aquatic species, especially marine mammals.[75] Ocean noise is now considered a marine pollutant of considerable potency,[76] with particular reservations expressed over the impact of oil and gas exploration and exploitation, especially with regard to seismic surveying of the seabed, as well as noise attendant to the installation and operation of windfarms.[77] In this regard, the SEA process could in principle be seen to exhibit considerable value in addressing anthropogenic noise proactively, identifying areas in which noise-creating activities are likely to be most prevalent, as well as locations of primary importance to sound-sensitive species, thus allowing for future licensing decisions to be taken in an informed and environmentally sympathetic manner. The SEAs conducted to date have observed the prospective problems posed by ocean noise, as well as a general dearth of data concerning the levels of anthropogenic sound in the marine environment and difficulties in assessing its precise effects upon affected species.

Nevertheless, in approving prospective offshore energy projects, considerable faith has been placed by the various SEA documents in the EIA process to address these problems and, in particular, in mitigation measures, which may include soft-start techniques, temporal or spatial restrictions and technical fixes. Scientific opinion has, however, proved to be rather more circumspect concerning the efficacy of such measures, the parameters of buffer zones and the preparedness of the industry to proactively implement mitigation strategies.[78] Moreover, concerns have been raised that subsequent EIAs have deployed flawed modelling processes to assess the prospective impacts of noise, offering little methodological transparency to decision-makers and stakeholders,[79] and ultimately failing to provide

[75] For a comprehensive analysis of the impacts of ocean noise, see W John Richardson et al, *Marine Mammals and Noise* (Cambridge, MA, Academic Press, 1995) 387–424.

[76] See especially Harm M Dotinga and Alex G Oude Elferink, 'Acoustic Pollution in the Oceans: The Search for Legal Standards' (2000) 31 *Ocean Development and International Law* 151; Alexander Gillespie, 'Noise Pollution, the Oceans, and the Limits of International Law' (2010) 21 *Yearbook of International Environmental Law* 114. Ocean noise is widely considered to meet the definition of 'pollution' prescribed under art 1(1)(d) LOSC as entailing the deleterious introduction of 'substances or energy' into the marine environment.

[77] Noise impacts include death, injury and hearing loss, habitat avoidance, stress and disruption to vital lifecycle events: John Harwood and Ben Wilson, 'The Implications of Developments on the Atlantic Frontier for Marine Mammals' (2001) 21 *Continental Shelf Research* 1073, 1087–88.

[78] Ross Compton et al, 'A Critical Examination of Worldwide Guidelines for Minimising the Disturbance to Marine Mammals during Seismic Surveys' (2008) 32 *Marine Policy* 255, 261–62.

[79] Adrian Farcas, Paul M Thompson and Nathan D Merchant, 'Underwater Noise Modelling for Environmental Impact Assessment' (2016) 57 *Environmental Impact Assessment Review* 114, 114 (noting that: 'In practice, noise modelling for EIAs is often carried out using simplistic models, with limited environmental data, and without field measurements to ground-truth predictions').

concerted protection against noise sources originally identified within the SEA processes. The limitations of certain elements of current mitigation strategies have been tacitly acknowledged within the recent OESEA 3 initiative, albeit in generally permissive terms—noting that the enhancement of existing measures 'should be considered'—and seemingly in the limited context of beaked whales.[80]

A matter of significant allied concern has been consideration of the cumulative effects of offshore activities, which is acknowledged to be 'challenging at project, industry and strategic levels, and is frequently raised by stakeholders as an issue'.[81] This has bedevilled SEA practices generally, not least since there is little consensus on a universal understanding of the meaning of this term.[82] This concept has accordingly proved difficult to capture coherently within pertinent legislation and guidelines, at both a domestic and EU level, generating longstanding uncertainties in methodology, outcome and procedure. Accordingly, the degree of assessment of cumulative impacts on the part of regulators and developers has traditionally been relatively low.[83] This has been particularly acute in the context of ocean noise, which the regulatory authorities consider to be 'fraught with difficulty',[84] yet may have considerable adverse implications for the wider marine environment. Additional commitments towards the prioritisation of research into the cumulative elements of ocean noise have been recently advanced in OESEA 3,[85] which may be further complemented by the ongoing development of pan-EU strategies to address this issue under the broader auspices of the Marine Strategy Framework Directive.[86]

The lack of a coherent strategy to inform cumulative impacts has nonetheless proved to be a considerable problem in many jurisdictions, not least since these 'are typically not detected within the footprint of any individual project assessment',[87] yet individual EIAs are continue to be considered to be a primary mitigation strategy for aggregated environmental effects. A particularly welcome recent initiative in this regard has been the establishment of a Cross-Government

[80] DECC, *UK Offshore Energy Strategic Environmental Assessment: Future Leasing/Licensing for Offshore Renewable Energy, Offshore Oil and Gas, Hydrocarbon Gas and Carbon Dioxide Storage and Associated Infrastructure: Environmental Report* (London, DECC, 2016) 474.

[81] DECC ibid 475.

[82] Indeed, 'there is neither a legal definition of cumulative and synergistic effects nor a uniform understanding in the specialist world about what is really to be understood by these terms': Ulrike Weiland, 'Strategic Environmental Assessment in Germany—Practice and Open Questions' (2010) 30 *Environmental Impact Assessment Review* 211, 212.

[83] Lourdes M Cooper and William R Sheate, 'Integrating Cumulative Effects Assessment into UK Strategic Planning: Implications of the European Union SEA Directive' (2004) 22 *Impact Assessment and Project Appraisal* 5, 7.

[84] DTI, *SEA6: Post-consultation Report* (London, DTI, 2006) 19.

[85] DECC (n 80) 474.

[86] Directive No. 2008/56/EC of 17 June 2008 establishing a framework for community action in the field of marine environmental policy [2008] OJ L164/19 [hereinafter 'the MSFD']. Consideration of the impacts of 'energy, including underwater noise' is an element of attaining the 'Good Environmental Status' required of EU marine areas under the MSFD: Qualitative Descriptor 11; listed in Annex I of the Directive.

[87] Noble et al (n 60) 298.

Cumulative Assessment Working Group under the auspices of the Department for Environment, Food and Rural Affairs (DEFRA). Comprising representatives from DEFRA, the BEIS and the Department for Transport, as well as the devolved administrations and an array of other advisory bodies including the MMO and Crown Estate, this forum aims to foster a more consistent and predictable assessment process for cumulative effects. This may in turn inspire a more central consideration of cumulative effects in future SEA procedures, which has been a significant shortcoming in such practices to date. Indeed, many prior SEA processes have ultimately endorsed potential development plans for UK offshore waters while concurrently lamenting substantial and substantive shortfalls in the data and the resultant inability to clearly project the full range of impacts arising from increased industrial activities. This position raises legitimate questions as to how strictly the stated objective of facilitating precautionary marine management through the SEA process has been applied in particular offshore areas within which there is little overall understanding of the cumulative impacts of the proposed development upon protected species and sites.

Assessment of Alternatives

One particular feature of SEA methodology that has proved problematic in reviewing offshore plans is the assessment of alternatives. A core requirement of the SEA process is the consideration of alternative development possibilities. However, this may be considered to be among the weaker aspects of current UK offshore SEA practices. Thus far, there has been relatively little deviation from the proposed licensing programmes. Indeed, the oil and gas licensing Rounds surveyed under SEAs 1–3, as well as the offshore windfarm surveys conducted under R2 endorsed the proposals in full. However, this is perhaps unsurprising since they addressed areas of significant pre-existing activity or, as in the case of SEA1, acreage for which extensive licensing had been approved in an adjacent location by a neighbouring state. Since SEA4, there has been a trend towards the broad endorsement of development proposals, balanced by the withdrawal of a limited amount of acreage from potential licensing activities.

Particular concerns have been raised by a perceived absence of meaningful discussion of alternatives. In earlier processes, alternatives were either virtually discounted[88] or relegated to a superficial table-based survey,[89] although a discernible commitment towards improving the process was made at SEA6.[90]

[88] For instance, the SEA processes conducted pursuant to R2 only sanctioned consideration of wind development in three specific sites. However, as is the case with joint EU-funded initiatives, the ability of SEA consultants to assess alternatives in government-directed projects is decidedly limited. This may be compared and contrasted to the onshore experience, as discussed by David Elvin in Ch 6 of this volume.

[89] As exemplified in SEA3: DTI, *Strategic Environmental Assessment of Parts of the Central & Southern North Sea: Assessment Document* (London, DTI, 2003) 197.

[90] DTI (n 84) 8.

Adjustments have been made in the subsequent SEAs, including the inclusion of a somewhat more nuanced explanation of the potential value of alternatives, although consideration of alternatives has generally continued to err on the side of brevity. This has been especially true in the context of the traditionally marginalised 'do nothing' option: consultees have consistently complained of a tacit bias towards the socio-economic benefits of production in the most widely read segments of SEA reports to the virtual exclusion of ecological merits,[91] while there has been peripheral consideration of the implications of eschewing development beyond a vague discussion of wilderness values in SEA1.[92] Indeed, in the context of renewable energy projects, concerns have been raised that the various OESEA processes 'were conducted not as enquiries into the environmental effects of plans for offshore wind farm development and how these might be minimised, but as information-gathering exercises to support future planning processes'.[93] Although an exhaustive appraisal of alternatives risks generating unfocused, sprawling and unwieldy documentation, there is nonetheless a clear case for a more extensive treatment of these issues as advocated by many stakeholders.

Data Generation and Management

As with comparable SEA regimes,[94] the UK offshore initiatives have generated an extensive array of data, while conversely demonstrating that the overall knowledge base concerning the marine environment ultimately remains variable and patchy. In this respect, the UK practice demonstrates a somewhat mixed record of managing development projects in the context of scientific uncertainty. On the one hand, a number of environmentally beneficial developments have subsequently emerged from the extensive research exercises that have characterised SEA practices in the offshore environment. Indeed, having established the unique ecological value of cold-water coral in the White Zone, a considerable proportion of the data yielded during SEA1 was ultimately submitted in support of the designation of the Darwin Mounds as a Special Area of Conservation (SAC) under the Habitats Directive.[95] Moreover, the SEA process has constituted a valuable, if irregular, source of governmental funding for marine environmental research in

[91] BERR, *SEA7: Post-consultation Report* (London, BERR, 2007) 6.

[92] DTI (n 72) 70–72.

[93] Olivia Woolley, 'Ecological Governance for Offshore Wind Energy in United Kingdom Waters: Has an Effective Legal Framework Been Established for Preventing Ecologically Harmful Development?' (2015) 30 *International Journal of Marine and Coastal Law* 765, 772–73.

[94] Doelle, Bankes and Porta (n 3) 111.

[95] SEA1 asserted that the area 'should be subject to stringent control measures to prevent direct and indirect effects': DTI, *Strategic Environmental Assessment of the Former White Zone: Volume 1—An Overview of SEA Process, Key Issues and Findings* (London, DTI, 2001) 21.

offshore waters.[96] Indeed, research has been conducted not only on the more obvious impacts of offshore energy production, but also on the wider threats facing key species to establish an overall picture of ecosystem health.[97]

Beyond strict environmental considerations, a somewhat unexpected beneficiary of the SEA process has been marine archaeology. Cultural heritage is perhaps one of the less prominent elements requiring consideration under the SEA Directive.[98] However, while archaeological requirements may constitute a more limited conservationist preoccupation, this is no trivial issue: judicial reconsideration of the concept of 'military remains' has ensured that a significantly larger number of war wrecks will require formal protection than had previously been considered the case.[99] Indeed, since SEA6, archaeological interests have gained a steady degree of prominence within the SEA process, with SEA requirements having since facilitated a closer engagement between archaeological interests and the offshore industry, for which some progress has been made towards the development of a future code of conduct for marine artefacts.[100]

Concerns have nonetheless been raised over the quality of certain aspects of the acquisition and dissemination of the data generated under the various offshore SEA initiatives conducted to date. There has been some question of the validity of the methodologies employed in the various SEAs, albeit that this is an occupational hazard inherent in any major scientific research. Stakeholders have regularly criticised the loose terminology used within particular SEAs in approving licensing activities.[101] There has also been a notable reluctance to consider the potential impacts of future decommissioning activities for installations that have reached the end of their economic utility, which represents a significant omission in current SEA practice. Likewise, while the offshore SEAs have addressed a number of environmental factors at sea, little consideration has been given to the onshore implications of servicing significant marine infrastructure projects.[102]

[96] This has been particularly valuable in marine mammal research, which is notoriously expensive to conduct on a widespread basis: BERR, *Environmental Report: Twenty-Fifth Offshore Oil and Gas Licensing Round* (London, BERR, 2007) 56.

[97] Most notably in the context of by-catches, widely considered to constitute the most pressing threat to marine mammals: DTI (n 89) 107–08.

[98] SEA Directive, Annex I(f).

[99] *R (Fogg and Another) v Secretary of State for Defence* [2006] EWCA Civ 1270. The judgment advanced a reinterpretation of the Protection of Military Remains Act 1986 to include merchant convoy casualties sustained while in service with the armed forces.

[100] BERR, *Post-consultation Report: Twenty-Fifth Offshore Oil and Gas Licensing Round* (London, BERR, 2007) 7.

[101] For instance, a number of documents refer to an 'acceptably low risk' of harm to the environment, without articulating further how a particular impact would be deemed acceptable: DTI, *Strategic Environmental Assessment Area North and West of Orkney and Shetland: Consultation Document* (London, DTI, 2004) 148. Likewise, OESEA Recommendation 3 suggests the 'bulk of' windfarm developments should be located offshore, without quantifying further what this might mean in practice.

[102] Terrestrial concerns have been conspicuous by their absence in many of the SEA documentation produced to date, while in OESEA 3 it was observed in response to stakeholder questions concerning implications for port activities that the developers had 'not commissioned specific work but build on that of others': DECC, *OESEA 3: Stakeholder Workshops* (London, DECC, 2016), 3.

However, of greatest concern in this regard, substantial knowledge gaps remain in relation to critical species, the core areas of habitat that may overlap with licensable areas and, as noted above, the cumulative impact of offshore activities upon the marine environment. The marine SEA initiatives have consistently illustrated the considerable practical challenges incumbent in gathering effective baseline data for a number of key species affected by offshore industrial activities. Indeed, many species of marine mammals defy attempts to monitor their movements effectively, since they may exhibit poor site fidelity and undertake extensive and erratic movements, while offshore conditions further render them difficult to identify and track.[103] There is a similar paucity of data on migratory birds due to the considerable research challenges experienced in monitoring the types of offshore locations suitable for windfarm development[104] and thereby in assessing optimal location and licensing options.

These shortcomings and challenges in offshore SEA processes have also exposed further difficulties in managing the data that has been generated within SEAs conducted to date and in identifying clear lines of responsibility for addressing information gaps. While deficiencies in the available data and resulting ongoing core research needs have been identified clearly within many of the SEAs conducted thus far, there has been little information within subsequent initiatives, or indeed the designated SEA platforms, as to whether these gaps have been filled and to what extent.[105] More recent SEAs have advanced a commendable commitment towards securing a more integrated approach to data collection between relevant government bodies, conservationists and independent researchers and offshore operators.[106] While the UK Joint Nature Conservation Committee (JNCC) has advocated that a willingness to engage with researchers ought to be an operative factor in determining the selection of licence holders,[107] operators have in turn raised legitimate concerns as to the commercial sensitivity of environmental information.[108] Significant problems have also been encountered in maintaining the data generated to date. There are few central databases and repositories for this material, which remains scattered among a wide range of outlets with varying degrees of public availability. There is some circularity in approaches to

[103] Clare B Embling et al, 'Using Habitat Models to Identify Suitable Sites for Marine Protected Areas for Harbour Porpoises' (2010) 143 *Biological Conservation* 267, 267–68.

[104] AD Fox et al, 'Information Needs to Support Environmental Impact Assessment of the Effects of European Marine Offshore Wind Farms on Birds' (2006) 148 *Ibis* 129, 141.

[105] This has also been a significant problem in comparable jurisdictions: Doelle, Bankes and Porta (n 3) 111.

[106] See OESEA, Recommendations 7, 8 and 21 and OESEA 2, Recommendation 17.

[107] BERR (n 91) 21.

[108] DECC, *OESEA: Post-consultation Report* (London, DECC, 2009) 112. OESEA 3 has also considered that research results should be made publicly available 'where ever possible': Recommendation 19 of OESEA 3. From the developer's perspective, aside from valid operational secrecy considerations, a further inhibiting factors is the strong risk that heavy investment in species monitoring might generate precisely the level of data that would justify withdrawing a commercially valuable site from industrial use.

the ultimate responsibility for data management: operators view this as a broad task of the JNCC, which has, in turn, stated that it lacks the resources of offshore operators in order to fulfil this function effectively.[109] Concerns have also been expressed over the lack of a clear forum to prioritise ongoing research needs, an issue that is likely to be addressed in future—to some extent at least—under the auspices of the MMO.[110]

Administration and Review

Despite questions as to the treatment of scientific uncertainty in the SEAs conducted to date, a particular strength of UK offshore practice has been reflected in clear commitments towards institutional review and the ongoing procedural refinement of the SEA process. In marked contrast to other domestic industrial initiatives subject to SEA requirements, the UK offshore energy sector has been subject to a strong degree of administrative oversight and reflective practice since SEA was introduced as a core requirement of the pre-licensing procedure. Unlike many other sectors, offshore energy has seen the establishment of a central repository of SEA documentation and a targeted forum for the review of both previous practice and ongoing requirements. This has allowed the process to evolve significantly since its inception by identifying and addressing shortcomings in methodology, structure and other institutional challenges encountered in the course of successive SEA proceedings.

By 2001, with the commencement of the initial investigations of SEA2, a dedicated Steering Group had been established to oversee the wider process of offshore SEA, comprising representatives of pertinent stakeholders, as well as experts in EIA practices, SEA processes, environmental management, conservation and industry regulation. The Steering Group was given the broad remit of providing 'objective technical and general advice to facilitate the DTI SEA process, to promote stakeholder involvement and to achieve timely preparation of quality documents to inform licensing decisions'.[111] While responsibility for the publication of the assessment documentation remains vested in the regulatory authority, the Steering Group plays a key role in the scoping phase of the SEA process and in

[109] ibid 101. More recently, mixed organisations encompassing a range of government and industrial representatives, such as UK Oil and Gas, have started to maintain additional databases of pertinent information with a greater degree of accessibility to external experts, a trend further encouraged under the most recent SEA initiative: Recommendation 21 of OESEA 3.

[110] DECC, *OESEA2: Post-consultation Report* (London, DECC, 2011) 61. Nevertheless, the MMO Offshore Renewables Research Steering Group currently provides automatic access only to public authorities and other budget holders, a position that will need to be reviewed to ensure a meaningful contribution from other experts.

[111] DTI, *Strategic Environmental Assessment of the Mature Areas of the Offshore North Sea: SEA 2—Consultation Document* (London, DTI, 2001) 8.

facilitating the circulation of information, securing public and expert participation, and reviewing the resulting documentation.

A strong commitment to reflective practice has served to refine the process significantly, to the considerable advantage of subsequent SEA procedures. A more integrated approach to offshore SEA can be seen to have emerged as a result, especially in relation to regulatory coordination to streamline governmental administration,[112] and to allay concerns over the shortcomings of an overly narrow sectoral focus.[113] Indeed, assessment undertaken for individual energy sectors in a multi-use environment is considered 'inherently restrictive and challenges the delivery of effective SEA'.[114] Accordingly, recent SEAs have adopted a more coordinated outlook, with the OESEA initiatives examining a range of energy options within the same broad location, an approach that is likely to characterise future SEA practices for the offshore sector. The Steering Group is also seemingly well placed to monitor the overall progress of SEA to date, especially the various recommendations that have been formulated throughout the process, not least in respect of identifying the extent to which data gaps have been addressed and in streamlining and improving administrative practices. Nevertheless, despite some initial progress towards mapping the outcomes of earlier recommendations, this process appears to have stalled more recently. Notwithstanding an ongoing commitment by the UK government to collate and publicise this information, little headway has been made since OESEA 2, hence progress towards the implementation of operative recommendations remains difficult to accurately assess.

Public and Stakeholder Participation

Consultation with public authorities and the general public, including relevant NGOs and other interested organisations[115] as well as neighbouring states that may be potentially affected by the development in question,[116] remains a key requirement under the SEA Directive. The precise arrangements for the transmission of information and the organisation of appropriate consultation are to be determined by the individual Member States.[117] The EU institutions have placed considerable emphasis upon the value of effective consultation at an early stage, but have noted that practice in this respect has been decidedly variable.[118] In the

[112] This was a particular concern of SEA3, identifying a need to coordinate SEA at several governmental levels 'to ensure the sharing of information and experience, the avoidance of duplication of effort and stakeholder confusion and fatigue': DTI (n 89) 197.

[113] ibid.

[114] Noble et al (n 60) 300.

[115] SEA Directive, art 6(4); see also recital 18.

[116] ibid, art 7.

[117] ibid, art 6(5).

[118] Commission (n 33) 5.

context of the UK offshore energy industry, a series of concerns have been raised over the consultation process, in relation to both public and expert participation.

Consultation practices have developed significantly since SEA1, which was considered with some understatement to be 'inadequate',[119] and are now streamlined to include both stakeholder and expert meetings. Engaging the general public with offshore SEA processes has proved challenging due to a general 'out of sight, out of mind' philosophy that is less apparent with terrestrial development.[120] Improvements have been made since SEA2, for which participants were considered 'too self-selecting',[121] and successive SEAs have identified the need to include additional participants from related sectors. Indeed, concerns have been raised at varying stages over a lack of engagement with environmental NGOs, local government, military authorities, archaeological specialists, the fishing industry, and leisure and tourism interests, all of whom have been duly canvassed and engaged in subsequent processes. Despite criticism over a lack of publicity for such events—in marked contrast to the apparent ability of developers to mobilise effective information campaigns—attendance from the general public has improved significantly in recent years. It may be speculated as to whether this is attributable to more effective outreach and a growing public appreciation of the SEA process or whether the inclusion of offshore wind in the latter SEA initiatives has provoked greater public mobilisation—the seascape implications of wind turbines having generally proved a considerably less palatable prospect than the trickle-down economic impact of the hydrocarbon industry in coastal communities. Stakeholder meetings have generally served to educate the public further about SEA initiatives, notwithstanding some suggestion that this enlightenment has been focused more on the SEA process generally than the specific developmental initiative at hand.[122]

The consultation processes have also generated a significant volume of information, although until SEA4, this documentation was confined to the rather cryptic internet domain of www.habitats-directive.org, an obscure designation that was seemingly derived from the titular focus of SEA1. From 2004, the more intuitive choice of www.offshore-sea.org.uk proved more readily identifiable and accessible, with such documentation now posted in full upon the general website of the UK government.[123] The substantial web traffic to such sites indicates that interested parties are accessing vital information, especially the non-technical

[119] DTI, *SEA2: Stakeholder Dialogue Meeting Report* (London, DTI, 2001) 4. Indeed, the process of consultation pursuant to SEA1 was largely an 'internal exercise': Fidler and Noble (n 59) 17.

[120] ibid 15.

[121] DTI (n 119) 42.

[122] DTI, *SEA3: Stakeholder Dialogue Meeting Report* (London, DTI, 2003)16; DTI, *SEA5: Stakeholder Dialogue Meeting Report* (London, DTI, 2005) 11.

[123] The relevant documentation is now posted at https://www.gov.uk/guidance/offshore-energy-strategic-environmental-assessment-sea-an-overview-of-the-sea-process. Additionally, the British Geological Survey retains data gathered in the course of previous SEA processes, with this archive available at http://www.bgs.ac.uk/data/sea/. SEA documents are now more readily accessible through search engines and social media fora than had been the case at the commencement of the offshore assessment process.

reports, which suggests engagement with a lay audience. The timing and structure of some public consultation meetings have, however, raised concerns—SEA3 was conducted at the height of the summer holiday period and duly secured minimal participation—while stakeholder and expert feedback suggests that meetings have to a degree lacked focus, been unduly brief, overly reliant upon prior electronic communication and conducted as if a pre-development formality.[124]

Conclusion

The UK offshore energy sector provides an illuminating case study of the role of SEA processes generally and their application to the marine environment specifically. Although UK offshore assessment practices pre-date the formal requirements of the SEA Directive by some margin, the impending EU legislation clearly exerted a strong influence on licensing decisions at the material time. Since the entry into force of the Directive, offshore SEA in the UK has evolved considerably. Notwithstanding certain ongoing challenges that are inherent to many comparable SEA processes, the UK offshore system represents an effective procedural model for the preliminary assessment of major infrastructure projects. A strong culture of reflective practice has helped to refine and streamline the process considerably, while there has been a steady improvement in baseline marine environmental data generated by these initiatives. These practices accordingly provide enhanced scope for offshore licensing decisions to proceed in a more environmentally informed manner, especially in relation to hydrocarbons, in line with the original legislative intent of the Directive.

However, significant challenges remain in ensuring that decision-making subsequent to the SEA process proceeds in a manner that is sensitive to the requirements of precaution and the ecosystem approach to the management of marine resources. In this respect, licensing decisions have often been made in the context of limited information as to the offshore ecosystem itself, as well as the prospective impact of specific pollution sources and the cumulative impacts of large-scale industrial developments. Strong concerns have been raised that approval has been granted to projects irrespective of the prevailing uncertainty surrounding potential threats to the marine environment, which accordingly impacts upon the ability of the pertinent authorities to design and implement appropriate mitigation measures and policies.[125]

[124] See BERR (n 91) 10 in the context of SEA7. Indeed, one prominent NGO equated the process to 'box-ticking': ibid 4.

[125] This has been particularly apparent in UK practices concerning offshore wind energy: see Woolley (n 93) 775.

Moreover, notwithstanding the laudable culture of institutional learning, procedural difficulties continue to create practical impediments to the effective discharge of SEA obligations. The more recent OESEA initiatives have strongly mandated a coordinated approach between developers and other marine interests; a degree of investment is accordingly necessary in maintaining central data requirements and in securing an effective and accessible platform for the review of environmental information. The assessment of alternatives would also appear to require further consideration, either as an extended standing appendix to SEA documentation or as a more overt theme within current reporting processes. Tracking the implementation of specific recommendations arising from previous SEA procedures and the progress of initiatives to address core data shortages are also significant operational and managerial tasks. Future SEA processes should also consider decommissioning issues more explicitly, which have been marginalised to date, as well as the onshore implications of offshore development projects.

In principle, the offshore energy SEA process may be considered to represent a broadly effective platform by which to guide future licensing decisions. Considerable faith has nonetheless been placed in the subsequent role of EIA and in technical solutions to address aspects of the environmental impacts identified within the combined SEA initiatives, neither of which offer the ecological panacea seemingly contemplated by the regulatory authorities in the offshore context. The acquisition and review of data as to the efficacy of these mitigation and assessment strategies will accordingly frame the environmental regulation of the offshore industries in the mid-term and will also guide the focus of future SEA processes and reassessments. If the OESEA processes are a reliable barometer of regulatory intent, future and more experimental industrial developments—such as fracking, CCS and other seabed activities—will be consolidated and coordinated through even broader SEA initiatives in the coming years. The UK has adopted a proactive national approach to emerging industries, for which the SEA requirements under associated EU provisions have been otherwise subject to some uncertainty. The further elaboration and clarification of SEA obligations in this regard is likely to be forthcoming through specific EU legislation for these industries, as evidenced by CCS issues and the nascent regulatory position on fracking. Offshore fisheries will, however, remain outside the purview of SEA requirements due to the nature of regulatory competences, a position that could merit legislative reconsideration in future revisions to the Common Fisheries Policy.

At the time of writing (August 2016), the UK electorate had rejected the prospect of continued membership of the EU, with the government tentatively commencing the unprecedented task of repatriating legislative competences after forty years of regional integration. While the so-called 'Brexit' process remains in its infancy, it is abundantly clear that it will have profound domestic legal implications, not least in the field of environmental regulation. However, as far as the oversight of SEA is concerned, especially in the offshore environment, withdrawal from the EU appears unlikely to exert a material impact upon current and future practices, irrespective of whichever model of regional cooperation is ultimately pursued. Prospective participation in the EEA would seemingly entail continued adherence to the SEA Directive, as exemplified by the marine practices of Iceland and Norway.[126] Moreover, as this chapter has sought to demonstrate, the UK offshore framework has moved substantially beyond the original 'minimal standards' intentions of the SEA Directive. Nevertheless, while national practices have evolved organically into a proactive and sophisticated regulatory regime, the role of the underlying objectives of the Directive—if not necessarily its specific provisions—in facilitating these developments should not be overlooked. At a time at which the conceptual merits of EU law are subject to profound national introspection, the SEA Directive and its offshore application represents an intriguing example of the regulatory value of overarching supranational principles.

[126] On Norwegian and Icelandic implementation of the SEA in their respective offshore waters see Johnstone (n 16) 171–73.

Part IV

The SEA Experience in Neighbouring Jurisdictions

14

Strategic Environmental Assessment in a Cold Climate: The Scottish Experience

COLIN REID AND DENIS EDWARDS

Introduction

The story of the Environmental Assessment (Scotland) Act 2005 draws together several threads of the legal and political consequences of devolution and the relationship between European Union (EU), UK and Scottish matters. The devolution settlement created the potential for a Scottish government to adopt a policy on strategic environmental assessment (SEA) different from and more all-embracing than that adopted by the UK government, and gave Scotland the power and procedures to give this legal effect. Meanwhile, the overriding need to ensure compliance with EU law and the mechanisms for this are shown by the brief interlude when SEA in Scotland merely mirrored the response taken elsewhere in the UK.

The SEA experience in Scotland is also worthy of note because of what it highlights about the state of public law and environmental law in Scotland. Although few Scottish cases have considered the implications of the SEA Directive, one case, namely *Walton v Scottish Ministers*,[1] has much to say about both the Directive and judicial review in Scotland. Indeed, *Walton* brings a satisfactory conclusion to a long-running problem in Scots law in relation to the test for standing in judicial review cases. The requirement for standing in Scottish judicial reviews had long been a need to show 'title and interest to sue'. This was applied by the Scottish courts, in effect, to make representative judicial review actions almost impossible. *Walton* has liberated the law from restrictive standing rules, both in environmental cases and generally, a change now codified by the Courts (Scotland) Act 2014. This Act makes other significant changes to Scottish judicial procedure, notably a new requirement for the Court's permission before a judicial review petition can proceed. It is too early to say what these changes will mean for public law and

[1] *Walton v Scottish Ministers* 2012 SC (UKSC) 67; [2012] UKSC 44.

environmental law in Scotland. What can be said is that Scottish judicial review procedure is likely to need more *Walton*-like changes before all of the potential of the Scottish implementation of the SEA Directive can be realised.

Background

There are three starting points to consider. Chronologically, the first is the European Communities Act 1972, which in section 2(2) confers a broad power to make delegated legislation to implement EU law.[2] This has been the predominant means by which European directives have been implemented in the UK. The second is the Scotland Act 1998, which created the Scottish Parliament and government,[3] and conferred on them powers to legislate for all matters within Scotland, including environmental matters, not expressly reserved for the UK authorities.[4] Third, there is the SEA Directive,[5] which required implementing legislation to be enacted within the UK and the other Member States by 21 July 2004.

The first two developments interact in the handling of EU matters in Scotland. The general transfer of powers to the Scottish ministers achieved by the Scotland Act extends to exercising the power under the European Communities Act 1972 to make delegated legislation to implement EU laws and the expectation is that Scotland will take responsibility for implementing EU laws within its sphere of competence.[6] Indeed, although it is the UK that is the Member State of the EU and thus the party liable to face any infringement proceedings and sanctions for failing to meet its EU obligations, the Memorandum of Understanding between the UK and the devolved authorities makes it clear that any financial consequences of non-compliance will be borne by the devolved administration.[7] Nevertheless, it is a feature of the devolution settlement, and one which differentiates it from a federal arrangement, that the UK authorities retain powers to intervene in

[2] The term 'EU' is used throughout the chapter, ignoring the formal evolution of the European structures from Communities to Community to Union.

[3] Known as the 'Scottish Executive' in the 1998 Act (s 44), but widely referred to as the 'Scottish government', especially since the Scottish National Party took power in 2007, a change now given official recognition by s 12 of the Scotland Act 2012.

[4] There are other limits on these powers, notably that neither Parliament nor government can lawfully make laws incompatible with EU law; Scotland Act 1998, ss 29(2)(d), 54.

[5] Directive 2001/42/EC of the European Parliament and of the Council on the assessment of the effects of certain plans and programmes on the environment [2001] OJ L197/30 (hereinafter 'the SED Directive').

[6] Scotland Act 1998, sch 5, para 7; see Andrea Ross and Hazel Nash, 'European Union Environmental Law: Who Legislates for Whom in a Devolved Great Britain' [2009] *Public Law* 564.

[7] Memorandum of Understanding and Supplementary Agreements between the United Kingdom Government, the Scottish Ministers, the Welsh Ministers, and the Northern Ireland Executive Committee (September 2012), para B4.26. See Stephen Ashworth and Rachael Herbert in Ch 5 of this volume for how the requirement for 'early and effective' public participation under the SEA Directive has been implemented in the different constituent parts of the UK.

devolved matters. One specific example of this is the express provision that, despite the transfer of powers to Scotland, the UK government can still exercise powers in Scotland to ensure the implementation of EU law, even within areas of devolved power.[8] Thus, despite the overall division of responsibilities, there is a large overlap of powers when it comes to implementing EU law.[9]

In responding to the SEA Directive, therefore, there was a choice to be made as to who was to legislate to give effect to its provisions in Scotland. In relation to matters that extended beyond Scotland alone, only the UK authorities could act, but matters within Scotland could be covered by Scottish or by UK legislation. The standard practice has been for Scotland to take on such a task,[10] making use of the powers under the 1972 Act. However, by the time the Directive's implementation was due, the decision had been taken in Scotland (as described below) to do more than just give effect to the Directive—which limits the requirement for environmental assessment to the categories of 'plans and programmes' specified therein—and to introduce a more far-reaching procedure.[11] This could not be achieved using the powers in the 1972 Act, since it involved not just implementing the terms of EU law, but also applying a similar requirement in situations well beyond its scope. Accordingly, primary legislation would be needed to achieve the result sought. Yet, in practice, this could not be put in place before the deadline for implementation and, in order to avoid breaching EU law, an interim measure was adopted.

At the UK level, the Environmental Assessment of Plans and Programmes Regulations 2004 were made,[12] under the 1972 Act, to give effect to the SEA Directive in relation to plans and programmes affecting England alone or England and any other part of the UK, but not those affecting Scotland alone. In Scotland, a parallel set of regulations was made, the Environmental Assessment of Plans and Programmes (Scotland) Regulations 2004,[13] covering plans and programmes applying to Scotland only and requiring an environmental assessment for those plans within the categories covered by the Directive. Both sets of regulations, and further ones for matters exclusive to Wales and Northern Ireland,[14] took effect just

[8] Scotland Act 1998, s 57.

[9] Colin Reid, 'The Limits of Devolved Power: Subordinate Legislation in Scotland' (2003) 24 *Statute Law Review* 187, 207–09.

[10] Ross and Nash (n 6).

[11] This is not the first time that the Scottish government has gone beyond the strict letter of what EU environmental legislation requires. See, eg, the Water Environment (Controlled Activities) (Scotland) Regulations 2011, SSI 2011/209, reg 27, providing for 'surrender' of permits. This has been held to prevent a liquidator disclaiming a pollution permit granted to a company which has become insolvent: see *Liquidators of the Scottish Coal Company Ltd* [2013] CSIH 108; *cf Re Celtic Extraction Ltd* [2001] Ch 475.

[12] SI 2004/1633.

[13] SSI 2004/258.

[14] Environmental Assessment of Plans and Programmes (Wales) Regulations 2004, SI 2004/1656; Environmental Assessment of Plans and Programmes Regulations (Northern Ireland) 2004, SR 2004/280.

before the deadline for implementing the Directive and ensured that its provisions were duly implemented in the UK. The Scottish regulations continued in force until February 2006, when they were replaced by the wider provisions of the Environmental Assessment (Scotland) Act 2005, but gave rise to no noteworthy legal issues during their brief life.

The interim nature of the Scottish regulations was the result of a process that began with the Liberal Democrats' manifesto for the elections to the Scottish Parliament in 2003. This called for the implementation of strategic environmental assessment 'across the range of the Scottish Executive's work'[15] and, when the party formed a coalition with Labour after the election, a commitment to introduce strategic environmental assessment for 'all new strategies, programmes and plans developed by the public sector' was part of the 'green thread' that ran through the coalition agreement.[16] The result was the Environmental Assessment (Scotland) Act 2005 (EASA), which came into force in February 2006 and considerably extends the scope of strategic environmental assessment in Scotland.

Environmental Assessment (Scotland) Act 2005

Since it follows that of the SEA Directive, the basic pattern of the EASA will be familiar to anyone who knows about SEA in Europe. The bodies responsible for creating a 'qualifying' plan or programme (the 'responsible authority') must carry out an SEA by producing an environmental report which is subject to consultation with specified 'consultation authorities' and the public before a decision is reached. There are provisions to determine whether certain plans should be exempt from this procedure ('screening') and for determining the range of topics to be addressed ('scoping'). The big difference is that the reach of this requirement is not limited to the categories of plans set out in the Directive, but applies to all strategies, plans and programmes prepared by public authorities. A consequence of this broader reach is the inclusion of a further 'pre-screening' stage to allow those plans that can be readily identified as being likely to have no or only a minimal effect on the environment to be excluded at an early stage through a simple process. These features and other aspects of the EASA are now considered.

The responsible authorities required to undertake an SEA are 'any person, body or office-holder exercising functions of a public character'.[17] Given the endless variety of ways in which what were once clearly public sector functions are now exercised—including through privatised utilities, publicly owned companies

[15] Scottish Liberal Democrats, 'Make the Difference: Fresh Thinking for Four More Years' (2003), www.scottishcorpus.ac.uk/document/?documentid=1418.

[16] Scottish Executive, *A Partnership for a Better Scotland: Partnership Agreement* (2003) 48.

[17] Environmental Assessment (Scotland) Act 2005 (EASA), s 2(1).

and arm's length bodies of many sorts at central and local government levels—identifying what are 'public' bodies is now a difficult and contested task.[18] This legal issue arises in several contexts, including human rights[19] and freedom of information,[20] but as yet does not appear to have been a disputed issue in this context. To provide some assistance here, the EASA specifies certain bodies[21] and gives the ministers power to make orders specifying further bodies for this purpose.[22]

The starting point in determining when an SEA must be carried out is that this requirement applies to all plans and programmes prepared and/or adopted by a responsible authority (including those adopted through a legislative procedure).[23] Modifications of plans are also included,[24] and it is expressly provided that the term 'plans and programmes' includes strategies;[25] hereinafter the term 'plans' is used for all of these. There are, though, several exclusions and exemptions. In the first place, and in keeping with the limits of devolved power, the Act applies only to plans which relate solely to the whole or any part of Scotland;[26] those of wider effect will be covered by the UK regulations, but only if they fall within any of the categories specified there. Second, plans count as 'qualifying plans' only to the extent that they 'relate to matters of a public character';[27] as noted above, identifying a 'public character' in the complex patchwork of public, private and third sector arrangements for serving the public may not always be straightforward, but no litigation has arisen as yet on this issue.[28] Third, certain plans are automatically excluded, namely those whose sole purpose is national defence or civil emergency, financial and budgetary plans and certain EU-funded plans.[29] Finally, certain other plans are exempted at the preliminary stage without there having to be any consideration of their likely impact on the environment. The only category listed is plans relating to an individual school (which are too local to be likely to have a significant impact), but the Act allows ministers to specify further categories,

[18] In practice, the Scottish government was responsible for over 80 per cent of assessments between 2004 and 2010, with local authorities for a further 11 per cent: Historic Scotland, Scottish Environment Protection Agency and Scottish Natural Heritage, 'The Scottish Strategic Environmental Assessment Review—A Summary' (2011) 13 (see n 48).

[19] eg, *YL v Birmingham City Council* [2008] 1 AC 95.

[20] eg, Case C-279/12 *Fish Legal and Shirley v The Information Commissioner* (CJEU, 19 December 2013).

[21] Scottish ministers and other members of the Scottish Administration and the Scottish Parliament and Parliamentary Corporate Body.

[22] EASA, s 2(4); no such order has been made. This is the same pattern as under the Freedom of Information (Scotland) Act 2002, where much more detail is provided and there have been specification orders made.

[23] ibid, s 4(1).

[24] ibid, s 4(2); see *Walton*, discussed below, on both the status of a plan and the issue of modification.

[25] ibid, s 4(4).

[26] ibid, s 4.

[27] ibid, s 5(2).

[28] Neither the original nor the recent Scottish guidance (see n 52 below and accompanying text) provides substantial assistance on this point.

[29] EASA, s 4(3).

provided that they are satisfied that the type of plan is likely to have no or minimal effect on the environment.[30]

These limited exclusions leave all other plans potentially subject to SEA, but the Act distinguishes between two groups, using first a definition which mirrors that in the SEA Directive to ensure the clarity of its implementation (including a list of the categories of project covered by the Directive) and then a residual group for all others (that is, the extended set of public plans that come within the Scottish regime).[31] Undertaking the thorough screening process called for under the Directive to ascertain whether a plan's likely environmental effects are such as to demand an SEA would be burdensome for the many plans where such effects are clearly absent, not least for the 'consultation authorities'—the Scottish ministers, the Scottish Environment Protection Agency (SEPA) and Scottish Natural Heritage (SNH)[32]—which must be involved in such screening. Accordingly, a simpler 'pre-screening' stage has been introduced for the extended set of public plans not covered by the Directive,[33] allowing the responsible authority alone to decide that a plan is exempt because it will have no or only minimal effect on the environment, bearing in mind the standard criteria for determining significant effects.[34] The fact that the authority is determining for itself that an SEA is unnecessary, without even the need for external consultation, inevitably gave rise to concerns over the rigour with which the task would be undertaken. To assuage these, two features are added: first, a requirement to notify the consultation authorities as soon as practicable once a decision is taken that no SEA is required; and, second, the placing of such decisions on a public register. Thus, although there is no external participation in the decision-making procedure, the fact that plans are being excluded will be publicised and they are available for scrutiny.

The rest of the Act follows the pattern under the SEA Directive, with provisions on:

- screening to determine whether a plan (unless already excluded as above) is likely to have significant effects, a more involved screening process that includes consultation with the consultation authorities, and publicity for the decision and its justification;[35]
- powers for ministers to make a screening direction;[36]
- the requirement to undertake an SEA for non-exempt plans before they can be adopted;[37]

[30] ibid, s 6.

[31] ibid, s 5(3)–(4) and sch 1.

[32] ibid, s 3.

[33] ibid, s 7. In order to comply with the Directive, there must be a standard screening for any plans which it covers, governed by EASA, s 8.

[34] Set out in EASA, sch 2.

[35] ibid, ss 8–10.

[36] ibid, s 11.

[37] ibid, s 12.

— the details of what the environmental report prepared by the authority must contain, including scoping procedures and decisions;[38]
— consultation arrangements with both the consultation authorities and the public;[39]
— the need to take account of the report and the outcome of consultation before deciding whether to adopt the plan;[40]
— publicity for the adoption of the plan;[41] and
— obligations in relation to post-adoption monitoring.[42]

There is no significant difference between these provisions and those in the SEA Directive and the English/UK regulations, although there are slight differences in wording.[43] For example, the Scottish ministers must ensure that the consultation authorities and public have an 'early and effective' opportunity to comment, not just an 'effective' one.[44] The assessment procedure itself, if not its scope, is therefore essentially the same for Scottish plans as for those governed by the English/UK regulations.

Gateway, Review and Guidance

In considering the implementation and effect of SEA in Scotland, three developments are worthy of consideration: the SEA Gateway established by the Scottish government; the review of SEA in Scotland completed in 2011; and the changing nature of the supporting guidance that has been provided. All of these aim to ensure that the SEA process is effective and that those involved have support and assistance whilst the process remains transparent.

Although the title itself is not now so prominent, the Scottish 'SEA Gateway' was established online to provide a single point of reference on SEA matters in Scotland.[45] In particular, it hosts the SEA Database, which records all the plans which have been subjected to SEA or considered but exempted from the process at the screening or pre-screening stages, and provides access to the plans themselves and the relevant documentation at each stage of SEA consideration. It is

[38] Ibid, ss 14–15 and sch 3.
[39] ibid, s 16.
[40] ibid, s 17.
[41] ibid, s 18.
[42] ibid, s 19.
[43] For a detailed analysis, see Veronica Burbridge, 'Strategic Environmental Assessment in Scotland: Implementation in a Devolved Administration' (LLM thesis, 2006, available from University of Dundee Library).
[44] EASA, s 16(3); *cf* Environmental Assessment of Plans and Programmes Regulations 2004, SI 2004/1633, reg 13(3).
[45] www.scotland.gov.uk/Topics/Environment/environmental-assessment/sea.

thus possible to see here the plans (almost 1,500 of them),[46] which have fallen within the scope of the EASA and the preceding regulations, and the decisions and supporting documents detailing whether an SEA has been deemed necessary and, if so, the environmental report, the considerations behind the eventual decision and the post-adoption monitoring arrangements. With this database and access to other relevant documents, including guidance and the annual reports from ministers statutorily required for the first five years of the Act being in force,[47] there is plenty of information readily accessible to enable understanding and scrutiny of the SEA process in Scotland.

Reflection on SEA was further undertaken in *The Scottish Strategic Environmental Assessment Review* completed by Historic Scotland, SEPA and SNH in 2011.[48] This substantial report[49] concluded that 'the fundamental components of SEA in Scotland ... are generally sound and fit for purpose', but that practice could be improved, particularly to ensure that there is earlier consideration of environmental matters in policy-making and to build SEA into the corporate culture of authorities across all sectors. Also recommended are the integration of SEA into the actual making and enhancement of plans, rather than acting as something applied to plans once completed; increased attention on using SEA to build in an effective framework for delivering mitigation measures; and greater use of the process to assist authorities fulfil their duties under the Climate Change (Scotland) Act 2009.[50] In terms of the actual process of undertaking SEA, recommendations include greater focus on key issues at the scoping stage, seeking earlier input from stakeholders, and a 'continuous engagement' approach between responsible and consulting authorities to provide enhanced support. The mechanics of SEA are thus in fairly good shape, but more can be done to make the process effective, efficient and proportionate, and to ensure full engagement by all relevant parties.[51]

The emphasis on embedding the culture of SEA within authorities is reflected in the most recent guidance that has been issued by the Scottish government to support SEA. The initial guidance took the form of the *SEA Tool Kit*,[52] which was 318 pages long and contained lots of flowcharts, templates and styles to assist those learning how to operate the SEA process. This has now been replaced by the

[46] Some are listed at more than one stage, but the scale of this figure shows the importance of pre-screening, with fewer than 600 instances of formal screening decisions or full SEA taking place between 2004 and 2010; 'The Scottish Strategic Environmental Assessment Review' (n 18) 13.

[47] EASA, s 20.

[48] The full report, a summary and supporting documents are available at www.scotland.gov.uk/Topics/Environment/environmental-assessment/sea/Review.

[49] The conclusions, recommendations and key findings are presented in the 30-page summary, with the full Report running to 170 pages with 11 additional appendices.

[50] Notably the duty to exercise functions 'in the way best calculated to contribute to the delivery of the targets set' in the Act: Climate Change (Scotland) Act 2009, s 44.

[51] Barbara Illsley, Tony Jackson and Neil Deasley, 'Spheres of Public Conversation: Experiences in Strategic Environmental Assessment' (2014) 44 *Environmental Impact Assessment Review* 1.

[52] Available at www.scotland.gov.uk/Publications/2006/09/13104943/0.

Strategic Environmental Assessment Guidance,[53] which is only a sixth of the length and 'spends more time on mindset than prescription'.[54] It is aimed at practitioners and emphasises the benefits of SEA and of close collaboration from the earliest stages between plan-makers, consultation authorities and stakeholders. There are still templates for screening and assessing the effects of a plan, but more attention is paid to how to get the best from the process rather than describing how to do it. In keeping with the wider mood of 'better regulation', there is also considerable emphasis on achieving proportionality in the process, one aspect of which is understanding where a plan lies within a hierarchy so that only the issues relevant at that level are addressed. A useful one-page list of 'Do's and Don'ts' appears near the end of the document.[55] The change in the nature of the guidance shows that SEA is now firmly established, but with the potential to make more of the opportunities it offers.

One further point to mention about the Scottish experience is the insistence on a separation between environmental assessment and wider forms of sustainability review. The EASA preserves an examination of the environmental consequences of plans, policies and strategies as a distinct process,[56] as opposed to submerging this in a broader sustainability appraisal.[57] This approach is reflected in other legislation where the two concepts are also kept apart, such as in the Transport (Scotland) Act 2005, which expressly requires regional transport strategies to show how transport will be operated 'to be consistent with the principle of sustainable development and to conserve and enhance the environment'.[58] Within the Scottish Parliament, the distinction has also been emphasised rather than allowing the wider concept of sustainability to subsume all the elements that contribute to its holistic view.[59] The benefits of the narrower focus of environmental assessment are not to be sacrificed in the attempt to have the one process consider all aspects of sustainability.

[53] Published in August 2013 and available at www.scotland.gov.uk/Publications/2013/08/3355.

[54] Frances McChlery, 'Strategic Environmental Assessment Guidance' (2013) 160 *Scottish Planning and Environmental Law* 130, 131.

[55] *Strategic Environmental Assessment Guidance* (n 53) 48.

[56] Although the position is slightly muddied by the requirement when determining the likely significance for the environment of a plan to have regard to 'the relevance of the plan or programme for the integration of environmental considerations in particular with a view to promoting sustainable development': EASA, sch 2, para 1.

[57] Sustainability appraisals are used in England and Wales under, eg, Planning and Compulsory Purchase Act 2004, ss 5, 19, 23; Planning Act 2008, ss 5–6; and Marine and Coastal Access Act 2009, sch 5, para 7. See further Jack Connah and Stephanie Knowles in Ch 7 of this volume.

[58] Transport (Scotland) Act 2005, s 5(2). See also Water Environment and Water Services (Scotland) Act 2003, s 2(4), (5).

[59] eg, during committee sessions concerning the drafting of the Nature Conservation (Scotland) Act 2004, the Minister stressed that the conservation measures were only part of the sustainable development strategy and should keep their distinct focus: Ross Finnie (Minister for Environment and Rural Development), Scottish Parliament, Official Report, Environment and Rural Development Committee, col 529 (26 November 2003).

SEA and the Scottish Courts

Several Scottish cases have considered the EASA and the SEA Directive, but it is only in *Walton* that detailed consideration of the SEA Directive, its terms and some of the CJEU's case law has taken place. The decisions of both the Inner House and the Supreme Court in *Walton* are of interest, specifically for what they say about the scope of the SEA Directive and more generally for what they say about judicial review procedure in Scotland.[60]

The background to *Walton* was the need to improve the road system around Aberdeen. For some time, the volume of traffic and congestion around Aberdeen had been the subject of various proposals for an improved road system. In 2001, the Scottish ministers and a number of regional authorities established a non-statutory partnership ('NESTRANS') to develop a regional transport strategy for northeast Scotland. In early 2003, the partnership had considered the possibilities and their preferred scheme was for a western peripheral route (WPR)—a road—around Aberdeen. In March 2003, the ministers announced that they would promote the WPR as a trunk road. This meant that the ministers became the roads authority for the purposes of the Roads (Scotland) Act 1984 (hereinafter 'the 1984 Act').

The proposal for the WPR generated a considerable amount of opposition, most of it focusing on part of the road's proposed path. This prompted the ministers to review part of the road's path, which eventually led to public consultation on five alternative options. Meanwhile, the ministers became interested in a sixth 'hybrid' option, one attraction of which was that it anticipated future increases in traffic on the road between Stonehaven and Aberdeen. In December 2005, the ministers announced that the WPR would now follow the route of the hybrid option, which thereafter became known as 'the fastlink'. As things had turned out, the fastlink as such had never been the subject of the public consultation, combining as it did almost all of one option with part of another of the options that had been consulted on.

In December 2006, the ministers published draft special road schemes under section 7 of the 1984 Act, draft trunk road orders under (inter alia) section 5 of the 1984 Act together with an Environmental Impact Assessment (EIA) prepared under section 20A of the 1984 Act. In around October 2007, the original EIA was withdrawn and replaced by a new EIA. By this time, however, some 10,000

[60] For further discussion, see Colin Reid, 'The End of the Road for *Walton*' 2013 *Juridical Review* 53; Robert McCracken and Denis Edwards, 'Standing and Discretion in Environmental Challenges: *Walton*, a Curate's Egg' (2014) *Journal of Planning and Environmental Law* 304. See further Gregory Jones and David Graham in Ch 11 of this volume for an examination of how the SEA Directive has applied to non-town and country plans or programmes. They identify that a weakness in the SEA Directive is that 'even where a systematic assessment of alternatives to a particular transport scheme is carried out, the objectives may be so narrowly defined that optimal solutions are not examined'.

objections to the WPR and fastlink scheme had been received, among them one from 'Road Sense', an organisation chaired by Mr Walton.

In October 2007, the ministers announced that a public local inquiry would be held into the WPR and fastlink scheme under section 139 of the 1984 Act. Road Sense was represented at the inquiry by counsel. The inquiry had been given a limited remit by the ministers, essentially foreclosing any questioning of the need for the WPR and the fastlink, and focusing only on 'the technical and environmental issues' associated with them. The reporters duly reported and, at the end of December 2009, the ministers announced their decision to proceed with the WPR and fastlink scheme, having considered all the objections, including those of Road Sense, and, as they were obliged by section 20A(5A) of the 1984 Act to do, all representations about the project and the EIA.

In March 2010, the Scottish Parliament approved the necessary orders to allow the road scheme. This prompted an appeal by the appellant against the scheme under paragraphs 2–4 of Schedule 2 to the 1984 Act. These provide:

> 2 If any person aggrieved by the scheme or order desires to question the validity thereof, or of any provision contained therein, on the grounds that it is not within the powers of this Act or that any requirement of this Act or of any regulations made thereunder has not been complied with in relation to the scheme or order, he may, within six weeks of—
>
> (a) the date on which the notice required by paragraph 1 above is first published … make an application as regards that validity to the Court of Session.
>
> 3 On any such application the Court—
>
> (a) may by interim order suspend the operation of the scheme or order or of any provision contained in it, either generally or in so far as it affects any property of the applicant, until the final determination of the proceedings; and
>
> (b) if satisfied that the scheme or order or any provision contained in it is not within the powers of this Act or that the interests of the applicant have been substantially prejudiced by failure to comply with any such requirement as aforesaid, may quash the scheme or order or any provision contained in it, either generally or in so far as it affects the property of the applicant.
>
> 4 Subject to paragraph 3 above, a scheme or order to which this Schedule applies shall not, either before or after it has been made or confirmed, be questioned in any legal proceedings whatever, and shall become operative on the date on which the notice required by paragraph 1 above is first published or on such later date, if any, as may be specified in the scheme or order.

The Lord Ordinary dismissed the appeal and the appellant appealed to the Inner House.[61] Before the Inner House, the appellant continued to maintain that there

[61] [2011] CSOH 131 and [2012] CSIH 19. By this time, Road Sense had already unsuccessfully complained to the Aarhus Compliance Committee about a breach of the UNECE Convention on Access to Information, Public Participation in Decision-Making and Access to Justice in Environmental Matters (Aarhus, 28 June 1998) 2161 UNTS 447; 38 ILM 517 (1999), in force 30 October 2001 (hereinafter 'the Aarhus Convention'): see *Walton* (n 1) [100]–[101] (Lord Carnwath).

had been breaches of the EIA Directive,[62] the Habitats Directive[63] and common law procedural fairness. In addition, he argued that the requirements of the SEA Directive had been breached because there had not been an SEA of the fastlink hybrid option.

The Inner House dismissed the appeal. In addition, the Inner House concluded that Mr Walton was not a 'person aggrieved' for the purposes of paragraph 2 of Schedule 2 to the 1984 Act, but that, even if he were and he could have shown that his challenges relying on EU law were well founded, he was not 'substantially prejudiced' by any breach of EU law so as to be entitled to a remedy under paragraph 3(b) of Schedule 2 to the 1984 Act. Accordingly, if a breach of EU law could have been established, the Court would have refused to quash the scheme. The reasoning of the Inner House was essentially based on a concern that if Mr Walton could be a person aggrieved and 'substantially prejudiced', then too much uncertainty would enter into planning decision-making if technical breaches of EU rules meant that schemes and orders had to be quashed at the instance of such a challenger.

Mr Walton appealed to the Supreme Court. By this time, he had abandoned his challenges relying on the EIA and Habitats Directives. His claim now focused mainly on whether the ministers' failure to perform an SEA on the fastlink was unlawful and whether there had been a breach of common law procedural fairness. *Walton* therefore presented the Supreme Court with an opportunity to consider the thresholds for the SEA Directive to apply and whether the ministers had unlawfully approved the fastlink by having failed to perform any strategic environmental assessment.

Walton and the SEA Directive

In essence, the main question for the Supreme Court was whether the changes to the WPR project between its initial stages and the form in which it was finally approved required an SEA. The central issue was therefore whether the fastlink was a modification of a 'plan and programme' for the purposes of the SEA Directive, thus requiring an SEA under Article 2(a) of the Directive.

The focus on the fastlink element rather than the transport proposals as a whole is largely explained by its timing. The initial strategy for the WPR was adopted before the SEA Directive took effect, but the changes to the strategy entailed by the fastlink occurred after the date of the SEA Directive's implementation.[64] However,

[62] Codified in European Parliament and Council Directive 2011/92/EU on the assessment of the effects of certain public and private projects on the environment [2012] OJ L28/1, and recently amended by European Parliament and Council Directive 2014/52/EU [2014] OJ L124/1.

[63] Council Directive 92/43/EEC on the conservation of natural habitats and of wild fauna and flora [1992] OJ 206/7.

[64] *Walton* (n 1) [57] (Lord Reed) and [148] (Lord Hope).

the focus on the fastlink is also the result of a further difficult issue, and one of current topical interest in light of the Supreme Court's decision in *HS2*,[65] namely whether the non-statutory nature of NESTRANS and its strategy for the WPR fell to be treated as a 'plan and programme' within the scope of the Directive.

The SEA Directive defines relevant 'plans and programmes' as essentially those 'which are required by legislative, regulatory or administrative provisions' and which 'set the framework for future development consent'.[66] In *Walton*, the Supreme Court left the issues concerning the origins and non-statutory nature of the proposals unresolved. Lord Reed appears to have been more disposed to accept that NESTRANS and its strategy fell under the SEA Directive, on the basis that they 'set the framework for future development consent of projects'.[67] However, Lord Carnwath was more sceptical:

> I should register my serious doubts on the point, even accepting the flexible approach required by the European authorities. I note … from *Inter-Environnement Bruxelles* … [that it] refers to regulation of plans and programmes by provisions 'which determine the competent authorities for adopting them and the procedure for preparing them …' There may be some uncertainty as to what in the definition is meant by 'administrative', as opposed to 'legislative or regulatory', provisions. However, it seems that some level of formality is needed: the administrative provisions must be such as to identify both the competent authorities and the procedure for preparation and adoption. Given the relatively informal character of the NESTRANS exercise, it is not clear to me what 'administrative provisions' could be relied on as fulfilling that criterion.[68]

In the light of the Supreme Court's subsequent decision in *HS2*, it is unlikely that if the point had required to be determined in *Walton*, the original proposals for the WPR would have been a plan or programme under the SEA Directive.

Having accepted for the purposes of *Walton* that the strategy for the WPR could be a plan or programme, the question then was whether the fastlink was a 'modification' to a 'plan or programme'. The Supreme Court avoided that question by concluding that the fastlink was instead a 'project', which implemented the WPR. Accordingly, the fastlink was subject to the procedures of the EIA Directive and not the SEA Directive. The change of route and other adjustments to the proposal for the WPR were properly seen as alterations to an individual project rather than as modifications to the framework within which future development would take place; there was not a modification to the plan and therefore no need to carry out a further SEA.

[65] *R (HS2 Action Alliance Ltd) v Secretary of State for Transport* [2014] UKSC 3. See further Valerie Fogleman (Ch 3 in this volume).

[66] SEA Directive, arts 2(a) and 3(2)(a).

[67] *Walton* (n 1) [61]–[63], quoting from AG Kokott in Joined Cases C-105/09 and C-110/09 *Terre Wallone ASBL v Région Wallone and Inter-Environnement Wallonie ASBL v Région Wallone* [2010] I-ECR 5611.

[68] *Walton* (n 1) [99]; see also Lord Hope at [149].

It followed that the procedure adopted for the fastlink was not unlawful. This conclusion was seen as consistent with a purposive interpretation of the relevant legislation, observing the distinction between the two forms of assessment but leaving no gaps, since the effects of the revised scheme on the environment were covered by the EIA to which the new road was subject as a project that helped to give effect to the WPR, which was, of course, the underlying transport plan.

The Supreme Court concluded that the environmental impact of the WPR and the amendment to the scheme entailed by the fastlink were properly to be assessed by an EIA. An EIA had been undertaken and there was no longer any complaint about the EIA process. The fastlink was neither a 'plan or programme' nor a modification to a plan or programme under the SEA Directive.

The contribution which *Walton* makes to the law on the SEA Directive is important as a forensic examination of the interaction between the SEA and EIA Directives. The Supreme Court's decision does not deal at any length with the fundamental purposes of the SEA Directive, which are aired more extensively in *HS2*. But *Walton* does lay the judicial groundwork for *HS2* and, in hindsight, there is little by way of surprise in the latter decision in the light of *Walton*.

Walton and Standing in Environmental Law Cases

The issue of standing to bring judicial review petitions in Scotland had for some time been a controversial issue.[69] The law had substantially remained unchanged since the House of Lords' 1915 decision in *D & J Nicol v Trustees of the Harbour of Dundee*.[70] In effect, Lord Dunedin's speech in that case became the model for *locus standi* in Scottish judicial reviews. As the doctrine developed, a petitioner had to show 'title and interest' to sue in order to challenge an act or decision.[71] These were two, cumulative qualifications.

In many cases, the problem for a petitioner was to demonstrate 'interest'. The Court of Session had repeatedly emphasised that this meant a 'real interest to enforce or protect'.[72] There can be little doubt that this approach to standing had a chilling effect on judicial reviews in Scotland, not least in the field of environmental law. In particular, the test made it difficult—almost impossible—for a judicial review to be raised by a representative body in which the *body* itself did not have an interest to 'enforce or protect' other than in a representative capacity.[73] Indeed, judicial review claims that could or should have been raised in the Scottish courts

[69] See Ian Cran, 'Towards Good Administration—The Reform of Standing in Scots Law' 1995 *Juridical Review* 332.

[70] *D & J Nicol v Trustees of the Harbour of Dundee* 1915 SC (HL) 7.

[71] See Lord Clyde and Denis Edwards, *Judicial Review* (London, W Green & Sons, 2000) ch 10.

[72] A formula taken from *Swanson v Mason* 1907 SC 426, 429 (Lord Ardwell).

[73] See, eg, *Scottish Old People's Welfare Council* 1987 SLT 179.

by international non-governmental organisations (NGOs), such as Greenpeace, were not brought there, almost certainly because of the restrictive approach to 'title and interest'.[74]

The Court of Session itself did not show much inclination to change the law and, perhaps surprisingly, the issue did not come before the House of Lords. This was despite reforms to Scottish judicial review procedure in 1985, having been prompted by the comments of Lord Fraser of Tulleybelton in *Brown v Hamilton District Council*[75] that Scotland might usefully consider having something akin to the (then) relatively new Order 53 procedure in England and Wales.[76]

It was not until the Supreme Court's decision in *AXA General Insurance Ltd v Lord Advocate*[77] that a change to the standing rules for Scottish judicial reviews was heralded. In *AXA*, the Supreme Court indicated that it was time to abandon 'title and interest to sue', which 'had too often obstructed the proper administration of justice … and ignored [the court's] constitutional function of maintaining the rule of law'.[78] Both Lord Hope and Lord Reed gave clear indications in their judgments that a test of 'sufficient interest' should be adopted for standing (as in England and Wales).[79]

Nevertheless, some decisions of the Court of Session appeared not to follow the new approach.[80] In *Walton* itself, the Inner House had robustly concluded that Mr Walton lacked standing to bring the appeal because he was not a 'person aggrieved'.[81] This conclusion led the Supreme Court to consider it necessary to say something about standing to bring statutory appeals and judicial reviews in environmental cases. In particular, the observations of the Inner House about Mr Walton's standing under the standard test for judicial review prompted Lord Reed to repeat his and Lord Hope's dicta on the approach for standing in judicial review:

> [T]here may also be cases in which any individual, simply as a citizen, will have sufficient interest to bring a public authority's violation of the law to the attention of the court, without having to demonstrate any greater impact upon himself than upon other members of the public. The rule of law would not be maintained if, because everyone was equally affected by an unlawful act, no-one was able to bring proceedings to challenge it.[82]

[74] See Mark Poustie, 'Sparring at Oil Rigs: Greenpeace, Brent Spar and Challenges to the Legality of Disposing of Oil Rigs at Sea' 1995 *Juridical Review* 542.

[75] *Brown v Hamilton District Council* 1983 SC (HL) 1.

[76] RSC Ord 53.

[77] *AXA General Insurance Ltd v Lord Advocate* [2011] UKSC 46.

[78] *Walton* (n 1) [90] (Lord Reed). There is some evidence that the test of title and interest to sue for locus standi in Scottish judicial reviews discouraged challenges in planning and environmental cases: see www.brodies.com/sites/default/files/pages/planning%20e-update%20report%20february%20 2013.pdf. This research confirms that few cases are brought by individuals and that few planning challenges succeed (about half the rate in England).

[79] Senior Courts Act 1981, s 31(3).

[80] See, eg, *Forbes v Aberdeenshire Council* [2010] CSOH 1.

[81] [2012] CSIH 19 [37]–[38].

[82] ibid [94].

In referring to the importance of vindicating the rule of law, Lord Reed here is echoing a point made in leading English cases where the need to take a broad view of standing has been stated.[83]

In *Walton*, since it was a statutory appeal, the standing test required the litigant to be a 'person aggrieved'. Here too, however, the Supreme Court stressed the need to avoid a restricted view. It was held that it is not only a person whose interests are prejudicially affected who should be regarded as being aggrieved. In particular, a person (such as Mr Walton) who has participated in the procedure leading to a decision should normally be entitled to make a challenge on the basis that the decision has not been properly made. Making objections or representations at the appropriate stage in the procedure is not, however, an absolute requirement. Thus, for example, the alleged procedural flaw may be a misdescription of the project leading to a party not participating, but this will ordinarily be a relevant factor.[84]

Lord Hope made further comments specifically about environmental cases, noting that environmental law proceeds on the basis that 'the quality of the natural environment is of legitimate concern to everyone'.[85] Some cases may involve an impact on private interests, but others will not, such as those involving disturbance to wildlife,[86] yet there should be someone able to invoke the law. Anyone coming to court must demonstrate a genuine interest in the environmental issue, and sufficient knowledge to qualify them to act in the public interest. Normally one would expect either a government agency or an established NGO to take the lead. Yet, there must be room for individuals 'who are sufficiently concerned, and sufficiently well-informed' to raise actions.[87]

The Supreme Court was unanimous in deciding that Mr Walton had standing as a person aggrieved. The opinions of Lord Reed and Lord Hope define the test for 'person aggrieved' in the broadest terms where environmental interests are in issue.[88] Moreover, *Walton* emphasises that a generous approach to standing is to be taken in all judicial review claims raising environmental issues.[89] Now that the Supreme Court's dicta on 'sufficient interest' as the test for standing in Scottish

[83] *Inland Revenue Commissioners v National Federation of Self-Employed and Small Businesses Ltd.* [1982] AC 617, 644 (Lord Diplock); *R v Secretary of State for Foreign and Commonwealth Affairs ex p World Development Movement Ltd* [1995] 1 WLR 386, 395 (Rose LJ).

[84] *Walton* (n 1) [87] (Lord Reed).

[85] ibid [152]; *cf* Case C 176/03 *Commission v Parliament and Council* [2005] ECR I-7879, Opinion of AG Colomer [67].

[86] ibid. The example Lord Hope gives is of development impeding an osprey's access to its fishing loch.

[87] ibid [153].

[88] But *cf Crawford-Brunt v Secretary of State for Communities and Local Government* [2015] EWHC 3580 (Admin), where the claimants who had not taken part in the planning appeal were found not to be 'persons aggrieved'. This decision may not be consistent with the tenor of all of Lord Reed's observations in *Walton*: see *Standing under the 1990 Act Section 288* [2016] JPEL 441.

[89] In the recent Scottish judicial review case *McGinty v Scottish Ministers* [2013] CSIH 78, the new approach of 'sufficient interest' is applied by the Court of Session. However, it appears that the test for interveners in Scottish judicial reviews remains influenced by stricter requirements to show a 'direct interest' in the outcome: see *Sustainable Shetland v Scottish Ministers* [2013] CSIH 116.

judicial reviews has been codified in section 27B of the Court of Session Act 1988,[90] there should be no more room for a more restrictive approach to standing in Scotland compared to elsewhere in the UK.

However, the terms in which the 'person aggrieved' test were explained in *Walton* prompted Lord Carnwath and Lord Hope to say something about the implications for wide standing rules for judicial remedies in environmental law cases. In short, the width of the person aggrieved requirement for standing comes with a judicial discretion to refuse relief to challengers, even in cases where the decision-maker has breached EU law. *Walton* has therefore been used, in particular by Lord Carnwath, to revisit the House of Lords' decision in *Berkeley v Secretary of State for the Environment (No 1)*, which had held that there was no discretion to refuse a remedy in cases of a breach of EU law.[91] Although there have been very few cases in Scotland where a remedy has been refused to an otherwise successful petitioner in a judicial review case, the Scottish courts appear to have embraced the existence of a discretion to refuse a remedy where a petitioner cannot establish that a possible irregularity would not have made any difference.[92] Now, following the Supreme Court's decision in *R (Champion) v North Norfolk District Council*,[93] where relief was refused on the grounds that the claimant had 'in practice' been able to enjoy the benefits of EU rules and had not suffered any 'substantial prejudice' by the breach, it is likely that Scottish courts will adopt the same, or an essentially similar, approach when considering to refuse a remedy to a petitioner.[94]

SEA and Environmental Judicial Reviews in Scotland

The clarification that *Walton* brings to the test for 'person aggrieved' in statutory appeals and, more generally, standing in judicial reviews will make pursuing environmental cases easier in Scotland, at least to the extent of removing one obstacle for petitioners. However, it would be wrong to think that liberalisation of the standing rules makes Scottish public law as accommodating to environmental cases as the law elsewhere.

One difficulty which will continue to be a problem concerns the funding of environmental judicial reviews. In England, the courts have developed the law on protective costs orders so that, in appropriate cases, a litigant is not deterred from pursuing an environmental claim solely because of the risk of being exposed to the

[90] Introduced by the Courts Reform (Scotland) Act 2014, s 89.

[91] *Berkeley v Secretary of State for the Environment (No 1)* [2001] 2 AC 603. For further discussion, see McCracken and Edwards (n 60).

[92] *McGinty* (n 89); *cf Scottish Old Peoples Welfare Council* 1987 SLT 179.

[93] *R (Champion) v North Norfolk District Council* [2015] 1 WLR 3710.

[94] One which, as *Champion* notes, is consistent with EU law: *cf Gemeinde Altrip, Gebrüder Hört GbR and Willi Schneider v Land Rheinland-Pfalz* (C-72/12); and *Commission v Germany* (C-137/14).

other side's costs if the claim fails. More recently, the Civil Procedure Rules (CPR) have been amended, with effect from 1 April 2013, to introduce a new CPR 45.41 so as to give effect to the Aarhus Convention.[95]

In Scotland, the courts eventually followed the English cases on protective expenses orders (PEOs), albeit with a sense of reluctance.[96] In addition, in 2013, the Rules of the Court of Session (broadly, the Court of Session's equivalent of the *White Book* in England and Wales)[97] were amended so as to provide for 'automatic' PEOs in Aarhus cases.[98]

While the new chapter 58A of the Rules expressly includes both judicial reviews and statutory appeals, the substantive scope of the new Scottish PEO rules in Aarhus cases was initially much narrower than CPR 45.41.[99] An 'Aarhus PEO' in Scotland was available only if the case raised an issue under the EIA Directive or the Industrial Emissions Directive, excluding SEA cases. In 2015, though, the scope was extended to 'proceedings which include a challenge to an act or omission on the grounds that it contravenes the law relating to environment'.[100] This means that now the Scottish rules should enable PEOs to be available in cases raising issues under the SEA Directive and should be compatible with the Aarhus Convention and EU law, although this will depend on their application in practice.[101]

Conclusion

The Scottish experience with SEA has presented interesting and, in the UK, unique issues concerning the interaction of domestic law, devolution and EU

[95] Civil Procedure (Amendment) Rules 2013, SI 2013/262, sch 1.

[96] *McGinty v Scottish Ministers* [2010] CSOH 5; see Sarah Pirie, 'Court Makes Protective and Restrictive Costs Order' (2010) 137 *Scottish Planning and Environmental Law* 20. More recent cases present a mixed picture: see *Carroll v Scottish Borders Council* [2014] CSOH 30; 2014 SLT 659 (PEO granted after rather elaborate procedure); and *Gibson v Scottish Ministers* [2016] CSIH 10 (PEO refused by Lord Ordinary, but granted on appeal to the Inner House, which indicated that PEO applications should be dealt with quickly and inexpensively). Environmental NGOs have had mixed success: *RSPB v Scottish Ministers* (P28-31/15, Outer House, 12 May 2015); *John Muir Trust, Petitioner* [2016] CSIH 33. For further discussion, see Tom Mullen, 'Public Interest Litigation in Scotland' (2015) *Juridicial Review* 363.

[97] *The White Book Service: Civil Procedure* (London, Sweet & Maxwell, 2014).

[98] Act of Sederunt (Rules of the Court of Session Amendment) (Protective Expenses Orders in Environmental Appeals and Judicial Reviews) 2013, SSI 2013/81.

[99] On the new English rules in CPR 45.41, see *Venn v Secretary of State for Communities and Local Government* [2013] EWHC 3546 (Admin), discussed by Sarah Skea in 'The Scope of Protective Costs Orders' (2014) 161 *Scottish Planning and Environmental Law* 13. The judge's decision to grant a PCO in *Venn* was overruled by the Court of Appeal: [2014] 1 WLR 2328. But the Court expressed concern that the limitation in CPR 45.41 to judicial review and not statutory appeals was inconsistent with art 9 of the Aarhus Convention. The UK government has proposed to include statutory appeals within the scope of CPR 45.41: *Costs Protection in Environmental Claims* (Ministry of Justice, September 2015).

[100] Rule 58A(1)(c); Act of Sederunt (Rules of the Court of Session 1994 Amendment) (No. 4) (Protective Expenses Orders) 2015, SSI 2015/408.

[101] See n 96 above.

law. Although there have been few Scottish cases on the SEA Directive, one case, namely *Walton*, has analysed the implications of the Directive for 'plans and programmes' at the margins of the definition of those terms.

More generally, SEA has played a significant role in the development of judicial review, with *Walton* confirming a fundamental change to the rules on standing in Scottish judicial review petitions. This is to be welcomed, particularly in environmental cases where representative actions are an important means by which environmental rights and interests can be raised in court.

Looking forward, the changes made by *Walton* to judicial review in Scotland have come at a time when even more fundamental changes to Scottish judicial review procedure are taking effect. In 2014 the Scottish Parliament enacted the Courts Reform (Scotland) Act 2014, which gives effect to the reforms to the Scottish courts proposed by the Gill review.[102] Among the reforms are the introduction of a leave or permission stage before a judicial review petition can proceed and a time limit of three months within which petitions can be brought.[103] Along with the changes made by *AXA* and *Walton* to standing, now codified in section 27B of the Court of Session Act 1988, and in light of the fact that the grounds for judicial review in Scotland are substantially the same as those elsewhere in the UK, it is thus possible to see a convergence of both the substance and procedure of judicial review with the other UK jurisdictions.[104]

The one area of difference continues to concern the scope of judicial review, with Scotland not having a 'public law' system such as that prevailing in England following *O'Reilly v Mackman*.[105] For example, decisions by sports clubs in Scotland can on occasions be challenged through judicial review in a way that is not possible south of the border.[106] However, that difference may be more apparent than real.

In terms of SEA itself, though, Scotland has chosen to go down a different path, expanding on the EU obligations in the SEA Directive to make SEA a standard part of all public planning. Not only does this avoid the difficulty of determining which plans do or do not fall within the categories subject to this process, it also fits better with the concept of sustainable development, which emphasises the need to consider the environmental consequences of everything we do. No

[102] *Report of the Scottish Civil Courts Review* (Scottish Civil Courts Review 2009).

[103] Courts Reform (Scotland) Act 2014, s 89. In *OKM v Secretary of State for the Home Department* [2015] CSOH 177 [6], Lady Wolffe comments that the new rules 'represent a step change in the presentation and conduct of petitions for judicial review'.

[104] Though the test for permission to seek judicial review in Scotland could turn out to be different from that in England: *cf Ochlemhen v Secretary of State for the Home Department* [2016] CSOH 20 [33]–[38].

[105] *O'Reilly v Mackman* [1983] 2 AC 237.

[106] Compare *R v Disciplinary Committee of the Jockey Club (ex p Aga Khan)* [1993] 1 WLR 909 and *Irvine v Royal Burgess Golfing Society of Edinburgh* 2004 SCLR 386.

plans are made without careful consideration of their financial consequences, and the wider reach of SEA may encourage us towards the position where the environmental consequences are similarly taken into account as a matter of course.

Be that as it may, the scope of the SEA Directive in Scotland may be a model for a wider approach to SEA throughout the UK, irrespective of whatever differences between the judicial review systems there continue to be.

15

Any *Seaport* in a Storm: The Northern Ireland SEA Experience

WILLIAM ORBINSON QC

Give me back my broken night
my mirrored room, my secret life
it's lonely here,
there's no one left to torture.[1]

Introduction

Effect was given to the SEA Directive[2] in Northern Ireland by the Environmental Assessment of Plans and Programmes Regulations (Northern Ireland) 2004.[3] Before the Regulations came into effect, nothing approaching SEA was conducted in the jurisdiction, with draft development plans undergoing a distinctly light-weight strategic environmental appraisal (SEA) in accordance with paragraph 41 of Planning Policy Statement 1: General Principles (PPS1).[4] It is safe to say that the introduction of formal SEA posed something of a challenge to the then centralised planning authority for the region, the Department of the Environment for Northern Ireland (DOE).

[1] From the lyrics of Leonard Cohen's 'The Future'.

[2] Directive 200142//EC [2001] OJ L197 on the assessment of the effects of certain plans and programmes on the environment (hereinafter 'the SEA Directive').

[3] SI 2004/1633.

[4] Paragraph 41 of PPS1 simply states that: 'The Department will carry out a strategic environmental appraisal in respect of all its development plans. This appraisal will identify the main environmental concerns of direct relevance to the plan area. It will assess the probable environmental impacts of the plan's policies or proposals. The appraisal process will help to pinpoint those options most likely to be environmentally beneficial. Where consequences adverse to the environment are anticipated possible mitigation measures may be considered. The appraisal will be published with the development plan.'

Be Careful What You Wish for

Having generated the seminal *Seaport/Magherafelt* decision[5] and then launched a series of SEA challenges to draft development plans that had the audacity to propose drawing in development limits at the peak of the greatest property boom the island of Ireland had ever seen, or will see, the planning lawyers of Northern Ireland (led by the author) might reasonably have expected SEA to blossom into a rose garden of fiscal opportunity. That was not to be. The response of the DOE was to down tools on emerging development plans until the boom became recessionary gloom and the enthusiasm for bringing down anti-development plans had withered. As a result, there have been only two SEA challenges since the initial flurry, neither of them against draft development plans. It follows that this chapter will be relatively short on legal analysis and relatively long on context.

Seaport/Magherafelt

Seaport/Magherafelt was the first full-blown challenge to a development plan on SEA grounds in the UK. Keith Lindblom QC and Gregory Jones BL (as they both then were) acted for Seaport, which wished to challenge the publication of the draft Northern Area Plan 2016. The author represented a consortium comprised mainly of developers, but led by Magherafelt District Council, which was keen to challenge the decision to publish the draft Magherafelt Area Plan 2015. Both draft plans hugely drew in development limits throughout the respective plan areas, both of which were prime areas of residential growth during the boom. That in itself might not have been much of a concern for the development industry, but because of prematurity concerns, neither the DOE nor the Planning Appeals Commission was prepared to grant planning permission for housing development on sites proposed to be excluded from the development limits. This was a huge concern for the then burgeoning and bullish development industry, with many hundreds of millions of pounds' worth of investment at stake. So the draft plans could not be allowed to stand.

The Northern Area Plan was accompanied by a document erroneously[6] described as a 'Strategic Environmental Assessment', and almost a year after the publication of the draft Magherafelt plan, the DOE issued a related document bearing the same erroneous title.

Both applicants for judicial review challenged the publication of the plans on broadly two grounds:

— failure properly to transpose the requirements of the SEA Directive in two respects;

[5] *Re Seaport Investments Ltd's and Another's Application for Judicial Review* [2007] NIQB 62.

[6] Erroneous because SEA is a process, not a document.

— non-compliance with the requirements of the Directive and its implementing Regulations.[7]

The First Transposition Issue: Article 6.3

Article 6.3 of the Directive provides that 'Member States shall designate authorities to be consulted which, by reason of their specific environmental responsibilities, are likely to be concerned by the environmental effects of implementing plans and programmes'.

This was transposed by regulation 4 of the implementing Regulations, which provides that:

> (1) Subject to paragraph (2), for the purposes of these Regulations, the Department of the Environment shall be the consultation body.
>
> (2) Where the Department of the Environment is at any time the responsible authority as regards a plan or programme, *it shall not at the same time exercise the functions under these Regulations of the consultation body in relation to the plan or programme*; and the references to the consultation body in the following provisions of these Regulations shall be construed accordingly. (emphasis added)

The problem for the DOE was that, as the then single planning authority for the region, it had sole responsibility for development plan-making. And yet it, and only it, was designated as the consultation body. So, said the applicants, Article 6.3 had not been transposed into the Regulations because there was no designated authority to be consulted on the environmental effects of implementing plans and programmes when those plans and programmes had been drawn up by the DOE. The DOE's response was that in preparing the two draft plans, it had had the input of its Environmental Heritage Service, a division of the DOE with the requisite expertise on environmental matters. Thus, contended the DOE, it was not required to create a new environmental authority for consultation purposes, and the principle of subsidiarity recognised in the SEA Directive permits the state to meet its environmental responsibilities within its existing structures.

Weatherup J identified the difficulties that this state of affairs inevitably posed for the transparent and robust consultation process stipulated by the SEA Directive:

> Recital 15 states that consultation is necessary 'in order to contribute to more transparent decision-making' and also 'with the aim of ensuring that the information supplied for the assessment is comprehensive and reliable'. Consultation with the designated authorities is required under art 5.4 when deciding on the scope and level of detail of the information that must be included in the environmental report. Consultation with the designated authorities is required by art 6.2 so that they might express their opinion on the draft plan or programme and the accompanying environmental report.[8]

[7] The Environmental Assessment of Plans and Programmes Regulations (Northern Ireland) 2004.
[8] *Re Seaport* (n 5) [14].

The applicants contended that the independence of the responsible authority and the consultation body is implicit in the required arrangements. The DOE contended that the arrangements are concerned to gather all appropriate expertise into the preparation of the documents, that the participation of an independent authority is not required and that the rationale of designating bodies with specific environmental responsibilities is to ensure that 'the left hand' of government knows what the 'right hand' of government knows. While the DOE recognised the need for separation, if not independence, between the responsible authority and the consultation authority, it contended that that was achieved in the present cases by the preparation of the draft plans by the DOE's Planning Service in consultation with the Environment and Heritage Service. Weatherup J did not buy that:

> By the terms of the Directive it is apparent, as the Department accepts, that there be separation between the responsible authority and the consultation body. In the present cases I am satisfied that no such separation occurred and that it was not achieved by the Planning Service and the Environmental and Heritage Service being separate divisions of the same Department. For all practical purposes there was integration between the Planning Service and the Environmental and Heritage Service in the preparation of the documents. In any event had there been a formal separation of roles between the Planning Service and the Environmental and Heritage Service I would not have been satisfied that there was sufficient separation for the purposes of the Directive while the two services remain part of the same Department and legal entity. I reject the Department's contention that the primary concern of the consultation process is access to expertise and consider that the purpose of the process relates not only to access to expertise but also to independence. Accordingly I am satisfied that the rationale of designating bodies with specific environmental responsibilities is not to ensure that all parts of Government are fully informed of the information available to all other parts. The necessity for consultation contributes to more transparent decision-making and to comprehensive and reliable information being available and these require not only expertise but independence. I consider it to be necessarily implicit in art 5.4 and art 6.3 that there be consultation with an authority with relevant environmental responsibilities which is external to the responsible body ... Accordingly it may become necessary to create such an authority if it is not already in existence in the domestic structures.[9]

As for the DOE's reliance on the principle of subsidiarity, that too was given short shrift. Weatherup J held that the margin of appreciation accorded to Member States must be consistent with securing the aim of the measure in question and observing the requirements of the Treaty, the aim of the measures in the case before him being directed to achieving an input from a consultation body which has sufficient expertise and which is independent of the body responsible for the preparation of the plan.

[9] ibid, [15] and [16].

The Second Transposition Issue: Article 6.2

Article 6.2 of the SEA Directive provides that:

> The authorities referred to in paragraph 3 and the public referred to in paragraph 4 shall be given *an early and effective opportunity within appropriate timeframes* to express their opinion on the draft plan or programme and the accompanying environmental report before the adoption of the plan or programme or its submission to the legislative procedure. (emphasis added)

This was transposed by regulation 12 of the implementing Regulations, the key feature of which for the purposes of the applicants' case was that it did not fix the timeframes for opinions to be obtained, but rather left them to the discretion of the DOE. That, said the applicants, was a failure in transposition, and the regulation should have fixed the timeframes. In response, the DOE relied on Article 6.5 of the SEA Directive, which provides that the detailed arrangements for consultation are to be determined by the Member States, and on what was suggested to be the broad elastic terminology in Article 6.2 of 'early and effective opportunity' and 'appropriate timeframes', which was said to be supported by Recital 15 and the reference to allowing 'sufficient time' for consultation. Again, the judge rejected the DOE's contentions:

> The nature of art 6.2 is such that it requires consultation with environmental authorities and the public in circumstances where appropriate timeframes are set that admit of sufficient time for consultation including the expression of opinion (recital 15). To achieve sufficient precision and clarity to satisfy the demands of legal certainty requires Member States to set the appropriate timeframes and not to pass to a public authority the responsibility for setting timeframes from case to case. Accordingly the requirement in art 6.2 of the Directive for consultation within appropriate timeframes has not been transposed by reg 12 which does not set appropriate timeframes.[10]

Non-compliant Environmental Reports

Weatherup J then went on to tackle the factually involved question of whether the 'Strategic Environmental Assessment'—more properly, the Environmental Report—for each of the two draft plans was substantially compliant with the SEA Directive. In short, they were not. There were serious shortcomings in the substance of each report when compared to what the Directive said they should include. Moreover, the Non-technical Summary for each report, which in each case was a model of brevity heavily focused on process, was inadequate.

Sequencing

Both applicants argued that in their case, there was a temporal disjunct between the publication of the Environmental Report and the related draft plan. In the

[10] ibid [23].

Northern area, a draft plan and an 'environmental appraisal' prepared in accordance with paragraph 41 of PPS1 were published in 2004, and the draft plan was described by the DOE as 'having reached an advanced stage' when the Regulations were introduced in July 2004. The supposed 'consultation body', the DOE's Environment and Heritage Service, had been involved in environmental appraisal in the emerging plan from an early stage in the process, and the DOE argued that the Environmental Report for the draft plan had built on that earlier environmental work. Weatherup J found that this was not in accordance with Articles 4 and 6 of the Directive: 'It is apparent that when the development of the draft plan had reached an advanced stage before the environmental report had been commenced there was no opportunity for the latter to inform the development of the former.'[11]

As for the Magherafelt area, the situation was even more stark, in that the Environmental Report issued for consultation after the draft plan was issued for consultation, so that there could be no parallel consultation on the draft plan and report, and the consultation on the report could not influence the draft plan. Weatherup J found that this was not in accordance with Articles 4 and 6 of the SEA Directive.

Remedies

So, on foot of this debacle was the publication of the draft plans quashed, as one might expect?

No. Just before the court decided on remedies, the DOE issued in each case a determination pursuant to Article 13(3) of the SEA Directive and regulation 6 of the implementing Regulations that it was not feasible to carry out SEA. The distinctly circular rationale for the determinations would have made Sir Humphrey Appleby very proud: in the light of the judge's ruling, it was not possible to secure full compliance with the Directive without starting the plan processes afresh. Given the determinations, Weatherup J simply issued declarations of the DOE's diverse errors and declined to quash. So the DOE's condemnation served as its salvation. Seaport later launched a judicial review of the Northern area determination; the Magherafelt consortium did not challenge the Magherafelt determination. Meanwhile, the DOE took the declarations on the inadequacy of the Environmental Reports and sequencing on the chin, but appealed to the Northern Ireland Court of Appeal on the transposition issues, which in turn referred those issues to the European Court under Article 267 of the Treaty.

Seaport *and the European Court of Justice Case C-474/10*

At the European Court of Justice, Advocate General Bot opined strongly that the purposes of the SEA Directive required the consultation body to be both separate

[11] ibid [51]. It should be noted that in the later case of *Cogent Land LLP v Rochford District Council* [2013] 1 P & CR 2, Singh J found that there is no absolute requirement for concurrent consultation.

from and independent of the planning authority and that, as a result, a new body wholly distinct from the DOE had to be designated as the consultation body. But in its ruling on Case C-474/10, the European Court was not prepared to go that far. Structural independence of the consultation body was not required and therefore no separate consultation body needed to be established. That said, in the sort of situation then obtaining in Northern Ireland:

> Article 6 does require that, within the authority usually responsible for consultation on environmental matters, a functional separation be organised so that an administrative entity internal to it has real autonomy, meaning, in particular, that it is provided with administrative and human resources of its own and is thus in a position to fulfil the tasks entrusted to authorities to be consulted as provided for in that Directive, and, in particular, to give an objective opinion on the plan or programme envisaged by the authority to which it is attached, which it is for the referring court to verify.[12]

So all that was required was that the consultation body had functional separation from the plan-making body and, as a result, sufficient autonomy to allow it to fulfil the role for the consultation body contemplated by the SEA Directive, including in particular the ability to express an objective view on the plan in question. As Professor Sharon Turner, then of the School of Law at Queen's University Belfast, commented:

> In effect, the Court of Justice proved unwilling to interpret Article 6(3) as imposing anything other than the most general constraints on Member States' discretion to use structural arrangements as a means of limiting the rigour of the consultation process between plan-making bodies and environmental authorities.[13]

Professor Turner also correctly noted that the European Court of Justice chose not to address the role of the consultation process as a guarantor of the effectiveness and credibility of the SEA regime, a factor which had seemed to weigh heavily with Advocate General Bot.

As for the question of whether Article 6(2) required national legislation transposing the SEA Directive to specify 'appropriate time-frames' for the purposes of consultation, both the Advocate General and the ECJ concluded that it did not, subject to the proviso that, as appeared to be the case in *Seaport/Magherafelt*, 'the period actually laid down for each consultation is such as to give them an early and effective opportunity to do so'.[14] Indeed, the Court saw potential advantage in the flexibility offered by leaving the fixing of timeframes to the national authority:

> Nonetheless, laying down the period within which such opinions can be expressed on a case-by-case basis may, in certain circumstances, allow for greater recognition of the

[12] *Re Seaport* (n 5) [42].

[13] Sharon Turner, 'The Strategic Environmental Assessment Directive: A Potential Lever for Independent Environmental Regulation in Northern Ireland?' (2012) 24(2) *Journal of Environmental Law* 357.

[14] *Re Seaport* (n 5) [48].

> complexity of a proposed plan or programme and lead, if appropriate, to the allowance of periods longer than those that might be laid down by law or regulation.[15]

These conclusions of the European Court of Justice meant that the DOE inevitably won before the Northern Ireland Court of Appeal. It is worth noting that, by the time the matter reached the European Court, both Seaport and the Magherafelt consortium had dropped out of the picture, so with the exception of Advocate General Bot, the UK government faced no opposition, and the only party familiar with the facts of the situation to make observations on the issues in play was the government.

Aftermath

So, then, ultimately both draft plans survived the *Seaport* and *Magherafelt* consortium challenges, and went on to public inquiry and adoption. But even by the beginning of the public inquiries, few cared very much about what the draft plans proposed, because with the worldwide property crash, the sky had fallen in on the Northern Ireland development industry. Even at the point of adoption, residential property development in both the Northern and Magherafelt areas remained at an all-time low, so the anti-development thrust of both plans was largely academic. Moreover, with the recent return of development planning to local government, the new 'super-councils' responsible for the two areas will no doubt bring forward their own development plans as a matter of priority, and those plans are almost certain to be more encouraging of development. The same applies in the other areas whose draft plans were challenged on the basis of Weatherup J's judgment, challenges which were ultimately withdrawn once it became clear that that judgment would not stand.

On a macro-level, the ultimate disposal of the case was a great disappointment to the green lobby in Northern Ireland, which saw it as a means of securing a genuinely independent environmental protection agency free of political influence and the perceived pressure not to impede much-needed development. Some, such as Professor Turner,[16] have speculated that the European Court of Justice might just have been influenced by the politically destabilising effect of diminishing the DOE by externalising the consultation role. While the present author doubts that that factor was in the mind of the European Court at all, the subtleties of our local squabbles rarely resonating quite so much with others as with ourselves, he agrees with the Professor that both the London government and the main parties in the Northern Ireland Executive—none of which would have felt any enthusiasm for an independent consultation body being at liberty to obstruct development, particularly in the then recessionary context—will have 'breathed a sigh of relief at the Court's refusal to repeat its normally purposive approach to legal interpretation in this context'.

[15] ibid [49].
[16] ibid.

What of the DOE's Environment and Heritage Service? It has been subsumed into the Northern Ireland Environment Agency, a notably well-staffed and well-resourced agency within the DOE. Notwithstanding continuing pressure from the green lobby, it is unlikely ever to become independent of the DOE. But time heals all wounds and the return of plan-making to local government has, finally, secured the structural independence and externality Weatherup J considered necessarily implicit in Articles 5.4 and 6.3, just as Northern Ireland climbs out of recession. As Angus Kerr of the DOE said at a recent SEA seminar organised by the Belfast Branch of the UK Environmental Law Association, that will be a decidedly 'better fit'.

What remains of *Seaport/Magherafelt*? The authors of future SEA Environmental Reports would do well to remind themselves of the trenchant criticisms levelled by Weatherup J at the two Environmental Reports before him. Those criticisms were never challenged by the DOE and never mulled over by the European Court of Justice, so that part of the judgment remains good and a launch pad for new challenges.

SEA and Regional Planning Policy: Never Knowingly Undersold

The guerilla war over the proposed John Lewis-anchored out-of-centre retail development at Sprucefield regional shopping centre, Lisburn has taken many turns, and key objectors are a consortium of commercial objectors known as the House of Fraser group, represented by the author,[17] and Central Craigavon Ltd. One detour taken by Central Craigavon was down the twisty SEA side road.

Draft Planning Policy Statement 5 on retail development was originally published by the Department for Regional Development in July 2006. This department acted beyond its lawful competence,[18] but once that became clear, draft PPS5 was adopted without change by the DOE. The draft policy explicitly accepted that it was subject to SEA, though in fact no SEA was ever conducted.

The draft policy not only stated that it represented a material planning consideration, but one that would 'prevail' over other material considerations. Draft PPS5 included Policy RRP2, which favoured the 'John Lewis' development at Sprucefield by removing the control on retail development at that location provided by the adopted PPS5 and by allowing any proposal to be judged on its merits. Unsurprisingly in that context, the inclusion of Policy RRP2 prompted a challenge by one

[17] So-called because a lead participant is House of Fraser, the anchor tenant of Victoria Square, which is a major Belfast City Centre retail-led development approved following a development scheme inquiry where the author was led by the then Keith Lindblom QC, now Lindblom J.

[18] As established in *Re Omagh District Council* [2007] NIQB 61.

of the objectors to the lawfulness of the decision to publish the draft PPS: *Central Craigavon Ltd v Department of the Environment for Northern Ireland.*[19]

A ground of challenge was that in the formulation of draft PPS5, the DOE had not complied with SEA requirements. The core issue on that ground was whether the draft PPS was a 'plan or programme' attracting SEA requirements. It will be recalled that the SEA Directive does not define 'plan or programme', which is a concept to be interpreted purposively just as with the rest of the Directive.[20]

At first instance in *Central Craigavon*,[21] the Lord Chief Justice had concluded that the Directive did not apply to the draft PPS essentially because the development plan covering Sprucefield was the Draft Belfast Metropolitan Area Plan, which had undergone environmental assessment, and that consistently with Recital 9 of the SEA Directive, there should not be duplication of assessment by requiring Draft PPS5 to undergo SEA. The Court of Appeal focused on three questions:

> (a) Did draft PPS5 constitute a plan or programme falling within art 2 of the Directive?
> (b) If so, was it a plan falling within art 3(2)(a) that is to say did it set the framework for future development consent of projects listed within Annexes I and II of Directive 85/337/EEC?
>
> Before a plan or programme falls within the definition in art 2 it must be one which is required by legislative, regulatory or administrative provisions. Accordingly, a third question arises as to whether a draft PPS5 was required by any such provisions.

Given the a priori nature of the third question, the Court of Appeal addressed it first. It will be recalled that Article 2 defines 'plans and programmes' in this way:

> [P]lans and programmes, including those co-financed by the European Community, as well as any modifications to them:
>
> — which are subject to preparation and/or adoption by an authority at national, regional or local level or which are prepared by an authority for adoption, through a legislative procedure by Parliament or Government, *and*
> — which are *required by legislative, regulatory or administrative provisions*. (emphasis added)

So, what does 'required' mean in Article 2? Central Craigavon suffered from the Court of Appeal judge giving the lead judgment, Girvan LJ, being an accomplished linguist:

> The word 'required' in English points clearly in the direction of interpreting art 2 as necessitating the existence of an obligatory duty on the part of the authority producing the plan or programme to produce such plan or programme. The French text (exigés)

[19] *Central Craigavon Ltd v Department of the Environment for Northern Ireland* [2012] NI 60. For a fuller discussion of the decision, see G Jones, N Westaway and R Watts, 'Why *Central Craigavon* was Wrongly Decided' [2013] *JPL* 1074.

[20] See the speech of Lord Reed in *Walton v Scottish Ministers* [2013] PTSR 51 at [20]–[21] and Sales J in *R (Cala Homes (South) Ltd) v Secretary of State (No 1)* [2010] EWHC 2866 (Admin) at [57].

[21] *Central Craigavon Ltd v Department of the Environment for Northern Ireland* [2010] NIQB 73.

and the German text (erstellt werden m‚ssen) are in equally strong terms pointing to a relevant provision demanding such a plan or programme. The Italian text is more ambiguous (previsti da dispozioni legislativi etc) since the verb prevedere may mean both prescribed by or provided for by legislative or other provisions. In reading a community text it is necessary to distil from all the language texts the true intent, no one text having priority. The Commission Guidance clearly confirms the sense emerging from the English, French and German texts where it distinguishes between plans which an authority shall prepare and a plan which it may prepare. The former is within art 2 but the latter not. The Commission's advice confirms the clear impression from the wording of the text that there must be an obligation or duty on the authority to produce the plan. This conclusion is clearly established in *Terre Wallonne*[22] in which the Court of Justice concluded that the relevant action programme in question was within art 2 because the Member State was required to implement and monitor it. The Advocate General at para 42 of her opinion considered it was based on a legislative obligation.[23]

According to the Northern Ireland Court of Appeal, then, for a plan or programme to be 'required' for SEA purposes meant that the domestic authority must be under an obligation or duty to produce that plan or programme—it is something that the authority *must* do and not something that it *may* do. The obvious difficulty with that analysis is that very few plans are actually required to be produced in the sense contemplated by the Court of Appeal, most being the children of discretion both in conception and in content. The Court of Appeal's analysis was, of course, reached before the European Court of Justice gave its decision in *Inter Environment Brussels ASBL and Others v Region of Brussels*,[24] where it rejected the suggestion from the Belgian, Czech and UK governments that a 'plan or programme' had to be required by law before it would attract SEA:

28. It must be stated that an interpretation which would result in excluding from the scope of the Directive to 001/42 all plans and programmes … whose adoption is in the various national legal systems regulated by rules of law solely because their adoption is not compulsory and in all circumstances cannot be upheld.

29. The interpretation of Article 2(a) of Directive 2001/42 that is relied upon by the abovementioned governments would have the consequence of restricting considerably the scope of the scrutiny, established by the Directive, of the environmental effects of plans and programmes concerning town and country planning of the Member States.

30. Consequently, such an interpretation of Article 2(a) of Directive 2001/42, by appreciably restricting the Directive's scope, would compromise, in part, the practical effect of the Directive, having regard to its objective, which consists in providing for a high level of protection of the environment (see, to this effect, Case C-295/10 *Valčiukienė and Others* [2011] ECR I-0000, paragraph 42). That interpretation would thus run counter

[22] Joined Cases C-105/09 and C-110/09 *Terre Wallonne ASBL and Inter-Environnement Wallonie ASBL v Région Wallonne* (4 March 2010, unreported), ECJ.

[23] *Re Seaport* (n 5) [36].

[24] Case C-567/10 *Inter Environment Brussels ASBL and Others v Region of Brussels*, decided on 22 March 2012.

to the Directive's aim of establishing a procedure for scrutinising measures likely to have significant effects on the environment, which define the criteria and the detailed rules for the development of land and normally concern a multiplicity of projects whose implementation is subject to compliance with the rules and procedures provided for by those measures.

31. It follows that plans and programmes whose adoption is regulated by National legislative or regulatory provisions which determines the competent authority adopting them and the procedures for preparing them must be regarded as 'required' within the meaning and for the application of Directive 2001/42 and accordingly subject to an assessment on their environmental effectives in the circumstances which it lays down.[25]

It seems, then, that the Court of Appeal's view on the meaning of 'required' is unsustainable.[26] Based on his view of what 'required' meant, the next question for Girvan LJ was whether the DOE was under an obligation or duty to publish draft PPS 5. It was not:

A draft PPS proposing to alter an earlier PPS is not something which the department was obliged to produce. It is a statement of evolving departmental policy thinking. While the DOE is required to formulate and coordinate policy for securing the orderly and consistent development of land and the planning of that development,[27] the ongoing duty to formulate policy did not oblige the Department to introduce draft PPS5 or to produce it in the form which it did. It represents a policy choice and, at this stage, it is a preliminary policy choice which will not be finalised until the consultation process is exhausted.

Lindblom J[28] in *Cala (No 2)*[29] points out:

The power of a minister to issue a statement articulating or confirming a policy commitment on the part of the Government does not derive from statute. As was noted by Cooke J in *Stringer* (at p 1295), Section 1 of the Town and Country Planning Act 1943 imposed on the minister a general duty to secure consistency and continuity in the framing and execution of national policy.

While art 3 of the Planning (Northern Ireland) Order 1991[30] imposes a general duty to formulate and coordinate planning policy it does not oblige the department to formulate a particular PPS or a particular policy within a PPS. Hence art 3 cannot provide the basis for an argument that a draft PPS5 was required by legislative, regulatory or administrative provisions.

[25] See *R (Wakil) v Hammersmith and Fulham London Borough Council* [2013] Env LR 3, where the English High Court held that the SEA Directive applies to a Supplementary Planning Document even though there is no obligation to publish this.

[26] The Supreme Court Blog tactfully commented that the decision was 'hard to reconcile' with *Inter Environment Brussels*, and in the later Northern Irish case of *Re Alternative A5 Alliance* discussed later in the text, Stephens J followed *Inter Environment Brussels*.

[27] Planning (Northern Ireland) Order 1991, art 3, as amended.

[28] Formerly Lindblom QC, who led Gregory Jones in *Seaport*, and the author in the major Victoria Square development scheme inquiry and in various other major development projects in Northern Ireland when he was a Junior.

[29] *Cala (No 2)* [2011] 1 P & CR 451 [50].

[30] Now s 1(1) of the Planning Act (Northern Ireland) 2011.

It can be argued that that analysis conflicts with paragraph 31 of the judgment in *Inter Environment Brussels*: it is enough for a plan or programme to be 'regulated' by national legislative or regulatory provisions, and the duty in Article 3 of the Planning (Northern Ireland) Order 1991[31] surely amounted to regulation. The point certainly applies to development plans, because their making is governed by the process laid down in the successor provision to the 1991 Order, the Planning Act (Northern Ireland) 2011.

The answer to the Court of Appeal's a priori third question being in the negative, arguably the Court of Appeal did not need to go on to address either of the other two questions. Nonetheless:

> We also conclude the draft PPS5 does not in fact constitute a plan or programme providing a framework within art 3(2)(a). The travaux préparatoires of the formulation of the Directive forms part of the relevant matrix for arriving at the intent of the Directive. They indicate that the word policy was specifically omitted from the text. In many situations policy choices will be reached by government in the exercise of governmental power rather than in the exercise of a specific duty, as we have noted in relation to draft PPS5 and such a policy thus does not qualify as a plan or programme within art 2(a). A policy formulated on foot of a statutory duty could in certain circumstances constitute a plan giving rise to a framework depending upon its precise provisions and context. The label attached to the document would not be determinative of that issue for as the Commission Guidance points out 'the name alone (plan, programme, strategy, guidelines etc) will not be a sufficiently reliable guide. Documents having all the characteristics of a plan or programme as defined in the Directive may be found under a variety of names'.[32]

Central Craigavon had accepted that not every draft planning policy statement would be a 'plan or programme', but had contended that draft PPS5 was, because it provided location-specific development control policy setting the framework for future development at Sprucefield that would fall within Annexes I and II to the Directive. This contention was rejected:

> [T]hat argument must fail for the reason that the draft PPS5 contains none of the necessary indicia of a framework governing such development. Draft PPS5 currently has no legal status until Executive Committee approval is obtained and, thus, cannot constitute even a material consideration of any weight in a planning application and for that reason even in [Central Craigavon's] argument it could not constitute a plan with a framework.[33]

To explain in merciful summary the reference to Executive Committee approval being necessary, the arcane constitutional arrangements for Northern Ireland following the Good Friday Agreement require a minister of the local Executive to bring to the Executive Committee for discussion and agreement any matter which is inter alia 'significant or controversial',[34] which some seasoned observers might

[31] ibid.
[32] *Re Seaport* (n 5) [39].
[33] ibid [40].
[34] Section 28 of the Northern Ireland Act 1998, as amended.

think apt to cover pretty much anything in the jurisdiction. At first instance, the Lord Chief Justice had concluded that the publication of the draft PPS was not significant or controversial since the policy had previously been promulgated by another government department and appeared to have raised no interest or contention at the Executive level. This conclusion was not challenged in the appeal. Of course, the traditional position elsewhere in the UK is that a draft policy can be a material consideration to which the decision-maker can give weight and, indeed, the Northern Irish Planning Policy Statement 1[35]—which pre-dated the Good Friday Agreement—took that line.

Appreciating perhaps the importance of its decision for the UK as a whole, the Court of Appeal went on to address the wider question of whether, had it been approved by the Executive Committee, the publication of draft PPS5 would have constituted a 'plan or programme' within Article 2(2), thus necessitating SEA. The Court adopted what Lindblom J said in *Cala (No 2)*, namely:

> Advice given by or on behalf of the Secretary of State that an intention or policy of the Government is a material consideration in a planning decision is not a 'plan or programme' or a 'modification' of a plan or programme; it is merely advice. The same may be said of the policy itself, whether it came into existence when announced in the coalition agreement or only in the statement and letter of 10 November 2010. Neither the policy nor the advice takes the form of a 'plan or programme'. Whether or not the statement and letter are to be regarded as national planning policy, they clearly do express 'freely taken political decisions on legislative proposals'. Furthermore they were not 'required' by any legislative regulatory or administrative provision.[36]

On that basis, the Court of Appeal concluded as follows:

> RRP2 does not lay down anything that would fall within what we would normally understand to be a framework or cadre, Rahmen or quadro in the French, German or Italian texts, these latter words indicating a frame. What it does do is to indicate that the material planning considerations to be taken account of were the contribution of the application to Sprucefield's Regional Development, consideration of the development's impact on Belfast City Centre and other retail centres and the provisions of policy RRP1 and 'detailed policy in a prevailing development plan'. It goes on in para 88 in the last sentence to state that 'the Belfast Metropolitan Area Plan presently in draft form sets out detailed policy for the Sprucefield Regional Shopping Centre'. The draft BMAP, albeit a draft and evolving plan (and now subject to criticism by the PAC), represents an existing material consideration. Pointing to existing material considerations cannot be said to lay down a framework for development. The planning decision-maker must give such weight (and perhaps none) to those considerations as he considers appropriate in the circumstances. Although [Central Craigavon] sought to argue that RRP2 constituted a clear shift in policy for Sprucefield by no longer subjecting it to the word 'control', such

[35] Since cancelled and replaced by the Strategic Planning Policy Statement for Northern Ireland of September 2015.

[36] *Cala (No 2)* (n 29) [99].

> shift as it created in policy was modest. In any event that shift emanated from the draft BMAP which had been subjected to an SEA. In reality PPS5 was a policy statement that the framework set out in the draft plan was the appropriate consideration. Draft PPS5 cannot be considered to be a plan within art 2.

It was thought by some in Northern Irish legal circles that this analysis did not sit terribly comfortably with *Terre Wallonne*,[37] where both the Advocate General and the European Court of Justice were perceived as having taken the view that it was enough that a plan or programme merely influence the granting of consents, not predetermine their granting. Surely even a 'modest' shift in policy in favour of the 'John Lewis' development at Sprucefield would be enough positively to influence the grant of planning permission? However, as Lord Carnwath pointed out in the *HS2* case,[38] the Advocate General in *Terre Wallonne* spoke of influence by way of contrast with the submissions before her, which suggested the need for the plan to be determinative, and the word 'influence' does not appear in the judgment of the European Court. So, held Lord Carnwath, 'setting a framework implies more than mere influence'.

In any event, Central Craigavon's appeal was dismissed. It then appealed to the Supreme Court, at which point Friends of the Earth successfully applied to intervene on the basis of the wider implications of the case, but the appeal was withdrawn by consent on the basis of undertakings by the DOE that it would not progress draft PPS5 and would give it no weight in decision-making. The DOE is now promoting new retail policy through the Strategic Planning Policy Statement for Northern Ireland, published in September 2015 (hereinafter 'the SPPS'). Ironically, the draft SPPS was accompanied by what purported to be an SEA Environmental Report, though whether this was done through an over-abundance of caution or—notwithstanding the *Central Craigavon* decision by the Court of Appeal—as a matter of perceived legal obligation remains opaque. Meanwhile, a series of notable developments have taken place. First, the Sprucefield application was withdrawn, pending 'clarification' of retail planning policy. Second, the Belfast Metropolitan Area Plan (BMAP), including policy constraining non-bulky retail development at Sprucefield, was adopted by the then Environment Minister Mark Durkan of the Social Democratic and Labour Party—a party with a strong commitment to protecting Belfast City Centre from threats from out-of-centre retailers—without Executive discussion and agreement. Third, the then Minister of Enterprise Trade and Investment, Arlene Foster[39] of the Democratic Unionist

[37] *Terre Wallonne* (n 22). Compare also *R (on the Application of Buckinghamshire County Council) v Secretary of State for Transport* [2013] EWHC 481 (Admin), where Ouseley J took a liberal approach to what a framework was; and *Re Alternative A5 Alliance*, considered below, where Stephens J thought it was enough that a plan or programme 'prospectively influence' the granting of consent, though he also went on to say that it had to 'define criteria and the detailed rules for the development of land', which seems a bit strong.

[38] *R (on the Application of HS2 Action Alliance Ltd) v Secretary of State for Transport and Another* [2014] UKSC 3 [41].

[39] Now Northern Ireland's First Minister and leader of the Democratic Unionist Party.

Party—which is known to favour the 'John Lewis' development at Sprucefield—challenged BMAP's adoption essentially because of that unilateral adoption. Fourth, in ruling on that challenge, Treacy J concluded that the Environment Minister had acted ultra vires in unilaterally adopting BMAP, but postponed the question of relief, presumably to see if the issue could be resolved at a political level.[40] Fifth, the judgment prompted the 'John Lewis' project developers to start formulating a fresh application for Sprucefield. Sixth, following the May 2016 elections, Mark Durkan was replaced as Minister with responsibility for the environment by Chris Hazzard[41] of Sinn Féin, a party which so far has had a notably 'light touch' engagement with the Sprucefield controversy, but which governs Northern Ireland in partnership with the pro-Sprucefield Democratic Unionist Party. So, BMAP's future—and the future of policy for retail development at Sprucefield—is likely to prove very interesting indeed.

A Road to Nowhere

Re Alternative A5 Alliance[42] underlines how wide a net is cast by the SEA Directive.[43] The case was a statutory challenge[44] to the decision of the Department for Regional Development for Northern Ireland to progress the £330 million 85 km A5 Western Transport Corridor dual-carriageway scheme. The scheme was regarded as economically important for the western counties of Northern Ireland, but provoked a substantial body of opposition by those adversely affected by it. There were multiple grounds of challenge, including that the project had not undergone SEA. The particular appeal of the SEA ground of challenge to the applicants, as perhaps hinted at by their name, was that the SEA Directive requires reasonable alternatives to be assessed, while the EIA Directive does not.[45] Were they to succeed on that ground, the scheme would obviously have to be put on prolonged hold while potentially better alternatives were explored. The SEA ground was therefore a great prize for the applicants.

The obvious difficulty for them was that, at least at first face, the proposed scheme was an individual project and not a 'plan or programme'. But, said the

[40] *The Minister of Enterprise Trade and Investment's Application* [2016] NIQB 26.

[41] Mr Hazzard is Minister for Infrastructure, and his department—the Department for Infrastructure—has been given the strategic planning functions previously residing in the DOE.

[42] *Re Alternative A5 Alliance* [2013] NIQB 30.

[43] See Robert McCracken and Ned Westaway at Ch 1 of this volume.

[44] Under art 67BA of the Roads (Northern Ireland) Order 1993, as amended.

[45] Compare the somewhat surprising suggestions to the contrary in the recent EU Commission guidance document 'Guidance on the Application of the Environmental Impact Assessment Procedure for Large-scale Transboundary Projects', http://ec.europa.eu/environment/eia/pdf/Transboundry%20EIA%20Guide.pdf.

applicants, things were a lot more subtle than that. The decision at the fifth plenary meeting of the North South Ministerial Council was to construct a dual carriageway, the Republic's government announced its intention to contribute £400 million towards the construction costs, and the Northern Ireland Executive confirmed its acceptance in principle to taking forward the provision of a dual carriageway as the improvement to the A5. This acceptance in principle was, contended the applicants, then incorporated into subsequent plans or programmes of the Northern Ireland Executive, none of which had undergone SEA, thereby setting the framework for future development consent of the scheme. It followed that SEA was required, but had not been done. In response, the DOE contended that none of the various documents relied on by the applicants could be said to be 'plans or programmes', so did not require SEA, that any challenge indirectly to the publication of those documents was massively out of time and that the High Court had a discretion not to quash the decisions to publish those documents given the lapse of time.

Stephens J reviewed the authorities and in particular the decision of the Court of Appeal in *Central Craigavon* and the later decision of the European Court of Justice in *Inter Environment Brussels*,[46] which, as we have seen, moved things on somewhat on the question of what 'required' meant. In the light of *Inter Environment Brussels*, Stephens J examined the terms of the Northern Ireland Act 1998, as amended, concluding that the Act obligated ministers to collaborate in the preparation of a Programme for Government and that, by extension, all of the documents relied on by the applicants were required by legislative, regulatory or administrative provisions. This took him to the question of what constituted a 'framework' for SEA purposes. In the light of *Central Craigavon*, *Terre Wallonne* and *Inter Environment Brussels*, Stephens J concluded that:

> A plan or programme which 'might' influence subsequent development consent does not set a framework. To set a framework a plan or programme has to prospectively influence a development consent and has to define criteria and the detailed rules for the development of land. However the degree of detail may be limited by the high strategic level of the plan or programme.[47]

Applying this conclusion to the facts of the case, Stephens J held that the documents relied on by the applicants did indeed set the framework for future development consent by proscribing a dual-carriageway solution and ruling out all other options. SEA was therefore required for those documents, but had not been carried out for any of them. But what of the delay point? Given that the documents dated back to 2008, some two years previously, that they could have been challenged at that time and that many tens of millions of pounds had since been spent

[46] *Inter Environment Brussels* (n 24).

[47] Compare this with what Lord Carnwath said in *HS2* (n 38), discussed above.

progressing the dual-carriageway scheme, Stephens J was not impressed by the applicant's inactivity, characterising it as 'an attempt to evade the ordinary judicial review time limits', which had caused 'substantial prejudice'. Moreover, later plans which had undergone SEA recognised the need to progress the dualling scheme. All this persuaded the judge that the proper course was simply to record his view that the documents relied on by the applicants ought to have undergone SEA but had not, and that even granting a formal declaration to that effect would serve no further purpose. Happily for the applicants, though, Stephens J was prepared to quash the decision to progress the A5 scheme because the minister had irrationally concluded that there was no doubt as to the efficacy of mitigation measures proposed in respect of the River Foyle and River Finn Special Areas of Conservation, and that an appropriate assessment under the Habitats Directive[48] ought to have been, but was not carried out.

The decision of Stephens J is notable for the breadth of view taken on what can constitute a 'plan or programme', but despite being received with surprise in some political circles in Northern Ireland, that breadth of view was not entirely novel, given that in *Walton v Scottish Ministers*,[49] Lord Reed had found it 'arguable' that the 'Delivering a Modern Transport System for North East Scotland' strategy document was a required 'plan or programme' regardless of the fact that it had not been published pursuant to any statutory function but voluntarily.

What now for the A5 scheme? The DOE did not appeal and conducted what then Minister Danny Kennedy called a 'more comprehensive'[50] assessment of the impact on the Special Areas of Conservation, with associated public consultation. In November 2015, the 'Fresh Start' agreement committed the Northern Ireland Executive and the Irish government to commencing the first section of the A5 in 2017, subject to the successful completion of the statutory processes. The scheme is due to go to public inquiry before the Planning Appeals Commission in the autumn of 2016. Interestingly, the Ministerial Announcement confirming the public inquiry mentioned in passing that the DOE had 'become aware' that the Non-technical Summary of the Environmental Statement did not fully reflect the content of the main body of the Environmental Statement, something that rather suggests that the DOE has had its various assessments under the microscope for fear of getting it wrong again.

[48] Council Directive 92/43/EEC of 21 May 1992 on the conservation of natural habitats and of wild fauna and flora.

[49] *Walton v Scottish Ministers* [2012] UKSC 44 [61]–[62]. Lord Carnwath was rather more sceptical on this point, but did not deny its arguability. In any event, the matter did not need to be resolved by the Supreme Court, the appeal failing on other grounds.

[50] *BBC News Northern Ireland*, 15 April 2013.

'Things Are Going to Slide, Slide in All Directions'[51]

Following the withdrawal of all the challenges to draft development plans subsequent to *Seaport/Magherafelt*, the DOE turned its hand to progressing to adoption a number of draft development plans, including both the plans that provoked the *Seaport/Magherafelt* challenge and others that had been put on ice. Northern Ireland is starting to experience growth in the construction and residential sectors, so the focus is likely soon to return to SEA. That must particularly be so in a context in which, after some 40 years of centralisation, development plan making has been restored to local government. And local government must be quaking at the thought of having to get SEA right when the DOE, with all its resources and expertise, contrived to get it so wrong.

Conclusion

Those who look over the Irish Sea to the dreary steeples of Fermanagh and Tyrone will be aware of the implosion of the Planning Bill because of a hugely controversial last-minute amendment promoted jointly by the two largest parties, the Democratic Unionist Party and Sinn Féin. This amendment—vaunted as having been agreed with Downing Street, presumably as a precursor to a similar manoeuvre in Great Britain—proposed restricting planning judicial reviews to European grounds. The objective was to expedite preferred major development projects such as the Sprucefield project much favoured by the Democratic Unionist Party, a number of which had been delayed because of successful judicial reviews. On advice from David Elvin QC that the amendment was a breach of the European Convention on Human Rights, the then Environment Minister Mark Durkan refused to progress the Bill. The irony of all this is that all the challenges to the favoured major development projects have involved European law points, so of course the amendment would not have achieved its purpose had the Bill made it into law. The amendment may be resurrected at some point in the future, though Brexit has probably killed it off once and for all. If it is resurrected, it is highly likely to be found unlawful by the courts, but even if it survives challenge, it cannot protect plan-makers at either the central or local government level from SEA challenges.

So, after a few fairly fallow SEA years, the legal landscape in Northern Ireland looks likely to produce a healthy crop of challenges—the answer to any planning barrister's prayer.

[51] Also from the lyrics of 'The Future', Leonard Cohen.

16

Strategic Environmental Assessment: The Irish Experience

ÁINE RYALL*

Introduction

A legislative framework governing strategic environmental assessment (SEA) has been in place in Ireland since July 2004. Twelve years on, an analysis of experience in practice reveals a gradual but significant evolution in the level of public authority engagement with SEA obligations. This positive development is due mainly to the strong advocacy role played by the Environmental Protection Agency (EPA) in highlighting to public authorities the added value of SEA in delivering integrated decision-making and better environmental outcomes. In many ways, the development of SEA law and practice over the years confirms wider issues with environmental governance in Ireland. These include fragmented legislation, structures and processes; a strong initial reluctance to acknowledge and integrate European Union (EU) and international environmental law obligations into national systems; and (still) limited access to justice to enforce environmental rights and obligations in an affordable and timely manner. It is well known that Ireland struggled over the years to deliver effective implementation and enforcement of EU environmental law.[1] The SEA experience provides an interesting case study of the challenges that must be tackled in order to integrate EU and international obligations successfully into the national system and to strengthen local enforcement mechanisms. This chapter provides a critical appraisal of efforts to implement

* I thank Eloise Scotford and in particular Tadhg O'Mahony, Senior Scientific Officer, SEA Section, Environmental Protection Agency, Ireland for very helpful comments on an earlier draft of this chapter. The views expressed here are mine alone. This chapter was finalised in August 2014; however, at the copyediting stage, I have attempted to include significant updates up to 1 July 2016.

[1] See generally, L Cashman, 'Commission Enforcement of EU Environmental Legislation in Ireland: A 20-Year Retrospective' in S Kingston (ed), *European Perspectives on Environmental Law and Governance* (Abingdon, Routledge, 2012).

the SEA Directive[2] in Ireland. The analysis is set against the challenges involved in implementing and enforcing EU environmental law more generally. The chapter also reflects on the potential of the Aarhus Convention[3] to deliver more effective environmental governance and to strengthen enforcement of environmental law. The first section opens with an account of how Ireland transposed the SEA Directive and the mechanisms available at the national level to enforce SEA obligations. This overview is followed in the next section by an analysis of the jurisprudence where the Irish courts have considered SEA principles in the context of challenges to the legality of plans and programmes. These decisions provide interesting insights into early judicial attitudes to SEA, public participation and access to justice. Drawing on the findings presented in a *Review of Effectiveness of SEA in Ireland*, published by the EPA in 2012,[4] the third section takes stock of SEA implementation. The chapter concludes that SEA is still at a relatively early stage of development in Ireland. While considerable work remains to be done to improve implementation and embed SEA successfully in national practice, based on the experience to date, the outlook for the future is generally positive.

Transposition of the SEA Directive into Irish Law

The National Legislative Framework Governing SEA

Following a comprehensive review of planning legislation initiated by the Department of the Environment, Heritage and Local Government (DEHLG) in 1997, the Planning and Development Act 2000 (PDA) aimed to consolidate Irish planning law and to modernise the planning code. The provisions of the PDA governing the making of Development Plans required the plan to contain 'information on the likely significant effects on the environment of implementing the plan'.[5] A similar requirement was put in place in respect of Local Area Plans and Regional Planning Guidelines.[6] These measures pre-dated the formal adoption of the SEA Directive in June 2001 and were obviously very basic. But they succeeded in generating an initial awareness among decision-makers of the forthcoming EU SEA obligations while the DEHLG prepared for formal transposition of the SEA Directive.

[2] Directive 2001/42/EC on the assessment of the effects of certain plans and programmes on the environment [2001] OJ L197/30 (hereinafter 'the SEA Directive').

[3] UN ECE Convention on Access to Information, Public Participation in Decision-Making and Access to Justice in Environmental Matters (Aarhus, 28 June 1998) 2161 UNTS 447; 38 ILM 517 (1999), in force 30 October 2001 (hereinafter 'the Aarhus Convention').

[4] Environmental Protection Agency, 'Review of Effectiveness of SEA in Ireland: Key Findings and Recommendations' (EPA, 2012) www.epa.ie/monitoringassessment/assessment/sea/#.Uu7fMWyYZdg (hereinafter 'the SEA Review').

[5] PDA, s 10(5)(a) as originally enacted.

[6] ibid, ss 19(4)(a) and 23(3)(a) as originally enacted.

On 14 July 2004, the Minister for the Environment, Heritage and Local Government made two statutory instruments designed to transpose the SEA Directive into Irish law.[7] The European Communities (Environmental Assessment of Certain Plans and Programmes) Regulations 2004[8] and the Planning and Development (Strategic Environmental Assessment) Regulations 2004[9] came into force on 21 July 2004—the formal deadline for transposition.[10] Both sets of regulations followed the general scheme set down in the SEA Directive. The first set of regulations (SI 2004/435) was designed to transpose SEA obligations as regards plans and programmes for the sectors listed in Article 3(2) of the SEA Directive—apart from land use planning. These regulations also provided the statutory basis for transposition of the SEA Directive in respect of land use planning by amending the relevant provisions of the PDA. The detailed provisions governing SEA in the land use planning context are found in the second set of regulations (SI 2004/436). These regulations set out procedures for the assessment of the environmental effects of implementing Development Plans,[11] Local Area Plans, Regional Planning Guidelines and Planning Schemes for Strategic Development Zones.

In May 2011, two further statutory instruments were made with the stated aim of giving 'further effect' to the SEA Directive in Irish law. The European Communities (Environmental Assessment of Certain Plans and Programmes) (Amendment) Regulations 2011 amended SI 2004/435, governing the SEA of sector-related (non-land use) plans.[12] The main changes included an amendment to the definition of 'plans and programmes' to align the wording of the regulations more closely with that of the SEA Directive, and new provisions to improve public participation, including a requirement that certain documents must be made available for inspection on the relevant public authority's website. The Planning and Development (Strategic Environmental Assessment) (Amendment)

[7] Ireland was one of only nine (out of the then 25) Member States to transpose the SEA Directive by the 21 July 2004 deadline. See European Commission, 'Report on the Application and Effectiveness of the Directive on Strategic Environmental Assessment' (Directive 2001/42/EC), COM (2009) 469, 14 September 2009, para 2.

[8] SI 2004/435. These regulations were made in exercise of the powers conferred on the Minister by s 3 of the European Communities Act 1972.

[9] SI 2004/436. These regulations were made in exercise of powers conferred on the Minister by ss 10(5), 13(12), 19(4), 23(3), 168(3) and 262 of the Planning and Development Act 2000.

[10] The DEHLG issued a Circular Letter to regional authorities, planning authorities and *An Bord Pleanála* (the Planning Appeals Board) to accompany the regulations: Circular Letter BC 8/2004, 16 July 2004. In November 2004, the DEHLG published guidelines for regional and planning authorities on the implementation of the SEA Directive, addressing the various stages of the SEA process and explaining how SEA requirements should be integrated into existing plan-making procedures. See DEHLG, 'Implementation of SEA Directive (2001/42/EC): Assessment of the Effects of Certain Plans and Programmes on the Environment—Guidelines for Regional Authorities and Planning Authorities', November 2004, http://environ.ie/en/DevelopmentHousing/PlanningDevelopment/EnvironmentalAssessment/EIASEAGuidance.

[11] The environmental effects of implementing variations to a Development Plan are also subject to assessment.

[12] SI 2011/200.

Regulations 2011 amended SI 2004/436 concerning SEA in the land use planning context.[13] Important changes here included: a reduction in the threshold to trigger mandatory SEA of a Local Area Plan (from a target population of more than 10,000 persons to 5,000 persons, or where the area covered by the plan is greater than 50 square kilometres, or where the plan is being prepared for a town and its environs); a new, explicit screening obligation requiring the public authority to make a determination on the need for SEA for a Local Area Plan with a target population under 5,000 persons or where the area covered by the plan is less than 50 square kilometres; expansion of the Minister for the Environment's role as a designated environmental authority for the purposes of SEA; and new provisions to improve public participation, including a requirement that certain documents must be made available for inspection on the public authority's website.[14] Although introduced almost seven years after the original transposition measures came into force, the amendments made in 2011 were very welcome in that they strengthened a number of fundamental aspects of the legislative framework governing SEA. In June 2013, the Department of Environment, Community and Local Government (DECLG)[15] issued a Circular Letter to remind planning and regional authorities of the requirements of Articles 8 and 9 of the SEA Directive.[16] These articles concern the obligation to take the Environmental Report and the views expressed by the public into account during the preparation of the relevant plan and to publish specified information once the plan has been adopted.

It is worth remarking on the method Ireland adopted to transpose the SEA Directive. As in the UK, it is common practice for the Irish authorities to deploy secondary legislation (statutory instruments) to transpose EU law obligations.[17] This approach is obviously faster—a significant factor when a deadline for transposition is looming or has already expired—and it involves far less external scrutiny than steering primary legislation through the *Oireachtas* (Parliament). Secondary legislation is, however, far from ideal as a means of transposing EU law. The quality of drafting generally tends to be poor and the lack of public scrutiny can lead to a minimalist approach to transposition and missed opportunities to identify potential problems while regulations are still at draft stage. Moreover, it is not uncommon in Ireland for statutory instruments to amend primary legislation. This was the case with one of the measures used to transpose the SEA Directive, where SI 2004/435 made a number of amendments to the PDA. Heavy reliance on secondary legislation as the preferred mode of transposing EU law

[13] SI 2011/201.

[14] A Circular Letter was issued to inform regional and planning authorities of the new regulations: Circular Letter PSSP 6/2011, 26 July 2011.

[15] Following a transfer of functions, with effect from 2 May 2011, the Department's name was changed to the Department of the Environment, Community and Local Government (DECLG).

[16] DECLG, Circular Letter PL 9/2013, 19 June 2013.

[17] On the use of secondary legislation to implement environmental obligations in the UK, see 'The State of UK Environmental Law in 2011–12: Is There a Case for Legislative Reform?', UK Environmental Law Association, King's College London and Cardiff University, May 2012, www.ukela.org/rte.asp?id=143 [3.22].

has led to a highly fragmented legislative framework in the field of planning and environmental law. The result is that extensive cross-referencing between multiple legal instruments is de rigueur and it is difficult, if not impossible at times, for even experienced practitioners to identify the rules currently in force. As things stand, the rules governing SEA in Ireland are found in the PDA (as amended on numerous occasions) and in four sets of statutory instruments. There is currently no unofficial consolidated text of the SEA regulations publicly available for ease of reference. This state of affairs inhibits public awareness of the rules governing SEA and risks undermining both public participation in the SEA process and the public's oversight role in ensuring that national and EU law obligations are met in practice.

Beyond formal transposition measures, whether or not SEA succeeds in informing and supporting the integration of environmental considerations in plans and programmes will depend on how forcefully the law is applied on a day-to-day basis. A range of problems and challenges that have surfaced with implementation of SEA law and policy is examined in the section entitled 'SEA in Practice' below. But the overarching governance structure in which SEA operates is also crucial to its success. Planning authorities and regional assemblies are responsible for SEA in relation to land use planning, while SEA for each of the other sectors listed in Article 3(2) of the SEA Directive is primarily the task of the relevant government department. There are five statutorily designated environmental authorities for SEA in Ireland: the DECLG; the Department of Arts, Heritage and the Gaeltacht; the Department of Agriculture, Food and the Marine; the Department of Communications, Energy and National Resources; and the EPA.[18] The EPA is the public authority with by far the most significant role in the wider implementation of SEA, including review and assessment of SEA notifications from the responsible authorities charged with plan-making. The EPA has proven itself to be a forceful advocate for the added value of SEA in terms of delivering improved environmental outcomes. In addition, it plays the lead role in preparing and developing SEA guidance, providing training for public authorities, raising awareness of SEA across the various sectors, and driving and supporting applied research in this field.

Enforcement of SEA Obligations at the National Level

An Enforcement Role for the EPA?

The EPA is not vested with any enforcement role as regards SEA. As a designated environmental authority for SEA, it responds to statutory SEA notifications,

[18] Note that the names of the government departments mentioned here are due to change shortly following a transfer of functions between various departments in the wake of the 2016 General Election and the formation of a minority government on 6 May 2016. The secondary legislation necessary to bring about these changes is pending at the time of writing.

provides advice on screening and scoping, and comments on Environmental Reports, but it does not have a statutory function or power to actually require a public authority to undertake SEA of a plan or programme in a particular case. However, competent authorities generally do take note of, and act on, EPA screening observations. With a view to underpinning SEA obligations firmly in the national system, assigning a formal statutory oversight and enforcement role to the EPA should be considered. An independent, expert Review Group appointed by the government in February 2010 to examine the legislation governing the EPA, together with its performance, mandate and resources, and to identify any necessary improvements, considered how SEA was operating in practice.[19] The Review Group reported in May 2011 and recommended a wider statutory role for the EPA in relation to SEA in order to strengthen practical implementation in a more uniform manner.[20] Given the significant potential of SEA as a regulatory tool to support the integration of environmental considerations in plan-making at an early stage in the process, it is disappointing to report that, five years on, the Review Group's recommendation has not gained any traction at a political level. Instead, following the publication of an EPA-commissioned review of the effectiveness of SEA in Ireland, a 'National SEA (Environmental Authority) Technical Forum' was established in 2012 to promote compliance with SEA obligations and to support and advance best practice in this field.[21] However, this body has no statutory basis and plays no role in SEA enforcement.

Judicial Review and SEA Enforcement

At present, the primary means of enforcing SEA obligations is by way of judicial review proceedings in the High Court. The legality of a plan or programme may be challenged on the basis of alleged non-compliance with the SEA Directive and/or the national SEA regulations. The SEA Directive itself is silent on enforcement. And, whilst judicial review is the primary means of enforcing SEA obligations in Ireland, it has also been an inaccessible means for doing so for most people, due largely to the expense and time involved in engaging in litigation. In this respect, it is notable that the SEA Directive has not been amended to reflect the access to justice obligations set down in the Aarhus Convention. Article 9 of the Convention essentially demands that the public, including environmental non-governmental organisations (NGOs), must have access to a review procedure to enforce the rights conferred by the Convention and to challenge alleged breaches of environmental law. Any such review procedure must not be 'prohibitively expensive',

[19] The author was a member of the EPA Review Group.

[20] Environmental Protection Agency Review Group, 'A Review of the Environmental Protection Agency', DECLG, May 2011, www.epa.ie/pubs/reports/other/corporate/areviewoftheepa.html#.Uu7fDGyYZdg (hereinafter 'the EPA Review') [3.6].

[21] The findings of the SEA Review (n 4) are considered in the section entitled 'SEA in Practice' below.

must be timely and must provide 'adequate and effective' remedies.[22] The Directive on Public Access to Environmental Information,[23] the Environmental Impact Assessment (EIA) Directive[24] and the Industrial Emissions Directive[25] (formerly the Integrated Pollution Prevention and Control (IPPC) Directive)[26] all contain specific access to justice clauses designed to implement Aarhus obligations. Notwithstanding the absence of an access to justice provision in the text of the SEA Directive, the principle of effective judicial protection developed by the Court of Justice of the European Union (CJEU) provides for a general right of access to the courts to enforce EU law rights.[27] This would obviously embrace the rights arising under the SEA Directive, including, for example, the public's right to specific sets of information, to participate effectively at an early stage in the SEA process and to have its views taken into account prior to the adoption of the plan or programme as per Article 8 of the SEA Directive. Nevertheless, an access to justice clause would be a valuable addition to the text of the SEA Directive. It would require Member States to provide specifically for effective and affordable access to justice to enforce SEA law and would, in turn, enable the national courts to adopt a more robust approach to the enforcement of SEA obligations. We have already seen, for example, how the access to justice clause in the EIA Directive (formerly Article 10a, now Article 11 of the consolidated EIA Directive) has generated a groundbreaking body of case law on standing rules and costs liability, in particular, at both the EU and national levels.[28] At the time of writing, this exciting body of case law continues to evolve.[29]

Environmental litigation in Ireland is expensive, time-consuming and unpredictable. Speaking in 2012 in an extra-judicial capacity, Peart J (at the time a judge of the High Court) observed that the cost of litigation in Ireland is 'a deterrent to any but the rich, the courageous and the foolhardy'.[30] The general position under

[22] Aarhus Convention (n 3) art 9(4).

[23] Parliament and Council Directive 2003/4/EC on public access to environmental information [2003] OJ L41/32.

[24] Parliament and Council Directive 2011/92/EU on the assessment of the effects of certain public and private projects on the environment (codification) [2011] OJ L26/1—formerly Directive 85/337/EEC as amended. Directive 2014/52/EU amending Directive 2011/92/EU on the assessment of the effects of certain public and private projects on the environment [2014] OJ L124/1 introduced a number of significant amendments to the text of the EIA Directive.

[25] Parliament and Council Directive 2010/75/EU on industrial emissions (integrated pollution prevention and control) (Recast) [2010] OJ L334/7.

[26] Council Directive 96/61/EC concerning integrated pollution prevention and control [1996] OJ L257/26.

[27] See generally Á Ryall, *Effective Judicial Protection and the Environmental Impact Assessment Directive in Ireland* (Oxford, Hart Publishing, 2009) 82–91.

[28] On the particularly thorny question of costs and the practical implications of the ban on 'prohibitive' expense see, in particular, Case C-260/11 *R (Edwards) v Environment Agency* (CJEU, 11 April 2013); Case C-530/11 *Commission v UK* (CJEU, 13 February 2014).

[29] See further Á Ryall, 'Aarhus Convention and Access to Justice in Environmental Matters: Some Critical Reflections' (2013) 20 *Irish Planning and Environmental Law Journal* 165.

[30] 'Litigation Costs a Deterrent to Any But the Rich, Says Judge' *Irish Times* (27 February 2012). Peart J currently serves as a member of the Court of Appeal of Ireland.

Irish law is that costs follow the event (in other words, the 'loser pays').[31] However, the courts hold the ultimate discretion to determine who should pay the costs of the proceedings.[32] Directive 2003/35/EC (the 'Public Participation' Directive) inserted specific access to justice clauses into the EIA and IPPC Directives with the aim of giving effect to Article 9(2)–(4) of the Aarhus Convention, including the requirement that review procedures must not be 'prohibitively expensive'.[33] Ireland took the view that its costs rules were already compatible with the new access to justice obligations and that there was no need for legislative intervention to transpose this aspect of the Public Participation Directive. The European Commission disagreed with the Irish authorities' assessment of the situation and infringement proceedings ensued. In July 2009, the CJEU ruled that Ireland had failed to transpose the obligation to ensure that costs in cases involving the EIA Directive and the IPPC Directive were 'not prohibitively expensive'.[34] More specifically, the Court determined that a judicial discretion to depart from the general rule that costs follow the event (that is, the 'loser pays' principle) did not constitute adequate transposition of the obligation that the costs involved in judicial review procedures must not be 'prohibitively expensive.' The CJEU also determined that Ireland had failed to fulfil the obligation to make practical information on access to administrative and judicial review procedures available to the public. Faced with this adverse ruling from Luxembourg, in the summer of 2010, Ireland moved to amend the PDA by introducing a special costs regime for certain categories of environmental litigation. The special costs regime applies to judicial review proceedings involving a challenge to a decision, act or failure to act under any provision of Irish law that gives effect to the EIA Directive, the IPPC Directive or the SEA Directive. It is interesting that the Irish authorities decided to extend the special costs rule to cover challenges involving the SEA Directive. Obviously, EIA and IPPC matters had to be included, given the express access to justice obligations in the Public Participation Directive, but the precise legal basis for deciding to include SEA matters remains unclear. Why were challenges involving SEA included, but not, for example, challenges involving the Habitats Directive[35] or other significant environmental directives? The parliamentary debates provide no hint as to the rationale behind the inclusion of the SEA Directive in the special costs regime.

[31] Rules of the Superior Courts 1986 (SI 1986/15) (as amended), Ord 99, rr 1(3) and (4).

[32] ibid, Ord 99, r 1(1).

[33] Parliament and Council Directive 2003/35/EC providing for public participation in respect of the drawing up of certain plans and programmes relating to the environment and amending with regard to public participation and access to justice Council Directives 85/337/EEC and 96/61/EC [2003] OJ L156/17.

[34] Case C-427/07 *Commission v Ireland* [2009] ECR I-6277.

[35] Council Directive 92/43/EEC on the conservation of natural habitats and of wild flora and fauna [1992] OJ L206/7.

The special costs rule governing challenges involving EIA, IPPC and SEA are found in section 50B of the PDA.[36] Essentially, the special costs regime introduced in 2010 established a general rule that each of the parties to the proceedings is to bear its own costs, subject to certain limited exceptions. The result is that the usual 'loser pays' principle does not apply in this particular category of proceedings. The special costs rule was subsequently amended and refined, pursuant to section 21 of the Environment (Miscellaneous Provisions) Act 2011 (hereinafter 'the 2011 Act'), to address the apparent injustice done to a successful party under the original section 50B, whereby the court was required to make no order for costs in its favour. The impact of the 2011 amendments is that the court now has discretion to award costs (or a portion of costs, as appropriate) to reflect the extent to which the applicant was successful in the proceedings.[37] The 2011 Act also extended the special costs regime beyond judicial review proceedings involving EIA, IPPC and SEA. Specifically, Part 2 of the 2011 Act extended the special costs rule to certain categories of civil proceedings aimed at the enforcement of planning and environmental law.[38] The special costs rule established in section 3 of the 2011 Act follows the template set down in section 50B of the PDA (as amended).

There is no doubt that, in the limited situations where it applies, the special costs rule has removed a significant deterrent to those contemplating environmental litigation. Previously, fear of liability for an opponent's (often substantial) costs had an undoubtedly 'chilling' effect on litigation. At the time of writing, the scope of the special costs regime, and its impact on access to environmental justice, still remains to be teased out fully by the Irish courts. Notwithstanding the special costs rule (which addresses liability for the other side's costs), a potential litigant will usually require expert legal advice of his/her own in order to mount a compelling case. The high price of legal services in Ireland, taken in conjunction with the very limited availability of civil legal aid, means that the cost of engaging legal advice may well be 'prohibitive' in cases where an individual or NGO has limited resources. This is an issue that the Irish courts will likely be called upon to consider in the future given that the Aarhus Convention and EU law provide for a right of access to a review procedure that is not 'prohibitively expensive'.[39] The next section of this chapter considers the limited number of cases involving SEA matters that have come before the Irish courts to date.

[36] Section 50B was inserted into the PDA pursuant to s 33 of the Planning and Development (Amendment) Act 2010.

[37] See, eg, *Tesco Ireland Ltd v Cork County Council* [2013] IEHC 580.

[38] Environment (Miscellaneous Provisions) Act 2011, ss 3 and 4.

[39] *Browne v Fingal County Council* [2013] IEHC 630 and *Coffey et al v EPA* [2013] IESC 31 demonstrate that litigants in Ireland are determined to test the scope of the obligation to deliver access to justice that is not 'prohibitively expensive' and, in particular, the extent to which this obligation requires the state to provide a measure of financial support towards the costs of a litigant's own legal representation. See also the analysis in *Commission v UK* (n 28) Opinion of AG Kokott (12 September 2013) [66]–[80].

The SEA Directive in the Irish Courts

Deficiencies in the SEA Directive, including the restrictive definition of 'plans and programmes' and the general manner in which many obligations are articulated[40] compromise its effectiveness as a regulatory tool. Beyond the Directive's weaknesses, the practical reality is that the public is far more inclined to engage in decision-making processes at a project level. Higher-level plan-making lacks the sense of urgency that usually arises when specific, identifiable (and potentially unwelcome) projects are on the horizon. Moreover, there is still limited awareness of SEA among the Irish public. The EIA Directive and the Habitats Directive are invoked regularly in environmental litigation. When compared with the SEA Directive, these directives have a sharper edge in terms of their impact and enforceability. Along with the access to justice concerns discussed earlier, it is not particularly surprising, therefore, to find that SEA-related matters have only been considered in three High Court decisions to date. Two of these decisions turned on the definition of 'plans and programmes', while the third concerned the SEA decision-making process, specifically the duty to give reasons for adopting a plan in a particular form. A fourth case, involving a high-profile challenge to Ireland's National Renewable Energy Action Plan (NREAP), is currently before the High Court.[41] This Irish SEA jurisprudence is considered in the following sections.

'Plans and Programmes' Subject to Assessment under the SEA Directive

The Irish courts have adopted a restrictive interpretation of the SEA Directive's scope to date, through their construction of what constitutes a 'plan or programme'. *Kavanagh v Ireland* involved a challenge to the legality of a series of decisions relating to the development of a major prison complex on a rural site at Thornton Hall in North County Dublin.[42] The specific decisions challenged were: (1) the decision to close Mountjoy Prison and build a new prison at Thornton Hall; (2) the decision to close and sell the existing Central Mental Hospital (CMH) at Dundrum and build a new CMH at Thornton Hall; (3) a combination of both

[40] See the contributions by Valerie Fogleman (Ch 3), Stephen Ashworth (Ch 5), and Simon Ricketts and Juliet Munn (Ch 4) in this volume.

[41] *Swords v Minister for Communications, Energy and Natural Resources, Ireland and the Attorney General* Record No 2013/4122P.

[42] *Kavanagh v Ireland* [2007] IEHC 296. The Thornton Hall site comprised 150 acres of land zoned for agricultural use. There was intense local opposition to the proposed development, which was dubbed 'a super prison'. Thornton Hall was described by local residents as 'a farm, not a prison site'. See Press Release, 'Rural North Dublin Community Fights to Save their Community and Environment from Unsustainable Development', 11 August, 2005, www.indymedia.ie/article/71474?userlanguage=ga&save_prefs=true.

these decisions; and (4) the inclusion of the decision to close Mountjoy Prison and build a new prison at Thornton Hall in the 'National Development Plan 2007 to 2013' (NDP)[43] adopted in January 2007.[44] Mr Kavanagh, a local resident, grounded his challenge on a number of points, including alleged breaches of the EIA and SEA Directives. Smyth J identified the SEA issues that fell to be determined by the High Court as follows: (1) were any of the contested decisions a 'plan' or 'programme' for the purpose of the SEA Directive?; (2) if so, were they concerned with 'town and country planning' or 'land use'?; and (3) did they set the framework for future development consent of projects listed in Annexes I and II of the EIA Directive?[45]

The lengthy and convoluted *Kavanagh* judgment is difficult to follow. A number of complex issues are intertwined throughout the text. The judgment is poorly structured and there is significant, unnecessary repetition. Ultimately, the High Court concluded, on the facts, that the plaintiff's case fell to be dismissed on the basis of 'inordinate and inexcusable delay' on his part.[46] For the present purposes, the High Court's main findings and conclusions on the SEA points raised by the plaintiff were as follows. First, the government's decision—taken on 3 February 2004—to replace Mountjoy Prison with a new prison complex at Thornton Hall was 'a stand-alone decision'.[47] It was not part of, or contingent on, 'a plan or programme of general prison development'—it was merely a decision 'in principle'.[48] Once the government had taken its decision to replace Mountjoy, references were made to that decision in subsequent documentation, including the NDP. Second, the NDP was:

> [E]ssentially a financial plan or framework setting out what the Government sees as the investment priorities for the next seven years, and how resources can be invested amongst different investment priorities. It [was] not designed or intended to set any kind of framework for the granting or refusing of permissions for the carrying out of projects or to have any influence on the physical planning process (even if planning authorities or *An Bord Pleanála* [the Planning Appeals Board] may note it or do have regard to it ... in their decisions).[49]

[43] Government of Ireland, *National Development Plan 2007–2013—Transforming Ireland: A Better Quality of Life for All* (Dublin, The Stationery Office, 2007) (hereinafter 'NDP').

[44] *Kavanagh* (n 42) section 2.

[45] ibid, section 3. The judgment records (section 7) that, at the outset of the proceedings, the plaintiff made an application to the High Court for a reference for a preliminary ruling to the CJEU on 'certain questions'. It is disappointing that the judgment does not reveal the nature of the questions that the plaintiff sought to have referred. In any event, Smyth J refused the application on the basis that: (1) the matter could be determined 'reasonably' without making a reference; and (2) the plaintiff had a direct right of appeal to the Supreme Court, which, the High Court noted, had 'its own body of expertise and experience of the European Court of Justice'. (This statement presumably refers to the fact that at the time of the *Kavanagh* judgment, three members of the Supreme Court of Ireland had previously served as either a Judge or Advocate General at the CJEU.)

[46] ibid, section 6.

[47] ibid, section 5.

[48] ibid.

[49] ibid.

Third, relying on Article 3(8) of the SEA Directive (which excludes 'financial or budget plans and programmes' from its scope), Smyth J concluded that the Directive had 'no application whatsoever to the NDP'.[50] The Directive was 'quite clear' that not all plans and programmes were subject to SEA—only those that meet the criteria specified in Article 3 require assessment. Referring to the guidelines on the implementation of the SEA Directive published by the European Commission,[51] Smyth J emphasised that 'the name alone ('plan', 'programme', 'strategy', 'guidelines' etc) will not be a sufficiently reliable guide: Documents having all of the characteristics of a plan or programme as defined in the Directive may be found under a variety of names'.[52] In the words of the High Court, a 'policy decision to build something in an urban or rural location does not amount to a plan or programme' within the meaning of the Directive.[53] A further obstacle to the plaintiff's case on the SEA Directive was the fact that the government's decision to replace Mountjoy was taken in February 2004, prior to the date on which Member States were required to transpose the SEA Directive and the date of entry into force of the national SEA regulations (21 July 2004).

The *Kavanagh* judgment is unsatisfactory in a number of respects. Although the judgment pre-dates the recent body of CJEU jurisprudence interpreting the SEA Directive in a purposive fashion, it is striking how Smyth J underplayed the role and impact of the NDP when competent authorities are determining applications for development consent. At the time, the NDP amounted to a 'roadmap' for Ireland's future, involving a €184 billion investment framework. It claimed to integrate 'strategic development frameworks for regional development, for rural communities, for all-island co-operation, and for protection of the environment with common economic and social goals'.[54] Yet it was never subjected to SEA. The High Court's conclusion that the NDP was not a 'plan' or 'programme' for the purposes of the SEA Directive confirms that the narrow definition deployed in the Directive is plainly problematic in practice. At a more general level, the best that can be said is that the convoluted and, at times, mystifyingly opaque judgment (together with the fact that the plaintiff was ultimately unsuccessful due to his delay in bringing the proceedings) means that *Kavanagh* is of limited value as a precedent.

But there is a further dimension to the Thornton Hall litigation. The High Court's subsequent determination on liability for the costs of the unsuccessful challenge merits consideration. *Kavanagh v Ireland (No 2)*[55] is an early example of the Irish courts grappling with the implications of the access to justice clause in the EIA Directive (at the time, Article 10a). (Mr Kavanagh had also alleged breach of the EIA Directive in relation to the Thornton Hall project.) Having been

[50] ibid, section 7.

[51] Commission, 'Guidance on the Implementation of Directive 2001/42/EC on the Assessment of the Effects of Certain Plans and Programmes on the Environment' (undated).

[52] *Kavanagh* (n 42) section 7, citing para 3.3 of the Commission Guidance (n 51).

[53] ibid, section 7.

[54] NDP (n 43) 15.

[55] *Kavanagh v Ireland (No 2)* [2007] IEHC 389.

unsuccessful in the proceedings and consequently facing a substantial costs order, Mr Kavanagh sought to rely on the access to justice clause in Article 10a of the EIA Directive. In a disappointing judgment, Smyth J ruled that the obligation to provide review procedures that are not 'prohibitively expensive' did not extend to an unsuccessful litigant's exposure to legal costs. The High Court reasoned that if the terms of the EIA Directive were 'applied literally in the abstract and devoid of context then every litigant no matter how vexatious should have carte blanche to engage without risk of basic responsibility—in short a *Crank's Charter*'. (emphasis added) Smyth J cited Article 3(8) of the Aarhus Convention and concluded that the Convention sought to ensure that the 'cost of entry' to litigation (specifically, court fees)—as opposed to legal costs—is not 'prohibitively expensive'. This unduly narrow interpretation of the Article 10a obligation has now been overtaken by the contemporary CJEU jurisprudence on costs and access to justice in environmental matters.[56] It is now beyond doubt that the access to justice provision in the EIA Directive has, in effect, created a ban on 'prohibitively expensive' legal costs, and the more interesting question is now how far access to justice requirements might apply in relation to the SEA Directive. It is also notable that in *Edwards*, the UK Supreme Court saw fit to make a reference for a preliminary ruling on the interpretation of Article 10a. In sharp contrast, in *Kavanagh (No 2)*, Smyth J opted to interpret this provision very narrowly without the benefit of a ruling from the Luxembourg Court. An early reference for a preliminary ruling would have provided valuable guidance to the Irish authorities on the implications of Article 10a for judicial review law and practice in environmental matters. *Kavanagh (No 2)* stands out as a missed opportunity to clarify the law.

More recently, a challenge to the decision to approve the Ballinasloe Town Enhancement Scheme led the High Court to consider the definition of 'plans and programmes' in *Ballinasloe Chamber of Commerce Ltd v Ballinasloe Town Council*.[57] Ballinasloe is a large town in East County Galway. The Chamber's primary concern was the extent to which the Enhancement Scheme made provision for car-parking spaces. The main plank to its challenge was that the Scheme was a 'plan' or 'programme' for the purposes of the SEA Directive and that the Council had failed to carry out an SEA. As regards remedies, the High Court agreed with the Chamber's submission that if an SEA was required, but had not been undertaken, then it would be appropriate to quash the decision to approve the Scheme.[58] Birmingham J recalled the objectives of the SEA Directive set out in Article 1 and then turned to consider the definition of 'plans and programmes' in Article 2(a). The High Court was satisfied that there was 'no doubt' that the Scheme 'was subject to preparation and/or adoption by an authority at local level pursuant to legislative provisions'.[59] Birmingham J referred to the Commission guidance on

[56] *Edwards* (n 28); *Commission v UK* (n 28).

[57] *Ballinasloe Chamber of Commerce Ltd v Ballinasloe Town Council* [2012] IEHC 273.

[58] ibid [16].

[59] ibid.

the implementation of the SEA Directive, which, although not binding, offered 'assistance' in determining whether or not the Directive applied.[60] The High Court relied on Smyth J's analysis of the meaning of the term 'plan' in *Kavanagh*. Smyth J considered that a 'plan':

> [I]s envisaged as a framework against which decisions are made concerning development consents: e.g. a development plan sets a framework against which individual planning permissions for specific projects are to be granted … which is the requirement of Article 3(2)(a) of the [SEA] Directive.[61]

Birmingham J concluded that the Enhancement Scheme did not meet this definition. In particular, there was no basis for suggesting that it set the framework for future development consents. It was a 'once-off operative project'.[62] In the words of the High Court, the Chamber's submission on the SEA point was 'misconceived'.

SEA and the Duty to Provide Reasons for Adopting a Plan

Notwithstanding the narrow interpretation of the scope of the SEA Directive, once it is found to apply, the Directive is taking hold within Irish public administration and the courts. An early example is provided by the third case involving the SEA Directive in the Irish courts, *Farrell and Forde v Limerick County Council*.[63] In this case, a challenge to the Local Area Plan (LAP) for Adare (a unique, historic and picturesque village in County Limerick) led the High Court to examine plan-making procedures. Under the draft LAP, the applicants' lands were zoned for agricultural use. The land owners challenged an order where the County Manager had ruled that a resolution passed by the elected Council members was invalid. The resolution purported to accept the Manager's Report in relation to the draft LAP, but subject to certain modifications. Under the terms of this resolution, one of the modifications to the draft plan would have resulted in the applicants' lands being rezoned for mixed-use development (which the applicant landowners supported). The Manager took the view that the resolution was invalid, particularly for failing to meet the requirements of the SEA Directive, and the High Court was invited to rule on this point.

The making of a LAP is a function of the executive of a local authority. The only circumstances in which the elected members can intervene in this situation are specified in section 20(3)(d) of the PDA (as amended). The High Court determined that the procedure set down in section 20(3)(d) had to be read in light of the obligations imposed on a planning authority under the SEA Directive and the

60 ibid [17].
61 *Kavanagh* (n 42) section 7.
62 *Ballinasloe* (n 57) [17].
63 *Farrell and Forde v Limerick County Council* [2009] IEHC 274.

national SEA regulations.[64] McGovern J agreed that a resolution passed by elected members purporting to modify the draft LAP would only be effective if it complied with the requirements of the SEA Directive and the regulations. The High Court noted the express obligation under Article 9 of the Directive to publish 'a statement' summarising how environmental considerations were integrated into the plan or programme, and how the environmental report and the results of consultations were taken into account, together with information explaining the reasons for choosing the plan or programme as adopted. The applicants submitted that the contested resolution contained sufficient reasons and was valid. McGovern J concluded that the resolution was made having regard to one consideration alone—the perceived need for more housing. The High Court found that the reasons why this particular decision was arrived at were not clear. Furthermore, the reasons behind the decision were not stated in the resolution itself. It followed that the resolution was not a valid and effective resolution in accordance with section 20(3)(d) of the PDA (as amended). The *Farrell and Forde* ruling demonstrates that the High Court is alert to the procedural requirements set down in the SEA Directive, which can have significant implications for the development of land use policy. In particular, it confirms the importance of compliance with the publication obligation in Article 9, including the duty to provide reasons, and that the High Court will not hesitate to quash any decisions taken in breach of this fundamental element of the SEA process.

Aarhus, SEA and Public Participation

Article 7 of the Aarhus Convention governs public participation concerning plans, programmes and policies relating to the environment. The public participation requirements mandated by Article 7 have come into sharp focus following the findings and recommendations of the Aarhus Convention Compliance Committee in a communication alleging non-compliance by the EU—Communication ACCC/C/2010/54.[65] The communication, which was lodged by Mr Swords, a chemical engineer based in Ireland, concerned the manner in which Ireland's National Renewable Energy Action Plan (NREAP) had been adopted (Ireland was not a party to the Convention at the time when Mr Swords lodged this communication with the Compliance Committee).[66] The Compliance Committee found that the NREAP constituted a plan or programme relating to the environment which was subject to Article 7 of the Convention. It followed from Article 7 that, where a NREAP is prepared, the requirements for public participation set

[64] ibid [13].

[65] Details of this communication are available via the data sheet published at: www.unece.org/env/pp/compliance/Compliancecommittee/54TableEU.html.

[66] Ireland was the last of the EU Member States to ratify the Convention. Ireland ratified on 20 June 2012 and only became subject to the Compliance Committee's jurisdiction from 18 September 2013.

out in Article 6(3), (4) and (8) of the Convention must be met. The Compliance Committee determined that the EU had failed to comply with Article 7 of the Convention: (1) by not having a proper regulatory framework in place to implement Article 7 in the context of the adoption of NREAPs by the Member States under Directive 2009/28/EC;[67] and (2) by not having properly monitored Ireland's implementation of Article 7 in the adoption of its NREAP.[68] The Committee also found non-compliance with Article 3(1) in that the EU did not have a proper regulatory framework in place to enforce Article 7 with respect to the adoption of NREAPs in the Member States.

Mr Swords had questioned the process leading up to the adoption of Ireland's NREAP, including alleged inadequate opportunities for public participation. The Compliance Committee found that the public consultation on the NREAP was conducted 'within a very short timeframe, namely two weeks'.[69] It added that a 'two week period is not a reasonable time frame for "the public to prepare and participate effectively", taking into account the complexity of the plan or programme'.[70] It recommended that the EU adopt a proper regulatory framework for implementing Article 7 with respect to NREAPs. Such a framework would include ensuring that the arrangements for public participation in the Member States are 'transparent and fair' and that the necessary information is provided to the public. Moreover, the framework put in place must ensure that Article 6(3), (4) and (8) of the Convention is satisfied.[71] The Committee's findings and recommendations in this case confirm its exacting approach to public participation and its concern to ensure that each specific element of the participation requirements set down in the Convention are delivered in practice at a local level.

Relying in part on the Compliance Committee's findings and recommendations in Communication ACCC/C/2010/54, Mr Swords subsequently initiated proceedings before the Irish courts alleging, inter alia, that Ireland adopted its NREAP in breach of both the Aarhus Convention and EU law (that is, the SEA Directive).[72] At the time of writing, these proceedings are before the High Court and the Irish authorities are defending this challenge to the NREAP vigorously. While it remains to be seen how the various arguments presented in *Swords* will be resolved by the Irish courts, it is heartening to see the public participation rights conferred by Article 7 of the Convention being deployed in litigation at the national level.

In parallel to the High Court proceedings, on 29 May 2014, three members of the public (including Mr Swords), representing seven Irish NGOs, submitted

[67] Parliament and Council Directive 2009/28/EC on the promotion of the use of energy from renewable sources [2009] OJ L140/16.

[68] UNECE Compliance Committee, 'Findings and Recommendations with regard to Communication ACCC/C/201/54 concerning Compliance by the European Union' (12 October 2012).

[69] ibid [83].

[70] ibid.

[71] ibid [98].

[72] *Swords v Minister for Communications, Energy and Natural Resources, Ireland and the Attorney General* Record No 2013/4122P.

a communication to the Aarhus Convention Compliance Committee alleging a failure by Ireland to comply with a range of obligations under the Convention, including Articles 3(1), 4, 5, 6, 7, 8 and 9 in connection with the implementation of Ireland's NREAP. This communication is currently under consideration by the Compliance Committee.[73]

SEA in Practice

This section examines the implementation of SEA in Ireland. By way of background, a report on the application and effectiveness of the SEA Directive, published by the Commission in September 2009, revealed varied experiences with implementation across the Member States.[74] Overall, the report cast SEA in a positive light, as successfully delivering better integration of environmental considerations at an early stage in the planning process. But the Commission's analysis signalled a number of problem areas, including: the identification and evaluation of reasonable alternatives; lack of attention to climate change impacts; the interaction between SEA and assessment requirements under other directives (for example, the EIA and Habitats Directives); and a lack of national guidance on monitoring methodologies. The report also acknowledged the need to develop capacity at the national level to support SEA implementation. The Commission's findings resonated with the experience in Ireland at the time.

Levels of SEA Activity in Ireland

The EPA collects and publishes data on SEA activity. The most recent data reflects SEA-related notifications and other documentation received by the EPA up to 30 June 2016 (for example, screening submissions, scoping submissions and Environmental Reports and information on decisions (SEA statements)). In the

[73] Details of this communication, ACCC/C/2014/112 Ireland, are available here: www.unece.org/environmental-policy/conventions/public-participation/aarhus-convention/tfwg/envppcc/envppcccom/acccc2014112-ireland.html. It is also notable in this context that on 28 October 2013, the European Platform against Windfarms (EPAW), represented by Mr Swords, submitted a communication to the Compliance Committee alleging breach of Convention obligations by the EU (including alleged breach of Article 7 of the Convention) as regards the adoption by the European Commission on 14 October 2013 of a list of 248 Projects of Common Interest. These projects essentially involve trans-national energy infrastructure projects, including a number of projects concerning Ireland. Details of this communication, ACCC/C/2013/96 European Union, which is currently under consideration by the Compliance Committee, are available here: www.unece.org/environmental-policy/conventions/public-participation/aarhus-convention/tfwg/envppcc/envppcccom/acccc201396-european-union.html.

[74] Commission, 'Report on the Application and Effectiveness of the Directive on Strategic Environmental Assessment (Directive 2001/42/EC)' COM (2009) 469.

period from July 2004 to 30 June 2016, a total of 450 SEAs were either completed or in progress.[75] The EPA data confirms that the vast majority of SEAs were (predictably) undertaken in the planning/land use sector (338). This was followed by water management (30), energy (24), fisheries (12), transport (11), waste management (8), agriculture (4), tourism (4), forestry (3), industry (3), telecommunications (1) and 'other cases' (12).

Review of SEA in Ireland

The EPA published its *Review of Effectiveness of SEA in Ireland* (hereinafter 'the SEA Review') in 2012.[76] This report presented a range of findings on SEA in practice at the time, as well as recommendations to support better implementation. The review was informed by a wide range of sources, including a stakeholder workshop, an online survey, a detailed analysis of a selection of SEA case studies, interviews with SEA practitioners and a review of SEA effectiveness studies in a number of other jurisdictions.[77] The SEA Review concluded that:

> SEA is fulfilling its role and is providing a vital tool for environmental protection in Ireland. SEA ensures that environmental considerations are taken into account in policy development and implementation, and is raising the profile of environmental issues in decision-making at plan level among those sectors applying SEA.[78]

Notwithstanding this overall positive assessment, the review also identified significant problems with SEA in practice. The main negative findings presented in the report included: failure to screen some sectoral plans systematically (such as in forestry and agriculture); failure to document adequately scoping responses and how those responses are addressed; lack of a central database of plans with the result that it is difficult to identify what other plans exist; significant base-line data gaps that need to be addressed at a national level; inadequate consideration of alternatives; inadequate treatment of certain categories of environmental effects (such as impacts on biodiversity and climate change impacts) and the interrelationship between effects; mitigation measures not always being taken into account in the plan or being documented poorly; limited public involvement in SEA; Environmental Reports not always focusing on key issues; non-technical summaries sometimes being of poor quality; environmental effects of amendments to plans generally being poorly considered; some SEA Statements either not being produced at all or being of poor quality; SEA-related monitoring of the environmental effects of plans seldom being undertaken; and that SEA and appropriate assessment could be integrated more effectively.

75 Source: data received by author from the EPA, July 2016.
76 SEA Review (n 4).
77 ibid vi.
78 ibid 62.

The SEA Review made a series of recommendations to improve implementation, with particular emphasis on the following: strengthening governance; providing detailed guidance on various aspects of SEA; ensuring that authorities have adequate resources to fulfil their obligations; and improving training and awareness. Following the publication of the SEA Review, a National SEA (Environmental Authority) Technical Forum was established. This Forum comprises the five statutory designated environmental authorities for SEA and meets on a quarterly basis.[79] It is not a statutory body and has no enforcement role.[80] The statutory environmental authorities jointly developed the *SEA Effectiveness Review in Ireland: Action Plan 2012–2016* to provide a roadmap to deliver the recommendations made in the SEA Review and to improve the effectiveness of SEA more generally.[81] The five authorities have 'shared responsibility' for the delivery of the recommendations.

It is heartening to see that there have been significant positive developments in practice since the publication of the SEA Review in 2012. Public authorities have learnt from their early experiences with SEA. All sectors now appear to be engaging with their SEA obligations at an early stage, including the agriculture and forestry sectors. This gradual change in attitude has led to a greater level of 'buy-in' to the value of the SEA process, which can be traced back to the strong advocacy role played by the EPA in promoting SEA. It is also likely that public authorities' attitudes to SEA have been influenced by the recent increase in litigation challenging development consents for individual projects, in particular proposed wind farm development and associated infrastructure, based on alleged breaches of environmental impact assessment and habitat protection obligations.[82] This increase in litigation, facilitated to some extent by the special costs rules, demonstrates sharply to public authorities the high risks involved (particularly in terms of unpredictable outcomes, increased costs and delay) in failing to engage with environmental obligations, including SEA, at an early stage. The ongoing litigation in the High Court challenging the NREAP (noted above) and the communications involving Ireland currently being considered by the Aarhus Convention Compliance Committee also serve to raise the profile and practical importance of SEA obligations among public authorities and members of the public generally.

[79] The five statutory authorities in question are: the DECLG; the Department of Arts, Heritage and the Gaeltacht; the Department of Agriculture, Food and the Marine; the Department of Communications, Energy and National Resources; and the EPA. As explained at n 18 above, the names of the government departments mentioned here are due to change shortly.

[80] It will be recalled from the first section of this chapter that the independent EPA Review Group, which reported in May 2011, recommended that the EPA should be assigned a wider statutory role as regards SEA with a view to strengthening implementation. This recommendation has not been acted upon to date and there is no indication of any plans to act on it in the near future.

[81] Environmental Protection Agency, 'SEA Effectiveness Review in Ireland: Action Plan 2012–2016', 2012, www.epa.ie/monitoringassessment/assessment/sea/#.Uu7fMWyYZdg.

[82] See generally Á Ryall, 'Delivering Energy Policy in Ireland: Politics, Protest and Law' in RJ Heffron and G Little (eds), *Delivering Energy Law and Policy in the EU and the US: A Reader* (Edinburgh, Edinburgh University Press, 2016).

As regards improving SEA methodologies and practice, the EPA has published detailed guidance on integrating climate change into SEA,[83] as well as guidance on developing and assessing alternatives.[84] It is anticipated that the EPA will prepare a follow-up SEA effectiveness review in 2017. In light of recent developments, it is likely that a fresh contemporary review of progress will confirm the gradual maturing of SEA in Ireland and document significant improvements in implementation. A number of key strategic plans have been subjected to SEA recently, including, for example, the *Offshore Renewable Energy Development Plan: A Framework for the Sustainable Development of Ireland's Offshore Renewable Energy Resource* published in 2014[85] and *Food Wise 2025*, a strategic plan for the agri-food sector over the next decade, published in 2015.[86] A significant number of other high-profile plans are emerging at the time of writing. These include the National Planning Framework,[87] preparation of new Regional and Economic Spatial Strategies by the three Regional Assemblies, and the Renewable Electricity Policy and Development Framework.[88]

Conclusion

SEA is still at a relatively early stage of development in Ireland. However, recent years have seen significant positive developments, in particular a growing acknowledgement by decision-makers of the added value of SEA in terms of delivering better environmental outcomes. While significant work remains to be done to improve implementation and embed SEA fully in national practice, the outlook for the future is generally positive. The EPA continues to play a vital advocacy role in relation to SEA and, through the National Technical Forum, is promoting greater shared responsibility for implementation between the designated environmental authorities. It also continues to develop capacity to improve SEA implementation by providing specialist advice, expert guidance and dedicated training for public authorities.

[83] EPA, *Integrating Climate Change into Strategic Environmental Assessment in Ireland: A Guidance Note*, 2014.

[84] EPA, *Developing and Assessing Alternatives in Strategic Environmental Assessment* (EPA Research Report No 157, 2015).

[85] The text of the *Offshore Renewable Energy Development Plan* and related documents, including the SEA Statement, the SEA Environmental Report and the Natura Impact Statement, are available here: www.dcenr.gov.ie/energy/en-ie/Renewable-Energy/Pages/OREDP-Landing-Page.aspx.

[86] The text of *Food Wise 2025*, together with SEA documentation and Natura Impact Statement and the *Food Wise 2025 Implementation Plan*, is available here: http://agriculture.gov.ie/foodwise2025.

[87] *Towards a National Planning Framework: A Roadmap for the Delivery of the National Planning Framework 2016*, December 2015, www.environ.ie/sites/default/files/publications/files/towards_a_national_planning_framework_december_2015.pdf.

[88] This policy framework is currently under preparation; see further www.dcenr.gov.ie/energy/en-ie/Renewable-Energy/Pages/Renewable-Electricity-Policy-and-Development-Framework.aspx.

There are strong indications of a shift in approach towards SEA obligations among public authorities (due to persistent EPA efforts) and a developing awareness of the risks associated with not engaging the SEA process when required. In fact, there has been a gradual movement away from treating SEA as a mere 'box-ticking' exercise towards a growing recognition that there are environmental constraints to development and, where significant impacts cannot be avoided, stringent controls and robust mitigation measures must be put in place. Overall, SEA practice in Ireland has matured significantly in recent years.

If SEA obligations are to be taken seriously, then robust governance and oversight mechanisms must be put in place. When public authorities fail to fulfil their legal obligations, tangible consequences and sanctions are necessary if SEA is to be integrated successfully into plan-making processes. The SEA Review published in 2012 suggested that 'an independent body' could evaluate SEAs, decide whether or not they are acceptable, and examine whether significant effects are being identified and mitigated. A better approach would be to assign to the EPA a statutory oversight and enforcement role in relation to SEA. The EPA is the public authority best placed to fulfil this role, subject to the necessary resources being assigned to it to fulfil any new responsibilities.

Looking to the future, as awareness of SEA continues to grow among the public and NGOs, we are likely to see SEA-related points surfacing more frequently in litigation and before the Aarhus Convention Compliance Committee. This is particularly likely since the special costs rule now applies to SEA challenges, although the high cost of legal services in Ireland remains problematic in terms of access to the courts in certain cases. High-profile litigation, including, for example, the current challenge to Ireland's National Renewable Energy Action Plan, increases the visibility of SEA and forces public authorities to consider the unpalatable consequences of a successful challenge. Litigation has no doubt served to concentrate decision-makers' minds on the value of compliance at the outset. It is heartening to see the gradual change in culture within public authorities and the emerging willingness to accept SEA as a means of improving the quality of decision-making rather than as an unwelcome constraint on development. As the Irish experience demonstrates, folding SEA successfully into national practice is a gradual and challenging process, particularly in the current climate when the government and public authorities are under intense pressure to generate jobs and to reinvigorate and grow the economy. Overall, based on the experience to date, we can be optimistic about the future of SEA in Ireland, but only if the government is prepared to invest the necessary resources to support a robust system of environmental governance.

17

Afterword: Aarhus and HS2

RICHARD MACRORY AND GREGORY JONES QC

Switzerland is a country where very few things begin, but many things end.[1]

Introduction

As discussed elsewhere in this volume, the challenge brought by way of judicial review by the HS2 Action Alliance (HS2AA)[2] and others of the Command Paper *High Speed Two: Decisions and Next Steps* (hereinafter 'the DNS'), in which the government set out its strategy for HS2 and the details of its proposed route for Phase 1 from London to the West Midlands, finally resulted in the Supreme Court's judgment in *R (HS2 Action Alliance Ltd) v Secretary of State for Transport v Secretary of State for Transport*.[3] In the course of those proceedings, the English courts held that the consultation leading to the DNS had not provided the public with sufficient information about the environmental impacts of HS2 and the reasonable alternatives to it so as to amount to a strategic environmental assessment (SEA) under the Directive, but that this did not render the DNS unlawful because the SEA Directive did not apply, as the DNS did not 'set the framework for development consent' for HS2 within the meaning of Article 3(2)(a) of the Directive, which was a necessary precondition for the applicability of the Directive.

Notwithstanding the loss in the UK Supreme Court and that court's refusal to make a reference to the Court of Justice to the European Union (CJEU), campaigners including HS2AA and the London Borough of Hillingdon have continued the battle, taking matters before the Aarhus Compliance Committee (ACCC) based in Geneva, Switzerland. This short afterword notes the position which has been reached in the Aarhus process at the date of writing.

[1] F Scott Fitzgerald from the short story, 'One Trip Abroad', first published in the Saturday Evening Post, October 11, 1930.

[2] https://www.hs2actionalliance.org.

[3] *R (HS2 Action Alliance Ltd) v Secretary of State for Transport v Secretary of State for Transport* [2014] 1 WLR 324.

The Aarhus Compliance Committee

The UNECE Aarhus Convention provides for Access to Information, Public Participation in Decision Making and Access to Justice in Environmental Matters. The Convention was adopted in June 1998 and was the first international treaty with the purpose of granting rights directly to the public with regard to protection of the environment. Its focus is not the protection of the environment of itself, but the procedural rights of individuals in society to participate in decision-making that relates to environmental matters. It links environmental rights and human rights and also recognises the right to a healthy environment for every individual.

Article 15 of the Aarhus Convention requires the Meeting of the Parties (MOP) to establish arrangements for reviewing compliance with the Convention. For that purpose, a 'Compliance Committee' (ACCC) has been tasked with discussing and deciding on possible violations of the Convention. The ACCC allows the public (individuals, non-governmental organisations (NGOs) and others) to report to it directly possible violations of the Convention to the committee is unique in international environmental law.[4] Campaigners against HS2 exercised this power to make complaints known as 'communications' against both the UK and the European Union (EU), both of whom are signatories to the Convention. The ACCC is, as its name makes clear, a 'committee.' It is not a court. It makes recommendations to the MOP.[5]

The Communications

The first Communication is against the UK. It alleges that the failure to provide sufficient environmental information about HS2 and its reasonable alternatives amounts to a breach by the UK of Article 7 of the Aarhus Convention, which requires effective public participation in plans or programmes relating to the environment, regardless of whether they 'set the framework for development consent'.

The second Communication is against the EU. It alleges that, on the Supreme Court's interpretation of the term 'set the framework for development consent' in the SEA Directive, the Directive's scope excludes a range of plans and programmes which are subject to Article 7 of the Convention and, in the absence of any other EU legislation requiring Member States to subject such plans to effective public participation, the EU has failed to comply with its obligations under Article 7

[4] http://www.unece.org/env/pp/cc.html

[5] For a useful explanation of the way in which the ACCC operates, see Veit Koester, 'The Compliance Committee of the Aarhus Convention: An Overview of Procedures and Jurisprudence' (2007) 37(2–3) *Environmental Policy and Law* 83, available at http://cmsdata.iucn.org/downloads/cel10_koester.pdf.

to put in place a regulatory framework for the public participation in such plans and programmes within the EU.

Preliminary Determination

On 2 July 2014, the ACCC declared both Communications to be admissible.[6] The threshold for admissibility is not excessively high. The ACCC's decisions on admissibility have regard to the merits and significance of the communication as well as whether domestic remedies have been exhausted.[7] The consequence of the rulings was that both communications proceeded to a full hearing in Geneva, at which the UK government and the EU were given the opportunity to set out their cases. The findings are not binding on the approach to be taken at the full hearing and, as noted below, the UK government has run a preliminary point as to an alleged failure to exhaust domestic remedies at the full hearing.

Full Hearing

Preliminary Issues

The hearing was conducted on 10 March 2016. The UK government also raised two preliminary issues before the ACCC hearing. The first concerns whether the complaint at issue qualifies as a communication under paragraph 18 of the annex to decision I/7 in relation to the Second Communicant, the London Borough of Hillingdon. It is the UK government's position that the London Borough of Hillingdon as a 'public authority' within Article 2(2) of the Convention is not a 'member of the public' on whom the Convention confers rights. One suspects that the UK government is motivated in taking this point in part as a way of helping it to overturn the Court of Appeal's ruling in *R (on the Application of HS2 Action Alliance Ltd) v Secretary of State for Transport*,[8] which confirmed that local authorities were entitled to costs cap protection in public law challenges before the courts of England and Wales involving Aarhus Convention cases.

[6] www.unece.org/fileadmin/DAM/env/pp/compliance/C2014-100/Determinationonadmissibility C100_UK.pdf.

[7] Guidance Document on the Aarhus Convention Compliance Mechanism, at www.unece.Aorg/fileadmin/DAM/env/pp/compliance/CC_GuidanceDocument.pdf.

[8] *R (on the Application of HS2 Action Alliance Ltd) v Secretary of State for Transport* [2015] EWCA Civ 203.

The second preliminary point concerns the alleged failure of the communicants to exhaust all domestic remedies prior to bringing this complaint contrary to paragraph 21 of the annex to decision I/7.[9] This relates to the fact that the complaints did not pursue all the grounds on appeal from the Court of Appeal to the Supreme Court.

UK Government Communication[10]

The communicants' case on this Communication is essentially that the UK government had failed to discharge its duties under Article 7 of the Aarhus Convention. In particular, they stressed that Article 7 includes express requirements that public participation in relation to plans and programmes must be: (1) during their preparation; (2) within 'a transparent and fair framework, having provided the necessary information to the public'; and (3) compliant with the standards set out in Article 6, paragraphs 3, 4 and 8, namely that the provision of 'reasonable time frames' which allow sufficient time 'for the public to prepare and participate effectively during the environmental decision-making' (Article 6, paragraph 3), the provision of 'early public participation, when all the options are open and effective public participation can take place' (Article 6, paragraph 4) and ensuring that the final decision takes due account of the outcome of the public participation (Article 6, paragraph 8).

The communicants, HS2AA and the London Borough of Hillingdon, reminded the Committee that in an earlier communication: *United Kingdom* ACCC/C/2011/61 (regarding the Crossrail project) it had held that Parliament in approving hybrid bills such as for the Crossrail and HS2 schemes was not acting 'in a legislative capacity', but as a 'public authority' (16). The present communication, they said, related to a plan/programme for a national infrastructure development on 'a once-in-a-generation scale, with acknowledged very wide-ranging and significant environmental impacts'. And they argued that the body given responsibility for determining whether to grant development consent is a national legislature. They further submitted that this also affects the level of environmental information necessary to provide effective public participation as required under Article 7 of the Convention. In particular, the communicants emphasised the following, namely: (1) there is no justification for concluding that the level of

[9] Decision I/7 Review of Compliance adopted at the first meeting of the parties held in Lucca, Italy, 21–23 October 2002, www.unece.org/fileadmin/DAM/env/pp/documents/mop1/ece.mp.pp.2.add.8.e.pdf.

[10] ACCC/C/2014/100 *United Kingdom*. Communication documents can be found at www.unece.org/environmental-policy/conventions/public-participation/aarhus-convention/tfwg/envppcc/envppcccom/acccc2014100-united-kingdom.html

environmental information required by Article 7 of the Convention is lower than that of the internationally recognised standards set out in the SEA Directive and the Kiev Protocol; and/or (2) even if, contrary to the communicants' primary case, the ACCC did not agree that an Article 7 analysis is required in all cases, at the very least it is is applicable in the present context.

According to HS2AA and the London Borough of Hillingdon, the consultation undertaken on the DNS document prior to its adoption in January 2012 did not comply with the standards of Article 7 of the Convention. In particular: (1) some of the options considered were ruled out without any prior public participation; (2) no information was given about the environmental effects of some of the options considered; and (3) the level of information provided about the Secretary of State for Transport's referred options for the plan or programme was not equivalent to the level of information provided about some of the other options considered.

In response, the UK government argued that it had discharged its duties under Article 7 by carrying out its consultation in 2011 under the common law principles governing consultation and that the consultation that it carried out satisfied these requirements. It reiterated the argument upon which it was successful before the Supreme Court, namely that the SEA Directive did not apply in these circumstances as the DNS did not set the framework for the subsequent decision-making process.

EU Communication[11]

HS2AA and the London Borough of Hillingdon presented a case against the EU on the basis that there was a gap in the EU's implementation of Article 7 as a result of the UK Supreme Court's decision that the DNS did not set the framework for the subsequent decision making process.

The main piece of EU legislation on public participation concerning plans and programmes relating to the environment is the SEA Directive. The communicants argued that a gap arises because the SEA Directive applies to plans and programmes prepared by EU Member States only where they are 'required by legislative, regulatory or administrative provisions' (Article 2(a)) and 'set the framework for development consent' (Article 3(2)). Accordingly, they said it follows that the consequences (if correct) of the UK Supreme Court judgment creates an EU-wide exemption from the SEA Directive for plans and programmes relating to a project for which the subsequent development consent is a national legislature. It was argued that, accordingly, the EU had failed to put in place an appropriate

[11] ACCC/C/2014/101 *European Union*. Communication documents can be found at www.unece.org/environmental-policy/conventions/public-participation/aarhus-convention/tfwg/envppcc/envppcccom/acccc2014101-european-union.html.

framework to ensure the implementation of Article 7 in light of the UK Supreme Court's decision.

The EU was of the view that it had discharged its obligations under Article 7 and that it was a matter for the UK government to comply with Article 7 where the EU framework did not cover circumstances such as those of the present case. However, it is interesting to note that the EU refused to be drawn when asked by the Committee Members as to whether it considered that the UK Supreme Court's decision was correct. Similarly, the ACCC also refused to be drawn on whether it was minded to take proceedings against the UK.

Conclusion

Following the March 2016 hearing, the ACCC was to write to the UK and the EU with some questions it would like to have answered. There has been some apparent delay in formulating and sending these questions. Upon receipt of these questions, the UK and the EU will be expected to respond. The ACCC will then deliberate before coming to its findings and possible recommendations, which will be published at one of its subsequent meetings.

The substantive outcome of these communications is, of course, difficult to predict. However, it is perhaps worth observing that, first, the UK government was keen to pursue the procedural preliminary points as to whether domestic remedies had been exhausted and, second, the EU was reluctant to express a view as to whether the UK Supreme Court's judgment was in breach of EU law. As to the latter, it is perhaps particularly unfortunate that the UK Supreme Court did not make a reference to the CJEU. The Supreme Court of Justice is a court of last instance subject to Article 267 of the Treaty on the Functioning of the EU.[12] The UK Supreme Court was obliged to make a reference unless the matters were *acte claire*.[13] The Supreme Court did not make a reference in this case. This was notwithstanding the fact Sullivan LJ who is a highly experienced judge in the field of town and country planning and its interaction with EU environmental law had delivered a powerfully reasoned descenting judgment in the Court of Appeal.[14] As

[12] '... Where any such question is raised in a case pending before a court or tribunal of a Member State against whose decisions there is no judicial remedy under national law, that court or tribunal shall bring the matter before the Court. ...'

[13] In accordance with the principles set down in Case C-283/81 *Srl CILFIT* et *Lanificio di Gavardo SpA v Ministero della sanità* [1982] ECR 3415 (ECJ).

[14] Since its creation, the UK Supreme Court has proved quite resilient in its reluctance to make references to the CJEU in the field of EU environmental law. A good example is its decision not to make a reference in *R (Morge) v Hampshire County Council* [2011] UKSC 2; [2011] 1 WLR 268 concerning the correct interpretation of the Habitats Directive. Of the five-person court deciding the substantive

a result, we now have a situation where, albeit indirectly, the UK's compliance with matters of EU law are being assessed by a committee of the Aarhus Convention rather than the CJEU itself.[15] One cannot help but feel that in this case, it might have been better in terms of legal certainty if the UK Supreme Court had made a reference to the CJEU. There is perhaps a further irony depending on the outcome of the Brexit negotiations following the referendum result in 2016. If the United Kingdom fully withdraws from the European Union, the UK courts will no longer have to consider references to the CJEU. Assuming that the UK remains a party to Aarhus, the only effective remedy for parties wishing to question the compatibility of UK legislation with Aarhus will then be a complaint to the Aarhus compliance committee.

appeal, Lord Kerr had dissented and the reasoning given by Lord Simon Brown as to why a reference should not be made did not appear to comply with the principles set down in *Srl CILFIT* (n 12). For a criticism of this approach, see G Jones (ed), *The Habitats Directive: A Developer's Obstacle Course?* (Oxford, Hart Publishing, 2012), especially Charles George and David Graham in Chapter 3, 'After *Morge*, Where are We Now? The Meaning of Disturbance' (at 60–61) and Denis Edwards in Chapter 12, 'Judicial Review, the Precautionary Principle and the Protection of Habitats: Do We Have a System of Administrative Law Yet?' (at 231).

[15] In relation to the EU, the Aarhus Compliance Committee has recently been quite bold. In June 2016 the Committee published its draft findings with regard to Communication ACCC/C/2008/32 finding that the EU legislation applying Aarhus to Community institutions and the jurisprudence of the Court of Justice concerning standing and access to the court was incompatible with Art 9 of Aarhus (access to justice).

APPENDIX

DIRECTIVE 2001/42/EC OF THE EUROPEAN PARLIAMENT AND OF THE COUNCIL

of 27 June 2001

on the assessment of the effects of certain plans and programmes on the environment

THE EUROPEAN PARLIAMENT AND THE COUNCIL OF THE EUROPEAN UNION,

Having regard to the Treaty establishing the European Community, and in particular Article 175(1) thereof,

Having regard to the proposal from the Commission [1],

Having regard to the opinion of the Economic and Social Committee [2],

Having regard to the opinion of the Committee of the Regions [3],

Acting in accordance with the procedure laid down in Article 251 of the Treaty [4], in the light of the joint text approved by the Conciliation Committee on 21 March 2001,

Whereas:

(1) Article 174 of the Treaty provides that Community policy on the environment is to contribute to, *inter alia*, the preservation, protection and improvement of the quality of the environment, the protection of human health and the prudent and rational utilisation of natural resources and that it is to be based on the precautionary principle. Article 6 of the Treaty provides that environmental protection requirements are to be integrated into the definition of Community policies and activities, in particular with a view to promoting sustainable development.

(2) The Fifth Environment Action Programme: Towards sustainability — A European Community programme of policy and action in relation to the environment and sustainable development [5], supplemented by Council Decision No 2179/98/EC [6] on its review, affirms the importance of assessing the likely environmental effects of plans and programmes.

(3) The Convention on Biological Diversity requires Parties to integrate as far as possible and as appropriate the conservation and sustainable use of biological diversity into relevant sectoral or cross-sectoral plans and programmes.

(4) Environmental assessment is an important tool for integrating environmental considerations into the preparation and adoption of certain plans and programmes which are likely to have significant effects on the environment in the Member States, because it ensures that such effects of implementing plans and programmes are taken into account during their preparation and before their adoption.

(5) The adoption of environmental assessment procedures at the planning and programming level should benefit undertakings by providing a more consistent framework in which to operate by the inclusion of the relevant environmental information into decision making. The inclusion of a wider set of factors in decision making should contribute to more sustainable and effective solutions.

(6) The different environmental assessment systems operating within Member States should contain a set of common procedural requirements necessary to contribute to a high level of protection of the environment.

(7) The United Nations/Economic Commission for Europe Convention on Environmental Impact Assessment in a Transboundary Context of 25 February 1991, which applies to both Member States and other States, encourages the parties to the Convention to apply its principles to plans and programmes as well; at the second meeting of the Parties to the Convention in Sofia on 26 and 27 February 2001, it was decided to prepare a legally binding protocol on strategic environmental assessment which would supplement the existing provisions on environmental impact assessment in a transboundary context, with a view to its possible adoption on the occasion of the 5th Ministerial Conference 'Environment for Europe' at an extraordinary meeting of the Parties to the Convention, scheduled for May 2003 in Kiev, Ukraine. The systems operating within the Community for environmental assessment of plans and programmes should ensure that there are adequate transboundary consultations where the implementation of a plan or programme being prepared in one Member State is likely to have significant effects on the environment of another Member State. The information on plans and programmes having significant effects on the environment of other States should be forwarded on a reciprocal and equivalent basis within an appropriate legal framework between Member States and these other States.

(1) OJ C 129, 25.4.1997, p. 14 and OJ C 83, 25.3.1999, p. 13.
(2) OJ C 287, 22.9.1997, p. 101.
(3) OJ C 64, 27.2.1998, p. 63 and OJ C 374, 23.12.1999, p. 9.
(4) Opinion of the European Parliament of 20 October 1998 (OJ C 341, 9.11.1998, p. 18), confirmed on 16 September 1999 (OJ C 54, 25.2.2000, p. 76), Council Common Position of 30 March 2000 (OJ C 137, 16.5.2000, p. 11) and Decision of the European Parliament of 6 September 2000 (OJ C 135, 7.5.2001, p. 155). Decision of the European Parliament of 31 May 2001 and Decision of the Council of 5 June 2001.
(5) OJ C 138, 17.5.1993, p. 5.
(6) OJ L 275, 10.10.1998, p. 1.

(8) Action is therefore required at Community level to lay down a minimum environmental assessment framework, which would set out the broad principles of the environmental assessment system and leave the details to the Member States, having regard to the principle of subsidiarity. Action by the Community should not go beyond what is necessary to achieve the objectives set out in the Treaty.

(9) This Directive is of a procedural nature, and its requirements should either be integrated into existing procedures in Member States or incorporated in specifically established procedures. With a view to avoiding duplication of the assessment, Member States should take account, where appropriate, of the fact that assessments will be carried out at different levels of a hierarchy of plans and programmes.

(10) All plans and programmes which are prepared for a number of sectors and which set a framework for future development consent of projects listed in Annexes I and II to Council Directive 85/337/EEC of 27 June 1985 on the assessment of the effects of certain public and private projects on the environment [1], and all plans and programmes which have been determined to require assessment pursuant to Council Directive 92/43/EEC of 21 May 1992 on the conservation of natural habitats and of wild flora and fauna [2], are likely to have significant effects on the environment, and should as a rule be made subject to systematic environmental assessment. When they determine the use of small areas at local level or are minor modifications to the above plans or programmes, they should be assessed only where Member States determine that they are likely to have significant effects on the environment.

(11) Other plans and programmes which set the framework for future development consent of projects may not have significant effects on the environment in all cases and should be assessed only where Member States determine that they are likely to have such effects.

(12) When Member States make such determinations, they should take into account the relevant criteria set out in this Directive.

(13) Some plans or programmes are not subject to this Directive because of their particular characteristics.

(14) Where an assessment is required by this Directive, an environmental report should be prepared containing relevant information as set out in this Directive, identifying, describing and evaluating the likely significant environmental effects of implementing the plan or programme, and reasonable alternatives taking into account the objectives and the geographical scope of the plan or programme; Member States should communicate to the Commission any measures they take concerning the quality of environmental reports.

(15) In order to contribute to more transparent decision making and with the aim of ensuring that the information supplied for the assessment is comprehensive and reliable, it is necessary to provide that authorities with relevant environmental responsibilities and the public are to be consulted during the assessment of plans and programmes, and that appropriate time frames are set, allowing sufficient time for consultations, including the expression of opinion.

(16) Where the implementation of a plan or programme prepared in one Member State is likely to have a significant effect on the environment of other Member States, provision should be made for the Member States concerned to enter into consultations and for the relevant authorities and the public to be informed and enabled to express their opinion.

(17) The environmental report and the opinions expressed by the relevant authorities and the public, as well as the results of any transboundary consultation, should be taken into account during the preparation of the plan or programme and before its adoption or submission to the legislative procedure.

(18) Member States should ensure that, when a plan or programme is adopted, the relevant authorities and the public are informed and relevant information is made available to them.

(19) Where the obligation to carry out assessments of the effects on the environment arises simultaneously from this Directive and other Community legislation, such as Council Directive 79/409/EEC of 2 April 1979 on the conservation of wild birds [3], Directive 92/43/EEC, or Directive 2000/60/EC of the European Parliament and the Council of 23 October 2000 establishing a framework for Community action in the field of water policy [4], in order to avoid duplication of the assessment, Member States may provide for coordinated or joint procedures fulfilling the requirements of the relevant Community legislation.

(20) A first report on the application and effectiveness of this Directive should be carried out by the Commission five years after its entry into force, and at seven-year intervals thereafter. With a view to further integrating environmental protection requirements, and taking into account the experience acquired, the first report should, if appropriate, be accompanied by proposals for amendment of this Directive, in particular as regards the possibility of extending its scope to other areas/sectors and other types of plans and programmes,

[1] OJ L 175, 5.7.1985, p. 40. Directive as amended by Directive 97/11/EC (OJ L 73, 14.3.1997, p. 5).
[2] OJ L 206, 22.7.1992, p. 7. Directive as last amended by Directive 97/62/EC (OJ L 305, 8.11.1997, p. 42).
[3] OJ L 103, 25.4.1979, p. 1. Directive as last amended by Directive 97/49/EC (OJ L 223, 13.8.1997, p. 9).
[4] OJ L 327, 22.12.2000, p. 1.

HAVE ADOPTED THIS DIRECTIVE:

Article 1

Objectives

The objective of this Directive is to provide for a high level of protection of the environment and to contribute to the integration of environmental considerations into the preparation and adoption of plans and programmes with a view to promoting sustainable development, by ensuring that, in accordance with this Directive, an environmental assessment is carried out of certain plans and programmes which are likely to have significant effects on the environment.

Article 2

Definitions

For the purposes of this Directive:

(a) 'plans and programmes' shall mean plans and programmes, including those co-financed by the European Community, as well as any modifications to them:

— which are subject to preparation and/or adoption by an authority at national, regional or local level or which are prepared by an authority for adoption, through a legislative procedure by Parliament or Government, and

— which are required by legislative, regulatory or administrative provisions;

(b) 'environmental assessment' shall mean the preparation of an environmental report, the carrying out of consultations, the taking into account of the environmental report and the results of the consultations in decision-making and the provision of information on the decision in accordance with Articles 4 to 9;

(c) 'environmental report' shall mean the part of the plan or programme documentation containing the information required in Article 5 and Annex I;

(d) 'The public' shall mean one or more natural or legal persons and, in accordance with national legislation or practice, their associations, organisations or groups.

Article 3

Scope

1. An environmental assessment, in accordance with Articles 4 to 9, shall be carried out for plans and programmes referred to in paragraphs 2 to 4 which are likely to have significant environmental effects.

2. Subject to paragraph 3, an environmental assessment shall be carried out for all plans and programmes,

(a) which are prepared for agriculture, forestry, fisheries, energy, industry, transport, waste management, water management, telecommunications, tourism, town and country planning or land use and which set the framework for future development consent of projects listed in Annexes I and II to Directive 85/337/EEC, or

(b) which, in view of the likely effect on sites, have been determined to require an assessment pursuant to Article 6 or 7 of Directive 92/43/EEC.

3. Plans and programmes referred to in paragraph 2 which determine the use of small areas at local level and minor modifications to plans and programmes referred to in paragraph 2 shall require an environmental assessment only where the Member States determine that they are likely to have significant environmental effects.

4. Member States shall determine whether plans and programmes, other than those referred to in paragraph 2, which set the framework for future development consent of projects, are likely to have significant environmental effects.

5. Member States shall determine whether plans or programmes referred to in paragraphs 3 and 4 are likely to have significant environmental effects either through case-by-case examination or by specifying types of plans and programmes or by combining both approaches. For this purpose Member States shall in all cases take into account relevant criteria set out in Annex II, in order to ensure that plans and programmes with likely significant effects on the environment are covered by this Directive.

6. In the case-by-case examination and in specifying types of plans and programmes in accordance with paragraph 5, the authorities referred to in Article 6(3) shall be consulted.

7. Member States shall ensure that their conclusions pursuant to paragraph 5, including the reasons for not requiring an environmental assessment pursuant to Articles 4 to 9, are made available to the public.

8. The following plans and programmes are not subject to this Directive:

— plans and programmes the sole purpose of which is to serve national defence or civil emergency,

— financial or budget plans and programmes.

9. This Directive does not apply to plans and programmes co-financed under the current respective programming periods [1] for Council Regulations (EC) No 1260/1999 [2] and (EC) No 1257/1999 [3].

(1) The 2000-2006 programming period for Council Regulation (EC) No 1260/1999 and the 2000-2006 and 2000-2007 programming periods for Council Regulation (EC) No 1257/1999.

(2) Council Regulation (EC) No 1260/1999 of 21 June 1999 laying down general provisions on the Structural Funds (OJ L 161, 26.6.1999, p. 1).

(3) Council Regulation (EC) No 1257/1999 of 17 May 1999 on support for rural development from the European Agricultural Guidance and Guarantee Fund (EAGGF) and amending and repealing certain regulations (OJ L 160, 26.6.1999, p. 80).

Article 4

General obligations

1. The environmental assessment referred to in Article 3 shall be carried out during the preparation of a plan or programme and before its adoption or submission to the legislative procedure.

2. The requirements of this Directive shall either be integrated into existing procedures in Member States for the adoption of plans and programmes or incorporated in procedures established to comply with this Directive.

3. Where plans and programmes form part of a hierarchy, Member States shall, with a view to avoiding duplication of the assessment, take into account the fact that the assessment will be carried out, in accordance with this Directive, at different levels of the hierarchy. For the purpose of, *inter alia*, avoiding duplication of assessment, Member States shall apply Article 5(2) and (3).

Article 5

Environmental report

1. Where an environmental assessment is required under Article 3(1), an environmental report shall be prepared in which the likely significant effects on the environment of implementing the plan or programme, and reasonable alternatives taking into account the objectives and the geographical scope of the plan or programme, are identified, described and evaluated. The information to be given for this purpose is referred to in Annex I.

2. The environmental report prepared pursuant to paragraph 1 shall include the information that may reasonably be required taking into account current knowledge and methods of assessment, the contents and level of detail in the plan or programme, its stage in the decision-making process and the extent to which certain matters are more appropriately assessed at different levels in that process in order to avoid duplication of the assessment.

3. Relevant information available on environmental effects of the plans and programmes and obtained at other levels of decision-making or through other Community legislation may be used for providing the information referred to in Annex I.

4. The authorities referred to in Article 6(3) shall be consulted when deciding on the scope and level of detail of the information which must be included in the environmental report.

Article 6

Consultations

1. The draft plan or programme and the environmental report prepared in accordance with Article 5 shall be made available to the authorities referred to in paragraph 3 of this Article and the public.

2. The authorities referred to in paragraph 3 and the public referred to in paragraph 4 shall be given an early and effective opportunity within appropriate time frames to express their opinion on the draft plan or programme and the accompanying environmental report before the adoption of the plan or programme or its submission to the legislative procedure.

3. Member States shall designate the authorities to be consulted which, by reason of their specific environmental responsibilities, are likely to be concerned by the environmental effects of implementing plans and programmes.

4. Member States shall identify the public for the purposes of paragraph 2, including the public affected or likely to be affected by, or having an interest in, the decision-making subject to this Directive, including relevant non-governmental organisations, such as those promoting environmental protection and other organisations concerned.

5. The detailed arrangements for the information and consultation of the authorities and the public shall be determined by the Member States.

Article 7

Transboundary consultations

1. Where a Member State considers that the implementation of a plan or programme being prepared in relation to its territory is likely to have significant effects on the environment in another Member State, or where a Member State likely to be significantly affected so requests, the Member State in whose territory the plan or programme is being prepared shall, before its adoption or submission to the legislative procedure, forward a copy of the draft plan or programme and the relevant environmental report to the other Member State.

2. Where a Member State is sent a copy of a draft plan or programme and an environmental report under paragraph 1, it shall indicate to the other Member State whether it wishes to enter into consultations before the adoption of the plan or programme or its submission to the legislative procedure and, if it so indicates, the Member States concerned shall enter into consultations concerning the likely transboundary environmental effects of implementing the plan or programme and the measures envisaged to reduce or eliminate such effects.

Where such consultations take place, the Member States concerned shall agree on detailed arrangements to ensure that the authorities referred to in Article 6(3) and the public referred to in Article 6(4) in the Member State likely to be significantly affected are informed and given an opportunity to forward their opinion within a reasonable time-frame.

3. Where Member States are required under this Article to enter into consultations, they shall agree, at the beginning of such consultations, on a reasonable timeframe for the duration of the consultations.

Article 8

Decision making

The environmental report prepared pursuant to Article 5, the opinions expressed pursuant to Article 6 and the results of any transboundary consultations entered into pursuant to Article 7 shall be taken into account during the preparation of the plan or programme and before its adoption or submission to the legislative procedure.

Article 9

Information on the decision

1. Member States shall ensure that, when a plan or programme is adopted, the authorities referred to in Article 6(3), the public and any Member State consulted under Article 7 are informed and the following items are made available to those so informed:

(a) the plan or programme as adopted;

(b) a statement summarising how environmental considerations have been integrated into the plan or programme and how the environmental report prepared pursuant to Article 5, the opinions expressed pursuant to Article 6 and the results of consultations entered into pursuant to Article 7 have been taken into account in accordance with Article 8 and the reasons for choosing the plan or programme as adopted, in the light of the other reasonable alternatives dealt with, and

(c) the measures decided concerning monitoring in accordance with Article 10.

2. The detailed arrangements concerning the information referred to in paragraph 1 shall be determined by the Member States.

Article 10

Monitoring

1. Member States shall monitor the significant environmental effects of the implementation of plans and programmes in order, *inter alia*, to identify at an early stage unforeseen adverse effects, and to be able to undertake appropriate remedial action.

2. In order to comply with paragraph 1, existing monitoring arrangements may be used if appropriate, with a view to avoiding duplication of monitoring.

Article 11

Relationship with other Community legislation

1. An environmental assessment carried out under this Directive shall be without prejudice to any requirements under Directive 85/337/EEC and to any other Community law requirements.

2. For plans and programmes for which the obligation to carry out assessments of the effects on the environment arises simultaneously from this Directive and other Community legislation, Member States may provide for coordinated or joint procedures fulfilling the requirements of the relevant Community legislation in order, *inter alia*, to avoid duplication of assessment.

3. For plans and programmes co-financed by the European Community, the environmental assessment in accordance with this Directive shall be carried out in conformity with the specific provisions in relevant Community legislation.

Article 12

Information, reporting and review

1. Member States and the Commission shall exchange information on the experience gained in applying this Directive.

2. Member States shall ensure that environmental reports are of a sufficient quality to meet the requirements of this Directive and shall communicate to the Commission any measures they take concerning the quality of these reports.

3. Before 21 July 2006 the Commission shall send a first report on the application and effectiveness of this Directive to the European Parliament and to the Council.

With a view further to integrating environmental protection requirements, in accordance with Article 6 of the Treaty, and taking into account the experience acquired in the application of this Directive in the Member States, such a report will be accompanied by proposals for amendment of this Directive, if appropriate. In particular, the Commission will consider the possibility of extending the scope of this Directive to other areas/sectors and other types of plans and programmes.

A new evaluation report shall follow at seven-year intervals.

4. The Commission shall report on the relationship between this Directive and Regulations (EC) No 1260/1999 and (EC) No 1257/1999 well ahead of the expiry of the programming periods provided for in those Regulations, with a view to ensuring a coherent approach with regard to this Directive and subsequent Community Regulations.

Article 13

Implementation of the Directive

1. Member States shall bring into force the laws, regulations and administrative provisions necessary to comply with this Directive before 21 July 2004. They shall forthwith inform the Commission thereof.

2. When Member States adopt the measures, they shall contain a reference to this Directive or shall be accompanied by such reference on the occasion of their official publication. The methods of making such reference shall be laid down by Member States.

3. The obligation referred to in Article 4(1) shall apply to the plans and programmes of which the first formal preparatory act is subsequent to the date referred to in paragraph 1. Plans and programmes of which the first formal preparatory act is before that date and which are adopted or submitted to the legislative procedure more than 24 months thereafter, shall be made subject to the obligation referred to in Article 4(1) unless Member States decide on a case by case basis that this is not feasible and inform the public of their decision.

4. Before 21 July 2004, Member States shall communicate to the Commission, in addition to the measures referred to in paragraph 1, separate information on the types of plans and programmes which, in accordance with Article 3, would be subject to an environmental assessment pursuant to this Directive. The Commission shall make this information available to the Member States. The information will be updated on a regular basis.

Article 14

Entry into force

This Directive shall enter into force on the day of its publication in the *Official Journal of the European Communities*.

Article 15

Addressees

This Directive is addressed to the Member States.

Done at Luxembourg, 27 June 2001.

For the European Parliament	*For the Council*
The President	*The President*
N. FONTAINE	B. ROSENGREN

ANNEX I

Information referred to in Article 5(1)

The information to be provided under Article 5(1), subject to Article 5(2) and (3), is the following:

(a) an outline of the contents, main objectives of the plan or programme and relationship with other relevant plans and programmes;

(b) the relevant aspects of the current state of the environment and the likely evolution thereof without implementation of the plan or programme;

(c) the environmental characteristics of areas likely to be significantly affected;

(d) any existing environmental problems which are relevant to the plan or programme including, in particular, those relating to any areas of a particular environmental importance, such as areas designated pursuant to Directives 79/409/EEC and 92/43/EEC;

(e) the environmental protection objectives, established at international, Community or Member State level, which are relevant to the plan or programme and the way those objectives and any environmental considerations have been taken into account during its preparation;

(f) the likely significant effects [1] on the environment, including on issues such as biodiversity, population, human health, fauna, flora, soil, water, air, climatic factors, material assets, cultural heritage including architectural and archaeological heritage, landscape and the interrelationship between the above factors;

(g) the measures envisaged to prevent, reduce and as fully as possible offset any significant adverse effects on the environment of implementing the plan or programme;

(h) an outline of the reasons for selecting the alternatives dealt with, and a description of how the assessment was undertaken including any difficulties (such as technical deficiencies or lack of know-how) encountered in compiling the required information;

(i) a description of the measures envisaged concerning monitoring in accordance with Article 10;

(j) a non-technical summary of the information provided under the above headings.

---

[1] These effects should include secondary, cumulative, synergistic, short, medium and long-term permanent and temporary, positive and negative effects.

ANNEX II

Criteria for determining the likely significance of effects referred to in Article 3(5)

1. The characteristics of plans and programmes, having regard, in particular, to
   - the degree to which the plan or programme sets a framework for projects and other activities, either with regard to the location, nature, size and operating conditions or by allocating resources,
   - the degree to which the plan or programme influences other plans and programmes including those in a hierarchy,
   - the relevance of the plan or programme for the integration of environmental considerations in particular with a view to promoting sustainable development,
   - environmental problems relevant to the plan or programme,
   - the relevance of the plan or programme for the implementation of Community legislation on the environment (e.g. plans and programmes linked to waste-management or water protection).
2. Characteristics of the effects and of the area likely to be affected, having regard, in particular, to
   - the probability, duration, frequency and reversibility of the effects,
   - the cumulative nature of the effects,
   - the transboundary nature of the effects,
   - the risks to human health or the environment (e.g. due to accidents),
   - the magnitude and spatial extent of the effects (geographical area and size of the population likely to be affected),
   - the value and vulnerability of the area likely to be affected due to:
     - special natural characteristics or cultural heritage,
     - exceeded environmental quality standards or limit values,
     - intensive land-use,
   - the effects on areas or landscapes which have a recognised national, Community or international protection status.

INDEX

Introductory Note

References such as '178–9' indicate (not necessarily continuous) discussion of a topic across a range of pages. Because the whole of this work is about 'strategic environmental assessment', use of this term (and certain others which occur throughout) as an entry point has been restricted. Please look under the appropriate detailed entries. Wherever possible in the case of topics with many references, these have either been divided into sub-topics or only the most significant discussions of the topic are listed.

www.ingramcontent.com/pod-product-compliance
Lightning Source LLC
LaVergne TN
LVHW052218200926
848481LV00001B/142